WARRIOR • 148

LONG RANGE DESERT GROUP PATROLMAN

The Western Desert 1940–43

TIM MOREMAN   ILLUSTRATED BY RAFFAELE RUGGERI

Series editor Marcus Cowper

OSPREY PUBLISHING
Bloomsbury Publishing Plc

PO Box 883, Oxford, OX1 9PL, UK
1385 Broadway, 5th Floor, New York, NY 10018, USA
Email: info@ospreypublishing.com

OSPREY is a trademark of Osprey Publishing, a division of
Bloomsbury Publishing Plc

First published in Great Britain in 2010

Transferred to digital print on demand 2018

First published 2010
6th impression 2017

Printed and bound by Cadmus Communications, USA

A CIP catalogue record for this book is available from the British Library.

ISBN: 978 1 84603 924 9
eBook ISBN: 978 1 84603 925 6

Editorial by Ilios Publishing Ltd, Oxford, UK (www.iliospublishing.com)
Cartography Map Studio, Romsey, UK
Page layout by Mark Holt
Index by Alan Thatcher
Typeset in Sabon and Myriad Pro
Originated by PDQ Digital Media Solutions, Suffolk, UK

ACKNOWLEDGMENTS

My thanks to Jack Valenti at the LRDG Preservation Society for some
extremely useful pointers about LRDG vehicles and Matthew Broadbridge
for information about the Indian Long Range Squadron. John Mussell at
Token Publishing kindly gave permission to quote from Brendan O'Carroll's
The Kiwi Scorpions (Honiton: 2008) and my thanks also to Pen & Sword for
permission to quote from David Lloyd Owen's *The Long Range Desert Group
1940–45: Providence their Guide* (London: 2001) and Alastair Timpson and
Andrew Gibson-Watt's *In Rommel's Backyard* (London: 2000).

ARTIST'S NOTE

Readers may care to note that the original paintings from which the colour
plates in this book were prepared are available for private sale.
The Publishers retain all reproduction copyright whatsoever. All enquiries
should be addressed to:

Raffaele Ruggeri,
Via Indipendenza 22,
Bologna, 40121,
Italy

The Publishers regret that they can enter into no correspondence upon
this matter.

THE IMPERIAL WAR MUSEUM COLLECTIONS

The photographs in this book come from the Imperial War Museum's huge
collections, which cover all aspects of conflict involving Britain and the
Commonwealth since the start of the twentieth century. These rich
resources are available online to search, browse and buy at
www.iwmcollections.org.uk. In addition to collections online, you can visit
the Visitor Rooms where you can explore over 8 million photographs,
thousands of hours of moving images, the largest sound archive of its kind
in the world, thousands of diaries and letters written by people in wartime,
and a huge reference library.

To make an appointment, call (020) 7416 5320, or e-mail mail@iwm.org.uk.
Imperial War Museum www.iwm.org.uk

THE WOODLAND TRUST

Osprey Publishing are supporting the Woodland Trust, the UK's leading
woodland conservation charity, by funding the dedication of trees.

ABBREVIATIONS

AA	Anti-Aircraft
AFV	Armoured Fighting Vehicles
AP	Armour Piercing
AT	Anti-Tank
HQ BTE	Headquarters British Troops Egypt
CO	Commanding Officer
CGS	Chief of the General Staff
DCM	Distinguished Conduct Medal
GHQ ME	General Headquarters, Middle East
GOC	General Officer Commanding
HE	High Explosive
HMG	Heavy Machine Gun
ILRS	Indian Long Range Squadron
LCP	Light Car Patrols
LMG	Light Machine Gun
LRDG	Long Range Desert Group
LRP	Long Range Patrol
MG	Machine Gun
MMG	Medium Machine Gun
NCO	Non-commissioned Officer
NZ	New Zealand
OC	Officer Commanding
PPA	Popski's Private Army
rpm	Rounds per minute
RSM	Regimental Sergeant Major
SAS	Special Air Service
SAA	Small-arms Ammunition
SMG	Sub-machine Gun
SMLE	Short Magazine Lee-Enfield
WE	War Establishment

CONTENTS

LONG RANGE DESERT GROUP PATROLMAN

INTRODUCTION

The Long Range Desert Group (LRDG) – the brainchild of Brigadier Ralph Bagnold (1896–1990) – was the very first special force raised by the UK during the Desert War. Initially under the command of this intrepid soldier-scientist-explorer, what was initially know as the Long Range Patrol (LRP) quickly proved itself as an elite intelligence-gathering unit. While the main British and Axis armies slogged it out along the coast, small LRDG patrols ranged virtually at will across the inner deserts of Egypt, Libya and later Tunisia, exploiting the Axis' open desert flank. Mounted aboard specially adapted trucks, LRDG patrolmen routinely travelled deep behind enemy lines to reconnoitre, carry out covert surveillance of roads, airfields and installations and gather topographical intelligence. Information sent back over vast distances by skilled radio operators often played a key part in

The vast sand seas found in parts of the inner Libyan Desert consisted of range after range of dunes up to 150m in height. They were formidable obstacles to all but LRDG patrols. (HU 16566)

decision-making in Middle East Command. The LRDG also preyed upon Axis lines of communication, airfields and isolated outposts, although raiding was always very much a subsidiary role. Other tasks included ferrying agents and other units to and from their objectives behind enemy lines, as well as rescuing downed aircrew and escaped POWs. Later it struck up a close relationship with other special forces – most notably the SAS – with whom it closely cooperated.

The LRDG fully justified its status as an elite special force and despite its small size it played a key contributory role in the Allied victory in North Africa. It repeatedly performed tasks beyond the knowledge and ability of regular Commonwealth troops. It had a unique organisation, was equipped with especially adapted arms and equipment and carried out specialist training to fit it for its role. A selective recruitment policy ensured it was always composed of skilled, self-reliant and highly motivated

A carefully posed group photograph of the Yeomanry Patrol celebrating at Kufra after a successful raid deep behind enemy lines. Back row from left to right: Trooper 'Tankie' Babb (Tank Corps); Corporal Jack Harris (Somerset Yeomanry); Gunner James Patch (Royal Artillery); Sergeant Derek Hutchins (Somerset Yeomanry); Lance Corporal Arthur Cave MM (Somerset Yeomanry); Lance Corporal Brian Springford (Somerset Yeomanry); Trooper Kenneth Tinckler (Cheshire Regiment); Craftsman Alf Tighe MM (REME); Trooper Armstrong. Front row (left to right): Private Devine (Seaforths); Private John McKay (Seaforths); Trooper F. Gordon Harrison (Yorkshire Hussars); Private William Fraser (Seaforths); Trooper L. D. Coombs (Somerset Yeomanry); Trooper Robert Davies (Yeomanry); Trooper Donald Cashin (Cheshire Yeomanry). (HU 25277)

volunteers. Overall this small force provided a massive return for investment in terms of the vital information it gathered. Its raiding activities diverted Axis troops and aircraft away from the main battle and prevented incursions into Egypt and the Sudan. Its early successes inspired a direct offshoot – the Indian Long Range Squadron (ILRS) – which the LRDG helped train and which later came under its direct command in 1942/43. The LRDG undoubtedly earned the respect of its opponents, with its ability to appear out of and then disappear into the desert. Indeed, the Italians dubbed them 'the ghost patrols'. As Brendan O'Carroll has written, the LRDG clearly lived up to its unofficial motto – 'Not by strength, but guile'.

The LRDG's impressive achievements were made possible only by its mastery of the vast inner deserts of Egypt, Libya and Tunisia where it lived, moved and fought. This arid, rugged and extremely inhospitable area formed its cradle and nursery, where the LRDG grew and matured. The Libyan Desert, part of the Sahara Desert, stretches over western Egypt, north-west Sudan and nearly all of Libya itself towards the border with Tunisia. It is roughly the same area in size as India, covering an area of 1,900 x 1,600km.

The Libyan Desert consists of two distinct areas. To the north lies an area of semi-desert atop the narrow coastal plateau – popularly known to British troops as the Western Desert – running along the Mediterranean littoral from El Alamein in the east to Tripoli in the west where most of the fighting took place. This area was mostly flat, open and lacked a civilian population, except in Gebel Akhdar and near the coast where some small towns and villages existed. Few regular units, however, operated farther than 80km inland due to the shortage of water, logistical constraints and the real and imagined difficulties of the broken desert terrain inland. The 'true', deep or inner desert where the LRDG was based, and which it used as a highway to and from its operational areas, lay farther to the south. A combination of the vast distances involved, a dearth of water and seas of towering sand dunes along its periphery meant that this huge expanse of desert was regarded as largely impassable.

The ordinary LRDG patrolman learnt by training and experience to overcome the myriad difficulties encountered when living and moving in the inner desert, where it fought a war as much against nature as against its Axis opponents, with heat, thirst and simply getting lost posing a near-constant threat to life. As Major-General David Lloyd Owen, a veteran of the Desert War and the LRDG's commanding officer between 1943 and 1945, has written: 'It was here that the LRDG found the disciplines and the challenges under which it grew into a unit which in its professionalism, its level of attainment in specialist skills, its internal coherence, its very high morale and its avoidance of the public eye was in my experience unique.'

CHRONOLOGY

1940

10 June	Italy declares war on the UK and France.
10 June	Major Ralph Bagnold proposes a desert patrol unit.
23 June	General Sir Archibald Wavell, Commander-in-Chief Middle East, approves formation of a Long Range Patrol unit.

The North African theatre of war, 1940–43

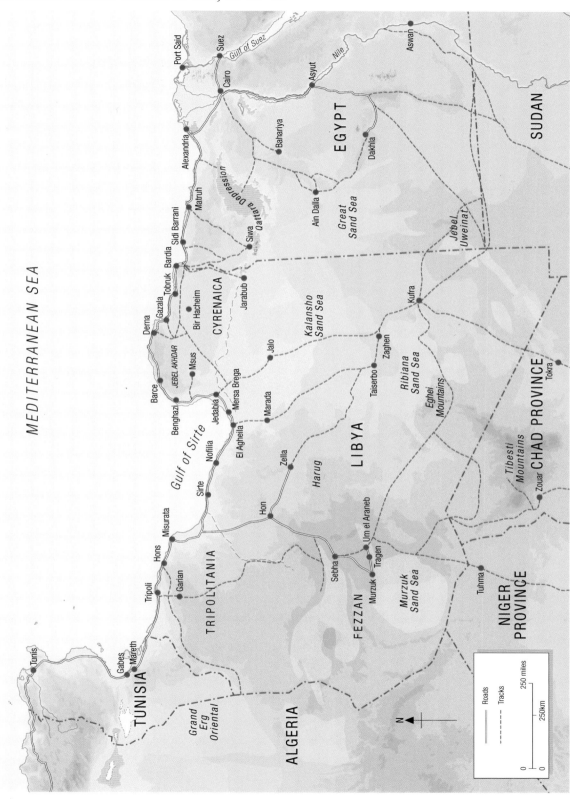

7 July	Formation of the LRP begins.
10 July	War Office cables provisional approval for LRP.
7–19 August	LRP reconnaissance of the Jalo–Kufra road.
27 August	LRP inspected by the C-in-C Middle East and reported ready for duty.
5 September	First LRP mission undertaken in Libya.
29 September	War Office authority received to double the size of the LRP.
9 November	LRP renamed the LRDG and reorganized with War Office approval into an HQ and two squadrons of three patrols each.
23 November	First LRDG Mission: W and R Patrols.
5 December	Officers and men of G Patrol arrive at the Citadel at Cairo.
27 December	G and T Patrols begin Fezzan Expedition.

1941

11 January	The LRDG and Free French capture Murzuk.
31 January	Southern Rhodesian Patrol formed.
9 March	Formation of Yeomanry Patrol completed.
21 March	Men of a new Royal Artillery section arrive.
12 February	Rommel and the advance guard of the Deutsches Afrika Korps reach Tripoli.
1st March	Free French capture Kufra.
9 April	The LRDG (less A Squadron) moves its base to Kufra Oasis.
April–July	A Squadron operates in Cyrenaica.
10 July	GHQ ME orders the Sudan Defence Force to relieve the LRDG at Kufra.
1 August	Lieutenant-Colonel Bagnold promoted to Colonel and leaves the LRDG. Lieutenant-Colonel Guy Prendergast assumes command.
1 November	The LRDG patrols are subdivided into two.
1 October	LRDG comes under GOC Western Army (later 8th Army).

9 November	LRDG concentrated at Siwa (with the exception of S Patrol).
18 November	All patrols, except one in reserve, are committed in support of Operation *Crusader*.
23 December	LRDG escorts SAS to targets at Sirte and Tamet.
28 December	ILRS formed.
30 December	Kufra ceases to be a base for the LRDG.

1942

21 January	Start of Rommel's offensive through Cyrenaica, which is halted at the Gazala Line.
26 January	Jalo evacuated by the HQ LRDG.
1 February	HQ LRDG reopens at Siwa.
2 March	Beginning of 'road watch' by LRDG.
26 May	Rommel begins his ultimately victorious offensive and breaches the Gazala Line.
23–26 June	LRDG withdraws from Siwa.
1 July	British make their stand at El Alamein.
13/14 September	Operations *Bigamy*, *Agreement*, *Nicety* and *Caravan* begin.
1 October	The remainder of the ILRS (HQ and two patrols) is placed under LRDG command.
23 October	Second Battle of El Alamein begins.
30 October	LRDG ceases to be under command of 8th Army and reverts to GHQ ME.
4 November	Axis forces retreat from El Alamein.
8 November	Operation *Torch* – the Anglo-American invasion of North Africa – begins.
20 November	8th Army reaches Benghazi.

1943

4 February	Advance units of 8th Army cross into Tunisia.
March–April	LRDG vehicles and personnel withdrawn to Egypt.
12 May	Axis forces surrender in North Africa.

THE CONCEPT, ROLE AND TRAINING

The British Army knew little about the Libyan Desert in 1939, although this had not always been the case. The challenges inherent in living, moving and fighting in the inner Libyan Desert had been encountered during World War I when the Light Car Patrols (LCPs), equipped with Model T Fords, had battled against Senussi tribesmen in 1916/17. Few of the lessons learnt about desert fighting using motor vehicles, however, were officially retained in terms of written 'doctrine'. Knowledge of the difficulties facing those operating in the inner desert and solutions to some of its problems was kept alive by a small band of intrepid British soldier-explorers led by Captain Ralph Bagnold, a Royal Signals officer, who had served in Egypt. A series of privately funded desert explorations during the 1920s and 1930s in Sinai, Palestine, Transjordan and then western Egypt taught these dedicated desert enthusiasts about the practicalities of living and travelling in the inner desert aboard suitably modified vehicles. Old lessons were relearned and valuable new experience gained in navigation, desert survival and travelling across rugged terrain.

The British Army was fortunate that Bagnold was posted to Egypt in 1939 following the intervention of the then shadowy Commander-in-Chief Middle East, General Sir Archibald Wavell, where his knowledge and experience could be put to better effect. Those lessons learnt by Bagnold and his friends were behind the highly imaginative concept he presented in two papers submitted to higher authority, discussing the possible use of a long-range reconnaissance force operating deep in Libya. A suitably trained, equipped and specially organized unit, he believed, could exploit the mobility of desert-worthy vehicles to evade enemy pursuit and hide in the vastness of the desert, operating for extended periods without support. Indeed, such reconnaissance patrols could carry out missions lasting for weeks at a time gathering vital information, communicating with base by radio, and by striking against isolated outposts divert troops and spread alarm. On both occasions, however, these ideas were firmly rejected because of a lack of resources, scepticism about their practicability and fear of provoking the Italians.

A group of LRDG men pose for a photograph in front of their vehicles, having become the first 8th Army unit to cross the Tunisian border. At this time, LRDG patrols were being tasked by Montgomery to reconnoitre the 'going' in southern Tunisia, in case the 8th Army had to bypass the strongly held Mareth Line. (HU 16497)

The Italian declaration of war in June 1940 proved a catalyst for the acceptance of Bagnold's visionary ideas, with Egypt and the Sudan now facing a direct threat from Libya. Finding out whether the Italians were planning an offensive from Kufra towards the undefended Upper Nile and Sudan was paramount. General Sir Archibald Wavell, always open to ideas about harrying the enemy by bold and unorthodox means, quickly saw the potential of Bagnold's ideas about deep desert operations when his paper was resubmitted on 19 June. On 23 June 1940 Wavell gave Bagnold virtual carte blanche to get a new unit operational before the end of the summer.

Bagnold displayed considerable drive, determination and willpower in raising, equipping and training what became known as No. 1 Long Range Patrol Unit or more simply as the Long Range Patrol (LRP). It initially consisted of an HQ and two fighting patrols (R and T), with a third (W) to carry supplies. Each patrol was capable of operating independently or with another. The fighting patrols were initially equipped with a 15cwt pilot car and ten 30cwt Chevrolet trucks. They fielded two officers, 28 other ranks and four replacements. These unarmoured vehicles were modified for desert travel by stripping unnecessary weight (windscreens, doors and bonnets), and adding 10in.-wide sand tyres, extra springs and water condensers. Brackets and other fittings were added for sun compasses, sand channels, sand mats and other specialized equipment. The lighter pilot car carried the patrol commander, a driver and a gunner. The remaining Chevrolet 30cwt trucks were organized into four troops, with each having three vehicles. Each truck had a crew of three men: a driver, gunner and another patrolman who doubled as either a navigator, a wireless operator, an ordnance fitter, a medical orderly or a cook. In total a patrol was armed with 11 Lewis machine guns, four Boys anti-tank rifles and a single portee-mounted 37mm Bofors anti-tank gun. A patrol carried sufficient ammunition, water and rations for three weeks and enough fuel to travel 2,400km over difficult terrain. The range and endurance of patrols was progressively extended by W Patrol, which established dumps of petrol, food and water deep in the desert.

Two LRDG patrols meet in the desert. All LRGD vehicles were normally loaded to the gunnels with water, fuel, ammunition and assorted equipment required while out on patrol. (E 12390)

The Long Range Desert Group, as the LRP was re-designated in November 1940, grew quickly in size with its strength peaking in mid 1942 at 350 men organized into a Group HQ and two squadrons, each having six patrols, equipped with 110 vehicles. The strength of each fighting patrol was originally half that. The Group's HQ included a specialized signal, light repair, artillery, air, survey and heavy section. Each of the latter had a vital role in support of the fighting patrols, especially the heavy section, whose lorries supplied bases and carried out a programme of building dumps in the desert.

The ILRS was the only other major addition to the LRDG's fighting strength. Originally raised to perform a similar role in Persia–Iraq Command, it came under the LRDG's direct command in North Africa between October 1942 and April 1943. Organized, equipped and trained on the same lines as the LRDG, whose officers had assisted with its training, its four patrols were a welcome addition at a time when the LRDG was badly overstretched.

Role

The LRDG's forte was always distant reconnaissance behind Axis lines throughout Tripolitania, Cyrenaica and later Tunisia. A wide range of tasks were carried out: patrols carefully observed enemy dispositions, monitored Axis reactions to British moves, tracked the flow of reinforcements and supplies and identified units by capturing prisoners and seizing documents. Each day vital tactical information was transmitted over vast distances by LRDG radio operators to Group HQ and then onwards to General Headquarters Middle East (GHQ ME). A particular intelligence-gathering task in which the LRDG excelled was 'road watch'. From 1941 onwards small parties of patrolmen covertly observed the Via Balbia – the only metalled road running between Tripoli and Benghazi – and other routes, tallying the troops, vehicles and supplies travelling to and from the front. This information played a key role in identifying trends and evaluating other intelligence sources.

The LRDG also collected vital topographical intelligence. With Italian maps of Libya inaccurate at best and with large areas unmapped, information was badly needed about areas likely to be the scene of future large-scale operations. This 'going' reconnaissance in particular assessed the

The LRDG's survey section, under the command of Capt. Ken Lazarus, corrected inaccurate Italian maps and produced new surveys of large parts of Libya for GHQ ME. (HU 69744 LRDG Collection)

suitability of the terrain for wheeled and tracked vehicles, as well as locating sites for landing grounds and the available water supply. Every LRDG patrol routinely mapped the terrain over which it travelled and this information was forwarded to GHQ ME. In 1941 a specialized survey section consisting of three vehicles, commanded by Captain Ken Lazarus, was added to the LRDG specifically for this task. Based on this information, GHQ ME produced the first detailed maps of Libya, which played a key part in staff planning and the operations of conventional units.

The LRDG regularly transported other special units – such as the Middle East Commandos, the Inter-Service Liaison Department (ISLD) or the Libyan Arab Force – and acted as pathfinders for conventional units, who were all far less well skilled or equipped for desert travel. As acknowledged experts in long-distance desert navigation the LRDG – dubbed 'Libyan Taxis Ltd' – regularly infiltrated, supplied and collected British and Arab agents deep behind enemy lines, as well as rescuing downed aircrew and escaped POWs.

An LRDG truck negotiates rough terrain near Haruz el Eswad, November–December 1942. The ability of LRDG patrols to travel over rugged desert terrain judged impassable by conventional units was a key reason for its success. (HU 24971 LRDG Collection)

The LRDG also acted as pathfinders by guiding conventional troops cross-country through desert terrain to distant objectives.

The LRDG also carried out a growing number of specifically ordered or opportunistic 'beat-ups' or raids that provided an exciting break from the less-spectacular reconnaissance work. These included hit-and-run attacks on Axis forts, supply dumps and lines of communication. Supply convoys were ambushed, bombs surreptitiously placed aboard vehicles, mines laid on tracks and telephone lines cut. Although the damage inflicted by the LRDG was small, Axis troops and aircraft had to be diverted to protect the rear areas. On occasion the LRDG mounted large-scale raids, such as those in Fezzan and Barce in September 1942.

The LRDG struck up a close partnership with other special forces, especially the newly formed L Detachment, Special Air Service Brigade, the Middle East Commandos and Popski's Private Army. Following several disastrous parachute drops, David Stirling, the OC SAS, realized in November 1941 that LRDG patrols were capable of transporting his men and dropping them with pinpoint accuracy at a given location. The LRDG henceforward provided vital communications and safely delivered SAS raiders to within walking distance of their objectives and then brought them home again. Joint offensive operations were carried out by the SAS and the LRDG, although this association exposed LRDG patrolmen to far greater risks than normal. This 'marriage' of special forces continued until the SAS acquired transport, signallers and navigators of its own.

Captain David Lloyd Owen at Ghetmir near Jalo, February 1942. (HU 25287 LRDG Collection)

Training

Those who volunteered for the LRP in July 1940 were already trained soldiers, albeit most were 'hostilities only' volunteers. Many were already also trained drivers, fitters and radio operators. Bagnold enjoyed considerable freedom when it came to training his new command in the knowledge and skills for living, moving and fighting in a hostile desert environment. The small size of the unit meant early patrolmen learnt primarily by word of mouth and example from Bagnold and his peers initially, and afterwards while 'on the job'. Indeed, the small band of New Zealand volunteers who first joined the LRP carried out only two desert training runs, under Bagnold's watchful eye, before being judged fit for operations. Later additions to the unit had more (albeit still limited) time for instruction. The Guards Patrol, for example, received only ten days' training before the Fezzan expedition began. Fortunately, Major Pat Clayton was at hand to teach such skills as driving, desert survival and using weapons during two days' practical instruction near Fayoum. Similarly, Bagnold and Captain Bill Kennedy Shaw taught S Patrol these skills. As one NCO recalled: 'We were very lucky to have Bagnold to instruct us and we learnt even more during the informal chats around the campfire in the evening.'

The new LRDG patrolmen first learnt the skills needed to safely live in and move through the inner Libyan Desert. This included accustoming them to the desert and such basic survival skills as strict water conservation and constructing shelters. The ever-present danger of becoming lost in the featureless desert meant every patrolman was schooled in navigation using differing types of compasses and in plotting locations and courses on maps. Patrolmen were taught that no individual should ever move out of direct vision of his fellows given the ease of becoming lost.

The ordinary patrolman also received instruction in skills required for the unit's specialized duties. All ranks were instructed in 'car track lore' – reading tracks left behind by Axis vehicles with the aim of determining their age and the direction in which they had travelled. Instruction was given in identifying differing types of friendly and enemy aircraft, armoured fighting vehicles (AFVs), wheeled transport and troops. Patrolmen were also instructed in camouflaging their trucks, disguising tyre tracks and building hides. All ranks were taught to use and maintain the various personal and crew-served weapons mounted aboard trucks. Men were instructed in how to engage both air and ground targets and how to fire when halted and on the move.

The drivers, navigators and signallers in each LRDG Patrol, upon whom so much depended for survival and the completion of missions, unsurprisingly received the most detailed instruction. Those men designated drivers bore considerable responsibility for safely driving across rugged terrain and day-to-day maintenance. Drivers were taught how to read the terrain, know when to alter tyre pressures, how to use gears in soft sand, how to start or stop gently and how to avoid tracks used by other vehicles to prevent bogging. The art of tackling dunes was covered as well as different methods of 'unsticking' trapped vehicles. Various formations used by patrols had to be mastered. Although each patrol had a fitter, drivers also needed to be skilled at vehicle maintenance.

The fact that LRDG patrols operated in areas where distances were vast, maps unreliable at best and landmarks few and far between meant accurate desert navigation was vital. It was a highly technical subject with three

ABOVE

The Bagnold sun compass proved vital for navigating LRDG patrols during daylight hours. Mounted on the dashboard of each LRDG vehicle, it indicated the true bearing on which a vehicle was moving using the shadow cast by the sun as a guide. (HU 71822)

ABOVE RIGHT

Bill Kennedy Shaw, the LRDG's intelligence officer, uses a theodolite to fix his patrol's position at Ain Ghetmir, February 1942. This vital piece of LRDG equipment was used each night to accurately fix a patrol's location in the desert. (HU 25143)

to six months normally allowed for training. In recognition of its complexity a new army trade – Land Navigator – was eventually authorized by the War Office, with an extra shilling a day paid to qualified men.

The intricacies of desert navigation were first taught by Bill Kennedy Shaw, aided by an early New Zealand volunteer – Corporal Dick Croucher – who had earned his ticket as a mate in the Merchant Navy. Each student was taught two ways of navigating: dead reckoning and the far more complex 'astrofix' method.

The essential tools that had to be mastered for dead reckoning navigation were the sun compass and speedometer on a vehicle. Indeed, the sun compass – a device invented by the LRP and refined by Bagnold – was an essential LRDG item of equipment since getting accurate bearings with a magnetic compass was impossible inside a metal vehicle. This simple device consisted of a small circular table, divided into 360 degrees, fixed to the dashboard of a vehicle with a central upright needle projecting from the centre that cast a shadow over the graduations. By rotating the circle throughout the course of a day to correspond with the movement of the sun, the shadow indicated a true bearing.

The LRDG used astronomical observations to fix a position far more accurately. Using a theodolite to accurately fix a latitude and longitude, however, required detailed instruction, although calculating a position was considerably simplified by using RAF air almanacs. A fix on a given star would be taken by the navigator using a theodolite (if possible this was done independently by two members of each patrol) and after an accurate time check was taken and a complex formula applied to the data an exact position could be plotted on a map. This provided a fix accurate to within 1.6km of a particular location.

The signaller, drawn from either the Royal Signals or the New Zealand Divisional Cavalry, was arguably the most important individual in each patrol, given that so much depended on maintaining contact with base and transmitting accurate, reliable and timely intelligence. Signallers in the LRDG

always required and received intensive training. The No. 11 HP Set used by LRDG patrols may well have been standard issue, but the skills needed to operate them deep in the desert were not. Originally designed for use over a distance of 32km, it was routinely used on patrol over distances of up to 1,600km. On occasion even further distances were achieved. All communication was normally by continuous wave (CW) transmission. A combination of the distances covered and atmospheric conditions in the desert, however, often made maintaining communications extremely difficult. All signallers underwent one to two months of specialized training, supervised by Captain Tim Heywood (LRDG Signals Officer from December 1940), before being judged fit for patrol work, and in that time learned how to pick up very weak signals from a background of atmospherics and interference. Instead of following normal practice LRDG signallers learnt French, Turkish and Egyptian commercial procedure so that an Axis radio operator listening in would confuse with a French station in Tunisia or others depending on the area a patrol was operating in. Last but by no means least, each signaller needed to be a trained and skilled technician capable of maintaining his set for weeks on end unaided.

The training of the LRDG patrolmen was put on a more formal basis when a properly constituted Group HQ was established following the unit's expansion. A series of detailed training instructions, following standard British practice, were issued by its HQ covering a wide range of tasks carried out by the LRDG as amended by practical experience. Training was always an ongoing process as new men arrived to fill gaps in the ranks and new arms and equipment were acquired. With heavy demands always being made on LRDG patrols, however, time for the 'luxury of training' was often short and was crammed in after periodic refits. Much, however, was still learnt during the course of operations, especially by individual replacements, who relied on word of mouth and the example set by their peers to master LRDG skills. As one officer put it: 'There was only one way to learn, and that was to get on with the job.'

RECRUITMENT

Bagnold quickly realized that the success or failure of the LRP depended on the quality of the available manpower. A special type of man was needed who was capable of withstanding the hardship involved in living, moving and fighting deep behind enemy lines. In Bagnold's own words: 'We had to have tough and self-reliant volunteers, but they had to be highly intelligent men too, capable of quick adaptation to entirely new ways of life, and absorbing a mass of desert lore that had taken us years to learn. Moreover, a high proportion must be technicians: fitters, gunners, wireless men, navigators, and the like.' Finding such men was a tall order since those qualified were in high demand in the Middle East in 1940.

Bagnold built up his LRP around a small experienced nucleus composed of former members of his pre-war 'desert club', who in 1940 were scattered across the Middle East. Pat Clayton and Bill Kennedy Shaw were hurriedly found and commissioned, while Teddy Mitford was transferred to the unit. All three were appointed as patrol commanders. Captain Rupert Harding-Newman, serving with the Military Mission to the Egyptian Army, also helped select suitable vehicles.

Bagnold was given a free hand by GHQ ME to find volunteers from amongst units serving in the Middle East. His first port of call was amongst those from the Dominions, believing it would be easier to find better-acclimatized, hardy and more self-reliant troops amongst them than those from the UK, as well as ones already skilled at driving and vehicle maintenance. A robust 'no' from the Australian GOC (who was under strict instructions to retain national control over all Australian troops), however, meant he turned instead to the New Zealand Division for his first recruits.

These Kiwi volunteers proved ideal. A combination of their physical toughness, individual initiative, self-reliance, knowledge of driving and vehicle maintenance (born of living an outdoor life as farmers) and willingness

G patrol, originally recruited from volunteers from the Coldstream and Scots Guards, prepares to move off on patrol from Siwa Oasis. (HU 16614)

to learn indeed made them readily adaptable to desert life. As Bill Kennedy Shaw later wrote: 'There can be no doubt whatsoever that much of the early and continued success of the LRDG was due to the speed and thoroughness with which the New Zealanders learned desert work and life.' The period of service for these men was fixed at six months, after which they would be returned. In practice the latter, however, was not strictly adhered to with some returning after only a few months and others staying with the LRDG for several years.

The recruitment of the LRDG remained highly selective for the duration of the Desert War, with Bagnold's views about the essential qualities required being shared by his successor. The LRDG was extremely fortunate, as throughout the Desert War it escaped the crippling losses suffered by many regular units fighting in the Western Desert and accordingly never needed large numbers of replacements at any one time. Indeed, it retained many of its highly experienced officers, NCOs and men throughout the Desert War. Since wastage from accidents, disease and enemy action (to which promotion should be added) was also limited, men steadily trickled into the unit. The LRDG, moreover, was able to call upon manpower from an ever-widening pool. Most still came from 'parent' units, and individuals to fill specialist posts or small groups eventually came from some 50 other units in Middle East Command. Indeed, the LRDG's burgeoning reputation and the desire of 'free spirits' seeking excitement and to escape red tape, drill, guard duty, fatigues and the hidebound discipline of regular troops meant it always maintained a long waiting list. Indeed, many men willingly dropped a rank to secure a billet.

While serving in the LRDG the threat of being 'RTUed' – returned to unit – hung over the heads of all ranks. Those officers, NCOs and men who failed to prove themselves left in ignominy. This fate nearly befell David Lloyd Owen himself, a future LRDG CO, when an NCO reported badly on him after his first outing in the Libyan Desert.

New Zealand members of the LRDG pause for a welcome cup of tea in the Western Desert, 27 March 1941. (E 2307)

The ILRS also relied on volunteers to fill its ranks. Under the command of Major Sam McCoy its four patrols were filled with British officers, Indian Viceroy's Commissioned Officers (VCOs) and other ranks, drawn from the 2nd Royal Lancers (Gardner's Horse), Prince Albert Victor's Own Cavalry and 18th King Edward's Own Cavalry (elements of 3rd Indian Motor Brigade), who had volunteered for special duty. It also appears likely that some officers and other ranks came from the 6th Cavalry. Like other units of the Indian Army its patrols were organized on class or ethnic lines: No. 1 Patrol consisted of Jats, No. 2 Patrol Muslims, No. 3 Patrol Rajputs and lastly No. 4 Patrol had Sikhs. Two of its British officers were 'hostilities only' but the others were pre-war regulars eager to make their mark. Since the Indian troops lacked the necessary skills, most specialist posts in the ILRS were filled by attached senior British NCOs.

BELIEF AND BELONGING

The officers, NCOs and men who served with the LRDG were always conscious that they belonged to an elite. A combination of its extremely dangerous and very specialized mission deep behind enemy lines, selective recruitment process and fiercely independent ethos set it well apart from conventional units. A deeply held belief in the LRDG's elite status had a direct concomitant of giving the unit extremely high morale and *esprit de corps* throughout its wartime existence and inspired a fierce desire to succeed at its designated tasks.

The LRDG as a whole remained throughout the Desert War a proud, happy and highly efficient organization, largely owing to the personality, skill, and foresight of its two COs. While neither possessed the charisma and showmanship of other British commanders, both Lt. Col. Ralph Bagnold and then Lt. Col. Guy Prendergast were brave, consummate professionals well versed at their chosen career and possessing detailed knowledge of living, moving and fighting in the desert. Although both were shy, reserved and quiet

A **INDIAN LONG RANGE SQUADRON (ILRS)**

The Indian Long Range Squadron (ILRS), under the LRDG's direct command between October 1942 and April 1943, remains the least known and arguably most misunderstood unit that served behind enemy lines in North Africa. Originally formed with the approval of the Commander-in-Chief Middle East, following a petition by Captain Sam McCoy (a regular Indian Army cavalry officer), as part of 9th Army during the winter of 1941/42 it was intended to perform duties similar to the LRDG in the Persia–Iraq Command if Axis troops broke through from the Caucasus. Under the command of McCoy its ranks were filled with British officers and Indian volunteers drawn from the 2nd Royal Lancers (Gardner's Horse), Prince Albert Victor's Own Cavalry, and 18th King Edward's Own Cavalry (elements of 3rd Indian Motor Brigade). It also appears that some officers and other ranks came from the 6th Cavalry.

The ILRS performed largely the same tasks as the LRDG during the Desert War. Under the overall command of Major Sam McCoy, it patrolled deep behind enemy lines from Siwa, Kufra and then Hon. The ILRS finally came into its own early in 1943 when 8th Army approached the border with Tunisia at a time when the LRDG was badly stretched and had suffered serious casualties. This included acting as a radio link with Free French forces as they advanced from Fezzan, attacking enemy road convoys south of Tripoli and carrying out ground reconnaissance.

This illustration shows a Willys jeep (**1**), part of No. 4 Patrol, carrying out a reconnaissance mission near the border with Tunisia. While a British officer (**2**) scans the horizon, a Viceroy's Commissioned Officer (**3**) checks the patrol's position on a map.

in character, each had a shrewd understanding of human nature and knew how to get the best out of the men under their command. From the outset Bagnold – affectionately dubbed 'Baggers' – won the respect and confidence of his new command by personal example, enthusiasm, detailed knowledge of the intricate details of desert travel and his ability to answer difficult questions. Both men knew the importance of quality equipment, regarded good communications as essential and were convinced that first-class manpower was vital for the LRDG to work. A strong sense of the possible meant they guarded against the LRDG being used for tasks for which it was unfit. Both men believed in detailed, thorough and proficient prior preparation and planning that ensured success and minimum casualties.

The close-knit nature of the LRDG meant that the relationship between officers and the men at lower levels was very different from the rest of the regular British Commonwealth armies. A remote style of command based on rigid discipline and 'bull' common to other units was marked by its absence, with an informality based on mutual respect and understanding taking its place. In some patrols the use of first names between officers and patrolmen was common. This was partly a product of the small size of the LRDG as a unit, the small size of patrols in which men lived, moved and fought and a careful selection process that ensured that like-minded, hand-picked and dedicated men worked well together. Junior officers were always of high quality and all ranks had combat experience before joining the LRDG. The self-reliance, adaptability, initiative and good humour prized by its officers when selecting personnel helped foster morale. The combination of a shared experience of physical hardship, working closely together and living at close quarters for long periods of time and the excitement of doing a valuable (albeit extremely dangerous) job deep behind enemy lines developed a confidence and close mutual respect between officers, NCOs and men in the LRDG. As David Lloyd Owen has written: 'Both officers and men were in the same situation, suffering the same privations, the same exhaustions, the same exhilarating thrill at the success of some operation, and the same agonising distress at some tragedy

BELOW

Lieutenant-Colonel Guy Prendergast (right), the quiet and reserved CO of the LRDG between 1941–43, and Capt. Jake Easonsmith discuss operations in the inner Libyan Desert. (HU 25158)

BELOW RIGHT

Men of Y Patrol enjoy rest and relaxation at Cleopatra's Pool at Siwa, April 1942. A swim in these clear natural pools was extremely welcome after long periods without washing and shaving on patrol. (HU 24963)

Captain David Lloyd Owen and members of Y1 Patrol standing next to one of their vehicles, September 1942. (HU 25286)

or disappointment, the same fears to a greater or lesser degree when threatened by enemy action, the same determination to survive, the same anxieties about their families and their friends.'

Many officers, moreover, were promoted from within the ranks of the LRDG as the Desert War progressed. While out on patrol all officers, NCOs and men 'mucked in' – with everyone working as part of a close-knit team placing considerable trust for their own survival in the hands of their fellow patrolmen. Each man knew his own job and was willing to help others with theirs. Last but by no means least the ordinary patrolman also owed a powerful sense of loyalty to his small band of personal 'mates', with whom he lived, moved and fought. A desire not to let down his patrol and friends was always a powerful fillip to combat effectiveness.

The press indirectly also played a part in building and maintaining LRDG *esprit de corps*, although initially their attention was actively discouraged. Following the end of the Fezzan Expedition in February 1941, the LRDG was the subject of a series of newspaper and magazine articles and even a radio programme. The fertile imagination of war correspondents directly fostered a 'swashbuckling' image of LRDG patrolmen as the 'pirates' of the Desert War, swooping down out of the vastness of the inner desert to carry out daring 'acts of piracy' before disappearing as fast as they had come.

APPEARANCE, WEAPONS AND VEHICLES

The 'ordinary' LRDG patrolman wore an eclectic mixture of headdress, clothing and equipment of his own choice whilst on patrol, with comfort always the key. As one officer has put it succinctly: 'The LRDG were no sticklers for uniformity.' Those men who volunteered for the LRDG brought with them and wore headgear, uniform, and webbing drawn from the stores of several Commonwealth countries. Initially much was of World War I vintage, including greatcoats and 1908-pattern webbing. As the Desert War progressed a limited degree of standardization was introduced, with replacement items being drawn from British stocks.

The headgear worn by the LRP patrolmen in 1940/41 included a mixture of 'lemon squeezer' felt hats, field service caps, khaki forage caps and 'Wolseley' pith helmets, with or without original insignia. Steel helmets were always carried on trucks. The distinctive mustard or sand-coloured Arab headdress or *keffiyeh,* held in place by an *agal,* was worn from 1941 onwards. It provided warmth, shade from the sun and (when wound around the face) protection from sand and dust. Its popularity waned, however, since it proved stuffy in hot weather and became easily entangled in working machinery and was usually reserved for formal parades. As one LRDG member wryly remarked: 'Very good for travelling in a dust storm and things like that, but a nuisance for working at odd jobs. Probably the reason why Arabs never work at odd jobs.' Instead, practical woollen cap comforters were widely used by patrolmen. By 1943 the Royal Tank Regiment (RTR) black beret had become almost by default the official LRDG headdress.

The clothing worn by LRDG patrolmen was very mixed. During the intense summer heat patrolmen normally wore little more than khaki drill shirts and either shorts or long trousers. Some simply wore only their shorts. Over this 'uniform' was worn 37-pattern webbing as required. When away from vehicles this normally consisted of a belt, shoulder straps, ammunition pouches with a water bottle or an RTR-pattern open-top or flap-type holster attached. A small pack loaded with a small-scale map, a compass, cigarettes, emergency rations and water was always kept close to hand.

The plummeting temperature at night and during the winter months meant patrolmen wore heavier and more layers of clothing. Standard-issue Khaki Drill (KD) battledress jackets and trousers were normally worn over shirts and woollen underwear. These were supplemented with lightweight woollen pullovers. Early LRDG members wore World War I-pattern greatcoats. The extremely warm kapok-lined Tropal coat replaced these and was one of the few distinctive items of clothing issued to the LRDG. Locally made Hebron coats, made from goatskin, were also worn to keep out the chill.

Footwear worn by the LRDG patrolmen initially consisted of standard-issue hobnailed ammunition boots, over warm woollen socks, which were sometimes worn with web anklets. *Chaplis* based on those worn by tribesmen on the north-western frontier of India were issued at Bagnold's direction.

A group of LRDG patrolmen, wearing Arab headdresses tightly wound around their heads, shelter from a violent dust storm in the lee of a truck. (HU 24964 LRDG Collection)

These leather sandals proved comfortable and were better suited for moving through hot, soft desert sand.

The officers, NCOs and men in the LRDG wore the same rank insignia as the rest of the British Commonwealth armies. The only other insignia worn by LRDG officers and men consisted of a cap badge, worn as a matter of choice on all types of headdress, and unit shoulder titles. These were seldom worn on campaign as a security measure.

Whilst on campaign the physical appearance of LRDG patrolmen rapidly deteriorated. With water in short supply soldiers seldom shaved or washed. By the end of most patrols nearly all men were coated with dust and sported ragged beards and shaggy haircuts. As one officer described:

> A stranger meeting an LRDG patrol returning from a month's trip in Libya would have been hard put to decide to what race or army, let alone to what unit, they belonged. In winter the use of battle dress made for some uniformity, but in summer, with a month-old beard thick with sand, with a month's dirt … skin burnt to the colour of coffee, and clad in nothing but a pair of torn shorts and chapplies [sic] a man looked like a creature from another world.

The LRDG always carried an extremely light scale of personal weapons. These included .38 revolvers, bolt-action .303 Short Magazine Lee-Enfield (SMLE) rifles, and American .45 Thompson sub-machine guns. Types of grenade used during LRDG operations included the No. 36 'Mills Bomb', No. 69 concussion grenade and No. 77 phosphorous grenade used primarily to produce smokescreens. Depending on the individual, the highly effective No. 36 grenade could be thrown a distance of around 25m.

The LRDG employed a wide assortment of vehicle-mounted automatic and anti-tank weapons that gave each patrol far greater firepower than any unit of comparable size. While most were officially issued, others were salvaged, begged, borrowed or stolen. The exact type, number of guns and means of mounting them was very much the choice of patrol commanders. Lighter automatic weapons were normally mounted on swan-neck mounts that fitted into sockets in the chassis and on either side of the cab. Heavier-calibre weapons were normally fired from a pillar mount in the rear of each vehicle.

The LRDG frequently used captured Axis weapons. In this posed photograph the man sitting beside the driver mans an Italian Breda machine gun, while the other crewman aims a Mk I Lewis Gun. (E 12380)

The gas-operated Mk 1 Lewis Gun, a US-designed veteran of World War I, was initially used by the LRDG since it was available in large numbers and more modern weapons were in short supply. With a distinctive wide tubular cooling shroud and round pan magazines, holding either 47 or 97 rounds, it had a rate of fire of 500–600rpm. It had a tendency to jam, however, unless frequently cleaned and the ammunition pans were vulnerable to windblown sand and dust. Later some sub-units of the LRDG and the ILRS were issued with the highly effective gas-operated Bren light machine gun, which was capable of firing single rounds or full automatic bursts. Based on a Czech design, this extremely reliable weapon was accurate at ranges of up to 550m. With a magazine of 30 rounds it had a practical rate of fire of 120rpm.

The LRDG's main source of sustained heavy fire support was the venerable .303 Vickers medium machine gun. The lightweight, gas operated and air-cooled .303 Vickers K (or Vickers VGO) machine guns were also widely used, either in a single or in a custom-designed twin mount. From March 1942 the LRDG also employed .50-cal. Browning HB Air Pattern machine guns. They proved highly successful and a total of 26 Mk IV versions were issued to the unit.

The 37mm Bofors 37mm anti-tank gun, mounted portee on the back of a Chevrolet 30cwt, provided LRDG patrols with a source of heavy fire support during the early part of the Desert War. It was unpopular with LRDG patrolmen, however, owing to its heavy weight. (E 2301)

The LRDG always equipped its patrols with anti-tank weapons that provided protection against enemy AFVs, as well as the extra punch needed against Italian forts. Initially the bolt-action .55-cal. Boys Anti-Tank Rifle, with a five-round magazine, was carried. A combination of its very limited effectiveness and heavy weight made it unpopular and it was eventually replaced by additional machine guns. The most effective anti-tank weapon initially used was a 37mm Bofors anti-tank gun mounted on a turntable on the back of a single truck in each patrol. A combination of its bulkiness and heavy weight, however, meant they were later replaced by the highly versatile 20mm Breda 20mm/65mm modello 35 anti-tank/anti-aircraft guns, captured from the Italians.

The LRDG patrolman was seldom ever far from his vehicle, on which his life largely depended whilst operating deep in the Libyan Desert. None were armoured since the extra weight would drastically reduce the range of patrols. Those vehicles used by LRDG in North Africa can be broadly divided into three types: pilot cars, patrol trucks and other more specialized load-carrying vehicles used by the heavy section. All underwent considerable modification at base workshops and by LRDG fitters to make them 'desert-worthy'. A range of more specialized vehicles were also employed.

The Ford 01 V8 was initially employed as a pilot car, with one in each patrol and several at HQ, after four Chevrolet 15cwts originally issued were found too light for desert work. Although these Fords performed remarkably well in rugged terrain, their V8 engines were easily damaged by penetrating sand. By the end of the year, nearly all the engines had worn out and the trucks had to be replaced – initially by a small number of short-wheel based 8cwt Ford WT and PU trucks. The 15cwt Chevrolet 1311X3 truck – a smaller variant of the 1533 – replaced the unsatisfactory Ford WT and PU trucks. A combination of extra low-ratio gears and a six-cylinder engine that produced lower petrol consumption made them ideal for work in the desert.

The first Willys MB 5cwt jeep used by the LRDG as a pilot car had initially been abandoned by the SAS. This salvaged vehicle proved far faster and lighter than its predecessors and in July 1942 six were issued as pilot cars. Further vehicles later replaced the 15cwt Chevrolets and were prized additions to the LRDG given their ruggedness, reliability and superior cross-country performance.

Bagnold initially selected the left-hand-drive 30cwt Chevrolet WB commercial truck, bought from a local General Motors dealer or the Egyptian Army, for use by the LRP as a standard patrol truck since nothing else in British service in 1940 was suitable. Eventually, 33 of these two-wheel drive trucks were employed after having their cabs removed and being equipped with large sand tyres.

The heavy wear and tear entailed during early LRP operations in the Fezzan area, however, meant that the 30cwt Chevrolet quickly needed

Two fully loaded LRDG Chevrolet 30cwt trucks, 25 May 1942. (E 12353)

replacing. The Canadian 1533X2 4x2 30cwt Chevrolet truck was the mainstay of the LRDG fleet from March 1942 onwards. With an open cab, full-width screen and steel ammunition body it was better suited to desert work than earlier vehicles. This rugged, sturdy and reliable truck proved highly resilient to wear and tear and the constant hard work the LRDG demanded of them in the Libyan Desert.

The heavy section was initially equipped with 6-ton Ford and Marmon Herrington 6x6 heavy trucks. These were replaced by four 10-ton 6x4 Whites that were then superseded by four Mack MR9s. They were later joined by 20 Ford F60 CMP trucks.

These assorted LRDG vehicles shared common characteristics in terms of appearance. While on patrol LRDG vehicles were normally loaded up to the gunnels, with over 2½ tons of water, fuel, arms and ammunition. On occasion

A column of Chevrolet 30cwt trucks move of out into the desert, 25 May 1942. These sturdy, reliable and well-built vehicles formed the mainstay of the LRDG from early 1942 onwards. (E 12376)

B

LRDG WEAPONS

The LRDG always enjoyed considerable freedom in choosing the types of personal and vehicle-mounted weapons it employed during the Desert War. Members of LRDG patrols largely carried standard British small arms: the .38 Enfield or Webley service revolvers (**1**), the tried-and-tested .303 Lee-Enfield Rifle (**2**) and the M1928 Thompson SMG (**3**). Unlike other Commonwealth units, the critical shortage of modern Bren light machine guns in 1940 meant patrols were issued initially with World War I-vintage Mk 1 Lewis light machine guns (**4**) capable of being fired from vehicles or from a bipod when dismounted. Although some Bren guns were used by LRDG patrols as the desert war progressed, only the ILRS was completely equipped with them. Indirect fire support was provided by 2in. mortars (**5**), along with some EY grenade-launching .303 SMLE rifles (**6**) that could fire Mills hand grenades (**7**).

The vehicle-mounted weapons used by the LRDG gave each patrol far greater firepower than other units of its size. A wide variety of weapons were employed by the LRDG during the desert war, including a mix of .303 Vickers medium machine guns (**8**), .5 Vickers medium machine guns (**9**) and later the .303 Browning and .5 Browning HB Air Pattern machine guns. The .303 Vickers Gas Operated or Vickers K (**10**), either in a single or double mount, originally salvaged from downed aircraft was widely used as it was capable of enormous volumes of automatic fire. It was not unusual for captured Axis machine guns, moreover, to be employed by the LRDG on operations. Several types of anti-tank weapon were also employed. The .55 Boys anti-tank rifle (**11**) was initially used by the LRDG, although its dubious effectiveness against anything better armoured than an armoured car meant that it was quickly abandoned. Each patrol initially had a single Bofors 37mm anti-tank gun fitted on the back of one truck, which was capable of destroying enemy light tanks and armoured cars and could damage forts. These were later replaced by highly effective captured Italian 20mm dual-purpose Breda guns, which were effective against both ground targets and Axis aircraft.

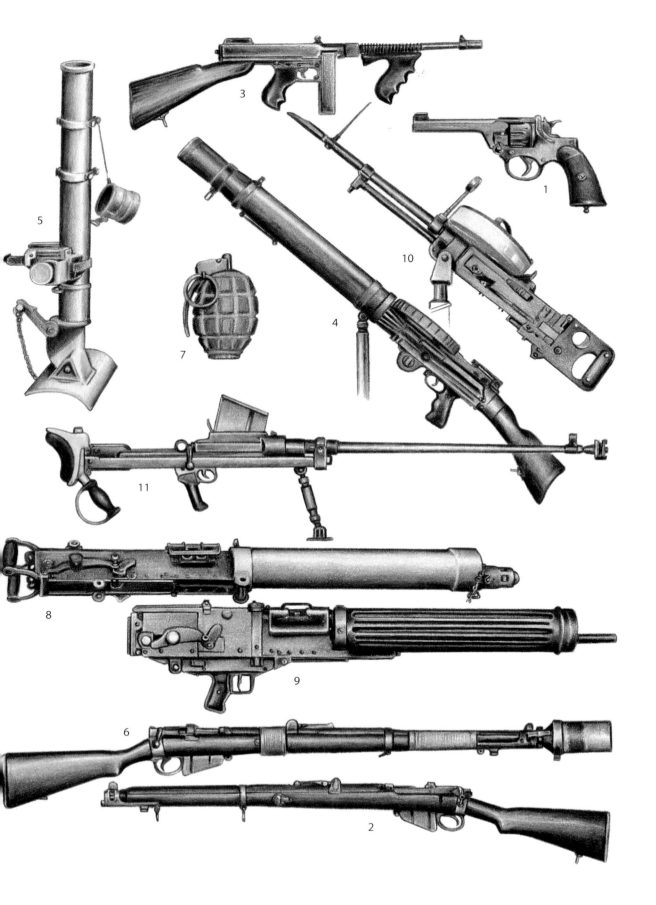

A group of LRDG patrolmen inspect newly issued Chevrolet 30cwt trucks at Cairo in May 1942. Extensive modifications were required to fit these vehicles for service deep in the desert. (E 12343)

far more was carried. The choice of camouflage was very much left to patrol commanders and considerable variations existed based on the availability of paint and personal theories about what worked best. Most vehicles had tactical markings and in some patrols vehicles bore individual names. The harsh conditions in the desert quickly weathered these vehicles, however, and most operated covered in a thick layer of dust.

LIFE ON CAMPAIGN

The life of an LRDG patrolman was extremely hard, normally characterized by long, gruelling journeys spent aboard a jolting lorry sitting amidst clouds of choking dust, with patrols travelling vast distances across the Libyan Desert. The war the LRDG fought was at times lonely, boring, and monotonous, with vast distances and difficult terrain separating patrols from outside support. On reconnaissance missions, for example, routine seldom differed for four days out of five. Throughout a patrol the threat of an encounter with Axis forces hung permanently over all ranks. For many LRDG members though, combat was quite rare with much time simply spent moving to and from patrol areas.

The vast, unmapped and hostile inner Libyan Desert formed the backdrop to everyday life. Whilst training familiarized patrolmen with the desert, a combination of its sheer immensity, eerie silence and the sense of loneliness and isolation it often instilled meant some men found it both oppressive and disorientating. For the majority the unsurpassed beauty of the clean and empty inner Libyan Desert, however, held great attraction and captivated many, especially at sunrise and sunset. Many found the panorama of twinkling stars stretching from horizon to horizon each night mesmerizing.

The unforgiving desert always posed threats to the unwary. The intense dry heat generated by the desert sun dominated everyday existence except during the cooler winter months. With little escape from the sun and the glare reflected from the sand, life was extremely unpleasant during daylight hours, with temperatures in the shade rising steadily towards 54 degrees celcius during the summer at midday. Heatstroke was a constant danger and until men developed deep tans sunburn was frequent. Thirst was a near-constant companion for patrolmen with the amount of water aboard each vehicle

strictly limited. Along with dehydration, heatstroke was a permanent risk. A combination of the heat and an inability to wash meant desert sores were suffered frequently, with these irritating and painful ulcers sometimes penetrating as deep as the bone. At night, temperatures plummeted, requiring patrolmen to don layers of clothing to remain warm.

The sand and dust storms that blew up in minutes out of nowhere were an unpleasant feature of desert life. In particular, the debilitating effect of the hot sand-laden Libyan Desert wind or *qibli* blowing northwards out of the deep desert or the similar *khamsin* wind in Egypt was keenly felt. As Bill Kennedy Shaw described the former: 'You don't merely feel hot, you don't merely feel tired, you feel as if every bit if energy had left you, as if your brain was thrusting its way through the top of your head and you want to lie in a stupor till the accursed sun has gone down.' Normal sandstorms, however, were fairly harmless, although they caused patrolmen to wear protective goggles and scarves, caused vehicles to halt or slow down and made navigation difficult.

The patrolman also had to guard against snakes, scorpions and insect life especially when he crawled into sleeping bags or got dressed. Extremely painful scorpion stings incapacitated victims for up to 36 hours. In some parts of the desert malaria-bearing mosquitoes caused casualties. Flies abounded in areas that had been the scene of fighting or home to the local Arab population.

An LRDG patrol departs into the immensity of the desert wastes at the beginning of a patrol. The appearance of LRDG patrolmen rapidly deteriorated, since washing and shaving were impossible because of strict water rationing. (HU 16490)

An LRDG patrol moves through rocky terrain on its way back to base at Kufra. Most LRDG patrolmen found the sheer beauty of the desert where they lived, moved and fought entrancing. (E 12384)

The cumulative effect of alternating extremes of heat and cold, shortages of water, fatigue and the general strain of everyday life were physically and mentally wearing and caused a particular LRDG disease – desert weariness or *cafard*. It was not fatal, however, with the afflicted cured by shade, rest and copious quantities of water to drink.

The average day for an LRDG soldier on patrol always began early to exploit the coolest daylight hours. The cook rose first and over an open fire boiled water for tea and prepared a hot breakfast. A pint of piping hot tea – using the first of the six pints of water allowed each day for all purposes – when ready would be carefully measured out into tin mugs closely supervised by the second-in-command or a senior NCO. The cook bore much responsibility for transforming the pre-packed daily rations into three appetizing meals. Fortunately the privations of desert life were such that the LRDG always enjoyed an extremely generous ration scale intended to overcome the

An LRDG patrol eats breakfast beside a vehicle, May 1942. The LRDG enjoyed an extremely generous scale of rations throughout the Desert War given the privations entailed by extended periods of life on patrol. (E 12406)

C   WACO AIRCRAFT

The vast distances covered by LRDG patrols and the extremely remote location of its forward base at Kufra caused serious command-and-control problems for its CO by early 1941. Since the RAF was unwilling or unable to provide suitable liaison aircraft, two WACO aircraft (built by the Western Aircraft Corporation of Ohio) were privately purchased by the LRDG, using its own funds, from a wealthy Egyptian businessman. These aircraft – dubbed affectionately Big WACO (AX 695) and Little WACO (AX 697) because of their different sizes – henceforward formed the LRDG's private air force and were flown and navigated, until others could be trained, by Lt. Col. Guy Prendergast and Sergeant (later Captain) Trevor Barker (a New Zealander), who both possessed private flying licences. Major overhauls of this 'private air force' were carried out in Cairo by Misr Airways. Despite the RAF's strenuous opposition, these suitably modified and camouflaged biplanes proved invaluable for liaison work, evacuating casualties and dropping mail, supplies and spare parts. Flying in the inner Libyan Desert, however, was extremely hazardous. Both aircraft were slow (with speeds of 225km/h and 185km/h respectively), lacked radios and initially suitable navigational equipment and bore more than a passing resemblance to Italian CR42 fighters. The dangers of ditching in the vast desert were such that both aircraft normally flew together at all times and dumps of food, fuel and water were located every 24km along well-travelled routes. This illustration depicts Little WACO (AX 697) (**1**) taxiing to a halt near a Chevrolet 1533X2 LRDG truck (**2**) to pick up a sick patrolman (**3**) for evacuation to a base hospital in Egypt.

debilitating effects of life in the desert. A typical breakfast, for example, consisted of porridge, fried tinned bacon and biscuits covered with margarine or jam. Other options included bacon and oatmeal cakes or bacon with oatmeal chapatis. When they were finished, tea dregs or drifts of soft sand were used to scour plates clean.

The departure of a patrol was delayed until the sun had risen at least 20 degrees or more above the horizon, which was sufficient to throw a sharp shadow on a sun-compass dial. Each crew member carefully packed any stores used overnight. Last-minute checks of fuel, oil and other consumables were carried out on each vehicle. The patrol signaller normally reported in to Group HQ at a pre-arranged time. Before departure patrolmen would be carefully briefed on the proposed direction of travel for the day ahead and on a series of agreed rendezvous if the patrol became separated. When operating near the coast all traces of the bivouac area would be carefully removed.

The lighter and faster pilot car, carrying the patrol commander, normally ranged ahead of the other trucks searching out easier routes or vantage points for observing the terrain ahead. If the enemy was sighted, a route change was required, a change in formation was needed or a sudden halt was necessary it was indicated using flags or hand signals.

The remainder of the HQ troop normally travelled not far behind the pilot car, leading the main body of the patrol. Sitting beside his driver, the patrol navigator in another vehicle was always busily employed maintaining the patrol's designated course using 'dead reckoning'. As Bill Kennedy Shaw has described: 'Sitting all day beside the driver in the navigating car, with one eye on the sun-compass, the other on the speedometer and the third on his watch he would record the course and the distance run, seizing his chance between the joltings of the truck to write down each bearing and mileage.' The radio truck normally travelled in close attendance, although its No. 11 HP set could not be used until it was stationary. The main body of a patrol – during the early years of the LRDP made up of three troops each of three trucks – followed behind, normally dispersed over as wide an area as the terrain allowed. The fitter's truck, heavily loaded with tools and spare parts, always travelled in the rear troop. Mechanical failure brought about by the heavy wear and tear on vehicles in the desert was common. If a vehicle halted because of a breakdown or a blown tyre the fitter's truck remained with

Members of Y Patrol rest near a Willys jeep following the Hon raid. These rugged and highly manoeuvrable vehicles were used as pilot cars by the LRDG during the last phases of the war in the desert. (HU 25080 LRDG Collection)

it while the remainder of the patrol moved on. The second-in-command brought up the rear of each patrol, carefully keeping an eye open for vehicles in difficulty or any signs of pursuit.

The formation in which a patrol moved depended in large part on the 'going' and the level of anticipated threat. The greatest potential danger facing a moving LRDG patrol was always being chanced upon by patrolling enemy aircraft. It was a relatively rare occurrence, however, given the vastness of the desert and the ability of LRDG to travel without being confined to recognized tracks except when operating close to the front line, near a regularly used air route or an Axis line

A camouflaged LRDG truck at Landing Ground 125, September 1942. The LRDG were highly skilful at disguising their vehicles from patrolling Axis aircraft. (HU 24967)

of communication. The likelihood of being spotted and then being subjected to bombing and strafing runs, however, was mitigated as far as possible by each patrol always travelling in an open and irregular 'air formation' across open terrain. This involved its HQ and the three fighting troops spreading out over a wide front, with a considerable gap intervening between each troop and also each vehicle.

The danger posed by marauding Axis aircraft was ever-present, however, especially since LRDG patrols normally threw up a vast plume of dust. A single crewman on each vehicle, acting as an air sentry, constantly scanned for approaching aircraft. If one was spotted or heard, the patrol commander was immediately alerted by whistle blasts, toots on the horn or flag signals. A series of pre-arranged drills would be implemented. Only if it was certain that a patrol had been sighted and an attack was imminent would a patrol halt, with trucks separated by at least by 100m, or slow down to reduce dust with vehicles using any undulations in the ground, shadows cast by rock walls or dunes and boulders for cover. Experience showed that a halted, widely dispersed and camouflaged LRDG patrol was extremely difficult to spot from the air. Indeed, patrols often escaped detection even when directly overflown.

An LRDG patrol normally had two responses if spotted by hostile aircraft. Bluff often proved highly effective. With Axis forces employing large numbers of captured British vehicles, patrolmen were adept at disguising their vehicles using fabricated German or Italian identification panels and waving jauntily at enemy pilots as if nothing untoward had happened. The nondescript clothing worn and captured headgear added to the illusion. If all else failed a patrol scattered over a wide area as soon as an aircraft began its strafing and bombing run, with vehicles moving off at speed in all directions and halting widely spaced apart in any cover available. Only a single vehicle could be attacked at a time by a fast-moving aircraft. This vehicle would spoil the aircraft's attack run by moving off at speed at the last possible moment upwind at right-angles to the line of movement of the aircraft as it made its run. Meanwhile, any other vehicles in range engaged it with automatic fire. The quick reactions of drivers and speed and mobility of vehicles made it difficult for aircraft to hit them. On occasion a patrol's concentrated firepower, moreover, convinced pilots of the wisdom of departing.

The speed and distance covered by an LRDG patrol each day depended on the type of 'going' over which it travelled. Over areas of hard sand and gravel *serrir* LRDG trucks were capable of up to 65–80km an hour with up to 320km a day possible. The speed at which an LRDG patrol moved across sand seas

An LRDG Chevrolet 30cwt truck is reloaded after a tyre change, 25 May 1942. Mechanical breakdowns and flat tyres were a frequent feature of life while out on patrol given the heavy wear and tear imposed on vehicles operating in the desert. (E 12357)

was in contrast far, far slower. The parallel lines of steep and often 90m-high dunes, normally running north to south, presented formidable obstacles, as well as posing deadly hazards to the unwary. As Michael Chrichton-Stuart described: 'The smooth rollers were called "whaleback" dunes. Where they rose to break into a sharp, twisting crest they were impassable. "Razorbacks" were the danger, presenting an innocent front which dropped like a cliff on the far side.' A special technique was developed to cross them. As Bagnold later recalled: 'To get a heavy truck up 200 or 300ft of soft sand at a slope of one in three you have to charge it very fast. But it takes a lot of confidence to charge at full speed into what looks like a vertical wall of dazzling yellow.' A well-driven fast-moving truck, with desert tyres partially deflated to improve traction, normally had little difficulty in reaching the top of a dune. It would then stop and its crew carefully select a route across the intervening trough and a good place to charge up the next dune.

The danger of heavily laden LRDG vehicles getting trapped in the embrace of soft sand was ever present. It was a predicament, however, that by dint of training and experience LRDG patrolmen were always well prepared. A first step was always to identify a patch of nearby hard ground capable of supporting a heavily laden truck. A vehicle was 'unstuck' using tried and tested methods: partially deflating sand tires to improve traction, digging troughs between the front and rear wheels into which a 1.8m perforated steel sand channel was laid with its rearmost ends almost underneath the rear tyre and laying a canvas and slatted wood sand mat in front of each of the front wheels. A driver would carefully release the clutch and the car would move forwards using the sand channels and mats for traction. By the time the rear tyres reached the end of the channels

D **FREEING A BOGGED-DOWN TRUCK**

LRDG patrols travelled vast distances across the inner Libyan Desert carrying out reconnaissance missions, surveillance work, taxiing other units, and carrying out raids between 1940 and 1943. The 'going' in large parts of the inner desert often proved a greater enemy than Axis forces or the climate by restricting progress to particular areas, causing serious delays or often badly damaging vehicles. A major task for LRDG officers and highly skilled drivers was carefully spying out the terrain ahead to find routes passable to heavily loaded vehicles. Despite their best efforts to spot areas of bad going, frequent halts were often required to free vehicles trapped in soft sand or mud or hung up on rocks. Damage caused by such incidents frequently required lengthy halts, moreover, so that a REME fitter, part of each patrol, and drivers could do running repairs. Halts caused by bad going were an extremely common feature of desert travel, with many often required during the course of a single day to extricate vehicles despite the efforts of patrol vehicles to find a practicable route. Fortunately specialist equipment had been devised by Bagnold and his peers during pre-war desert explorations to assist in extricating vehicles.

This illustration shows the crew of a badly bogged-down Ford F30 struggling to free the vehicle from the sand's embrace. Freeing a vehicle from the desert sand was often a very hot, time-consuming, arduous and generally unpleasant process as patrolmen dug away sand in front of each tyre, laid sand channels in front of the rear wheels and laid sand mats in front of the front wheels to give greater purchase when the truck was restarted and the engine gunned into life. Quite often the entire contents of a heavily laden vehicle had to be unloaded and piled to one side by the unfortunate hot, sweating and struggling crew.

it normally had enough speed and momentum to carry it forward hopefully until it reached firm ground. A good push by hot, sweating and increasingly exhausted crew members was also normally essential to provide further momentum. If badly bogged the entire cargo had to be unloaded and then reloaded once a truck was free. 'Unsticking' was always backbreaking and exhausting work, especially on hot days when the steel channels would be almost too hot to handle. This process often had to be repeated again and again. As one soldier recalled: 'Occasionally in particularly bad going could we could look back a couple of miles at suppertime and see the ration tins at the spot where we had breakfast before setting out in the morning!'

The progress of an LRDG patrol halted when the sun neared its zenith, as the short shadow it cast on the sun compass made accurate navigation impossible. Driving became difficult, moreover, since the absence of shadows meant undulations in the ground or patches of soft sand were difficult to spot. The vehicles would halt dispersed as far apart as possible, and patrolmen sheltered from the burning sun and glare under a vehicle. The majority of patrolmen would lie as still as possible to conserve energy or else talked quietly. Lunch was eaten cold and normally consisted of biscuits spread with various types of spread, cheese, oatmeal cake or oatmeal and date biscuits. A further pint of water was issued to each man, which was slowly sipped to replace water lost by sweating. Although not always possible, the wireless operator normally listened in for signals from LRDG HQ at a scheduled time.

The patrol resumed travel in the mid-afternoon as soon as a sun compass could be used again, and as the temperature slowly dropped life once again became bearable. An LRDG patrol normally travelled on for as long as light remained to maximize the distance it covered each day.

The LRDG followed an established routine for making camp each night. A suitable site was carefully selected by a patrol commander towards sunset, looking for low ground that shielded fires and lights from view, provided a camouflage background, offered easy concealment of tracks and provided defence against a ground attack. Ideally a drift of sand provided material for cleaning cooking utensils, to 'wash' with and a soft bed at night. The wireless truck formed a central hub around which the other vehicles halted, with the pilot car and on the other side and the cook's truck parked nearby.

Two LRDG patrolmen lay sand mats In front of an LRDG Chevrolet 30cwt truck crossing an area of soft sand, 25 May 1942. Along with steel sand channels these were essential items of LRDG equipment and were used repeatedly on patrol to 'unstick' bogged down vehicles. (E 12396)

The limited shade underneath LRDG vehicles often provided the only escape from the burning desert sun at midday halts. This stop was essential since the shadow cast by the sand compass was too short to provide an accurate reading needed for desert navigation. (HU 71344)

The remaining vehicles would take up a position in a rough circle with trucks facing out in different directions in case a quick getaway was needed

The initial halt was followed by a period of frenetic activity as patrol members carried out their pre-assigned duties. If fresh water was available, however, the first priority was always refilling receptacles in case a hasty departure was made. The cook immediately lit an open fire and 'brewed up'. The luxury of a blazing campfire for warmth each night, using surplus petrol-soaked wooden packing cases as fuel, was something LRDG patrols frequently enjoyed when operating deep in the desert. Alternatively a three-ring Primus stove or a smaller fire inside a four-gallon tin was used, into which two round two-gallon pots were lowered to cook food. Within 15 minutes each man had a refreshing mug of tea using the final pint of water allowed to each man per day. The evening ration of a tot of strong service rum, issued at the same time as the tea, was a highlight of the day for many patrolmen and an LRDG custom. Some men drank it in their tea while others had it neat. The Rhodesian patrol developed their own cocktail, rum mixed with Rose's Lime Juice, which was drunk either as a 'sundowner' or as an 'anti-*qibli* pick-me-up'. This custom was later adopted by other patrols. Following this welcome refreshment, the cook immediately prepared a hot supper, using as little water as possible, while other patrol members returned to their duties.

The care and maintenance of vehicles always occupied much time, with vehicle commanders having responsibility for keeping them desert-worthy. Drivers refilled tanks, checked the mileage of their charges, adjusted tyre pressures and checked petrol and oil consumption. Loads would also be carefully readjusted taking account of the amount of fuel, oil and rations consumed each day. Fitters assisted with any maintenance required. Gunners carefully cleaned all weapons of the sand and grit thrown up during a long day's drive, as well as checking the interior fittings of their truck.

The second-in-command of each patrol, who acted as a patrol quartermaster, carefully took stock each day of the remaining fuel, oil and supplies as reported by truck commanders, as well as overseeing vehicle maintenance as transport officer. Based on this daily check the patrol commander was informed how much farther a patrol could travel and for how many more days. Each evening (or after breakfast the next day depending on the patrol) a further two pints of water, for sipping next day, were measured out to each man again under close supervision.

The signaller manning the WT truck was always extremely busy, initially erecting the bulky Wyndham aerials. Messages to Group HQ had to be carefully enciphered before transmission, which itself often took considerable time owing to atmospheric effects.

The senior patrol navigator would also immediately complete his dead reckoning plot on the map. This would be checked against the readings taken independently by a second patrol navigator. The senior navigator then used a theodolite to take shots of two stars at an exact time, with a 'booker' standing beside him carefully noting down the details, before using his dead reckoning, the angle of the stars and aircraft navigation tables to plot the position of the patrol in the desert. This would be scrupulously checked by the second navigator and finally an exact position for the bivouac agreed.

Meanwhile, the remaining patrol members – apart from those on sentry duty – prepared beds for the night. Trucks would normally park side-on to the prevailing wind and in their lee three shallow coffin-like trenches were dug into the sand. A tarpaulin would be stretched out from the side of the vehicle and pinned to the ground using spare tyres to form both a wind-shelter and groundsheet. On top of this bedding rolls were laid out, providing sufficient warmth to counter the plunging temperature.

The patrol would eat the evening meal, normally a stew with or without curry powder, after completing their work. Occasionally official rations were supplemented by captured food or by what could be foraged from the

UNIFORM

The ordinary LRDG patrolman enjoyed great freedom when it came to what 'uniform' was worn whilst on patrol. With LRDG members coming from over 50 different units and several different British Commonwealth countries, a wide variety of headgear, uniform and equipment was the norm. Indeed, the only restrictions were those placed on them by individual patrol commanders keen to maintain the individual identity of his patrol. Much depended on the season and time of day when it came to what was worn, with temperatures normally plunging after nightfall. During the summer months many wore little more than a hat to keep off the sun, a pair of standard-issue KD shorts and leather *chaplis* in an attempt to remain cool in the blistering heat of the day. The glare off the desert sand was so intense, moreover, that goggles were normally worn. During the winter, conditions were normally much cooler during daylight hours with warmer headgear and heavier clothing the norm. At night men bundled up against the rising chill. This illustration shows a bearded LRDG patrolman on sentry duty in the early evening wearing a mixture of clothing to keep warm. A thick Tropal coat is worn over battledress along with a *keffiyeh* (Arab headdress). In the background two men wearing battledress prepare to take a star shoot. By the winter of 1942/43 most men wore either Royal Tank Regiment black berets, cap comforters or balaclavas while out on operations. Uniform then mainly consisted of battledress blouses and trousers, with either a Tropal coat or greatcoat worn on top, giving LRDG patrols some degree of uniformity they had often lacked before. Although sometimes worn on patrol for warmth, the distinctive LRDG *keffiyeh* was normally reserved for wearing at base or while on leave. The physical appearance of those on patrol rapidly deteriorated while in the desert. A strict embargo on the amount of water each day meant shaving and washing were largely impossible. By the end of a patrol most men sported unkempt beards, dirty faces and clothing that was heavily worn by the rigours of desert life.

surrounding area. For those not immediately retiring for a well-earned rest, the small receiving set carried by the WT truck was used to listen to the 8.00pm BBC news and popular shows such as *The Crazy Gang* and Tommy Handley's *ITMA*. Others read or played cards. Some patrol members with pressing work to complete on wayward vehicles or a signaller struggling with poor atmospheric conditions, however, laboured on well into the night before bedding down.

EXPERIENCE IN BATTLE

The LRDG and 'road watch'

The LRDG carried out a range of covert intelligence-gathering missions during the Desert War. What became known as 'road watch' was arguably the most daring, difficult and dangerous of these and has always been regarded as the most important. For many months LRDG patrols travelled deep behind enemy lines and covertly observed the main Axis lines of communication. From a camouflaged 'hide' located within 300m of chosen roads, patrolmen carefully noted down the number and details of every Axis tank, lorry and other vehicle travelling to and from the front line. This information was quickly relayed to GHQ ME. It was a specialized mission very specific to the Desert War, and possible only because the Axis forces were dependent on a very limited number of deep-water ports – Tripoli and to a far lesser extent Benghazi – for offloading tanks, reinforcements, petrol and supplies. These were transported in turn along the only metalled road – the Via Balbia – to frontline units. By far the most successful and longest road watch was that carried out on the Tripoli–Benghazi road. From 2 March to 21 July 1942 and 30 October to 29 December 1942 this route was kept under near-continuous observation by LRDG patrols.

The intelligence-gathering potential of covertly observing the Axis lines of communication, as a means of assessing enemy strengths, intentions and general conditions, became apparent to senior LRDG officers early in the Desert War. It was a task that fitted the LRDG's capabilities perfectly given its

ability to penetrate deep behind enemy lines using the inner desert as a route to and from a suitable observation post (OP) and communicate back information over long distances by radio. The LRDG, moreover, was capable of doing what aerial reconnaissance could not – provide intelligence of considerable accuracy, detail and timeliness unaffected by weather conditions. A search for a suitable vantage point overlooking the Via Balbia began during a reconnaissance mission in July–August 1941 in the Sirte Desert, carried out by T Patrol. With typical thoroughness Bill Kennedy Shaw, the LRDG's intelligence officer, identified and made careful notes about an upland area offering suitable vantage points and good cover lying just to the south of the Via Balbia 56km west of El Agheila near Ras Lanuf. It was near an imposing triumphal arch called the Arae Philaenorum, which straddled the Via Balbia at the boundary point between Tripolitania and Cyrenaica. This striking edifice, visible for miles, was quickly dubbed 'Marble Arch' by British soldiers, given its resemblance to a similar edifice at Park Lane in London. This position also had a suitable place to conceal patrol vehicles nearby – an area of scrub in a shallow wadi bed running from the low hills towards the coast, located 4km from the road and 8km from Marble Arch. The broken terrain also provided good cover for vehicles approaching and leaving the position.

The LRDG began its first trial traffic census in September 1941 when S2 Patrol, commanded by Second Lieutenant John Olivey, carefully reconnoitred the coast road westwards of El Agheila. A census of road traffic was carefully taken by his Rhodesians between 18 and 25 September 1941 from atop a low hill, despite the surveillance party being discovered by some wandering Arabs, enemy convoys camping overnight near the hidden observers on two occasions and the patrol harbour nearly being spotted by a reconnaissance aircraft. During the 168 hours S2 Patrol spent watching the road it noted, for example, that 1,218 lorries, 131 military and civil cars, 111 DR motorcycles and 556 motorcycles and motorcycle combinations belonging to German fighting units had travelled eastbound. A smaller number travelled westbound: 764 lorries, 59 military and civilian cars and 13 motorcycles. Some 30 four-wheeled armoured cars, 27 tanks and 44 guns had also travelled eastbound.

The sheer immensity of desert wastes through which the LRDG patrolled in itself provided considerable protection from enemy attack, except when patrols operated near the coastal plateau. (E 12385)

This valuable experience and the quality of the intelligence collected taught Lt. Col. Prendergast and his intelligence officer much about the limitations of LRDG observers, especially that they lacked training to recognize specific types of enemy AFV and lorry. Further experience helped refine methods of noting down information. A further reconnaissance of the coast road between 9 and 16 October 1941 was carried out by a party of S Patrol, on orders from GHQ ME, using the same location. On this occasion, during daylight hours the observers occupied a shallow sand pit 500m south of the road to get more accurate information, in addition to maintaining a continuous watch from a hill 3km away. A detailed questionnaire provided by GHQ ME asked for specific details about the construction of AFVs, artillery and trailers. It also asked about the nature of any convoys seen and about the types of headgear worn by enemy troops. As a result, the traffic census compiled by Captain Holliman was far more detailed than that done before, carefully cataloguing the different types of vehicle, as well as describing

Lieutenant-Colonel Guy Prendergast, Maj. Bill Kennedy Shaw (the intelligence officer) and another member of the LRDG enjoy a meal at the command post. (HU25097)

 ROAD WATCH

'Road watch' was a vital task carried out by the LRDG and arguably the most significant of its intelligence-gathering duties during the Desert War. Patrols were regularly tasked with observing Axis road traffic using the Via Balbia (and other routes) around the clock up to 965km behind enemy lines and recording the details over long periods of time for onward transmission to Cairo. In effect a 'census' was taken of different types of vehicles, condition and their loads. LRDG patrolmen became highly skilled at identifying AFVs, different types of vehicles and what they carried. Normally, detached parties of two men spent 24 hours lying up within a few hundred metres of a road at a suitable carefully camouflaged vantage point before being relieved by other men and returning to a nearby bivouac where the rest of the patrol was laid up. This illustration shows two LRDG patrolmen lying doggo behind cover observing an Axis supply convoy. Both are heavily clothed against the chill of a winter's day, with one wearing a Tropal coat and the other a shaggy, rather grubby and unkempt Hebron goatskin jacket over battledress. Road watch often entailed considerable hardship since those on surveillance duty had to lie without moving in the fierce heat or cold for fear of alerting the enemy to their presence. It required a strong nerve, moreover, with Axis troops in such close proximity. On occasion wandering Arabs compromised LRDG observers, while the danger of Axis troops suddenly moving off the road to camp or rest nearby was a constant concern.

A bearded LRDG patrolman, wearing a woollen cap comforter, sits at the wheel of his truck. The decision about what was worn on patrol was always left to individual LRDG patrolmen, with comfort being the key. (CBM 1212)

every group of vehicles spotted giving its direction, the date and time when it was seen and whether troops or loads were being transported.

The value of road watch as an intelligence-gathering tool had been clearly established and the fact that the LRDG evaded detection was judged particularly remarkable. The intelligence staff at GHQ ME was not slow to take advantage of this new source of information. Indeed, the need for reliable, accurate and timely intelligence about Axis strengths and intentions was pressing in January 1942 when Rommel launched a devastating counterstroke against 8th Army and surged forwards to the Gazala Line.

Those LRDG patrols committed to road watch during early 1942 were far better prepared for this highly specialized task than their predecessors, with specific training and other preparations carried out to improve the accuracy of information provided by surveillance teams. Before each mission LRDG patrolmen were given recognition pamphlets and detailed photographs of different types of Axis vehicle. Visits were carried out to collections of captured Axis motor transport. To improve record taking, GHQ provided a detailed memorandum and album of photographs, along with Captain Enoch Powell (a university professor of such evident learning that he became known as 'Grey Matter' to patrolmen) to explain them. A mimeographed notebook given to each patrol listed technical designations, model numbers and had silhouettes of differing types of Axis vehicle. To improve record taking it also contained blank pages for listing numbers and types of enemy units, types of cargo and any information about special vehicle markings. These changes enabled LRDG patrolmen to give a far better running score of the type and volume of traffic heading eastwards towards the front, as well as westward-bound returning traffic.

The LRDG patrols carrying out road-watch duties at Marble Arch followed a set routine. Each patrol did a stint of ten to 14 days on duty given the acknowledged boredom, monotony and mental strain it always involved. An incoming LRDG patrol would be met at a rendezvous point far from the actual bivouac area, into which it was then carefully guided. When a patrol arrived its first task was to carefully conceal its vehicles from view from the air and ground, using scrim nets and interwoven foliage in the wadi bed. All tyre tracks visible from the air were carefully brushed away by hand. Overnight patrol commanders formally handed over while the first pair of new observers plus an additional member of the incoming patrol were taken to the OP by a guide. This guide then returned to the bivouac area along with the additional patrolman, who had now seen the hide and the route to it in both directions and thus could safely guide his own surveillance teams into position.

The observation of the road was always carried out by a two-man team that spent 24 hours on duty. Each team was normally woken at 0330hrs by a sentry. Following a hot cup of tea and a bite of food under cover of darkness they walked 3km down to the plain, carrying all the equipment, food and water required for the day. Before dawn the two men relieved those on duty and occupied a camouflaged hide, a shallow pit with overhead cover just high enough to remain hidden from view and provide some shade from the sun for men lying flat on their stomachs, where they remained for the rest of the day.

It was located 300m from the road on the plain in an area largely devoid of cover apart from some scattered scrub and Spinafex tufts. Road traffic could be observed through a small slit using binoculars or a telescope. Other patrolmen selected their own vantage point overlooking the road, however, believing that discovery in a carefully constructed hide might compromise their cover story of being lost in the desert. Apart from rolling over onto their backs, the danger of being spotted by traffic moving on the road or wandering Arabs meant movement by the observation team was impossible until darkness fell. A combination of this inability to move, blowing sand, intense heat during the summer or cold during the winter months made it an extremely testing and tiring experience. Time always dragged. The two men tasked with identifying and noting down Axis road traffic could not relax, except for a few brief periods when traffic on the road was marked by its absence. As David Lloyd Owen has described: 'It was an exacting task, for we were expected to give the details of every tank, the calibre of every gun, the classification of every vehicle, the number of troops or tonnage of stores in them and whether the truck was covered or uncovered, German or Italian, as well as the actual number of vehicles that went past our hiding place.' To provide details of divisional signs and unit designations patrolmen carefully approached to within 30–40m of the road when darkness fell.

Road watch was always extremely hazardous for the men on duty. Apart from being spotted by traffic using the roads or by parties of workmen, Axis convoys might at any time move off-road for a meal or to bivouac nearby. As one report noted: 'Reports on the day are accurate up to 1230hrs. From then onwards until darkness the road pickets were unable to look up or move … as a convoy pulled in behind with the nearest vehicle at 150 yards.' The LRDG observers, moreover, might at any time be compromised by bands of nomadic Bedouin grazing their flocks. A real danger of being betrayed to Axis troops always existed since the inhabitants of Tripolitania often proved unfriendly. On one occasion, for example, an Arab tried to extract a bribe to keep quiet. On another occasion a bus full of children pulled off the road and played a game of rounders around the hide. If capture appeared likely each surveillance detachment was briefed to bury its notebook or else

LRDG patrolmen were highly skilled at building camouflaged hides to conceal their positions while carrying out covert road-watch duties deep behind Axis lines. (HU 24993)

tear up the pages. Indeed, in recognition that effective resistance was impossible without prejudicing the safety of the remainder of the patrol, some went unarmed and equipped with a carefully prepared cover story about being the lost survivors of an overrun British unit. If this ruse was successful the remainder of the patrol could then simply relocate its surveillance post.

The two-man road-watch team remained at their post until relieved at dawn the next day. While they enjoyed breakfast followed by a well-earned rest, the report they had carefully compiled was analysed by the patrol commander and compared with information gathered earlier. If a particularly important convoy or a concentration of Axis AFVs was spotted it was reported immediately by radio. If this was necessary the radio truck normally drove away from the bivouac area into the desert before transmitting to Group HQ in case an Axis radio-detection team operated nearby. Otherwise a longer and far more detailed report was sent when a patrol's stint of road watch had ended and it was en route to base. Immediately upon the return to base the patrol commander wrote up a detailed report complete with all traffic census information. Each patrol report normally ran into dozens of closely typed pages during busy periods on the roads, offering intelligence analysts at GHQ a rich fund of information for analysis.

Those patrolmen left in the hidden bivouac area always suffered badly from boredom, with a stint on picquet duty the only break from the monotony. The danger of being spotted from the air or by hostile Arabs meant movement around the wadi was strictly restricted and food was eaten cold as fires were forbidden. Apart from talking, playing cards, reading or listening to the radio, there was little to do apart from sleep or endure the heat under the shade provided by the camouflaged vehicles. To add to the discomfort, flies abounded in the wadi.

Road watch was always an extremely expensive commitment for the LRDG in terms of manpower keeping three complete patrols tied up at any one time. While one patrol carried out road-watch duties another was returning to base and a third was either en route or preparing to depart. The 965km

A column of LRDG vehicles in the Nile Valley while en route to Kufra, August 1942. The oasis at Kufra provided the LRDG with a vital base deep in the Libyan Desert, from where its patrols ranged across Cyrenaica and Tripolitania. (E 12376)

from Siwa to Marble Arch might take anything up to a week to cover depending on the route taken and the level of enemy activity.

The road watch carried out by LRDG patrolmen with such daring, boldness and skill was one of the great intelligence-gathering success stories of the Desert War. The simple fact that it was successfully maintained without interruption for such a long period was a tribute to the professionalism of the LRDG and its skill at covert intelligence gathering. Overall, the road watch provided a massive return on the investment of comparatively few officers, men and vehicles, although it was a heavy commitment given the small size of the LRDG and constant calls on its services. Ironically it was by far the most hated duty performed by the LRDG because of its monotony.

The road watch was regarded at the time and immediately after the war as of crucial importance in determining Axis strengths and general

An LRDG Chevrolet 30cwt truck belonging to T Patrol gets ready to leave Cairo, 25 May 1942. The bars, clubs and sights of this bustling city provided LRDG patrolmen with a welcome break from life in the desert. (E 2348)

intentions. The true significance of the intelligence gathered, however, can only be accurately gauged when compared with that garnered from other sources. What LRDG officers and most early historians of the desert war did not know was that the road watch played only a supporting role in GHQ Middle East's efforts to build up an accurate intelligence assessment of Axis forces. Indeed, the main purpose of the road watch was providing accurate empirical information that helped verify and assess intelligence obtained from Top Secret Y Service radio intercepts and ULTRA decrypts. Since the spring of 1940 British HQ had routinely intercepted and decrypted German high level radio traffic encoded through the use of the supposedly unbreakable Enigma code. As a result it enjoyed an enormous advantage conferred by having detailed knowledge of the composition, strength and location of Axis forces, as well as vital information about enemy intentions. This flow of high-level information was not without its limitations, however, and the trustworthy information provided by the LRDG helped counterbalance this information and accurately confirm how Axis forces would actually be employed at the tactical level. The road watch, moreover, offered continuity and certainty at times when signals intelligence was unreliable. Lastly, LRDG road watch teams also provided a perfect cover to which intelligence obtained from ULTRA could otherwise be attributed.

The raid on Barce, September 1942

The sharply deteriorating military situation in early autumn 1942 prompted GHQ ME to plan four ambitious raids deep behind enemy lines. Intended to disrupt Rommel's vulnerable ever-lengthening lines of communication, these included large-scale raids by commandos and the Special Air Service (SAS) respectively on the vital enemy supply ports of Benghazi and Tobruk, and also on Jalo Oasis four days later by the Sudan Defence Force. The LRDG provided guides for all these ambitious ventures, as well as carrying out a subsidiary diversionary raid – Operation *Caravan* – on its own on the Italian-held town and airfield at Barce in Gebel Akhdar in northern Cyrenaica. The key to all these disparate operations was surprise, careful coordination and detailed prior preparation and planning.

The LRDG raiding force chosen for the Barce raid consisted of the New Zealanders of T1 Patrol (led by Captain Nick Wilder) and the British guardsmen of G1 Patrol (led by Captain Alastair Timpson), under the overall command of Major Jake Easonsmith with assistance in gathering last-minute intelligence provided by Major Vladimir 'Popski' Peniakoff and two Senussi other ranks from the Libyan Arab Force. A small detachment from B Squadron's HQ also participated, including the medical officer, Captain Dick Lawson. To carry the 47 attackers the 1,860km from Faiyum in Egypt to the objective, 12 trucks and five jeeps were employed. Two 10-ton Mack NR trucks from the heavy section accompanied them to Ain Dalla to refill fuel tanks. Captain John Olivey's S2 Patrol travelled with them before departing on its own mission.

Operation *Caravan* began on 1 September when the raiding force left Faiyum in Egypt, beginning a 1,850km journey far to the south, and then across the Great and Kalansho Sand Seas before swinging northwards to the Gebel Akhdar. By autumn 1942 it was a well-trodden route. As always, desert travel proved hazardous. During the crossing of the Egyptian Sand Sea a jeep carrying Capt. Alastair Timpson and his driver shot over the blind side of a razorback dune and plunged downward a distance of 6m. The impact fractured the patrol commander's skull and knocked out several teeth. Guardsman Thomas Wann suffered a fractured spine that paralysed him from the waist downwards for life. Fortunately the LRDG's medical officer, Capt. Lawson, was at hand and after being transported to Big Cairn two days later they were evacuated by air to Egypt. Patrols G1 and T1, meanwhile, moved to Howard's Cairn where they rendezvoused with part of the heavy section loaded with additional fuel and stores. Captain Lawson hurriedly caught up with the main body and S2 Patrol departed on its own mission as part of Operation *Bigamy* at Benghazi.

The rest of the approach march to Barce passed largely without incident, with the column crossing the arch linking the Egyptian and Kalansho Sand Seas via Garet Khod and then the northern gravel plain. En route a 'spare' Chevrolet 30cwt truck, loaded with food, water and petrol, was hidden near Bir el Gerrari as an emergency rendezvous. Despite earlier delays the LRDG strike force reached Benia, 24km from Barce Township, by 13 September, the day scheduled for the attack, and Maj. Easonsmith transported Peniakoff and two Senussi tribesmen to within 3km of the outskirts for a brief

The successful raid on Barce was carried out by G and T patrols in September 1942 by a mixed force of Willys jeeps and Chevrolet trucks. Major Jake Easonsmith, leader of the raid, is sitting behind the wheel of the nearest jeep. (HU 16666)

The Barce Raid, September 1942

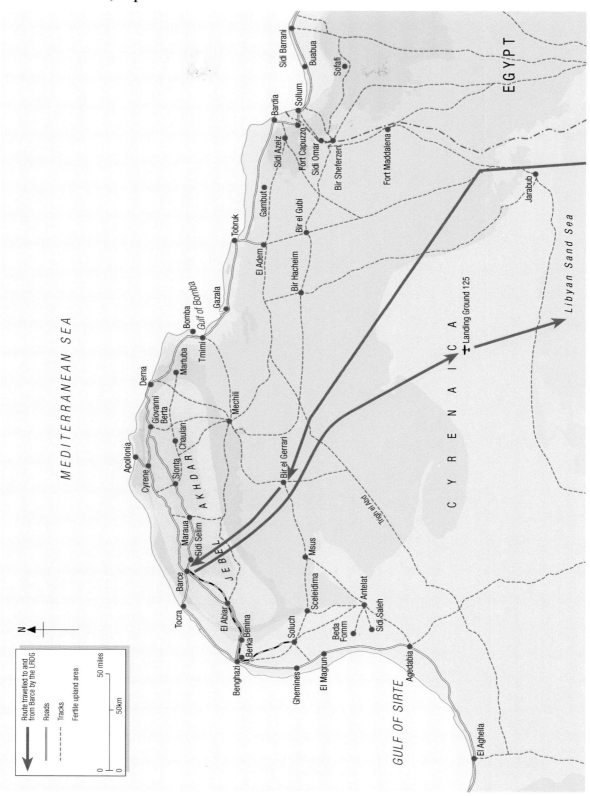

MEDITERRANEAN SEA

EGYPT

Sidi Barrani
Buabua
Sofafi
Sollum
Bardia
Sidi Azeiz
Fort Capuzzo
Sidi Omar
Bir Sheferzen
Fort Maddalena
Jarabub

Libyan Sand Sea

Gambut
Tobruk
El Adem
Bir el Gubi
Bir Hacheim
Gazala
Bomba
Gulf of Bomba
Martuba
Tmimi
Derna
Giovanni Berta
Chaulan
Mechili
Apollonia
Cyrene
Slonta
Bir el Gerrari
Maraua
Sidi Selim
J E B E L   A K H D A R
Barce
Tocra
El Abiar
Berka Benina
Benghazi
Soluch
Ghemines
El Magrun
Sceleidima
Msus
Antelat
Beda Fomm
Sidi Saleh
Agedabia
El Agheila

Landing Ground 125

C Y R E N A I C A

Trigh el Abd

GULF OF SIRTE

Legend

Route travelled to and from Barce by the LRDG
Roads
Tracks
Fertile upland area

N

0 ——— 50 miles
0 ——— 50km

51

reconnaissance. Unknown to the raiders, the LRDG column had already been spotted and nearby Italian units alerted by Barce Sector Command. Following a day spent in preparation, hidden amidst some olive trees and stunted pines, the two LRDG patrols set off as dusk gathered.

The LRDG column made steady progress towards its objective, after cutting nearby telephone lines, before encountering a police post at Sidi bu Raui. Trooper Mahomed Bu Masaud on duty outside the small post was quickly relieved of his rifle and bundled aboard one of the trucks. An NCO who investigated the noise was killed and Sergeant Dennis threw several grenades into the post before the convoy left, albeit leaving behind two damaged trucks that had collided in the darkness. An Italian machine gun, however, opened up shortly afterwards, though the column quickly silenced it. Clearly the element of surprise had been lost. Major Peniakoff rejoined them at Sidi Selim although both Arabs failed to appear. As planned, the valuable WT truck and medical officer were left behind to act as an emergency rendezvous.

The LRDG column, driving with headlights blazing in imitation of an Italian convoy, moved towards the town at approximately 2330hrs. A few miles outside Barce at the top of an escarpment two Italian light tanks were encountered parked on either side of the main road. Dazzled by the beams, however, neither of their sleepy crews realized that the enemy were upon them until each received a broadside from each LRDG truck as they passed unscathed between them.

Patrols T1 and G1 separated at midnight at a fork in the road immediately outside Barce: T1 Patrol went to the left to attack the airfield and G1 Patrol, now commanded by Sgt. Dennis, went straight on to the Campo Maddalena barracks to neutralize its occupants, cut telephone lines and then damage the railway station. Two hours were allocated for each task. Independently, Maj. Easonsmith drove into the centre of the town with two heavily armed Willys jeeps.

The attack on Barce airfield proved a resounding success. A gate barring entry was quickly opened and T Patrol, consisting of a Willys jeep and four 30cwt Chevrolet trucks, drove into the base. A fuel dump, petrol tanker and trailer were set alight and the resulting flames belched unchecked, illuminating the surrounding area. Several hand grenades were thrown into a nearby building. The LRDG vehicles, moving in single file, then drove around the airfield firing mixed tracer and ball ammunition from their machine guns at parked aircraft. To ensure complete destruction, a corporal in the last vehicle planted incendiary time bombs on any aircraft not already engulfed in flame. An hour later a delighted T1 Patrol finally withdrew, having destroyed or damaged 35 enemy aircraft without suffering a single casualty. Success was largely due to the overwhelming firepower produced by T1 Patrol's massed machine guns and the gunners' skill.

Elsewhere, the situation was also highly encouraging. With Sgt. Dennis at its head, G1 Patrol entered Barce, where it quickly pulled down some telephone lines and killed two Italian sentries. Noise from the airfield, however, had already alerted the barracks. A small group of Italians standing outside on the low veranda were showered with grenades and then intense Vickers K and 20mm Breda gunfire was pumped into the building's interior. Some return fire was experienced from several Italian soldiers who had leapt into nearby slit trenches. A lull in the firing, a shortage of grenades and the clear success of the airfield attack convinced Sgt. Dennis that it was time to

withdraw. Two Italian L3 light tanks blocking the only exit from the barracks, however, caused a sudden rethink. Following a brief game of 'cat and mouse' with an Italian L3, a gap was found in the perimeter wall. Although the escaping guardsmen successfully crossed an anti-tank ditch barring the way, a jeep was lost in the process. A truck also became separated from the main body in the confusion. This badly damaged vehicle did not get far, although the four-man crew escaped on foot. Two men were eventually rescued, another was captured and the final patrolman found shelter with friendly Bedouin. The main body of the patrol then withdrew as planned to Sidi Selim.

The Italian reaction to the LRDG raid slowly gathered strength, intensity and momentum. With his ammunition supply dwindling Capt. Wilder decided to withdraw T1 Patrol from the airfield. As it withdrew through the town, four L3 light tanks were encountered firing up and down the main streets. By driving at full tilt an Italian light tank was rammed out of the way by Capt. Wilder's 30cwt truck, although it was wrecked as it cannoned into another. This manoeuvre had the desired effect, however, of clearing the way for the vehicles behind. Following further attempts to destroy the tanks by throwing grenades under them, Capt. Wilder and his crew quickly boarded a jeep. While moving at great speed Capt. Wilder's Willys jeep overturned, pinning its unconscious or wounded occupants underneath. The crew of the following Chevrolet quickly disentangled them from the wreckage and revived them before they reached the rendezvous. The rammed Italian tank was immobilized by the crew of another truck, meanwhile, who jumped upon it and put it out of action using grenades. Unfortunately, grenade fragments injured a New Zealand patrolman before the truck finally made good its escape. The last LRDG truck was cut off by an Italian Autoblinda 41 armoured car and set on fire as it raced along the streets, and it eventually crashed into a concrete roadside shelter. The gunner and two other injured crew members were taken prisoner. Although the driver initially escaped, he was later captured.

Major Easonsmith led his two jeeps into Barce to cause as much chaos and confusion as possible by attacking targets of opportunity. Fortunately, they avoided two Italian light tanks and threw grenades at Italian troops and into various occupied buildings. Ten parked lorries and a tanker and trailer

ABOVE LEFT
An LRDG truck armed with a .55in. Boys anti-tank rifle and a Mk 1 Lewis Gun drives carefully down a sandy hill. These weapons were issued early during the Desert War and were later replaced by other automatic weapons. (E 2298)

ABOVE
An LRDG patrolman poses with a single gas-operated Vickers K machine gun mounted in the cab of a Chevrolet 30cwt truck. These fearsome weapons, originally salvaged from wrecked RAF aircraft, produced a massive volume of firepower. (E 12410)

were destroyed by machine-gun fire. Major Easonsmith then rejoined the rest of the withdrawing raiding force.

The LRDG strike force – now with only three jeeps and seven Chevrolet trucks – rendezvoused at the crossroad as planned, before withdrawing down the main road and then southwards towards the rallying point at Sidi Selim. However, G Patrol's top-heavy 20mm Breda truck toppled over suddenly in the darkness, and it was not until just before dawn that it was righted and the column picked up the medical officer and wireless truck at Sidi Selim. Much valuable time and the hours of darkness had been lost. Just before dawn, as they reached Peniakoff's original drop-off point, they were ambushed by approximately 150–180 Tripolitanian infantrymen belonging to the 7th Savari Cavalry. Although a truck was damaged and three men were wounded, the Italian attack was poorly handled and Sgt. Dennis kept the advancing enemy at bay in his jeep until the truck's damaged wheel was changed. The LRDG successfully ran the gauntlet without further loss. After reaching the police post the two other trucks abandoned during the approach march were taken in tow.

The LRDG column was given little respite when it briefly halted to brew up, treat the wounded and repair the three vehicles in tow. A group of mounted Tripolitanian cavalry suddenly appeared out of the darkness, followed soon afterwards by infantry, while overhead two CR.42 Falco fighter-bombers appeared. Major Easonsmith successfully drove off an impromptu ground attack by charging the enemy aboard a Willys jeep. This act of bravery bought sufficient time for stores to be offloaded, time bombs to be placed aboard the three damaged vehicles and for the LRDG to break contact.

The escaping LRDG vehicles were spotted by a Ca311 reconnaissance aircraft, however, after G Patrol's wireless truck broke down on an exposed hillside. At 1030hrs six CR.42 fighter-bombers appeared overhead just after the LRDG had hidden its remaining vehicles under thick low-branched trees. From mid-morning until dusk relays of fighter-bombers attacked, who picked

G **'BEAT-UPS'**

LRDG patrols carried out 'beat-ups' or raids comparatively infrequently when compared with their other duties of reconnaissance, surveillance and intelligence gathering. They took many forms: hit-and-run attacks on Axis lines of communication, airfields, other base installations, isolated outposts and transport, with the LRDG ruthlessly exploiting surprise and the firepower and mobility of their heavily armed trucks to wreak havoc and then disappear into the vastness of the desert. In this image a representative LRDG patrol attacks a small convoy utilizing surprise and the devastating firepower produced by its vehicle-mounted automatic weapons to inflict as much damage and demoralization as possible. A heavily loaded 20mm Breda Gun truck brings up the rear of the column. On other occasions patrols set up ambushes or laid mines on key routes to disrupt road traffic. LRDG patrols also participated in several large-scale raids, most notably at Murzuk and later at Barce in September 1942. For some time a close 'raiding partnership' was struck up between the LRDG and the newly formed Special Air Service, with the former navigating and transporting the latter to their objectives deep behind enemy lines. For many patrolmen such direct action was a welcome break and fillip to morale from the normal monotony and boredom associated with LRDG patrols.

The majority of these very small-scale raids against Axis troops were undertaken in direct support of 8th Army (or its predecessors). During Operation *Crusader* for example, LRDG patrols operated offensively against Axis supply convoys supporting the main battle. Such 'acts of piracy' and 'freebooting' often had an impact far out of proportion to their size, causing the diversion of enemy troops to rear areas, but carried with them the serious risk of losing valuable and very difficult-to-replace LRDG personnel and vehicles during attacks or the inevitable Axis reaction. The growing strength and mobility of the SAS ultimately meant that the LRDG carried out fewer and fewer of these direct actions, largely incompatible with their primary role, and concentrated instead on surveillance and intelligence gathering.

off LRDG vehicles one by one and then strafed patrolmen hiding nearby. Everything that could be saved was removed from the burning vehicles in the 20-minute gap between air attacks. By last light only two jeeps and two trucks remained desert-worthy. When it appeared the Italians had finally departed, salvaged food and water were loaded aboard T1 Patrol's wireless truck, but unfortunately shortly afterwards two aircraft unexpectedly returned and left it a burning wreck. It had been an extremely difficult day for the raiding force. During the attacks Capt. Wilder was shot through both legs and another guardsman injured, increasing the number of wounded men to six. No radio remained intact to call for help.

Major Easonsmith and his men faced a daunting task in making good their escape, but he was convinced Prendergast would realize something was amiss and dispatch a patrol to his aid. As soon as darkness fell the 33 exhausted surviving LRDG patrolmen departed southwards towards Bir el Gerrari. Only two jeeps and one Chevrolet, loaded with the wounded and everything salvageable, remained serviceable to make the 1,125km journey to Kufra. Food and water were in short supply. The plight of the wounded together with the need to make a smaller target in case of air attack convinced Maj. Easonsmith that the party should separate. A jeep carrying Capt. Lawson and Maj. Peniakoff and the remaining truck loaded with the wounded departed southwards. The remainder of the party – 14 men and one jeep loaded with stores – plodded onwards to the same objective independently.

The walking party led by Maj. Easonsmith steadily trudged southwards. Unfortunately, during the first night it separated into two parties and a New Zealand medical orderly went missing. A combination of the intense heat and a shortage of water made life extremely trying, and many men, used to travelling in vehicles, suffered badly from sore feet. On 15 September they encountered an Arab encampment where a lamb was purchased. Although no water could be spared enough milk was drunk to revitalize the patrol long enough until a well was found the following day. Early on the morning of 17 September, following a footsore march of 130km, Maj. Easonsmith, Sgt. Dennis and four guardsmen met S2 Patrol returning from Operation *Bigamy*. The encounter occurred purely by chance. The patrol immediately travelled to Bir el Gerrari, but no sign was found of the other walking party. Leaving Maj. Easonsmith behind with vehicles to search for his remaining stragglers, three trucks carried the survivors of the Barce raid to Kufra.

The second walking party led by Trooper Jopling, a navigator, made its own way towards Bir El Gerrari. With only a silk escape map, a dim memory of what had been seen on a larger map and the stars, navigation was a constant problem for the badly wounded trooper. A chance encounter with some Bedouins secured some water, and more water and food was found the following day. The party plodded slowly onwards despite the burning heat and growing exhaustion. Jopling's leg wound, however, meant that he and another exhausted guardsman lagged behind. On 19 September Maj. Easonsmith and S2 Patrol found three guardsmen near Bir El Gerrari and five more were located shortly afterwards. Jopling and Gutteridge, however, were in acute difficulty. A combination of his now-gangrenous foot, a lack of water and the belief that they were too late to make the rendezvous finally convinced Jopling and his companion to stop. Both men entered an Arab encampment whose occupants handed them over the Italians.

Major Easonsmith's determination to keep searching for survivors paid off, when two of the missing guardsmen from the G Patrol truck lost in Barce

were picked up near Bir el Gerrari. On 21 September, however, the search for remaining walkers was finally abandoned.

The poor terrain initially meant that the vehicle party led by the medical officer made slow progress. A bullet hole through the jeep's radiator led to its abandonment since water could not be spared. As soon as level terrain was reached the heavily overloaded truck drew away. The broken terrain and darkness, however, made driving extremely hazardous. When the vehicle left the Gebel Akhdar on 15 September it made rapid progress over the gravel plain. At 1600hrs Capt. Lawson reached Bir el Gerrrari where he collected food, water and a spare tyre from the hidden truck before continuing onwards to an emergency landing strip (LG 125) near the Kalansho Sand Sea that had often been used as a rallying point and where it was hoped they would encounter an LRDG patrol. Without a working theodolite or radio the party relied on dead reckoning alone to find the landing strip. Luck was with them. On 17 September Capt. Lawson bumped into Capt. Owen's Y1 Patrol, who had been directed there by LRDG HQ after being alerted to Lawson's plans by Maj. Easonsmith, who had been picked up earlier that day. On 18 September the wounded were evacuated to Kufra by a Bristol Bombay transport aircraft.

Unlike the failed raids carried out on Benghazi, Tobruk and Jalo, the Barce raid was a complete success, inflicting considerable material and psychological damage on the Italian defenders, who paid a heavy price for their complacency. Although Italian and LRDG accounts differ about the exact number, an impressive number of aircraft were destroyed on the ground. Whether the raid had successfully diverted Italian troops away from the other objectives targeted for raids that night, however, is more difficult to ascertain. Even so, the Barce raid was a considerable feat of arms for the LRDG and was its most successful 'beat-up' of the Desert War. As Brendan Carroll has observed: 'The operation encompassed all the elements common to the success of other LRDG operations: overcoming the difficulties

An LRDG truck moves back through Gebel Akhdar following the Barce raid in September 1942. This well-watered area had farmland and a comparatively large population. (HU 71335)

of desert travel, good navigation, independent action, fortitude, evasion and survival against the odds. Typically the role of the LRDG had been like that of the scorpion: to hide, watch and wait. This time they were out in the open and able to fully demonstrate the devastating sting in their tail.'

For their gallantry during the Barce raid and the ensuing withdrawal Maj. Easonsmith and Capt. Wilder were both awarded the Distinguished Service Order, Capt. Lawson the Military Cross and three New Zealanders from T1 Patrol were given the Military Medal. The Barce raid was not, however, without cost, with eight patrolmen wounded in action, three injured and 11 others taken prisoner. Although no fatalities were suffered, considerable hardship was experienced by the wounded during the long march home.

AFTERMATH

The LRDG without doubt had fought a very successful Desert War. It had been almost constantly in the field – only 15 days passed without a patrol operating behind or on the flanks of the enemy between 26 December 1940 and 10 April 1943 – fully exploiting its unchallenged mastery of the inner Libyan Desert.

The greatest contribution it, and to a lesser degree its offshoot the ILRS, had made to victory was without doubt in terms of deep reconnaissance and intelligence gathering, including the road watch, in which it excelled. This unique special force provided a flow of unrivalled accurate, timely and reliable tactical and topographical intelligence. This information greatly aided staff planning at GHQ ME and directly contributed to the course and ultimately successful conduct of the hard-fought main battle. The topographical intelligence the LRDG provided, impossible to secure by any other means, was alone of extreme importance and arguably justified the existence of the unit.

The precise contribution made by intelligence provided by the LRDG is difficult to quantify, however, since this was not the only source of information upon which GHQ ME relied, and also until the apparatus for collecting and disseminating detailed, accurate and timely intelligence had been surmounted at GHQ ME it was not always fully exploited. Albeit always important, the significance of the information provided by road watch, for example, must be re-evaluated in light of the quality and quantity of information provided by ULTRA. Undoubtedly it was not as decisive as some commentators, writing before the existence of ULTRA was known, have claimed. The intelligence provided by the LRDG was used primarily to verify information obtained from ULTRA, although the intelligence provided by road-watch teams had some clear advantages in terms of continuity, certainty and reliability, especially at times when signals intelligence was incomplete and unpredictable.

The value of the information the LRDG provided in the final analysis far, far outstripped the physical damage inflicted by 'beat-ups' carried out by the LRDG alone, apart from the difficult-to-quantify diversion of enemy troops, vehicles and aircraft to protect rear areas. It had undoubtedly been worthwhile in 1940, by spreading alarm and diverting Italian forces away from the main battle, especially during Operation *Compass*. However, although offensive operations were dramatic and the tangible destruction of enemy vehicles and troops undoubtedly provided a 'tonic' to jaded LRDG patrolmen, the actual damage inflicted between 1941 and 1943 was always minimal. A question mark remains in final analysis regarding whether

Members of Y Patrol read mail from home at Siwa Oasis in May 1942. Letters from home nearly always provided a boost to morale. (CBM 2219)

'beat-ups' justified the risk to and actual losses to the highly trained LRDG men and specialist vehicles they often entailed.

The LRDG also played an important role in path-finding for conventional formations and other units, as well as transporting various special forces to and from their objectives. This was a direct corollary of its acknowledged skill at desert navigation and travel. Without the LRDG's assistance in this respect and general guidance the SAS would undoubtedly have struggled to find its feet. Most notable was the final LRDG contribution to the Desert War as part of Operation *Pugilist*, when a small detachment from T2 Patrol guided the New Zealand Corps to victory.

The LRDG's successes were ultimately very much down to the young, fit and enthusiastic 'ordinary' patrolmen – officers, NCOs and men – that filled its ranks. These specially selected and courageous patrolmen willingly withstood protracted and extreme hardship, adapted to living, moving and fighting deep in the Libyan Desert and accepted without demur all the perils near-constant behind-the-lines work entailed. While individually the death of each patrolman was a tragic loss, overall the unit paid a remarkably low price in casualties during the Desert War. Nearly a third of its men won honours and awards during this time, giving testimony to the bravery and skill with which the LRDG had carried out its challenging mission.

World War II was far from over for the LRDG, with a new role found in southern Europe and the Balkans by mid-summer. As David Lloyd Owen later summed up: 'Our role was recce, shipping and aircraft reporting, and communications and liaison with partisans.' During the summer of 1943 the LRDG reorganized, re-equipped and retrained in Lebanon on the basis it would deploy small patrols (one officer and ten men) primarily operating on foot capable of operating and maintaining communications 160km behind enemy lines. Before completing its training, the LRDG was committed in September 1943 as part of the ill-conceived Aegean campaign. Fighting in an infantry role the LRDG lost heavily. During the course of a single operation on the island of Levita on 24 October 1943, for example, the LRDG lost more men – two officers and 39 men – than it had during the entire Desert War. Worse followed on Leros where many highly experienced and irreplaceable old 'desert hands' were either killed in action, posted missing or captured when in November 1943 the Germans seized the island.

The resurrected LRDG took to the field again on 16 May 1944, although by then it was a very different unit. For the rest of the war it carried out a series of long-range reconnaissance missions in Italy, Yugoslavia, Albania and Greece demonstrating its continued effectiveness at behind-the-lines operations.

The LRDG did not outlive the end of hostilities in Europe. Although its transfer to the Far East had been mooted, in June 1945 the War Office informed its CO that it was surplus to requirements. Although this news shocked many LRDG veterans, it was largely unsurprising. As David Lloyd Owen recorded in his personal diary: 'There is perhaps some consolation in feeling that we are going out on the crest of a wave when our star could not have been brighter.' Without further fanfare, on 1 August 1945 – five years and 14 days after it had been formed in Cairo – the LRDG officially disbanded.

The ILRS lingered on for a while, although it had fared far less well than its 'parent' unit following the end of the North African campaign. In mid-1943 it had returned to India hoping it would serve in Burma. Instead, the ILRS spent the rest of the war in Baluchistan and East Persia reconnoitring routes, performing escort duties and patrolling the Persian–

Afghan border to discourage Soviet infiltration. In 1947 this direct offshoot of the LRDG was also disbanded.

An LRDG patrol crosses the sand sea on the return journey from Tobruk. (HU 24989 LRDG Collection)

The LRDG has left an enduring legacy in terms of its guiding principles, tactical methods and sheer professionalism. As Julian Thompson has written: 'Theirs was a yardstick by which one should gauge those [special forces] that came after them.' Undoubtedly its early successes acted as a fillip to the formation of the other special forces in British service, most notably the SAS with whom the LRDG established a close bond. Indeed, it remains a role model and inspiration for the modern-day British SAS and similar special forces as a covert long-range reconnaissance and surveillance unit capable of operating deep in the enemy's rear for protracted periods. Indeed, many of the skills learnt by the LRDG during its long desert patrols have had to be relearnt in post-war counterinsurgency campaigns. In Saddam Hussein's Iraq, for example, the small SAS motorized columns that ranged across the desert displayed an uncanny resemblance to the LRDG desert patrols.

MUSEUMS AND COLLECTIONS

The main archival repository for documents relating to the LRDG in North Africa can be found in the National Archives at Kew in London. This includes policy documents relating to the organization and planning for LRDG operations in the WO 203 series, as well as war diaries and similar documents perhaps of greater interest to the general public. The files contain useful reports, for example, related to the LRDG's activities, including several dealing with the Barce raid. A caveat should be added about the war diaries, however, since they vary greatly in coverage and quality and often the original documents contained in appendices to each monthly report have gone missing. A lengthy and detailed history prepared by Brigadier H. W. Wynter, written for the Historical Section of the War Cabinet, outlining the activities of the LRDG in North Africa is also available, but fortunately it has also recently been published by the National Archive along with an account of the activities of the SAS (see bibliography). The main source of information elsewhere is located at the Imperial War Museum at Lambeth in London. Several manuscript or typescript accounts of service with the LRDG have been deposited with the museum that throw light on the everyday life of patrolmen. By far the most important source are the papers and photographs deposited by Maj. Gen. David Lloyd Owen and the now sadly defunct Long Range Desert Group Association, which contain a wealth of information about the raising, organizing and training of the LRDG. The National Army Museum in Chelsea also has some material and displays relating to the LRDG.

The availability of LRDG ephemera with good provenance for collectors is far more limited. This is a direct product of the small size of the unit and its short-lived wartime existence. While items of uniform, webbing and other equipment similar to that worn by LRDG patrolmen on active service have survived the war, very little is what was actually worn on patrol (apart from within a few private collections). Those on offer at auction houses and on eBay should be treated with considerable care. Items of insignia – cap badges and shoulder titles – are perhaps the most widely available of items relating to the LRDG, but should be treated with caution given the large number of fakes and reproductions on the market. Similarly, the regrettable British and Rhodesian decision to issue campaign medals without naming them to the recipient means single medals or groups attributed to the LRDG should be treated with considerable circumspection unless accompanied by supporting paperwork, or unless they include a named gallantry award. Fortunately, the New Zealand government was not so penny-pinching.

BIBLIOGRAPHY

Special Forces in the Desert War (PRO: London, 2001)

Bagnold, R. A., 'Early Days of the Long Range Desert Group' in *The Geographical Journal*, Vol. 105 (Jan–Feb 1945) pp.30–42

——, *Sand, Wind & War: Memoirs of a Desert Explorer* (University of Arizona Press: Tuscon, 1990)

Clayton, Peter, *Desert Explorer: A Biography of Colonel P. A. Clayton* (Zerzura Press, 1998)

Constable, Trevor, 'Bagnold's Bluff: The Little Known Figure Behind Britain's Daring Long Range Desert Patrols' in *Hidden Heroes* (Arthur Barker: London, 1971)

Crichton-Stuart, Michael, *G Patrol: The Story of the Guards Patrol of The Long Range Desert Group* (Purnell Book Services: London, 1976)

Fourie, Craig, Pittaway, Jonathan and Broster, Alison, *LRDG Rhodesia: Rhodesians in the Long Range Desert Group* (Dandy Agencies: Durban, 2002)

Gordon, John W., *The Other Desert War: British Special Forces in North Africa, 1940–1943* (Greenwood Press: New York, 1987)

Griffith, Paddy, *World War II Desert Tactics* (Osprey Publishing: Oxford, 2008)

Gross, Kuno, Charvetto, Roberto and O'Carroll, Brendan, *Incident at Gebel Sherif: In Search of the First Clash of Special Forces 1941/2009* (Kuno Gross: Singapore, 2009)

Hargreaves, Andrew L., 'The Advent, Evolution and Value of British Specialist Formations in the Desert War 1940–43' in *Global War Studies* (Forthcoming 2010)

Jenner, Robin, List, David, Sarson, Peter and Badrocke, Mike, *The Long Range Desert Group 1940–1945* (Osprey Publishing: Oxford, 1999)

Kay, R. L., *Long Range Desert Group in the Mediterranean* (Official: Wellington, 1949)

Kelly, Saul, *The Lost Oasis: The Desert War and the Hunt for Zerzura* (John Murray: London, 2002)

Kennedy Shaw, W. B., *Long Range Desert Group* (Collins: London, 1945)

Owen, David Lloyd, *Desert My Dwelling Place: With the Long Range Desert Group in North Africa* (Arms and Armour: London, 1986)

Owen, David Lloyd and Keegan, John, *The Long Range Desert Group 1940–1945: Providence Their Guide* (Pen and Sword: London, 2001)

Molinari, Andrea, *Desert Raiders: Axis and Allied Special Forces 1940–44* (Osprey Publishing: Oxford, 2007)

Moreman, Tim, *Desert Rats: British 8th Army in North Africa 1941–43* (Osprey Publishing: Oxford, 2007)

Morgan, Mike, *The Sting of the Scorpion: In Action with the Long Range Desert Group* (Sutton: London, 2000)

O'Carroll, Brendan, *Bearded Brigands: The LRDG in the Diaries/Photographs of Trooper Frank Jopling* (Pen and Sword: London, 2003)

——, *Barce Raid. The Long Range Desert Group's Most Daring Exploit in World War II*, (Ngaio Press: Wellington, 2005)

——, *The Kiwi Scorpions: The Story of the New Zealanders in the Long Range Desert Group* (Token Publishing: London, 2000)

Peniakoff, Vladimir, *Private Army* (Jonathan Cape: London, 1950)

Swinson, Arthur, *The Raiders: Desert Strike Force* (McDonald and Co: London, 1968)

Thompson, Julian, *The Imperial Museum Book Of War Behind Enemy Lines* (Sidgwick and Jackson: London, 1998)

Thorne, Colin R. and Soar, Philip, 'R. A. Bagnold: A Biography and Extended Bibliography' in *Earth Surface Processes and Landforms*, 21 (1996), pp.987–91

Timpson, Alastair and Gibson-Watt, Andrew, *In Rommel's Backyard: Behind the Lines with the LRDG* (Pen and Sword: London, 2000)

Online Sources

Long Range Desert Group Preservation Society http://www.lrdg.org

Long Range Desert Group http://www.lrdg.de/main.htm

INDEX

References to illustrations are shown in **bold**.

A·N·N·U·A·L E·D·I·T·I·O·N·S

PERSONAL GROWTH AND BEHAVIOR 01/02

Twenty-First Edition

WITHDRAWN

EDITOR

Karen G. Duffy
SUNY College, Geneseo

Karen G. Duffy holds a doctorate in psychology from Michigan State University and is currently a professor of psychology at SUNY at Geneseo. She sits on the executive board of the New York State Employees Assistance Program and is a certified community and family mediator. She is a member of the American Psychological Society and the Eastern Psychological Association.

McGraw-Hill/Dushkin
530 Old Whitfield Street, Guilford, Connecticut 06437

Visit us on the Internet
http://www.dushkin.com

Credits

1. Becoming a Person: Foundations
Unit photo—© 2001 by Cleo Freelance Photography.
2. Determinants of Behavior: Motivation, Environment, and Physiology
Unit photo—Courtesy World Health Organization.
3. Problems Influencing Personal Growth
Unit photo—Courtesy of McGraw-Hill/Dushkin.
4. Relating to Others
Unit photo—© 2001 by Cleo Freelance Photography.
5. Dynamics of Personal Adjustment: The Individual and Society
Unit photo—Courtesy of Louis Raucci.
6. Enhancing Human Adjustment: Learning to Cope Effectively
Unit photo—© 2001 by Cleo Freelance Photography.

Cataloging in Publication Data
Main entry under title: Annual Editions: Personal Growth and Behavior. 2001/2002.
1. Personality—Periodicals. 2. Adjustment (Psychology)—Periodicals.
I. Duffy, Karen G., *comp.* II. Title: Personal growth and behavior.
ISBN 0–07–243373–6   ISSN 0732-0779   155′.2′05   75–20757

Twenty-First Edition

Cover image © 2001 by PhotoDisc, Inc.

Printed in the United States of America   1234567890BAHBAH54321   Printed on Recycled Paper

Copyright

In publishing ANNUAL EDITIONS we recognize the enormous role played by the magazines, newspapers, and journals of the public press in providing current, first-rate educational information in a broad spectrum of interest areas. Many of these articles are appropriate for students, researchers, and professionals seeking accurate, current material to help bridge the gap between principles and theories and the real world. These articles, however, become more useful for study when those of lasting value are carefully collected, organized, indexed, and reproduced in a low-cost format, which provides easy and permanent access when the material is needed. That is the role played by ANNUAL EDITIONS.

Have you ever watched children on a playground? Some children are reticent; watching the other children play, they sit demurely and shun becoming involved in the fun. Some children readily and happily interact with their playmates. They take turns, share their toys, and follow the rules of the playground. Other children are bullies who brazenly taunt the playing children and aggressively take others' possessions. What makes each child so different? Do childhood behaviors forecast adult behaviors? Can children's (or adults') antisocial behaviors be changed?

These questions are not new. Lay persons and social scientists alike have always been curious about human nature. The answers to our questions, though, are incomplete, because attempts to address these issues are relatively new or just developing. Psychology, the science that can and should answer questions about individual differences, is the primary focus of this book, and has existed for just over 100 years. That may seem old to you, but it is young when other disciplines are considered. Mathematics, medicine, and philosophy are thousands of years old.

By means of psychology and related sciences, this anthology will help you explore the issues of individual differences and their origins, methods of coping, personality changes, and other matters of human adjustment. The purpose of this anthology is to compile the newest, most complete and readable articles that examine individual behavior and adjustment as well as the dynamics of personal growth and interpersonal relationships. The readings in this book offer interesting insights into both the everyday and scientific worlds, a blend welcomed by most of today's specialists in human adjustment.

This anthology is revised each year to reflect both traditional viewpoints and emerging perspectives about people's behavior. Thanks to the editorial board's valuable advice, the current edition has been completely revised and includes a large number of new articles representing the latest thinking in the field.

Annual Editions: Personal Growth and Behavior 01/02 is comprised of six units, each of which serves a distinct purpose. The first unit is concerned with theories and philosophies related to self-identity. For example, one theory, humanism, hypothesizes that self-concept,

our feelings about who we are and how worthy we are, is the most valuable component of personality. This unit includes articles that supplement the theoretical articles by providing applications of, or alternate perspectives on, popular theories about personal growth and human adjustment. These include all of the classic and major theories of personality: humanistic, psychoanalytic, behavioral, and trait theories.

The second unit provides information on how and why a person develops in a particular way—in other words, what factors determine or direct individual growth: physiology, heredity, experience, or some combination. The third unit pertains to problems commonly encountered in the different stages of development: infancy, childhood, adolescence, middle age, and adulthood.

The fourth and fifth units are similar in that they address social problems of adjustment—problems that occur in interpersonal relationships and problems that are created for individuals by society or culture. Unit 4 concerns interpersonal topics such as friendship and shyness, while unit 5 discusses broader societal issues such as racism, gender roles, and cults. The final unit focuses on adjustment or on how most people cope with problems of daily existence.

Annual Editions: Personal Growth and Behavior 01/02 will challenge you and interest you in a variety of topics. It will provide you with many answers, but it will also stimulate many questions. Perhaps it will inspire you to continue your study of the burgeoning field of psychology, which is responsible for exploring personal growth and behavior. As has been true in the past, your feedback on this edition would be valuable for future revisions. Please take a moment to fill out and return the postage-paid *article rating form* on the last page. Thank you.

Karen Grover Duffy

Karen G. Duffy
Editor

Contents

UNIT 1

Becoming a Person: Foundations

Six selections discuss the psychosocial development of an individual's personality. Attention is given to values, emotions, lifestyles, and self-concept.

The concepts in bold italics are developed in the article. For further expansion please refer to the Topic Guide, the Glossary, and the Index.

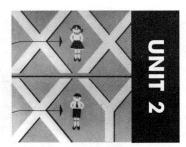

The concepts in bold italics are developed in the article. For further expansion please refer to the Topic Guide, the Glossary, and the Index.

UNIT 3

Problems Influencing Personal Growth

Ten articles consider aging, development, self-image, and social interaction, and their influences on personal growth.

UNIT 4

Relating to Others

Ten articles examine some of the
dynamics involved in relating to
others. Topics discussed include
friendship, love, the importance of
family ties, and self-esteem.

The concepts in bold italics are developed in the article. For further expansion please refer to the Topic Guide, the Glossary, and the Index.

UNIT 5

Dynamics of Personal Adjustment: The Individual and Society

Six selections discuss some of the problems experienced by individuals as they attempt to adjust to society.

UNIT 6

Enhancing Human Adjustment: Learning to Cope Effectively

Six selections examine some of the ways an individual learns to cope successfully within today's society. Topics discussed include therapy, depression, and interpersonal relations.

The concepts in bold italics are developed in the article. For further expansion please refer to the Topic Guide, the Glossary, and the Index.

The concepts in bold italics are developed in the article. For further expansion please refer to the Topic Guide, the Glossary, and the Index.

This topic guide suggests how the selections in this book relate to the subjects covered in your course.

The Web icon (☻) under the topic articles easily identifies the relevant Web sites, which are numbered and annotated on the next two pages. By linking the articles and the Web sites by topic, this ANNUAL EDITIONS reader becomes a powerful learning and research tool.

TOPIC AREA	TREATED IN	TOPIC AREA	TREATED IN
Adolescents	22. World of Their Own 23. How Well Do You Know Your Kid? 37. Teening of Childhood ☻ *1, 9, 13, 14, 16, 17, 18,* *22, 24, 25*	**Death**	26. Start the Conversation ☻ *17*
		Decisions	45. Bad Choices: Why We Make Them, How to Stop ☻ *21, 23*
Aging	24. Road Ahead: A Boomer's Guide to Happiness 25. Live to 100? No Thanks 27. Friendships and Adaptation Across the Life Span ☻ *15, 26, 27, 28, 29*	**Development**	17. Seven Stages of Man 18. Fetal Psychology 19. Four Things You Need to Know About Raising Baby 20. Why Children Turn Out the Way They Do 21. Invincible Kids 22. World of Their Own 23. How Well Do You Know Your Kid? 24. Road Ahead: A Boomer's Guide to Happiness 25. Live to 100? No Thanks 27. Friendships and Adaptation Across the Life Span ☻ *1, 7, 9, 12, 13, 14, 15, 16*
Anxiety/Anxiety Disorder	46. Chronic Anxiety ☻ *27, 28, 29, 31*		
Apologies/ Forgiveness	33. Discover the Power of Forgiveness ☻ *14, 20*		
Autism	11. Autism Is Likely to Be Linked to Several Genes ☻ *15, 18, 27, 29, 31*		
Behavior/ Behaviorism	2. Last Interview of Abraham Maslow 4. Private Lives: Discipline and Knowing Where to Draw the Line ☻ *3, 7, 13*	**Emotional Intelligence**	28. Emotional Intelligence: Do You Have It? ☻ *19, 20, 21*
		Emotions	13. Biology of Joy 30. What's in a Face? 35. Prescription for Passion 46. Chronic Anxiety ☻ *15, 16, 29*
Biochemistry	13. Biology of Joy ☻ *6, 7, 10, 11*		
Biological Cycles	14. Tick-Tock of the Biological Clock ☻ *7, 10, 11*	**Fetus**	18. Fetal Psychology ☻ *1, 7, 8, 10, 11*
Brain	12. Future of the Brain 13. Biology of Joy 14. Tick-Tock of the Biological Clock ☻ *6, 7, 8, 10, 11*	**Forgiveness**	33. Discover the Power of Forgiveness ☻ *14, 20*
		Freud, Sigmund	3. Psychoanalyst: Sigmund Freud ☻ *3, 5*
Children	11. Autism Is Likely to Be Linked to Several Genes 17. Seven Stages of Man 18. Fetal Psychology 19. Four Things You Need to Know About Raising Baby 20. Why Children Turn Out the Way They Do 21. Invincible Kids 22. World of Their Own 23. How Well Do You Know Your Kid? 37. Teening of Childhood ☻ *1, 12, 14, 15*	**Gender**	8. Gender Blur 38. Betrayal of the American Man ☻ *8, 10, 12, 21*
		Genes	8. Gender Blur 9. Personality Genes 10. Decoding the Human Body 11. Autism Is Likely to Be Linked to Several Genes ☻ *11, 30, 31*
		Groups	36. Coping With Crowding 40. Lure of the Cult ☻ *15, 22, 29*
Circadian Rhythms	14. Tick-Tock of the Biological Clock ☻ *6, 7, 10, 11*	**Health**	16. Faith & Healing 48. Mind Over Medicine ☻ *12, 14, 15, 27, 28, 29*
Computers	29. Shyness: The New Solution ☻ *31*		
Crowding	36. Coping With Crowding ☻ *15, 29*	**Humanistic Psychology**	2. Last Interview of Abraham Maslow ☻ *3*
Cults	40. Lure of the Cult ☻ *22*	**Interpersonal Relationships**	27. Friendship and Adaptation Across the Life Span 28. Emotional Intelligence: Do You Have It? 29. Shyness: The New Solution 30. What's in a Face? 31. How to Spot a Liar 32. Revealing Personal Secrets
Culture	6. How Culture Molds Habits of Thought 37. Teening of Childhood 38. Betrayal of the American Man ☻ *5, 20, 21*		

● AE: Personal Growth and Behavior

The following World Wide Web sites have been carefully researched and selected to support the articles found in this reader. The sites are cross-referenced by number and the Web icon (●) in the topic guide. In addition, it is possible to link directly to these Web sites through our DUSHKIN ONLINE support site at *http://www.dushkin.com/online/*.

The following sites were available at the time of publication. Visit our Web site—we update DUSHKIN ONLINE regularly to reflect any changes.

General Sources

1. National Institute of Child Health and Human Development (NICHD)
http://www.nichd.nih.gov
The NICHD conducts and supports research on the reproductive, neurobiologic, developmental, and behavioral processes that determine and maintain the health of children and adults.

2. Psychnet
http://www.apa.org/psychnet/
Get information on psychology from this Web site through the site map or by using the search engine. Access *APA Monitor*, the American Psychological Association newspaper; APA Books on a wide range of topics; PsychINFO, an electronic database of abstracts on over 1,350 scholarly journals; and HelpCenter for information on dealing with modern life problems.

Becoming a Person: Foundations

3. Abraham A. Brill Library
http://plaza.interport.net/nypsan/service.html
The Abraham A. Brill Library, perhaps the largest psychoanalytic library in the world, contains data on over 40,000 books, periodicals, and reprints in psychoanalysis and related fields. Its holdings span the literature of psychoanalysis from its beginning to the present day.

4. JungWeb
http://www.cgjungboston.com
Dedicated to the work of Carl Jung, this site is a comprehensive resource for Jungian psychology. Links to Jungian psychology, reference materials, graduate programs, dreams, multilingual sites, and related Jungian themes are available.

5. Sigmund Freud and the Freud Archives
http://plaza.interport.net/nypsan/freudarc.html
Internet resources related to Sigmund Freud can be accessed through this site. A collection of libraries, museums, and biographical materials, as well as the Brill Library archives, can be found here.

Determinants of Behavior: Motivation, Environment, and Physiology

6. American Psychological Society (APS)
http://www.psychologicalscience.org
APS membership includes a diverse group of the world's foremost scientists and academics working to expand basic and applied psychological science knowledge. Links to teaching, research, and graduate studies resources are available.

7. Federation of Behavioral, Psychological, and Cognitive Science
http://www.am.org/federation/
At this site you can hotlink to the National Institutes of Health's medical database, government links to public information on mental health, a social psychology network, and the Project on the Decade of the Brain.

8. Max Planck Institute for Psychological Research
http://www.mpipf-muenchen.mpg.de/BCD/bcd_e.htm
Several behavioral and cognitive development research projects are available on this site.

9. The Opportunity of Adolescence
http://www.winternet.com/~webpage/adolescencepaper.html
This paper calls adolescence the turning point, after which the future is redirected and confirmed, and goes on to discuss the opportunities and problems of this period to the individual and society, using quotations from Erik Erikson, Jean Piaget, and others.

10. Psychology Research on the Net
http://psych.hanover.edu/APS/exponnet.html
Psychologically related experiments on the Internet can be found at this site. Biological psychology/neuropsychology, clinical psychology, cognition, developmental psychology, emotions, general issues, health psychology, personality, sensation/perception, and social psychology are addressed.

11. Serendip
http://serendip.brynmawr.edu/serendip/
Organized into five subject areas (brain and behavior, complex systems, genes and behavior, science and culture, and science education), Serendip contains interactive exhibits, articles, links to other resources, and a forum area for comments and discussion.

Problems Influencing Personal Growth

12. Ask NOAH About: Mental Health
http://www.noah-health.org/index.html
This enormous resource contains information about child and adolescent family problems, mental conditions and disorders, suicide prevention, and much more.

13. Biological Changes in Adolescence
http://www.personal.psu.edu/faculty/n/x/nxd10/biologic2.htm
This site offers a discussion of puberty, sexuality, biological changes, cross-cultural differences, and nutrition for adolescents, including obesity and its effects on adolescent development.

14. Facts for Families
http://www.aacap.org/info_families/index.htm
The American Academy of Child and Adolescent Psychiatry provides concise, up-to-date information on issues that affect teenagers and their families. Fifty-six fact sheets include many teenager's issues.

World Wide Web Sites

DUSHKIN ONLINE

15. Mental Health Infosource: Disorders
  http://www.mhsource.com/disorders/
This no-nonsense page lists hotlinks to psychological disorders pages, including anxiety, panic, phobic disorders, schizophrenia, and violent/self-destructive behaviors.

16. Mental Health Risk Factors for Adolescents
  http://education.indiana.edu/cas/adol/mental.html
This collection of Web resources is useful for parents, educators, researchers, health practitioners, and teens. It covers a great deal, including abuse, conduct disorders, and stress.

17. Suicide Awareness: Voices of Education
  http://www.save.org
This is the most popular suicide site on the Internet. It is very thorough, with information on dealing with suicide (both before and after), along with material from the organization's many education sessions.

Relating to Others

18. CYFERNET-Youth Development
  http://www.cyfernet.mes.umn.edu/youthdev.html
An excellent source of many articles on youth development, this site includes a statement on the concept of normal adolescence and impediments to healthy development.

19. Hypermedia, Literature, and Cognitive Dissonance
  http://www.uncg.edu/~rsginghe/metastat.htm
This article, subtitled *The Heuristic Challenges of Connectivity*, discusses EQ (emotional intelligence) in adults and offers an interactive study, the Metatale Paradigm, that is linked to story sources. Click on *http://www.uncg.edu/~rsginghe/metatext.htm* for access.

20. Emotional Intelligence Discovery
  http://www.cwrl.utexas.edu/~bump/Hu305/3/3/3/
This site has been set up by students to talk about and expand on Daniel Goleman's book, *Emotional Intelligence*. There are links to many other EI sites.

21. The Personality Project
  http://personality-project.org/personality.html
The Personality Project of William Revelle, director of the Graduate Program in Personality at Northwestern University, is meant to guide those interested in personality theory and research to the current personality research literature.

Dynamics of Personal Adjustment: The Individual and Society

22. AFF Cult Group Information
  http://www.csj.org/index.html
Information about cults, cult groups, and psychological manipulation is available at this page sponsored by the secular, not-for-profit, tax-exempt research center and educational organization, American Family Foundation.

23. Explanations of Criminal Behavior
  http://www.uaa.alaska.edu/just/just110/crime2.html
An excellent outline of the causes of crime, including major theories, which was prepared by Darryl Wood at the University of Alaska, Anchorage, can be found at this site.

24. National Clearinghouse for Alcohol and Drug Information
  http://www.health.org
This is an excellent general site for information on drug and alcohol facts that might relate to adolescence and the issues of peer pressure and youth culture. Resources, referrals, research and statistics, databases, and related Internet links are among the options available at this site.

25. Schools Health Education Unit (SHEU)
  http://www.ex.ac.uk/~dregis/sheu.html
SHEU is a research unit that offers survey, research, and evaluation services on health and social development for young people.

Enhancing Human Adjustment: Learning to Cope Effectively

26. John Suler's Teaching Clinical Psychology Site
  http://www.rider.edu/users/suler/tcp.html
This page contains Internet resources for clinical and abnormal psychology, behavioral medicine, and mental health.

27. Health Information Resources
  http://www.health.gov/nhic/Pubs/tollfree.htm
Here is a long list of toll-free numbers that provide health-related information. None offer diagnosis and treatment, but some do offer recorded information; others provide personalized counseling, referrals, and/or written materials.

28. Knowledge Exchange Network (KEN)
  http://www.mentalhealth.org
The CMHS National Mental Health Services Exchange Network (KEN) provides information about mental health via toll-free telephone services, an electronic bulletin board, and publications. It is a one-stop source for information and resources on prevention, treatment, and rehabilitation services for mental illness, with many links to related sources.

29. Mental Health Net
  http://www.mentalhealth.net
This comprehensive guide to mental health online features more than 6,300 individual resources. It covers information on mental disorders, professional resources in psychology, psychiatry, and social work, journals, and self-help magazines.

30. Mind Tools
  http://www.psychwww.com/mtsite/
Useful information on stress management can be found at this Web site.

31. NetPsychology
  http://netpsych.com/index.htm
This site explores the uses of the Internet to deliver mental health services. This is a basic cybertherapy resource site.

We highly recommend that you review our Web site for expanded information and our other product lines. We are continually updating and adding links to our Web site in order to offer you the most usable and useful information that will support and expand the value of your Annual Editions. You can reach us at:

Unit Selections

1. **A Dance to the Music of the Century: Changing Fashions in 20th–Century Psychiatry,** David Healy
2. **The Last Interview of Abraham Maslow,** Edward Hoffman
3. **Psychoanalyst: Sigmund Freud,** Peter Gay
4. **Private Lives: Discipline and Knowing Where to Draw the Line,** Jan Parker and Jan Stimpson
5. **The Stability of Personality: Observations and Evaluations,** Robert R. McCrae and Paul T. Costa Jr.
6. **How Culture Molds Habits of Thought,** Erica Goode

Key Points to Consider

❖ Can you trace the history of psychological thought? Where do you think psychological and psychiatric thinking will head in the future?

❖ What does Abraham Maslow propose about self in his theory? How can his humanistic theory help us produce a more peaceful world and strengthen positive human attributes?

❖ Do you think self-concept is the most important human construct? Do you think that the development of self is driven by biology? Why or why not?

❖ Do you believe in the unconscious? Why or why not? If yes, can you provide examples from your own life of its influence? What other concepts are important to Sigmund Freud's conceptualization of humans?

❖ What is behaviorism? To what general principles do behavioral theorists subscribe? Should we utilize punishment to alter or manage children's behaviors? Which is most preferred—reinforcement or punishment? What general principles should we follow when we administer punishment? What principles should we follow when we provide reward or reinforcement? Why is punishment so much more controversial than reinforcement?

❖ What is a personality trait? Do you think personality traits remain stable over a lifetime? Do traits remain stable across situations; that is, are they carried from church to school, for example? From where do personality traits originate? Are they biological or learned? Do traits collectively comprise self-concept or is self comprised of more than traits?

❖ Which theory of human personality (humanistic, behavioral, psychoanalytic, or trait) do you think is best and why? How do these theories differ from one another; for example, how does each deal with the "nature" (goodness or badness) of humans? What part of our life experience is most important according to each theory? On what other dimensions can we contrast these theories?

❖ What role does culture play in shaping our mental life? Are there differences among cultures? How so? Do any of the above theories take culture into account? If not, should they? How can we use research to explore mental life, especially when theorists such as the Freudians and behaviorists indicate that it is inaccessible?

 **Links**   **www.dushkin.com/online/**

3. **Abraham A. Brill Library**
   http://plaza.interport.net/nypsan/service.html
4. **JungWeb**
   http://www.cgjungboston.com
5. **Sigmund Freud and the Freud Archives**
   http://plaza.interport.net/nypsan/freudarc.html

These sites are annotated on pages 4 and 5.

A baby sits in front of a mirror and looks at himself. A chimpanzee sorts through photographs while its trainer carefully watches its reactions. A college student answers a survey on how she feels about herself. What does each of these events share with the others? All are examples of techniques used to investigate self-concept.

That baby in front of the mirror has a red dot on his nose. Researchers watch to see if the baby reaches for the dot in the mirror or touches his own nose. Recognizing the fact that the image he sees in the mirror is his own, the baby touches his real nose, not the nose in the mirror.

The chimpanzee has been trained to sort photographs into two piles—human pictures or animal pictures. If the chimp has been raised with humans, the researcher wants to know into which pile (animal or human) the chimp will place its own picture. Is the chimp's concept of itself animal or human? Or does the chimp have no concept of self at all?

The college student taking the self-survey answers questions about her body image, whether or not she thinks she is fun to be with, whether or not she spends large amounts of time in fantasy, and what her feelings are about her personality and intelligence.

These research projects are designed to investigate how self-concept develops and steers our behaviors and thoughts. Most psychologists believe that people develop a personal identity or a sense of self, which is a sense of who we are, our likes and dislikes, our characteristic feelings and thoughts, and an understanding of why we behave as we do. Self-concept is our knowledge of our gender, race, and age, as well as our sense of self-worth and more. Strong positive or negative feelings are usually attached to this identity. Psychologists are studying how and when this sense of self develops. Most psychologists do not believe that infants are born with a sense of self but rather that children slowly develop self-concept as a consequence of their experiences.

This unit delineates some of the popular viewpoints regarding how sense of self, personality, and behavior develop and how, or whether, they guide behavior. This knowledge of how self develops provides an important foundation for the rest of the units in this book. This unit explores four major theories or forces in psychology: self or humanistic, behavioral, psychoanalytic, and trait theories. The last article is included because it references an important element which many of these theories ignore—culture.

The first article reviews the interesting and circuitous history of theories in the area of personal growth and development. David Healy not only provides information about themes related to human adjustment, he also attempts to predict which theories will survive the test of time and continue to influence psychological thinking.

The next series of articles introduces the reader to some of the various theories about human nature. In the next unit article related to humanistic psychology, Abraham Maslow, one of the founders of this philosophical orientation to self-concept, gives an inspired last interview on his philosophy of human nature. In the interview, Maslow talks about his philosophy and its potential for peaceful living and other positive outcomes for humans.

The article that follows relates to a different theory, the psychoanalytic theory of Sigmund Freud. Psychoanalysis, a theory as well as a form of therapy, proposes that individuals possess a dark, lurking unconscious that often motivates negative behaviors such as guilt and defensiveness. This notion is quite a contrast to the more positive thinking of the humanists. This article reviews the theory, its contributions, and its criticisms.

The next article pertains to a third theory—behaviorism. Behaviorism expunges thought, emotion, and abstract concepts such as self from psychological philosophy. In "Private Lives: Discipline and Knowing Where to Draw the Line," the authors discuss how, using principles from operant conditioning, parents and teachers can better manage a child's behavior. Jan Parker and Jan Stimpson provide guidelines on how and when to use reinforcement and punishment, with punishment being the most controversial and least desirable of the two.

The unit's next essay offers a contrasting viewpoint of human nature, known as the trait or dispositional approach. Trait theories in general hold that personality is comprised of various traits that perhaps are bound together by our self-concept. This review of relevant research claims that most personality traits remain constant over time, a view that is in sharp contrast to the growth theory of Abraham Maslow, the psychoanalytic stage theory of Freud, and the behavior change model of behaviorism.

Finally, this unit would not be complete without an article on culture. Most of the above theories (humanism, psychoanalysis, behaviorism, and trait theory) are laced with Western thought. However, cross-cultural psychologists are teaching us that there are other ways of construing the world and the self such that these theories might not be universally applicable. In "How Culture Molds Habits of Thought," several studies are highlighted which demonstrate that culture, rather than any single over-arching theoretical principle, influences mental life.

Becoming a Person: Foundations

A dance to the music of the century:

Changing fashions in 20th-century psychiatry

David Healy, Director

North Wales Department of Psychological Medicine, Hergest Unit, Bangor LL57 2PW

Modern psychiatry began in the early 19th century from a social psychiatric seed. The early alienists, Pinel and Tuke, Esquirol and Connolly believed that managing the social milieu of the patient could contribute significantly to their chances of recovery. These physicians produced the first classificatory systems in the discipline. At the turn of the century, university psychiatry, which was biologically oriented, began to impact on psychiatry, especially in Germany. This is seen most clearly in the work and classificatory system of Emil Kraepelin (Healy, 1997). At the same time, a new psychodynamic approach to the management of nervous problems in the community was pioneered most notably by Sigmund Freud. This led to yet another classification of nervous problems.

In the first half of the century, unlike German and French psychiatry, British psychiatry remained largely aloof from the influences of both university and psychodynamic approaches. It became famously pragmatic and eclectic. Edward Mapother, the first director of the Maudsley Hospital typified the approach. Aubrey Lewis who succeeded him, as well as David Henderson in Edinburgh, both of whom trained with Adolf Meyer in the USA, were committed to Meyer's biopsychosocial approach (Gelder, 1991). The social psychiatry that stemmed from this was to gain a decisive say in European and world psychiatry in the decades immediately following the Second World War.

Things at first unfolded no differently in that other bastion of English-speaking psychiatry—America. In the first decade of the 20th century, Meyer introduced Kraepelin's work to North America, where it had a modest impact, failing to supplant Meyer's own biopsychosocial formulations. In 1909, Freud visited the USA. He appears to have regarded it as an outpost of the civilised world, one particularly prone to enthusiasms. At this point, Freudian analysis restricted itself to handling personalities and their discontents. It initially made little headway in the USA.

There was another development in the USA that was to have a decisive impact on British and world psychiatry in due course. In 1912, the USA legislature passed the Harrison's Narcotics Act, the world's first piece of legislation which made drugs available on prescription only, in this case, opiates and cocaine. While substance misuse was not at the time a part of psychiatry, which confined itself worldwide almost exclusively to the management of the psychoses, this move to prescription-only status by involving medical practitioners in managing the problem almost by necessity meant that the issue of personalities and their disorders would at some point become part of psychiatry.

The years before the Second World War led to two sets of developments. First, there was a migration of psychoanalysts from Europe to North America, so that by the 1940s a majority of the world's analysts lived there. In America, what had been a pessimistic worldview was recast with an optimistic turn, in part perhaps because the War demonstrated that nervous disorders could be environmentally induced and at the same time genetic research was temporarily eclipsed. This new remodelled psychoanalysis abandoned Freud's reserve about treating psychosis. It triumphed and drove American psychiatry to a view that everyone was at least latently ill, that everyone was in need of treatment and that the way to put the world's wrongs right was not just to treat mental illness, but to resculpt personalities and promote mental health (Menninger, 1959).

Second, sulphonamides were discovered and the War stimulated research, which made penicillin commercially available. The success that stemmed from these led to explosive growth in the pharmaceutical sector. The search for other antibiotics led to the discovery in France of antihistamines, one of which turned out to be chlorpromazine. The Food and Drug Administration in the USA responded to these new drugs by making all new drugs available on prescription only. European countries followed suit. This was to bring not only problems of personality but also the vast pool of community nervousness within the remit of non-analytic psychiatry.

The psychoanalysts gained control of American psychiatry in the decade before the introduction of the psychotropic drugs. By 1962, 59 of 82 psychiatric departments were headed by analysts, all graduate programmes were based on analytical principles and 13 of the 17 most recommended texts were psychoanalytical (Shorter, 1996). As a director of the National Institute of Mental Health put it:

> "From 1945 to 1955, it was nearly impossible for a non-psychoanalyst to become a chairman of a department or professor of psychiatry" (Brown, 1976).

As early as 1948, three-quarters of all committee posts in the American Psychiatric Association (APA) were held by analysts (Shorter, 1996).

One of the features of these developments was that a rootless patois of dynamic terms seeped out into the popular culture to create a psychobabble, with untold consequences for how we view ourselves. Another feature, that is regularly cited was the way the analytical totalitarianism that resulted handled failures of patients to get well or of critics to come on side. These were turned around and viewed as further indicators of the psychopathology afflicting patients and critics respectively (Dolnick, 1998).

Walter Reich (1982) argued that this style was a defence against pessimism that stemmed at least in part from America's peculiar needs for solutions to complexity. He was writing at a time of change, just after the publication of DSM-III (American Psychiatric Association, 1980). DSM-III, which is commonly cited as marking the triumph of a neo-Kraepelinian revolution in American psychiatry, was widely seen as changing the rules to favour a newly emerging biological psychiatry. Its message that psychiatry's business was to treat diseases, was a counter to perceptions that the analytical agenda had become a crusade that had taken "psychiatrists on a mission to change the world which had brought the profession to the verge of extinction" (Bayer & Spitzer, 1985).

Part of the stimulus to DSM-III had come from participation in the International Pilot Study of Schizophrenia, where American psychiatrists had felt keenly the disdain with which their diagnostic views were regarded by their European counterparts, who were British or who, like Norman Sartorius, Assen Jablensky and others, had close links with the Maudsley (Spitzer, 2000). The DSM-III was fiercely resisted in the UK, whose leading authorities had been the key figures behind the international system of classification (ICD) for several decades. The new system was dismissed—"serious students of nosology will continue to use the ICD" (Shepherd, 1981). But an empire was slipping from British hands (Spitzer, 2000). The World Psychiatric Association took as its banner for its 1996 meeting the slogan "One World, One Language". Few people, attending the meeting at least, thought this language was anything other than biological or neo-Kraepelinian.

Reich (1982) commented on the change in American psychiatry from analysis to a more biologically-based discipline but this change, he suggested, was likely to be governed by similar dynamics to those that drove the earlier turn to psychoanalysis. By the 1990s, the rise of psychopharmacology and biological psychiatry was complete. The chances of a non-neuroscientist becoming a head of a psychiatric department in the USA was highly unlikely and not much more likely in the UK. The standard textbooks were heavily neuroscientific in their emphasis. Where once the APA was controlled by analysts, annual meetings now generated millions of dollars—largely from pharmaceutical company sponsored satellite symposia, of which there were 40 in 1999, at approximately $250 000 per symposium in addition to fees for exhibition space and registration fees for several thousand delegates brought to the meeting by pharmaceutical companies, as well as several million dollars per annum from sales of successive versions of the DSM.

The UK, which had once stood dismissive of American trends and diagnoses, increasingly followed American leads. Fashions in recovered memory therapies or fluoxetine-taking rapidly crossed the Atlantic, influenced in part perhaps by the ever-increasing attendance of British psychiatrists at APA meetings. By 1999, it was possible that greater numbers of British psychiatrists, sponsored largely by pharmaceutical companies, attended the APA meeting than the annual meeting of the Royal College of Psychiatrists, a development that would have been incredible a decade before.

Biological psychiatry, meanwhile, had not restricted itself to the psychoses from whence it came. By the end of the century, the complete transformation of personality rather than simply the treatment of disease was becoming the goal. This was most clearly articulated in Peter Kramer's *Listening to Prozac* (Kramer, 1993). Where once the psychiatric concern had been for symptoms as these reflected diseases, the emphasis was increasingly on the management of problems by biological means. The extent to which community nervousness stems from social arrangements rather than diseases is clearly uncertain, but where the best estimates of annual prevalence rates of depressive disease stood at between 50 and 100 per million in 1950, by the mid-1990s they had risen to 100 000 per million for depressive disorders as defined by the DSM, with even higher rates for depressive symptoms (Healy, 1997).

Despite the neo-Kraepelinian revolution, some American opinion leaders were beginning to argue that the profession faced disaster if it did not stop offering to solve social ills and if it did not pull back to a medical

focus (Detre & McDonald, 1997). Where once blame had been put on families, or mothers in particular, the 1990s became the decade of blaming the brain (Valenstein, 1998). By the end of the decade, the psychobabble of yesteryear was fast being replaced by a newly minted biobabble. *The Guardian* newspaper ran a feature on "Oh no! We're not really getting more depressed are we?" in which a psychologist, Oliver James, pondered whether the British have become a low-serotonin people (James, 1997). Finally, an ever increasing emphasis on long-term treatment with psychotropic agents, along with difficulties with withdrawal from them (a perennial British concern), inevitably recalls Karl Kraus' quip about analysis becoming the illness it purported to cure.

The mass treatment of problems with psychotropic drugs could not but in itself run into problems. Reports of suicides, homicides and other events while taking fluoxetine (Healy *et al*, 1999) led Eli Lilly to devise a strategy to manage criticism which involved blaming the disease, not the drug (Cornwell, 1996). On 20 April 1999, two students took firearms into a high school in Littleton, Colorado, killing 12 students, one staff member and then themselves. Within days of suggestions that one of the teenagers had an antidepressant in their blood stream, the APA Website carried a statement from the Association's president:

> "Despite a decade of research, there is little valid evidence to prove a causal relationship between the use of antidepressant medications and destructive behavior. On the other hand, their [sic] is ample evidence that undiagnosed and untreated mental illness exacts a heavy toll on those who suffer from these disorders as well as those around them" (American Psychiatric Association, 1999).

Many of those who take up psychiatry as a career might be thought to do so for fairytale or romantic reasons. At some point they will have nourished fantasies of helping patients with neuroses or psychoses to recover to the point of being invited to participate in the ball of life once more. In the course of a century, psychiatrists attending the ball have elegantly changed partners on a number of occasions. It is less clear that those who are not invited to the ball have seen much difference as a consequence of changes on the dance floor. When the clock strikes for the new millennium, are any of the dancers likely to be bothered by a stray glass slipper or does that just happen in fairytales?

References

AMERICAN PSYCHIATRIC ASSOCIATION (1980) *Diagnostic and Statistical Manual of Mental Disorders* (3rd edn) (DSM-III). Washington, DC: American Psychiatric Association.

AMERICAN PSYCHIATRIC ASSOCIATION (1999) *Online News Stand*, release no. 99–19. www.psych.org/news.stand/nr.990428.html.

BAYER R. & SPITZER, R. L. (1985) Neurosis, psychodynamics and DSM-III. *Archives of General Psychiatry*, **25**, 123–130.

BROWN, B. S. (1976) The life of psychiatry. *American Journal of Psychiatry*, **133**, 489–495.

CORNWELL, J. (1996) *The Power to Harm. Mind, Medicine and Money on Trial.* London: Viking Press.

DETRE, T. & McDONALD, M. C. (1997) Managed care and the future of psychiatry. *Archives of General Psychiatry*, **54**, 201–204.

DOLNICK, E. (1998) *Madness on the Couch. Blaming the Victim in the Heyday of Psychoanalysis.* New York: Simon & Schuster.

GELDER, M. (1991) Adolf Meyer and his influence in British psychiatry. In *150 Years of British Psychiatry 1841–1991* (eds G. E. Berrios & H. Freeman), pp. 419–435. London: Gaskell.

JAMES, O. (1997) Oh no! We're not really getting more depressed are we? *The Guardian, G2,* pp. 1–3. Monday 15 September.

HEALY, D. (1997) *The Antidepressant Era.* Cambridge, MA: Harvard University Press.

HEALY, D., LANGMAACK, C. & SAVAGE, M. (1999) Suicide in the course of the treatment of depression. *Journal of Psychopharmacology*, **13**, 94–99.

KRAMER, P. (1993) *Listening to Prozac.* New York: Viking Press.

MENINGER, K. (1959) Hope. *American Journal of Psychiatry*, **116**, 481–491.

REICH, W. (1982) American psychoideology. *Psychiatric Bulletin*, **6**, 43.

SHEPHERD, M. (1981) Diagnostic and Statistical Manual, 3rd Edition. American Psychiatric Association Press. *Psychological Medicine*, **11**, 215.

SHORTER, F. (1996) *A History of Psychiatry. From the Age of the Asylum to the Era of Prozac.* New York: John Wiley & Sons.

SPITZER, R. (2000) A manual for diagnosis and statistics. In *The Psychopharmacologists*, volume 3 (ed. D. Healy). London: Arnold.

VALENSTEIN, E. S. (1998) *Blaming the Brain.* New York: Free Press.

The Last Interview of
ABRAHAM
MASLOW

When Abraham Maslow first shared his pioneering vision of a "comprehensive human psychology" in this magazine in early 1968, he stood at the pinnacle of his international acclaim and influence.

Edward Hoffman, Ph.D.

About the author: Edward Hoffman received his doctorate from the University of Michigan. A clinical psychologist on New York's Long Island, he is the author of several books, including The Right to be Human: A Biography of Abraham Maslow (*Tarcher*).

HIS ELECTION AS PRESIDENT OF THE AMERIcan Psychological Association some months before capped an illustrious academic career spanning more than 35 productive years, during which Maslow had steadily gained the high regard—even adulation—of countless numbers of colleagues and former students. His best-known books, *Motivation and Personality* and *Toward a Psychology of Being*, were not only being discussed avidly by psychologists, but also by professionals in fields ranging from management and marketing to education and counseling. Perhaps even more significantly, Maslow's iconoclastic concepts like peak experience, self-actualization, and synergy had even begun penetrating popular language.

Nevertheless, it was a very unsettling time for him: Recovering from a major heart attack, the temperamentally restless and ceaselessly active Maslow was finding forced convalescence at home to be almost painfully unbearable. Suddenly, his extensive plans for future research, travel, and lecturing had to be postponed. Although Maslow hoped for a speedy recovery, frequent chest pains induced a keen sense of his own mortality. As perhaps never before, he began to ponder his career's accomplishments and his unrealized goals.

In 1968 PSYCHOLOGY TODAY was a precocious one-year-old upstart, but such was its prestige that it was able to attract perhaps the country's most famous psychologist for an interview.

Maslow likely regarded the PT interview as a major opportunity to outline his "comprehensive human psychology" and the best way to actualize it. At 60, he knew that time permitted him only to plant seeds (in his own metaphor) of research and theory—and hope that later generations would live to see the flowering of human betterment. Perhaps most prescient at a time of global unrest is Maslow's stirring vision of "building a psychology for the peace table." It was his hope that through psychological research, we might learn how to unify peoples of differing racial and ethnic origins, and thereby create a world of peace.

Although the complete audiotapes of the sessions, conducted over three days, disappeared long ago under mysterious circumstances, the written condensation that remains provides a fascinating and still-relevant portrait of a key thinker at the height of his prowess. Intellectually, Maslow was decades ahead of his time; today the wide-ranging ideas he offers here are far from outdated. Indeed, after some twenty-odd years, they're still on the cutting edge of American psychology and social science. Emotionally, this interview is significant for the rare—essentially unprecedented—glimpse it affords into Maslow's personal history and concerns: his ancestry and upbringing; his mentors and ambitions; his courtship, marriage, and fatherhood; and even a few of his peak experiences.

Maslow continued to be puzzled and intrigued by the more positive human phenomenon of self-actualization. He was well aware that his theory about the "best of humanity" suffered from methodological flaws. Yet he had become ever more convinced of its intuitive validity, that self-actualizers provide us with clues to our highest innate traits: love and compassion, creativity and aesthetics, ethics and spirituality. Maslow longed to empirically verify this lifelong hunch.

In the two years of his life that remained, this gifted psychologist never wrote an autobiography, nor did he ever again bare his soul in such a public and wide-ranging way. It may have been that Maslow regarded this unusually personal interview as a true legacy. More than 20 years later, it remains a fresh and important document for the field of psychology.

Mary Harrington Hall, for PSYCHOLOGY TODAY: A couple of William B. Yeats's lines keep running through my head: "And in my heart, the daemons and the gods wage an eternal battle and I feel the pain of wounds, the labor of the spear." How thin is the veneer of civilization, and how can we understand and deal with evil?

Abraham H. Maslow: It's a psychological puzzle I've been trying to solve for years. Why are people cruel and why are they nice? Evil people are rare, but you find evil behavior in the majority of people. The next thing I want to do with my life is to study evil and understand it.

PT: By evil here, I think we both mean destructive action without remorse. Racial prejudice is an evil in our society which we must deal with. And soon. Or we will go down as a racist society.

> # All the goals of objectivity, repeatability, and preplanned experimentation are things we have to move toward. The more reliable you make knowledge, the better it is.

Maslow: You know, when I became A.P.A. president, the first thing I wanted to do was work for greater recognition for the Negro psychologists. Then I found that there were no Negroes in psychology, at least not many. They don't major in psychology.

PT: Why should they? Why would I think that psychology would solve social problems if I were a Negro living in the ghetto, surrounded by despair?

Maslow: Negroes have really had to take it. We've given them every possible blow.

If I were a Negro, I'd be fighting, as Martin Luther King fought, for human recognition and justice. I'd rather go down with my flag flying. If you're weak or crippled, or you can't speak out or fight back in some way, then people don't hesitate to treat you badly.

PT: Could you look at evil behavior in two ways: evil from below and evil from above? Evil as a sickness and evil as understood compassionately?

Maslow: If you look at evil from above, you can be realistic. Evil exists. You don't give it quarter, and you're a better fighter if you can understand it. You're in the position of a psychotherapist. In the same way, you can look at neurosis. You can see neurosis from below—as a sickness—as most psychiatrists see it. Or you can understand it as a compassionate man might: respecting the neurosis as a fumbling and inefficient effort toward good ends.

PT: You can understand race riots in the same way, can't you?

Maslow: If you can only be detached enough, you can feel that it's better to riot than to be hopeless, degraded, and defeated. Rioting is a childish way of trying to be a man, but it takes time to rise out of the hell of hatred and frustration and accept that to be a man you don't have to riot.

PT: In our society, we see all behavior as a demon we can vanquish and banish, don't we? And yet good people do evil things.

Maslow: Most people are nice people. Evil is caused by ignorance, thoughtlessness, fear, or even the desire for popularity with one's gang. We can cure many such causes of evil. Science is progressing, and I feel hope that psychology can solve many of these problems. I think that a good part of evil behavior bears on the behavior of the normal.

PT: How will you approach the study of evil?

Maslow: If you think only of evil, then you become pessimistic and hopeless like Freud. But if you think there is no evil, then you're just one more deluded Pollyanna. The thing is to try to understand and realize how it's possible for people who are capable of being angels, heroes, or saints to be bastards and killers. Sometimes, poor and miserable people are hopeless. Many revenge themselves upon life for what society has done to them. They enjoy hurting.

PT: Your study of evil will have to be subjective, won't it? How can we measure evil in the laboratory?

Maslow: All the goals of objectivity, repeatability, and preplanned experimentation are things we have to move toward. The more reliable you make knowledge, the better it is. If the salvation of man comes out of the advancement of knowledge—taken in the best sense—then these goals are part of the strategy of knowledge.

PT: What did you tell your own daughters, Ann and Ellen, when they were growing up?

Maslow: Learn to hate meanness. Watch out for anybody who is mean or cruel. Watch out for people who delight in destruction.

PT: How would you describe yourself? Not in personality, because you're one of the warmest and sweetest men I've ever met. But who are you?

Maslow: I'm someone who likes plowing new ground, then walking away from it. I get bored easily. For me, the big thrill comes with the discovering.

PT: Psychologists all love Abe Maslow. How did you escape the crossfire?

Maslow: I just avoid most academic warfare. Besides, I had my first heart attack many years ago, and perhaps I've been unconsciously favoring my body. So I may have avoided real struggle. Besides, I only like fights I know I can win, and I'm not personally mean.

PT: Maybe you're just one of the lucky few who grew up through a happy childhood without malice.

Maslow: With my childhood, it's a wonder I'm not psychotic. I was the little Jewish boy in the non-Jewish neighborhood. It was a little like being the first Negro enrolled in the all-white school. I grew up in libraries and among books, without friends.

Both my mother and father were uneducated. My father wanted me to be a lawyer. He thumbed his way across the whole continent of Europe from Russia and got here at the age of 15. He wanted success for me. I tried law school for two weeks. Then I came home to my poor father one night after a class discussing "spite fences" and told him I couldn't be a lawyer. "Well, son," he said, "what do you want to study?" I answered: "Everything." He was uneducated and couldn't understand my passion for learning, but he was a nice man. He didn't understand either that at 16, I was in love.

PT: All 16-year-olds are in love.

Maslow: Mine was different. We're talking about my wife. I loved Bertha. You know her. Wasn't I right? I was extremely shy, and I tagged around after her. We were too young to get married. I tried to run away with her.

PT: Where did you run?

Maslow: I ran to Cornell for my sophomore year in college, then to Wisconsin. We were married there when I was 20 and Bertha was 19. Life didn't really start for me until I got married.

I went to Wisconsin because I had just discovered John B. Watson's work, and I was sold on behaviorism. It was an explosion of excitement for me. Bertha came to pick me up at New York's 42nd Street library, and I was dancing down Fifth Avenue with exuberance. I embarrassed her, but I was so excited about Watson's behaviorist program. It was beautiful. I was con-fident that here was a real road to travel: solving one problem after another and changing the world.

PT: A clear lifetime with built-in progress guaranteed.

Maslow: That was it. I was off to Wisconsin to change the world. I went there to study with psychologist Kurt Koffka, biologist Hans Dreisch, and philosopher Alexander Meiklejohn. But when I showed up

> I've devoted myself to developing a theory of human nature that could be tested by experiment and research. I wanted to prove that humans are capable of something grander than war, prejudice, and hatred.

on the campus, they weren't there. They had just been visiting professors, but the lying catalog had included them anyway.

Oh, but I was so lucky, though. I was young Harry Harlow's first doctoral graduate. And they were angels, my professors. I've always had angels around. They helped me when I needed it, even fed me. Bill Sheldon taught me how to buy a suit. I didn't know anything of amenities. Clark Hull was an angel to me, and later, Edward L. Thorndike.

PT: You're an angelic man. I've heard too many stories to let you deny it. What kind of research were you doing at Wisconsin?

Maslow: I was a monkey man. By studying monkeys for my doctoral dissertation, I found that dominance was related to sex, and to maleness. It was a great discovery, but somebody had discovered it two months before me.

PT: Great ideas always go in different places and minds at the same time.

Maslow: Yes, I worked on it until the start of World War II. I thought that working on sex was the easiest way to help mankind. I felt if I could discover a way to improve the sexual life by even one percent, then I could improve the whole species.

One day, it suddenly dawned on me that I knew as much about sex as any man living—in the intellectual sense. I knew everything that had been written; I had made discoveries with which I was pleased; I had done therapeutic work. This was about 10 years before the Kinsey report came out. Then I suddenly burst into laughter. Here was I, the great sexologist, and I had never seen an erect penis except one, and that was from my own bird's-eye view. That humbled me considerably.

PT: I suppose you interviewed people the way Kinsey did?

Maslow: No, something was wrong with Kinsey. I really don't think he liked women, or men. In my research, I interviewed 120 women with a new form of interview. No notes. We just talked until I got some feeling for the individual's personality, then put sex against that background. Sex has to be considered in regard to love, otherwise it's useless. This is because behavior can be a defense—a way of hiding what you feel—particularly regarding sex.

I was fascinated with my research. But I gave up interviewing men. They were useless because they boasted and lied about sex. I also planned a big research project involving prostitutes. I thought we could learn a lot about men from them, but the research never came off.

PT: You gave up all your experimental research in these fields.

Maslow: Yes, around 1941 I felt I must try to save the world, and to prevent the horrible wars and the awful hatred and prejudice. It happened very suddenly. One day just after Pearl Harbor, I was driving home and my car was stopped by a poor, pathetic parade. Boy Scouts and old uniforms and a flag and someone playing a flute off-key.

As I watched, the tears began to run down my face. I felt we didn't understand—not Hitler, nor the Germans, nor Stalin, nor the Communists. We didn't understand any of them. I felt that if we could understand, then we could make progress. I had a vision of a peace table, with people sitting around it, talking about human nature and hatred, war and peace, and brotherhood.

I was too old to go into the army. It was at that moment I realized that the rest of my life must be devoted to discovering a psychology for the peace table. That moment changed my whole life. Since then, I've devoted myself to developing a theory of human nature that could be tested by experiment and research. I wanted to prove that humans are capable of something grander than war, prejudice, and hatred. I wanted to make science consider all the people: the best specimen of mankind I could find. I found that many of them reported having something like mystical experiences.

PT: Your work with "self-actualizing" people is famous. You have described some of these mystical experiences.

Maslow: Peak experiences come from love and sex, from aesthetic moments, from bursts of creativity, from moments of insight and discovery, or from fusion with nature.

I had one such experience in a faculty procession here at Brandeis University. I saw the line stretching off into a dim future. At its head was Socrates. And in the line were the ones I love most. Thomas Jefferson was there. And Spinoza. And Alfred North Whitehead. I was in the same line. Behind me, that infinite line melted into the dimness. And there were all the people not yet born who were going to be in the same line.

I believe these experiences can be studied scientifically, and they will be.

PT: This is all part of your theory of metamotivation, isn't it?

Maslow: But not all people who are metamotivated report peak experiences. The "nonpeakers" are healthy, but they lack poetry and soaring flights of the imagination. Both peakers and nonpeakers can be self-actualized in that they're not motivated by basic needs, but by something higher

PT: Real self-actualization must be rare. What percentage of us achieve it?

Maslow: I'd say only a fraction of one percent.

PT: People whose basic needs have been met, then, will pursue life's ultimate values?

Maslow: Yes, the ultimate happiness for man is the realization of pure beauty and truth, which are the ultimate values. What we need is a system of thought—you might even call it a religion—that can bind humans together. A system that would fit the Republic of Chad as well as the United States: a system that would supply our idealistic young people with something to believe in. They're searching for something they can pour all that emotion into, and the churches are not much help.

PT: This system must come.

Maslow: I'm not alone in trying to make it. There are plenty of others working toward the same end. Perhaps their efforts, aided by the hundreds of youngsters who are devoting their lives to this, will develop a new image of man that rejects the chemical and technological views. We've technologized everything.

PT: The technologist is the person who has fallen in love with a machine. I suppose that has also happened to those in psychology?

Maslow: They become fascinated with the machine. It's almost a neurotic love. They're like the man who spends Sundays polishing his car instead of stroking his wife.

> **Good psychology should include all the methodological techniques, without having loyalty to one method, one idea, or one person.**

PT: In several of your papers, you've said that you stopped being a behaviorist when your first child was born.

Maslow: My whole training at Wisconsin was behaviorist. I didn't question it until I began reading some other sources. Later, I began studying the Rorschach test.

At the same time, I stumbled into embryology and read Ludwig von Bertalanffy's *Modern Theories of Development*. I had already become disillusioned with Bertrand Russell and with English philosophy generally. Then, I fell in love with Alfred North Whitehead and Henri Bergson. Their writings destroyed behaviorism for me without my recognizing it.

When my first baby was born, that was the thunderclap that settled things. I looked at this tiny, mysterious thing and felt so stupid. I felt small, weak, and feeble. I'd say that anyone who's had a baby couldn't be a behaviorist.

PT: As you propose new ideas, and blaze new ground, you're bound to be criticized, aren't you?

Maslow: I have worked out a lot of good tricks for fending off professional attacks. We all have to do that. A good, controlled experiment is possible only when you already know a hell of a lot. If I'm a pioneer by choice and I go into the wilderness, how am I going to make careful experiments? If I tried to, I'd be a fool. I'm not against careful experiments. But rather, I've been working with what I call "growing tip" statistics.

With a tree, all the growth takes place at the growing tips. Humanity is exactly the same. All the growth takes place in the growing tip: among that one percent of the population. It's made up of pioneers, the beginners. That's where the action is.

PT: You were the one who helped publish Ruth Benedict's work on synergy. What's it about?

Maslow: That it's possible to set up social institutions that merge selfishness and unselfishness, so that you can't benefit yourself without benefiting others. And the reverse.

PT: How can psychology become a stronger force in our society?

Maslow: We all should look at the similarities within the various disciplines and think of enlarging psychology. To throw anything away is crazy. Good psychology should include all the methodological techniques, without having loyalty to one method, one idea, or one person.

PT: I see you as a catalyst and as a bridge between many disciplines, theories, and philosophies.

Maslow: My job is to put them all together. We shouldn't have "humanistic psychology." The adjective should be unnecessary. I'm not antibehaviorist. I'm antidoctrinaire.

PT: Abe, when you look back on your own education, what kind would you recommend for others?

Maslow: The great educational experiences of my life were those that taught me most. They taught me what kind of a person I was. These were experiences that drew me out and strengthened me. Psychoanalysis was a big thing for me. And getting married. Marriage is a school itself. Also, having children. Becoming a father changed my whole life. It taught me as if by revelation. And reading particular books. William Graham Sumner's *Folkways* was a Mount Everest in my life: It changed me.

My teachers were the best in the world. I sought them out: Erich Fromm, Karen

Horney, Ruth Benedict, Max Wertheimer, Alfred Adler, David Levy, and Harry Harlow. I was there in New York City during the 1930s when the wave of distinguished émigrés arrived from Europe.

PT: Not everyone can have such an illustrious faculty.

Maslow: It's the teacher who's important. And if this is so, then what we are doing with our whole educational structure—with credits and the idea that one teacher is as good as another? You look at the college catalog and it says English 342. It doesn't even bother to tell you the instructor's name, and that's insane. The purpose of education—and of all social institutions—is the development of full humaneness. If you keep that in mind, all else follows. We've got to concentrate on goals.

PT: It's like the story about the test pilot who radioed back home: "I'm lost, but I'm making record time."

Maslow: If you forget the goal of education, then the whole thing is lost.

PT: If a rare, self-actualizing young psychologist came to you today and said, "What's the most important thing I can do in this time of crisis?" what advice would you give?

Maslow: I'd say: Get to work on aggression and hostility. We need the definitive book on aggression. And we need it now. Only the pieces exist: the animal stuff, the psychoanalytic stuff, the endocrine stuff. Time is running out. A key to understanding the evil which can destroy our society lies in this understanding.

There's another study that could be done. I'd like to test the whole, incoming freshman class at Brandeis University in various ways: psychiatric interviews, personality tests, everything. I want to follow them for four years of college. For a beginning, I want to test my theory that emotionally healthy people perceive better.

PT: You could make the college study only a preliminary, and follow them through their whole life span, the way Lewis Terman did with his gifted kids.

Maslow: Oh yes! I'd like to know: How good a father or mother does this student become? And what happens to his/her children? This kind of long-term study would take more time than I have left. But that ultimately doesn't make any difference. I like to be the first runner in the relay race. I like to pass on the baton to the next person.

PSYCHOANALYST
SIGMUND FREUD

He opened a window on the unconscious—where, he said, lust, rage and repression battle for supremacy—and changed the way we view ourselves

By PETER GAY

There are no neutrals in the Freud wars. Admiration, even downright adulation, on one side; skepticism, even downright disdain, on the other. This is not hyperbole. A psychoanalyst who is currently trying to enshrine Freud in the pantheon of cultural heroes must contend with a relentless critic who devotes his days to exposing Freud as a charlatan. But on one thing the contending parties agree: for good or ill, Sigmund Freud, more than any other explorer of the psyche, has

> **BORN** May 6, 1856, Freiberg, Moravia
>
> **1881** Earns medical degree
>
> **1885** Receives appointment as lecturer in neuropathology, University of Vienna
>
> **1886** Begins private neurology practice in Vienna; marries Martha Bernays
>
> **1900** Publishes *The Interpretation of Dreams*
>
> **1910** Establishes International Psychoanalytic Association
>
> **1938** Emigrates from Vienna to London
>
> **1939** Dies Sept. 23 in London

shaped the mind of the 20th century. The very fierceness and persistence of his detractors are a wry tribute to the staying power of Freud's ideas.

There is nothing new about such embittered confrontations; they have dogged Freud's footsteps since he developed the cluster of theories he would give the name of psychoanalysis. His fundamental idea—that all humans are endowed with an unconscious in which potent sexual and aggressive drives, and defenses against them, struggle for supremacy, as it were, behind a person's back—has struck many as a romantic, scientifically unprovable notion. His contention that the catalog of neurotic ailments to which humans are susceptible is nearly always the work of sexual maladjustments, and that erotic desire starts not in puberty but in infancy, seemed to the respectable nothing less than obscene. His dramatic evocation of a universal Oedipus complex, in which (to put a complicated issue too simply) the little boy loves his mother and hates his father, seems more like a literary conceit than a thesis worthy of a scientifically minded psychologist.

Freud first used the term psychoanalysis in 1896, when he was already 40. He had been driven by ambition from his earliest days and encouraged by his doting parents to think highly of himself. Born in 1856 to an impecunious Jewish family in the Moravian hamlet of Freiberg (now Pribor in the Czech Republic), he moved with the rest of a rapidly increasing brood to Vienna. He was his mother's firstborn, her "golden Siggie." In recognition of his brilliance, his parents privileged him over his siblings by giving him a room to himself, to study in peace. He did not disappoint them. After an impressive career in school, he matriculated in 1873 in the University of Vienna and drifted from one philosophical subject to another until he hit on medicine. His choice was less that of a dedicated healer than of an inquisitive explorer determined to solve some of nature's riddles.

As he pursued his medical researches, he came to the conclusion that the most intriguing mysteries lay concealed in the complex operations of the mind. By the early 1890s, he was specializing in "neurasthenics" (mainly severe hysterics); they taught him much, including the art of patient listening. At the same time he was beginning to write down his dreams, increasingly convinced that they might offer clues to the workings of the unconscious, a notion he borrowed from the Romantics. He saw himself as a scientist taking material both from his patients and from himself, through introspection. By the mid-1890s, he was launched on a full-blown self-analysis, an enterprise for which he had no guidelines and no predecessors.

The book that made his reputation in the profession—although it sold poorly—was *The Interpretation of Dreams* (1900), an indefinable masterpiece—part dream analysis, part autobiography, part theory of the mind, part history of contemporary Vienna. The principle that underlay this work was that mental experiences and entities, like physical ones, are part of nature. This meant that Freud could admit no mere accidents in mental procedures. The most nonsensical notion, the most casual slip of the tongue, the most fantastic dream, must have a meaning and can be used to unriddle the often incomprehensible maneuvers we call thinking.

Although the second pillar of Freud's psychoanalytic structure, *Three Essays on the Theory of Sexuality* (1905), further alienated him from the mainstream of contemporary psychiatry, he soon found loyal recruits. They met weekly to hash out interesting case histories, converting themselves into the Vienna Psychoanalytic Society in 1908. Working on the frontiers of mental science, these often eccentric pioneers had their quarrels. The two best known "defectors" were Alfred Adler and Carl Jung. Adler, a Viennese physician and socialist, developed his own psychology, which stressed the aggression with which those people lacking in some quality they desire—say manliness—express their discontent by acting out. "Inferiority complex," a much abused term, is Adlerian. Freud did not regret losing

TODAY WE ALL SPEAK FREUD

His ideas—or ideas that can be traced, sometimes circuitously, back to him—have permeated the language

PENIS ENVY Freud's famous theory—not favored by feminists—that women wish they had what men are born with

FREUDIAN SLIP A seemingly meaningless slip of the tongue that is really e-mail direct from the unconscious

UNCONSCIOUS Repressed feelings, desires, ideas and memories that are hidden from the conscious mind

REPRESSION Involuntary blocking of an unsettling feeling or memory from conscious thought

OEDIPUS COMPLEX In classic Freudian theory, children in their phallic phase (ages three to six) form an erotic attachment to the parent of the opposite sex, and a concomitant hatred (occasionally murderous) of the parent of the same sex

CASTRATION ANXIETY A boy's unconscious fear of losing his penis, and his fantasy that girls have already lost theirs

SUBLIMATION Unconscious shifting of an unacceptable drive (lust for your sister, say) into culturally acceptable behavior (lust for your friend's sister)

TRANSFERENCE Unconscious shifting of feelings about one person (e.g., a parent) to another (e.g., your analyst)

ID The part of the mind from which primal needs and drives (e.g., lust, rage) emerge

SUPEREGO The part of the mind where your parents' and society's rules reside; the original guilt trip

EGO The mind's mechanism for keeping in touch with reality, it referees the wrestling match between id and superego

PHALLIC SYMBOLS Almost anything can look like a penis, but sometimes, as Freud is supposed to have remarked, "a cigar is just a cigar"

Adler, but Jung was something else. Freud was aware that most of his acolytes were Jews, and he did not want to turn psycho-analysis into a "Jewish science." Jung, a Swiss from a pious Protestant background, struck Freud as his logical successor, his "crown prince." The two men were close for several years, but Jung's ambition, and his growing commitment to religion and mysticism—most unwelcome to Freud, an aggressive atheist—finally drove them apart.

Freud was intent not merely on originating a sweeping theory of mental functioning and malfunctioning. He also wanted to develop the rules of psychoanalytic therapy and expand his picture of human nature to encompass not just the couch but the whole culture. As to

the first, he created the largely silent listener who encourages the analysand to say whatever comes to mind, no matter how foolish, repetitive or outrageous, and who intervenes occasionally to interpret what the patient on the couch is struggling to say. While some adventurous early psychoanalysts thought they could quantify just what proportion of their analysands went away cured, improved or untouched by analytic therapy, such confident enumerations have more recently shown themselves untenable. The efficacy of analysis remains a matter of controversy, though the possibility of mixing psychoanalysis and drug therapy is gaining support.

Freud's ventures into culture—history, anthropology, literature, art, sociology, the study of religion—

"If often he was wrong and, at times, absurd, to us he is no more a person now but a whole climate of opinion."

W. H. AUDEN,
after Freud's death
in 1939

have proved little less controversial, though they retain their fascination and plausibility and continue to enjoy a widespread reputation. As a loyal follower of 19th century positivists, Freud drew a sharp distinction between religious faith (which is not checkable or correctable) and scientific inquiry (which is both). For himself, this meant the denial of truth-value to any religion whatever, including Judaism. As for politics, he left little doubt and said so plainly in his late—and still best known—essay, *Civilization and Its Discontents* (1930), noting that the human animal, with its insatiable needs, must always remain an enemy to organized society, which exists largely to tamp down sexual and aggressive desires. At best, civilized living is a compromise between wishes and repression—not a comfortable doctrine. It ensures that Freud, taken straight, will never become truly popular, even if today we all speak Freud.

In mid-March 1938, when Freud was 81, the Nazis took over Austria, and after some reluctance, he immigrated to England with his wife and his favorite daughter and colleague Anna "to die in freedom." He got his wish, dying not long after the Nazis unleashed World War II by invading Poland. Listening to an idealistic broadcaster proclaiming this to be the last war, Freud, his stoical humor intact, commented wryly, "*My* last war."

Yale historian Peter Gay's 22 books include Freud: A Life for Our Times

POST-FREUDIAN ANALYSIS

Other psychologists continued the work that Freud began, though not always in ways that he would have approved

CARL JUNG A former disciple of Freud's, Jung shared his mentor's enthusiasm for dreams but not his obsession with the sex drive. Jung said humans are endowed with a "collective unconscious" from which myths, fairy tales and other archetypes spring.

ALFRED KINSEY A biologist who knew little about sex and less about statistics, Kinsey nonetheless led the first large-scale empirical study of sexual behavior. The Kinsey reports shocked readers by documenting high rates of masturbation and extramarital and homosexual sex.

BENJAMIN SPOCK One of the first pediatricians to get psychoanalytic training, Dr. Spock formed commonsense principles of child rearing that helped shape the baby-boom generation. Since 1946 his book on baby care has sold 50 million copies.

B. F. SKINNER A strict behaviorist who avoided all reference to internal mental states, Skinner believed that behavior can best be shaped through positive reinforcement. Contrary to popular misconception, he did not raise his daughter in the "Skinner box" used to train pigeons.

Private Lives: Discipline and knowing where to draw the line

Jan Parker and Jan Stimpson

NO MATTER what you do, how hard you try, there may be times when your child behaves appallingly.

Managing these times so that your child's behaviour improves can be difficult and stressful, but leaving the behaviour unchallenged is worse. Only when you show where you draw the line can a child know which side of it she should be on.

To do this constructively, in ways that bring the results you both need without terrifying or crushing your child in the process, you will sometimes need to be gentle, sometimes tough, often both, and always strong enough to stand your ground.

Thinking ahead and considering your options will make it easier to deal calmly with your child's worst moments. Choosing which discipline strategies, if any, best suit your circumstances is also easier if you know the difference between discipline and punishment.

Discipline is an investment. It teaches children what they have done wrong, the consequences of their behaviour and how they could modify it. It encourages self-discipline and motivates them to do better. It is not a soft option, but can be astonishingly effective.

Punishment involves making children suffer for misbehaviour in an attempt to control it. It aims to shame, frighten or otherwise force children into compliance without them necessarily understanding why. It therefore risks teaching children to modify their behaviour for the wrong reasons, such as the risk of being caught.

The distinction between the two is not always clear-cut and some strategies may involve an element of both, but your *ability* to recognise the type and likely outcome of each approach will help you decide how best to proceed.

Effective discipline strategies

As ever, only consider those approaches that feel right for you and are appropriate to your child's age, understanding and temperament. If any strategy does not work as you hoped, or loses its effectiveness, change it.

Learning to challenge

Challenging is a key skill for turning around a child's behaviour. It takes practice. To those who have never tried it, it may sound too "reasonable" to work in the heat of the moment, but both parents and professionals vouch for its *ability* to stop children in their tracks and praise its effectiveness.

It works on the principle that most children will stop behaving unacceptably if they are told in no uncertain terms how it is affecting others and are given the opportunity to change course without loss of face.

Saying no and meaning it

If you mean it, really mean it, your child is much more likely to get the message. If you don't really mean it your child will pick this up in your expression and body *language* and either ignore you or provoke you until you do.

If you do mean "No", say it in a way that increases its effectiveness. Sometimes you may need to be sharp and stern.

To help your child know you mean business, try getting down to her level so you at least have a chance of eye contact.

Try to stay relaxed and say, calmly but firmly: "No. You are to stop that now—no more." This stops you getting drawn into negotiations and keeps you on very certain ground. Children often echo their parents' emotions; staying in control in an otherwise fiery situation may help them follow suit.

Removing the victim, not the culprit

This is especially useful in educating very young children not to hurt others. It denies the aggressor the attention that may fuel her behaviour and also makes the victim feel safer with you than being left alone.

If your child is hurting another, always explain why you do not like that behaviour and how you would like her to behave instead.

Consequences

Helping children understand the natural consequences of their actions is crucial to their improving their behaviour and learning self-control. This approach can also be used when your child is displaying behaviour you need to stop. For example: Parent (firmly and calmly): "Joe, if you throw your toys someone will get hurt, and you don't want that to happen. Play without throwing, or put it down."

This is often all that is needed to help a child *think* through the consequences of an action—and stop. But what happens when you have told your child the natural consequences of an action and she carries on doing it? Or when you have reminded her of a family rule and she still breaks it? To make it very clear where you draw the line, you may have to impose an (artificial) consequence for crossing it. Eg:

The weapons rule

You may have a family rule that no toys are to be used as weapons to hurt or frighten other children. Whenever necessary, you remind her of it and tell her the natural consequence of breaking it (ie "You will hurt"). You may even challenge her behaviour. But two minutes later she hits her brother on the head with a drumstick. What next?

Three strikes and it's out

1. Any toy used as a weapon (ie to hurt or frighten others) is immediately removed (for an hour, for the afternoon, for the rest of the day—the older the child the longer the time can be).

2. If it happens again, it is removed again, for longer.

3. If it happens a third time, it is put in the bin.

Standing back

If you react to every misdemeanour you could spend most of your time reining in your child's behaviour, which, by the law of diminishing returns, means she will take less notice and you will become increasingly frustrated and angry.

Liberate yourself by choosing times not to react immediately. At the very least, this will allow you time to assess what you want your child to do and how important it is that they do it, or whether you can let it go. If it is behaviour that you feel you must challenge, a considered response is generally much more effective than a knee-jerk one.

'Raising Happy Children' by Jan Parker and Jan Stimpson (Hodder & Stoughton, pounds 9.99)

The Stability of Personality: Observations and Evaluations

Robert R. McCrae and Paul T. Costa, Jr.

Robert R. McCrae is Research Psychologist and **Paul T. Costa, Jr.,** is Chief, Laboratory of Personality and Cognition, both at the Gerontology Research Center, National Institute on Aging, National Institutes of Health. Address correspondence to Robert R. McCrae, Personality, Stress and Coping Section, Gerontology Research Center, 4940 Eastern Ave., Baltimore, MD 21224.

"There is an optical illusion about every person we meet," Ralph Waldo Emerson wrote in his essay on "Experience":

> In truth, they are all creatures of given temperament, which will appear in a given character, whose boundaries they will never pass: but we look at them, they seem alive, and we presume there is impulse in them. In the moment it seems impulse; in the year, in the lifetime, it turns out to be a certain uniform tune which the revolving barrel of the music-box must play.[1]

In this brief passage, Emerson anticipated modern findings about the stability of personality and pointed out an illusion to which both laypersons and psychologists are prone. He was also perhaps the first to decry personality stability as the enemy of freedom, creativity, and growth, objecting that "temperament puts all divinity to rout." In this article, we summarize evidence in support of Emerson's observations but offer arguments against his evaluation of them.[2]

EVIDENCE FOR THE STABILITY OF ADULT PERSONALITY

Emerson used the term temperament to refer to the basic tendencies of the individual, dispositions that we call personality traits. It is these traits, measured by such instruments as the Minnesota Multiphasic Personality Inventory and the NEO Personality Inventory, that have been investigated in a score of longitudinal studies over the past 20 years. Despite a wide variety of samples, instruments, and designs, the results of these studies have been remarkably consistent, and they are easily summarized.

1. The mean levels of personality traits change with development, but reach final adult levels at about age 30. Between 20 and 30, both men and women become somewhat less emotional and thrill-seeking and somewhat more cooperative and self-disciplined—changes we might interpret as evidence of increased maturity. After age 30, there are few and subtle changes, of which the most consistent is a small decline in activity level with advancing age. Except among individuals with dementia, stereotypes that depict older people as being withdrawn, depressed, or rigid are unfounded.
2. Individual differences in personality traits, which show at least some continuity from early childhood on, are also essentially fixed by age 30.

Stability coefficients (test-retest correlations over substantial time intervals) are typically in the range of .60 to .80, even over intervals of as long as 30 years, although there is some decline in magnitude with increasing retest interval. Given that most personality scales have short-term retest reliabilities in the range from .70 to .90, it is clear that by far the greatest part of the reliable variance (i.e., variance not due to measurement error) in personality traits is stable.

3. Stability appears to characterize all five of the major domains of personality—neuroticism, extraversion, openness to experience, agreeableness, and conscientiousness. This finding suggests that an adult's personality profile as a whole will change little over time, and studies of the stability of configural measures of personality support that view.
4. Generalizations about stability apply to virtually everyone. Men and women, healthy and sick people, blacks and whites all show the same pattern. When asked, most adults will say that their personality has not changed much in adulthood, but even those who claim to have had major changes show little objective evidence of change on repeated administrations of personality questionnaires. Important exceptions to this generalization include people suffering from dementia and certain

From *Current Directions in Psychological Science*, December 1994, pp. 173–175. © 1994 by the American Psychological Society. Reprinted by permission of Blackwell Publishers.

categories of psychiatric patients who respond to therapy, but no moderators of stability among healthy adults have yet been identified.[3]

When researchers first began to publish these conclusions, they were greeted with considerable skepticism—"I distrust the facts and the inferences" Emerson had written—and many studies were designed to test alternative hypotheses. For example, some researchers contended that consistent responses to personality questionnaires were due to memory of past responses, but retrospective studies showed that people could not accurately recall how they had previously responded even when instructed to do so. Other researchers argued that temporal consistency in self-reports merely meant that individuals had a fixed idea of themselves, a crystallized self-concept that failed to keep pace with real changes in personality. But studies using spouse and peer raters showed equally high levels of stability.[4]

The general conclusion that personality traits are stable is now widely accepted. Some researchers continue to look for change in special circumstances and populations; some attempt to account for stability by examining genetic and environmental influences on personality. Finally, others take the view that there is much more to personality than traits, and seek to trace the adult developmental course of personality perceptions or identity formation or life narratives.

These latter studies are worthwhile, because people undoubtedly do change across the life span. Marriages end in divorce, professional careers are started in mid-life, fashions and attitudes change with the times. Yet often the same traits can be seen in new guises: Intellectual curiosity merely shifts from one field to another, avid gardening replaces avid tennis, one abusive relationship is followed by another. Many of these changes are best regarded as variations on the "uniform tune" played by individuals' enduring dispositions.

ILLUSORY ATTRIBUTIONS IN TEMPORAL PERSPECTIVE

Social and personality psychologists have debated for some time the accuracy of attributions of the causes of behavior to persons or situations. The "optical illusion" in person perception that Emerson pointed to was somewhat different. He felt that people attribute behavior to the live and spontaneous person who freely creates responses to the situation, when in fact behavior reveals only the mechanical operation of lifeless and static temperament. We may (and we will!) take exception to this disparaging, if common, view of traits, but we must first concur with the basic observation that personality processes often appear different when viewed in longitudinal perspective: "The years teach much which the days never know."

Consider happiness. If one asks individuals why they are happy or unhappy, they are almost certain to point to environmental circumstances of the moment: a rewarding job, a difficult relationship, a threat to health, a new car. It would seem that levels of happiness ought to mirror quality of life, and that changes in circumstances would result in changes in subjective well-being. It would be easy to demonstrate this pattern in a controlled laboratory experiment: Give subjects $1,000 each and ask how they feel!

But survey researchers who have measured the objective quality of life by such indicators as wealth, education, and health find precious little association with subjective well-being, and longitudinal researchers have found surprising stability in individual differences in happiness, even among people whose life circumstances have changed markedly. The explanation is simple: People adapt to their circumstances rapidly, getting used to the bad and taking for granted the good. In the long run, happiness is largely a matter of enduring personality traits.[5] "Temper prevails over everything of time, place, and condition, and . . . fix[es] the measure of activity and of enjoyment."

A few years ago, William Swann and Craig Hill provided an ingenious demonstration of the errors to which too narrow a temporal perspective can lead. A number of experiments had shown that it was relatively easy to induce changes in the self-concept by providing self-discrepant feedback. Introverts told that they were really extraverts rated themselves higher in extraversion than they had before. Such studies supported the view that the self-concept is highly malleable, a mirror of the evaluation of the immediate environment.

Swann and Hill replicated this finding, but extended it by inviting subjects back a few days later. By that time, the effects of the manipulation had disappeared, and subjects had returned to their initial self-concepts. The implication is that any one-shot experiment may give a seriously misleading view of personality processes.[6]

The relations between coping and adaptation provide a final example. Cross-sectional studies show that individuals who use such coping mechanisms as self-blame, wishful thinking, and hostile reactions toward other people score lower on measures of well-being than people who do not use these mechanisms. It would be easy to infer that these coping mechanisms detract from adaptation, and in fact the very people who use them admit that they are ineffective. But the correlations vanish when the effects of prior neuroticism scores are removed; an alternative interpretation of the data is thus that individuals who score high on this personality factor use poor coping strategies and also have low well-being: The association between coping and well-being may be entirely attributable to this third variable.[7]

Psychologists have long been aware of the problems of inferring causes from correlational data, but they have not recognized the pervasiveness of the bias that Emerson warned about. People tend to understand behavior and experience as the result of the immediate context, whether intrapsychic or environmental. Only by looking over time can one see the persistent effects of personality traits.

THE EVALUATION OF STABILITY

If few findings in psychology are more robust than the stability of personality, even fewer are more unpopular. Gerontologists often see stability as an affront to their commitment to continuing adult development; psychotherapists sometimes view it as an alarming challenge to their ability to help patients;[8] humanistic psychologists and transcendental philosophers think it degrades human nature. A popular account in *The Idaho Statesman* ran under the disheartening headline "Your Personality—You're Stuck With It."

In our view, these evaluations are based on misunderstandings: At worst, stability is a mixed blessing. Those individuals who are anxious, quarrelsome, and lazy might be understandably distressed to think that they are likely to stay that way, but surely those who are imaginative, affectionate, and carefree at age 30 should be glad to hear that they will probably be imaginative, affectionate, and carefree at age 90.

Because personality is stable, life is to some extent predictable. People can make vocational and retirement choices with some confidence that their current interests and enthusiasms will not desert them. They can choose friends and mates with whom they are likely to remain compatible. They can vote on the basis of candidates' records, with some assurance that future policies will resemble past ones. They can learn which co-workers they can depend on, and which they cannot. The personal and social utility of personality stability is enormous.

But it is precisely this predictability that so offends many critics. ("I had fancied that the value of life lay in its inscrutable possibilities," Emerson complained.) These critics view traits as mechanical and static habits and believe that the stability of personality traits dooms human beings to lifeless monotony as puppets controlled by inexorable forces. This is a misunderstanding on several levels.

First, personality traits are not repetitive habits, but inherently dynamic dispositions that interact with the opportunities and challenges of the moment.[9] Antagonistic people do not yell at everyone; some people they flatter, some they scorn, some they threaten. Just as the same intelligence is applied to a lifetime of changing problems, so the same personality traits can be expressed in an infinite variety of ways, each suited to the situation.

Second, there are such things as spontaneity and impulse in human life, but they are stable traits. Individuals who are open to experience actively seek out new places to go, provocative ideas to ponder, and exotic sights, sounds, and tastes to experience. Extraverts show a different kind of spontaneity, making friends, seeking thrills, and jumping at every chance to have a good time. People who are introverted and closed to experience have more measured and monotonous lives, but this is the kind of life they choose.

Finally, personality traits are not inexorable forces that control our fate, nor are they, in psychodynamic language, ego alien. Our traits characterize us; they are our very selves;[10] we act most freely when we express our enduring dispositions. Individuals sometimes fight against their own tendencies, trying perhaps to overcome shyness or curb a bad temper. But most people acknowledge even these failings as their own, and it is well

that they do. A person's recognition of the inevitability of his or her one and only personality is a large part of what Erik Erikson called ego integrity, the culminating wisdom of a lifetime.

Notes

1. All quotations are from "Experience," in *Essays: First and Second Series*, R.W. Emerson (Vintage, New York, 1990) (original work published 1844).

2. For recent and sometimes divergent treatments of this topic, see R.R. McCrae and P.T. Costa, Jr., *Personality in Adulthood* (Guilford, New York, 1990); D. C. Funder, R.D. Parke, C. Tomlinson-Keasey and K. Widaman, Eds., *Studying Lives Through Time: Personality and Development* (American Psychological Association, Washington, DC, 1993); T. Heatherton and J. Weinberger, *Can Personality Change?* (American Psychological Association, Washington, DC, 1994).

3. L.C. Siegler, K.A. Welsh, D.V. Dawson, G.G. Fillenbaum, N.L. Earl, E.B. Kaplan, and C.M. Clark, Ratings of personality change in patients being evaluated for memory disorders, *Alzheimer Disease and Associated Disorders, 5,* 240–250 (1991); R.M.A. Hirschfeld, G.L. Klerman, P. Clayton, M.B. Keller, P. McDonald-Scott, and B. Larkin, Assessing personality: Effects of depressive state on trait measurement, *American Journal of Psychiatry, 140,* 695–699 (1983); R.R. McCrae, Moderated analyses of longitudinal personality stability, *Journal of Personality and Social Psychology, 65,* 577–585 (1993).

4. D. Woodruff, The role of memory in personality continuity: A 25 year follow-up, *Experimental Aging Research, 9,* 31–34 (1983); P.T. Costa, Jr., and R.R. McCrae, Trait psychology comes of age, in *Nebraska Symposium on Motivation: Psychology and Aging,* T.B. Sonderegger, Ed.

(University of Nebraska Press, Lincoln, 1992).

5. P.T. Costa, Jr., and R.R. McCrae, Influence of extraversion and neuroticism on subjective well-being: Happy and unhappy people, *Journal of Personality and Social Psychology, 38,* 668–678 (1980).

6. The study is summarized in W.B. Swann, Jr., and C.A. Hill, When our identities are mistaken: Reaffirming self-conceptions through social interactions, *Journal of Personality and Social Psychology, 43,* 59–66 (1982). Dangers of single-occasion research are also discussed in J.R. Council, Context effects in personality research, *Current Directions in Psychological Science, 2,* 31–34 (1993).

7. R.R. McCrae and P.T. Costa, Jr., Personality, coping, and coping effectiveness in an adult sample, *Journal of Personality, 54,* 385–405 (1986).

8. Observations in nonpatient samples show what happens over time under typical life circumstances; they do not rule out the possibility that psychotherapeutic interventions can change personality. Whether or not such change is possible, in practice much of psychotherapy consists of helping people learn to live with their limitations, and this may be a more realistic goal than "cure" for many patients. See P.T. Costa, Jr., and R.R. McCrae, Personality stability and its implications for clinical psychology, *Clinical Psychology Review, 6,* 407–423 (1986).

9. A. Tellegen, Personality traits: Issues of definition, evidence and assessment, in *Thinking Clearly About Psychology: Essays in Honor of Paul E. Meehl,* Vol. 2, W. Grove and D. Cicchetti, Eds. (University of Minnesota Press, Minneapolis, 1991).

10. R.R. McCrae and P.T. Costa, Jr., Age, personality, and the spontaneous self-concept, *Journals of Gerontology: Social Sciences, 43,* S177–S185 (1988).

How Culture Molds Habits of Thought

By ERICA GOODE

For more than a century, Western philosophers and psychologists have based their discussions of mental life on a cardinal assumption: that the same basic processes underlie all human thought, whether in the mountains of Tibet or the grasslands of the Serengeti.

Cultural differences might dictate what people thought about. Teenage boys in Botswana, for example, might discuss cows with the same passion that New York teenagers reserved for sports cars.

But the habits of thought—the strategies people adopted in processing information and making sense of the world around them— were, Western scholars assumed, the same for everyone, exemplified by, among other things, a devotion to logical reasoning, a penchant for categorization and an urge to understand situations and events in linear terms of cause and effect.

Recent work by a social psychologist at the University of Michigan, however, is turning this long-held view of mental functioning upside down.

In a series of studies comparing European Americans to East Asians, Dr. Richard Nisbett and his colleagues have found that people who grow up in different cultures do not just think about different things: they think differently.

"We used to think that everybody uses categories in the same way, that logic plays the same kind of role for everyone in the understanding of everyday life, that memory, perception, rule application and so on are the same," Dr. Nisbett said. "But we're now arguing that cognitive processes themselves are just far more malleable than mainstream psychology assumed."

A summary of the research will be published next winter in the journal Psychological Review, and Dr. Nisbett discussed the findings Sunday at the annual meetings of the American Psychological Association in Washington.

In many respects, the cultural disparities the researchers describe mirror those described by anthropologists, and may seem less than surprising to Americans who have lived in Asia. And Dr. Nisbett and his colleagues are not the first psychological researchers to propose that thought may be embedded in cultural assumptions: Soviet psychologists of the 1930's posed logic problems to Uzbek peasants, arguing that intellectual tools were influenced by pragmatic circumstances.

But the new work is stirring interest in academic circles because it tries to define and elaborate on cultural differences through a series of tightly controlled laboratory experiments. And the theory underlying the research challenges much of what has been considered gospel in cognitive psychology for the last 40 years.

"If it's true, it turns on its head a great deal of the science that many of us have been doing, and so it's sort of scary and thrilling at the same time," said Dr. Susan Andersen, a professor of psychology at New York University and an associate editor at Psychological Review.

In the broadest sense, the studies—carried out in the United States, Japan, China and Korea—document a familiar division. Easterners, the researchers find, appear to think more "holistically," paying greater attention to context and relationship, relying more on experience-based knowledge than abstract logic and showing more tolerance for contradiction. Westerners are more "analytic" in their thinking, tending to detach objects from their context, to avoid contradictions and to rely more heavily on formal logic.

In one study, for example, by Dr. Nisbett and Takahiko Masuda, a graduate student at Michigan, students from Japan and the United States were shown an animated underwater scene, in which one larger "focal" fish swam among smaller fishes and other aquatic life.

Asked to describe what they saw, the Japanese subjects were much more likely to begin by setting the scene, saying for example, "There was a lake or pond" or "The bottom was rocky," or "The water was green." Americans, in contrast, tended to begin their descriptions with the largest fish, making statements like

"There was what looked like a trout swimming to the right."

Over all, Japanese subjects in the study made 70 percent more statements about aspects of the background environment than Americans, and twice as many statements about the relationships between animate and inanimate objects. A Japanese subject might note, for example, that "The big fish swam past the gray seaweed."

"Americans were much more likely to zero in on the biggest fish, the brightest object, the fish moving the fastest," Dr. Nisbett said. "That's where the money is as far as they're concerned."

But the greater attention paid by East Asians to context and relationship was more than just superficial, the researchers found. Shown the same larger fish swimming against a different, novel background, Japanese participants had more difficulty recognizing it than Americans, indicating that their perception was intimately bound with their perception of the background scene.

When it came to interpreting events in the social world, the Asians seemed similarly sensitive to context, and quicker than the Americans to detect when people's behavior was determined by situational pressures.

Psychologists have long documented what they call the fundamental attribution error, the tendency for people to explain human behavior in terms of the traits of individual actors, even when powerful situational forces are at work. Told that a man has been instructed to give a speech endorsing a particular presidential candidate, for example, most people will still believe that the speaker believes what he is saying.

Yet Asians, according to Dr. Nisbett and his colleagues, may in some situations be less susceptible to such errors, indicating that they do not describe a universal way of thinking, but merely the way that Americans think.

In one study, by Dr. Nisbett and Dr. Incheol Choi, of Seoul National

What Americans notice: the biggest, fastest and shiniest.

University in Korea, the Korean and American subjects were asked to read an essay either in favor of or opposed to the French conducting atomic tests in the Pacific. The subjects were told that the essay writer had been given "no choice" about what to write. But subjects from both cultures still showed a tendency to "err," judging that the essay writers believed in the position endorsed in the essays.

When the Korean subjects were first required to undergo a similar experience themselves, writing an essay according to instructions, they quickly adjusted their estimates of how strongly the original essay writers believed what they wrote. But Americans clung to the notion that the essay writers were expressing sincere beliefs.

One of the most striking dissimilarities found by the researchers emerged in the way East Asians and Americans in the studies responded to contradiction. Presented with weaker arguments running contrary to their own, Americans were likely to solidify their opinions, Dr. Nisbett said, "clobbering the weaker arguments," and resolving the threatened contradiction in their own minds. Asians, however, were more likely to modify their own position, acknowledging that even the weaker arguments had some merit.

In one study, for example, Asian and American subjects were presented with strong arguments in favor of financing a research project on adoption. A second group was presented both with strong arguments in support of the project and weaker arguments opposing it.

Both Asian and American subjects in the first group expressed strong

support for the research. But while Asian subjects in the second group responded to the weaker opposing arguments by decreasing their support, American subjects increased their endorsement of the project in response to the opposing arguments.

In a series of studies, Dr. Nisbett and Dr. Kaiping Peng of the University of California at Berkeley found that Chinese subjects were less eager to resolve contradictions in a variety of situations than American subjects. Asked to analyze a conflict between mothers and daughters, American subjects quickly came down in favor of one side or the other. Chinese subjects were more likely to see merit on both sides, commenting, for example, that, "Both the mothers and the daughters have failed to understand each other."

Given a choice between two different types of philosophical argument, one based on analytical logic, devoted to resolving contradiction, the other on a dialectical approach, accepting of contradiction, Chinese subjects preferred the dialectical approach, while Americans favored the logical arguments. And Chinese subjects expressed more liking than Americans for proverbs containing a contradiction, like the Chinese saying "Too modest is half boastful." American subjects, Dr. Nisbett said, found such contradictions "rather irritating."

Dr. Nisbett and Dr. Ara Norenzayan of the University of Illinois have also found indications that when logic and experiential knowledge are in conflict, Americans are more likely than Asians to adhere to the rules of formal logic, in keeping with a tradition that in Western societies began with the Ancient Greeks.

For example, presented with a logical sequence like, "All animals with fur hibernate. Rabbits have fur. Therefore rabbits hibernate," the Americans, the researchers found, were more likely to accept the validity of the argument, separating its formal structure, that of a syllogism, from its content, which might or might not be plausible. Asians, in contrast, more frequently judged such syllogisms as invalid based on their implausibility—not all animals with fur do in fact hibernate.

While the cultural disparities traced in the researchers' work are substantial, their origins are much less clear. Historical evidence suggests that a divide between Eastern and Occidental thinking has existed at least since ancient times, a tradition of adversarial debate, formal logical argument and analytic deduction flowering in Greece, while in China an appreciation for context and complexity, dialectical argument and a tolerance for the "yin and yang" of life flourished.

How much of this East-West difference is a result of differing social and religious practices, different languages or even different geography is anyone's guess. But both styles, Dr. Nisbett said, have advantages, and both have limitations. And neither approach is written into the genes: many Asian-Americans, born in the United States, are indistinguishable in their modes of thought from European-Americans.

Dr. Alan Fiske, an associate professor of anthropology at the University of California at Los Angeles, said that experimental research like Dr. Nisbett's "complements a lot of ethnographic work that has been done."

"Anthropologists have been describing these cultures and this can tell you a lot about everyday life and the ways people talk and interact," Dr. Fiske said. "But it's always difficult to know how to make sense of these qualitative judgments, and they aren't controlled in the same way that an experiment is controlled."

Yet not everyone agrees that all the dissimilarities described by Dr. Nisbett and his colleagues reflect fundamental differences in psychological process.

Dr. Patricia Cheng, for example, a professor of psychology at the University of California at Los Angeles, said that many of the researchers' findings meshed with her own experience. "Having grown up in a traditional Chinese family and also being in Western culture myself," she said, "I do see some entrenched habits of interpretation of the world that are different across the cultures, and they do lead to pervasive differences."

But Dr. Cheng says she thinks that some differences—the Asian tolerance for contradiction, for example—are purely social. "There is not a difference in logical tolerance," she said.

Still, to the extent that the studies reflect real differences in thinking and perception, psychologists may have to radically revise their ideas about what is universal and what is not, and to develop new models of mental process that take cultural influences into account.

Unit 2

Unit Selections

Key Points to Consider

❖ What evidence do we have that biology is not the only influence on our psychological being? How much of a role do you think the environment plays compared to biology?

❖ Based on your experience observing children, what would you say most contributes to personal growth: physiological or environmental factors?

❖ Name some bona fide differences between the sexes that are controlled by the brain and that have been discovered by scientists. What sex differences are due to stereotypes and are therefore untrue?

❖ What is a gene? Why is it important to study heredity? How is genetic research conducted and why is it important to psychologists? What is the human genome project? What do you think this project holds for the future of humankind?

❖ How do the genes influence specific human features, such as personality traits? Can you think of any traits that are probably controlled by genes?

❖ If we can map genes, can we "map" the brain? Do you know the various parts of the brain? Explain whether or not and how you could ascribe certain behaviors to certain parts of the brain.

❖ What is the biology of joy? What are endorphins? What other biochemical actions influence our moods, emotions, and behaviors? Do you think most moods and emotions are the result of biochemistry?

❖ Do we have a biological clock? What does this clock control? What controls the clock? How can the study of human body rhythms help us lead healthier or better lives?

❖ What is meant by the term "motivation?" Are great athletes different in motivation level than average athletes? How else do they differ, if at all?

❖ Can our minds affect our physical health? How? Can you offer data to support your position? If the mind does affect the body, what can we do to keep ourselves mentally and physically well?

 **Links** | # www.dushkin.com/online/

These sites are annotated on pages 4 and 5.

On the front page of every newspaper, in practically every televised newscast, and on many magazine covers the problems of substance abuse in America haunt us. Innocent children are killed when caught in the crossfire of the guns of drug lords or even of their own classmates. Prostitutes selling their bodies for drug money spread the deadly AIDS virus. The white-collar middle manager loses his job because he embezzled company money to support his cocaine habit.

Why do people turn to drugs? Why doesn't the publicity about the ruination of human lives diminish the drug problem? Why can some people consume two cocktails and stop, while others feel helpless against the inebriating seduction of alcohol? Why do some people crave heroin as their drug of choice, while others choose cigarettes or caffeine?

The causes of individual behavior such as drug and alcohol abuse are the focus of this section. If physiology—either biochemistry, the nervous system or genes—is the determinant of our behavior, then solutions to such puzzles as alcoholism lie in the field of psychobiology, the study of behavior in relation to biological processes. However, if experience as a function of our environment and learning histories creates personality and coping ability and thus causes subsequent behavior, normal or not, then researchers must take a different tack and explore features of the environment responsible for certain behaviors. A third explanation is that ability to adjust to change is produced by some complex interaction or interplay between experience and biology. If this interaction accounts for individual differences in personality and ability to cope, scientists then have a very complicated task ahead of them.

Conducting research designed to unravel the determinants of behavior is difficult. Scientists must call upon their best design skills to develop studies that will yield useful and replicable findings. A researcher hoping to examine the role of experience in personal growth and behavior needs to be able to isolate one or two stimuli or environmental features that seem to control a particular behavior. Imagine trying to delimit the complexity of the world sufficiently so that only one or two events stand out as the cause of an individual's alcoholism. Likewise, researchers interested in psychobiology also need refined, technical knowledge. Suppose a scientist hopes to show that a particular form of mental illness is inherited. She cannot merely examine family genetic histories, because family members can also learn maladaptive behaviors from one another. The researcher's ingenuity will be challenged; she must use intricate techniques such as comparing children to their adoptive as well as to their biological parents. Volunteer subjects may be difficult to find, and, even then, the data may be hard to interpret.

The first two articles in this unit offer general information on the interaction of nature and nurture. In "Human Nature: Born or Made?" Erica Goode explores the joint contributions of nature and nurture. The article discusses the contributions of genes as well as the relative influence of the environment. Goode clearly but succinctly provides a general overview of the nature/nurture controversy. A companion article discusses gender as an exemplar of the nature/nurture issue. From where do gender differences and similarities come? Deborah Blum argues in "The Gender Blur" that the boundaries are becoming less crisp and therefore there are more similarities than differences between the two sexes, a situation that makes the study of the origin of gender more complicated.

The role of nature, in particular of genetics in determining our behaviors, is examined next. In "Decoding the Human Body," Sharon Begley provides an overview of the exciting project designed to map and decode human genes—the Human Genome Project. This project may offer insight into which genes contribute to various psychological disorders and health problems that plague a large part of our population.

The companion piece on personality assesses how DNA exerts an influence on our developing personalities, one particular aspect of human nature. In "The Personality Genes," the article concludes with the understanding that genes do exert significant influence.

A related essay, "Autism Is Likely to Be Linked to Several Genes," discusses how such a disorder is usually not tied to the action of a single gene but rather is influenced by multiple genes. The article is also interesting because it divulges information about a baffling but intriguing disorder—autism.

The nervous system is also an important component of the biological determinants of our personal tendencies and behaviors. Three articles provide information about the brain, which is the focal point of the nervous system. In the first article, "The Future of the Brain," the author discusses how special techniques are helping us better understand the functioning of the brain. Such techniques allow physicians and scientists to conduct research and do surgery on the brain with less damage than older, more invasive methods.

The influence of the brain on the expression of specific aspects of the human behavior is discussed in the next two articles. In the first article, "The Biology of Joy," hormones, neurotransmitters, and parts of the brain affect the whole nervous system and thus affect human behavior. Author Jeremiah Creedon discusses the role of biopsychology with regard to one particular and delightful emotion—joy. Psychologists and biologists have discovered certain neurotransmitters related to joy, which they labeled endorphins, and have found these substances to be secreted during pleasurable events.

A companion article also delves into the role of the brain in regulating our daily lives (see "The Tick-Tock of the Biological Clock). Scientists have discovered a biological clock that is controlled by the brain. Knowledge of this regulation and the role the brain plays in it helps us understand why, for example, heart attacks are more likely during one part of the day than another.

We next turn our attention away from psychobiology to human motivation—an entirely different determinant of human behavior and growth. James Bauman, in "The Gold Medal Mind," examines what makes a great athlete different from the more mundane athlete. Highly successful athletes possess certain traits that motivate, focus, and relax them better than the rest of us.

In the final unit article, we stray far from the laboratory and athletic field but remain within the realm of motivation. In "Faith & Healing," Claudia Wallis suggests that people are turning more and more to alternative forms of healing than to medicine and psychology. Some individuals turn to religion as an inspiration; others look inward and examine their private feelings and attitudes. In any event, new research is demonstrating that there is indeed a mind-body connection, and that, for example, those in whose lives faith plays a part are healthier than those who do not.

In summary, this unit covers factors that determine our behavior, in other words, factors that are moderated by genes, the nervous system, biochemicals, motives, or some combination of the these.

Human Nature: Born or Made?

Evolutionary Theorists Provoke an Uproar

By ERICA GOODE

When two scientists proposed in a recent book that rape was best viewed as a sexual act with its roots in evolution, it set off a squall of protest from feminists and social scientists, won the researchers appearances on programs like "Dateline NBC," and became the talk of the cocktail party circuit. Even last week the controversy continued, with the book's authors engaging in a rancorous exchange over a critical review in the scientific journal Nature.

But the case put forward by Dr. Randy Thornhill and Dr. Craig Palmer in "A Natural History of Rape: Biological Bases of Sexual Coercion," published last month by the MIT Press, was not, as some assumed, a fringe theory developed by a pair of renegade researchers.

Rather, the arguments made by Dr. Thornhill and Dr. Palmer fit into a larger theoretical framework, the work of a group of scientists who have ushered Darwin into new and provocative areas, including sexual attraction between men and women, parenting, jealousy and violence, as well as less touchy regions like the learning of language and the organization of perception.

And while some of these researchers, who call their approach "evolutionary psychology" (other scientists view it as only one way of approaching evolutionary psychology), would quibble with some of the methods used and conclusions drawn by the authors of the rape book, most would endorse the larger principles that underlie the work.

The general notion that much of what humans do today evolved in the Pleistocene has seeped into popular culture, and some findings have achieved the status of sound bites: "Men are polygamous, women monogamous," for example, or "Women rank wealth and status higher in selecting a mate; men put a higher priority on reproductive potential." The actor Michael Douglas may have had such precepts in mind when he was asked in a recent interview about his engagement to an actress much younger than he. "It's something that has existed as long as time," he replied. "As long as history, there have been older men with younger women."

The scientists whose work is reflected in such statements, albeit in oversimplified form, are not just trying to attract public attention. They are trying to reshape psychology, placing at its center the question of how the mind was "designed" by evolution millions of years ago to solve specific problems faced by human ancestors in an environment very different from the modern world.

In constructing this new psychology, evolutionary psychologists have crafted a novel approach that differs in crucial respects from other, more traditional ways of viewing the mind, and from methods of other evolutionary scientists who study human behavior.

For example, the researchers dispute the view that the human mind is a "general purpose computer" that is programmed by parents, schools and other cultural influences only after birth. They see the mind as preprogrammed, made up of specialized mechanisms—"modules" or "organs"—that predispose all human beings to think and act in certain ways, especially when it comes to basic endeavors like selecting a mate, fighting off sexual competitors or deciding what is safe to eat.

The genes for these complex mental mechanisms, the argument goes,

Evolutionary Psychology: The Landscape

Few scientific enterprises evoke more interest, debate and hostility than evolutionary psychology, the effort to use the principles of evolutionary biology in studying the human mind.

Evolution

All life evolved through a process of "natural selection": Organisms with traits that promoted survival or reproduction passed on those traits to future generations: others died off. Natural selection remains the central feature of evolutionary biology.

CHARLES DARWIN
The naturalist's 1859 book, "On the Origin of Species by Means of Natural Selection," changed the scientific world forever.

Cognitive Science

Applies the idea of a "designed" mind.

In the last few decades, scientists in a variety of fields, including psychology, have harnessed concepts from computer science to understand how people take in information, process it and use it to solve problems.

Evolutionary Psychology

Applies natural selection to behavior.

It holds that the human mind is not a "blank slate," but instead, comprises specialized mental mechanisms for solving problems faced long ago. The question is, are these mechanisms limited to functions like vision, or do they extend to complex behaviors?

LEDA COSMIDES AND JOHN TOOBY
Considered by many as among the intellectual leaders of evolutionary psychology, they have articulated many of its basic tenets and have studied cooperation and other aspects of social interaction.

MARGO WILSON AND MARTIN DALY
Their studies of infanticide and spousal murder have become classics in evolutionary psychology.

DONALD SYMONS
One of the first to study sexual attractions and other aspects of human sexuality from an evolutionary perspective.

STEVEN PINKER
He maintains that humans have an instinctive ability to learn language, that all people learn language similar ways and that languages evolve in predictable fashion.

DAVID M. BUSS
His controversial studies find that women looking for mates rank wealth and status higher while men put a higher priority on reproductive potential.

Sociobiology

Adopts natural selection as a partial explanation for social behavior.

The systematic study of the biological basis of social behavior; it attempts to explain animal behavior in light of natural selection and other biological processes.

EDWARD O. WILSON
A renowned entomologist, his 1975 book "Sociobiology," laid a foundation for the field. Though most of it dealt with animals, its final chapter brought evolution into the realm of human affairs, where critics said he was on shaky ground.

GEORGE C. WILLIAMS
In 1966, he refuted the idea that adaptions arise for the good of the species or group. Rather, he said, adaptions are the result of successful genes spreading themselves through the population.

WILLIAM D. HAMILTON
His work brought mathematical rigor to the study of evolution and offered a genetic basis for altruism, behavior that had baffled naturalists from Darwin onward. Wilson called Hamilton's work "pivotal."

A Shadow Over the Field

Distorts Darwin's theory to justify class differences.

SOCIAL DARWINISM
The 19th-Century theory distorted Darwin's scientific message to justify social inequities. Though scientists generally agree that social Darwinism has nothing to do with reputable evolutionary science, some theorists find themselves tarred with the term.

were passed on through the generations because they were adaptive, enhancing survival or reproductive success, and eventually, they spread widely and became standard equipment.

But in the year 2000, such mechanisms may or may not be adaptive, and may or may not represent aspects of behavior that society wants to encourage. For example, even if rape was adaptive in the distant past, a notion that even many of Dr. Thornhill and Dr. Palmer's like-minded colleagues think dubious, that would not mean that it is excusable or should not be heavily punished.

Evolutionary psychologists argue that their job is to approach the mind as an ancient engineering project, developing and testing out hypotheses about what "design problems" needed solving, and what universal mental structures might have been designed, by the pressures to survive and reproduce, to solve them.

Such an approach, they assert, offers a badly needed bridge between psychology and the natural sciences, and will ultimately provide a much firmer foundation for the understanding of human behavior.

"Psychologists should be interested in evolutionary biology for the same reason that hikers should be interested in an aerial map of an unfamiliar territory that they plan to explore on foot," wrote Dr. Leda Cosmides, Dr. John Tooby and Dr. John Barkow in the introduction to "The Adapted Mind: Evolutionary Psychology and the Generation of Culture" (Oxford, 1992). "If they look at the map, they are much less likely to lose their way."

Dr. Cosmides and her husband, Dr. Tooby, both professors at the University of California at Santa Barbara, are widely regarded as intellectual leaders of the evolutionary psychology school. Joined by several other scientists, including Dr. Donald Symons, also at Santa Barbara, and Dr. Margo Wilson and Dr. Martin Daly, both of McMaster University in Hamilton, Ontario, they

hammered out the basic principles of their approach in the mid-1980's in a series of meetings at a hotel in Palm Desert, Calif.

In the intervening years, this nucleus has expanded to encompass a wide variety of researchers in different areas, including Dr. David M. Buss, a psychologist at the University of Texas, Dr. Thornhill at the University of New Mexico and Dr. Steven Pinker, a psychologist at the Massachusetts Institute of Technology and the author of "Words and Rules: The Ingredients of Language" (Basic Books, 1999) and "How The Mind Works," (W. W. Norton, 1997).

Evolutionary psychologists have not always carried on their campaign quietly.

They have issued a noisy assault on the way the social sciences have done business for the last 50 years, asserting that social scientists have a collective phobia about possible biological influences on behavior and an obsession with more "politically correct" environmental explanations. Some researchers have thrust their work into the spotlight by pursuing topics that seem guaranteed to push people's emotional buttons, rape being only the latest example.

In the process, the scientists have gained a reputation for a self-confidence bordering on arrogance, and a style of scholarly debate so unapologetic and uncompromising that, as one observer put it, "They just make people mad."

Perhaps as a result, the scientists' work and occasionally the scientists themselves have attracted no shortage of criticism, from social scientists and within evolutionary science itself.

Critics have assailed their scientific methods, suggested that some work is tinged by sexism and disputed most of the major tenets of the scientists' approach. And some worry that the studies will be misused by politicians and advocacy groups, who are often quick to blur the distinction between theory and fact.

"The fact is," said Dr. Jerry Coyne, an evolutionary biologist at the University of Chicago and a co-author of the critical review of Dr. Thornhill and Dr. Palmer's book in Nature, "that evolutionary psychology, except for its barest claims, remains highly controversial, and there are ideological agendas on both sides."

The Background

A Disturbing Legacy Of Twisting Darwin

At the most basic level, some critics oppose any effort to link evolution and human behavior.

"There are a whole bunch of people who think it's dehumanizing to talk about humans in biological terms," said Dr. Robert Boyd, an evolutionary anthropologist at the University of California at Los Angeles. "They think it's just kind of distasteful."

In some cases, people confuse the "biological" approach of evolutionary science, which seeks to understand how genes contributed to the evolution of humans as a species, with the field of behavioral genetics, which investigates to what extent heredity accounts for how traits like shyness or schizophrenia vary from person to person.

But biology, applied to human behavior, also has a disturbing history of misuse. College students in introductory courses are taught the perils of "social Darwinism," a 19th-century theory that borrowed catch words of evolutionary thinking and twisted them into a justification for class differences: the struggle for wealth and power, social Darwinists argued, was a battle for "survival of the fittest," a term coined by Herbert Spencer, an English philosopher.

Darwin's theory, stretched and distorted in various ways, was also called upon by the Nazis as a rationale for genocide, and has been a staple of forced sterilization campaigns and racist propaganda.

In the decades after World War II, the record of these abuses created a distrust of biological explanations for human behavior.

But sensitivity could also turn into virtual censorship, as Dr. E. O. Wilson, a renowned entomologist at Harvard, discovered after publishing his now-classic book, "Sociobiology," in 1975. The book, mostly devoted to a discussion of animal behavior, included a final chapter extending evolutionary theory into the realm of human affairs. It was heavily criticized, and in 1978, as Dr. Wilson began to speak about his theories at a meeting of the American Association for the Advancement of Science in Washington, protesters heckled him and dumped a pitcher of water on his head.

Dr. Stephen Jay Gould, a paleontologist, and Dr. Richard Lewontin, a population geneticist, both of Harvard, have been the most vocal and prolific of sociobiology's critics, writing a famous 1979 paper, "The Spandrels of San Marco and the Panglossian Paradigm: A Critique of the Adaptationist Program."

Dr. Gould, in particular, has continued to find fault with the work of scientists, including evolutionary psychologists, who seek to explain traits as "adaptations." In fact, he argues, many traits are not the products of natural selection, favored because they enhance reproduction or survival, but are simply random byproducts of other evolutionary developments.

The Issues

Controversial Task, Abundance of Critics

Some evolutionary biologists have also historically opposed applying Darwinian principles to humans, not because they have moral misgivings about such research, but because they think the task is simply too complicated.

Trying to determine the evolutionary forces that shaped animal behavior is hard enough, they argue. But to tease out the legacy of evolution from the effects of thousands of years of human culture presents almost insurmountable obstacles, particularly given the limits on the kinds of experiments that can be done with people.

Yet in the last 20 years, advances in genetics and molecular science have made it impossible to ignore the evidence that biology has at least some impact on how people behave and have made the discussion of genetic influences more widely accepted.

And evolutionary scientists, able to go about their work in a more tolerant climate, have begun to develop a variety of methods for applying Darwinian principles to humans. Evolutionary psychology, as defined by Dr. Cosmides, Dr. Tooby and others, might involve laboratory experiments, cross-cultural studies and other approaches.

Other researchers use mathematical models to study foraging and other behavior in modern hunter-gatherer societies. Still others do comparative studies, looking for similarities and differences between humans and animals.

And the Human Behavior and Evolution Society, founded 15 years ago, counts 1,000 members from a wide variety of disciplines, including biology, psychology, anthropology, law and medicine, who study topics as diverse as the way pheromones coordinate female menstrual cycles and hunting practices among the Ache of Paraguay.

Still, some evolutionary psychologists feel their arguments for biology must overcome substantial resistance.

"There is a flagrant double standard that's applied to the evidence," said Dr. Buss, whose latest book, "The Dangerous Passion" (Free Press, 2000) deals with jealousy, and who has recently proposed that human beings may have a specialized mental module for murder.

"If it's an evolutionary hypothesis, you have to document mountains of evidence before anyone will take it seriously, and even then it will be dismissed," Dr. Buss said. "On the contrary, if you say there is a sex difference and it's all due to media violence, then the standards are low and everyone accepts it without any evidence."

The Real Question

Not a Simple Matter Of Nature/Nurture

The nature/nurture dichotomy, however, is in many ways spurious. No evolutionary scientist would dispute that culture is a powerful influence, or that environmental forces shape behavior. Darwin himself was in a sense a "nurturist": it was the environment, after all, with all of its threats, possibilities and complications, that in his theory ultimately determined which traits were "successful" and passed on to future generations, and which were not.

A more sophisticated debate, and one central to many of the most knowledgeable critiques of evolutionary psychology, revolves around more subtle distinctions, like the timing of evolutionary change, the criteria used to decide whether something is an adaptation. Then there is the question of the relative balance of culture and genes in determining how humans behave.

Dr. Cosmides and Dr. Tooby argue that the complex mechanisms, or "design features," that they believe make up the structure of the human mind evolved over millions of years, as combinations of genes proved successful at reproducing themselves, and gradually spread through the species, eventually becoming universal.

Because of this, they assert, it makes little sense to study traits that vary from group to group, or society to society. Humans are basically all the same, they argue, with only a "dusting" of difference. Nor, they say, is it worthwhile to ask whether a particular behavior is adaptive—in the sense of producing more off-spring—in the modern world. Doing so, they say, can lead scientists wildly astray.

In an example given by Dr. Cosmides, a scientist might argue that smoking cigarettes is "adaptive" for teenage girls because it causes boys to think they are cool. The boys are then more likely to choose them as sexual partners.

Instead, researchers should ask what purpose behavior might have served during the period in which it evolved, a time evolutionary psychologists refer to as the Environment of Evolutionary Adaptedness and sometimes pinpoint in the Pleistocene Era, when human ancestors lived in hunter-gatherer groups.

In the modern world, Dr. Cosmides, Dr. Tooby and others argue, humans are not "fitness maximizers," continually strategizing to make the most of their chances at reproduction and survival.

Rather, they are "adaptation executors," carrying out programs written into the mind's machinery long ago. "The machinery doesn't know its own programming," Dr. Cosmides and Dr. Tooby are fond of saying.

Other scientists, however, object that this view is much too narrow, that it requires assumptions that are impossible to test and ignores the possibility that evolution might in some cases have proceeded at a faster pace.

They also find the notion of studying only universal traits perplexing: in studies of animal behavior, a standard procedure is to study how traits vary in different environmental circumstances and to explore the effects of different traits on reproduction.

"We don't have a time machine," said Dr. Patricia Adair Gowaty, professor of ecology at the University of Georgia. "We don't even know for the Pleistocene what the social and environmental conditions were. The only evidence we have for these things is the behavior itself."

The work of Dr. Gowaty, who studies birds, Dr. Sarah Blaffer Hrdy,

a professor emerita at the University of California at Davis who studies primates, and other researchers, some of whom study humans, offers an evolutionary view of male-female relations that differs sharply from that painted by evolutionary psychologists like Dr. Buss.

"It really is frustrating to me," Dr. Gowaty said, "when I read these evolutionary psychologists saying that you can't look at selective process in real-time environments, because these novel environments might not be like environments of the past. That might be so. Then again, that might not be so."

The Dissent

Saying That Culture Plays a Greater Role

Other critics complain that evolutionary psychologists often underemphasize the extent to which culture influences human behavior, and ignore equally plausible cultural explanations for their data.

Dr. Alice Eagly, for example, a social psychologist at Northwestern University, has been critical of Dr. Buss's research showing that women rank wealth and status higher in choosing a sexual partner, while men put a higher priority on physical attractiveness.

"I wouldn't argue that there are no differences between men and women," Dr. Eagly said. "But there remains a big question whether things as specific as a preference for money are built in genetically."

Dr. Boyd, of U.C.L.A., also said that culture's impact on behavior was often underplayed in evolutionary psychologists' work.

While Dr. Tooby, Dr. Cosmides and others have written extensively about the ways in which culture might be shaped by the mental mechanisms humans have evolved, for example, they have spent far less time on the reverse proposition, that culture itself transmits knowledge

about how to solve problems from generation to generation.

"From my research perspective," Dr. Boyd said, "evolutionary psychologists place a much smaller emphasis on cultural variation than I think is empirically going on. I'm inclined to think of cultures as evolving over fairly long periods of time, accumulating information, some of it adaptive, some not adaptive. I still take an evolutionary perspective, but I don't think we have to have it all coded in the genes."

For their part, Dr. Cosmides and Dr. Tooby respond that theirs is "the first intellectual community that does know what to do with culture," and that can truly address the way biology and culture interact in creating human societies.

In fact, Dr. Tooby said, he entered graduate school in anthropology at Harvard in part because "I was interested in cracking the problem of culture, in what was the underlying mechanism."

Yet the word "mechanism" is in itself controversial. The notion that the mind is specialized is considered gospel by the "Santa Barbara Church," as one scientist jokingly referred to Dr. Tooby, Dr. Cosmides and their colleagues. But many researchers remain skeptical that the same specialization that has been demonstrated for some brain functions—vision, for example—holds when it comes to complex patterns of behavior.

Dr. Boyd, for example, said: "I am convinced that we don't understand the brain well enough to make these assumptions. I've read the two sides of this argument, and it seems to me that it's an open question."

The Future

A Young Field Still Taking Shape

Many scientific disciplines are riddled with internal disagreements. Physicists fight about why particles have different masses. Climatologists do battle over global warming.

Yet the intensity of emotion that infuses any discussion of evolutionary psychology is unusual, even among scientists.

In part, the reason may be that the star actors in this scientific drama are human beings, and the question at issue is the nature of being human.

Dr. Tooby says he sometimes worries "that evolutionary psychology will die because of sociological reasons."

"Almost all that anyone has heard about evolutionary psychology has to do with sex and violence," he said. "But there is insight to be found for hundreds of really critical topics."

Other evolutionary scientists who study human behavior say they, too, are worried: they worry that the controversy is dividing researchers who should be working together, and that the work of a relatively small group of scholars is inviting a hostility that the field—just recovering from two decades of embattled debate—hardly needs.

The antidote to such fears, many say, is the faith that constructive scientific argument often leads to greater knowledge, and the belief that, for a field still in its infancy, patience is a virtue.

"I don't think we really know how to do evolutionary psychology yet," said Dr. Randolph Nesse, director of the Evolution and Human Adaptation Program at the Institute for Social Research at the University of Michigan. "I think we have great trouble formulating our hypotheses, and even more trouble figuring out how to test them. We know we have a powerful principle, that will eventually provide a foundation for a deeper and richer psychology. But we have a lot of work to do."

Once there were only two: male and female. Men, mostly, were the big ones, with deep voices and sturdy shoes, sitting with legs splayed. Women, mostly, were the smaller ones, with dainty high heels, legs crossed tightly at the ankle, and painted mouths. It was easy to tell them apart. These days, it's not so easy. Men wear makeup and women smoke cigars; male figure skaters are macho—but Dennis Rodman wears a dress. We can be one gender on the Internet and another in bed. Even science, bastion of the rational, can't prove valid the lines that used to separate and define us. Although researching the biology of gender has answered some old questions, it has also raised important new one. The consensus? Gender is more fluid than we ever thought. Queer theorists call gender a social construct, saying that when we engage in traditional behaviors and sexual practices, we are nothing but actors playing ancient, empty roles. Others suggest that gender is performance, a collection of masks we can take on and off at will. So are we witnessing the birth of thrilling new freedoms, or the disintegration of the values and behaviors that bind us together? Will we encounter new opportunities for self-realization, or hopeless confusion? Whatever the answers, agreeing that our destinies aren't preordained will launch a search that will profoundly affect society, and will eventually engage us all.

—The Editors

By Deborah Blum

The Gender Blur

where does biology end and society take over ?

I was raised in one of those university-based, liberal elite families that politicians like to ridicule. In my childhood, every human being—regardless of gender—was exactly alike under the skin, and I mean exactly, barring his or her different opportunities. My parents wasted no opportunity to bring this point home. One Christmas, I received a Barbie doll and a softball glove. Another brought a green enamel stove, which baked tiny cakes by the heat of a lightbulb, and also a set of steel-tipped darts and competition-quality dart-board. Did I mention the year of the chemistry set and the ballerina doll?

It wasn't until I became a parent—I should say, a parent of two boys—that I realized I had been fed a line and swallowed it like a sucker (barring the part about opportunities, which I still believe). This dawned on me during my older son's dinosaur phase, which began when he was about 2 ½. Oh, he loved dinosaurs, all right, but only the blood-swilling carnivores. Plant-eaters were wimps and losers, and he refused to wear a T-shirt marred by a picture of a stegosaur. I looked down at him one day, as he was snarling around my feet and doing his toddler best to gnaw off my right leg, and I thought: This goes a lot deeper then culture.

Raising children tends to bring on this kind of politically-incorrect reaction. Another friend came to the same conclusion watching a son determinedly bite his breakfast toast into the shape of a pistol he hoped would blow away—or at least terrify—his younger brother. Once you get past the guilt part—Did I do this? Should I have bought him that plastic allosaur with the oversized teeth?—such revelations can lead you to consider the far more interesting field of gender biology, where the questions take a different shape: Does love of carnage begin in culture or genetics, and which

drives which? Do the gender roles of our culture reflect an underlying biology, and, in turn, does the way we behave influence that biology?

The point I'm leading up to—through the example of my son's innocent love of predatory dinosaurs—is actually one of the most straightforward in this debate. One of the reasons we're so fascinated by childhood behaviors is that, as the old saying goes, the child becomes the man (or woman, of course.) Most girls don't spend their preschool years snarling around the house and pretending to chew off their companion's legs. And they—mostly—don't grow up to be as aggressive as men. Do the ways that we amplify those early differences in childhood shape the adults we become? Absolutely. But it's worth exploring the starting place—the faint signal that somehow gets amplified.

"There's plenty of room in society to influence sex differences," says Marc

From *Utne Reader,* September/October 1998, pp. 44-48. Reprinted by permission of International Creative Management, Inc. © 1998 by Deborah Blum.

Breedlove, a behavioral endocrinologist at the University of California at Berkeley and a pioneer in defining how hormones can help build sexually different nervous systems. "Yes, we're born with predispositions, but it's society that amplifies them, exaggerates them. I believe that—except for the sex differences in aggression. Those [differences] are too massive to be explained simply by society."

Aggression does allow a straightforward look at the issue. Consider the following statistics: Crime reports in both the United States and Europe record between 10 and 15 robberies committed by men for every one by a woman. At one point, people argued that this was explained by size difference. Women weren't big enough to intimidate, but that would change, they predicted, with the availability of compact weapons. But just as little girls don't routinely make weapons out of toast, women—even criminal ones—

sexual encounters, more offspring, more genetic future. For the female—especially in a species like ours, with time for just one successful pregnancy a year—what's the genetic advantage in brawling?

Thus the issue becomes not whether there is a biologically influenced sex difference in aggression—the answer being a solid, technical "You betcha"—but rather how rigid that difference is. The best science, in my opinion, tends to align with basic common sense. We all know that there are extraordinarily gentle men and murderous women. Sex differences are always generalizations: They refer to a behavior, with some evolutionary rationale behind it. They never define, entirely, an individual. And that fact alone should tell us that there's always—even in the most biologically dominated traits—some flexibility, an instinctive ability to respond, for better and worse, to the world around us.

mal matches. One is that even with this apparently precise system, there's nothing precise—or guaranteed—about the physical construction of male and female. The other point makes that possible. It appears that sex doesn't matter in the early states of embryonic development. We are unisex at the point of conception.

If you examine an embryo at about six weeks, you see that it has the ability to develop in either direction. The fledgling embryo has two sets of ducts—Wolffian for male, Muellerian for female—an either/or structure, held in readiness for further development. If testosterone and other androgens are released by hormone- producing cells, then the Wolffian ducts develop into the channel that connects penis to testes, and the female ducts wither away.

Without testosterone, the embryo takes on a female form; the male ducts vanish and the Muellerian ducts expand into oviducts, uterus, and vagina. In other words, in humans, anyway (the opposite is true in birds), the female is the default sex. Back in the 1950s, the famed biologist Alfred Jost showed that if you castrate a male rabbit fetus, choking off testosterone, you produce a completely feminized rabbit.

We don't do these experiments in humans—for obvious reasons—but there are naturally occurring instances that prove the same point. For instance: In the fetal testes are a group of cells, called Leydig cells, that make testosterone. In rare cases, the fetus doesn't make enough of these cells (a defect known as Leydig cell hypoplasia). In this circumstance we see the limited power of the XY chromosome. These boys have the right chromosomes and the right genes to be boys; they just don't grow a penis. Obstetricians and parents often think they see a baby girl, and these children are routinely raised as daughters. Usually, the "mistake" is caught about the time of puberty, when menstruation doesn't start. A doctor's examination shows the child to be internally male; there are usually small testes, often tucked within the abdomen. As the researchers put it, if the condition had been known from the beginning, "the sisters would have been born as brothers."

Just to emphasize how tricky all this body-building can get, there's a peculiar genetic defect that seems to be clustered by heredity in a small group of villages in the Dominican Republic. The result of the defect is a failure to produce an enzyme that concentrates testosterone, specifically for building

will that wonderful, unpredictable, flexible biology that we have been given allow a shift, so that one day, we will literally be far more alike?

don't seem drawn to weaponry in the same way that men are. Almost twice as many male thieves and robbers use guns as their female counterparts do.

Or you can look at more personal crimes: domestic partner murders. Three-fourths of men use guns in those killings; 50 percent of women do. Here's more from the domestic front: In conflicts in which a woman killed a man, he tended to be the one who had started the fight—in 51.8 percent of the cases, to be exact. When the man was the killer, he again was the likely first aggressor, and by an even more dramatic margin. In fights in which women died, they had started the argument only 12.5 percent of the time.

Enough. You can parade endless similar statistics but the point is this: Males are more aggressive, not just among humans but among almost all species on earth. Male chimpanzees, for instance, declare war on neighboring troops, and one of their strategies is a warning strike: They kill females and infants to terrorize and intimidate. In terms of simple, reproductive genetics, it's an advantage of males to be aggressive: You can muscle your way into dominance, winning more

This is true even with physical characteristics that we've often assumed are nailed down by genetics. Scientists now believe height, for instance, is only about 90 percent heritable. A person's genes might code for a six-foot-tall body, but malnutrition could literally cut that short. And there's also some evidence, in girls anyway, that children with stressful childhoods tend to become shorter adults. So while some factors are predetermined, there's evidence that the prototypical male/female body design can be readily altered.

It's a given that humans, like most other species—bananas, spiders, sharks, ducks, any rabbit you pull out of a hat—rely on two sexes for reproduction. So basic is that requirement that we have chromosomes whose primary purpose is to deliver the genes that order up a male or a female. All other chromosomes are numbered, but we label the sex chromosomes with the letters X and Y. We get one each from our mother and our father, and the basic combinations are these: XX makes female, XY makes male.

There are two important—and little known—points about these chromoso-

the genitals. One obscure little enzyme only, but here's what happens without it: You get a boy with undescended testes and a penis so short and stubby that is resembles an oversized clitoris.

In the mountain villages of this Caribbean nation, people are used to it. The children are usually raised as "conditional" girls. At puberty, the secondary tide of androgens rises and is apparently enough to finish the construction project. The scrotum suddenly descends, the phallus grows, and the child develops a distinctly male body—narrow hips, muscular build, and even slight beard growth. At that point, the family shifts the child over from daughter to son. The dresses are thrown out. He begins to wear male clothes and starts dating girls. People in the Dominican Republic are so familiar with this condition that there's a colloquial name for it: *guevedoces,* meaning "eggs (or testes) at 12."

stances, behave differently than if the individual was a female."

Do the ways that we amplify physical and behavioral differences in childhood shape who we become as adults? Absolutely. But to understand that, you have to understand the differences themselves—their beginning and the very real biochemistry that may lie behind them.

Here is a good place to focus on testosterone—a hormone that is both well-studied and generally underrated. First, however, I want to acknowledge that there are many other hormones and neurotransmitters that appear to influence behavior. Preliminary work shows that fetal boys are a little more active than fetal girls. It's pretty difficult to argue socialization at that point. There's a strong suspicion that testosterone may create the difference.

And there are a couple of relevant animal models to emphasize the point.

consensus seems to be that full-blown "I'm a girl" or "I'm a boy" instincts arrive between the ages of 2 and 3. Research shows that if a family operates in a very traditional, Beaver Cleaver kind of environment, filled with awareness of and association with "proper" gender behaviors, the "boys do trucks, girls do dolls" attitude seems to come very early. If a child grows up in a less traditional family, with an emphasis on partnership and sharing—"We all do the dishes, Joshua"—children maintain a more flexible sense of gender roles until about age 6.

In this period, too, relationships between boys and girls tend to fall into remarkably strict lines. Interviews with children find that 3-year-olds say that about half their friendships are with the opposite sex. By the age of 5, that drops to 20 percent. By 7, almost no boys or girls have, or will admit to having, best friends of the opposite sex. They still hang out on the same playground, play on the same soccer teams. They may be friendly, but the real friendships tend to be boy-to-boy or girl-to-girl.

do the ways that we amplify differences in childhood shape who we become as adults?

It's the comfort level with this slip-slide of sexual identity that's so remarkable and, I imagine, so comforting to the children involved. I'm positive that the sexual transition of these children is less traumatic than the abrupt awareness of the "sisters who would have been brothers." There's a message of tolerance there, well worth repeating, and there are some other key lessons too.

These defects are rare and don't alter the basic male-female division of our species. They do emphasize how fragile those divisions can be. Biology allows flexibility, room to change, to vary and grow. With that comes room for error as well. That it's possible to live with these genetic defects, that they don't merely kill us off, is a reminder that we, male and female alike, exist on a continuum of biological possibilities that can overlap and sustain either sex.

Marc Breedlove points out that the most difficult task may be separating how the brain responds to hormones from how the brain responds to the *results* of hormones. Which brings us back, briefly, below the belt: In this context, the penis is just a result, the product of androgens at work before birth. "And after birth," says Breedlove, "virtually everyone who interacts with that individual will note that he has a penis, and will, in many in-

Back in the 1960s, Robert Goy, a psychologist at the University of Wisconsin at Madison, first documented that young male monkeys play much more roughly than young females. Goy went on to show that if you manipulate testosterone level—raising it in females, damping it down in males—you can reverse those effects, creating sweet little male monkeys and rowdy young females.

Is testosterone the only factor at work here? I don't think so. But clearly we can argue a strong influence, and, interestingly, studies have found that girls with congenital adrenal hypoplasia—who run high in testosterone—tend to be far more fascinated by trucks and toy weaponry than most little girls are. They lean toward rough-and-tumble play, too. As it turns out, the strongest influence on this "abnormal" behavior is not parental disapproval, but the company of other little girls, who tone them down and direct them toward more routine girl games.

And that reinforces an early point: If there is indeed a biology to sex differences, we amplify it. At some point—when it is still up for debate—we gain a sense of our gender, and with it a sense of "gender-appropriate" behavior.

Some scientists argue for some evidence of gender awareness in infancy, perhaps by the age of 12 months. The

There's some interesting science that suggests that the space between boys and girls is a normal part of development; there are periods during which children may thrive and learn from hanging out with peers of the same sex. Do we, as parents, as a culture at large, reinforce such separation? Is the pope Catholic? One of my favorite studies looked at little boys who asked for toys. If they asked for a heavily armed action figure, they got the soldier about 70 percent of the time. If they asked for a "girl" toy, like a baby doll or a Barbie, their parents purchased it maybe 40 percent of the time. Name a child who won't figure out how to work *that* system.

How does all this fit together—toys and testosterone, biology and behavior, the development of the child into the adult, the way that men and women relate to one another?

Let me make a cautious statement about testosterone: It not only has some body-building functions, it influences some behaviors as well. Let's make that a little less cautious: These behaviors include rowdy play, sex drive, competitiveness, and an in-your-face attitude. Males tend to have a higher baseline of testosterone than females—in our species, about seven to ten times as much—and therefore you would predict (correctly, I think) that all of those behaviors would be more generally found in men than in women.

But testosterone is also one of my favorite examples of how responsive biology is, how attuned it is to the way we live our lives. Testosterone, it turns out, rises in response to competition and threat. In the days of our ancestors, this might have been hand-to-hand combat or high-risk hunting endeavors. Today, scientists have measured testosterone rise in athletes preparing for a game, in chess players awaiting a match, in spectators following a soccer competition.

If a person—or even just a person's favored team—wins, testosterone continues to rise. It falls with a loss. (This also makes sense in an evolutionary perspective. If one was being clobbered with a club, it would be extremely unhelpful to have a hormone [under] one to battle on.) Testosterone also rises in the competitive world of dating, settles down with a stable and supportive relationship, climbs again if the relationship starts to falter.

It's been known for years that men in high-stress professions—say, police work or corporate law—have higher testosterone levels than men in the ministry. It turns out that women in the same kind of strong-attitude professions have higher testosterone than women who choose to stay home. What I like about this is the chicken-or-egg aspect. If you argue that testosterone influenced the behavior of those women, which came first? Did they have high testosterone and choose the law? Or did they choose the law, and the competitive environment ratcheted them up on the androgen scale? Or could both be at work?

And, returning to children for a moment, there's an ongoing study by Pennsylvania researchers, tracking that question in adolescent girls, who are being encouraged by their parents to engage in competitive activities that were once for boys only. As they do so, the researchers are monitoring, regularly, two hormones: testosterone and cortisol, a stress hormone. Will these hormones rise in response to this new, more traditionally male environment?

What if more girls choose the competitive path; more boys choose the other? Will female testosterone levels rise, male levels fall? Will that wonderful, unpredictable, flexible biology that we've been given allow a shift, so that one day, we will literally be far more alike?

We may not have answers to all those questions, but we can ask them, and we can expect that the answers will come someday, because science clearly shows us that such possibilities exist. In this most important sense, sex differences offer us a paradox. It is only through exploring and understanding what makes us different that we can begin to understand what binds us together.

Deborah Blum is a Pulitzer Prize-winning science writer, a professor of journalism at the University of Wisconsin-Madison, and author of Sex on the Brain: The Biological Differences Between Men and Women *(Penguin, 1997).*

THE PERSONALITY GENES

Does DNA shape behavior? A leading researcher's behavior is a case in point

By J. MADELEINE NASH

MOLECULAR BIOLOGIST Dean Hamer has blue eyes, light brown hair and the goofy sense of humor of a stand-up comic. He smokes cigarettes, spends long hours in a cluttered laboratory at the National Institutes of Health, and in his free time clambers up cliffs and points his skis down steep, avalanche-prone slopes. He also happens to be openly, matter-of-factly gay.

What is it that makes Hamer who he is? What, for that matter, accounts for the quirks and foibles, talents and traits that make up anyone's personality? Hamer is not content merely to ask such questions; he is trying to answer them as well. A pioneer in the field of molecular psychology, Hamer is exploring the role genes play in governing the very core of our individuality. To a remarkable extent, his work on what might be called the gay, thrill-seeking and quit-smoking genes reflects his own genetic predispositions.

That work, which has appeared mostly in scientific journals, has been gathered into an accessible and quite readable form in Hamer's provocative new book, *Living with Our Genes* (Doubleday; $24.95). "You have about as much choice in some aspects of your personality," Hamer and coauthor Peter Copeland write in the introductory chapter, "as you do in the shape of your nose or the size of your feet."

Until recently, research into behavioral genetics was dominated by psychiatrists and psychologists, who based their most compelling conclusions about the importance of genes on studies of identical twins. For example, psychologist Michael Bailey of Northwestern University famously demonstrated that if one identical twin is gay, there is about a 50% likelihood that the other will be too. Seven years ago, Hamer picked up where the twin studies left off, homing in on specific strips of DNA that appear to influence everything from mood to sexual orientation.

Hamer switched to behavioral genetics from basic research; after receiving his Ph.D. from Harvard, he spent more then a decade studying the biochemistry of metallothionein, a protein that cells use to metabolize heavy metals like copper and zinc. As he was about to turn 40, however, Hammer suddenly realized he had learned as much about metallothionein as he cared to. "Frankly, I was bored," he remembers, "and ready for something new."

Instrumental in Hamer's decision to switch fields was Charles Darwin's *The Descent of Man, and Selection in Relation to Sex.* "I was fascinated to learn that Darwin seemed so convinced that behavior was partially inherited," he remembers, "even though when he was writing, genes had not been discovered, let alone DNA." Homosexual behavior, in particular, seemed ripe for exploration because few scientists had dared tackle such an emotionally and politically charged subject. "I'm gay," Hamer says with a shrug, "but that was not a major motivation. It was more of a question of intellectual curiosity—and the fact that no one else was doing this sort of research."

The results of Hamer's first foray into behavioral genetics, published by the journal *Science* in 1993, ignited a furor that has yet to die down. According to Hamer and his colleagues, male homosexuality appeared to be linked to a stretch of DNA at the very tip of the X chromosome, the chromosome men inherit from their mothers. Three years later, in 1996, Hamer and his collaborators at NIH seconded an Israeli group's finding that linked a gene on chromosome 11 to the personality trait psychologists called novelty seeking. That same year Hamer's lab helped pinpoint another gene, this time on chromosome 17, that appears to play a role in regulating anxiety.

Unlike the genes that are responsible for physical traits, Hamer emphasizes, these genes do not cause people to become homosexuals, thrill-seeking rock climbers or anxiety-ridden worrywarts. The biology of personality is much more complicated than that. Rather, what genes appear to do, says Hamer, is subtly bias the psyche so that different individuals react to similar experiences in surprisingly different ways.

Intriguing as these findings are, other experts caution that none has been unequivocally replicated by other research teams. Why? One possibility is that, despite all of Hamer's work, the links between these genes and these particular personality traits do not, in fact, exist. There is, however, another, more tantalizing possibility. Consider the genes that give tomatoes their flavor, suggests Hamer's colleague Dr. Dennis Murphy of the National Institute of Mental Health. Even a simple trait like acidity is controlled not by a single gene but by as many as 30 that operate in concert. In the same way, he speculates, many genes are involved in setting up temperamental traits and psychological vulnerabilities; each gene contributes just a little bit to the overall effect.

Hunting down the genes that influence personality remains a dauntingly difficult business. Although DNA is constructed out of a mere four chemicals—adenine, guanine, cytosine, thymine—it can take as many as a million combinations to spell out a single human gene. Most of these genes vary from individual to individual by only one chemical letter in a thousand, and it is precisely these minute differences that Hamer and his colleagues are trying to identify. Of particular interest are variations that may affect the operation of such brain chemicals as dopamine and serotonin, which are well-known modulators of mood. The so-called novelty-seeking gene, for example, is thought to affect how efficiently nerve cells absorb dopamine. The so-called anxiety gene is postulated to affect serotonin's action.

How can this be? After all, as Hamer and Copeland observe in their book, " . . . genes are not switches that say 'shy' or 'outgoing' or 'happy' or 'sad.' Genes are simply chemicals that direct the combination of more chemicals." What genes do is order up the production of proteins in organs like the kidney, the skin and also the brain. Thus, Hamer speculates, one version of the novelty-seeking gene may make a protein that is less efficient at absorbing dopamine. Since dopamine is the chemical that creates sensations of pleasure in response to intense experiences, people who inherit this gene might seek to stimulate its production by seeking out thrills.

Still, as critics emphasize and Hamer himself acknowledges, genes alone do not control the chemistry of the brain. Ultimately, it is the environment that determines how these genes will express themselves. In another setting, for example, it is easy to imagine that Hamer might have become a high school dropout rather than a scientist. For while he grew up in an affluent household in Montclair, N.J., he was hardly a model child. "Today," he chuckles, "I probably would have been diagnosed with attention-deficit disorder and put on Ritalin." In his senior year in high school, though,

Hamer discovered organic chemistry and went from being an unruly adolescent to a first-rate student. What people are born with, Hamer says, are temperamental traits. What they can acquire through experience is the ability to control these traits by exercising that intangible part of personality called character.

Over the coming decade, Hamer predicts, scientists will identify thousands of genes that directly and indirectly influence behavior. A peek inside the locked freezer in the hallway outside his own lab reveals a rapidly expanding stash of plastic tubes that contain DNA samples form more than 1,760 volunteers. Among them: gay men and their heterosexual brothers, a random assortment of novelty seekers and novelty avoiders, shy children and now a growing collection of cigarette smokers.

Indeed, while Hamer has maintained a professional distance from his studies, it is impossible to believe he is not also driven by a desire for self-discovery. Soon, in fact, his lab will publish a paper about a gene that makes it harder or easier for people to stop smoking. Judging by the pack of cigarettes poking out of his shirt pocket, Hamer would seem to have drawn the wrong end of that genetic stick. He has tried to stop smoking and failed, he confesses, dozens of times. "If I quit," he says, "it will be an exercise of character." And not, it goes without saying, of his genes.

Nature or Nurture?

Many aspects of personality may have a genetic component—such as sexual orientation, anxiety, a tendency to take chances and . . .

ILLUSTRATIONS FOR TIME BY SCOTT MENCHIN

DECODING THE
HUMAN BODY

The secrets of life: It is the most expensive, most ambitious biology mission ever. The Human Genome Project, at $250 million and counting, is biology's moon shot. In the eyes of boosters, it promises to provide no less than the operating instructions for a human body, and will revolutionize the detection, prevention and treatment of conditions from cancer to depression to old age itself. In the eyes of critics, it threatens to undermine privacy and bring on 'genetic discrimination' in insurance and employment. Near the finish line, one effect is indisputable: the genome has reignited the biotech industry. Explaining the genome—and what it means for you.

By Sharon Begley

EVERY FRIDAY morning at 11, the directors of the five labs leading the race to decipher the human genome confer by phone to assess their progress. In mid-March, it was clear they were closing in on the next big milestone: reading the 2 billionth chemical "letter" in human DNA. But since some of those letters were redundant, a count of 2 billion would not really tell how close they were to the finish line of 3.2 billion.

Greg Schuler, a molecular biologist turned computer jock at the National Institutes of Health, had just spent the weekend, sitting on the sofa with his laptop in front of his fireplace at home, writing a 674-line program to reanalyze the overlaps. When he sicced it on the redundant sequences, the answer popped out: the Human Genome Project had *already* passed the 2 billion mark, on March 9. It had taken four years to determine the first billion letters in the human genome, but only four months for what Schuler calls "that next odometer moment." The actual chemical letter was—drumroll, please—T.

All right, so it didn't really matter which of the four letters making up DNA claimed position number 2,000,000,000 in the largest, most expensive, most ambitious biology project ever undertaken. But after 13 years and $250 million, through the work of some

1,100 biologists, computer scientists and technicians at 16 (mostly university) labs in 6 countries, the announcement meant that the Human Genome Project was two thirds of the way toward its goal of determining the exact chemical sequence that constitutes the DNA in every cell of every human body. With competitors in the private sector goading them on, scientists in the public project have tripled their pace, sequencing 12,000 letters every minute of every day, 24/7. By last weekend the project, financed by the U.S. government and Britain's Wellcome Trust, had sequenced 2,104,257,000 chemical letters. At this rate, it will complete its "working draft"—90 percent of the genome, with an accuracy of 99.9 percent—in June. And Science will know the blueprint of human life, the code of codes, the holy grail, the source code of *Homo sapiens*. It will know, Harvard University biologist Walter Gilbert says, "what it is to be human."

That knowledge promises to revolutionize medicine and vault the biotech industry into the Wall Street stratosphere. But just as no one foresaw eBay or Amazon when Apple unveiled the first home computer in 1977, so there is no crystal ball clear enough to reveal how knowing the entire human genome will change the way we live and even the way we think about who we are. It is a pretty good bet, though, that doctors will

drip droplets of our genes onto a biochip to figure out if we have the kind of prostate cancer that will kill or not, or to figure out if ours is the kind of leukemia that responds to this drug rather than that one. They will analyze our children's genes to rank their chances of succumbing to heart disease or Alzheimer's. Scientists will learn which genes turn on when a wound heals, when a baby's fingers grow, when a scalp becomes bald or a brow wrinkled, when a song is learned or a memory formed, when hormones surge or stress overwhelms us—and they will learn how to manipulate those genes. Babies will be designed before conception. Employers will take your genetic profile before they offer you a job or withdraw an offer if they don't like the cut of your DNA. The human genome sequence "will be the foundation of biology for decades, centuries or millennia to come," says John Sulston, director of the Sanger Centre, the genome lab near Cambridge, England, where a spiral staircase in the lobby twists upward like the double helix itself.

And all of it will emerge from something like this: ATGCCGCGGCTCCTCC . . . on and on, for about 3.2 billion such letters. Each letter represents a molecule—adenine, cytosine, guanine, thymine. Every cell of every human body, from skin to muscle to liver and everything in between (except red

From *Newsweek*, April 10, 2000, pp. 50–57. © 2000 by Newsweek, Inc. All rights reserved. Reprinted by permission.

blood cells), contains a copy of the same DNA. The totality of DNA present in the cells of a species is its genome. Although the genetic age has brought incessant reports about genes "for" homosexuality, risk-taking, shyness, anxiety, cancer, Alzheimer's and more, the only thing a gene is actually "for" is a protein. The A's, T's, C's and G's constitute a code. Each triplet of letters instructs special machinery inside a cell to grab onto a particular amino acid. TGG, for instance, snatches the amino acid tryptophan. If you string together enough amino acids, you have a protein—a stomach enzyme that digests food, insulin that metabolizes carbohydrates, a brain chemical that causes depression, a sex hormone that triggers puberty. A gene, then, is an instruction, like the directions in a bead-making kit but written in molecule-ese. Humans have perhaps 80,000 genes, and we are 99.9 percent identical. That is, at only one in 1,000 chemical letters does the genome of, say, Woody Allen differ from that of Stone Cold Steve Austin.

Even at its inception, the creators of the Human Genome Project suspected that it would transform biology, vaulting it past physics as the hot science. But at the moment of its creation, the project was an unwanted child. Charles DeLisi, newly arrived at the Department of Energy, was in charge of research into the biological effects of radiation. In October 1985, he was reading a government report on technologies for detecting heritable mutations, such as those in the survivors of Hiroshima. It hit him: given the slow pace at which biologists were deciphering genes, which you need to do in order to assess mutations, they would finish . . . oh, about when humans had evolved into a new species. "We just weren't going to get there," says DeLisi. So he dashed off memos, ordered up reports, begged scientists to serve on planning committees—and got responses like "I don't want to spin my wheels" on a project that had little chance of happening.

For biologists and the genome, it was far from love at first sight. Critics pointed out that some 97 percent of the human genome—3.1 billion of the 3.2 billion A's, T's, C's and G's—does not spell out a gene. Why bother sequencing this "junk" DNA, whose presence no one can explain, especially when there was no known way to tell what was junk and what was a gene? But when a panel of leading scientists, including skeptics, unanimously endorsed the project in 1988, and it wrested funding from Congress, the Human Genome Project was out of the gate, headed toward a completion date of 2005 at a nice, sedate pace. It didn't last. In May 1998, gene-hunter extraordinaire J. Craig Venter and his newly formed Celera Genomics vowed to trounce the public project by finishing the human genome sequence in just three years. That made Francis Collins, director of the National Human Genome Research Institute, scramble. His

The Public Genome Team Races . . .

Going public: Collins has led the publicly financed genome project since 1993. This year he rebuffed an offer from the biotech firm Celera to join forces and thus speed up the work: he feared Celera would keep the results private, available only to those who pay, for too long. So the public project goes it alone, posting its discoveries every 24 hours (except weekends) at www.ncbi.nlm.nih.gov/genome/seq.

. . .The Upstart Master Of the Gene-iverse

To the swift: Venter's teams have sequenced the genomes of more organisms than anyone else. His policy of keeping data secret for six months ($5 million buys companies instant access for five years) riles some academics. But Venter's speed means that everyone gets data months sooner.

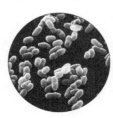

What We Know So Far

Fly boys: It took 195 scientists to decode *Drosophila's* genome. Why bother? Of 289 human-disease genes, 177 have analogs in the fly, including 68% of cancer genes.

Almost human? Half of the known human-disease genes have analogs in the genes of the worm *C. elegans,* raising hopes for the discovery of treatments

Tiny trailblazer: *Haemophilus influenzae,* a bacterium, was the first organism whose genome was fully sequenced

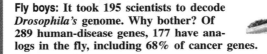

Photos by Baylor College of Medicine in Houston; Jones King—Holmes Science Photo Library, Photo Researchers; Oliver Meckes, Photo Researchers (2).

labs had sequenced less than 3 percent of the genome at the original halfway point, so he ordered everyone to forget about the double-checking and the exploring of cool scientific puzzles and just churn out the *#@*ing A's, T's, C's and G's. It worked. In October 1998 Collins announced that his team would have a rough draft in 2001; in March 1999 he pushed it to this spring.

What will it mean to know the complete human genome? Eric Lander of MIT's Whitehead Institute compares it to the discovery of the periodic table of the elements in the late 1800s. "Genomics is now providing biology's periodic table," says Lander. "Scientists will know that every phenome-non must be explainable in terms of this measly list"—which will fit on a single CD-ROM. Already researchers are extracting DNA from patients, attaching fluorescent molecules and sprinkling the sample on a glass chip whose surface is speckled with 10,000 known genes. A laser reads the fluorescence, which indicates which of the known genes on the chip are in the mystery sample from the patient. In only the last few months such "gene-expression monitoring" has diagnosed a muscle tumor in a boy thought to have leukemia, and distinguished between two kinds of cancer that require very different chemotherapy. Soon, predicts Patrick Brown of Stanford University, ex-

The Human Parts List

Scientists have identified more than 8,000 human genes, including those linked to breast and colon cancers and Alzheimer's disease. Figuring out how the genes work promises to lead to preventions and treatments. Some of the genes identified:

Chromo 1

Each human cell contains DNA organized into 23 pairs of chromosomes. Every chromosome has hundreds to thousands of codes for building proteins.

GBA
Gaucher disease
Absence of fat-breaking enzyme; can lead to jaundice or anemia.

HPC1
Prostate cancer

GLC1A
Glaucoma

PS2 (AD4)
Alzheimer's disease

Chromo 2

ETM2
Essential tremor
A common symptom of neurological disorders such as Parkinson's disease and stroke

MSH2
Colon cancer

*CREB
Memory
Mice without this gene can't learn simple tasks

PAX3
Waardenburg syndrome
Associated with deafness and mismatched eye colors

*PRESUMPTIVE LOCATION.

Chromo 3

VHL
Von Hippel-Lindau
Abnormal growth of blood vessels. Growth may develop in the retina, in the spinal cord, in certain areas of the brain or in the adrenal glands.

SCLC1
Lung cancer

MLH1
Colon cancer
Some 160,400 Americans died from the disease in 1997

ETM1
Essential tremor

Chromo 4

HD
Huntington disease
An inherited degenerative brain disease that leads to dementia

EVC
Ellis-van Creveld syndrome
Malformation of the wrist bones, partial harelip and prenatal teeth eruption

Alpha-synuclein
Parkinson's disease
Only recently discovered to be hereditary

Chromo 5

SRD51A
Steroid 5-alpha reductase 1
May lead to baldness and acne

*CSA
Cockayne syndrome
Premature aging

DTD
Diastrophic dysplasia
Malformations in joints

*PRESUMPTIVE LOCATION.

Chromo 6

SCA1
Spinocerebellar atrophy
Results in loss of muscle coordination and spasticity

IDDM1
Diabetes
A chronic disorder that greatly increases the risk of heart disease and kidney failure

EPM2A
Epilepsy

Chromo 7

GCK
Diabetes

ELN
Williams syndrome
Physical- and mental-development disorder

Pendrin
Pendred syndrome

CFTR
Cystic fibrosis

OB
Obesity

Chromo 8

WRN
Werner syndrome
Premature aging occurring during adolescence

MYC
Burkitt lymphoma
A rare form of cancer

Chromo 9

CDKN2
Malignant melanoma

ABC1
Tangier disease

ABL
Chronic myeloid leukemia

TSC1
Tuberous sclerosis

Chromo 10

PAHX
Refsum disease
One symptom is failure of muscle coordination

OAT
Gyrate atrophy
An error of metabolism known to cause progressive loss of vision

Locating Genes Within the Body...

The Human Genome Project is two-thirds completed. Scientists now know the exact identity of 2 billion of the 3 billion chemical "letters" that make up human DNA.

In a cell ... are chromosomes ... made of DNA strands ... wrapped around protein balls ... stretching to five feet

Photos by T. Ried–NHGRI–NIH

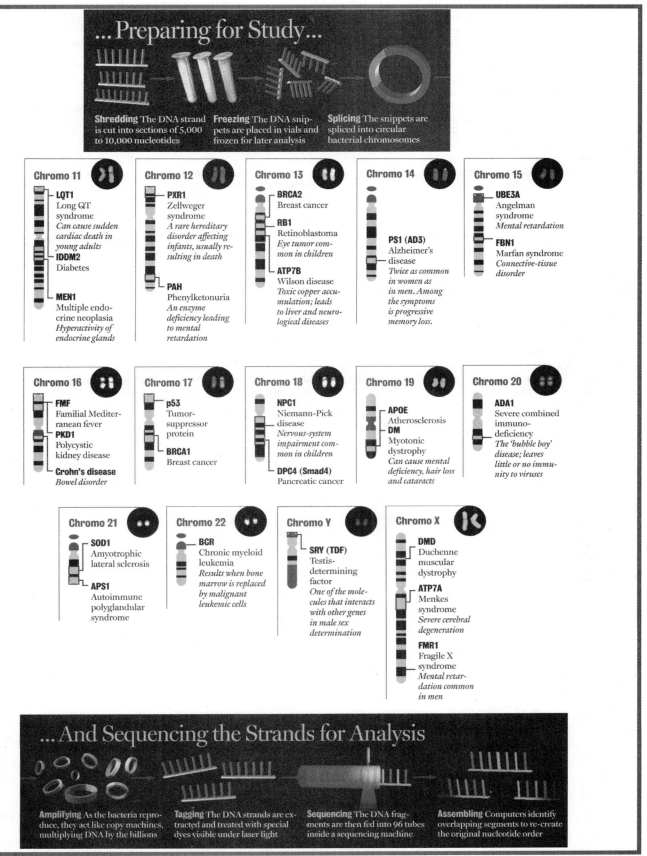

... Preparing for Study...

Shredding The DNA strand is cut into sections of 5,000 to 10,000 nucleotides

Freezing The DNA snippets are placed in vials and frozen for later analysis

Splicing The snippets are spliced into circular bacterial chromosomes

Chromo 11
LQT1
Long QT syndrome
Can cause sudden cardiac death in young adults
IDDM2
Diabetes
MEN1
Multiple endocrine neoplasia
Hyperactivity of endocrine glands

Chromo 12
PXR1
Zellweger syndrome
A rare hereditary disorder affecting infants, usually resulting in death
PAH
Phenylketonuria
An enzyme deficiency leading to mental retardation

Chromo 13
BRCA2
Breast cancer
RB1
Retinoblastoma
Eye tumor common in children
ATP7B
Wilson disease
Toxic copper accumulation; leads to liver and neurological diseases

Chromo 14
PS1 (AD3)
Alzheimer's disease
Twice as common in women as in men. Among the symptoms is progressive memory loss.

Chromo 15
UBE3A
Angelman syndrome
Mental retardation
FBN1
Marfan syndrome
Connective-tissue disorder

Chromo 16
FMF
Familial Mediterranean fever
PKD1
Polycystic kidney disease
Crohn's disease
Bowel disorder

Chromo 17
p53
Tumor-suppressor protein
BRCA1
Breast cancer

Chromo 18
NPC1
Niemann-Pick disease
Nervous-system impairment common in children
DPC4 (Smad4)
Pancreatic cancer

Chromo 19
APOE
Atherosclerosis
DM
Myotonic dystrophy
Can cause mental deficiency, hair loss and cataracts

Chromo 20
ADA1
Severe combined immuno-deficiency
The 'bubble boy' disease; leaves little or no immunity to viruses

Chromo 21
SOD1
Amyotrophic lateral sclerosis
APS1
Autoimmune polyglandular syndrome

Chromo 22
BCR
Chronic myeloid leukemia
Results when bone marrow is replaced by malignant leukemic cells

Chromo Y
SRY (TDF)
Testis-determining factor
One of the molecules that interacts with other genes in male sex determination

Chromo X
DMD
Duchenne muscular dystrophy
ATP7A
Menkes syndrome
Severe cerebral degeneration
FMR1
Fragile X syndrome
Mental retardation common in men

... And Sequencing the Strands for Analysis

Amplifying As the bacteria reproduce, they act like copy machines, multiplying DNA by the billions

Tagging The DNA strands are extracted and treated with special dyes visible under laser light

Sequencing The DNA fragments are then fed into 96 tubes inside a sequencing machine

Assembling Computers identify overlapping segments to re-create the original nucleotide order

GRAPHICS ON LAST TWO PAGES: SOURCES: NATIONAL CENTER FOR BIOTECHNOLOGY INFORMATION, NATIONAL LIBRARY OF MEDICINE, NATIONAL INSTITUTES OF HEALTH

RESEARCH BY FE CONWAY AND STEPHEN TOTILO, DESIGN BY BONNIE SCRANTON, GENE-SEQUENCING ILLUSTRATIONS BY CHRISTOPH BLUMRICH--NEWSWEEK.

pression analysis will distinguish prostate cancers that kill from prostate cancers that don't, neurons in a depressed brain from neurons in a normal brain—all on the basis of which genes are active.

Humankind's history is also written in its DNA. "Rare spelling differences in DNA can be used to trace human migrations," says Lander. "Scientists can recognize the descendants of chromosomes that ancient Phoenician traders left behind when they visited Italian seaports." Genetic data support the oral tradition that the Bantu-speaking Lemba of southern Africa are descendants of Jews who migrated from the Middle East 2,700 years ago. And they suggest that 98 percent of the Irish men of Connaught are descended from a single band of hunter-gatherers who reached the Emerald Isle more than 4,000 years ago.

But decoding the book of life poses daunting moral dilemmas. With knowledge of our genetic code will come the power to re-engineer the human species. Biologists will be able to use the genome as a parts list—much as customers scour a list of china to replace broken plates—and may well let prospective parents choose their unborn child's traits. Scientists have solid leads on genes for different temperaments, body builds, statures and cognitive abilities. And if anyone still believes that parents will recoil at playing God, and leave their baby's fate in the hands of nature, recall that couples have already created a frenzied market in eggs from Ivy League women.

Beyond the profound ethical issues are practical concerns. The easier it is to change ourselves and our children, the less society may tolerate those who do not, warns Lori Andrews of Kent College of Law. If genetic tests in utero predict mental dullness, obesity, short stature—or other undesirable traits of the moment—will society disparage children whose parents let them be born with those traits? Already, Andrew finds, some nurses and doctors blame parents for bringing into the world a child whose birth defect was diagnosable before delivery; how long will it be before the same condemnation applies to cosmetic imperfections? An even greater concern is that well-intentioned choices by millions of individual parents-to-be could add up to unforeseen consequences for all of humankind. It just so happens that some disease genes also confer resistance to disease: carrying a gene for sickle cell anemia, for instance, brings resistance to malaria. Are we smart enough, and wise enough, to know how knocking out "bad" genes will affect our evolution as a species?

From the inception of the genome project, ethicists warned that genetic knowledge would be used against people in insurance and employment. Sorting out whether this is happening is like judging whether HMOs provide quality care. Systematic surveys turn up few problems, but horror stories abound. One man underwent a genetic test and learned that he carried a marker for the blood disorder hemochromatosis. Although he was being successfully treated, his insurer dropped him on the ground that he might stop treatment and develop the disease. Another had a job offer withdrawn for "lying" during a pre-employment physical. He was healthy, but carried a gene for kidney disease. And last December Terri Seargent, 43, was fired from her job as an office manager after she tested positive for the genetic disease that killed her brother. She began receiving preventive treatments. When her self-insured employer got the first bill, she was fired.

So far 39 states prohibit, at least in part, discrimination in health insurance based on genetic tests; 15 have some ban on discrimination in employment. But many of the laws have loopholes. (One of the 15 is North Carolina, where Seargent lives). Employers still, apparently, want genetic information about their workers. A 1999 survey by the American Management Association found that 30 percent of large and midsize firms obtain such information on employees. Seven percent use it in hiring and promotions. "It is still possible to have information about the genome used to take away your health insurance or your job," says Collins. "As yet, we have not seen effective federal legislation [to prevent this]. With genes getting discovered right and left, the opportunities for mischief are on an exponential curve."

Perhaps the greatest unknown is how the completion of the Human Genome Project—not just getting C's, G's, T's and A's, but learning the function of every gene—will shape our views of what we are. There is a great risk of succumbing to a naive biological determinism, ascribing to our genes such qualities as personality, intelligence, even faith. Studies of twins have already claimed (to great criticism, but claimed nonetheless) that genes even shape whether an individual will favor or oppose capital punishment. "We do ascribe some sort of quasi-religious significance to our DNA," says Collins. "We have a tendency to be more deterministic than we should." For now, the power, and the limits, of the genome can only be guessed at. The stage is set. The players are ready. After millions of dollars and millions of hours, the curtain is rising on what our children will surely, looking back in awe, see as the dawn of the century of the genome.

With THOMAS HAYDEN, WILLIAM UNDERHILL *in London and* GREGORY BEALS

Autism is likely to be linked to several genes

Researchers are close to identifying several genes that influence different aspects of autism.

By Hugh McIntosh

Ever since a study revealed that if one identical twin had autism, the other was likely to have it too, researchers have been searching for genes that cause autism. Now, after 20 years of looking, scientists believe they're closing in on a handful of genes and chromosomal "hot spots" that may be responsible for different aspects of the disorder.

Identification of specific autism-related genes would reveal the proteins the genes produce—knowledge that will boost researchers' ability to diagnose autism and to discover more effective treatments for the disorder, which is characterized by communication problems, social impairment, and unusual or repetitive behaviors.

The discovery of such genes has been hampered by the complex nature of autism. Because the symptoms of people with autism vary dramatically in degree and form, researchers believe the condition might involve two or more of a large number of genes. In fact, a person with autism may have mutations in several of perhaps 20 possible genes. Thus, two people

with the disorder might have mutations in two completely different sets of genes.

In the past two years, scientists have identified several candidate genes. Some might alter the effects on the brain of neurotransmitters, others might compromise the immune system enough to allow viral infections that may cause autism, and another may influence embryonic development of the nervous system.

Chromosome 15

Among the most promising findings, say experts, are reports that an autism gene may be on the long arm of chromosome 15, near the centromere—an indented point that holds the two sides of a chromosome together. This region is a well-known spot for genetic abnormalities, including duplications of parts of the chromosome's DNA. Short duplications cause no apparent harm. But longer duplications are associated with about a 50 percent risk for autism.

Last year, the research team of child psychiatrist Edwin Cook, MD,

of the University of Chicago, reported that the autism risk associated with longer duplications appears to come through the mother.

Cook suspects that genes in this region of chromosome 15, which encode receptors for the neurotransmitter gamma-amino butyric acid (GABA), might be involved with autism. In fact, three genes for three GABA receptor subunits all are good candidates because they are associated with seizures and anxiety, which are common among autistic children, Cook says.

His team found moderately strong evidence for an association between one GABA subunit and autism—about one of every 70 children studied had a chromosome 15 duplication including this gene. Their study is published in the *American Journal of Human Genetics* (Vol. 62, No. 5, p. 1077–1083).

Duke University researchers say an autism gene might be a little farther away from chromosome 15's centromere, just beyond the GABA receptor genes. A genetic screening of about 50 families with autistic chil-

In the past two years, scientists have identified several candidate genes. Some might alter the effects on the brain of neurotransmitters, others might compromise the immune system enough to allow viral infections that may cause autism, and another may influence embryonic development of the nervous system.

dren turned up three positive markers in this area, says molecular geneticist John Gilbert, PhD. An autism susceptibility gene may lie between these markers and the GABA receptor genes. Exactly what that gene might do is still unknown.

To examine the link between chromosome 15 duplications and autism more closely, researchers at the University of California, Los Angeles, hope next year to launch a nationwide study of 100 children with these duplications. Researchers will look for molecular differences that might explain why half the people with this duplication have autism and half do not, says geneticist Carolyn Schanen, MD, PhD. They will also try to determine whether autistic children with this duplication are more likely to have severe language problems.

"In the kids that I know . . . it essentially wipes out language to have this extra piece," Schanen says. In the study, a psychologist will travel around the country to assess the children's phenotype, as well as to collect blood samples for genetic analysis.

A serotonin transporter gene?

Researchers have long found that many autistic persons have elevated blood levels of the neurotransmitter serotonin. This finding suggests that people with autism have a defect in the gene that produces serotonin transporter—a substance that sweeps serotonin from the space between two nerve cells, thus ending its effect on the cells.

In the general population, the transporter gene occurs in either a long or a short form. Last year Cook and his colleagues reported finding that children with autism inherited the short form more frequently than expected, based on typical inheritance patterns. This pattern of inheritance, called "preferential transmission," suggests that the gene is a susceptibility gene— one that plays a role in whether a person gets the disorder.

Research groups in France and Germany, however, found preferential transmission of the long form. Though conflicting, these results represent some of the stronger evidence to date for a genetic role in autism.

However, Yale University neurochemist George Anderson, PhD, says that, to him, the findings of the three studies suggest that the serotonin transporter gene may not be a susceptibility gene. Rather, it may be a "quantitative trait locus," which affects the degree of a genetic trait in someone who already has the disorder.

Cook agrees with that possibility but offers another explanation for the findings: The three samples studied may have contained different mixes of autism subtypes. The two other studies, he says, may have enrolled higher proportions of children referred for treatment of severe behavior problems such as aggression. In contrast, his group's sample contained a high proportion of people referred for communication or socialization problems rather than severe behavior problems. To test this possibility, his group has begun collecting data about aggression in people in their sample.

Nervous-system genes

Another autism candidate gene may lie among the genes involved with early development of the nervous system. This idea emerged from a Swedish study of 100 people whose mothers had taken thalidomide during pregnancy.

The study found that five of the 15 people exposed to thalidomide during days 20 to 24 of gestation had autism, says embryologist Patricia Rodier, PhD, of the University of Rochester. This suggests that the damage leading to autism occurred during the development of the hindbrain, long before the cortex and other parts of the forebrain developed. These and other findings have led Rodier and her colleagues to look for mutations in several well-known developmental genes.

"If you have mutations in some of these genes that are critical in the early stages of the development of the nervous system, that in itself may be sufficient to cause the kinds of neuroanatomical changes that we think underlie autism," Rodier says. "But it could also be that that just makes you more sensitive to environmental agents at that time."

For example, the investigators hypothesize that embryonic environmental factors—such as the presence of thalidomide—may act during early embryonic development on the genes being studied.

Immune deficiency?

Gene-environment interaction is the idea behind another candidate autism gene, called C4B, on the short arm of chromosome 6. This gene produces complement C4 protein, which works with the antibody immunoglobulin A to fight viruses. Deficiencies in either of these substances reduce the immune system's ability to respond to viral infection.

"Autistic children are chronically ill, which is an indication that they have a deficiency in their immune system," says immunologist Roger Bur-

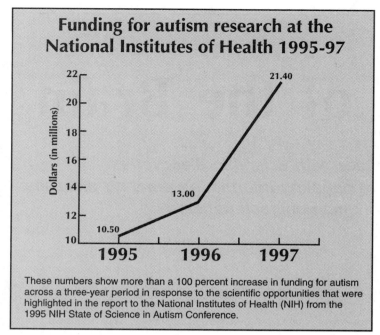

Funding for autism research at the National Institutes of Health 1995-97

Dollars (in millions)

21.40

13.00

10.50

1995   1996   1997

These numbers show more than a 100 percent increase in funding for autism across a three-year period in response to the scientific opportunities that were highlighted in the report to the National Institutes of Health (NIH) from the 1995 NIH State of Science in Autism Conference.

Angela e. Terry

ger, PhD, at Utah State University in Logan.

Immune deficiency might contribute to some cases of autism by allowing a virus to damage the brain or trigger an auto-immune response that causes brain injury, Burger says. Damage might also occur in utero if the mother has an immune deficiency. People with autism have an unusually high frequency of a form of the C4B gene that produces no protein.

Working together

While the University of Utah research team and others follow interest-ing leads, the National Institutes of Health (NIH) is funding five major collaborative groups to conduct genome screens of families with autism. Earlier this year, one of these consortiums reported in the journal *Human Molecular Genetics* (Vol. 7, No. 3, p. 571–578) that they'd found a hot spot on chromosome 7.

"We think it's a susceptibility gene," says geneticist Anthony Monaco, MD, PhD, of the University of Oxford. "But what gene . . . or what type of gene, we really have no idea." The suspect region includes genes expressed in the brain during development.

Supporting their finding is evidence from another collaborative group headquartered at Duke University. The researchers screened about 50 families and turned up "a number of interesting regions" on chromosome 7, says Duke geneticist Margaret Pericak-Vance, PhD.

A group at the University of Iowa has evidence for a link between autism and chromosome 13. The group is also exploring the idea that there is a broad autism phenotype that includes people with milder autism-like symptoms, as well as those with classic autistic disorder.

"We're seeing some pretty large pedigrees where there are maybe two autistic kids and an autistic first cousin, and then in between a lot of people who we think have the broad phenotype," says child psychiatrist Joseph Piven, MD. "These pedigrees . . . look more like single-gene disorders" than multigene disorders.

Although a single gene might explain autism in one family, the number of tantalizing prospects turning up from the genome screens suggests several genes are involved in autism, says Marie Bristol-Power, PhD, coordinator of the NIH autism network. She notes that the five collaborative groups together are expected to enroll more than 1,000 families with autistic children, generating plenty of statistical power to root out the genetics of this complex disorder.

Hugh McIntosh is a writer in Chicago.

The Future of the Brain

The pairing of innovative technologies with scientific discoveries about the brain opens new ways of handling information, treating diseases, and possibly creating robots with human characteristics.

Norbert R. Myslinski

For I dipp'd into the future,
far as human eye could see,
Saw the Vision of the world,
and all the wonder that
would be.

—**Alfred, Lord Tennyson**

An understanding of the brain helps us understand our nature. Over the course of evolution, the brain has acquired greater functions and higher consciousness. The reptilian brain, for instance, exerts control over vegetative functions, such as eating, sleeping, and reproduction. Development of the mammalian brain added the ability to express emotions. The human brain has the additional powers of cognition—such as reasoning, judgment, problem solving, and creativity. The latter functions, which are controlled by an area of the brain called the prefrontal cortex (located behind the forehead), distinguish us from other forms of life and represent the flower of our humanity. They have allowed us to re-create ourselves and decide our destiny.

Besides these long-term changes, our brains undergo short-term modifications during our lifetime. Not only does the brain control behavior, but one's behavior leads to changes in the brain, in terms of both structure and function. Subjective experiences play a major role in brain functions and the manifestation of one's mind, consciousness, and personal values. Thus the brain adapts to each individual's changing world.

Modern society and technology have given us the time, protection, and freedom to focus on the higher powers of the brain. As individual freedoms and the free enterprise system are extended around the world, we will see a continuing rise of innovative ventures and scientific exploration. In addition, our success at eliminating brain diseases and expanding brain functions will depend on the uniquely human characteristics of the brain. Given the finances and technology, we will need vision and creativity.

But modern technology also raises a number of questions about our future. For instance, how will the continuing information explosion challenge the powers of our brains? What does the next century have in store for us regarding memory drugs, brain surgery, brain regeneration, and other treatments for brain disorders? How will the relationships between mind and body or brain and machine evolve? More important, are we prepared to handle such challenges, socially, psychologically, and ethically?

The Information Explosion

Information technologies have been increasingly successful in helping us acquire and communicate large new areas of knowledge. But the same success challenges the brain's capacity. How will the brain continue to cope with this information explosion? It will probably employ the same techniques it always has: filtering, organizing, and selective forgetting [see "Sherlock Holmes' Lesson," THE WORLD & I, June 2000, p. 316].

> **Our brains allow us to exert such uniquely human powers as reasoning, judgment, problem solving, and creativity—thereby guiding our own development and destiny.**

Already, the brain filters out more than 99 percent of all sensory input before it reaches consciousness. In the future, it will be even more important to filter out the repetitive, boring, and unnecessary, and retain the novel, relevant, and necessary information. Actually, the brain is not good at remembering isolated facts but is great at organizing and associating thoughts and ideas. This ability will help it handle new information without suffering overload.

Just as important as the biology inside the brain is the technology

This article appeared in the August 2000 issue of *The World & I,* pp. 152-159. *The World & I,* a publication of The Washington Times Corporation. © 2000.

As the human genome is mapped, scientists hope to find cures for many genetically linked diseases, including those that affect the brain.

outside. First with the introduction of books, and now computers, we have become increasingly reliant on artificial means of storing information. Thus the relative need for long-term (storage) memory in the brain and the time span for storage have decreased. As this trend continues, we will make greater use of our working memory and less use of our storage memory [see "Now Where Did I Put Those Keys?" THE WORLD & I, November 1998, p. 160].

Help for our memories may also come in the form of a pill. Research related to Alzheimer's disease has already produced a drug that can improve normal memory in small, healthy animals.

Furthermore, the rate at which we access and share information will most likely continue to accelerate. As a result, our brains will be challenged to think faster and make decisions more quickly. Anything less will be inefficient. Bureaucracy and red tape will be our enemies. We may be compelled to place greater emphasis on intuition and "gut feelings."

Treating hereditary brain disorders

In living organisms, another type of memory occurs in the form of genetic material known as DNA (deoxyribonucleic acid). It is the blueprint for the body and the chemical memory for traits that are passed down from generation to generation. The DNA representing the human genome (complete set of genetic information) consists of over 3 billion subunits (base pairs) and contains

the coding for anywhere between 40,000 and 100,000 genes.

Scientists are already tackling the ambitious goal of determining the sequence of base pairs and mapping the genes of the entire human genome. Two groups—a publicly funded, international consortium (whose work is known as the Human Genome Project) and the private company Celera Genomics Corporation (based in Rockville, Maryland)—have just recently submitted "working drafts," with the promise of more detailed, high-quality results in the near future.

The human genetic map will help locate biomarkers for the diagnosis and treatment of hereditary disorders, including those affecting the brain. One type of treatment, known as gene therapy, is directed toward replacing defective genes with un-

for further refinements to the technique. In the meantime, a promising new strategy called *chimeraplasty*, in which the cell is stimulated to repair its own defective genes, has emerged [see "The Promise of Genetic Cures," THE WORLD & I, May 2000, p. 147]. Either approach may also be used to fight noninherited disorders by increasing the body's production of substances (such as interleukin or interferon) that protect the body.

The genetic information will probably lead to tests performed *in utero* or early in life to detect markers that suggest predispositions to such conditions as obesity and alcoholism, or such diseases as schizophrenia and Alzheimer's. People would then have the opportunity to get genetic counseling and design a lifestyle that integrates medical surveillance to stay healthy. At the same

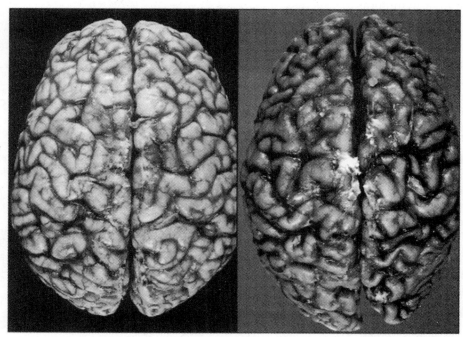

BOTH IMAGES COURTESY OF THE NATIONAL INSTITUTE OF NEUROLOGICAL DISORDERS AND STROKE/NIH

Convolutions in the brain of an Alzheimer's patient show considerable shrinkage (*right*) compared with those in a normal brain (*left*). Cures for Alzheimer's and other brain diseases may be found through such approaches as genetic engineering or neural cell regeneration.

damaged ones [see "Doctoring Genes to Beat Disease," THE WORLD & I, December 1997, p. 178]. But the many gene therapy trials conducted over the past 10 years have met with a low success rate, indicating the need

time, however, we need to improve our system of laws to prevent discrimination against people—particularly in employment and insurance coverage—based on this information. In February this year, President

Environment and behavior can alter our brains; free will can influence our behavior.

Clinton prohibited federal employers from requiring or requesting genetic tests as a condition of being hired or receiving benefits.

Moreover, knowledge of a person's genotype (gene structure and organization) will not necessarily enable us to predict his phenotype (body structure), which is the manifestation of not only the genetic information but environmental influences and life experiences as well. The phenotype for a brain disease, for example, could range anywhere from no symptoms to total disability. Even identical twins are not 100 percent concordant for most brain disorders. The health and character of the human brain (and the rest of the body) are neither predetermined nor inevitable. Environment and behavior can alter our brains; free will can influence our behavior.

It is also possible that a treatment that alters one gene may affect many traits, even those that we do not wish to change. The same gene linked to a brain disorder might also influence intelligence or creativity. The risk involved in altering a gene is especially great for disorders associated with multiple genes.

Vaccines, drugs, surgery, and brain regeneration

We have grown up in a world of miracle drugs, but most alleviate just the symptoms. The next century will focus on prevention and cures. Scientists are already working on oral vaccines that would attack the pathological plagues and tangles of Alzheimer's disease, decrease brain damage after a stroke or seizure, and lower the number of seizures in epileptics. We will be able to administer

specific substances (called trophic factors) that will stimulate brain cells to multiply and replace cells degenerating because of brain diseases such as Parkinson's and Huntington's.

The trail-and-error method of finding effective drugs is now being replaced by the use of computers to design molecules that will precisely fit into specific receptors for the purpose of treating diseases. In the future, we will also be able to manufacture and use larger quantities of disease-fighting chemicals—such as interleukins, interferon, and brain trophic factors—that occur naturally in the body.

One strategy for making large quantities of specific antibodies is called the monoclonal antibody technique. Antibodies of a particular type are produced in large quantities by fusing the specific antibody-producing cells with tumor cells that grow and proliferate indefinitely. We could even piggyback drugs onto

rected at protecting crops and improving their taste and nutritional value. About two dozen companies are now working to enhance the availability and lower the cost of drugs by genetically engineering plants to produce them. Some of the drugs may be ingested by simply eating the plant food.

With the improvement of brain imaging and robotics, brain surgery will improve and become less invasive. The brain is ideally suited for robotic surgery. It is enclosed in a firm skull that's appropriate for mounting instruments and providing fixed reference points by which to navigate the brain. Robotics and microscopic brain imaging will be used for higher precision, fewer mistakes, and minimally invasive surgical techniques.

While pharmacological and surgical treatments improve, another approach that's gaining in importance is the regeneration of neural tissue. This approach has become possible

---

On Being Human

According to futurist Alvin Toffler, the new millennium will challenge our understanding of what it means to be human. The fusion of computer technology, genetic engineering, and research on the brain will allow us to control our own evolution. For instance, electronic microchips may be placed in our brains to repair lost functions or create new ones. Scientists can now make microchips that are part organic. What about computers that are part protoplasm? When do we stop calling them machines and start calling them life?

There is currently a debate about the ethics of producing human clones or designer babies with "better" abilities. Can we also modify the genes of animals to give them human intelligence? Or can we create robots that take on human characteristics, such as human behavior or even self-replication? If so, should they be considered part human?

Whatever the answers may turn out to be, our differing views of what it means to be human are likely to polarize society because of conflicting causes taken up by political, religious, and scientific groups. We may experience a moral divide that could exceed that seen with slavery or abortion.

—N.R.M.

---

antibodies that target specific parts of the brain, thereby reducing the drug dosage and minimizing side effects.

Another approach currently being pursued is genetically engineering plants to produce pharmaceuticals. Until recently, efforts have been di-

because of recent research on stem cells and trophic factors, along with the discovery that adult brain cells can divide and multiply. Neural regeneration is the hope for those who suffer from such disorders as paralysis, Lou Gehrig's disease (amyotrophic lateral sclerosis), Down syndrome, retina degeneration, and Parkinson's disease.

The mind-body relationship

Charles Schultz, the beloved creator of Charlie Brown and author of the comic strip *Peanuts* for 50 years, died this year on the very day that his farewell strip was published. It was as if he stayed alive just long enough to see it end. Was that just a coincidence?

Warm, loving relationships, as well as isolation, can influence longevity and the will to live. How often have we heard of a person dying soon after his spouse dies? The body is not a biological machine operating independently of the mind. Even Hippocrates proposed that health was a balance of mind and body in the proper environment.

The mind has a powerful effect on our physical health by influencing our immune, cardiovascular, and endocrine systems. It can change the levels of such body substances as cortisol, adrenaline, and natural killer cells. Happy people get sick less often. Angry people have more health problems. Stress, anger, depression, and loneliness suppress the immune system, overexert the heart, raise blood pressure, enhance blood clotting, increase bone loss, harden the arteries, and increase cholesterol and abdominal fat. These factors can increase the incidence and severity of cancer, heart disease, stroke, arthritis, and even the common cold.

Western medicine, however, has underappreciated this mind-body

---

Robotics and microscopic brain imaging will be used for higher precision, fewer mistakes, and minimally invasive surgical techniques.

Brain Doctors

Technology will enable drugs to be more selective and surgeries to be more exact. But what about the doctors? How will they change? Their early training will involve greater use of virtual reality and less use of animals. They will emphasize prevention and cure rather than the treatment of symptoms. They will have to be genetic counselors and focus on the whole person rather than symptoms. They must put humanity back into medicine.

Today's neurologists tend to be technicians more than healers. They are trained primarily to diagnose and fix defective brains. Their success is determined by how effective they are at minimizing symptoms, restoring functions, and curing diseases. Although most patients are grateful, many find the doctor's help to be insufficient or lacking. Substituting a side effect for a symptom, or prolonging a life of pain and distress, may not be an improvement in the patient's quality of life.

In addition, the psychological and spiritual needs of the patient often go unattended. Patients need someone to appreciate their distress and relate to them on a human level. Recognizing these needs, medical education is now increasing its emphasis on treating the whole person. Doctors are realizing that the way to a healthy body is through the mind.

—N.R.M.

---

relationship. Now that brain imaging can be used to observe the effect of the mind on the body, we will see the medical establishment embrace this concept as the basis of a legitimate form of therapy. Support groups, meditation, and relaxation therapy will be prescribed to ward off disease and dampen its devastating effects.

Research has shown that people who derive strength and comfort from religion live healthier and longer lives [see "Is Religion Good for Your Health?" THE WORLD & I, February 1996, p. 291]. The benefits of religion go beyond social contact or the encouragement of healthier habits. It can be a mechanism to help cope with life and stressful situations. Faith in a Higher Being has been shown to be an important part of the successful Twelve Steps program of Alcoholics Anonymous—a program that has been extended to treat other addictions, such as gambling and overeating [see "Spirituality in Healing," THE WORLD & I, May 2000, p. 153]. Doctors will use it to increase the compliance of patients with the treatments prescribed for a wide range of acute and chronic medical problems.

People get better because they believe they will. This is called the pla-

cebo effect. A patient's belief that he is receiving effective medicine will alleviate his symptoms. The stronger his belief, the stronger the relief. This effect has been known and used by doctors for many years. It must be taken into account when testing new medicines and therapies.

The placebo effect is based on the brain's ability to anticipate the future and prepare for it. For example, the brain analyzes trajectories of objects in motion and predicts their future location, or it analyzes environmental temperatures and predicts the body's future temperature. Also, our senses are notorious for seeing what we hope to see and tasting what we expect to taste. The brain produces a placebo effect by stimulating cells and releasing hormones that start the healing process in anticipation of getting better.

The brain-machine connection

Over the past century, we have aided our vision and hearing with lenses and amplifiers. During the next century, we will probably replace eyes and ears with light and sound detectors and computer chips that send signals to the brain.

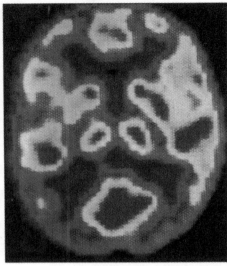 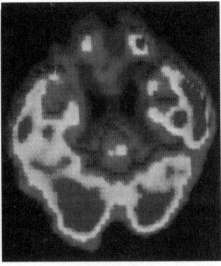

COURTESY OF THE NATIONAL INSTITUTE OF NEUROLOGICAL DISORDERS AND STROKE/NIH

Just as current PET scans (*above*) reveal general activity in the brain, future techniques may show microscopic details. *Left:* The brain of a young man listening intently to a story uses a great deal of glucose in the auditory cortex (gray areas near the ears). *Right:* An image at a different level of the same brain shows activity in the hippocampus (gray spots at short distances in from the sides), where short-term learning is converted to long-term memory.

We need to find ways to understand consciousness and how the brain is involved in the powers of reasoning, creativity, and love.

Every year, the International NAISO Congress on Information Science Innovations holds a Robot Soccer Competition. Winners are those who create robots that can "see" with greater acuity, "think" more perceptively, and move faster and with greater agility. Software companies are already making advertising claims that their programs can "think." Will molecular electronics and nanotechnology, combined with genetic engineering, give us the power to create sentient robots?

If so, a modern-day Pandora's box is being opened. Unlike scientific breakthroughs of the past, the robots and engineered organisms of the future could have the potential for self-replication. While the uncontrolled replication of mischievous programs on the Internet—as seen with the "Melissa" and "I Love You" viruses—can cause a lot of damage, the uncontrolled replication of senti-ment robots may pose a threat to our humanity. Will this evolution come suddenly, like the news about cloning the first mammal, or gradually, so that we will get used to it? Or will modern-day Luddites have the courage and foresight to say no and steer us in another direction?

We began the twentieth century looking at the brain's structure through a simple microscope and ended by examining its functions with such techniques as PET (positron emission tomography) and MRI (magnetic resonance imaging). We went through the stages of neuroanatomy, neurophysiology, and neurochemistry. We learned how the brain controls movement and processes sensory information. We scratched the surface in our attempts to clarify intelligence and emotions. Among the challenges of the new century will be to find ways to understand consciousness and how the brain is in-volved in the powers of reasoning, creativity, and love.

Speculating about the future, however, is daunting, even for experts. In a 1987 survey, medical scientists predicted that by the year 2000 we would probably have a cure for two-thirds of all cancers, AIDS would be eliminated, and coronary bypass surgery would be replaced by less invasive techniques.

Distinguishing between fact and fiction is difficult even today. On the first day of my neuroscience course in graduate school, our instructor told us that half of what he would teach us that semester would eventually prove to be wrong—the problem was, he could not tell which half was wrong. Since then, I have repeatedly witnessed the truth of that statement. Revisions of our knowledge will continue in the twenty-first century. We must keep testing our view of the world, and if it fails, replace it with a better one. We must remain flexible in our beliefs, just as our brains remain flexible in their structure and function.

Norbert R. Myslinski is associate professor of neuroscience at the University of Maryland and director of Maryland Brain Awareness Week.

THE BIOLOGY OF *Joy*

By Jeremiah Creedon

Scientists are unlocking the secrets of pleasure— and discovering what poets already knew

Pleasure, like fire, is a natural force that from the beginning humans have sought to harness and subdue. We've always sensed that pleasure is somehow crucial to life, perhaps the only tangible payoff for its hardships. And yet many have discovered that unbridled pleasure can also be dangerous, even fatal. Since ancient times, philosophers and spiritual leaders have debated its worth and character, often comparing it unfavorably to its more stable sibling, happiness. No one, however, saint or libertine, has ever doubted which of the pair would be the better first date.

Happiness is a gift for making the most of life. Pleasure is born of the reckless impulse to forget life and give yourself to the moment. Happiness is partly an abstract thing, a moral condition, a social construct: The event most often associated with happiness, some researchers say, is seeing one's children grow up to be happy themselves. How nice. Pleasure, pure pleasure, is a biological reflex, a fleeting "reward" so hot and lovely you might sell your children to get it. Witness the lab rat pressing the pleasure bar until it collapses. Or the sad grin of the crack addict as the molecules of mountain shrub trip a burst of primal gratitude deep in a part of the human brain much like a rat's. Both know all too well that pleasure, uncaged, can eat you alive.

Some scientists claim they're close to knowing what pleasure is, biologically speaking. Their intent is to solve the riddle of pleasure much as an earlier generation unleashed the power of the atom. Splitting pleasure down to its very molecules will have many benefits, they say, including new therapies for treating drug abuse and mental illness. Others note that research on the biology of pleasure is part of a wider trend that's exploding old ideas about the human brain, if not the so-called "Western biomedical paradigm" in general, with its outmoded cleaving of body from mind.

The assumption is that somehow our lives will be better once this mystery has been unraveled. Beneath that is the enduring belief that we can conquer pleasure as we've conquered most everything else, that we can turn it into a docile beast and put it to work. That we've never been able to do so before, and yet keep trying, reveals a lot about who we are, as creatures of a particular age—and species.

Of all the animals that humans have sought to tame, pleasure most resembles the falcon in its tendency to revert to the wild. That's why we're often advised to keep it hooded. The Buddha warned that to seek pleasure is to chase a shadow; it only heightens the unavoidable pain of life, which has to be accepted. Nevertheless, most have chosen to discover that for

From *Utne Reader*, November/December 1997, pp. 66-71, 106. © 1997 by Jeremiah Creedon. Reprinted by permission.

themselves. The early Greek hedonists declared pleasure the ultimate good, then immediately began to hedge. Falling in love, for instance, wasn't really a pleasure, given the inevitable pain of falling out of it. The hedonists thought they could be masters of pleasure, not its slaves; yet their culture's literature is a chronicle of impetuous, often unspeakable pleasures to be indulged at any cost.

When the Christians crawled out of the catacombs to make Rome holy, they took revenge on pagan pleasure by sealing it in—then pretended for centuries not to hear its muffled protests. Eclipsed was the Rose Bowl brilliance of the Roman circus, where civic pleasure reached a level of brutal spectacle unmatched until the advent of *Monday Night Football*. Pleasure as a public function seemed to vanish.

The end of the Dark Ages began with the Italian poet Dante, who, for all his obsession with the pains of hell, endures as one of the great, if ambivalent, students of pleasure. His *Inferno* is but a portrait of the enjoyments of his day turned inside out, like a dirty sock. For every kind of illicit bliss possible in the light of the world above, Dante created a diabolically fitting punishment in his theme-park hell below. We can only guess what terrible eternity he has since devised for his countryman, the pleasure-loving Versace, felled in what Dante would have considered the worst of ways—abruptly, without a chance to confess his sins. At the very least he's doomed to wear Armani.

Dante's ability to find a certain glee in the suffering of others—not to mention in the act of writing—goes to the heart of the problem of pleasure. Let's face it: Pleasure has a way of getting twisted. Most people, most of the time, are content with simple pleasures: a walk on the beach, fine wine, roses, cuddling, that sort of thing. But pleasure can also be complicated, jaded, and sick. The darker aspects of pleasure surely lie dormant in many of us, like the Minotaur in the heart of the labyrinth waiting for its yearly meal of pretty flesh. In the words of the Mongol ruler Genghis Khan, "Happiness lies in conquering one's enemies, in driving them in front of oneself, in taking their property, in savoring their despair, in outraging their wives and daughters." He meant pleasure, of course, not happiness—but *you* tell him.

In the Age of Reason, the vain hope that humans could reason with pleasure returned. Thinkers like Jeremy Bentham took up the old Greek idea of devising a "calculus" of pleasure—complex equations for estimating what pleasure really is, in light of the pain often caused by the quest for it. But the would-be moral engineers, rational to a fault, found the masses oddly attached to the older idea of pleasure being a simple sum of parts, usually private parts. As for the foundlings thus multiplied, along with certain wretched venereal ills, well, who would have figured?

The first "scientists of mind" were pretty sure that the secrets of pleasure, and the emotions in general, lay locked beyond their reach, inside our heads. Throughout the 19th century, scientists could only speculate about the human brain and its role as "the organ of consciousness." Even more galling, the era's writers and poets clearly speculated so much better—especially those on drugs.

Two of them, Samuel Taylor Coleridge and Thomas De Quincey, both opium addicts, also may have been early explorers of the brain's inner geography. Images of a giant fountain gushing from a subterranean river in Coleridge's most famous poem—"Kubla Khan; or, A Vision in a Dream" bear an odd resemblance to modern models of brain function, especially brains steeped in mind-altering chemicals. Writing in *The Human Brain* (BasicBooks, 1997), Susan A. Greenfield, professor of pharmacology at Oxford University, describes the "fountainlike" nerve-cell structures that arise in the brain stem and release various chemical messengers into the higher brain areas. As Greenfield notes, and Coleridge perhaps intuited, these geysers of emotion are "often the target of mood-modifying drugs."

De Quincey describes a similar terrain in *Confessions of an English Opium Eater (1821)*. He even suggests that the weird world he envisioned while he was on the drug might have been his own fevered brain projected, a notion he fears will seem "ludicrous to a medical man." Not so. Sherwin B. Nuland, National Book Award winner and clinical professor of surgery at Yale, expresses an updated version of that concept in *The Wisdom of the Body* (Knopf, 1997). In Nuland's view, we may possess an "awareness" distinct from rational thought, a kind of knowledge that rises up from our cells to "imprint itself" on how we interpret the world. "It is by this means that our lives . . . and even our culture come to be influenced by, and are the reflection of, the conflict that exists within cells," he writes.

Maybe De Quincey really could see his own brain. Maybe that's what many artists see. Think of Dante's downward-spiraling hell, or the Minotaur in the labyrinth, even the cave paintings at Altamira and Lascaux. The first known labyrinth was built in Egypt nearly 4,000 years ago, a convoluted tomb for both a pharaoh's remains and those of the sacred crocodiles teeming in a nearby lake. It's an odd image to find rising up over and over from the mind's sunless sea, of subterranean passages leading ever deeper to an encounter with . . . the Beast. In an age when high-tech imaging devices can generate actual images of the brain at work, it's intriguing to think that artists ventured to the primordial core of that process long ago. And left us maps.

Today, Paul D. MacLean, National Institute of Mental Health scientist and author of *The Triune Brain in Evolution* (Plenum, 1990), describes a similar geography. He theorizes that the human brain is "three-brains-in-one," reflecting its "ancestral relationship to reptiles, early mammals, and recent mammals." Peter C. Whybrow, director of the Neuropsychiatric Institute at UCLA, uses this model to explain what he calls "the anatomical roots of emotion." Writing in A *Mood Apart* (BasicBooks, 1997), his study of depression and other "afflictions of the self," Whybrow notes: "The behavior of human beings is more complicated than that of other animals . . . but nonetheless we share in common with many creatures such behaviors as sexual courtship, pleasure-seeking, aggression, and the defense of territory. Hence it is safe to conclude that the evolution of human behavior is, in part, reflected in the evolution and hierarchical development of other species."

Sensuous LIKE ME

How I got back in my body through my nose

Some mornings my head is like a little dog panting, whimpering, and straining at his leash. *Let's go, let's go, let's go!* My head gets me up and leads me around all day. Sometimes it's dinnertime before I remember that I have a body.

And the idea that this body can give me pleasure—well, that's a really hard one. I used to think that because I read hip French books about sexual ecstasy I had somehow escaped my Calvinist heritage—the idea that the body is shameful and only a narcissistic lazybones would pay any attention to it. No such luck. My version of Calvinist body-denial was compulsive reading, and the more I read about French people's ecstasies, which are usually pretty cerebral anyway—the more I hid out from my own body. A body that, let's face it, is plumper, paler, and more easily winded than I would prefer.

Falling in love changed things. Intimacy with a woman who was learning to accept and even love her body gave me new eyes to see (and new nerve endings to feel) my own. I started—just started—to think of my body as a means of communication with the world, not a sausage case for Great Thoughts. I wanted to go further.

It was my wife who found Nancy Conger, professor of the five senses. A slender young woman with apparently bottomless reserves of energy and optimism, she lives in an old farmhouse in western Wisconsin, plays the violin, and teaches people how to get out of debt, simplify their lives, and use their senses for entertainment and joy. She even teaches a one-night class called "Sensuous Living." Laurie and I enrolled.

A class in sensuousness. An idea not without irony, amazing that we actually have to study this stuff. Five perfectly sensible-looking adults perched on plastic chairs in a drab little classroom in Minneapolis, with Nancy presiding in a sleeveless black jumpsuit. On two tables toward the front: nasturtiums in a vase, a strip of fur, a piece of sandpaper, a twig, a violin, a seashell.

"Lick your forearm," said Nancy, "and smell yourself."

Lick my forearm and smell myself?

I looked around me. The matronly woman in the purple blouse and matching shoes was licking her forearm. So was the shy, 40ish guy with the salt-and-pepper beard, and the thin, Italian-looking young woman with the big braid. Finally, feeling uncomfortably canine, I licked myself. I sniffed ("Little, short sniffs, like perfumers use," said Nancy). Hmm. A faintly metallic aroma. Sniff, sniff. Beneath it, something breadlike.

Like a wine, I had a bouquet.

Then Nancy got us out of our chairs to wander around and "smell what doesn't seem to have a smell." I put my nose right up next to a big pad of paper on an easel. Faint wheaty aroma like my school tablets in fifth grade. All the sunshiny, chalk-dusty, gentle boredom of elementary school came back, like a tune.

A brick gave off a mysterious musty tang, charged with the past. A quarter smelled sour, a metal door bitter and somehow sad.

"Smell detours right around your thinking brain, back to the limbic system at the bottom of the brain, where memory is,"

Nancy told us. She also explained that smell can be hugely improved, made more subtle and precise, if you keep sniffing. "Smell dishes. Smell clothes. Smell everything," she exhorted.

I did want to keep on smelling, but we were on to a trust-and-touch experiment. We paired off (I went with the big-braid woman) and took turns blindfolding and leading each other. I put my partner's hand on a brick, a door, a seashell, a twig.

Then I put on the blindfold (it smelled powdery and lusciously feminine), and she led me. Without any visual clues to tell me what things were supposed to feel like, I met each surface with a small thrill of tactile freshness. A metal door, I discovered, was studded with sharp little grains. A twig was as rough as sandpaper, and the sandpaper itself practically made me jump out of my skin. With most of the objects, I enjoyed a few wonderful seconds of pure sensation before the thinking brain clicked in and gave the thing a name. But click in it did; and that's when the magic ended.

The evening concluded with experiments in sound (Nancy played her violin very near each of us so we could feel the vibration in our bodies) and taste (we passed around a loaf of focaccia), but as we drove home I was still hung up on the smell and touch thing.

My nose, which I had mostly used as a passive receiver of pretty large and often alarming signals (skunk crushed on an Iowa road, underarms needing immediate attention, and so on) felt amazingly discriminating, having actually sniffed the difference between a door and a quarter. My fingers still tingled with the thrill of sandpaper and brick and (blessed relief!) fur.

The part of my head that names, makes distinctions, and is vigilant against stupidities pointed out that five middle-class white folks in a certain demographic had just spent three hours rubbing, if not exactly gazing at, their navels.

The honorable side of my Calvinism (as a kid I lived on Calvin Avenue in Grand Rapids, Michigan, just down the street from Calvin College) bridled at the idea of stroking my nerve endings like some French decadent poet, while an entire society—an entire world—splits along economic fault lines.

A third part of me rejoiced: I had discovered the cleverest answer yet to television. It was the exquisite entertainment technology of a body—my body. Anyone's body. It is—or could be—an immediate rebuke and alternative to the technologies of consumerism, which coarsen, obscure, jack up, deny, extend beyond reason, and in general do numbing violence to the subtle, noble equipment for receiving the joys of life that we were all issued at birth.

Anyone can sniff a leaf or reach out to the rough bark of a tree. Anyone can listen for a little while to the world. And anyone can do it now, at the kitchen table, in the schoolroom, at the racetrack, in the hospital bed. And we can keep doing it until we believe again in the wondrous beauty of our own equipment (absolutely no amplification from Sony required).

— Jon Spayde

Deciphering the code of art into the language of modern science took most of two centuries. One discipline after another tried to define what feelings like pleasure were, and from where they arose, only to fall short. Darwin could sense that emotions were important in his evolutionary scheme of things, but he was limited to describing how animals and humans expressed them on the outside, using their bodies, especially faces. William James, in a famous theory published in 1884, speculated that the brain only translates various sensations originating below the neck into what we think of as, say, joy and fear. Others saw it the other way around—emotions begin in the brain and the bodily reactions follow. Without knowing what pleasure actually is, Freud could see that the inability to feel it is a kind of disease, or at least a symptom, that he traced to (you guessed it) neurotic conflict.

By then, though, many people were fed up with all the talking. The study of mind had reached that point in the movie where the gung-ho types shove aside the hostage negotiator and shout, *We're going in*." And with scalpels drawn, they did. In 1872, Camillo Golgi, a young doctor working at a "home for incurables" in an Italian village, discovered the basic component of brain tissue, the neuron. During the 1920s, German scientist Otto Loewi, working with frog hearts, first identified neurotransmitters: chemical messengers that carry information across the gap between the neurons—the synapse—to receptors on the other side. Meanwhile, the Canadian neurosurgeon Wilder Penfield, operating on conscious patients with severe epilepsy, managed to trigger various emotions and dreamlike memories by electrically stimulating their brains. Such work gave rise to the idea that various mental functions might be "localized" in particular brain areas.

In 1954, psychologists James Olds and Peter Milner made a remarkable breakthrough—by accident. While researching the alerting mechanism in rat brains, they inadvertently placed an electrode in what they soon identified as a rat's pleasure-and-reward center: the so-called limbic system deep inside the brain. When the rats were later wired in a way that let them press a lever and jolt themselves, they did so as many as 5,000 times an hour.

This became the basis for current research on the "biology of reward." Scientists like Kenneth Blum have linked what they call reward deficiency syndrome to various human behavioral disorders: alcoholism, drug abuse, smoking, compulsive eating and gambling. Blum traces these disorders to genetically derived flaws in the neurotransmitters and receptors now associated with pleasure, including the pathways tied to the brain chemicals serotonin and dopamine, and the endorphins. Other researchers aren't so sure.

We all know by now that endorphins are the "body's own natural morphine." The discovery of endorphins in the early '70s marked the start of what some have declared the golden age of modern neuroscience. The impact was clear from the beginning to Candace B. Pert, whose work as a young scientist was crucial to the discovery. A few years earlier, she had helped identify the receptors that the endorphins fit into, as a lock fits a key, thus popping the lid of pleasure. According to Pert, "it didn't matter if you were a lab rat, a First Lady, or a dope addict—everyone had the exact same mechanism in the brain for creating bliss and expanded consciousness." As she recounts in *Molecules of Emotion* (Scribner, 1997), her early success led to a career at the National Institute of Mental Health identifying other such messenger molecules, now known as neuropeptides.

Pert's interest in the natural opiates soon took her into uncharted territory—sexual orgasm. Working with Nancy Ostrowski, a scientist "who had left behind her desire to become a nun and gone on instead to become an expert on the brain mechanisms of animal sex," Pert turned her clinical gaze on the sexual cycle of hamsters. "Nancy would inject the animals with a radioactive opiate before copulation, and then, at various points in the cycle, decapitate them and remove the brains," Pert writes. "We found that blood endorphin levels increased by about 200 percent from the beginning to the end of the sex act." She doesn't say what happened to their own endorphin levels while they watched—but Dante has surely kept a log.

Modern students of pleasure and emotion have their differences. Pert, for instance, having worked so much with neuropeptides, doesn't buy the idea that emotions are localized in certain brain areas. "The hypothalamus, the limbic system, and the amygdala have all been proposed as the center of emotional expression," she writes. "Such traditional formulations view only the brain as important in emotional expressivity, and as such are, from the point of view of my own research, too limited. From my perspective, the emotions are what link body and mind into bodymind."

This apparent reunion of body and mind is, in one sense, Pert's most radical conjecture. And yet, oddly, it's the one idea that many modern researchers do seem to share, implicitly or otherwise, to varying degrees. Most would agree that the process of creating human consciousness is vastly complex. It is also a "wet" system informed and modulated by dozens of neurochemical messengers, perhaps many more, all moving at incredible speeds. Dare we call it a calculus? Not on your life. Any analogy of the brain that summons up a computer is definitely uncool. For now.

There also seems to be a shared sense, not always stated, that some sort of grand synthesis may be, oh, 20 minutes away. In other words, it's only a matter of time before the knowledge of East and West is melded back into oneness, a theory that reunifies body and mind—and, as long as we're at it, everything else. That may be. But given that a similar impulse seems so prevalent throughout the culture, could it be that what we're really seeing is not purely science, but a case of primal yearning, even wishful thinking? A generation of brilliant scientists, their sensibilities formed in the psychedelic '60s, could now be looking back to the vision of mystical union they experienced, or at least heard about over and over again, in their youth. Perhaps they long to reach such a place, abstract though it is, for the same reason a salmon swims to the placid pool where its life began. We, like all creatures, are driven by the hope of an ultimate reward, a pleasure that has no name, a pleasure that in fact may not be ours to feel. Thus, we never conquer pleasure; pleasure conquers us. And for its own reasons, both wondrous and brutal.

THE NEW
Pleasure PRINCIPLE

This just in: Pain is not the route to happiness

Don't worry. Be happy.

The philosophy is simple, but living it is not, especially in our achievement-oriented society. According to Los Angeles-based therapist Stella Resnick, that's because we focus on the pain in our lives—getting through it, around it, or over it. Pleasure, the "visceral, body-felt experience of well-being," is a better path to growth and happiness, she contends in her book *The Pleasure Zone* (Conari Press, 1997). If only we knew how to feel it.

Resnick had to learn, too. Her childhood was unpleasant; her father left when she was 5, and, for 10 years, she endured beatings from her stepfather. She hung out on street corners and dated a gang leader. By age 32, she'd had two brief marriages and was involved in another stormy relationship. Although she'd built a successful San Francisco therapy practice, she was lonely and miserable. Nothing helped: not yoga, nor meditation, nor exercise, nor a vegetarian diet. "I was a very unhappy young woman," she recalls. "I'd had the best therapy from the best therapists, but even with all the work I had done on myself, something was missing."

What was missing, she discovered, was the ability to enjoy herself. At 35, after she lost her mother to cancer, she moved to a small house in the Catskill Mountains, where she lived alone for a year and, for the first time, paid attention to what felt good. At first she cried and felt sorry for herself. But by year's end, she was dancing to Vivaldi and the Temptations, and finding creativity in cooking and chopping wood.

She soon realized that most of her patients shared the same pleasure deprivation. "Our whole society diminishes the value of pleasure," she writes. "We think of it as fun and games, an escape from reality—rarely a worthwhile end in itself. Amazingly, we don't make the connection between vitality—the energy that comes from feeling good—and the willingness to take pleasure in moment-by-moment experience."

Therapy too often concentrates on pain and what the mind thinks; Resnick focused on pleasure and what the body feels. But when she first published her ideas in 1978, epithets were hurled: "narcissist," "hedonist," "icon for the Me Decade." It wasn't until research on the positive effects of pleasure and the negative effects of stress began to accumulate in the '80s that people became more receptive. "This is not about creating a society of me-first people," she says of her work. "There's no joy in hoarding all the goodies for our lonesome."

To help people understand pleasure, Resnick divides it into eight "core" categories: primal (the feeling of floating); pain relief (being touched and soothed); elemental (childlike laughter, play, movement, and voice); mental (the fun of learning); emotional (the feeling of love); sensual (the five senses, plus imagination); sexual (arousal, eroticism, orgasm); and spiritual (empathy, morality, and altruism).

Her prescription is body-based and simple. Listen to a fly buzz. Float on your back. Tell a dream. Her number-one tip for falling and staying in love is . . . breathe. Conscious breathing enhances relationships, she claims, because it allows us to let go in sweet surrender, rather than fighting or resisting ourselves or each other.

Experiencing pleasure opens the body, releasing enormous energy, says Resnick. Ironically, this flow is what scares us, causing us to tense up and shut down, because we don't know what to do with it. We can miss the healing power of great sex, for example, by wanting to release the energy as soon as we get turned on. She advises allowing the excitement to build and circulate so that "it's something you feel in your heart. And in your big toes."

Repressing one's desire for pleasure was once considered virtuous, a sign of moral superiority. But Resnick questions whether it's good to continue in that vein. "We have poor race relations, poor man-woman relations, whole segments of society that have problems with parents and institutions," she says. "Could we do better if we enjoyed our relationships more, if people knew how to encourage and inspire themselves instead of being motivated by shame, guilt, and other negative emotions?"

Resnick doesn't advocate always succumbing to immediate gratification—there's pleasure in yearning—or fear and anger, which can inform and protect us. But using negative means to pursue positive ends simply doesn't work. "The secret to success in all things—business, creativity, art, relationships, family, spirituality—is to be relaxed during challenging times," she says. "Don't hold yourself in, or brace yourself for what might go wrong." And if you don't get it at first, don't worry. Even Resnick has to remind herself to breathe.

— *Cathy Madison*

None of which makes the alleged new paradigm any less real. As the poets of our day, for better or worse, the modern scientists of mind have already shaped our reality with their words and concepts. Who hasn't heard of the endorphin-driven runner's high, or traced a pang of lover's jealousy to their reptilian brain? On *Star Trek Voyager,* a medical man of the future waves his magic wand over a crewmate emerging from a trance and declares, "His neuropeptides have returned to normal!"

You didn't have to be a Darwin to see that the news gave Captain Janeway a certain . . . pleasure.

Jeremiah Creedon is a senior editor of Utne Reader.

The **Tick-Tock** of the **Biological Clock**

Biological clocks count off 24-hour intervals in most forms of life. Genetics has revealed that related molecular timepieces are at work in fruit flies, mice and humans

by Michael W. Young

You have to fight the urge to fall asleep at 7:00 in the evening. You are ravenous at 3 P.M. but have no appetite when suppertime rolls around. You wake up at 4:00 in the morning and cannot get back to sleep.

This scenario is familiar to many people who have flown from the East Coast of the U.S. to California, a trip that entails jumping a three-hour time difference. During a weeklong business trip or vacation, your body no sooner acclimatizes to the new schedule than it is time to return home again, where you must get used to the old routine once more.

Nearly every day my colleagues and I put a batch of *Drosophila* fruit

THE BASICS
THE BIOLOGICAL CLOCK
THE AUTHOR ANSWERS SOME KEY QUESTIONS

Where is the biological clock? In mammals the master clock that dictates the day-night cycle of activity known as circadian rhythm resides in a part of the brain called the suprachiasmatic nucleus (SCN). But cells elsewhere also show clock activity.

What drives the clock? Within individual SCN cells, specialized clock genes are switched on and off by the proteins they encode in a feedback loop that has a 24-hour rhythm.

Is the biological clock dependent on the normal 24-hour cycle of light and darkness? No. The molecular rhythms of clock-gene activity are innate and self-sustaining. They persist in the absence of environmental cycles of day and night.

What role does light play in regulating and resetting the biological clock? Bright light absorbed by the retina during the day helps to synchronize the rhythms of activity of the clock genes to the prevailing environ-

mental cycle. Exposure to bright light at night resets circadian rhythms by acutely changing the amount of some clock-gene products.

How does the molecular clock regulate an individual's day-night activity? The fluctuating proteins synthesized by clock genes control additional genetic pathways that connect the molecular clock to timed changes in an animal's physiology and behavior.

flies through the jet lag of a simulated trip from New York to San Francisco or back. We have several refrigerator-size incubators in the laboratory: one labeled "New York" and another tagged "San Francisco." Lights inside these incubators go on and off as the sun rises and sets in those two cities. (For consistency, we schedule sunup at 6 A.M. and sundown at 6 P.M. for both locations.) The temperature in the two incubators is a constant, balmy 77 degrees Fahrenheit.

The flies take their simulated journey inside small glass tubes packed into special trays that monitor their movements with a narrow beam of infrared light. Each time a fly moves into the beam, it casts a shadow on a phototransistor in the tray, which is connected to a computer that records the activity. Going

from New York to San Francisco time does not involve a five-hour flight for our flies: we simply disconnect a fly-filled tray in one incubator, move it to the other one and plug it in.

We have used our transcontinental express to identify and study the functions of several genes that appear to be the very cogs and wheels in the works of the biological clock that controls the day-night cycles of a wide range of organisms that includes not only fruit flies but mice and humans as well. Identifying the genes allows us to determine the proteins they encode—proteins that might serve as targets for therapies for a wide range of disorders, from sleep disturbances to seasonal depression.

The main cog in the human biological clock is the suprachiasmatic

nucleus (SCN), a group of nerve cells in a region at the base of the brain called the hypothalamus. When light hits the retinas of the eyes every morning, specialized nerves send signals to the SCN, which in turn controls the production cycle of a multitude of biologically active substances. The SCN stimulates a nearby brain region called the pineal gland, for instance. According to instructions from the SCN, the pineal rhythmically produces melatonin, the so-called sleep hormone that is now available in pill form in many health-food stores. As day progresses into evening, the pineal gradually begins to make more melatonin. When blood levels of the hormone rise, there is a modest decrease in body temperature and an increased tendency to sleep.

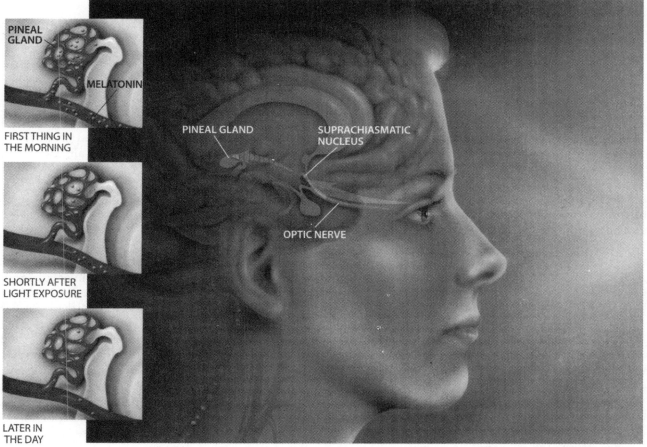

PINEAL GLAND — MELATONIN

FIRST THING IN THE MORNING

SHORTLY AFTER LIGHT EXPOSURE

LATER IN THE DAY

PINEAL GLAND

SUPRACHIASMATIC NUCLEUS

OPTIC NERVE

CYNTHIA TURNER

LIGHT HITTING THE EYE causes the pineal gland of the brain to taper its production of melatonin (*insets*), a hormone that appears to play a role in inducing sleep. The signal to reduce melatonin secretion is relayed from the retina, through the optic nerve, to a structure called the suprachiasmatic nucleus (SCN). The connection from the SCN to the pineal is indirect.

The Human Clock

Although light appears to "reset" the biological clock each day, the day-night, or circadian, rhythm continues to operate even in individuals who are deprived of light, indicating that the activity of the SCN is innate. In the early 1960s Jürgen Aschoff, then at the Max Planck Institute of Behavioral Physiology in Seewiesen, Germany, and his colleagues showed that volunteers who lived in an isolation bunker—with no natural light, clocks or other clues about time—nevertheless maintained a roughly normal sleep-wake cycle of 25 hours.

More recently Charles Czeisler, Richard E. Kronauer and their colleagues at Harvard University have determined that the human circadian rhythm is actually closer to 24 hours—24.18 hours, to be exact. The scientists studied 24 men and women (11 of whom were in their 20s and 13 of whom were in their 60s) who lived for more than three weeks in an environment with no time cues other than a weak cycle of light and dark that was artificially set at 28 hours and that gave the subjects their signals for bedtime.

They measured the participants' core body temperature, which normally falls at night, as well as blood concentrations of melatonin and of a stress hormone called cortisol that drops in the evening. The researchers observed that even though the subjects' days had been abnormally extended by four hours, their body temperature and melatonin and cortisol levels continued to function according to their own internal 24-hour circadian clock. What is more, age seemed to have no effect on the ticking of the clock: unlike the results of previous studies, which had suggested that aging disrupts circadian rhythms, the body-temperature and hormone fluctuations of the older subjects in the Harvard study were as regular as those of the younger group.

CLOCKS EVERYWHERE
THEY ARE NOT JUST IN THE BRAIN

Most of the research on the biological clocks of animals has focused on the brain, but that is not the only organ that observes a day-night rhythm.

Jadwiga Giebultowicz of Oregon State University has identified PER and TIM proteins—key components of biological clocks—in the kidneylike malpighian tubules of fruit flies. She has also observed that the proteins are produced according to a circadian cycle, rising at night and falling during the day. The cycle persists even in decapitated flies, demonstrating that the malpighian cells are not merely responding to signals from the insects' brains.

In addition, Steve Kay's research group at the Scripps Research Institute in La Jolla, Calif., has uncovered evidence of biological clocks in the wings, legs, oral regions and antennae of fruit flies. By transferring genes that direct the production of fluorescent PER proteins into living flies, Kay and his colleagues have shown that each tissue carries an independent, photoreceptive clock. The clocks even continue to function and respond to light when each tissue is dissected from the insect.

And the extracranial biological clocks are not restricted to fruit flies. Ueli Schibler of the University of Geneva showed in 1998 that the *per* genes of rat connective-tissue cells called fibroblasts are active according to a circadian cycle.

The diversity of the various cell types displaying circadian clock activity suggests that for many tissues correct timing is important enough to warrant keeping track of it locally. The findings might give new meaning to the term "body clock."—*M.W.Y.*

As informative as the bunker studies are, to investigate the genes that underlie the biological clock scientists had to turn to fruit flies. Flies are ideal for genetic studies because they have short life spans and are small, which means that researchers can breed and interbreed thousands of them in the laboratory until interesting mutations crop up. To speed up the mutation process, scientists usually expose flies to mutation-causing chemicals called mutagens.

The first fly mutants to show altered circadian rhythms were identified in the early 1970s by Ron Konopka and Seymour Benzer of the California Institute of Technology. These researchers fed a mutagen to a few fruit flies and then monitored the movement of 2,000 of the progeny, in part using a form of the same apparatus that we now use in our New York to San Francisco experiments. Most of the flies had a normal 24-hour circadian rhythm: the insects were active for roughly 12 hours a day and rested for the other 12 hours. But three of the flies had mutations that caused them to break the pattern. One had a 19-hour cycle, one had a 28-hour cycle, and the third fly appeared to have no circadian rhythm at all, resting and becoming active seemingly at random.

Time Flies

In 1986 my research group at the Rockefeller University and another led by Jeffrey Hall of Brandeis University and Michael Rosbash of the Howard Hughes Medical Institute at Brandeis found that the three mutant flies had three different alterations in a single gene named *period*, or *per*, which each of our teams had independently isolated two years earlier. Because different mutations in the same gene caused the three behaviors, we concluded that *per* is somehow actively involved both in producing circadian rhythm in flies and in setting the rhythm's pace.

After isolating *per,* we began to question whether the gene acted alone in controlling the day-night cycle. To find out, two postdoctoral fellows in my laboratory, Amita Sehgal and Jeffrey Price, screened more than 7,000 flies to see if they could identify other rhythm mutants. They finally found a fly that, like one of the *per* mutants, had no apparent circadian rhythm. The new mutation turned out to be on chromosome 2, whereas *per* had been mapped to the X chromosome. We knew this had to be a new gene, and we named it *timeless,* or *tim.*

But how did the new gene relate to *per*? Genes are made of DNA, which contains the instructions for making proteins. DNA never leaves the nucleus of the cell; its molecular recipes are read out in the form of messenger RNA, which leaves the nucleus and enters the cytoplasm, where proteins are made. We used the *tim* and *per* genes to make PER and TIM proteins in the laboratory. In collaboration with Charles Weitz of Harvard Medical School, we observed that when we mixed the two proteins, they stuck to each other, suggesting that they might interact within cells.

In a series of experiments, we found that the production of PER and TIM proteins involves a clock-like feedback loop. The *per* and *tim* genes are active until concentrations of their proteins become high enough that the two begin to bind to each other. When they do, they form complexes that enter the nucleus and shut down the genes that made them. After a few hours enzymes degrade the complexes, the genes start up again, and the cycle begins anew.

Moving the Hands of Time

Once we had found two genes that functioned in concert to make a molecular clock, we began to wonder how the clock could be reset. After all, our sleep-wake cycles fully adapt to travel across any number of time zones, even though the adjustment might take a couple of days or weeks.

That is when we began to shuttle trays of flies back and forth between the "New York" and "San Francisco" incubators. One of the first things we and others noticed was that whenever a fly was moved from a darkened incubator to one that was brightly lit to mimic daylight, the TIM proteins in the fly's brain disappeared—in a matter of minutes.

Even more interestingly, we noted that the direction the flies "traveled" affected the levels of their TIM proteins. If we removed flies from "New York" at 8 P.M. local time, when it was dark, and put them into "San Francisco," where it was still light at 5 P.M. local time, their TIM levels plunged. But an hour later, when the lights went off in "San Francisco," TIM began to reaccumulate. Evidently the flies' molecular clocks were initially stopped by the transfer, but after a delay they resumed ticking in the pattern of the new time zone.

In contrast, flies moved at 4 A.M. from "San Francisco" experienced a premature sunrise when they were placed in "New York," where it was 7 A.M. This move also caused TIM levels to drop, but this time the protein did not begin to build up again because the molecular clock was advanced by the time-zone switch.

We learned more about the mechanism behind the different molecular responses by examining the timing of the production of *tim* RNA. Levels of *tim* RNA are highest at about 8 P.M. local time and lowest between 6 A.M. and 8 A.M. A fly moving at 8 P.M. from "New York" to "San Francisco" is producing maximum levels of *tim* RNA, so protein lost by exposure to light in "San Francisco" is easily replaced after sunset in the new location. A fly traveling at 4 A.M. from "San Francisco" to "New York," however, was making very little *tim* RNA before departure. What the fly experiences as a premature sunrise eliminated

TIM and allows the next cycle of production to begin with an earlier schedule.

Not Just Bugs

Giving flies jet lag has turned out to have direct implications for understanding circadian rhythm in mammals, including humans. In 1997 researchers led by Hajime Tei of the University of Tokyo and Hitoshi Okamura of Kobe University in Japan—and, independently, Cheng Chi Lee of Baylor College of Medicine—isolated the mouse and human equivalents of *per.* Another flurry of work, this time involving many laboratories, turned up mouse and human forms of *tim* in 1998. And the genes were active in the suprachiasmatic nucleus.

Studies involving mice also helped to answer a key question: What turns on the activity of the *per* and *tim* genes in the first place? In 1997 Joseph Takahashi of the Howard Hughes Medical Institute at Northwestern University and his colleagues isolated a gene they called *Clock* that when mutated yielded mice with no discernible circadian rhythm. The gene encodes a transcription factor, a protein that in this case binds to DNA and allows it to be read out as messenger RNA.

Shortly thereafter a fly version of the mouse *Clock* gene was isolated, and various research teams began to introduce combinations of the *per, tim* and *Clock* genes into mammalian and fruit fly cells. These experiments revealed that the CLOCK protein targets the *per* gene in mice and both the *per* and *tim* genes in flies. The system had come full circle: in flies, whose clocks are the best understood, the CLOCK protein—in combination with a protein encoded by a gene called *cycle*—binds to and activates the *per* and *tim* genes, but only if no PER and TIM proteins are present in the nucleus. These four genes and their proteins con-

BODY CHANGES OVER 24-HOUR PERIOD

1:00 A.M.
- Pregnant women are most likely to go into labor.
- Immune cells called helper T lymphocytes are at their peak.

2:00 A.M.
- Levels of growth hormones are highest.

4:00 A.M.
- Asthma attacks are most likely to occur.

6:00 A.M.
- Onset of menstruation is most likely.
- Insulin levels in the bloodstream are lowest.
- Blood pressure and heart rate begin to rise.
- Levels of the stress hormone cortisol increase.
- Melatonin levels begin to fall.

7:00 A.M.
- Hay fever symptoms are worst.

8:00 A.M.
- Risk for heart attack and stroke is highest.
- Symptoms of rheumatoid arthritis are worst.
- Helper T lymphocytes are at their lowest daytime level.

Noon
- Level of hemoglobin in the blood is at its peak.

3:00 P.M.
- Grip strength, respiratory rate and reflex sensitivity are highest.

4:00 P.M.
- Body temperature, pulse rate and blood pressure peak.

6:00 P.M.
- Urinary flow is highest.

9:00 P.M.
- Pain threshold is lowest.

11:00 P.M.
- Allergic responses are most likely.

stitute the heart of the biological clock in flies, and with some modifications they appear to form a mechanism governing circadian rhythms throughout the animal kingdom, from fish to frogs, mice to humans.

Recently Steve Reppert's group at Harvard and Justin Blau in my laboratory have begun to explore the specific signals connecting the mouse and fruit fly biological clocks to the timing of various behaviors, hormone fluctuations and other functions. It seems that some output genes are turned on by a direct interaction with the CLOCK protein. PER and TIM block the ability of CLOCK to turn on these genes at the same time as they are producing the oscillations of the central feedback loop—setting up extended patterns of cycling gene activity.

An exciting prospect for the future involves the recovery of an entire system of clock-regulated genes in organisms such as fruit flies and mice. It is likely that previously uncharacterized gene products with intriguing effects on behavior will be discovered within these networks. Perhaps one of these, or a component of the molecular clock itself, will become a favored target for drugs to relieve jet lag, the side effects of shift work, or sleep disorders and related depressive illnesses. Adjusting to a trip from New York to San Francisco might one day be much easier.

MICHAEL W. YOUNG is a professor and head of the Laboratory of Genetics at the Rockefeller University. He also directs the Rockefeller unit of the National Science Foundation's Science and Technology Center for Biological Timing, a consortium that connects laboratories at Brandeis University, Northwestern University, Rockefeller, the Scripps Research Institute in La Jolla, Calif., and the University of Virginia. After receiving a Ph.D. from the University of Texas in 1975, Young took a postdoctoral fellowship at the Stanford University School of Medicine to study gene and chromosome structure. In 1978 he joined the faculty of Rockefeller, where members of his research group have isolated and deciphered the functions of four of the seven genes that have been linked to the fruit fly biological clock.

Further Information

THE MOLECULAR CONTROL OF CIRCADIAN BEHAVIORAL RHYTHMS AND THEIR ENTRAINMENT IN DROSOPHILA. Michael W. Young in Annual Review of Biochemistry, Vol. 67, pages 135–152; 1998.

MOLECULAR BASES FOR CIRCADIAN CLOCKS. Jay C. Dunlap in Cell, Vol. 96, No. 2, pages 271–290; January 22, 1999.

TIME, LOVE, MEMORY: A GREAT BIOLOGIST AND HIS QUEST FOR THE ORIGINS OF BEHAVIOR. J. Weiner. Alfred Knopf, 1999.

A tutorial on biological clocks—including ideas for home and classroom activities—can be found on the National Science Foundation's Science and Technology Center for Biological Timing's site at http://cbt4pc.bio.virginia.edu/tutorial/TUTORIALMAIN.html on the World Wide Web.

THE GOLD MEDAL **MIND**

ANY COMPETITIVE ATHLETE WILL TELL YOU THAT WHAT SEPARATES THE GREAT HOPEFULS FROM THE GREAT ACHIEVERS IS THE KNOWLEDGE AND APPLICATION OF MENTAL SKILLS. HERE, U.S. OLYMPIC TRAINING CENTER SPORT PSYCHOLOGIST **JAMES BAUMAN, PH.D.,** REVEALS JUST WHAT IT WILL TAKE TO SUCCEED IN SYDNEY THIS SUMMER— OR AT LEAST JUST IMPRESS EVERYONE AT THE GYM.

The day before Jonathan Jordan was to compete in the 1996 NCAA Track and Field Indoor Championships in Bakersfield, he got food poisoning and had to be rushed to the hospital. His coach tried to convince him to withdraw from the next day's race, but with the championship on the line, Jordan refused to quit.

The next morning, the 26-year-old triple and long jumper from suburban Chicago focused all his energy on the one good jump he knew he had to make. "I put everything into it," he said. "I was more relaxed than I ever was." When the jump measured an expansive 23 feet, a surprised Jordan said, "Oh my God." He had placed first, in spite of his weakened condition.

"In such situations I have found myself asking: 'How can I compete now?' But you concentrate and dig for something you didn't know you had," says Jordan, who will head for the Olympic Trials in Sacramento this summer.

A computer with all the gigabytes in the world is useless without the software to make it run. And so it is with the Olympian, whose mind is the software controlling that collection of hardware known as flesh and bone and muscle. Aside from their astounding physical prowess, it is the Olympians' mental muscles—and how they flex them—that really sets them apart from everyday athletes.

"The difference between you and the guy next to you is almost completely mental," says Curt R. Clausen, 32, the six-foot-one former public administrator whose newly shaved head will stand out in the 50-kilometer

Olympic race walk in Sydney. "At the highest level," says Clausen, who is ranked No. 1 in the United States and fourth in the world, "that's what makes the difference."

In my more than 10 years of working with hundreds of athletes, as the sport psychologist at Washington State University and one of four sports psychologists for the Sport Science and Technology Division of the U.S. Olympic Committee, I have seen how "mental management" contributes to an athlete's performance. Some Olympians even say it accounts for 90% of their success. While it's difficult to quantify percentages, we do know from years of research and hundreds of studies just how important psychological preparation is to optimum athletic performance.

It can even conquer the worst of distractions, as it did for Kathy Ann Colin, who overcame physical injuries, the distraction of college and a family disaster before becoming the No. 1 kayaker in the U.S.

Colin has had her eyes on the Olympics since she was 6, thinking she'd get there through gymnastics. But after tearing a ligament in her right knee when she was 12, she turned to kayaking. She had to give that up, too, when she left her hometown of Kailua, Hawaii, to attend the University of Washington. But after graduating from college and landing a good job with Boeing, Colin knew that if she were ever to compete in the Olympics, she had to train full time. Three years ago, she moved to the U.S. ARCO Olympic Training Center in Chula Vista, California, to work out with the national team.

When finally, last summer, the day came for her to qualify for the 2000 Olympics, tragedy struck. Colin's parents, who had flown all the way from Hawaii, were robbed at the airport and left with nothing but the clothes on their backs.

"I spent the whole day crying and rounding up clothes from teammates," the athlete recalls.

On top of that, she and kayak pair teammate Tamara Jenkins were having trouble balancing, and their warm-ups were "awful." When experts predicted that the race would be the fastest anyone had seen in 20 years, the pair was distracted, nervous and excited—all at once.

"I knew what I had to do," says Colin. "I had put too much time and effort into this." So with all the tenacity her five-foot-eight, 145-pound body could muster, she turned to Jenkins and said: "We can do this. Focus and relax and don't worry about anything else. Just do what we do."

And they did. Colin and Jenkins will be paddling for the gold in the K-2 in Sydney this summer.

Numerous studies over the years confirm that successful athletes are better able than the rest of us to deal with distractions. Olympic athletes in particular find ways to remain focused on an event to the exclusion of negative influences such as unruly crowds, inclement weather, even family problems. In his 1986 comparative study, Stanford University's Albert Bandura, Ph.D., internationally known for his work in personality and social learning theory, showed that while the vast majority of us spend lots of time worrying about things we can't control, successful athletes attend primarily to those cues or stimuli that are relevant, or within their control.

And where mental ability counts most is in preparation.

In addition to the intense concentration or focus of a Jordan, Clausen or Colin, "mental management" involves a number of techniques, including imaging, comparing performances, positive self-talk, mental relaxation, and achieving what athletes call "flow." And you don't have to be Olympic material to benefit from them. While the rest of us may lack the dream or the gift to compete in Sydney this summer, we can still use our minds to improve our sports performance.

MENTAL REHEARSAL is when athletes not only picture their movements but imagine feeling them as well. In 1988, Canadian sport psychologists Terry Orlick, Ph.D., and John Partington, Ph.D., found that 99% of the 235 athletes they surveyed rely on this technique to prepare for a high stakes race. Studies by the U.S. Olympic Training Center show that 94% of coaches use mental rehearsal for training and competition.

Colin describes how she glides through the waters in her mind as she lies in bed at night: "I focus on the feel of the boat and on my paddling. I am in the race. I get nervous energy. My muscles are triggered as I simulate a stroke in my mind. The boat is picking up; it's gliding and I'm gliding with it."

During warm-ups on the water, Colin's visualizations are key: "I'll hold a stop watch and imagine the start. My strategy is to figure out the number of strokes I need to win. I tell myself I want to get 152—and then I make the plan. I know exactly where I'll be when I stop, and I'll be within a second of my goal. So when the race comes, there's nothing new."

It's not as easy to mind-map a four-hour race. But Curt Clausen has his own way of visualizing the 50-kilometer race walk.

"I start by saying, 'I want to win this race.' Then I make a detailed plan with contingencies, strategies and coping methods. I take that plan, visualize the whole

---

TAKING IT TO THE GYM

You may not have the physical attributes to perform at the level of an Olympian, but you can get the most out of whatever you do to stay in shape by adapting the same mental techniques athletes use.

• *Set realistic goals.* Be specific about what you want to accomplish, whether it's walking five miles or biking once a week. Devise steps to achieve the goal and commit to a start-date.
• *Build self-confidence* by maintaining a clear and honest inventory of your skills. You're obviously not going to shoot a curl first thing in the morning if you haven't been on a surfboard in 10 years. But you *can* build on what you have accomplished before and believe in the untapped potential that is yours.
• *Relax.* There are a lot of ways to do it. Think about things that put you at ease. Breathe easily and fully. Picture the muscles in your body as being loose and limber.

Conjure up soothing images—scenes that make you feel genuinely good.
• *Imagine your performance.* Rehearse in your mind what it will look like and how you will feel as you break that sweat, run that extra half-mile, curl 10 more pounds. See yourself doing it; then do it.
• *Positive self-talk your way to success.* First, stop berating yourself for a less than stellar performance. Instead, tell yourself that you will accomplish your goal because you do have the skills to do it. Keep coaxing yourself. And, above all, listen to your self-talk.
• *Control distractions* by making a quick checklist of everything that might derail you from accomplishing your goal. Eliminate the things you can't control, like the weather, and focus on those you can, like having the proper shoes or equipment for your sport. Then concentrate on the here and now, because what you do right now and how you do it are the only true parameters of performance.

thing and then enter the race with it so that it's running through my head over and over."

An academic All-American with a bachelor's degree in criminal justice and a master's degree in forensic science, Jonathan Jordan talks to elementary school children about the importance of education as well as the preparation needed to become an Olympic athlete.

He begins his visualization two days before an event, he tells them. "I see myself on the runway. Then, I'm taking off on the board. From there, I'm holding my phases, and then I'm landing. If I get prepared like that beforehand," he explains, "then when I get there I don't worry about it. That's something I've been doing for 10 years."

By now he even does it subconsciously. While walking through his hometown shopping mall, Jordan has startled himself by suddenly leaping in the air. "I caught myself doing that one day. I was doing it for quite a bit of time before I realized."

According to Brent Rushall, Ph.D., in his 1991 book *Imagery Training in Sports: A Handbook for Athletes, Coaches and Sport Psychologists*, effective performance imagery involves the ability to:

- Focus on the most desirable aspects of the performance;
- Emphasize the feeling of the activity by including all senses that come into play;
- Conjure the image several times;
- Envision the whole environment, including the arena;
- Incorporate competition strategies into the image.

"Each successful imagery trial should be followed by covert positive reinforcement," Rushall wrote. "The combination of trials and reinforcement is critical for the mental skill to work."

COMPARING PERFORMANCES with competitors of the same caliber helps athletes build confidence.

"I try to match my mental abilities with the best in the world," said Andrew Hermann, 29, who will compete in his first Olympic games in the 50-kilometer race walk this summer in Sydney. Hermann ran distance and cross-country at Willamette College in Oregon before turning to race walking, competing in both 20- and 50-kilometer events. He placed second in the Olympic Trials in February.

Right before that, he took a number of tests to gauge his performance against other champions in his field. Afterward, he thought: "I'm just as tough as the best. Why can't I compete and put on a world-class performance?

Kathy Ann Colin was already a top-ranked junior kayaking champion when she went to the U.S. Nationals in Sacramento eight years ago, but it wasn't until she competed in the Olympic trials for the first time in 1996 that she had a true measure of her abilities.

"I remember driving to the airport. Everyone thought I did well, but I was upset because I knew I could do better," she said. "Up to that point, I was just having fun. But then when I was there, I was jealous because I knew I could do it." A year later, she began training full time at the ARCO Olympic Training Center.

When Jonathan Jordan first compared himself with others, the prognosis wasn't good. But when he tried out for the U.S. track and field team in 1996 and didn't make it, the failure strengthened his resolve.

"I had never gone up against guys who had competed for the U.S. for so many years," recalls Jordan. "I said, 'Man, am I supposed to be here?' " Now he knows what to expect. "With a field like that, you either jump well or you don't. I know I'm going to jump well because I know the competition."

POSITIVE SELF-TALK is another self-esteem builder. This internal dialogue, while not the stuff of Hamlet or Macbeth, helps athletes assess their performance; they use it to monitor, instruct and encourage.

"Sometimes I'm having problems with focus, where I'm just not up to it," says Colin. "So, I say, 'Come on. Just do it.' " She urges herself on, saying "ten strokes for power," then "ten for rhythm," then "ten for legs." At one point during the race she'll be thinking, "Legs, legs, legs" with such ferocity that she'll blurt it out, much to the chagrin of teammate Jenkins.

During a race, Curt Clausen carries on conversations with himself about his splits, his heart rate, the effort he's making, how fast he's going, how hard he can push. "More importantly," he says, "I repeat key words: relax, smile, low arms—all little techniques."

Based on their comprehensive study of Olympic gymnasts, Michael Mahoney, Ph.D., and M. Avener, Ph.D., reported in the *Canadian Journal of Sport Sciences* in 1992 that the more positive the self-talk, the easier it is for athletes to excel. In a separate study, published in *Cognitive Therapy and Research* in 1977, they found that athletes who made the U.S. men's gymnastics team used more positive self-talk than those who didn't.

Negative self-talk, on the other hand, is worse than no talk at all. In 1987, pioneering psychologist and founder of rational emotive therapy Albert Ellis, Ph.D., identified general irrational beliefs that can interfere with athletes reaching their potential. They include statements such as: "If I don't do well, I'm an incompetent person," or "I must do well to gain the approval of others." This can result in emotional distraction and decreased performance.

"It's a battle with yourself," says Jordan. "I tell myself, 'Jonathan, you trained too hard for this. That's why you're going to win it.' It's not being arrogant. It's just a statement of fact."

RELAXATION is especially important when even the slightest deviation from the norm can throw Olympians off. "The worst part about a race is the stress," says Clausen. "You tend to turn that into muscular tension, which detracts from your performance. I do deep breathing to trigger relaxation throughout my entire body."

Race-walker Andrew Hermann relaxes by visualizing a soothing blue liquid running through his body, from his head to his toes. "If I'm really in a jam," he says, "I picture brown sugar and pouring water over it. I see it dissolve and it makes the tensions dissolve wherever they are."

Von Ware, 24, ranked No. 3 in the United States in the triple jump, will prepare for his Olympic trials in Sacramento this July as he has prepared for past meets, by listening to music, strumming his guitar, tapping on a set of drums or fiddling with his laptop. A self-described "computer graphics nut," he hopes to own his own software company someday. Right now, though, he has his eyes on the prize—Olympic victory.

"The triple jump is structured. It's very technical, very rhythmic," says Ware. "And relaxation definitely helps."

Ware's abilities to jump, climb, run and perform a variety of athletic moves were recognized at an early age, especially after he broke the high school long jump record of 51 feet in 1994. At that point, Ware abandoned football, his sport of choice, and began to make the Olympics more than a dream.

What makes him happiest, he says, is seeing his mother smiling in the stands as he competes.

"For me," he says, "that's total bliss."

"FLOW" sums up the feelings of bliss, euphoria and contentment that athletes feel when they're on a roll, when the physical and mental aspects of performance are completely synchronized. In that state, nothing else, not even the crowd in the stands, matters.

"For me, it's almost an out-of-body experience," says Ware. "It's as if you can't feel your arms or legs or anything. I see nothing but the runway and pit, and my body just responds."

According to 1999 studies by Susan Jackson, Ph.D., of the Queensland University of Technology in Australia, and Mihaly Csikszentmihalyi, Ph.D., of Claremont Graduate University in California, the relationship between an athlete's confidence and the challenge being faced is a main factor in determining whether or not the athlete experiences competitive flow.

Jackson, in a 1992 study published in the *Journal of Applied Sport Psychology*, interviewed 28 elite athletes across seven different sports and found that the key factors contributing to flow are confidence, focus, how the performance felt and progressed, optimal motivation and arousal levels. She also found that athletes perceived the flow state to be within their control.

Flow is "a relaxed, fluid feeling, where my technique is better than anyone's," says Clausen. "I'm smiling. I'm scanning my competitors. I'm saying, 'I got these guys here today.' This is fun. Until this season, I was unable to do that."

James Bauman, Ph.D., is a sports psychologist at the U.S. Olympic Training Center in Chula Vista, California.

READ MORE ABOUT IT

In Pursuit of Excellence: How to Win in Sport and Life Through Mental Training, Third Ed., Terry Orlick, Ph.D. (Human Kinetics, 2000).
Flow In Sports, Susan Jackson, Ph.D., and Mihaly Csikszentmihalyi, Ph.D. (Human Kinetics, 1999).

FAITH & HEALING

Can prayer, faith and spirituality really improve your physical health?
A growing and surprising body of scientific evidence says they can.

Claudia Wallis

DRAPED IN EMBROIDERED CLOTH, laden with candles, redolent with roses and incense, the altar at the Santa Fe, New Mexico, home of Eetla Soracco seems an unlikely site for cutting-edge medical research. Yet every day for 10 weeks, ending last October, Soracco spent an hour or more there as part of a controlled study in the treatment of AIDS. Her assignment: to pray for five seriously ill patients in San Francisco.

Soracco, an Estonian-born "healer" who draws on Christian, Buddhist and Native American traditions, did not know the people for whom she was praying. All she had were their photographs, first names and, in some cases, T-cell counts. Picturing a patient in her mind, she would ask for "permission to heal" and then start to explore his body in her mind: "I looked at all the organs as though it is an anatomy book. I could see where things were distressed. These areas are usually dark and murky. I go in there like a white shower and wash it all out." Soracco was instructed to spend one hour a day in prayer, but the sessions often lasted twice as long. "For that time," she says, "It's as if I know the person."

Soracco is one of 20 faith healers recruited for the study by Dr. Elisabeth Targ, clinical director of psychosocial oncology research at California Pacific Medical Center in San Francisco. In the experiment, 20 severely ill AIDS patients were randomly selected; half were prayed for, half were not. None were told to which group they had been assigned. Though Targ has not yet published her results, she describes them as sufficiently "encouraging" to warrant a larger, follow-up study with 100 AIDS patients.

Twenty years ago, no self-respecting M.D. would have dared to propose a dou-

ble-blind, controlled study of something as intangible as prayer. Western medicine has spent the past 100 years trying to rid itself of remnants of mysticism. Targ's own field, psychiatry, couldn't be more hostile to spirituality: Sigmund Freud dismissed religious mysticism as "infantile helplessness" and "regression to primary narcissism." Today, while Targ's experiment is not exactly mainstream, it does exemplify a shift among doctors toward the view that there may be more to health than blood-cell counts and EKGS and more to healing than pills and scalpels.

"People, a growing number of them, want to examine the connection between healing and spirituality," says Jeffrey Levin, a gerontologist and epidemiologist at Eastern Virginia Medical School in Norfolk. To do such research, he adds, "is no longer professional death." Indeed, more and more medical schools are adding courses on holistic and alternative medicine with titles like Caring for the Soul. "The majority, 10 to 1, present the material uncritically," reports Dr. Wallace Sampson of Stanford University, who recently surveyed the offerings of every U.S. medical school.

This change in doctors' attitudes reflects a broader yearning among their patients for a more personal, more spiritual approach to health and healing. As the 20th century draws to an end, there is growing disenchantment with one of its greatest achievements: modern, high-tech medicine. Western medicine is at its best in a crisis—battling acute infection, repairing the wounds of war, replacing a broken-down kidney or heart. But increasingly, what ails America and other prosperous societies are chronic illnesses, such as high blood pressure, backaches, cardiovascular disease, arthritis, depression and acute illnesses that become chronic, such as

cancer and AIDS. In most of these, stress and life-style play a part.

"Anywhere from 60% to 90% of visits to doctors are in the mind-body, stress-related realm," asserts Dr. Herbert Benson, president of the Mind/Body Medical Institute of Boston's Deaconess Hospital and Harvard Medical School. It is a triumph of medicine that so many of us live long enough to develop these chronic woes, but, notes Benson, "traditional modes of therapy—pharmaceutical and surgical—don't work well against them."

Not only do patients with chronic health problems fail to find relief in a doctor's office, but the endless high-tech scans and tests of modern medicine also often leave them feeling alienated and uncared for. Many seek solace in the offices of alternative therapists and faith healers—to the tune of $30 billion a year, by some estimates. Millions more is spent on best-selling books and tapes by New Age doctors such as Deepak Chopra, Andrew Weil and Larry Dossey, who offer an appealing blend of medicine and Eastern-flavored spirituality.

Some scientists are beginning to look seriously at just what benefits patients may derive from spirituality. To their surprise, they are finding plenty of relevant data buried in the medical literature. More than 200 studies that touch directly or indirectly on the role of religion have been ferreted out by Levin of Eastern Virginia and Dr. David Larson, a research psychiatrist formerly at the National Institutes of Health and now at the privately funded National Institute for Healthcare Research. Most of these studies offer evidence that religion is good for one's health. Some highlights:

• A 1995 study at Dartmouth-Hitchcock Medical Center found that one of the best predictors of survival among 232 heart-surgery patients was the degree to which the patients said they drew comfort and strength from religious faith. Those who did not had more than three times the death rate of those who did.

• A survey of 30 years of research on blood pressure showed that churchgoers have lower blood pressure than nonchurchgoers— 5 mm lower, according to Larson, even when adjusted to account for smoking and other risk factors.

• Other studies have shown that men and women who attend church regularly have half the risk of dying from coronary-artery disease as those who rarely go to church. Again, smoking and socioeconomic factors were taken into account.

• A 1996 National Institute on Aging study of 4,000 elderly living at home in North Carolina found that those who attend religious services are less depressed and physically healthier than those who don't attend or who worship at home.

• In a study of 30 female patients recovering from hip fractures, those who regarded God as a source of strength and comfort and who attended religious services were able to walk farther upon discharge and had lower rates of depression than those who had little faith.

• Numerous studies have found lower rates of depression and anxiety-related illness among the religiously committed. Nonchurchgoers have been found to have a suicide rate four times higher than church regulars.

There are many possible explanations for such findings. Since churchgoers are more apt than nonattendees to respect religious injunctions against drinking, drug abuse, smoking and other excesses, it's possible that their better health merely reflects these healthier habits.

Some of the studies, however, took pains to correct for this possibility by making statistical adjustments for life-style differences. Larson likes to point out that in his own study the benefits of religion hold up strongly, even for those who indulge in cigarette smoking. Smokers who rated religion as being very important to them were one-seventh as likely to have an abnormal blood-pressure reading as smokers who did not value religion.

Churchgoing also offers social support— which numerous studies have shown to have a salutary effect on well-being. (Even owning a pet has been shown to improve the health of the lonesome.) The Dartmouth heart-surgery study is one of the few that attempts to tease apart the effects of social support and religious conviction. Patients were asked separate sets of questions about their participation in social groups and the comfort they drew from faith. The two factors appeared to have distinct benefits that made for a powerful combination. Those who were *both* religious and socially involved had a 14-fold advantage over those who were isolated or lacked faith.

Could it be that religious faith has some direct influence on physiology and health? Harvard's Herbert Benson is probably the most persuasive proponent of this view. Benson won international fame in 1975 with his best-selling book, *The Relaxation Response.* In it he showed that patients can successfully battle a number of stress-related ills by practicing a simple form of meditation. The act of focusing the mind on a single sound or image brings about a set of physiological changes that are the opposite of the "fight-or-flight response." With meditation, heart rate, respiration and brain waves slow down, muscles relax and the effects of epinephrine and other stress-related hormones diminish. Studies have shown that by routinely eliciting this "relaxation response," 75% of insomniacs begin to sleep normally, 35% of infertile women become pregnant and 34% of chronic-pain sufferers reduce their use of painkilling drugs.

In his latest book, *Timeless Healing* (Scribner; $24), Benson moves beyond the purely pragmatic use of meditation into the realm of spirituality. He ventures to say humans are actually engineered for religious faith. Benson bases this contention on his work with a subgroup of patients who report that they sense a closeness to God while meditating. In a five-year study of patients using meditation to battle chronic illnesses, Benson found that those who claim to feel the intimate presence of a higher power had better health and more rapid recoveries.

"Our genetic blueprint has made believing in an Infinite Absolute part of our nature," writes Benson. Evolution has so equipped us, he believes, in order to offset our uniquely human ability to ponder our own mortality: "To counter this fundamental angst, humans are also wired for God."

In Benson's view, prayer operates along the same biochemical pathways as the relaxation response. In other words, praying affects epinephrine and other corticosteroid messengers or "stress hormones," leading to lower blood pressure, more relaxed heart rate and respiration and other benefits.

Recent research demonstrates that these stress hormones also have a direct impact on the body's immunological defenses against disease. "Anything involved with meditation and controlling the state of mind that alters hormone activity has the potential to have an impact on the immune system," says David Felten, chairman of the Department of Neurobiology at the University of Rochester.

It is probably no coincidence that the relaxation response and religious experience share headquarters in the brain. Studies show that the relaxation response is controlled by the amygdala, a small, almond-shaped structure in the brain that together with the hippocampus and hypothalamus makes up the limbic system. The limbic system, which is found in all primates, plays a key role in emotions, sexual pleasure, deep-felt memo-

ries and, it seems, spirituality. When either the amygdala or the hippocampus is electrically stimulated during surgery, some patients have visions of angels and devils. Patients whose limbic systems are chronically stimulated by drug abuse or a tumor often become religious fanatics. "The ability to have religious experiences has a neuroanatomical basis," concludes Rhawn Joseph, a neuroscientist at the Palo Alto VA Medical Center in California.

Many researchers believe these same neuronal and hormonal pathways are the basis for the renowned and powerful "placebo effect." Decades of research show that if a patient truly believes a therapy is useful— even if it is a sugar pill or snake oil—that belief has the power to heal. In one classic 1950 study, for instance, pregnant women suffering from severe morning sickness were given syrup of ipecac, which induces vomiting, and told it was a powerful new cure for nausea. Amazingly, the women ceased vomiting. "Most of the history of medicine is the history of the placebo effect," observes Benson in *Timeless Healing.*

Though Benson devotes much of his book to documenting the power of the placebo effect—which he prefers to call "remembered wellness"—he has come to believe the benefits of religious faith are even greater. "Faith in the medical treatment," he writes, "[is] wonderfully therapeutic, successful in treating 60% to 90% of the most common medical problems. But if you so believe, faith in an invincible and infallible force carries even more healing power . . . It is a supremely potent belief."

Do the faithful actually have God on their side? Are their prayers answered? Benson doesn't say. But a true scientist, insists Jeffrey Levin, cannot dismiss this possibility: "I can't directly study that, but as an honest scholar, I can't rule it out."

A handful of scientists have attempted to study the possibility that praying works through some supernatural factor. One of the most cited examples is a 1988 study by cardiologist Randolph Byrd at San Francisco General Hospital. Byrd took 393 patients in the coronary-care unit and randomly assigned half to be prayed for by born-again Christians. To eliminate the placebo effect, the patients were not told of the experiment. Remarkably, Byrd found that the control group was five times as likely to need antibiotics and three times as likely to develop complications as those who were prayed for.

Byrd's experiment has never been replicated and has come under some criticism for design flaws. A more recent study of intercessory prayer with alcoholics found no benefit, while Elisabeth Targ's study of AIDS patients is still too small to produce significant results.

Science may never be able to pin down the benefits of spirituality. Attempts by Benson and others to do so are like "trying to nail Jell-O to the wall," complains William Jarvis, a public-health professor at California's Loma Linda University and the president of the National Council Against Health Fraud. But it may not be necessary to understand how prayer works to put it to use for patients. "We often know something works before we know why," observes Santa Fe internist Larry Dossey, the author of the 1993 best seller *Healing Words*.

A TIME/CNN poll of 1,004 Americans conducted last week by Yankelovich Partners found that 82% believed in the healing power of prayer and 64% thought doctors should pray with those patients who request it. Yet even today few doctors are comfortable with that role. "We physicians are culturally insensitive about the role of religion," says David Larson, noting that fewer than two-thirds of doctors say they believe in God. "It is very important to many of our patients and not important to lots of doctors."

Larson would like physicians to be trained to ask a few simple questions of their seriously or chronically ill patients: Is religion important to you? Is it important in how you cope with your illness? If the answers are yes, doctors might ask whether the patient would like to discuss his or her faith with the hospital chaplain or another member of the clergy. "You can be an atheist and say this," Larson insists. Not doing so, he argues, is a disservice to the patient.

Even skeptics such as Jarvis believe meditation and prayer are part of "good patient management." But he worries, as do many doctors, that patients may become "so convinced of the power of mind over body that they may decide to rely on that, instead of doing the hard things, like chemotherapy."

In the long run, it may be that most secular of forces—economics—that pushes doctors to become more sensitive to the spiritual needs of their patients. Increasingly, American medicine is a business, run by large HMOs and managed-care groups with a keen eye on the bottom line. Medical businessmen are more likely than are scientifically trained doctors to view prayer and spirituality as low-cost treatments that clients say they want. "The combination of these forces—consumer demand and the economic collapse of medicine—are very powerful influences that are making medicine suddenly open to this direction," observes Andrew Weil, a Harvard-trained doctor and author of *Spontaneous Healing*.

Cynics point out that there is an even more practical reason for doctors to embrace spirituality even if they don't believe. The high cost of malpractice insurance gives physicians an incentive to attend to their patients' spiritual needs—and, if necessary, get on their knees and pray with them. Not only might it help restore their image as infallible caregivers, but if something does go wrong, patients who associate their doctors with a higher power might be less likely to sue.

—Reported by Jeanne McDowell/
Los Angeles, Alice Park/ New York and
Lisa H. Towle/Raleigh

Unit Selections

Key Points to Consider

❖ Individuals face challenges at every phase of development. What are some of the phases or stages of development? What challenges are typical of each stage, as mentioned in this unit? What are other challenges that have not been mentioned?

❖ What are the various factors that can influence fetal development? If drugs and other addictive substances have detrimental effects on the fetus, should we hold addicted parents responsible for the care and treatment of their addicted and possibly deformed or developmentally delayed infants? Why or why not?

❖ What are four myths about infancy? Just how capable is an infant? What types of research can you provide to support your answer to the last question? How can we conduct research with infants who cannot always respond back to us?

❖ Are parents necessary to child development according to Judith Harris? What other individuals do you think have an impact on a child's development? According to Harris, what role do genes play in development? What role does the environment play? Do they play an equal role?

❖ What is an invincible kid? Why do some children suffer the detrimental effects of trauma and others don't? What is resiliency? How could knowledge of resiliency assist parents in raising their children?

❖ Are teens today different from teens of their parents' generation? How so? If you believe that today's teens are different, to what aspects of society can you point to explain these differences?

❖ Why do you think there has been an epidemic of violence in our high schools? What can parents do to protect their teens from this violence?

❖ What is a boomer? How and why can boomers shape and mold our society? If you were middle-aged, what could you do to stay happy? Do you believe in a midlife crisis? Why or why not?

❖ What myths do we hold about old age? What truth is there to these myths? Can we live longer? Do people want to live longer? Should we live longer? What must we do to live longer?

❖ Why is the topic of death so stigmatized in American society? What can we do to become more comfortable with the issue of death? What can you offer a friend who asked you to help him or her cope with the impending death of a loved one?

 **Links** **www.dushkin.com/online/**

These sites are annotated on pages 4 and 5.

At each stage of development from infancy to old age, humans are faced with new challenges. The infant has the rudimentary sensory apparatus for seeing, hearing, and touching but needs to begin coordinating stimuli into meaningful information. For example, early in life the baby begins to recognize familiar and unfamiliar people and usually becomes attached to the primary caregivers. In toddlerhood, the same child must master the difficult skills of walking, talking, and toilet training. This energetic, mobile, and sociable child also needs to learn the boundaries set on his or her behavior by others. As the child matures, not only do physical changes continue to take place, but the family composition may change when siblings are added, parents divorce, or mother and father work outside the home. Playmates become more influential, and others in the community, such as day-care workers and teachers, have an increasing influence on the child. The child eventually may spend more time at school than at home. The demands in this new environment require that the child sit still, pay attention, learn, and cooperate with others for long periods of time—behaviors perhaps never before extensively demanded of him or her.

In adolescence the body changes noticeably. Peers may pressure the individual to indulge in new behaviors such as using illegal drugs or engaging in premarital sex. Some older teenagers are said to be faced with an identity crisis when they must choose among career, education, and marriage. The pressures of work and family life exact a toll on less mature youths, while others are satisfied with the workplace and home.

Adulthood, middle age, and old age may bring contentment or turmoil as individuals face career peaks, empty nests, advancing age, and perhaps the death of loved ones, such as parents or spouses. Again, some individuals cope more effectively with these events than do others.

At any step in the developmental sequence, unexpected stressors challenge individuals. These stressors include major illnesses, accidents, natural disasters, economic recessions, and family or personal crises. It is important to remember, however, that an event need not be negative to be stressful. Any major life change may cause stress. As welcome as weddings, new babies, and job promotions may be, they, too, can be stressful because of the changes in daily life that they demand. Each challenge and each change must be met and adjusted to if the individual is going to move successfully to the next stage of development. Some individuals continue along their paths unscathed; others do not fare so well.

This unit of the book examines problems in various stages of life from before birth to death. The first article commences with and forecasts our chronological look at issues of development. In "The Seven Stages of Man," Costanza Villalba offers an overview of what can go right or wrong for both males and females in various life eras.

We next look at several stages in more detail. Janet Hopson, in "Fetal Psychology," reveals why fetal life is so important and so delicate. Drugs, alcohol, and other substances can adversely affect the fetus. Hopson suggests that problems for our development exist even before birth.

We next turn to childhood. In "Four Things You Need to Know About Raising Baby," Joanna Lipari explains that babies are not passive recipients of sensory information. Babies, in fact, are far more capable than we first believed. Lipari tackles myths about infancy by enlisting scientific evidence to the contrary.

Judith Rich Harris authored a controversial book on whether children are influenced most by genetics or by the experiences their parents provide for them. In excerpts from the book (see "Why Children Turn Out the Way They Do"), Harris suggests that genes are of utmost importance in child development. In other words, she insists that criminals are born—not made. Harris does suggest, however, that the environment pressures us to express what our genes have given us.

Continuing our developmental theme, "Invincible Kids" compares children who are traumatized and later do not do well with children who suffer trauma but are able to thrive. The latter are known as "resilient children." Psychologists are just beginning to understand what makes these children so hardy.

We move next to adolescence. In "A World of Their Own," Sharon Begley discusses why teens today are so different from past generations. Many of the differences are blamed on the modern media and on technology, especially the Internet.

No American who has lived through the last few years escaped hearing about the violent shootings in America's high schools. Barbara Kantrowitz and Pat Wingert examine this timely issue in "How Well Do You Know Your Kid?" They suggest that caring parents will be involved enough with their teens so that the teens will not become violent.

Middle age is the next developmental milestone undertaken in this unit. As the baby boomers swell the ranks of the middle aged, some are bound to be disappointed and others content with midlife. In "The Road Ahead: A Boomer's Guide to Happiness," the author discusses what issues face boomers and how boomers can find happiness at midlife.

Old age is the central issue in "Live to 100? No Thanks." Do people seek the fountain of youth? How long can we really live? What factors induce people to live to older ages? Do people really want to live to 100? The answer is a resounding "no." In a survey of elderly, results demonstrate that people prefer a high quality life over longevity.

The ultimate developmental stage is death. Death is a topic that both fascinates and frightens most of us. In "Start the Conversation," the veil of stigma that surrounds the issue of death is lifted. The article is designed to help people come to grips with their own fears and thus accept their own or another's death more comfortably.

Problems Influencing Personal Growth

The Seven Stages of Man

Men are often portrayed as big boys, differing from their younger selves only in the sums of money they spend on their toys. Indeed, because men can reproduce well into old age, and do not experience cyclical hormonal changes, their health is regarded as fairly static. But medical experts are learning that between the boy and the man stand a variety of genetic, biological and social changes. Understanding these factors may help men prepare for the stages that await them.

CONSTANZA VILLALBA

INFANCY

At the precise moment when a single sperm wiggles its way into an awaiting egg, the sex of the developing baby is defined. If that sperm carries a portly X chromosome, the egg turned embryo will give rise to a baby girl. If that sperm carries a diminutive Y chromosome, the baby will be a boy. With the blueprint for the male architecture, however, come several, often unfortunate genetic predispositions: hemophilia and Duchenne's Muscular Dystrophy afflict boys and men almost exclusively, while boys are more likely than girls to suffer from Fragile-X Syndrome, the nation's leading cause of mental retardation.

But being born a boy also comes with perks. Baby boys are an animated lot who display a marked curiosity about the world. Compared with girls, they are more alert and emotionally interactive with caretakers. They begin suppressing their emotions later in life, suggesting that masculine stoicism is learned, not hard-wired.

BOYHOOD

Once in school, boys tend to excel at mathematics and other tasks controlled by the brain's right side, or hemisphere. These natural aptitudes may be strengthened by the spike of testosterone that infant boys experience before and right after birth. But the biological machinery that gives boys an advantage in math and spatial tasks may predispose them to learning and developmental disorders: that is, in boys the left brain hemisphere, which controls language and facilitates socialization, may be underdeveloped.

On the playground, school-age boys resist playing with girls. They enjoy rough-and-tumble play and have inherent skill at games involving hit-the-target motor and navigational challenges. This time spent among other boys relays lessons—not all of them healthy—about what it means to be male. Chase and target games, for example, may be an evolutionary throwback to when men had to be good hunters.

ADOLESCENCE

Testosterone's effects on boys' development become most obvious during adolescence. As their soprano voices morph into tenors, boys squawk. Muscles begin replacing baby fat. Male hormones are also responsible for teen-age boys' novel interest in sex. Unfortunately, this interest is not always coupled with mature attitudes about safety and promiscuity. Data show that adolescents account for one-quarter of the 12 million cases of sexually transmitted diseases reported each year. The good news is that teen-agers may be getting the message. Gonorrhea among adolescent boys has been decreasing over the last seven years.

But boys' interest in girls is not purely sexual. Compared with previous generations, teen-age boys are more likely to have Platonic relationships with girls and to agree with survey statements like "Boys and girls should both be allowed to express feelings."

The hormones that pique boys' interest in sex goad them toward risky and aggressive behavior. At the same time, parental and societal expectations about masculinity may prevent them from expressing confusion or fear about the changes befalling them. These factors make teen-age boys 2.5 times more likely than girls to die of an unintentional injury and 5 times more likely to die from a homicide or suicide.

YOUNG ADULTHOOD

Men are physically in their prime. This period is characterized by a drive for achievement and by the realization that the foolhardiness of youth has unavoidable consequences. Fatherhood gives men the opportunity to redefine masculinity in a healthful way for themselves and their children.

Bad habits, like smoking, become less appealing but more difficult to shake; more than 80 percent of adults who ever smoked began doing so before age 18. Still, men are smoking less than they did and the incidence of lung cancer in men is falling. Although the incidence of smoking—28.8 percent for black men, 27.1 percent for white men—is similar, black men are at much higher risk of lung cancer than white men.

H.I.V. infection, the leading cause of death among men between ages 25 and 44, is often contracted during adolescence, when boys are experimenting with sex and are oblivious to the risks of infection. But with advances in drug therapies, the incidence of H.I.V.-related deaths has declined over the last four years.

MIDDLE AGE

Beginning in their early 40's, men experience a decline in testosterone of 1 percent each year. These reductions coincide with increased depressive symptoms, including anxiety and sexual dissatisfaction. While some doctors consider this stage tantamount to "male menopause," others argue that the hormonal changes are too subtle to account for these symptoms. They note, too, that impotence and other conditions associated with middle age can be caused by ailments that tend to strike men in this age group, like diabetes.

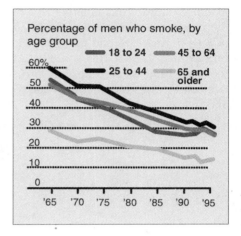

Percentage of men who smoke, by age group

The risk of heart disease, hypertension and diabetes is exacerbated by obesity, and middle age is when men are likely to be overweight. They lose 3 percent to 5 percent of their muscle mass for every decade after age 25. Reduced muscle mass and physical activity conspire to decrease men's resting metabolic rate. As men age, then, they burn less energy while resting and can gain weight even without changing their eating habits. And they do gain—2 to 3 pounds for every year over age 30.

Heart disease continues to be the leading cause of death for men in the United States. But the rate of heart disease-related deaths among men has decreased more than 50 percent since 1950; those who die of heart disease are dying later in life.

EARLY OLD AGE

Because men continue to produce testosterone throughout life, they are protected from—though not immune to—conditions like Alzheimer's Dis-

Reported cases of gonorrhea, per 100,000, for boys ages 15 to 19.

800
600
400
200
0
'92 '93 '94 '95

ease and osteoporosis. Their larger bone size also helps protect against this bone-weakening illness. Men can further maintain their mental acuity by engaging in intellectual activities. They can strengthen their bones and stem bone loss by undertaking weight-bearing exercise. The continued production of testosterone, however, can also adversely affect men. Testosterone aggravates hair loss and stimulates growth of the prostate gland. Noncancerous enlargement of the prostate occurs in more than half of men in their 60's and up to 90 percent of men in their 70's and 80's. At the same time, 80 percent of all prostate cancer cases occur in men age 65 and over.

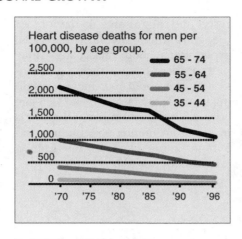

Heart disease deaths for men per 100,000, by age group.
- 65 - 74
- 55 - 64
- 45 - 54
- 35 - 44

LATER OLD AGE

Studies indicate that men are less likely than women to have difficulty maintaining normal routines, like bathing, dressing and using the toilet, as they age.

Still, the trend among the elderly in general is that they become less active, and so need fewer calories. Their appetites diminish, yet their nutritional needs increase because their bodies have lost the ability to synthesize and absorb important vitamins and nutrients. Their skin, for example, no longer easily synthesizes vitamin D when exposed to the sun. The benefits of avoiding potentially harmful foods, such as those high in cholesterol, lessen with age. Maintaining weight and making sure the right nutrients are present in the diet become more important.

PFSEYTCAHLOLOGY

Behaviorally speaking, there's little difference between a newborn baby and a 32-week-old fetus. A new wave of research suggests that the fetus can feel, dream, even enjoy *The Cat in the Hat*. **The abortion debate may never be the same.**

By Janet L. Hopson

The scene never fails to give goose bumps: the baby, just seconds old and still dewy from the womb, is lifted into the arms of its exhausted but blissful parents. They gaze adoringly as their new child stretches and squirms, scrunches its mouth and opens its eyes. To anyone watching this tender vignette, the message is unmistakable. Birth is the beginning of it all, ground zero, the moment from which the clock starts ticking. Not so, declares Janet DiPietro. Birth may be a grand occasion, says the Johns Hopkins University psychologist, but "it is a trivial event in development. Nothing neurologically interesting happens."

Armed with highly sensitive and sophisticated monitoring gear, DiPietro and other researchers today are discovering that the real action starts weeks earlier. At 32 weeks of gestation—two months before a baby is considered fully prepared for the world, or "at term"—a fetus is behaving almost exactly as a newborn. And it continues to do so for the next 12 weeks.

As if overturning the common conception of infancy weren't enough, scientists are creating a startling new picture of intelligent life in the womb. Among the revelations:

• By nine weeks, a developing fetus can hiccup and react to loud noises. By the end of the second trimester it can hear.

• Just as adults do, the fetus experiences the rapid eye movement (REM) sleep of dreams.

• The fetus savors its mother's meals, first picking up the food tastes of a culture in the womb.

A fetus spends hours in the rapid eye movement sleep of dreams.

Reprinted with permission from *Psychology Today*, September/October 1998, pp. 44-48, 76. © 1998 by Sussex Publishers, Inc.

• Among other mental feats, the fetus can distinguish between the voice of Mom and that of a stranger, and respond to a familiar story read to it.

• Even a premature baby is aware, feels, responds, and adapts to its environment.

• Just because the fetus is responsive to certain stimuli doesn't mean that it should be the target of efforts to enhance development. Sensory stimulation of the fetus can in fact lead to bizarre patterns of adaptation later on.

The roots of human behavior, researchers now know, begin to develop early—just weeks after conception, in fact. Well before a woman typically knows she is pregnant, her embryo's brain has already begun to bulge. By five weeks, the organ that looks like a lumpy inchworm has already embarked on the most spectacular feat of human development: the creation of the deeply creased and convoluted cerebral cortex, the part of the brain that will eventually allow the growing person to move, think, speak, plan, and create in a human way.

At nine weeks, the embryo's ballooning brain allows it to bend its body, hiccup, and react to loud sounds. At week ten, it moves its arms, "breathes" amniotic fluid in and out, opens its jaw, and stretches. Before the first trimester is over, it yawns, sucks, and swallows as well as feels and smells. By the end of the second trimester, it can hear; toward the end of pregnancy, it can see.

FETAL ALERTNESS

Scientists who follow the fetus' daily life find that it spends most of its time not exercising these new abilities but sleeping. At 32 weeks, it drowses 90 to 95% of the day. Some of these hours are spent in deep sleep, some in REM sleep, and some in an indeterminate state, a product of the fetus' immature brain that is different from sleep in a baby, child, or adult. During REM sleep, the fetus' eyes move back and forth just as an adult's eyes do, and many researchers believe that it is dreaming. DiPietro speculates that fetuses dream about what they know—the sensations they feel in the womb.

Closer to birth, the fetus sleeps 85 to 90% of the time, the same as a newborn. Between its frequent naps, the fetus seems to have "something like an awake alert period," according to developmental psychologist William Fifer, Ph.D., who with his Columbia University colleagues is monitoring these sleep and wakefulness cycles in order to identify patterns of normal and abnormal brain development, including potential predictors of sudden infant death syndrome. Says Fifer, "We are, in effect, asking the fetus: 'Are you paying attention? Is your nervous system behaving in the appropriate way?'"

FETAL MOVEMENT

Awake or asleep, the human fetus moves 50 times or more each hour, flexing and extending its body, moving its head, face, and limbs and exploring its warm wet compartment by touch. Heidelise Als, Ph.D., a developmental psychologist at Harvard Medical School, is fascinated by the amount of tactile stimulation a fetus gives itself. "It touches a hand to the face, one hand to the other hand, clasps its feet, touches its foot to its leg, its hand to its umbilical cord," she reports.

Als believes there is a mismatch between the environment given to preemies in hospitals and the environment they would have had in the womb. She has been working for years to change the care given to preemies so that they can curl up, bring their knees together, and touch things with their hands as they would have for weeks in the womb.

Along with such common movements, DiPietro has also noted some odder fetal activities, including "licking the uterine wall and literally walking around the womb by pushing off with its feet." Laterborns may have more room in the womb for such maneuvers than first babies. After the initial pregnancy, a woman's uterus is bigger and the umbilical cord longer, allowing more freedom of movement. "Second and subsequent children may develop more motor experience in utero and so may become more active infants," DiPietro speculates.

Fetuses react sharply to their mother's actions. "When we're watching the fetus on ultrasound and the mother starts to laugh, we can see the fetus, floating upside down in the womb, bounce up and down on its head, bum-bum-bum, like it's bouncing on a trampoline," says DiPietro. "When mothers watch this on the screen, they laugh harder, and the fetus goes up and down even faster. We've wondered whether this is why people grow up liking roller coasters."

FETAL TASTE

Why people grow up liking hot chilies or spicy curries may also have something to do with the fetal environment. By 13 to 15 weeks a fetus' taste buds already look like a mature adult's, and doctors know that the amniotic fluid that surrounds it can smell strongly of curry, cumin,

By 15 weeks, a fetus has an adult's taste buds and may be able to savor its mother's meals.

What's the Impact on Abortion?

Though research in fetal psychology focuses on the last trimester, when most abortions are illegal, the thought of a fetus dreaming, listening and responding to its mother's voice is sure to add new complexity to the debate. The new findings undoubtedly will strengthen the convictions of right-to-lifers—and they may shake the certainty of pro-choice proponents who believe that mental life begins at birth.

Many of the scientists engaged in studying the fetus, however, remain detached from the abortion controversy, insisting that their work is completely irrelevant to the debate.

"I don't think that fetal research informs the issue at all," contends psychologist Janet DiPietro of Johns Hopkins University. "The essence of the abortion debate is: When does life begin? Some people believe it begins at conception, the other extreme believes that it begins after the baby is born, and there's a group in the middle that believes it begins at around 24 or 25 weeks, when a fetus can live outside of the womb, though it needs a lot of help to do so.

"Up to about 25 weeks, whether or not it's sucking its thumb or has personality or all that, the fetus cannot survive outside of its mother. So is that life, or not? That is a moral, ethical, and religious question, not one for science. Things

can behave and not be alive. Right-to-lifers may say that this research proves that a fetus is alive, but it does not. It cannot."

"Fetal research only changes the abortion debate for people who think that life starts at some magical point," maintains Heidelise Als, a psychologist at Harvard University. "If you believe that life begins at conception, then you don't need the proof of fetal behavior." For others, however, abortion is a very complex issue and involves far more than whether research shows that a fetus hiccups. "Your circumstances and personal beliefs have much more impact on the decision," she observes.

Like DiPietro, Als realizes that "people may use this research as an emotional way to draw people to the pro-life side, but it should not be used by belligerent activists." Instead, she believes, it should be applied to helping mothers have the healthiest pregnancy possible and preparing them to best parent their child. Columbia University psychologist William Fifer, Ph.D., agrees. "The research is much more relevant for issues regarding viable fetuses—preemies."

Simply put, say the three, their work is intended to help the babies that live—not to decide whether fetuses should.—*Camille Chatterjee*

garlic, onion and other essences from a mother's diet. Whether fetuses can taste these flavors isn't yet known, but scientists have found that a 33-week-old preemie will suck harder on a sweetened nipple than on a plain rubber one.

"During the last trimester, the fetus is swallowing up to a liter a day" of amniotic fluid, notes Julie Mennella, Ph.D., a biopsychologist at the Monell Chemical Senses Center in Philadelphia. She thinks the fluid may act as a "flavor bridge" to breast milk, which also carries food flavors from the mother's diet.

FETAL HEARING

Whether or not a fetus can taste, there's little question that it can hear. A very premature baby entering the world at 24 to 25 weeks responds to the sounds around it, observes Als, so its auditory apparatus must already have been functioning in the womb. Many pregnant women report a fetal jerk or sudden kick just after a door slams or a car backfires.

Even without such intrusions, the womb is not a silent place. Researchers who have inserted a hydrophone into the uterus of a pregnant woman have picked up a noise level "akin to the background noise in an apartment," according to DiPietro. Sounds include the whooshing of blood in the mother's vessels, the gurgling and rumbling of her stomach and intestines, as well as the tones of her voice filtered through tissues, bones, and fluid, and the

voices of other people coming through the amniotic wall. Fifer has found that fetal heart rate slows when the mother is speaking, suggesting that the fetus not only hears and recognizes the sound, but is calmed by it.

FETAL VISION

Vision is the last sense to develop. A very premature infant can see light and shape; researchers presume that a fetus has the same ability. Just as the womb isn't completely quiet, it isn't utterly dark, either. Says Fifer: "There may be just enough visual stimulation filtered through the mother's tissues that a fetus can respond when the mother is in bright light," such as when she is sunbathing.

Japanese scientists have even reported a distinct fetal reaction to flashes of light shined on the mother's belly. However, other researchers warn that exposing fetuses (or premature infants) to bright light before they are ready can be dangerous. In fact, Harvard's Als believes that retinal damage in premature infants, which has long been ascribed to high concentrations of oxygen, may actually be due to overexposure to light at the wrong time in development.

A six-month fetus, born about 14 weeks too early, has a brain that is neither prepared for nor expecting signals from the eyes to be transmitted into the brain's visual cortex, and from there into the executive-branch frontal lobes, where information is integrated. When the fetus

> ## A fetus prefers hearing Mom's voice over a stranger's—speaking in her native, not a foreign tongue—and being read aloud familiar tales rather than new stories.

is forced to see too much too soon, says Als, the accelerated stimulation may lead to aberrations of brain development.

FETAL LEARNING

Along with the ability to feel, see, and hear comes the capacity to learn and remember. These activities can be rudimentary, automatic, even biochemical. For example, a fetus, after an initial reaction of alarm, eventually stops responding to a repeated loud noise. The fetus displays the same kind of primitive learning, known as habituation, in response to its mother's voice, Fifer has found.

But the fetus has shown itself capable of far more. In the 1980s, psychology professor Anthony James DeCasper, Ph.D., and colleagues at the University of North Carolina at Greensboro, devised a feeding contraption that allows a baby to suck faster to hear one set of sounds through headphones and to suck slower to hear a different set. With this technique, DeCasper discovered that within hours of birth, a baby already prefers its mother's voice to a stranger's, suggesting it must have learned and remembered the voice, albeit not necessarily consciously, from its last months in the womb. More recently, he's found that a newborn prefers a story read to it repeatedly in the womb—in this case, *The Cat in the Hat*—over a new story introduced soon after birth.

DeCasper and others have uncovered more mental feats. Newborns can not only distinguish their mother from a stranger speaking, but would rather hear Mom's voice, especially the way it sounds filtered through amniotic fluid rather than through air. They're xenophobes, too: they prefer to hear Mom speaking in her native language than to hear her or someone else speaking in a foreign tongue.

By monitoring changes in fetal heart rate, psychologist Jean-Pierre Lecanuet, Ph.D., and his colleagues in Paris have found that fetuses can even tell strangers' voices apart. They also seem to like certain stories more than others. The fetal heartbeat will slow down when a familiar French fairy tale such as *"La Poulette"* ("The Chick") or *"Le Petit Crapaud"* ("The Little Toad"), is read near the mother's belly. When the same reader delivers another unfamiliar story, the fetal heartbeat stays steady.

The fetus is likely responding to the cadence of voices and stories, not their actual words, observes Fifer, but the conclusion is the same: the fetus can listen, learn, and remember at some level, and, as with most babies

and children, it likes the comfort and reassurance of the familiar.

FETAL PERSONALITY

It's no secret that babies are born with distinct differences and patterns of activity that suggest individual temperament. Just when and how the behavioral traits originate in the womb is now the subject of intense scrutiny.

In the first formal study of fetal temperament in 1996, DiPietro and her colleagues recorded the heart rate and movements of 31 fetuses six times before birth and compared them to readings taken twice after birth. (They've since extended their study to include 100 more fetuses.) Their findings: fetuses that are very active in the womb tend to be more irritable infants. Those with irregular sleep/wake patterns in the womb sleep more poorly as young infants. And fetuses with high heart rates become unpredictable, inactive babies.

"Behavior doesn't begin at birth," declares DiPietro. "It begins before and develops in predictable ways." One of the most important influences on development is the fetal environment. As Harvard's Als observes, "The fetus gets an enormous amount of 'hormonal bathing' through the mother, so its chronobiological rhythms are influenced by the mother's sleep/wake cycles, her eating patterns, her movements."

The hormones a mother puts out in response to stress also appear critical. DiPietro finds that highly pressured mothers-to-be tend to have more active fetuses—and more irritable infants. "The most stressed are working pregnant women," says DiPietro. "These days, women tend to work up to the day they deliver, even though the implications for pregnancy aren't entirely clear yet. That's our cultural norm, but I think it's insane."

Als agrees that working can be an enormous stress, but emphasizes that pregnancy hormones help to buffer both mother and fetus. Individual reactions to stress also matter. "The pregnant woman who chooses to work is a different woman already from the one who chooses not to work," she explains.

She's also different from the woman who has no choice but to work. DiPietro's studies show that the fetuses of poor women are distinct neurobehaviorally—less active, with a less variable heart rate—from the fetuses of middle-class women. Yet "poor women rate themselves as less stressed than do working middle-class women," she notes. DiPietro suspects that inadequate nutrition and exposure to pollutants may significantly affect the fetuses of poor women.

Stress, diet, and toxins may combine to have a harmful effect on intelligence. A recent study by biostatistician Bernie Devlin, Ph.D., of the University of Pittsburgh, suggests that genes may have less impact on IQ than previously thought and that the environment of the womb may account for much more. "Our old notion of nature influencing the fetus before birth and nurture after birth needs an update," DiPietro insists. "There is an antenatal environment, too, that is provided by the mother."

Parents-to-be who want to further their unborn child's mental development should start by assuring that the antenatal environment is well-nourished, low-stress, drug-free. Various authors and "experts" also have suggested poking the fetus at regular intervals, speaking to it through a paper tube or "pregaphone," piping in classical music, even flashing lights at the mother's abdomen.

Does such stimulation work? More importantly: Is it safe? Some who use these methods swear their children are smarter, more verbally and musically inclined, more physically coordinated and socially adept than average. Scientists, however, are skeptical.

"There has been no defended research anywhere that shows any enduring effect from these stimulations," asserts Fifer. "Since no one can even say for certain when a fetus is awake, poking them or sticking speakers on the mother's abdomen may be changing their natural sleep patterns. No one would consider poking or prodding a newborn baby in her bassinet or putting a speaker next to her ear, so why would you do such a thing with a fetus?"

Als is more emphatic: "My bet is that poking, shaking, or otherwise deliberately stimulating the fetus might alter its developmental sequence, and anything that affects the development of the brain comes at a cost."

Gently talking to the fetus, however, seems to pose little risk. Fifer suggests that this kind of activity may help parents as much as the fetus. "Thinking about your fetus, talking to it, having your spouse talk to it, will all help prepare you for this new creature that's going to jump into your life and turn it upside down," he says—once it finally makes its anti-climactic entrance.

FOUR THINGS
YOU NEED TO KNOW
ABOUT RAISING BABY

*New thinking about the newborn's brain, feelings
and behavior are changing the way we look at parenting*

BY JOANNA LIPARI, M.A.

Bookstore shelves are crammed with titles purporting to help you make your baby smarter, happier, healthier, stronger, better-behaved and everything else you can imagine, in what I call a shopping-cart approach to infant development. But experts are now beginning to look more broadly, in an integrated fashion, at the first few months of a baby's life. And so should you.

Psychological theorists are moving away from focusing on single areas such as physical development, genetic inheritance, cognitive skills or emotional attachment, which give at best a limited view of how babies develop. Instead, they are attempting to synthesize and integrate all the separate pieces of the infant-development puzzle. The results so far have been enlightening, and are beginning to suggest new ways of parenting.

The most important of the emerging revelations is that the key to stimulating emotional and intellectual growth in your child is your own behavior—what you do, what you don't do, how you scold, how you reward and how you show affection. If the baby's brain is the hardware, then you, the parents, provide the software. When you understand the hardware (your baby's brain), you will be better able to design the software (your own behavior) to promote baby's well-being.

The first two years of life are critical in this regard because that's when your baby is building the mental foundation that will dictate his or her behavior through adulthood. In the first year alone, your baby's brain grows from about 400g to a stupendous 1000g. While this growth and development is in part predetermined by genetic force, exactly how the brain grows is dependent upon emotional interaction, and that involves you. "The human cerebral cortex adds about 70% of its final DNA content after birth," reports Allan N. Schore, Ph.D., assistant clinical professor of psychiatry and biobehavioral sciences at UCLA Medical School, "and this expanding brain is directly influenced by early environmental enrichment and social experiences."

Failure to provide this enrichment during the first two years can lead to a lifetime of emotional disability, according to attachment theorists. We are talking about the need to create a relationship and environment that allows your child to grow up with an openness to learning and the ability to process, understand and experience emotion with compassion, intelligence and resilience. These are the basic building blocks of emotional success.

Following are comparisons of researchers' "old thinking" and "new thinking." They highlight the four new insights changing the way we view infant development. The sections on "What To Do" then explain how to apply that new information.

1 FEELINGS TRUMP THOUGHTS

It is the emotional quality of the relationship you have with your baby that will stimulate his or her brain for optimum emotional and intellectual growth.

OLD THINKING: In this country, far too much emphasis is placed on developing babies' cognitive abilities. Some of this push came out of the promising results of the Head Start program. Middle-class families reasoned that if a little stimulation in an underendowed home environment is beneficial, wouldn't "more" be better? And the race to create the "superbaby" was on.

Gone are the days when parents just wished their child were "normal" and could "fit in" with other kids. Competition for selective schools and the social pressure it generates has made parents feel their child needs to be "gifted." Learning exercises, videos and educational toys are pushed on parents to use in play with their children. "Make it fun," the experts say. The emphasis is on developing baby's cognitive skills by using the emotional reward of parental attention as a behavior-training tool.

THE NEW THINKING: Flying in the face of all those "smarter" baby books are studies suggesting that pushing baby to learn words, numbers, colors and shapes too early forces the child to use lower-level thinking processes, rather than develop his or her learning ability. It's like a pony trick at the circus: When the pony paws the ground to "count" to three, it's really not counting; it's simply performing a stunt. Such "tricks" are not only not helpful to baby's learning process, they are potentially harmful. Tufts University child psychologist David Elkind, Ph.D., makes it clear that putting pressure on a child to learn information sends the message that he or she needs to "perform" to gain the parents' acceptance, and it can dampen natural curiosity.

Instead, focus on building baby's emotional skills. "Emotional development is not just the foundation for important capacities such as intimacy and trust," says Stanley Greenspan, M.D., clinical professor of psychiatry and pediatrics at George Washington University Medical School and author of the new comprehensive book *Building Healthy Minds.* "It is also the foundation of intelligence and a wide variety of cognitive skills. At each stage of development, emotions lead the way, and learning facts and skills follow. Even math skills, which appear [to be] strictly an impersonal cognition, are initially learned through the emotions: 'A lot' to a 2-year-old, for example, is more than he would expect, whereas 'a little' is less than he wants."

It makes sense: Consider how well you learn when you are passionate about a subject, compared to when you are simply required to learn it. That passion is the emotional fuel driving the cognitive process. So the question then becomes not "what toys and games should I use to make my baby smarter?" but "how should I interact with my baby to make him 'passionate' about the world around him?"

WHAT TO DO: When you read the baby "milestone" books or cognitive development guides, keep in mind that the central issue is your baby's *emotional* development. As Greenspan advises, "Synthesize this information about milestones and see them with emotional development as the central issue. This is like a basketball team, with the coach being our old friend, emotions. Because emotions tell the child what he wants to do—move his arm, make a sound, smile or frown. As you look at the various 'milestone components'—motor, social and cognitive skills—look to see how the whole mental team is working together."

Not only will this give you more concrete clues as to how to strengthen your emotional relationship, but it will also serve to alert you to any "players" on the team that are weak or injured, i.e., a muscle problem in the legs, or a sight and hearing difficulty.

2 **NOT JUST A SCREAMING MEATLOAF: BIRTH TO TWO MONTHS** It's still largely unknown how well infants understand their world at birth, but new theories are challenging the traditional perspectives.
OLD THINKING: Until now, development experts thought infants occupied some kind of presocial, precognitive, preorganized life phase that stretched from birth to two months. They viewed newborns' needs as mainly physiological—with sleep-wake, day-night and hunger-satiation cycles, even calling the first month of life "the normal autism" phase, or as a friend calls it, the "screaming meatloaf" phase. Certainly, the newborn has emotional needs, but researchers thought they were only in response to basic sensory drives like taste, touch, etc.

THE NEW THINKING: In his revolutionary book, *The Interpersonal World of the Infant,* psychiatrist Daniel Stern, Ph.D., challenged the conventional wisdom on infant development by proposing that babies come into this world as social beings. In research experiments, newborns consistently demonstrate that they actively seek sensory stimulation, have distinct preferences and, from birth, tend to form hypotheses about what is occurring in the world around them. Their preferences are emotional ones. In fact, parents would be unable to establish the physiological cycles like wake-sleep without the aid of such sensory, emotional activities as rocking, touching, soothing, talking and singing. In turn, these interactions stimulate the child's brain to make the neuronal connections she needs in order to process the sensory information provided.

WHAT TO DO: "Take note of your baby's own special biological makeup and interactive style," Greenspan advises. You need to see your baby for the special individual he is at birth. Then, "you can deliberately introduce the world to him in a way that maximizes his delight and minimizes his frustrations." This is also the time to learn how to help your baby regulate his emotions, for example, by offering an emotionally overloaded baby some soothing sounds or rocking to help him calm down.

3 **THE LOVE LOOP: BEGINNING AT TWO MONTHS** At approximately eight weeks, a miraculous thing occurs—your baby's vision improves and for the first time, she can fully see you and can make direct eye contact. These beginning visual experiences of your baby play an important role in social and emotional development. "In particular, the mother's emotionally expressive face is, by far, the most potent visual stimulus in the infant's environment," points out UCLA's Alan Schore, "and the child's intense interest in her face, especially in her eyes, leads him/her to track it in space to engage in periods of intense mutual gaze." The result: Endorphin levels rise in the baby's brain, causing pleasurable feelings of joy and excitement. But the key is for this joy to be interactive.

OLD THINKING: The mother pumps information and affection into the child, who participates only as an empty receptacle.

THE NEW THINKING: We now know that the baby's participation is crucial to creating a solid attachment bond. The loving gaze of parents to child is reciprocated by the baby with a loving gaze back to the parents, causing their endorphin levels to rise, thus completing a closed emotional circuit, a sort of "love loop." Now, mother (or father) and baby are truly in a dynamic, interactive system. "In essence, we are talking less about what the mother is doing to the baby and more about how the mother is being with the baby and how the baby is learning to be with the mother," says Schore.

The final aspect of this developing interactive system between mother and child is the mother's development of an "emotional synchronization" with her child. Schore defines this as the mother's ability to tune into the baby's internal states and respond accordingly. For example: Your baby is quietly lying on the floor, happy to take in the sights and sounds of the environment. As you notice the baby looking for stimulation, you respond with a game of "peek-a-boo." As you play with your child and she responds with shrieks of glee, you escalate the emotion with bigger and bigger gestures and facial expressions. Shortly thereafter, you notice the baby turns away. The input has reached its maximum and you sense your child needs you to back off for awhile as she goes back to a state of calm and restful inactivity. "The synchronization between the two is more than between their behavior and thoughts; the synchronization is on a biological level—their brains and nervous systems are linked together," points out Schore. "In this process, the mother is teaching and learning at the same time. As a result of this moment-by-moment matching of emotion, both partners increase their emotional connection to one another. In addition, the more the mother fine-tunes her activity level to the infant during periods of play and interaction, the more she allows the baby to disengage and recover quietly during periods of nonplay, before initiating actively arousing play again."

Neuropsychological research now indicates that this attuned interaction—engaged play, disengagement and restful nonplay, followed by a return to play behavior—is especially helpful for brain growth and the development of cerebral circuits. This makes sense in light of the revelation that future cognitive development depends not on the cognitive stimulation of flashcards and videos, but on the attuned, dynamic and emotional interactions between parent and child. The play periods stimulate baby's central nervous system to excitation, followed by a restful period of alert inactivity in which the developing brain is able to process the stimulation and the interaction.

In this way, you, the parents, are the safety net under your baby's emotional highwire; the act of calming her down, or giving her the opportunity to calm down, will help her learn to handle ever-increasing intensity of stimulation and thus build emotional tolerance and resilience.

WHAT TO DO: There are two steps to maximizing your attunement ability: spontaneity and reflection. When in sync, you and baby will both experience positive emotion; when out of sync, you will see negative emotions. If much of your interactions seem to result in negative emotion, then it is time to reflect on your contribution to the equation.

In these instances, parents need to help one another discover what may be impeding the attunement process. Sometimes, on an unconscious level, it may be memories of our own childhood. For example, my friend sings nursery rhymes with a Boston accent, even though she grew up in New York, because her native Bostonian father sang them to her that way. While the "Fahmah in the Dell" will probably not throw baby into a temper tantrum, it's a good example of how our actions or parenting style may be problematic without our realizing it.

But all parents have days when they are out of sync with baby, and the new perspective is that it's not such a bad thing. In fact, it's quite valuable. "Misattunement" is not a bioneurological disaster if you can become attuned again. The process of falling out of sync and then repairing the bond actually teaches children resilience, and a sense of confidence that the world will respond to them and repair any potential hurt.

Finally, let your baby take the lead. Schore suggests we "follow baby's own spontaneous expression of himself," which lets the child know that another person, i.e., mom or dad, can understand what he is feeling, doing, and even thinking. Such experiences, says Schore, assist in the development of the prefrontal area, which controls "empathy, and therefore that which makes us most 'human.' "

4 THE SHAME TRANSACTION
Toward the end of the first year, as crawling turns to walking, a shift occurs in the communication between child and parents. "Observational studies show that 12-month-olds receive more positive responses from mothers, while 18-month-olds receive more instructions and directions," says Schore. In one study, mothers of toddlers expressed a prohibition—basically telling the child "no"—approximately every nine minutes! That's likely because a mobile toddler has an uncanny knack for finding the most dangerous things to explore!

Yesterday, for example, I walked into the living room to find my daughter scribbling on the wall with a purple marker. "NO!" shot out of my mouth. She looked up at me with stunned shock, then realized what she had done. Immediately, she hung her head, about to cry. I babbled on a bit about how markers are only for paper, yada-yada and then thought, "Heck, it's washable." As I put my arm around my daughter, I segued into a suggestion for another activity: washing the wall! She brightened and raced to get the sponge. We had just concluded a "shame transaction."

OLD THINKING: Researchers considered all these "no's" a necessary byproduct of child safety or the socialization process. After all, we must teach children to use the potty rather than wet the bed, not to hit another child when mad, to behave properly in public. Researchers did not consider the function of shame vis-a-vis brain development. Instead, they advised trying to limit situations in which the child would feel shame.

NEW THINKING: It's true that you want to limit the shame situations, but they are not simply a necessary evil in order to civilize your baby. Neurobiological studies indicate that episodes of shame like the one I described can actually stimulate the development of the right hemisphere, the brain's source of creativity, emotion and sensitivity, as long as the shame period is short and followed by a recovery. In essence, it's not the experience of shame that can be damaging, but rather the inability of the parent to help the child recover from that shame.

WHAT TO DO: It's important to understand "the growth-facilitating importance of small doses of shame in the socialization process of the infant," says Schore. Embarrassment (a component of shame) first emerges around 14 months, when mom's "no" results in the child lowering his head and looking down in obvious sadness. The child goes from excited (my daughter scribbling on the wall) to sudden deflation (my "NO!") back to excitement ("It's okay, let's wash the wall together"). During this rapid process, various parts of the brain get quite a workout and experience heightened connectivity, which strengthens these systems. The result is development of the orbitofrontal cortex (cognitive area) and limbic system (emotional area) and the ability for the two systems to interrelate emotional resiliency in the child and the ability to self-regulate emotions· and impulse control.

What is important to remember about productive shame reactions is that there must be a quick recovery. Extended periods of shame result in a child learning to shut down, or worse, become hyperirritable, perhaps even violent. It's common sense: Just think how you feel when someone embarrasses you. If that embarrassment goes on without relief, don't you tend to either flee the situation or rail against it?

From these new research findings, it's clear that successful parenting isn't just about intuition, instinct and doing what your mother did. It's also not about pushing the alphabet, multiplication tables or violin lessons. We now believe that by seeing the newborn as a whole person—as a thinking, feeling creature who can and should participate in his own emotional and cognitive development—we can maximize the nurturing and stimulating potential of our relationship with a newborn baby.

Joanna Lipari is pursuing a Psy.D. at Pepperdine University in Los Angeles.

READ MORE ABOUT IT
The Irreducible Needs of Children: What Every Child Must Have to Grow, Learn and Flourish, T. Berry Brazelton, M.D., and Stanley Greenspan, M.D. (Perseus Books, 2000).

Building Healthy Minds, Stanley Greenspan, M.D. (Perseus Books, 1999).

WHY CHILDREN TURN OUT THE WAY THEY DO

Hint: A child's peers matter more than you think.

by Judith Rich Harris

Behavioral genetic studies have proved beyond a shadow of a doubt that heredity is responsible for a sizable portion of the variations in people's personalities. Some people are more hot-tempered or outgoing or meticulous than others, and these variations are a function of the genes they were born with, as well as the experiences they had after they were born. The exact proportion—how much is due to the genes, how much to the experiences—is not important; the point is that heredity cannot be ignored.

But usually it is ignored. Consider the case of Amy, an adopted child. It wasn't a successful adoption; Amy's parents regarded her as a disappointment and favored their older child, a boy. Academic achievement was important to the parents, but Amy had a learning disability. Simplicity and emotional restraint were important to them, but Amy went in for florid role-playing and feigned illnesses. By the time she was ten, she had a serious, though vague, psychological disorder. She was

pathologically immature, socially inept, shallow of character, and extravagant of expression.

Well, naturally. Amy was a rejected child. What makes this case interesting is that Amy had an identical twin, Beth, who was adopted into a different family. Beth was not rejected—on the contrary, she was her mother's favorite. Her parents were not particularly concerned about education, so the learning disability (which she shared with her twin) was no big deal. Beth's mother, unlike Amy's, was empathic, open, and cheerful. Nevertheless, Beth had the same personality problems that Amy did. The psychoanalyst who studied these girls admitted that if he had seen only one of them, it would have been easy to fetch up some explanation in terms of the family environment. But there were two of them. Two, with matching symptoms but very different families.

Matching symptoms and matching genes: unlikely to be a coincidence. Something in the genes that Amy and Beth received from their biological parents—from the woman who gave them up for adoption and the man who got her pregnant—must have predisposed the twins to develop their unusual set of symptoms. If I say that Amy and Beth "inherited" this predisposition from

their biological parents, don't misunderstand me: their biological parents may have had none of these symptoms. Slightly different combinations of genes can produce very different results, and only identical twins have exactly the same combination. Fraternal twins can be surprisingly dissimilar, and the same is true of parents and children: a child can have characteristics seen in neither of her parents. But there is a statistical connection—a greater-than-chance likelihood that a person with psychological problems has a biological parent or a biological child with similar problems.

Heredity is one of the reasons that parents with problems often have children with problems. It is a simple, obvious, undeniable fact; and yet it is the most ignored fact in all of psychology. Judging from the lack of attention paid to heredity by developmental and clinical psychologists, you would think we were still in the days when John Watson was promising to turn a dozen babies into doctors, lawyers, beggar men, and thieves.

Thieves. A good place to begin. Let's see if I can account for criminal behavior in the offspring without blaming it on the environment provided by the parents—on the parents' child-rearing methods or the lack thereof. Don't worry. I am not

Judith Rich Harris is a former writer of college textbooks on child development. Her latest book, *The Nurture Assumption*, brings together insights from psychology, sociology, anthropology, primatology, and evolutionary biology.

From the *Saturday Evening Post*, May/June 1999, pp. 50-53. Reprinted with the permission of The Free Press, a division of Simon & Schuster, from *The Nurture Assumption*. © 1998 by Judith Rich Harris.

going to pin it all on heredity. But I can't do it without heredity, so if that bothers you, go and take a cold shower or something.

How would you go about making a child into a thief? Fagin, of Charles Dickens' *Oliver Twist*, could have told Watson a thing or two. Take four or five hungry boys, make them into an *us*, give them a pep talk and a course in pocket-picking, and sic 'em on *them*, the rich folk. It's intergroup warfare, a tradition of our species, and the potential for it can be found in almost any normal human, particularly those of the male variety. Your schoolboy with his shining morning face is but a warrior in thin disguise.

But Fagin's method, which had worked flawlessly on the London slum children who were his other pupils, didn't work on Oliver. Dickens seemed to think it was because Oliver was born good, but there is another possibility: Oliver didn't identify with the other boys in Fagin's ring. They were Londoners, and he was not. They spoke in a thieves' argot that was almost a foreign language to him. There were too many differences, and Oliver's run-in with the law came too soon to allow him to adapt to his new companions.

Oliver Twist was published in 1838, a time when it was still politically correct to believe that people could be born good or born bad—when it was still politically correct, in fact, to believe that badness could be predicted on the basis of one's racial or ethnic group membership. It was by no means the worst of times, but it was certainly not the best of times.

Today, both the individual explanation—that certain children are born bad—and the group explanation are held to be politically incorrect. Western culture has swung back to the view associated with the philosopher Rousseau: that all children are born good and it is society—their environment—that corrupts them. I'm not sure if this is

optimism or pessimism, but it leaves too much unexplained.

Though we no longer say that some children are born bad, the facts are such, unfortunately, that a euphemism is needed. Now psychologists say that some children are born with "difficult" temperaments—difficult for their parents to rear, difficult to socialize. I can list for you some of the things that make a child difficult to rear and difficult to socialize: a tendency to be active, impulsive, aggressive, and quick to anger; a tendency to get bored with routine activities and to seek excitement; a tendency to be unafraid of getting hurt; an insensitivity to the feelings of others; and, more often than not, a muscular build and an IQ a little lower than average. All of these characteristics have a significant genetic component.

Developmentalists have described how things go wrong when a child who is difficult to manage is born to a parent with poor management skills—something that happens, thanks to the unfairness of nature, more often than it would if genes were dealt out randomly to each new generation. The boy (usually it's a boy) and his mother (often there is no father) get into a vicious spiral in which bad leads to worse. The mother tells the boy to do something or not to do something; he ignores her; she tells him again; he gets mad; she gives up. Eventually, she gets mad, too, and punishes him harshly, but too late and too inconsistently for it to have any educational benefits. Anyway, this is a child who is not very afraid of getting hurt—at least it relieves his boredom.

The dysfunctional family. Oh yes, such families exist—there is no question about it! They are no fun to visit, and you wouldn't want to live there. Even the biological father of this child doesn't want to live there. There's an old joke that goes like this:

Psychologist: You should be kind to Johnny. He comes from a broken home.

Teacher: I'm not surprised. Johnny could break any home.

Difficult for their parents to rear, difficult to socialize. For most psychologists these two phrases are virtually synonymous because socialization is assumed to be the parents' job. For me, they are two different things. It is true that there tends to be a correlation between them, due to the fact that children take their inherited characteristics with them wherever they go. But the correlation is not strong, because the social context within the home, where the rearing goes on, is very different from the social context outside the home, where the socializing goes on. Children who are obnoxious at home are not necessarily obnoxious outside the home. Johnny may be obnoxious everywhere he goes, but fortunately such kids are uncommon.

The word *socialization* is most often used to refer to the training in morality that children are presumed to get at home. Parents are held to be responsible for teaching their children not to steal, not to lie, not to cheat. But here again, there is little correlation between how children behave at home and how they behave elsewhere. Children who were observed to break rules at home when they thought no one was looking were not noticeably more likely than anyone else to cheat on a test at school or in a game on the playground. Morality, like other forms of learned social behavior, is tied to the context in which it is acquired.

Was Dickens right? Are some children born good? Let us do an experiment that John Watson would have approved of. Place in adoptive homes a bunch of infant boys whose biological parents had been convicted (or will later be convicted) of crimes, and a second bunch whose biological parents were, as far as anyone knows, honest. Mix them up: place some of each bunch in homes with honest adoptive parents and let others be reared by crooks. A dastardly experiment, you say?

Well, that's what adoption agencies do. Of course, they don't purposely put babies in the homes of criminals, but sometimes it works out that way, and in places where careful records are kept both of adoptions and of criminal convictions—Denmark, for example—it's possible to study the results. Researchers were able to obtain background data on over 4,000 Danish men who had been placed for adoption in infancy.

As it turned out, criminal convictions were numerous among the biological parents of the adoptees but infrequent among their adoptive parents. Thus, there were not many cases of boys who had honest biological parents being reared in the homes of crooks. Of this small group, 15 percent became criminals. But almost the same percentage (14 percent) was found among the adoptees whose biological parents were honest and whose adoptive parents were also honest. It seems that being reared in a criminal home does not make a criminal out of a boy who wasn't cut out for the job.

The story is a little different for the boys whose biological parents were criminals. Of those who were reared by honest folk, 20 percent became criminals. And of the small group who came up unlucky both times—criminal biological fathers *and* criminal adoptive fathers—almost 25 percent went wrong. So it's not just heredity: it looks like the home environment does count for something after all.

Not so fast. It turns out that the ability of a criminal adoptive family to produce a criminal child—given suitable material to work with—depends on where the family happens to live. The increase in criminality among Danish adoptees reared in criminal homes was found only for a minority of the subjects in this study: those who grew up in or around Copenhagen. In small towns and rural areas, an adoptee reared in a criminal home was no more likely to become a criminal than one reared by honest adoptive parents.

It wasn't the criminal adoptive parents who made the biological son of criminals into a criminal: it was the *neighborhood in which they reared him*. Neighborhoods differ in rates of criminal behavior, and I would guess that neighborhoods with high rates of criminal behavior are exceedingly hard to find in rural areas of Denmark.

People generally live in places where they share a lifestyle and a set of values with their neighbors; this is due both to mutual influence and, especially in cities, to birds of a feather flocking together. Children grow up with other children who are the offspring of their parents' friends and neighbors. These are the children who form their peer group. This is the peer group in which they are socialized. If their own parents are criminals, the friends' parents may also be inclined in that direction. The children bring to the peer group the attitudes and behaviors they learned at home, and if these attitudes and behaviors are similar, in all probability the peer group will retain them.

I have told you about an adoption study of criminality; there are also twin and sibling studies. Behavioral genetic studies of twins or siblings usually show that the environment shared by children who grow up in the same home has little or no effect, but we've come to one of the exceptions. Twins or siblings who grow up in the same home are more likely to match in criminality—to both be criminals or both be honest. This correlation is often attributed to the home environment that the twins or siblings share—in other words, to the influence of the parents. But kids who share a home also share a neighborhood and, in some cases, a peer group. The likelihood that two siblings will match in criminality is higher if they are the same sex and close together in age. It is higher in twins (even if they're not identical) than in ordinary siblings, and higher in twins who spend a lot of time together outside the home than in those who lead separate lives.

The evidence shows that the environment has an effect on criminality but it doesn't show that the relevant environment is the home; in fact, it suggests a different explanation. When both twins or both siblings get into trouble, it is due to their influence on each other and to the influence of the peer group they belong to.

Are some people born bad? A better way of putting it is that some people are born with characteristics that make them poor fits for most of the honest jobs available in most societies, and so far we haven't learned how to deal with them. We are at risk of becoming their victims, but they are victims, too—victims of the evolutionary history of our species. No process is perfect, not even evolution. Evolution gave us big heads, but sometimes a baby has a head so big it can't fit through the birth canal. In earlier times these babies invariably died, as did their mothers. In the same way, evolution selected for other characteristics that sometimes overshoot their mark and become liabilities, rather than assets. Almost all the characteristics of the "born criminal" would be, in slightly watered-down form, useful to a male in a hunter-gatherer society and useful to his group. His lack of fear, desire for excitement, and impulsiveness make him a formidable weapon against rival groups. His aggressiveness, strength, and lack of compassion enable him to dominate his group mates and give him first shot at hunter-gatherer perks.

Unlike the successful hunter-gatherer, however, the career criminal tends to be below average in intelligence. I take this to be a hopeful sign: it suggests that temperament can be overridden by reason. Those individuals born with the other characteristics on the list but who also have above-average intelligence are evidently smart enough to figure out that crime does not pay and to find other ways of gratifying their desire for excitement.

CULTURE & IDEAS

INVINCIBLE KIDS

*Why do some children survive
traumatic childhoods unscathed?
The answers can help every child*

Child psychologist Emmy Werner went looking for trouble in paradise. In Hawaii nearly 40 years ago, the researchers began studying the offspring of chronically poor, alcoholic, abusive and even psychotic parents to understand how failure was passed from one generation to the next. But to her surprise, one third of the kids she studied looked nothing like children headed for disaster. Werner switched her focus to these "resilient kids," who somehow beat the odds, growing into emotionally healthy, competent adults. They even appeared to defy the laws of nature: When Hurricane Iniki flattened Kauai in 1992, leaving nearly 1 in 6 residents homeless, the storm's 160-mpg gusts seemed to spare the houses of Werner's success stories.

Werner's "resilient kids," in their late 30s when Iniki hit, helped create their own luck. They heeded storm warnings and boarded up their properties. And even if the squall blew away their roofs or tore down their walls, they were more likely to have the financial savings and insurance to avoid foreclosure—the fate of many of Iniki's victims. "There's not a thing you can do personally about being in the middle of a hurricane," says the University of California–Davis's Werner, "but [resilient kids] are planners and problem solvers and picker-uppers."

For many of America's children, these are difficult times. One in five lives in poverty. More than half will spend some of their childhood living apart from one parent—the result of divorce, death or out-of-wedlock birth.

Child abuse, teen drug use and teen crime are surging. Living in an affluent suburb is no protection: Suburban kids are almost as likely as those in violent neighborhoods to report what sociologists call "parental absence"—the lack of a mother and father who are approachable and attentive, and who set rules and enforce consequences.

In the face of these trends, many social scientists now are suggesting a new way of looking at kids and their problems: Focus on survivors, not casualties. Don't abandon kids who fail, but learn from those who succeed.

Such children, researchers find, are not simply born that way. Though genes play a role, the presence of a variety of positive influences in a child's environment is even more crucial; indeed, it can make the difference between a child who founders and one who thrives.

The implications of such research are profound. The findings mean that parents, schools, volunteers, government and others can create a pathway to resiliency, rather than leaving success to fate or to hard-wired character traits. Perhaps most important, the research indicates that the lessons learned from these nearly invincible kids can teach us how to help *all* kids—regardless of their circumstances—handle the inevitable risks and turning points of life. The Search Institute, a Minneapolis-based children's research group, identified 30 resiliency-building factors. The more of these "assets" present in a child's environment, the more likely the child was to avoid school problems, alco-

hol use, early sexual experimentation, depression and violent behavior.

Like the factors that contribute to lifelong physical health, those that create resilience may seem common-sensical, but they have tremendous impact. Locate a resilient kid and you will also find a caring adult—or several—who has guided him. Watchful parents, welcoming schools, good peers and extracurricular activities matter, too, as does teaching kids to care for others and to help out in their communities.

From thug to Scout. The psychologists who pioneered resiliency theory focused on inborn character traits that fostered success. An average or higher IQ was a good predictor. So was innate temperament—a sunny disposition may attract advocates who can lift a child from risk. But the idea that resiliency can be molded is relatively re-

ROBERT DOLE. He came of age during the tough years of the Great Depression. Later, he overcame a nearly fatal war injury.

"Why me, I demanded? ... Maybe it was all part of a plan, a test of endurance and strength and, above all, of faith."

From *U.S. News & World Report*, November 11, 1996, pp. 60–71. © 1996 by U.S. News & World Report. Reprinted by permission.

cent. It means that an attentive adult can turn a mean and sullen teenage thug—a kid who would smash in someone's face on a whim—into an upstanding Boy Scout.

That's the story of Eagle Scout Rudy Gonzalez. Growing up in Houston's East End barrio, Gonzalez seemed on a fast track to prison. By the time he was 13, he'd already had encounters with the city's juvenile justice system—once for banging a classmate's head on the pavement until blood flowed, once for slugging a teacher. He slept through classes and fought more often than he studied. With his drug-using crew, he broke into warehouses and looted a grocery store. His brushes with the law only hardened his bad-boy swagger. "I thought I was macho," says Gonzalez. "With people I didn't like, [it was], 'Don't look at me or I'll beat you up.'"

Many of Gonzalez's friends later joined real gangs. Several met grisly deaths; others landed in prison for drug dealing and murder. More than a few became fathers and dropped out of school. Gonzalez joined urban scouting, a new, small program established by Boy Scouts of America to provide role models for "at risk" youth. At first glance, Gonzalez's path could hardly seem more different than that of his peers. But both gangs and Boy Scouts offer similar attractions: community and a sense of purpose, a hierarchical system of discipline and a chance to prove loyalty to a group. Gonzalez chose merit badges and service over gang colors and drive-by shootings.

Now 20, Gonzalez wears crisply pressed khakis and button-down shirts and, in his sophomore year at Texas A&M, seems well on his way to his goal of working for a major accounting firm. Why did he succeed when his friends stuck to crime? Gonzalez's own answer is that his new life is "a miracle." "Probably, God chose me to do this," he says.

There were identifiable turning points. Scoutmaster John Trevino, a city policeman, filled Gonzalez's need for a caring adult who believed in him and could show him a different way to be a man. Gonzalez's own father was shot and killed in a barroom fight when Rudy was just 6. Fate played a role, too. At 14, using survival skills he'd learned in scouting, Gonzalez saved the life of a younger boy stuck up to his chin in mud in a nearby bayou. The neighborhood hero was lauded in the newspaper and got to meet President Bush at the White

House. Slowly, he began to feel the importance of serving his community—another building block of resiliency. For a Scout project he cleaned up a barrio cemetery.

Something special. Once his life started to turn around, Gonzalez felt comfortable enough to reveal his winning personality and transcendent smile—qualities that contributed further to his success. "When I met him, I wanted to adopt him," says his high school counselor, Betty Porter. "There's something about him." She remembers Gonzalez as a likable and prodigious networker who made daily visits to her office to tell her about college scholarships—some she didn't even know about.

BILL CLINTON. He lost his father in an auto wreck before he was born. Later, he coped with an alcoholic, occasionally violent stepfather.

"My mother taught me about sacrifice. She held steady through tragedy after tragedy and, always, she taught me to fight."

A little bit of help—whether an urban scouting program or some other chance to excel—can go a long way in creating resiliency. And it goes furthest in the most stressed neighborhoods, says the University of Colorado's Richard Jessor, who directs a multimillion-dollar resiliency project for the John D. and Catherine T. MacArthur Foundation. Looking back, Gonzalez agrees. "We were just guys in the barrio without anything better to do," he says. "We didn't have the YMCA or Little League, so we hung out, played sports, broke into warehouses and the school." Adds Harvard University's Katherine Newman: "The good news is that kids are motivated. They want to make it. The bad news is that there are too few opportunities."

Resiliency theory brightens the outlook for kids. Mental health experts traditionally have put the spotlight on children who emerge from bad childhoods damaged and scarred. But statistics show that many—if not most—children born into unpromising

circumstances thrive, or at least hold their own. Most children of teen mothers, for example, avoid becoming teen parents themselves. And though the majority of child abusers were themselves abused as children, most abused children do not become abusers. Similarly, children of schizophrenics and children who grew up in refugee camps also tend to defy the odds. And many Iowa youths whose families lost their farms during the 1980s farm crisis became high achievers in school.

Living well. A person who has faced childhood adversity and bounced back may even fare *better* later in life than someone whose childhood was relatively easy—or so Werner's recently completed follow-up of the Kauai kids at age 40 suggests. Resilient children in her study reported stronger marriages and better health than those who enjoyed less stressful origins. Further, none had been on welfare, and none had been in trouble with the law. Many children of traumatic, abusive or neglectful childhoods suffer severe consequences, including shifts in behavior, thinking and physiology that dog them into adulthood. But though Werner's resilient kids turned adults tended to marry later, there was little sign of emotional turmoil. At midlife, these resilient subjects were more likely to say they were happy and only one third as likely to report mental health problems.

Can any child become resilient? That remains a matter of debate. Some kids, researchers say, simply may face too many risks. And the research can be twisted to suggest that there are easy answers. "Resiliency theory assumes that it's all or nothing, that you have it or you don't," complains Geoffrey Canada, who runs neighborhood centers for New York's poorest youth. "But for some people it takes 10,000 gallons of water, and for some kids it's just a couple of little drops."

In fact, as Canada notes, most resilient kids do not follow a straight line to success. An example is Raymond Marte, whom Canada mentored, teaching the youth karate at one of his Rheedlen Centers for Children and Families. Today, Marte, 21, is a freshman at New York's Bard College. But only a few years ago, he was just another high school dropout and teenage father, hanging out with gang friends and roaming the streets with a handgun in his pocket. "This is choice time," Canada told

DR. RUTH WESTHEIMER. The sex therapist fled the Nazis at 10; her parents died in the Holocaust, and she grew up in a Swiss orphanage.

"The values my family [instilled] left me with the sense I must make something out of my life to justify my survival."

Marte after five of the boy's friends were killed in three months. Marte re-enrolled in school, became an Ameri-Corps volunteer and won a college scholarship. Today, when he walks the streets of his family's gritty Manhattan neighborhood, he is greeted as a hero, accepting high-fives from friends congratulating the guy who made it out.

Good parenting can trump bad neighborhoods. That parents are the first line in creating resilient children is no surprise. But University of Pennsylvania sociologist Frank Furstenberg *was* surprised to find that adolescents in the city's most violence prone, drug-ridden housing projects showed the same resilience as middle-class adolescents. The expectation was that the worst neighborhoods would overwhelm families. Inner-city housing projects do present more risk and fewer opportunities. But good parenting existed in roughly equal proportions in every neighborhood.

Sherenia Gibbs is the type of dynamo parent who almost single-handedly can instill resiliency in her children. The single mother moved her three children from a small town in Illinois to Minneapolis in search of better education and recreation. Still, the new neighborhood was dangerous, so Gibbs volunteered at the park where her youngest son, T. J. Williams, played. Today, six years later, Gibbs runs a city park, where she has started several innovative mentoring programs. At home, Gibbs sets aside time to spend with T. J., now 14, requires him to call her at work when he gets home from school or goes out with friends and follows his schoolwork closely. Indeed, how often teens have dinner with their family and whether they have a curfew are two of the best predictors of teen drug use, according to

the National Center on Addiction and Substance Abuse at Columbia University. How often a family attends church—where kids are exposed to both values and adult mentors—also makes a difference. Says Gibbs: "The streets will grab your kids and eat them up."

Some resiliency programs study the success of moms like Gibbs and try to teach such "authoritative parenting" skills to others. When a kid has an early brush with the law, the Oregon Social Learning Center brings the youth's whole family together to teach parenting skills. Not only is the training effective with the offending youth, but younger brothers and sisters are less likely to get in trouble as well.

Despite the crucial role of parents, few—rich or poor—are as involved in their children's lives as Gibbs. And a shocking number of parents—25 percent—ignore or pay little attention to how their children fare in school, according to Temple University psychology professor Laurence Steinberg. Nearly one third of students across economic classes say their parents have no idea how they are doing in school. Further, half the parents Steinberg surveyed did not know their children's friends, what their kids did after school or where they went at night. Some schools are testing strategies for what educator Margaret Wang, also at Temple, calls "educational resilience."

One solution: teaching teams, which follow a student for a few years so the child always has a teacher who knows him well. In Philadelphia, some inner-city schools have set up "parents' lounges," with free coffee, to encourage moms and dads to be regular school visitors.

Given the importance of good parenting, kids are at heightened risk when parents themselves are troubled. But it is a trait of resilient kids that in such circumstances, they seek out substitute adults. And sometimes they become substitute adults themselves, playing a parental role for younger siblings. That was true of Tyrone Weeks. He spent about half his life without his mother as she went in and out of drug rehabilitation. Sober now for three years, Delores Weeks maintains a close relationship with her son. But Tyrone was often on his own, living with his grandmother and, when she died, with his basketball coach, Tennis Young. Young and Dave Hagan, a neighborhood priest in north

Philadelphia, kept Weeks fed and clothed. But Weeks also became a substitute parent for his younger brother, Robert, while encouraging his mother in her struggle with cocaine. Says Weeks, "There were times when I was lost and didn't want to live anymore."

Like many resilient kids, Weeks possessed another protective factor: a talent. Basketball, he says, gave him a self-confidence that carried him through the lost days. Today, Weeks rebounds and blocks shots for the University of Massachusetts. Obviously, not all kids have Weeks's exceptional ability. But what seems key is not the level of talent but finding an activity from which they derive pride and sense of purpose.

Mon Ye credits an outdoor leadership program with "keeping me out of gang life." Born in a Cambodian refugee camp, Ye has lived with an older brother in a crime-ridden Tacoma, Wash., housing project since his mother's death a few years ago. Outdoor adventure never interested him. But then parks worker LeAnna Waite invited him to join a program at a nearby recreation center (whose heavy doors are dented with bullet marks from gang fights). Last year, Ye led a youth climb up Mount Rainier and now plans to go to college to become a recreation and park supervisor.

It helps to help. Giving kids significant personal responsibility is another way to build resiliency, whether it's Weeks pulling his family together or Ye supervising preteens. Some of the best youth programs value both service to others and the ability to plan and make choices, according to Stanford University's Shirley Brice Heath. The Food Project—in which kids raise 40,000 pounds of vegetables for Boston food kitchens—is directed by the young par-

KWEISI MFUME. The NAACP chief's stepdad was abusive. After his mom died, he ran with gangs and had five sons out of wedlock.

"We're all inbred with a certain amount of resiliency. It's not until it's tested . . . that we recognize inner strength."

ticipants, giving them the chance to both learn and then pass on their knowledge. Older teens often find such responsibility through military service.

Any program that multiplies contacts between kids and adults who can offer advice and support is valuable. A recent study of Big Brothers and Big Sisters found that the nationwide youth-mentoring program cuts drug use and school absenteeism by half. Most youth interventions are set up to target a specific problem like violence or teen sex—and often have little impact. Big Brothers and Big Sisters instead succeeds with classic resiliency promotion: It first creates supportive adult attention for kids, then expects risky behavior to drop as a consequence.

The 42,490 residents of St. Louis Park, Minn., know all about such holistic approaches to creating resiliency. They've made it a citywide cause in the ethnically diverse suburb of Minneapolis. Children First is the city's call for residents to think about the ways, big and small, they can help all kids succeed, from those living in the city's Meadowbrook housing project to residents of parkside ranch houses. The suburb's largest employer, HealthSystem Minnesota, runs a free kids' health clinic. (Doctors and staff donate their time.) And one of the smallest businesses, Steve McCulloch's flower shop,

DIANNE FEINSTEIN. The California senator was raised in privilege, but her mother was mentally ill and at times violent.

"I've never believed adversity is a harbinger of failure. On the contrary, [it] can provide a wellspring of strength."

gives away carnations to kids in the nearby housing project on Mother's Day. Kids even help each other. Two high school girls started a Tuesday night baby-sitting service at the Reformation Lutheran Church. Parents can drop off their kids for three hours. The cost: $1.

The goal is to make sure kids know that they are valued and that several adults outside their own family know and care about them. Those adults might include a police officer-volunteering to serve lunch in the school cafeteria line. Or Jill Terry, one of scores of volunteers who stand at school bus stops on frigid mornings. Terry breaks up fights, provides forgotten lunch money or reassures a sad-faced boy about his parents' fighting. The adopt-a-bus-stop program

was started by members of a senior citizens' group concerned about an attempted abduction of a child on her way to school.

Another volunteer, Kyla Dreier, works in a downtown law firm and mentors Angie Larson. The 14-year-old has long, open talks with her mother but sometimes feels more comfortable discussing things with another adult, like Dreier.

Spreading out. St. Louis Park is the biggest success story of over 100 communities nationwide where the Search Institute is trying to develop support for childhood resiliency. In a small surburb, it was relatively easy to rally community leaders. Now Search is trying to take such asset building to larger cities like Minneapolis and Albuquerque, N.M.

In St. Louis Park, resiliency is built on a shoestring budget. About $60,000 a year—all raised from donations—covers the part-time staff director and office expenses. But that's the point, says Children First Coordinator Karen Atkinson. Fostering resiliency is neither complicated nor costly. It's basic common sense—even if practiced too rarely in America. And it pays dividends for all kids.

By Joseph P. Shapiro with Dorian Friedman in New York, Michele Meyer in Houston and Margaret Loftus

A World Of Their Own

**They're spiritual, optimistic and ambitious.
How teens want to shape the future.**

By Sharon Begley

THE TEMPTATION, OF COURSE, IS to seek The Teen, the one who can stand as a symbol of this generation, who exemplifies in a single, still-young life the aspirations, the values, the habits and outlook of the 22 million other Americans 13 to 19. Who, then, shall we offer up? Perhaps Vanesa Vathanasombat, 17, of Whittier, Calif., who spends her free time going to the beach and hanging at malls with friends. "You are who you hang around with," she says. "Before, parents made you who you are. Now, teens are pretty much defined by their friends. I see my mom maybe an hour a day and not at all on weekends." Or maybe Zoe Ward, 15, of Shoreline, Wash., who takes road trips with a friend (they sleep in the car) and sells her poetry on the street: "I can't decide if I want to be famous or if I want to go live in the mountains. That's what it's like for a lot of high-school kids: we don't know how to get there, what it's really going to be like." Or, finally, Marcus Ruopp, 16, of Newton, Mass., who would like to be an engineer or maybe a teacher after the Peace Corps, in order to "give back to the community."

No one teen incorporates all the attitudes and characteristics that the teachers who teach them, the parents who raise them, the researchers who study them and the kids who *are* them name as the identifying marks of this generation. In large part that is because "today's teens may have less in common with each other than those in generations past," says psychologist William Damon of Stanford University. "[Some] are absolutely on track: they're bright-eyed, genuine and ambitious. But a significant number are drifting or worse." Innumerable teens, then, will not recognize themselves in the portraits that follow. Yes, of course there are teens for whom adults are a strong presence, and teens who seldom volunteer. There are teens who are emotional wrecks, or even mentally ill. There are teens to whom "Instant Message" means Mom's telling them right away who phoned while they were out. And there are teens who belong to no clique—or "tribe." But, according to a new NEWSWEEK Poll as well as sociologists who have studied tens of thousands of the kids born between 1981 and 1987, those teens are the exceptions. As much as is possible when you are talking about 22 million human beings, a portrait of the millennial generation is emerging.

They were born at a time when the very culture was shifting to accommodate them—changing tables in restrooms, BABY ON BOARD signs and minivans. Yet, as a group, they lead lives that are more "adult-free" than those of previous generations. "Adolescents are not a tribe apart because *they* left *us,* as most people assume," says Patricia Hersch, author of the 1998 book "A Tribe Apart." "We left them. This generation of kids has spent more time on their own than any other in recent history."

When today's teens are not with their friends, many live in a private, adult-free world of the Web and videogames. Aminah McKinnie, 16, of Madison, Miss., attends church, loves gospel hip-hop and hopes to work in the computer industry. She doesn't "hang out," she says. "I shop on the Internet and am looking for a job on the Internet. I do homework, research, e-mail and talk to my friends on the Internet." She is not unusual. Data released last year from the Alfred P. Sloan Study of Youth and Social Development found that teens spend 9 percent of

Style counts

Teen cliques are more fluid than adults think, but each has its own distinctive tribal markings, from hippie chic to body art to buttoned-down prep

their waking hours outside school with friends. They spend 20 percent of their waking hours alone. "Teens are isolated to an extent that has never been possible before," says Stanford's Damon. "There is an ethic among adults that says, 'Kids want to be autonomous; don't get in their face.' "

This generation is strongly peer-driven. "This is much more a team-playing generation," says William Strauss, coauthor of the 1997 book "The Fourth Turning." "Boomers may be bowling alone, but Millennials are playing soccer in teams." That makes belonging so crucial that it can be a matter of life and death. In Littleton, Colo., a year ago, the two teenage shooters stood apart, alienated from the jock culture that infused Columbine High School. Yet in a landmark study of 7,000 teens, researchers led by Bar-

Sound and Fury

"There's a lot of anger in my generation. You can hear it in the music. Kids are angry for a lot of reasons, but mostly because parents aren't around."

Robertino Rodriquez, 17

bara Schneider of the University of Chicago found that teen social groups are as fluid and hard to pin down as a bead of mercury. "Students often move from one group to another, and friendships change over a period of a few weeks or months," they write in "The Ambitious Generation." "Best friends are few." As a group, today's teens are also in-fused with an optimism not seen among kids in decades (it doesn't hurt to have grown up in a time of relative peace and the longest economic expansion in U.S. history). "I think a lot of adolescents now are being taught that they can make a difference," says Sophie Mazuroski, 15, of Portland, Maine. "Children of our generation want to. I am very optimistic." Still the law of teenage angst is still on the books: 4.3 percent of ninth graders make suicide attempts serious enough to require medical treatment.

This generation of teens is more spiritual than their parents, but often less conventionally so. Many put together their own religious canon as they would a salad from a salad bar. Yet despite their faith, teens, as well as those who study them, say that "lying and cheating are standard behavior," as Trisha Sandoval, 17, of Santa Fe Springs, Calif., puts it—more so than for earlier generations. Elsewhere on the values front, teens today are less likely than those in 1992 "to get somebody pregnant, drive drunk or get into fights," says Kevin Dwyer, president of the National Association of School Psychologists. And teens, says Strauss, "had harsher opinions about the Clinton-Lewinsky scandal than any other group." Coming of age in a time of interracial marriages, many

---

A Snapshot of a Generation

In the Internet age, teens seem to be coming of age ever earlier. A recent NEWSWEEK Poll explores what concerns today's youth and asks if their parents have a clue.

• **Stress: Do teens today face more problems than their parents did as teens?**

	TEENS
More	70%
Fewer	5
Same	24

• **Family: Do your parents spend enough time with you?**

	TEENS
Enough	61%
Too little	24
Too much	15

• 48% of teens say they use a computer almost every day at home

• 21% have looked at something on the Internet that they wouldn't want their parents to know about

• **Identity: How much peer pressure from friends do you feel (does your teen feel) today to do the following?**

THOSE RESPONDING 'A LOT'	TEENS	PARENTS
Have sex	10%	20%
Grow up too fast	16	34
Steal or shoplift	4	11
Use drugs or abuse alcohol	10	18
Defy parents or teachers	9	16
Be mean to kids who are different	11	14

If you had to choose between fitting in with friends or becoming outstanding in some way, which would you (your teen) choose?

	TEENS	PARENTS
Fitting in	26%	43%
Becoming out-standing	69	50

• **Worries: How concerned are you about the following?**

THOSE RESPONDING 'A LOT'	TEENS	PARENTS
Not having enough money to buy the things you (they) want	34%	35%
The cost of your (their) college education	54	68
Violence in society	59	82
Not being sure about your (their) future job opportunities	43	49
Your (their) getting into trouble with drugs	25	66
Your (their) drinking or abusing alcohol	26	64
Sexual permissiveness in society	33	72
Sexually transmitted diseases	58	75

• **Hostility: Many teens these days feel a lot of anger. How angry are you?**

	TEENS
Very	3%
Somewhat	25
Not too	43
Not at all	29

• **Faith: How important is religion in your life today?**

	TEENS
Very	43%
Somewhat	35
Not too	14
Not at all	8

• 17% of teens and 37% of parents say they worry a lot about safety at school

• 21% of teenagers polled say that most of the teens they know have already had sex

FOR THIS SPECIAL NEWSWEEK POLL, PRINCETON SURVEY RESEARCH ASSOCIATES INTERVIEWED A NATIONAL SAMPLE OF TEENS 13–19 AND 509 PARENTS OF SUCH TEENS BY TELEPHONE APRIL 20–28. THE MARGIN OF ERROR IS +/– 5 PERCENTAGE POINTS FOR PARENTS; +/– 6 FOR ALL TEENS; COPYRIGHT 2000 BY NEWSWEEK, INC.

In Living Colors

"We don't care about skin, man. I know a lot about my heritage, about who I am. I'm more than just some black dude who is good at sports. I'm the future."

Marcus Robinson, 17

eschew the old notions of race; maturing at Internet speed, they are more connected than any generation. Both may bode well for tol-erance. "Prejudice against homosexuals, bi-sexuals, African-Americans, Latinos—this is a big issue," says Kathryn Griffin, 18, of Palo Alto, Calif., who hopes to make a career in advertising or marketing. "It's insane that people have these feelings [about other peo-ple] when they don't even know them."

What do they want out of life? Schneider and coauthor David Stevenson found that to-day's teens "are the most occupationally and educationally ambitious generation" ever. Most plan to attend college, and many aspire to work as professionals. A majority identify "happiness" as a goal, along with love and a long and enjoyable life. But many doubt that marriage and career will deliver that, so they channel their energies more broadly. About half of teens perform community service once a month by, for instance, deliv-ering meals to the homeless or reading to the elderly. But does their volunteer work reflect real compassion, or meeting a school requirement?

Regardless of what their terrified parents suspect, the belief that today's teens "are more sexual, rebellious and inebriated is flat-out wrong," says pediatrician Victor Stras-burger of the University of New Mexico. In 1997, 48 percent of high-school students had had sexual intercourse, compared with 54 percent in 1991, according to the CDC. More are smoking (36 percent, compared with 28 percent in 1991), but the percentage who are drinking alcohol remains at 51 per-cent. The social surround, though, may be different now. "A lot of my friends are into drinking a lot," says Marcus Ruopp. "Kids don't see it as a big problem. It's a regular thing, not like they're rebelling. There is no pressure to drink."

Some sociologists believe that each gen-eration assumes the societal role of the gen-eration that is dying, as if something in the Zeitgeist whispers to the young what is be-ing lost, what role they can fill. Those now passing away are the children of the Depres-sion and of World War II. They were tested, and they emerged with optimism, and pur-pose, and a commitment to causes larger than themselves. As Trisha Sandoval puts it, "We want to accomplish something with our lives." Teens today, with their tattoos and baggy shorts, could not seem more different from their grandparents. But every genera-tion has a chance at greatness. Let this one take its shot.

With PAT WINGERT *in Washington,* HOPE WHITE SCOTT *in Boston,* ANA FIGUEROA *in Los Angeles and* DEVIN GORDON, SUSANNAH MEADOWS *and* MICHAEL CRONIN *in New York*

BEYOND LITTLETON

How Well Do You Know Your Kid?

The new teen wave is bigger, richer, better educated and healthier than any other in history. But there's a dark side, and too many parents aren't doing their job.

By Barbara Kantrowitz and Pat Wingert

JOCKS, PREPS, PUNKS, GOTHS, GEEKS. They may sit at separate tables in the cafeteria, but they all belong to the same generation. There are now 31 million kids in the 12-to-19 age group, and demographers predict that there will be 35 million teens by 2010, a population bulge bigger than even the baby boom at its peak. In many ways, these teens are uniquely privileged. They've grown up in a period of sustained prosperity and haven't had to worry about the draft (as their fathers did) or cataclysmic global conflicts (as their grandparents did). Cable and the Internet have given them access to an almost infinite amount of information. Most expect to go to college, and girls, in particular, have unprecedented opportunities; they can dream of careers in everything from professional sports to politics, with plenty of female role models to follow.

But this positive image of American adolescence in 1999 is a little like yearbook photos that depict every kid as happy and blemish-free. After the Littleton, Colo., tragedy, it's clear there's another dimension to this picture, and it's far more troubled. In survey after survey, many kids—even those on the honor roll—say they feel increasingly alone and alienated, unable to connect with their parents, teachers and sometimes even classmates. They're desperate for guidance, and when they don't get what they need at home or in school, they cling to cliques or immerse themselves in a universe out of their parents' reach, a world defined by computer games, TV and movies, where brutality

is so common it has become mundane. The parents of Eric Harris and Dylan Klebold have told friends they never dreamed their sons could kill. It's an extreme case, but it has made a lot of parents wonder: do we really know our kids?

Many teens say they feel overwhelmed by pressure and responsibilities. They are juggling part-time jobs and hours of homework every night; sometimes they're so exhausted that they're nearly asleep in early-morning classes. Half have lived through their parents' divorce. Sixty-three percent are in households where both parents work outside the home, and many look after younger siblings in the afternoon. Still others are home by themselves after school. That unwelcome solitude can extend well into the evening; mealtime for this generation too often begins with a forlorn touch of the microwave.

In fact, of all the issues that trouble adolescents, loneliness ranks at the top of the list. University of Chicago sociologist Barbara Schneider has been studying 7,000 teenagers for five years and has found they spend an average of $3\frac{1}{2}$ hours alone *every day*. Teenagers may claim they want privacy, but they also crave and need attention—and they're not getting it. Author Patricia Hersch profiled eight teens who live in an affluent area of northern Virginia for her 1998 book, "A Tribe Apart." "Every kid I talked to at length eventually came around to saying without my asking that they wished they had more adults in their lives, especially their parents," she says.

Loneliness creates an emotional vacuum that is filled by an intense peer culture, a critical buffer against kids' fear of isolation. Some of this bonding is normal and appropriate; in fact, studies have shown that the human need for acceptance is almost a biological drive, like hunger. It's especially intense in early adolescence, from about 12 to 14, a time of "hyper self-consciousness," says David Elkind, a professor of child development at Tufts University and author of "All Grown Up and No Place to Go." "They become very self-centered and spend a lot of time thinking about what others think of them," Elkind says. "And when they think about what others are thinking, they make the error of thinking that everyone is thinking about *them*." Dressing alike is a refuge, a way of hiding in the group. When they're 3 and scared, they cling to a security blanket; at 16, they want body piercings or Abercrombie shirts.

If parents and other adults abdicate power, teenagers come up with their own rules. It's "Lord of the Flies" on a vast scale. Bullying has become so extreme and so common that many teens just accept it as part of high-school life in the '90s. Emory University psychologist Marshall Duke, an expert on children's friendships, recently asked 110 students in one of his classes if any of them had ever been threatened in high school. To his surprise, "they all raised their hand." In the past, parents and teachers served as mediating forces in the classroom jungle. William Damon, director of the Stanford University Center for Adolescence, re-

From *Newsweek*, May 10, 1999, pp. 36–40. © 1999 by Newsweek, Inc. All rights reserved. Reprinted by permission.

Peril and Promise: Teens by the Numbers

They watch too much television, and their parents may not be around enough, but today's teenagers are committing fewer crimes, having fewer babies and generally staying out of serious trouble. Here's a look at who they are—and what they're up to:

Demographics

THE BREAKDOWN
Teenagers account for roughly 10 percent of the U.S. population.

Teens (13–19)

White	18,199,000	66%
Black	3,992,000	15
Hispanic	3,723,000	14
Asian, Pac. Islander	1,030,000	4
American Indian, Eskimo and Aleut	275,000	1

KIDS HAVING KIDS: A TREND ON THE DECLINE
The birthrate among teens has fallen dramatically, down 16 percent overall.

Birthrates for females 15–19

Percent change, 1991–97	■ –20% or more	▨ –5 to –14.9%
	▨ –15 to –19.9%	

PARENTS AT WORK
Parents work more, so their teenagers are often left unsupervised.

Families with employed parents

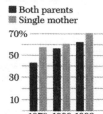

■ Both parents
▨ Single mother

70% 50 30 10
1978 1988 1998

DROP IN CRIME
In 1997, kids were responsible for 17 percent of violent-crime arrests.

Arrests per 100,000 juveniles 10–17

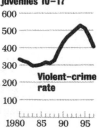

600 500 400 300 200 100

Violent–crime rate

1980 85 90 95

Lifestyle

SEXUAL ACTIVITY
Almost one out of five teenagers is still a virgin by the age of 20.

Percentage of teens who have had sexual intercourse, 1995

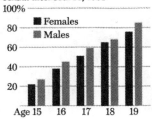

100% 80 60 40 20

■ Females
▨ Males

Age 15 16 17 18 19

COOLEST BRANDS

Boys	Girls
Nike	Nike
Sony	adidas
Tommy Hilfiger	Tommy Hilfiger
Nintendo	The Gap
adidas	Old Navy

FAVORITE TV SHOWS

Boys	Girls
'The Simpsons'	'Dawson's Creek'
'South Park'	'Friends'
'MTV'	'7th Heaven'
'Home Improve.'	'The Simpsons'
'Friends'	'Buffy the V.S.'

LESS OF THE BAD STUFF: SMOKING, DRINKING AND DOING DRUGS
Today, teens say, they misbehave less than kids in the recent past. The percentage who, in the last 30 days, admit to having used ...

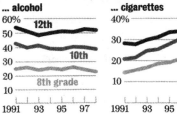
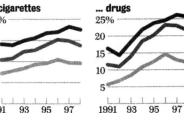

... alcohol
60% 50 40 30 20 10
12th
10th
8th grade
1991 93 95 97

... cigarettes
40% 30 20 10
1991 93 95 97

... drugs
25% 20 15 10 5
1991 93 95 97

calls writing a satirical essay when he was in high school about how he and his friends tormented a kid they knew. Damon got an "A" for style and grammar, but the teacher took him aside and told him he should be ashamed of his behavior. "That's what is supposed to happen," Damon says. "People are supposed to say, 'Hey, kid, you've gone too far here'." Contrast that with reports from Littleton, where Columbine students described a film class nonchalantly viewing a murderous video created by Eric Harris and Dylan Klebold. In 1999 this apparently was not remarkable behavior.

When they're isolated from parents, teens are also more vulnerable to serious emotional problems. Surveys of high-school students have indicated that one in four considers suicide each year, says Dr. David Fassler, a child and adolescent psychiatrist in Burlington, Vt., and author of "Help Me, I'm Sad: Recognizing, Treating and Preventing Childhood and Adolescent Depression." By the end of high school, many have actually tried to kill themselves. "Often the parents or teachers don't realize it was a suicide attempt," he says. "It can be something ambiguous like an overdose of nonprescription pills from the medicine cabinet or getting drunk and crashing the car with suicidal thoughts."

Even the best, most caring parents can't protect their teenagers from all these problems, but involved parents can make an enormous difference. Kids do listen. Teenage drug use (although still high) is slowly declining, and even teen pregnancy and birthrates are down slightly—largely because of improved education efforts, experts say. More teens are delaying sex, and those who are sexually active are more likely to use contraceptives than their counterparts a few years ago.

In the teenage years, the relationship between parents and children is constantly evolving as the kids edge toward independence. Early adolescence is a period of transition, when middle-school kids move from one teacher and one classroom to a different teacher for each subject. In puberty, they're moody and irritable. "This is a time

when parents and kids bicker a lot," says Laurence Steinberg, a psychology professor at Temple University and author of "You and Your Adolescent: A Parents' Guide to Ages 10 to 20." "Parents are caught by surprise," he says. "They discover that the tricks they've used in raising their kids effectively during childhood stop working." He advises parents to try to understand what their kids are going through; things do get better. "I have a 14-year-old son," Steinberg says, "and when he moved out of the transition phase into middle adolescence, we saw a dramatic change. All of a sudden, he's our best friend again."

IN MIDDLE ADOLESCENCE, ROUGHLY THE first three years of high school, teens are increasingly on their own. To a large degree, their lives revolve around school and their friends. "They have a healthy sense of self," says Steinberg. They begin to develop a unique sense of identity, as well as their own values and beliefs. "The danger in this time would be to try to force them to be something you want them to be, rather than help them be who they are." Their relationships may change dramatically as their interests change; in Schneider's study, almost three quarters of the closest friends named by seniors weren't even mentioned during sophomore year.

Late adolescence is another transition, this time to leaving home altogether. "Par-

Online

HOOKED UP
47% of teens are using the computer to go online this year.

Percentage of teens who go online

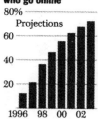

1996 98 00 02

Projections

WHAT DO THEY DO?
They keep up with each other—and what's out there.

Top 10 activities

E-mail	83%
Search engine	78
Music sites	59
General research	58
Games	51
TV/movie sites	43
Chat room	42
Own Web page	38
Sports sites	35

EVERY MOVE THEY MAKE
With age comes online freedom. Here's how parents say they monitor their kids while they're on the Net.

	Age 11–15	16–18
Sit with them while online	38%	9%
Kids can log on only with an adult	34	5
Mainly use for online games	28	15
Limit hours for kids' use	47	21
Know which Web sites kids can visit	68	43
Kids are online whenever they want	54	75
Use the Net more than watching TV	19	22

Home life

PASSING THE HOURS
Kids spend more time partying than studying each week. They also like tube time.

Activity	percentage of teens/hours	
Watching TV	98%	11.0
Listening to CDs, tapes, etc.	96	9.9
Doing chores	84	4.1
Studying	59	3.7
Going to parties	58	4.0
Going to religious functions	51	2.5
Working at a regular paid job	32	4.7

WHAT WERE WE TALKING ABOUT?
Parents and kids both say they're discussing important life issues.

Issue discussed	parents/kids	
Alcohol/drugs	98%	90%
How to handle violent situations	83	80
Basic facts of reproduction	76	80
AIDS	78	75

● **85%** of teens said that **Mom** cares 'very much' about them. **58%** said the same about **Dad.**

● **25%** of teens said that their **mom** is 'always' **home** when they return from school. **10%** said their **dad** was.

● Do parents let teenagers make their own decisions about weekend **curfew**? **66%** said no.

● How much are teens '**understood**' by their family members? **35%** said 'quite a bit.'

SPENDING HABITS
Teens average just under $100 in total weekly spending.

Weekly spending
■ Allowance ■ Own

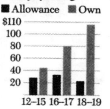

12–15 16–17 18–19

RESEARCH BY BRET BEGUN. SOURCES: CENSUS BUREAU; BLS; NAT'L CENTER FOR JUVENILE JUSTICE; NCHS; TEENAGE RESEARCH UNLIMITED; MONITORING THE FUTURE STUDY, UNIV. OF MICHIGAN; KAISER FAMILY FOUNDATION; NAT'L LONGITUDINAL STUDY OF ADOLESCENT HEALTH; JUPITER COMMUNICATIONS; GREENFIELD ONLINE; THE ALAN GUTTMACHER INST.

ents have to be able to let go," says Steinberg, and "have faith and trust that they've done a good enough job as parents that their child can handle this stuff." Contrary to stereotypes, it isn't mothers who are most likely to mourn in the empty nest. They're often relieved to be free of some chores. But Steinberg says that fathers "suffer from thoughts of missed chances."

That should be the ultimate lesson of tragedies like Littleton. "Parents need to share what they really believe in, what they really think is important," says Stanford's Damon. "These basic moral values are more important than math skills or SATs." Seize any opportunity to talk—in the car, over the breakfast table, watching TV. Parents have to work harder to get their points across. Ellen Galinsky, president of the Families and Work Institute, has studied teenagers' views of parents. "One 16-year-old told us, 'I am proud of the fact that [my mother] deals with me even though I try to push her away. She's still there'." So pay attention now. The kids can't wait.

With ANNE UNDERWOOD

The Road Ahead: A Boomer's Guide to Happiness

THE NEW MIDDLE AGE: The baby boom has always made its own rules, and now it's redefining growing old. From work to family to money, here's how boomers are writing the next chapter.

BY BARBARA KANTROWITZ

THE 50 THING STARTED HITTING KATE DONOHUE AT 49.5. "I DON'T want to be that old," says the San Francisco psychologist. "It's a half century." But when the big day came in January, Donahue decided to see it as a chance to fix the things in her life she didn't like. She made three resolutions: to worry less, to "make more space" for herself by not being so busy and to be more adventurous—more like the woman she was in her 20s and 30s when she routinely set off on solo trekking and biking trips. In August, she will head off to Africa to learn more about West African dance, a longtime passion. Procrastination is not an option. Her 83-year-old father is in the advanced stages of Parkinson's disease; her mother, 79, is active but suffers from a heart condition and glaucoma. "Seeing my parents get so tiny is the way it hits me," Donohue says. "How many more years do I have?"

For so long, the generation born between 1946 and 1964 (an estimated 78 million Americans) has been in collective denial as the years added up. Boomers couldn't be getting older—although, amazingly, everyone else seemed to. But while they're still inclined to moments of self-

By the Numbers: A Boomer's Life

The front line of this much-analyzed cohort hits 55 next year. Where have they been, and what's in store? A look at the stats that define this trendsetting generation.

Your job

- **71%** of boomer households had both spouses working in 1998. In 23% of the households, only the husband worked; in 4%, only the wife.
- **32%** of boomers age 35 to 44 worked at home in 1997, as did 27% of those 45 to 54
- **39%** of boomer households made $60,000 or more in 1997

Median income, in thousands, of boomers 35 to 44 in 1997

Your money

Average annual spending, in thousands, of households, 1997

	AGE 35-44	45-54
Housing	$13.4	$13.9
Transp.	7.3	8.7
Food	5.7	6.0
Taxes	4.3	4.9
Entertain.	2.1	2.4
Apparel	2.1	2.1
Health care	1.6	1.9

- **71%** of boomers owned their homes in 1998
- **92%** of boomers 35 to 44 had financial assets averaging $11,600 in 1995; 92% of those 45 to 54 had more than double the assets at $24,800
- **$90,500** was the net worth of householders 45 to 54 in 1995

Your health

- **37%** of boomers polled in 1992 said they suffer from muscle aches and pains, 37% from headaches, 28% from fatigue and 18% from anxiety
- **21%** of men and 33% of women 30 to 39 said in 1995 that they rarely or never exercise
- **27%** of men and 41% of women 40 to 49 said they rarely or never exercise

Adults who say they are in excellent health

AGE	1976	1996
18-29	44%	36%
30-39	41	35
40-49	27	32
50-59	23	30
60-69	18	23
70+	17	17

Your parents

Those who, at age 16, were living with both their parents

AGE NOW	1996
18-24	60%
25-34	60
35-44	74
45-54	76
55-64	71
65-74	70
75+	74

- **6%** of male boomers lived with their parents in 1998; 3% of female boomers did
- **19%** of boomers were raised by their mothers only; 5% were raised only by their fathers
- **65%** of boomers 45 to 54 still had their mothers living in 1994; 34% had fathers living

Your kids

- **36%** of married boomers in 1998 had no children under 18 living at home; 14% had three or more children at home
- **63%** of Hispanic boomer households had children at home in 1998, compared with 50% of whites and 46% of blacks
- **12%** of male boomers lived alone in 1997; 9% of female boomers lived alone

Boomer households with children at home by age of child, 1998

Any age	61%
under 18	50
under 12	32
under 6	14
under 1	2

SOURCE: "THE BABY BOOM, AMERICANS AGED 35 TO 54," CHERYL RUSSELL

Future Imperfect

With 78 million members in their generation, boomers have wielded a lot of economic and social power. Here's what they had to say in a recent Heinz/NEWSWEEK Poll.

- **69%** are satisfied with their current standard of living
- **69%** have some form of health insurance for all members of their families; 30% have one or more family members uninsured

Nonretirees: are you saving enough for retirement?

- Not sure 4%
- Not regularly saving 26%
- Yes 36%
- Not saving enough 34%

- **47%** of boomers believe that, in their communities, moral and ethical standards are sinking even lower
- **60%** believe we should have a third major political party in this country

- **62%** of boomers are concerned about having to care for an aging parent or relative
- **64%** worry about being able to afford health care for a family member who becomes sick

Over the past five years, have you or your family ...?

	ANSWERING "YES"
Felt stressed out from too much debt	46%
Been unable to pay loans	34
Maxed out your credit cards	27
Declared personal bankruptcy	9

FOR THIS SPECIAL HEINZ FAMILY PHILANTHROPIES/NEWSWEEK POLL, PRINCETON SURVEY RESEARCH ASSOCIATES INTERVIEWED A RANDOM NATIONAL SAMPLE OF 1,501 ADULTS BY TELEPHONE IN ENGLISH OR SPANISH FEB. 18—MARCH 5, 2000. THE MARGIN OF ERROR IS +/-3 PERCENTAGE POINTS, +/-4 POINTS FOR 617 IN THE 35–54 BOOMER AGE GROUP. COPYRIGHT © 2000 BY NEWSWEEK, INC.   ILLUSTRATIONS BY JAMES STEINBERG

'Nick at Twilight'
An imaginary guide to classic boomer TV, at midlife. **By Mark O'Donnell**

Lassie: After Large Timmy buries the seventh Lassie, he's gripped by a sudden sense of his own mortality and halfheartedly plans to visit Tibet. Guest appearance by, amazingly, June Lockhart. Large Timmy's trophy wife: Jennifer Lopez. Lassie Eight: a shiny red Lamborghini.

delusion ("No one would ever guess that I'm 50"), they can no longer escape intimations of their own mortality. The oldest boomers will turn 55 next year, an age when many people begin thinking seriously about retirement. Even the youngest members of this overchronicled cohort are on the cusp of Grecian Formula time.

Their own parents are aging and dying, making many of them the elders in their families. "There's the feeling that you're the next in line, and there's nothing between you and the abyss," says Linda Waite, director of the Center on Aging at the University of Chicago. When they look in the mirror, they see gray hair and wrinkles. Their bodies are beginning to creak and they're worried that all those years of avoiding the gym and stuffing their faces with Big Macs may add up.

At work, they're feeling the threat of a new generation fluent in technology and willing to work 24/7. Corporate America seems to value experience less, and has come to view older workers in the same way investors view Old Economy stocks: sure, they perform at a steady pace, but these younger, untested companies/employees have so much *potential*.

But don't expect boomers to go quietly into boring and predictable senescence. They're likely to transform the last decades of life just as they have already demolished other conventional milestones. There are 50-year-olds lugging toddlers and 40-year-olds retiring early after cashing out piles of dot-com stock. Settling down is anathema. Boomers switch jobs, and even careers (not to mention spouses) in a never-ending search for fulfillment. "The first generation to grow up with remote controls, we invented channel-surfing and attention-deficit living," says journalist Michael Gross in his new book, "My Generation." "That taught us to be infinitely adaptable, even in the baby-boom cliché of 'diminished expectations.' "

It helps that they're better educated and richer than previous generations and, as their parents die, expected to benefit from the largest transfer of inherited wealth in history. In a new Heinz Family Philanthropies/NEWSWEEK Poll, nearly half of all boomers said their personal financial situation was "good" or "excellent." Unlike their parents, they don't have to rely on Social Security or limited pensions. A healthy economy and a strong stock market give them new options as they phase out of full-time employment. They may decide to freelance, work part time or start their own companies.

At the same time, they're likely to embrace their more spiritual side, motivated by a need to give back—an echo of the anti-materialism of the '60s. Marialice Harwood, 53, a marketing executive with the Minneapolis Star Tribune, had her moment of reckoning three years ago when her brother, then 51, died of a heart attack. "My faith is more important to me," says Harwood, a Roman Catholic. "I care about different things." She's downsized to a town house now that her kids are grown and, although she intends to work until she's 65, "when I retire, I don't see myself in a resort community. I see myself in the inner city working with kids. That's my dream."

California gerontologist Ken Dychtwald, who has written extensively about boomers, says many "will age rebelliously," resisting stereotypes and convention. Paul Fersen celebrated turning 50 by getting a tattoo and putting down a deposit on a Harley. "I always wanted a tattoo and I got one, a striped bass," says Fersen, a marketing manager for Orvis, the fly-fishing outfitters based in Manchester, Vt. But that's just one of the changes he sees in his future. "Some people say my job could be voted best on the planet," Fersen says, given that he gets paid for fishing all over the country. But, he says, "I'm still working for somebody else." He has a quieter, more independent vision for his future: "There's a little country store in the next town. It's got two gas pumps and it's a deer weigh-in station. It's the main fo-

cal point of the town. I'd like to finish out my days by owning that store."

While their parents—seared by the Depression and war—craved security, boomers have always embraced the new and the unknown. Boomer women, in particular, have learned to march ahead without a road map. "Ours was the generation that broke the rules," says Jeanne Giordano, 51, an urban planner in Manhattan. "Anything was possible. You could speak back to your parents. You didn't have to get married." She found meaning in her work, including designing the master plan for the restoration of Grand Central Terminal. Now, like many boomers, she's thinking closer to home. "What I would like is to have a relationship that takes me into my final chapters," she says. "I no longer look at it as an imposition. The one thing I haven't done is rely on someone, trust someone to be a part of my life."

Unfinished business is a persistent theme. Dreams interrupted or delayed, regrets about relationships that fizzled. Staring at the abyss, many boomers are reordering their priorities. "You recognize that life is really very short," says Terry Patten, 49. In 1998 he sold his company, Tools for Exploration, and he's now working out of his house in Marin County, Calif., writing a book on improving intelligence. His marriage of 22 years broke up three years ago but he's committed to a new, "wonderful, loving" relationship. He's doing yoga, lifting weights and running. Like many boomers, he's also a prodigious consumer of products that claim to extend life and takes 25 supplements, including DHEA. Says Patten, "I'm just trying to optimize my quality of life as I embrace the inevitable." In other words, going out with a bang—and just a little bit of a whimper.

With PATRICIA KING *in San Francisco,* SARAH DOWNEY *in Chicago and* HOPE WHITE SCOTT *in Boston*

Live to 100? No thanks

Most people opt for quality, not quantity, in later years

BY SUSAN L. CROWLEY

Despite stunning medical advances that can extend life, most Americans do not want to live to be 100. They fear the disabilities, impoverishment and isolation commonly thought to accompany old age.

The finding emerged in a wide-ranging AARP survey on attitudes toward longevity. When asked how long they want to live, 63 percent of the 2,032 respondents opted for fewer than 100 years.

"What this says to me," notes Constance Swank, director of research at AARP, "is that people are more interested in the quality of their lives than the length. They don't want to be encumbered by poor health and financial worries in their older years."

Survey respondents reported they would like to live to an average of about 91 years, but expect to live to 80. According to the U.S. Census Bureau, the life expectancy for a child born in 1997 is 76.5 years. A person turning 65 in 1997 could expect to live another 17.6 years.

The telephone survey, conducted from April 9 to 14 for AARP by Market Facts, Inc. of McLean, Va., also found that a huge majority of people are aware that their behavior and habits can affect how well they age.

This was "the real take-home message for me," says Terrie Wetle, deputy director of the National Institute on Aging. "It was very good news that more than 90 percent recognized that they had some control over how they age."

Harvard neuropsychologist Margery Hutter Silver, who is associate director of the New England Centenarian Study, agrees: "Just the fact of thinking you have control is going to have tremendous impact."

Over eight out of 10 respondents reported doing things to stay healthy. Seventy percent said they exercise, 33 percent watch their diets, 10 percent watch their weight and 10 percent maintain a positive attitude.

Most Americans are also optimistic that life will be better for the typical 80-year-old in 2050 and that medical advances will lead to cures for cancer, heart disease, AIDS and Alzheimer's disease.

Yet, even though they are taking steps to age well and are upbeat about the future, most people are still leery of what might befall them if they live to be 100.

That shouldn't come as a surprise, people of all ages told the Bulletin.

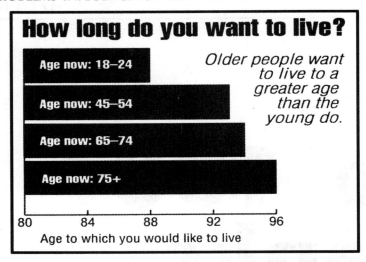

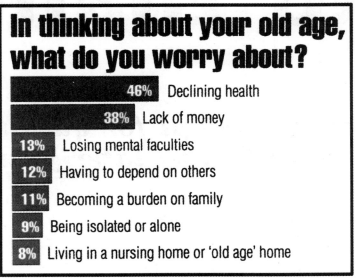

AARP SURVEY BY MARKET FACTS, INC. MCLEAN, VA.

"Our society bases its economy on young stars and young entrepreneurs," says Lynda Preble, 28, who works for a public relations firm in San Francisco. "I'm sure most people don't understand where they fit in once they are older."

"I was not surprised," says writer and publicist Susan Hartt, 57, of Baltimore. "As the saying goes, 'Old age is not for sissies.'"

Even though disability rates among the old are declining, chronic health problems and poverty are still more likely to appear in advanced age, Wetle says, and "people know that."

"I'm going to hang it up when I'm restricted to bed," say Marion Ballard, 59, a former software company owner in Bethesda, Md.

"A slow mental decline scares me the most," says Lilavati Sinclair, a 32-year-old mother in Bothell, Wash. For Peter Winkert, 47, a sales executive in Cazenovia, N.Y., "running out of income is my biggest concern."

Others express fear of being alone, burdening their families, living in a nursing home or, as one person puts it, "losing my joy and will to keep on living."

How old a person is tends to influence his or her views on age and aging. Among those ages 18 to 24, a person is "old" at 58, according to the survey, while those 65 or older think "old" starts at 75.

"I used to think I would be dead at 30," jokes one woman who just turned 30. "Now that I know I'll be around a while, I want to enjoy life as long as possible."

Not unexpectedly, older people hope and expect to live to greater ages than the young. Survey respondents 75 and older want to live to 96, but for 18- to 24-year-olds, 88 is enough.

Julie Vermillion, 24, who is a public affairs assistant in Washington, D.C., and Erin Laughlin, 23, a dog trainer in Sebastopol, Calif., say that living to 85 is about right.

Yet 85-year-old Lucille Runkel of Cochranton, Pa., is still in good shape and still active. "I wouldn't mind living to be 100 if I'm in good health," she says, "but I don't want to be dependent on my children."

"If I feel well enough," says lawyer Lester Nurick, 84, of Potomac, Md., "I could go on forever. . . .but I would never put a number on it."

"Young people deal with the mythology instead of the reality of aging," says AARP's Swank. "Older people are living it, and many embrace the challenges, the joys. No one wants to be debilitated, but for many, the later years are highly satisfying. So why walk away from it?"

Older people have also witnessed the development of life-saving vaccines, drugs and surgical techniques and are more confident of continuing medical breakthroughs. "What we see here," Swank says, "is the wisdom of age."

Writer Hartt says she wouldn't mind putting up with some infirmities to achieve such wisdom. "So what was adolescence—a day at the beach?"

Lack of information helps fuel the myths of old age. For example, only 28 percent of survey respondents know that the 85-plus age group is the fastest-growing segment of the population.

And many people don't know that most Americans over 65 live independently, with fewer than 5 percent in nursing homes, adds Harvard's Silver.

Other survey highlights:

• On average, people with a college education hope to live longer (to age 92) than those with a high-school education (to 89).

• Fifty-two percent of those with a yearly household income of over $50,000 worry about poor health in old age, compared to 41 percent among those with incomes lower than $50,000.

• Those who say they are doing things to stay healthy and active expect to live to 81, while others expect to live to 76.

Given new findings about centenarians—whose numbers in the United States grew to more than 62,000 by 1998 and by some estimates could reach 1 million by 2050—aiming for the century mark is not unreasonable.

Living to 100 doesn't mean you'll be in poor health, says Silver, who is co-author with Thomas T. Perls, M.D., of "Living to 100" (Basic Books, 1999). To the contrary, centenarians are often healthier than people in their 80s.

But there's a trick, according to their book: "One must stay healthy the vast majority of one's life in order to live to 100."

Some think it's a worthy goal.

"It would be cool to live for over a century, just because of the history involved," says one 30-something. "I can't even guess what will come."

Start the Conversation

The MODERN MATURITY guide to end-of-life care

The Body Speaks

Physically, dying means that "the body's various physiological systems, such as the circulatory, respiratory, and digestive systems, are no longer able to support the demands required to stay alive," says Barney Spivack, M.D., director of Geriatric Medicine for the Stamford (Connecticut) Health System. "When there is no meaningful chance for recovery, the physician should discuss realistic goals of care with the patient and family, which may include letting nature take its course. Lacking that direction," he says, "physicians differ in their perception of when enough is enough. We use our best judgment, taking into account the situation, the information available at the time, consultation with another doctor, or guidance from an ethics committee."

Without instructions from the patient or family, a doctor's obligation to a terminally ill person is to pro-

vide life-sustaining treatment. When a decision to "let nature take its course" has been made, the doctor will remove the treatment, based on the patient's needs. Early on, the patient or surrogate may choose to stop interventions such as antibiotics, dialysis, resuscitation, and defibrillation. Caregivers may want to offer food and fluids, but those can cause choking and the pooling of dangerous fluids in the lungs. A dying patient does not desire or need nourishment; without it he or she goes into a deep sleep and dies in days to weeks. A breathing machine would be the last support: It is uncomfortable for the patient, and may be disconnected when the patient or family finds that it is merely prolonging the dying process.

The Best Defense Against Pain

Pain-management activists are fervently trying to reeducate physicians about the importance and safety of making patients comfortable. "In medical school 30 years ago, we worried a lot about creating addicts,"

In Search of a Good Death

If we think about death at all, we say that we want to go quickly, in our sleep, or, perhaps, while fly-fishing. But in fact only 10 percent of us die suddenly. The more common process is a slow decline with episodes of organ or system failure. Most of us want to die at home; most of us won't. All of us hope to die without pain; many of us will be kept alive, in pain, beyond a time when we would choose to call a halt. Yet very few of us take steps ahead of time to spell out what kind of physical and emotional care we will want at the end.

The new movement to improve the end of life is pioneering ways to make available to each of us a good death—as we each define it. One goal of the movement is to bring death through the cultural process that childbirth has achieved; from an unconscious, solitary act in a cold hospital room to a situation in which one is buffered by pillows, pictures, music, loved ones, and the solaces of home. But as in the childbirth movement, the real goal is choice—here, to have the death you want. Much of death's sting can be averted by planning in advance, knowing the facts, and knowing what options we all have. Here, we have gathered new and relevant information to help us all make a difference for the people we are taking care of, and ultimately, for ourselves.

says Philadelphia internist Nicholas Scharff. "Now we know that addiction is not a problem: People who are in pain take pain medication as long as they need it, and then they stop." Spivack says, "We have new formulations and delivery systems, so a dying patient should never have unmet pain needs."

In 1999, the Joint Commission on Accreditation of Healthcare Organizations issued stern new guidelines about easing pain in both terminal and nonterminal patients. The movement intends to take pain seriously: to measure and treat it as the fifth vital sign in hospitals, along with blood pressure, pulse, temperature, and respiration.

The best defense against pain, says Spivack, is a combination of education and assertiveness. "Don't be afraid to speak up," he says. "If your doctor isn't listening, talk to the nurses. They see more and usually have a good sense of what's happening." Hospice workers, too, are experts on physical comfort, and a good doctor will respond to a hospice worker's recommendations. "The best situation for pain management," says Scharff, "is at home with a family caregiver being guided by a hospice program."

The downsides to pain medication are, first, that narcotics given to a fragile body may have a double effect: The drug may ease the pain, but it may cause respiratory depression and possibly death. Second, pain medication may induce grogginess or unconsciousness when a patient wants to be alert. "Most people seem to be much more willing to tolerate pain than mental confusion," says senior research scientist M. Powell Lawton, Ph.D., of the Philadelphia Geriatric Center. Dying patients may choose to be alert one day for visitors, and asleep the next to cope with pain. Studies show that when patients control their own pain medication, they use less.

Final Symptoms

Depression This condition is not an inevitable part of dying but can and should be treated. In fact, untreated depression can prevent pain medications from working effectively, and antidepressant medication can help relieve pain. A dying patient should be kept in the best possible emotional state for the final stage of life. A combination of medications and psychotherapy works best to treat depression.

Anorexia In the last few days of life, anorexia—an unwillingness or inability to eat—often sets in. "It has a protective effect, releasing endorphins in the system and contributing to a greater feeling of well-being," says Spivack. "Force-feeding a dying patient could make him uncomfortable and cause choking."

Dehydration Most people want to drink little or nothing in their last days. Again, this is a protective mechanism, triggering a release of helpful endorphins.

Hospice: The Comfort Team

Hospice is really a bundle of services. It organizes a team of people to help patients and their families, most often in the patient's home but also in hospice residences, nursing homes, and hospitals:

■ Registered nurses who check medication and the patient's condition, communicate with the patient's doctor, and educate caregivers.
■ Medical services by the patient's physician and a hospice's medical director, limited to pain medication and other comfort care.
■ Medical supplies and equipment.
■ Drugs for pain relief and symptom control.
■ Home-care aides for personal care, homemakers for light housekeeping.
■ Continuous care in the home as needed on a short-term basis.
■ Trained volunteers for support services.
■ Physical, occupational, and speech therapists to help patients adapt to new disabilities.
■ Temporary hospitalization during a crisis.
■ Counselors and social workers who provide emotional and spiritual support to the patient and family.
■ Respite care—brief noncrisis hospitalization to provide relief for family caregivers for up to five days.

■ Bereavement support for the family, including counseling, referral to support groups, and periodic check-ins during the first year after the death.

Hospice Residences Still rare, but a growing phenomenon. They provide all these services on-site. They're for patients without family caregivers; with frail, elderly spouses; and for families who cannot provide at-home care because of other commitments. At the moment, Medicare covers only hospice services; the patient must pay for room and board. In many states Medicaid also covers hospice services (see How Much Will It Cost?). Keep in mind that not all residences are certified, bonded, or licensed; and not all are covered by Medicare.

Getting In A physician can recommend hospice for a patient who is terminally ill and probably has less than six months to live. The aim of hospice is to help people cope with an illness, not to cure it. All patients entering hospice waive their rights to curative treatments, though only for conditions relating to their terminal illness. "If you break a leg, of course you'll be treated for that," says Karen Woods, executive director of the Hospice Association of America. No one is forced to accept a hospice referral, and patients may leave and opt for curative care at any time. Hospice programs are listed in the Yellow Pages. For more information, see Resources.

Drowsiness and Unarousable Sleep In spite of a coma-like state, says Spivack, "presume that the patient hears everything that is being said in the room."

Agitation and Restlessness, Moaning and Groaning The features of "terminal delirium" occur when the patient's level of consciousness is markedly decreased; there is no significant likelihood that any pain sensation can reach consciousness. Family members and other caregivers may interpret what they see as "the patient is in pain" but as these signs arise at a point very close to death, terminal delirium should be suspected.

The Ultimate Emotional Challenge

A dying person is grieving the loss of control over life, of body image, of normal physical functions, mobility and strength, freedom and independence, security, and the illusion of immortality. He is also grieving the loss of an earthly future, and reorienting himself to an unknowable destiny.

At the same time, an emotionally healthy dying person will be trying to satisfy his survival drive by adapting to this new phase, making the most of life at the moment, calling in loved ones, examining and appreciating his own joys and accomplishments. Not all dying people are depressed; many embrace death easily.

Facing the Fact

Doctors are usually the ones to inform a patient that he or she is dying, and the end-of-life movement is training physicians to bring empathy to that conversation in place of medspeak and time estimates. The more sensitive doctor will first ask how the patient feels things are going. "The patient may say, 'Well, I don't think I'm getting better,' and I would say, 'I think you're right,' " says internist Nicholas Scharff.

At this point, a doctor might ask if the patient wants to hear more now or later, in broad strokes or in detail. Some people will need to first process the emotional blow with tears and anger before learning about the course of their disease in the future.

"Accept and understand whatever reaction the patient has," says Roni Lang, director of the Geriatric Assessment Program for the Stamford (Connecticut) Health System, and a social worker who is a longtime veteran of such conversations. "Don't be too quick with the tissue. That sends a message that it's not okay to be upset. It's okay for the patient to be however she is."

Getting to Acceptance

Some patients keep hoping that they will get better. Denial is one of the mind's miracles, a way to ward off painful realities until consciousness can deal with them. Denial may not be a problem for the dying person, but it can create difficulties for the family. The dying person could be leaving a lot of tough decisions, stress, and confusion behind. The classic stages of grief outlined by Elisabeth Kübler-Ross—denial, anger, bargaining, depression, and acceptance—are often used to describe post-death grieving, but were in fact delineated for the process of accepting impending loss. We now know that these states may not progress in order. "Most people oscillate between anger and sadness, embracing the prospect of death and unrealistic episodes of optimism," says Lang. Still, she says, "don't place demands on them to accept their death. This is not a time to proselytize." It is enough for the family to accept the coming loss, and if necessary, introduce the idea of an advance directive and health-care proxy, approaching it as a "just in case" idea. When one member of the family cannot accept death, and insists that doctors do more, says Lang, "that's the worst nightmare. I would call a meeting, hear all views without interrupting, and get the conversation around to what the patient would want. You may need another person to come in, perhaps the doctor, to help 'hear' the voice of the patient."

What Are You Afraid Of?

The most important question for doctors and caregivers to ask a dying person is, What are you afraid of? "Fear aggravates pain," says Lang, "and pain aggravates fear." Fear of pain, says Spivack, is one of the most common problems, and can be dealt with rationally. Many people do not know, for example, that pain in dying is not inevitable. Other typical fears are of being separated from loved ones, from home, from work; fear of being a burden, losing control, being dependent, and leaving things undone. Voicing fear helps lessen it, and pinpointing fear helps a caregiver know how to respond.

How to Be With a Dying Person

Our usual instinct is to avoid everything about death, including the people moving most rapidly toward it. But, Spivack says, "In all my years of working with dying people, I've never heard one say 'I want to die alone.' " Dying people are greatly comforted by company; the benefit far outweighs the awkwardness of the visit. Lang offers these suggestions for visitors:

■ Be close. Sit at eye level, and don't be afraid to touch. Let the dying person set the pace for the conversation. Allow for silence. Your presence alone is valuable.

■ Don't contradict a patient who says he's going to die. Acceptance is okay. Allow for anger, guilt, and fear, without trying to "fix" it. Just listen and empathize.

Survival Kit for Caregivers

A study published in the March 21, 2000, issue of **Annals of Internal Medicine** shows that caregivers of the dying are twice as likely to have depressive symptoms as the dying themselves.

No wonder. Caring for a dying parent, says social worker Roni Lang, "brings a fierce tangle of emotions. That part of us that is a child must grow up." Parallel struggles occur when caring for a spouse, a child, another relative, or a friend. Caregivers may also experience sibling rivalry, income loss, isolation, fatigue, burnout, and resentment.

To deal with these difficult stresses, Lang suggests that caregivers:

■ Set limits in advance. How far am I willing to go? What level of care is needed? Who can I get to help? Resist the temptation to let the illness always take center stage, or to be drawn into guilt-inducing conversations with people who think you should be doing more.

■ Join a caregiver support group, either disease-related like the Alzheimer's Association or Gilda's Club, or a more general support group like The Well Spouse Foundation. Ask the social services department at your hospital for advice. Telephone support and online chat rooms also exist (see Resources).

■ Acknowledge anger and express it constructively by keeping a journal or talking to an understanding friend or family member. Anger is a normal reaction to powerlessness.

■ When people offer to help, give them a specific assignment. And then, take time to do what energizes you and make a point of rewarding yourself.

■ Remember that people who are critically ill are self-absorbed. If your empathy fails you and you lose patience, make amends and forgive yourself.

■ Give the patient as much decision-making power as possible, as long as possible. Allow for talk about unfinished business. Ask: "Who can I contact for you?"

■ Encourage happy reminiscences. It's okay to laugh.

■ Never pass up the chance to express love or say good-bye. But if you don't get the chance, remember that not everything is worked through. Do the best you can.

Taking Control Now

Sixty years ago, before the invention of dialysis, defibrillators, and ventilators, the failure of vital organs automatically meant death. There were few choices to be made to end suffering, and when there were—the fatal dose of morphine, for example—these decisions were made privately by family and doctors who knew each other well. Since the 1950s, medical technology has been capable of extending lives, but also of prolonging dying. In 1967, an organization called Choice in Dying (now the Partnership for Caring: America's Voices for the Dying; see Resources) designed the first advance directive—a document that allows you to designate under what conditions you would want life-sustaining treatment to be continued or terminated. But the idea did not gain popular understanding until 1976, when the parents of Karen Ann Quinlan won a long legal battle to disconnect her from respiratory support as she lay for months in a vegetative state. Some 75 percent of Americans are in favor of advance directives, although only 30–35 percent actually write them.

Designing the Care You Want

There are two kinds of advance directives, and you may use one or both. A Living Will details what kind of life-sustaining treatment you want or don't want, in the event of an illness when death is imminent. A durable power of attorney for health care appoints someone to be your decision-maker if you can't speak for yourself. This person is also called a surrogate, attorney-in-fact, or health-care proxy. An advance directive such as Five Wishes covers both.

Most experts agree that a Living Will alone is not sufficient. "You don't need to write specific instructions about different kinds of life support, as you don't yet know any of the facts of your situation, and they may change," says Charles Sabatino, assistant director of the American Bar Association's Commission on Legal Problems of the Elderly.

The proxy, Sabatino says, is far more important. "It means someone you trust will find out all the options and make a decision consistent with what you would want." In most states, you may write your own advance directive, though some states require a specific form, available at hospital admitting offices or at the state department of health.

When Should You Draw Up a Directive?

Without an advance directive, a hospital staff is legally bound to do everything to keep you alive as long as possible, until you or a family member decides otherwise. So advance directives are best written before emergency status or a terminal diagnosis. Some people write them at the same time they make a will. The process begins with discussions between you and your family and doctor. If anybody is reluctant to discuss the subject, Sabatino suggests starting the conversation with a story. "Remember what happened to Bob Jones and what his family went through? I want us to be different. . . ." You can use existing tools—a booklet or questionnaire (see Resources)—to keep the conversation moving. Get your doctor's commitment to support your wishes. "If you're asking for something that is against your doctor's conscience" (such as prescribing a lethal dose of pain medication or removing life support at a time he considers premature), Sabatino says, "he may have an obligation to transfer you to another doctor." And make sure the person you name as surrogate agrees to act for you and understands your wishes.

Filing, Storing, Safekeeping . . .

An estimated 35 percent of advance directives cannot be found when needed.

■ Give a copy to your surrogate, your doctor, your hospital, and other family members. Tell them where to find the original in the house—not in a safe deposit box where it might not be found until after death.

■ Some people carry a copy in their wallet or glove compartment of their car.

■ Be aware that if you have more than one home and you split your time in several regions of the country, you should be registering your wishes with a hospital in each region, and consider naming more than one proxy.

■ You may register your Living Will and health-care proxy online at uslivingwillregistry.com (or call 800-548-9455). The free, privately funded confidential service will instantly fax a copy to a hospital when the hospital requests one. It will also remind you to update it: You may want to choose a new surrogate, accommodate medical advances, or change your idea of when "enough is enough." M. Powell Lawton, who is doing a study on how people anticipate the terminal life stages, has discovered that "people adapt relatively well to states of poor health. The idea that life is still worth living continues to readjust itself."

Assisted Suicide: The Reality

While advance directives allow for the termination of life-sustaining treatment, assisted suicide means supplying the patient with a prescription for life-ending medication. A doctor writes the prescription for the medication; the patient takes the fatal dose him- or herself. Physician-assisted suicide is legal only in Oregon (and under consideration in Maine) but only with rigorous preconditions. Of the approximately 30,000 people who died in Oregon in 1999, only 33 received permission to have a lethal dose of medication and only 26 of those actually died of the medication. Surrogates may request an end to life support, but to assist in a suicide puts one at risk for charges of homicide.

Good Care: Can You Afford It?

The ordinary person is only one serious illness away from poverty," says Joanne Lynn, M.D., director of the Arlington, Virginia, Center to Improve Care of the Dying. An ethicist, hospice physician, and health-services researcher, she is one of the founding members of the end-of-life-care movement. "On the whole, hospitalization and the cost of suppressing symptoms is very easy to afford," says Lynn. Medicare and Medicaid will help cover that kind of acute medical care. But what is harder to afford is at-home medication, monitoring, daily help with eating and walking, and all the care that will go on for the rest of the patient's life.

"When people are dying," Lynn says, "an increasing proportion of their overall care does not need to be done by doctors. But when policymakers say the care is nonmedical, then it's second class, it's not important, and nobody will pay for it."

Bottom line, Medicare pays for about 57 percent of the cost of medical care for Medicare beneficiaries. Another 11 percent is paid by Medicaid, 20 percent by the patient, 10 percent from private insurance, and the rest from other sources, such as charitable organizations.

Medi-what?

This public-plus-private network of funding sources for end-of-life care is complex, and who pays for how much of what is determined by diagnosis, age, site of care, and income. Besides the private health insurance that many of us have from our employers, other sources of funding may enter the picture when patients are terminally ill.

■ **Medicare** A federal insurance program that covers health-care services for people 65 and over, some disabled people, and those with end-stage kidney disease. Medicare Part A covers inpatient care in hospitals, nursing homes, hospice, and some home health care. For most people, the Part A premium is free. Part B covers doctor fees, tests, and other outpatient medical services. Although Part B is optional, most people choose to enroll through their local Social Security office and pay the monthly premium ($45.50). Medicare beneficiaries share in the cost of care through deductibles and co-insurance. What Medicare does not cover at all is outpatient medication, long-term nonacute care, and support services.

■ **Medicaid** A state and federally funded program that covers health-care services for people with income or assets below certain levels, which vary from state to state.

■ **Medigap** Private insurance policies covering the gaps in Medicare, such as deductibles and co-payments, and in some cases additional health-care services, medical supplies, and outpatient prescription drugs.

Many of the services not paid for by Medicare can be covered by private long-term-care insurance. About 50 percent of us over the age of 65 will need long-term care at home or in a nursing home, and this insurance is an extra bit of protection for people with major assets to protect. It pays for skilled nursing care as well as non-health services, such as help with dressing, eating, and bathing. You select a dollar amount of coverage per day (for example, $100 in a nursing home, or $50 for at-home care), and a coverage period (for example, three years—the average nursing-home stay is 2.7 years). Depending on your age and the benefits you choose, the insurance can cost anywhere from around $500 to more than $8,000 a year. People with pre-existing conditions such as Alzheimer's or MS are usually not eligible.

How Much Will It Cost?

Where you get end-of-life care will affect the cost and who pays for it.

■ **Hospital** Dying in a hospital costs about $1,000 a day. After a $766 deductible (per benefit period), Medicare reimburses the hospital a fixed rate per day, which varies by region and diagnosis. After the first 60 days in a hospital, a patient will pay a daily deductible ($194) that goes up (to $388) after 90 days. The patient is responsible for all costs for each day beyond 150 days. Medicaid and some private insurance, either through an employer or a Medigap plan, often help cover these costs.

■ **Nursing home** About $1,000 a week. Medicare covers up to 100 days of skilled nursing care after a three-day hospitalization, and most medication costs during that time. For days 21–100, your daily co-insurance of $97 is usually covered by private insurance—if you have it. For nursing-home care not covered by Medicare, you must use your private assets, or Medicaid if your assets run out, which happens to approximately one-third of nursing-home residents. Long-term-care insurance may also cover some of the costs.

■ **Hospice care** About $100 a day for in-home care. Medicare covers hospice care to patients who have a life expectancy of less than six months. (See Hospice: The Comfort Team.) Such care may be provided at home, in a hospice facility, a hospital, or a nursing-home. Patients may be asked to pay up to $5 for each prescription and a 5 percent co-pay for in-patient respite care, which is a short hospital stay to relieve caregivers. Medicaid covers hospice care in all but six states, even for those without Medicare.

About 60 percent of full-time employees of medium and large firms also have coverage for hospice services, but the benefits vary widely.

Five Wishes

Five Wishes is a questionnaire that guides people in making essential decisions about the care they want at the end of their life. About a million people have filled out the eight-page form in the past two years. This advance directive is legally valid in 34 states and the District of Columbia. (The other 16 require a specific state-mandated form.)

The document was designed by lawyer Jim Towey, founder of Aging With Dignity, a nonprofit organization that advocates for the needs of elders and their caregivers. Towey, who was legal counsel to Mother Teresa, visited her Home for the Dying in Calcutta in the 1980s. He was struck that in that haven in the Third World, "the dying people's hands were held, their pain was managed, and they weren't alone. In the First World, you see a lot of medical technology, but people die in pain, and alone." Towey talked to MODERN MATURITY about his directive and what it means.

What are the five wishes? Who do I want to make care decisions for me when I can't? What kind of medical treatment do I want toward the end? What would help me feel comfortable while I am dying? How do I want people to treat me? What do I want my loved ones to know about me and my feelings after I'm gone?

Why is it so vital to make advance decisions now? Medical technology has extended longevity, which is good, but it can prolong the dying process in ways that are almost cruel. Medical schools are still concentrating on curing, not caring for the dying. We can have a dignified season in our life, or die alone in pain with futile interventions. Most people only discover they have options when checking into the hospital, and often they no longer have the capacity to choose. This leaves the family members with a guessing game and, frequently, guilt.

What's the ideal way to use this document? First you do a little soul searching about what you want. Then discuss it with people you trust, in the living-room instead of the waiting room—before a crisis. Just say, "I want a choice about how I spend my last days," talk about your choices, and pick someone to be your health-care surrogate.

What makes the Five Wishes directive unique? It's easy to use and understand, not written in the language of doctors or lawyers. It also allows people to discuss comfort dignity, and forgivness, not just medical concerns. When my father filled it out, he said he wanted his favorite afghan blanket in his bed. It made a huge difference to me that, as he was dying, he had his wishes fulfilled.

For a copy of Five Wishes in English or Spanish, send a $5 check or money order to Aging With Dignity, PO Box 1661, Tallahassee, FL 32302. For more information, visit www.agingwithdignity. org.

■ **Home care without hospice services** Medicare Part A pays the full cost of medical home health care for up to 100 visits following a hospital stay of at least three days. Medicare Part B covers home health-care visits beyond those 100 visits or without a hospital stay. To qualify, the patient must be home-bound, require skilled nursing care or physical or speech therapy, be under a physician's care, and use services from a Medicare-participating home-health agency. Note that this coverage is for medical care only; hired help for personal nonmedical services, such as that often required by Alzheimer's patients, is not covered by Medicare. It is covered by Medicaid in some states.

A major financial disadvantage of dying at home without hospice is that Medicare does not cover out-patient prescription drugs, even those for pain. Medicaid does cover these drugs, but often with restrictions on their price and quantity. Private insurance can fill the gap to some extent. Long-term-care insurance may cover payments to family caregivers who have to stop work to care for a dying patient, but this type of coverage is very rare.

Resources

MEDICAL CARE

For information about pain relief and symptom management:
Supportive Care of the Dying
(503-215-5053; careofdying.org).

For a comprehensive guide to living with the medical, emotional, and spiritual aspects of dying:
Handbook for Mortals
by Joanne Lynn and Joan Harrold, Oxford University Press.

For a 24-hour hotline offering counseling, pain management, downloadable advance directives, and more:
The Partnership for Caring
(800-989-9455; www.partnershipforcaring.org).

EMOTIONAL CARE

To find mental-health counselors with an emphasis on lifespan human development and spiritual discussion:
American Counseling Association
(800-347-6647; counseling.org).

For disease-related support groups and general resources for caregivers:
Caregiver Survival Resources
(caregiver911.com).

For AARP's online caregiver support chatroom, access **America Online** every Wednesday night, 8:30–9:30 EST (keyword: AARP).

Education and advocacy for family caregivers:
National Family Caregivers Association
(800-896-3650; nfcacares.org).

For the booklet,
Understanding the Grief Process
(D16832, EEO143C), e-mail order with title and numbers to member@aarp.org or send postcard to AARP Fulfillment, 601 E St NW, Washington DC 20049. Please allow two to four weeks for delivery.

To find a volunteer to help with supportive services to the frail and their caregivers:
National Federation of Interfaith Volunteer Caregivers (816-931-5442; nfivc.org).

For information on support to partners of the chronically ill and/or the disabled:
The Well Spouse Foundation
(800-838-0879; www.wellspouse.org).

LEGAL HELP

AARP members are entitled to a free half-hour of legal advice with a lawyer from **AARP's Legal Services Network.**
(800-424-3410; www.aarp.org/lsn).

For **Planning for Incapacity,** *a guide to advance directives in your state,* send $5 to Legal Counsel for the Elderly, Inc.,
PO Box 96474,
Washington DC 20090-6474.
Make out check to LCE Inc.

For a **Caring Conversations** *booklet on advance-directive discussion:*
Midwest Bioethics Center
(816-221-1100; midbio.org).

For information on care at the end of life, online discussion groups, conferences:
Last Acts Campaign
(800-844-7616; lastacts.org).

HOSPICE

To learn about end-of-life care options and grief issues through videotapes, books, newsletters, and brochures:
Hospice Foundation of America
(800-854-3402; hospicefoundation.org).

For information on hospice programs, FAQs, and general facts about hospice:
National Hospice and Palliative Care Organization
(800-658-8898; nhpco.org).

For **All About Hospice: A Consumer's Guide**
(202-546-4759; www.hospice-america.org).

FINANCIAL HELP

For **Organizing Your Future,** *a simple guide to end-of-life financial decisions,* send $5 to Legal Counsel for the Elderly, Inc., PO Box 96474, Washington DC 20090-6474. Make out check to LCE Inc.

For **Medicare and You 2000** *and a* **2000 Guide to Health Insurance for People With Medicare**
(800-MEDICARE [633-4227]; medicare.gov).
To find your State Agency on Aging: **Administration on Aging,U.S. Department of Health and Human Services**
(800-677-1116; aoa.dhhs.gov).

GENERAL

For information on end-of-life planning and bereavement: (www.aarp.org/endoflife/).

For health professionals and others who want to start conversations on end-of-life issues in their community: Discussion Guide: On Our Own Terms: Moyers on Dying, based on the PBS series, airing September 10–13. The guide provides essays, instructions, and contacts. From PBS, www.pbs.org/onourownterms Or send a postcard request to On Our Own Terms Discussion Guide, Thirteen/WNET New York, PO Box 245, Little Falls, NJ 07424-9766.

Funded with a grant from The Robert Wood Johnson Foundation, Princeton, N.J.
Editor Amy Gross   *Writer* Louise Lague
Designer David Herbick

Unit Selections

Key Points to Consider

❖ What is a friend? Do friendships change as we mature? How so? What kinds of people attract us to them?

❖ What is emotional intelligence? How does it develop? How can we tell if we possess it? How do people with EQ differ from people without it? Do you have EQ? If not, can you do anything to cultivate it? Explain.

❖ Why are some people painfully shy? Are you shy, so shy that you avoid certain social situations? What are the causes of shyness? How might others perceive shy individuals? How can shyness be overcome?

❖ Why is the face important to emotional expression and social interactions? How do researchers study the face and emotionality? Why is it important for lay persons to understand the emotions and moods of others?

❖ How do you feel when you know that someone has lied to or deceived you? Can you spot a liar? How? Are humans the only creatures who use deception? How do other organisms use and detect deception?

❖ What is a secret? Do you typically reveal your secrets to friends? Under what circumstances do we reveal secrets? When are we likely to keep secrets to ourselves?

❖ When we are betrayed or deceived by someone else, what are the typical ways we respond? Which response do you usually adopt?

❖ How do scientists study marriage? What makes a marriage high quality? How do happy couples and unhappy couples differ in their interactions? Can we predict whose marriage will end in divorce? What are some of the signs of an unhappy marriage? Do you think such marriages can be saved?

❖ What is jealousy? Is jealousy normal or not? Do you think jealousy is a necessary part of romance and intimacy? Can jealousy ever promote positive emotions or passion in couples?

❖ What is crowding? How does crowding differ from other concepts such as density? Is crowding more negative than it is positive? Why might early research be incorrect about the effects of crowding?

❖ In summary, this unit examines close relationships, including friends and lovers. For each, which factors make the relationship better, and which make it worse?

 **Links** # www.dushkin.com/online/

These sites are annotated on pages 4 and 5.

People can be seen everywhere in groups: couples in love, parents and their children, teachers and students, gatherings of friends, church groups, theatergoers. People have much influence on one another when they congregate in groups.

Groups spend a great deal of time communicating with members and nonmembers. The communication can be intentional and forceful, such as when protesters demonstrate against a totalitarian regime in a far-off land. Or communication can be more subtle, for example, when fraternity brothers reject a prospective brother who refuses to wear the symbols of membership.

In some groups, the reason a leader emerges is clear—perhaps the most skilled individual in the group is elected leader by the group members. In other groups, for example, as during a spontaneous nightclub fire, the qualities of the rapidly emerging, perhaps self-appointed, leader are less apparent. Nonetheless, the followers flee unquestioningly in the leader's direction. Even in dating couples, one person may seem to lead or be dominant over the other.

Some groups, such as formalized business corporations, issue formal, written rules; discipline for rule breaking is also formalized. Other groups, families or trios of friends, for example, possess fewer and less formalized rules and disciplinary codes, but their rules are still quickly learned by and are important to all unit members.

Some groups are large but seek more members, such as nationalized labor unions. Other groups seek to keep their groups small and somewhat exclusive, such as teenage cliques. Groups exist that are almost completely adversarial with other groups. For example, conflict between youth gangs is receiving much media attention today. Other groups pride themselves on their ability to remain cooperative, such as neighbors who band together in a community crime watch.

Psychologists are so convinced that interpersonal relationships are important to the human experience that they have intensively studied them. There is ample evidence that contact with other people is a necessary part of human existence. Research has shown that most individuals do not like being isolated from other people. In fact, in laboratory experiments in which subjects experience total isolation for extended periods, they begin to hallucinate the presence of others. In prisons, solitary confinement is often used as a form of punishment because of its aversive effect. Other research has shown that people who must wait under stressful circumstances prefer to wait with others, even if the others are total strangers, rather than wait alone.

This unit examines smaller and therefore fairly interpersonal relationships such those among friends, dating partners, and married couples. The next unit examines the effects of larger groups, specifically, society at large.

The first article provides a general introduction to the unit. In "Friendships and Adaptation Across the Life Span," the authors discuss why friendship is so important. They also disclose how friendship is construed differently by children and adults. The authors explain why we are attracted to various types of individuals. It is no surprise that we are most attracted to competent, mentally healthy individuals.

In the next two articles various factors that color our relationships are discussed. The first article reviews a new and important issue: emotional intelligence, or EQ. Emotional intelligence relates to our ability to get along with and be sensitive to other people's needs and emotions. Emotional intelligence may be more important to our success in life than any other aspect of our being. In fact, there exists research that indicates EQ may be more predictive of our life trajectory than IQ or intelligence.

While those with EQ thrive in social situations, others are not so fortunate. Shyness overwhelms them and sometimes prevents them from making and keeping friends. Bernardo Carducci writes about shyness and how to overcome it in "Shyness: The New Solution." He explains, for example, that the Internet offers an opportunity to meet and interact with others without being overwhelmed by social anxiety.

The next pair of articles in the series is about how the average person perceives others with whom they are in an interpersonal relationship. The first article is about the importance of the face as a nonverbal barometer of others' moods, emotional states, and inner thoughts. In "What's in a Face?" Beth Azar discusses just how important reading people's faces is.

Another concept related to the importance of the face is the ability to detect deception on the part of others. James Geary, in "How to Spot a Liar," examines how nature has provided a way for members of various species to deceive others. Similarly, nature usually also provides clues that point to these very same deceptions so as to help the deceived detect the delusion. In the human, the face is one of the best lie detectors. The next two articles are about special types of interpersonal relationships. In "Revealing Personal Secrets," the author discloses why and when we tell others our secrets. The article would not be complete, though, without reference to the times when we decide to keep information to ourselves and why.

Once in a while, we learn a secret that may be so appalling that we are angry with, disgusted with, or avoidant of the person we think promulgated the secret or awful event. In the essay "Discover the Power of Forgiveness," Ellen Michaud discusses how we typically cope with others who anger or harm us. In the end she concludes that forgiveness is the most powerful and healthy response to betrayal.

In the section that follows, some very close and intimate interpersonal relationships are addressed. "Welcome to the Love Lab" discusses research by renowned expert John Gottman (with co-author Sybil Carrere). Gottman contends that he can detect which relationships are headed for trouble even at their beginning. A discussion on jealousy, an emotion that can signal problems in a romantic relationship, is presented in a companion piece, "Prescription for Passion." David Buss takes the approach that jealousy is normal and might, in fact, hold couples together rather than drive them apart.

The final unit article, "Coping with Crowding," discusses both early and more recent research on the effects of crowding. The early research, now less credible, showed that crowding was probably detrimental. The newer research suggests that we are much better at coping with environmental changes (such as an increase in number of people present) than earlier believed.

Relating to Others

Friendships and Adaptation Across the Life Span

Willard W. Hartup[1] and Nan Stevens

Institute of Child Development, University of Minnesota, Minneapolis, Minnesota (W.W.H.),
and Department of Psychogerontology, University of Nijmegen, Nijmegen, The Netherlands (N.S.)

Abstract

Friends foster self-esteem and a sense of well-being, socialize one another, and support one another in coping with developmental transitions and life stress. Friends engage in different activities with one another across the life span, but friendship is conceived similarly by children and adults. Friends and friendships, however, are not all alike. The developmental significance of having friends depends on the characteristics of the friends, especially whether the friends are antisocial or socially withdrawn. Outcomes also depend on whether friendships are supportive and intimate or fractious and unstable. Among both children and adults, friendships have clear-cut developmental benefits at times but are mixed blessings at other times.

Keywords

friendships; life-span development; relationships

Friendships are important to the well-being of both children and adults. Parents worry if their children do not have friends; adolescents are anxious and upset when they lose their friends; and older adults go to considerable lengths to maintain old friendships and establish new ones. People who have friends generally feel better about themselves and others than do people who do not have friends. Recent studies, however, show that over the life span, the dynamics of friendship are complicated. These relationships sometimes contain a "dark side," and in these instances, developmental benefits are mixed.

In this report, we begin by showing that understanding friendships across the life span requires thinking about these relationships from two perspectives: It is necessary to consider, first, what friendships mean to both children and adults and, second, what distinctive patterns of social interaction characterize friendships. We then suggest that, in order to appreciate the significance of friends over the life span, one must take into account (a) whether a person does or does not have friends, (b) characteristics of the person's friends, and (c) the quality of these relationships.

HOW TO THINK ABOUT FRIENDSHIPS IN LIFE-SPAN PERSPECTIVE

The significance of friendship across the life span can be established only by examining what children and adults believe to be the social meaning (essence) of these relationships, as well as the social exchanges they actually have with their friends. When researchers examine what people believe friendships to be, or what elements constitute a friendship, reciprocity is always involved. Friends may or may not share likes and dislikes, but there is always the sense that one supports and sustains one's friends and receives support in return. Most people do not describe the relation between friends narrowly as a *quid pro quo,* but rather describe the relationship broadly as *mutuality*—that is, friendship involves social giving and taking, and returning in kind or degree. Children, adolescents, newlyweds, middle-aged adults, and soon-to-be retirees differ relatively little from one another in their emphasis on these reciprocities when asked to describe an ideal friend (Weiss & Lowenthal, 1975). Older people describe their friendships more elaborately and with greater subtlety than children do, but then older people generally describe other persons in more complex terms than younger persons do. Consequently, we can assert that the meaning structure specifying friendships changes relatively little from the preschool years through old age; social reciprocities are emphasized throughout the life span (Hartup & Stevens, 1997).

The actual exchanges that occur between friends change greatly with age. Social reciprocities between toddlers are reflected in the time they spend together and the connectedness of their interaction; reciprocities between kindergartners are more elaborated but remain basically concrete ("We play"). Among adolescents, friends engage in common activities (mainly socializing) and social disclosure; among young adults, friendships become "fused" or "blended" with work and parenting. Among older persons, friendships are separated from work once again and centered on support and companionship. The behavioral structures associated with friendship thus change greatly across the life span, generally in accordance with the distinctive tasks or challenges that confront persons at different ages.

HAVING FRIENDS

Occurrence

As early as age 3 or 4, children show preferences for interacting with particular children, and the word "friend" enters their vocabularies. About 75% of preschool-aged children are involved in mutual friendships as identified by mothers or nursery school teachers or measured in terms of the time the children spend together. Mutual friends among school-aged children and older persons are usually identified by asking individuals to name their "best friends," "good friends," or "casual friends," categories differentiated in terms of time spent together and intimacy. Among teenagers, 80% to 90% report having mutual friends, usually including one or two best friends and several good friends. The proportion of people who have friends remains high through adulthood, then declines in old age. More older persons, however, have friends than do not. Small numbers of individuals, about 7%, have no friends in adulthood; after age 65, this friendless group increases to 12% for women and 24% for men.

Friendship networks vary in size according to age and sex. During the nursery school years, boys have an average of two friends, whereas girls have one; during the school years, the number of best friends varies from three to five. Girls' networks are usually smaller and more exclusive than boys' during childhood; this situation reverses, however, in adolescence. Number of friends remains fairly constant through adolescence and early adulthood. Newlyweds have the largest numbers of friends, with fewer friendships being maintained during middle age. Friendship networks increase again before retirement, but a decline occurs following retirement, owing primarily to the loss of casual friends. Close friendships, however, are frequently retained into old, old age (Hartup & Stevens, 1997).

The amount of time spent with friends is greatest during middle childhood and adolescence; in fact, teenagers spend almost a third of their waking time in the company of friends. The percentage of time spent with friends declines until middle age, when adults spend less than 10% of their time with friends. A slight increase occurs at retirement, although it is not as great as one might expect (Larson, Zuzanek, & Mannell, 1985).

Behavior With Friends and Nonfriends

More positive engagement (i.e., more talk, smiling, and laughter) is observed among friends than among nonfriends in childhood and adolescence. Friends also have more effective conflict management and a more mutual orientation when working together (Newcomb & Bagwell, 1995). Differences in behavior between friends and mere acquaintances are similar in adulthood: Self-disclosure occurs more frequently and involves more depth of disclosure among friends than nonfriends; friends are more directive and authoritative with one another than nonfriends.

Companionship and talk continue to distinguish interactions between friends in middle and old age. Sharing, exchange of resources, and emotional support remain salient, especially during crises, such as divorce. Problem solving involves more symmetrical interaction between friends than between nonfriends; conflicts are more effectively managed. Adults' conflicts with friends center on differences in values and beliefs, as well as lifestyles. Conflicts between older friends mainly concern expectations related to age and resource inequities.

Developmental Significance

From early childhood through old age, people with friends have a greater sense of well-being than people without friends. Friendlessness is more common among people who seek clinical assistance for emotional and behavioral problems than among better adjusted persons (Rutter & Garmezy, 1983). But these results mean relatively little: They do not clarify whether friends contribute to well-being or whether people who feel good about themselves have an easier time making friends than those who do not.

Longitudinal studies show that children entering first grade have better school attitudes if they already have friends and are successful both in keeping old ones and making new ones (Ladd, 1990). Similarly, among adolescents, psychological disturbances are fewer when school changes (e.g., from grade to grade or from primary school to middle school) occur in the company of friends than when they do not (Berndt & Keefe, 1992). Once again, the direction of influence is not clear: Does

merely having friends support successful coping with these transitions, or are those people who are better able to cope with these transitions also able to make friends more easily?

Despite these difficulties in interpretation, well-controlled longer term studies extending from childhood into adulthood show similar patterns, thereby strengthening the conclusion that friendships are in some way responsible for the outcome. Self-esteem is greater among young adults who had friends while they were children than among those who did not, when differences in childhood self-esteem are controlled for statistically. Social adjustment in adulthood, however, is more closely related to having been generally liked or disliked by classmates than to having had mutual friends (Bagwell, Newcomb, & Bukowski, 1998).

CHARACTERISTICS OF ONE'S FRIENDS

Although friends may support positive developmental outcomes through companionship and social support, these outcomes depend on who one's friends are. Friendships with socially well-adjusted persons are like money in the bank, "social capital" that can be drawn upon to meet challenges and crises arising every day. In contrast, poorly adjusted friends may be a drain on resources, increasing one's risk of poor developmental outcomes.

Children of divorce illustrate these dynamics: Preadolescents, adolescents, and young adults whose parents have divorced are at roughly three times the risk for psychosocial problems as their peers whose parents are not divorced. Preadolescents who have positive relationships with both custodial and noncustodial parents have a significantly reduced risk if the parents are well-adjusted; friends do not provide the same protection. In contrast, resilience among adolescents whose parents are divorced is influenced by friends as well as family. Specifically, adolescent children of divorce are more resilient (better adapted) if they have both family and friends who have few behavior problems and who are socially mature. Friends continue to promote resilience among the offspring of divorce during early adulthood, but again friends provide this benefit only if they are well-adjusted themselves (Hetherington, in press). Two conclusions can be drawn: First, social capital does not reside merely in having friends, but rather resides in having socially competent friends; and second, whether friends are a protective factor in social development depends on one's age.

Research indicates that the role of friendships as a risk factor also depends on one's age. Friendship risks are especially evident among antisocial children and adolescents. First, antisocial children are more likely to have antisocial friends than other children. Second, antisocial behavior increases as a consequence of associating with antisocial friends. Antisocial children have poor social skills and thus are not good models. Relationships between antisocial children are also problematic: Interactions are more contentious and conflict-ridden, more marked by talk about deviance and talk that is deviant in its social context (e.g., swearing), and more lacking in intimacy than exchanges between nonaggressive children (Dishion, Andrews, & Crosby, 1995). Other studies show that behavior problems increase across the transition from childhood to adolescence when children have stable relationships with friends who have behavior problems themselves (Berndt, Hawkins, & Jiao, in press).

FRIENDSHIP QUALITY

Friendships are not all alike. Some are marked by intimacy and social support, others by conflict and contention. Some friends engage in many different activities, others share narrower interests. Some friendships are relatively stable, others are not. These features of friendships differentiate relationships among both children and adolescents, and define some of the ways that relationships differ from one another among adults.

Friendship quality is related to the psychological well-being of children and adolescents and to the manner in which they manage stressful life events. During the transition from elementary to secondary school, for example, sociability and leadership increase among adolescents who have stable, supportive, and intimate friendships, but decline or do not change among other adolescents. Similarly, social withdrawal increases among students with unstable, poor-quality friendships, but not among students who have supportive and intimate friendships (Berndt et al., in press).

Friendship quality contributes to antisocial behavior and its development. Conflict-ridden and contentious relationships are associated with increases in delinquent behavior during adolescence, especially among young people with histories of troublesome behavior; increases in de-

linquent behavior are smaller for youngsters who have supportive and intimate friends (Poulin, Dishion, & Haas, in press). Friendship quality is also important to the adaptation of young women from divorced families: Those who have supportive and intimate friendships tend to be resilient, but those who have nonsupportive friendships tend not to be resilient (Hetherington, in press).

Among older adults, support from friends also compensates for missing relationships (e.g., partners). Emotional support and receiving assistance from friends are among the most important protections against loneliness for persons without partners (Dykstra, 1995). There may be two sides to this coin, however: Older widows with "problematic" social ties (e.g., widows with friends who break promises, invade their privacy, and take advantage of them) have lower psychological well-being than widows whose social ties are not problematic (Rook, 1984). In other words, the absence of problematic qualities in these relationships may be as important as the presence of positive qualities.

CONCLUSION

Friendships are developmentally significant across the life span. The meaning assigned to these relationships changes relatively little with age, although the behavioral exchanges between friends reflect the ages of the individuals involved. Whether friendships are developmental assets or liabilities depends on several conditions, especially the characteristics of one's friends and the quality of one's relationships with them.

Recommended Reading

Blieszner, R., & Adams, R. G. (1992). *Adult friendship*. Newbury Park, CA: SAGE.

Bukowski, W. M., Newcomb, A. F., & Hartup, W. W. (Eds.). (1996). *The company they keep: Friendship in childhood and adolescence.* New York: Cambridge University Press.

Hartup, W. W., & Stevens, N. (1997). (See References)

Matthews, S. H. (1986). *Friendships through the life course.* Beverly Hills, CA: SAGE.

Note

1. Address correspondence to Willard W. Hartup, Institute of Child Development, University of Minnesota, 51 E. River Rd., Minneapolis, MN 55455.

References

Bagwell, C. L., Newcomb, A. F., & Bukowski, W. M. (1998). Preadolescent friendship and peer rejection as predictors of adult adjustment. *Child Development, 69*, 140–153.

Berndt, T. J., Hawkins, J. A., & Jiao, Z. (in press). Influences of friends and friendships on adjustment to junior high school. *Merrill-Palmer Quarterly.*

Berndt, T. J., & Keefe, K. (1992). Friends' influence on adolescents' perceptions of themselves in school. In D. H. Schunk & J. L. Meece (Eds.), *Students' perceptions in the classroom* (pp. 51–73). Hillsdale, NJ: Erlbaum.

Dishion, T. J., Andrews, D. W., & Crosby, L. (1995). Anti-social boys and their friends in early adolescence: Relationship characteristics, quality, and interactional process. *Child Development, 66*, 139–151.

Dykstra, P. (1995). Loneliness among the never and formerly married: The importance of supportive friendships and a desire for independence. *Journals of Gerontology: Psychological Sciences and Social Sciences, 50B*, S321–S329.

Hartup, W. W., & Stevens, N. (1997). Friendships and adaptation in the life course. *Psychological Bulletin, 121*, 355–370.

Hetherington, E. M. (in press). Social capital and the development of youth from nondivorced, divorced, and remarried families. In W. A. Collins & B. Laursen (Eds.), *Minnesota Symposia on Child Psychology: Vol. 30. Relationships as developmental contexts.* Hillsdale, NJ: Erlbaum.

Ladd, G. W. (1990). Having friends, keeping friends, making friends, and being liked by peers in the classroom: Predictors of children's early school adjustment? *Child Development, 61*, 1081–1100.

Larson, R., Zuzanek, J., & Mannell, R. (1985). Being alone versus being with people: Disengagement in the daily experience of older adults. *Journal of Gerontology, 40*, 375–381.

Newcomb, A. F., & Bagwell, C. (1995). Children's friendship relations: A meta-analytic review. *Psychological Bulletin, 117*, 306–347.

Poulin, F., Dishion, T. J., & Haas, E. (in press). The peer paradox: Relationship quality and deviancy training within male adolescent friendships. *Merrill-Palmer Quarterly.*

Rook, K. S. (1984). The negative side of social interaction: Impact on psychological well-being. *Journal of Personality and Social Psychology, 46*, 1156–1166.

Rutter, M., & Garmezy, N. (1983). Developmental psychopathology. In P. H. Mussen (Series Ed.) & E. M. Hetherington (Vol. Ed.), *Handbook of child psychology: Vol. 4. Socialization, personality, and social development* (4th ed., pp. 775–911). New York: Wiley.

Weiss, L., & Lowenthal, M. F. (1975). Life-course perspectives on friendship. In M. F. Lowenthal, M. Thurnher, & D. Chiriboga (Eds.), *Four stages of life: A comparative study of women and men facing transitions* (pp. 48–61). San Francisco: Jossey-Bass.

Emotional Intelligence:

Do You Have It?

Are your employees making you angry? What if it's not what they are doing wrong, but rather your reaction to the problem? Here's how you can become emotionally intelligent.

by Phillip M. Perry

Fran bristles when you ask if a job is getting done. David sabotages projects when you criticize his work. And Oliver snaps when you pile on too many assignments.

You must deal with these employees, but how?

You've gotten where you are today because of your cognitive intelligence, technical competence, and analytical skills. But you're starting to get a funny feeling that those capabilities are not enough. Why don't they work when you try to turn around these problem individuals?

Worse yet: Why are you starting to feel angry toward these employees? You're tempted to just up and yell at them.

Well, here's some good news. You have already made a great start toward resolving these knotty workplace problems, because you recognize how you feel. That's the first step toward achieving a new set of skills that business psychologists now say are required to deal with today's workplace problems.

Taken as a group, the new skills comprise "emotional intelligence." That's the ability to recognize your emotions and those of the people around you, and the competence to work with those emotions to resolve employee problems.

From *Floral Management*, October 1998, pp. 24-29. © 1998 by Phillip M. Perry. Reprinted by permission.

Ignore this new intelligence at your own risk. "There is a cost to the bottom line from low levels of emotional intelligence on the job," says Daniel P. Goleman, author of *Emotional Intelligence,* the best-seller that recently got people buzzing about the topic. Goleman says that success at work is 20 percent dependent on intellectual ability, and 80 percent dependent on emotional intelligence.

Odd thing is, we've had a clue to the importance of this knowledge for many years. We've known all along that customers buy for emotional reasons. They purchase to fill an inner need, then they rationalize it later. Up until now, though, we haven't recognized that employees act from similar motives. At work, people behave in ways that express their inner feelings. Later, they justify their actions.

This explains why some employees stubbornly resist your logical exhortations to change. When your directives do not address individuals' emotions, you are destined to fail. That's why it's vital to learn these new skills today.

Here's what business psychologists say to do to resolve common workplace situations.

Fran the Foot-dragger

Despite Fran's enthusiasm, skills and intelligence, she's slogging through molasses as she works on that project that you need done in two days. The task seems simple enough: Give a facelift to the drieds and permanent botanicals section. She makes attempt after attempt, then has to start over. And she constantly comes to you with small questions. You start screaming inside: "Why doesn't she just get the job done?" The last straw comes when she asks if she can start over again using the ancient Chinese Feng Shui philosophy of space and energy. You explode: "Get back to the sales floor and get it done! I need it done now!"

Listen Up

Good listening skills are key to a productive work environment. Sharpen yours by using a procedure called RECE, developed by Toni Bernay, a clinical psychologist and executive coach in Beverly Hills, Calif.

Here are the elements of RECE, which stands for **R**ecognize, **E**ngage, **C**ollaborate, and **E**mpower, and how to use them in response to the "Fran the Foot dragger" situation.

1. Recognize the employee. When an individual enters your work area, stop what you are doing and look directly at the person. Act as though you are glad to see the individual, not as though you are being distracted from your work.

2. Engage the employee. Communicate well by listening to the individual's words and responding appropriately. Here's how you might respond to Fran:

"Gosh, that's a creative solution. My problem is that I am very familiar with conventional merchandis-ing and not with Feng Shui, and I am the one who has to deal with the merchandising and display throughout this and our other stores. Let's try Feng Shui next month, so I can get prepared for it. Right now I am under the gun and would appreciate if you would use conventional display techniques.

3. Collaborate. Work with the employee to solve the current problem and plan ahead so the problem does not occur again. With Fran, try having her work with an experienced display co-worker. Ask Fran to set an appointment with you to discuss how your shop can migrate to Feng Shui.

4. Empower. Encourage the employee to take the initiative, and reward any creative solutions. Fran already feels empowered because you have acknowledged her initiative, and you have asked her to make an appointment with you so you can learn more about the newer merchandising method.

—P. P.

Barking orders at a subordinate may get the task accomplished, but at tremendous cost. Employee self-image and morale plummet. Your employees will hesitate to approach you again. Bottom line: The work ends up being sub-par.

So what to do? Toni Bernay, a clinical psychologist and executive coach in Beverly Hills, Calif., suggests the classic two-stepped approach of emotional intelligence:

1. Become aware of your own emotions. In this case, there is likely a combination of emotions. There is anger grown from frustration. There is fear that a critical task will not get done and you will look ineffective to your own supervisor.

2. Develop an action plan to resolve those troubling emotions. "Perhaps you have not learned the skills of delegation well," offers Bernay. "Or perhaps you have not learned to slow down and work with people closely when you launch a project." Further, perhaps you have not communicated well with Fran during the first stages of the project when she was sending you signals that not all was well. "Maybe you need to take stock and work on listening skills," says Dr. Bernay. (For more on listening skills, see sidebar, right.)

David, the Chronic Saboteur

Fran was a one-shot. Now, how about David, who has been simmering on the back burner for many months? While David has been a valuable worker, he seems to have developed a prima donna complex lately. Any slight criticism seems to set him off: He starts making demands that other departments cannot meet. When he doesn't get his way he always seems to find some "good excuse" why his tasks don't

Anger in the Workplace: Good or Bad?

Suppose you are a manager for whom anger is a driving force through the day. Are you being destructive by expressing anger in the workplace?

Not necessarily, says John Mayer, a University of New Hampshire psychologist who was one of the original formulators of the emotional intelligence concept.

"There are fair ways to exhibit temper," says Mayer. "Be sure to be angry at what happened rather than at the individual. Be angry that a job didn't get done or that an employee jeopardized his own future."

Make sure the employee understands the target of your anger by expressing yourself in terms such as "I'm angry that this job did not get done."

get done. Things have finally reached a head. You're furious. What to do?

Don't take it personally. Don't call a meeting right away, suggests John Mayer, a University of New Hampshire psychologist who was one of the original formulators of the emotional intelligence concept. "First, figure out what is making you angry ahead of time. Then call the meeting when you calm down."

Ask yourself why you have become angry at David. Because he makes you look like a bad manager? Because you lost a company competition due to poor performance? Because you feel David is targeting you personally?

"Try to separate the employee's actions from what you do," says Mayer. "Understand that you were a good supervisor and this person did not live up to it. You can at least realize that whatever is going on is not a direct reflection on you. This

will help calm you down." Then you can approach David with the same rational questions as you did with Fran (see sidebar, above).

Start a dialog. In this case, start early by keeping a work diary of the specific actions David has taken, including his unreasonable demands and the late work, or tasks that have fallen through the cracks. Then, ask David what you can do to help keep this pattern from repeating.

In recalling a specific outburst from David, you might say something like, "It seems to me you must have been feeling frustrated that you did not have the tools you asked for to get the job done."

Notice that the "seems to me" statement does not attempt to say with certainty how David was feeling. And just as important, you are not agreeing that he needed the tools to get his work done. But you are starting a dialog. Now, encourage David to open up and talk with you about what steps the two of you can take together to resolve the continuing problem.

Don't psychoanalyze. What if you sense that David has built up lots of resentments, and you want to encourage him to express them? Mayer cautions against going too far when dealing with sources of emotions. The employee may be experiencing problems at home that may be causing angry outbursts in the office, for example, but he may not want to share this information with you.

"The manager does not have a contract to psychoanalyze the employee," cautions Mayer. "Be sensitive enough that you do not create emotional turmoil that gets in the way of progress, but avoid going so far as to intrude on what may be none of your business. Figure out the boundary."

Overworked Oliver Has an Outburst

You've been piling on the work, thanks to an unforeseen barrage of

weddings. You know your employees are under stress. Then something snaps. Oliver bursts into your office and yells at you: "How can you tell us to do all of this extra work? There's just no time to get it all done. Don't you know how to manage?"

How you respond in the next five to 10 seconds is critical, according to David R. Caruso, a consultant with Harris McCully Associates, a New York-based human resources firm. Caruso suggests the following steps:

1. Identify feelings. "First, you need to calm down and control your feelings," says Caruso. "Don't assume this is an attack on you personally."

Then identify the feelings of the employee. "Read the emotions expressed in the face, the body language and tone of voice," says Caruso. "It's probably not pure anger. It's frustration. There may be some fear of not being effective."

2. Deal with the problem. If you have time to deal with the problem on the spot, invite the employee to sit down, then close the door. Don't take any interruptions, or answer the phone. Say, "I have a few minutes if you want to talk about it."

Let the person talk for the first minute or so, says Caruso. "Then always reflect on what the individual has said." Caruso suggests language such as this:

"Well, you have said that the workload is way too much. You said that you are feeling stressed out, and that the quality of the work is going to suffer. I appreciate your telling me these things. It's difficult for people to deliver bad news, and as a manager I cannot be effective without information, so I want to thank you first. I don't know what I can do now, but we need to spend time together and figure out what is happening and what can be done. I cannot promise an easy solution and maybe there is no solution. But it's certainly worth trying to come up with one."

You have echoed and interpreted what the individual has said. It is important not to deny emotions by ignoring them. But once again, don't tell people how they are feeling: "You're really angry." This will just make them angrier because your easy interpretation seems to belittle the complex emotions they have. Instead tell them how it "seems to you" they are feeling.

You use this initial meeting to buy time rather than to solve the problem on the spot. Make an appointment with a time frame so it does not fall through the cracks, causing further frustration. Say something like: "This is a serious enough issue that I want to discuss it in detail. Do you have time later today when we can go through all of your concerns?"

You have calmed down the person, taken them seriously and given them hope. Before your next meeting, do your research. Talk with other employees and get a sense of what the staff is feeling. Then you will be prepared with possible solutions when you meet with the employee.

Don't Miss the Boat

There is no one perfect solution to any problem. Emotional intelligence is a learned process rather than a preordained set of steps.

Some managers say they don't want to spend time calming down employees or becoming "amateur psychologists." These managers are missing the boat in a changing world where technical skills are no longer sufficient for success. Says Caruso: "Managers become successful when they start to view themselves as managers of people, not just as technicians."

Phillip M. Perry is a freelance writer based in New York City and a regular contributor to Floral Management.

Shyness:
The New Solution

The results of a recent survey are shaking up our ideas about shyness and pointing to a surprising new approach for dealing with it.

BY BERNARDO CARDUCCI, PH.D.

At the core of our existence as human beings lies a powerful drive to be with other people. There is much evidence that in the absence of human contact people fall apart physically and mentally; they experience more sickness, stress and suicide than well-connected individuals. For all too many people, however, shyness is the primary barrier to that basic need.

For more than two decades, I have been studying shyness. In 1995, in an article in PSYCHOLOGY TODAY, I, along with shyness pioneer Philip Zimbardo, Ph.D., summed up 20 years of shyness knowledge and research, concluding that rates are rising. At the same time, I ran a small survey that included five open-ended questions asking the shy to tell us about their experiences.

The thousands of responses we received have spawned a whole new generation of research and insight. In addition to the sheer volume of surveys, my colleague and I were surprised at the depth of the comments, often extending to five or 10 handwritten pages. It was as if we had turned on a spigot, allowing people to release a torrent of emotions. They understood that we were willing to listen. For that reason, perhaps, they were not at all shy about answering. This article represents the first analysis of their responses.

The New View

"My ex-wife picked me to marry her, so getting married wasn't a problem. I didn't want to get divorced, even though she was cheating on me, because I would be back out there trying to socialize. [But] I have a computer job now, and one of my strengths is that I work well alone."

Traditionally, shyness is viewed as an intrapersonal problem, arising within certain individuals as a result of characteristics such as excessive self-consciousness, low self-esteem and anticipation of rejection. The survey responses have shown, however, that shyness is also promoted by outside forces at work in our culture, and perhaps around the globe.

In addition, our research has led us to conclude that there is nothing at all wrong with being shy. Certainly shyness can control people and make them ineffective in classroom, social and business situations. Respondents told us that they feel imprisoned by their shyness. It is this feeling that seems to be at the core of their pain. But ironically, we find that the way to break out of the prison of shyness may be to embrace it thoroughly. There are many steps the shy can take to develop satisfying relationships without violating their basic nature.

The Cynically Shy

"My shyness has caused major problems in my personal/social life. I have a strong hate for most people. I also have quite a superiority complex. I see so much stupidity and ignorance in the world that I feel superior to virtually everyone out there. I'm trying [not to], but it's hard."

Of the many voices of shy individuals we "heard" in response to our survey, one in particular emerged very clearly. Among the new patterns our analysis identified was a group I call the cynically shy. These are people who have been rejected by their peers because of their lack of social skills. They

The Eight Habits of Highly Popular People

By Hara Estroff Marano

If you were ever the last person picked for a team or asked to dance at a party, you've probably despaired that popular people are born with complete self-confidence and impeccable social skills. But over the past 20 years, a large body of research in the social sciences has established that what was once thought the province of manna or magic is now solidly our own doing—or undoing. Great relationships, whether friendships or romances, don't fall out of the heavens on a favored few. They depend on a number of very sophisticated but human-scale social skills. These skills are crucial to developing social confidence and acceptance. And it is now clear that everyone can learn them.

And they should. Recent studies illustrate that having social contact and friends, even animal ones, improves physical health. Social ties seem to impact stress hormones directly, which in turn affect almost every part of our body, including the immune system. They also improve mental health. Having large social networks can help lower stress in times of crisis, alleviate depression and provide emotional support.

Luckily, it's never too late to develop the tools of the socially confident. Research from social scientists around the world, including relationship expert John Gottman, Ph.D., and shyness authority Bernardo Carducci, Ph.D., show that the most popular people follow these steps to social success:

1. Schedule Your Social Life

It is impossible to hone your social skills without investing time in them. Practice makes perfect, even for the socially secure. Accordingly, the well-liked surround themselves with others, getting a rich supply of opportunities to observe interactions and to improve upon their own social behaviors.

You need to do the same. Stop turning down party invitations and start inviting people to visit you at home. Plan outings with close friends or acquaintances you'd like to know better.

2. Think Positive

Insecure people tend to approach others anxiously, feeling they have to prove that they're witty or interesting. But self-assured people expect that others will respond positively—despite the fact that one of the most difficult social tasks is to join an activity that is already in progress.

3. Engage in Social Reconnaissance

Like detectives, the socially competent are highly skilled at information gathering, always scanning the scene for important details to guide their actions. They direct their focus outward, observing others and listening actively.

Socially skilled people are tuned in to people's expression of specific emotions, sensitive to signals that convey such information as what people's interests are, whether they want to be left alone or whether there is room in an activity for another person.

To infer correctly what others must be feeling, the socially confident are also able to identify and label their own experience accurately. That is where many people, particularly men, fall short.

Good conversationalists make comments that are connected to what is said to them and to the social situation. The connectedness of their communication is, in fact, one of its most outstanding features. Aggressive people actually make more attempts to join others in conversation but are less successful at it than the socially adept because they call attention to themselves, rather than finding a way to fit into ongoing group activity. They might throw out a statement that disrupts the conversation, or respond contentiously to a question. They might blurt something about the way they feel, or shift the conversation to something of interest exclusively to themselves.

"You don't have to be interesting. You have to be interested," explains John Gottman, Ph.D., professor of psychology at the University of Washington. "That's how you have conversations."

4. Enter Conversations Gracefully

Timing is everything. After listening and observing on the perimeter of a group they want to join, the socially competent look for an opportunity to step in, knowing it doesn't just happen. It usually appears as a lull in the conversation.

Tuned in to the conversational or activity theme, the deft participant asks a question or elaborates on what someone else has already said. This is not the time to shift the direction of the conversation, unless it comes to a dead halt. Then it might be wise to throw out a question, perhaps something related to events of the day, and, if possible, something tangentially related to the recent discussion. The idea is to use an open-ended question that lets others participate. "Speaking of the election, what does everybody think about so-and-so's decision not to run?"

"People admire the person who is willing to take a risk and throw out a topic for conversation, but you have to make sure it has general appeal," says Bernardo Carducci, Ph.D., director of the Shyness Research Institute at Indiana University Southeast. Then you are in the desirable position of having rescued the group, which confers immediate membership and acceptance. Once the conversation gets moving, it's wise to back off talking and give others a chance. Social bores attempt to dominate a discussion. The socially confident know that the goal is to help the group have a better conversation.

5. Learn to Handle Failure

It is a fact of life that everyone will sometimes be rejected. Rebuffs happen even to popular people. What distinguishes the socially confident from mere mortals is their reaction to rejection. They don't attribute it to internal causes, such as their own unlikability or inability to make friends. They assume it can result from many factors—incompatibility, someone else's bad mood, a misunderstanding. And some conversations are just private.

Self-assured people become resilient, using the feedback they get to shape another go at acceptance. Studies show that when faced with failure, those who are well-liked turn a negative response into a counterproposal. They say things like, "Well, can we make a date for next week instead?" Or they move onto another group in the expectation that not every conversation is closed. (continued)

And should they reject others' bids to join with them, they do it in a polite and positive way. They invariably offer a reason or counter with an alternative idea: "I would love to talk with you later."

6. Take Hold of Your Emotions

Social situations are incredibly complex and dynamic. One has to pay attention to all kinds of verbal and nonverbal cues, such as facial expression and voice tone, interpret their meaning accurately, decide on the best response for the scenario, and then carry out that response—all in a matter of microseconds. No one can pay attention to or correctly interpret what is going on, let alone act skillfully, without a reasonable degree of control over their own emotional states, especially negative emotions such as anger, fear, anxiety—the emotions that usually arise in situations of conflict or uncertainty.

Recently, studies have found that people who are the most well-liked also have a firm handle on their emotions. It isn't that they internalize all their negative feelings. Instead, they shift attention away from distressing stimuli toward positive aspects of a situation. In other words, they have excellent coping skills. Otherwise, they become overly reactive to the negative emotions of others and may resort to aggression or withdraw from social contact.

7. Defuse Disagreements

Since conflict is inevitable, coping with confrontations is one of the most critical of social skills. It's not the degree of conflict that sinks relationships, but the ways people resolve it. Disagreements, if handled well, can help people know themselves better, improve language skills, gain valuable information and cement their relationships.

Instead of fighting fire with fire, socially confident people stop conflict from escalating; they apologize, propose a joint activity, make a peace offering of some kind, or negotiate. And sometimes they just change the subject. That doesn't mean that they yield to another's demands. Extreme submissiveness violates the equality basic to healthy relationships—and a sense of self-worth.

As people gain social competence, they try to accommodate the needs of both parties. Managing conflict without aggression requires listening, communicating—arguing, persuading—taking the perspective of others, controlling negative emotions, and problem-solving. Researchers have found that when people explain their point of view in an argument, they are in essence making a conciliatory move. That almost invariably opens the door for a partner to offer a suggestion that ends the standoff.

8. Laugh A Little

Humor is the single most prized social skill, the fast track to being liked—at all ages. Humor works even in threatening situations because it defuses negativity. There's no recipe for creating a sense of humor. But even in your darkest moments, try to see the lighter side of a situation.

If you need more help, call the American Psychological Association at 1-800-964-2000 for a referral to a therapist near you. For further resources check http://www.shyness.com/.

---

do not feel connected to others—and they are angry about it. They feel a sense of alienation. And like the so-called trench coat mafia in Littleton, Colorado, they adapt a stance of superiority as they drift away from others.

Their isolation discourages them from having a sense of empathy, and this leads them to dehumanize others and take revenge against them. This process is the same one used by the military to train young boys to kill. The difference is, the military is now in your house, on your TV, in your video games.

Inside the Shy Mind

"As we talked, I felt uneasy. I worried about how I looked, what I said, how I said what I said, and so forth. Her compliments made me uncomfortable."

One of the solutions to shyness is a greater understanding of its internal dynamics. It is important to note that a critical feature of shyness is a slowness to warm up. Shy people simply require extra time to adjust to novel or stressful situations, including even everyday conversations and social gatherings.

They also need more time to master the developmental hurdles of life. The good news is that shy people eventually achieve everything that everyone else does—they date, marry, have children. The bad news is, it takes them a little longer.

An unfortunate consequence of the shy being on this delayed schedule is that they lack social support through many important life experiences. When they start dating and want to talk about first-date jitters, for example, their peers will be talking about weddings. As a result, the shy may need to take an especially active role in finding others who are in their situation. One way is to build social support by starting groups of like-minded people. Another is to seek out existing groups of shy people, perhaps via the Internet. While technology often works against the shy, it can also lend them an unexpected helping hand.

Our research reveals the fact that the shy tend to make unrealistic social comparisons. In a room full of others, their attention is usually drawn to the most socially outstanding person, the life of the party—against whom they compare themselves, unfavorably, of course. This is just a preemptive strike. Typically, they compound the negative self-appraisal by attributing their own comparatively poor performance to enduring and unchangeable internal characteristics—"I was born shy" or "I don't have the gift of gab." Such attributions only heighten self-consciousness and inhibit performance.

The shy are prone to such errors of attribution because they believe that they are always being evaluated by others. Self-consciously focused on their own shortcomings, they fail to look around and notice that most people are just like them—listeners, not social standouts. Our surveys show that 48% of people are shy. So not only are the shy not alone, they probably have plenty of company at any social function.

The No. 1 problem area for the shy is starting a relationship. Fifty-eight percent told us they have problems with introductions; they go to a party but nothing happens. Forty percent said their problem was social; they had trouble developing friendships. Only seven percent of the shy have a problem with intimacy. If you get into an intimate relationship, shyness no longer seems to be a problem. Unfortunately, it's hard to get there.

The New Cultural Climate

It is no secret that certain technological advances—the Internet, e-mail, cell phones—are changing the conditions of the culture we live in, speeding it up and intensifying its complexity. This phenomenon, dubbed hyperculture, has trickled down to alter the nature of day-to-day interactions, with negative consequences for the shy. In this cultural climate, we lose patience quickly because we've grown accustomed to things happening faster and faster. We lose tolerance for those who need time to warm up. Those who are not quick and intense get passed by. The shy are bellwethers of this change: They are the first to feel its effects. And so it's not surprising that hyperculture is actually exacerbating shyness, in both incidence and degree.

Another effect of hyperculture is what I call identity intensity. Our society is not only getting faster, it is getting louder and brighter. It takes an increasingly powerful personality to be recognized. We see this in the emergence of shock jocks like Howard Stern and outrageous characters like Dennis Rodman. People have to call attention to themselves in ways that are more and more extreme just to be noticed at all. That, of course, puts the shy at a further disadvantage.

We are also undergoing "interpersonal disenfranchisement." Simply put, we are disconnecting from one another. Increasingly, we deal with the hyperculture cacophony by cocooning—commuting home with headphones on while working on our laptops. We go from our cubicle to the car to our gated community, maintaining contact with only a small circle of friends and family. As other people become just e-mail addresses or faceless voices at the other end of electronic transactions, it becomes easier and easier to mistreat and disrespect them. The cost of such disconnection is a day-to-day loss of civility and an increase in rudeness. And, again, the shy pay. They are the first to be excluded, bullied or treated in a hostile manner.

As we approach the limits of our ability to deal with the complexities of our lives, we begin to experience a state of anxiety. We either approach or avoid. And, indeed, we are seeing both phenomena—a polarization of behavior in which we see increases in both aggression, marked by a general loss of manners that has been widely observed, and in withdrawal, one form of which is shyness. Surveys we have conducted reliably show that over the last decade and a half, the incidence of shyness has risen from 40% to 48%.

So it is no accident that the pharmaceutical industry has chosen this cultural moment to introduce the antidepressant Paxil as a treatment for social phobia. Paxil is touted as a cure for being "allergic to people." One of the effects of hyperculture is to make people impatient for anything but a pill that instantly reduces their anxiety level.

The use of Paxil, however, operates against self-awareness. It makes shyness into a medical or psychiatric problem, which it has never been. It essentially labels as pathology what is a personality trait. I think it is a mistake for doctors to hand out a physiological remedy when we know that there are cognitive elements operating within individuals, communication difficulties existing between individuals, and major forces residing outside of individuals that are making it difficult for people to interact.

It is much easier for the shy to take a pill, doctors figure, than for them to take the time to adjust to their cautious tendencies, modify faulty social comparisons or learn to be more civil to others. The promise of Paxil does not include teaching the shy to develop the small talk skills they so desperately need.

Strategies of the Shy

"I have tried to overcome my shyness by being around people as much as possible and getting involved in the conversation; however, after a few seconds, I become quiet. I have a problem keeping conversation flowing."

In our survey, we asked people what they do to cope with their shyness. What we found surprised us. The shy put a lot of effort into overcoming their shyness, but the strategies they use are largely ineffective, sometimes even counterproductive. Occasionally their solutions are potentially dangerous.

Ninety-one percent of shy respondents said they had made at least some effort to overcome their shyness. By far, the top technique they employ is forced extroversion. Sixty-seven percent of them said they make themselves go to parties, bars, dances, the mall—places that will put them in proximity to others. That is good. But unfortunately, they expect the others to do all the work, to approach them and draw them out of their isolation. Simply showing up is not enough. Not only is it ineffective, it cedes control of interactions to others.

But it exemplifies the mistaken expectations the shy often have about social life. Hand in hand with the expectation that others will approach them is their sense of perfectionism. The shy believe that anything they say has to come out perfect, sterling, supremely witty, as if everyday life is some kind of sitcom. They believe that everybody is watching and judging them—a special kind of narcissism.

> **Once the shy learn to focus more on the lives of other people, shyness no longer controls them.**

Their second most popular strategy is self-induced cognitive modification: thinking happy thoughts, or the "Stuart Smalley Effect"—remember the sketch from *Saturday Night Live?* "I'm

> # Shy people tend either to reveal information about themselves too quickly, or hold back and move too slowly.

good enough, I'm smart enough, and, doggone it, people like me." Twenty-two percent of the shy try to talk themselves into not being shy. But just talking to yourself doesn't work. You have to know how to talk to other people. And you have to be around other people. The shy seldom combine extroversion with cognitive modification.

Fifteen percent of the shy turn to self-help books and seminars, which is great. But not enough people do it.

And about 12 % of the shy turn to what I call liquid extroversion. They are a distinct population of people, who, often beginning in adolescence, ingest drugs or alcohol to deal with their shyness. They self-medicate as a social lubricant, to give them courage. And while it may remove inhibitions, it doesn't provide them with what they desperately need—actual social skills, knowledge about how to be with others. Further, drinking interferes with their cognitive functioning.

Liquid extroversion poses the great danger of overconsumption of alcohol. Indeed, we have found in separate studies that a significant proportion of problem drinkers in the general population are shy.

But "shy alcoholics" tell us they do not like having to drink to perform better; they feel uneasy and lack confidence in their true selves. They begin to believe that people will like them only if they are outgoing, not the way they really are. Interestingly, the largest program for problem drinkers, Alcoholics Anonymous, works squarely against shy people. Whereas the shy are slow to warm up, AA asks people to stand up right away, to be highly visible, to immediately disclose highly personal information. It is my belief that there needs to be an AA for the shy, a program that takes into consideration the nature and dynamics of shyness. A meeting might, for example, begin by having a leader speak for the first 45 minutes while people get comfortable, followed by a break in which the leader is available to answer questions. That then paves the way for a general question-and-answer period.

Cyberbonding

"I can be anyone I want to be on the Internet and yet mostly be myself, because I know I will never meet these people I'm talking with and can close out if I get uncomfortable."

"I think the Internet hinders people in overcoming their shyness. You can talk to someone but you don't have to actually interact with them. You can sit in your room and not REALLY socialize."

Another strategy of the shy is electronic extroversion. The Net is a great social facilitator. It enables people to reach out to many others and join in at their own speed, perhaps observing in a chat room before participating. Still, Internet interaction requires less effort than face-to-face interaction, so it may increase their frustration and cause difficulties in real-life situations where social skills are not only required, but born and learned.

We know that people start out using the Internet for informational purposes, then progress to use that is social in nature, such as entering chat rooms; some then progress to personal use, talking about more intimate topics and disclosing information about themselves. The danger of electronic extroversion is that anonymity makes it easy for the shy to misrepresent themselves and to deceive others, violating the trust that is the foundation of social life.

And talk about disconnecting. The irony of a World Wide Web packed with endless amounts of information is that it can also be isolating. As individuals head to their own favorite bookmarked sites, they cut out all the disagreement of the world and reinforce their own narrow perspective, potentially leading to alienation, disenfranchisement and intolerance for people who are different.

In addition, the shy are more vulnerable to instant intimacy because of their lack of social know-how. Normally, relationships progress by way of a reasonably paced flow of self-disclosure that is reciprocal in nature. A disclosure process that moves too

SHYNESS SURVEY

- 64% of shy individuals view their shyness as a result of external factors beyond their control, such as early family experiences, overprotective parents or peer victimization.

- 24% attribute shyness to internal factors within their control, such as intrapersonal difficulties, like low self-esteem and high self-consciousness, or interpersonal difficulties, like poor social skills and dating difficulties.

- 62% experience feelings of shyness daily.

- 82% report shyness as an undesirable experience.

- **Types of Individuals who make the shy feel shy:**

  75% strangers
  71% persons of the opposite sex, in a group
  65% persons of the opposite sex, one-on-one
  56% persons of the same sex, in a group
  45% relatives, other than immediate family
  38% persons of the same sex, one-on-one
  22% their parents
  20% siblings

- 46% believe their shyness can be overcome.

- 7.2% do not believe their shyness can be overcome.

- 85% are willing to work seriously at overcoming shyness.

quickly—and computer anonymity removes the stigma of getting sexually explicit—doesn't just destroy courtship; it is a reliable sign of maladjustment. Shy people tend either to reveal information about themselves too quickly, or hold back and move too slowly.

Like most cultural influences, the Internet is neither devil nor angel. It's a social tool that works in different ways, depending on how it's used.

The Solution to Shyness

"I was very shy as a kid. Every situation scared me if it required interacting with others. After high school and into college, I became much less shy. I consciously made each interaction an exercise in overcoming shyness. Just talking to people I didn't know, getting a part-time job, volunteering. I had always been afraid to sing in front of people, but now I sing all the time. That's a big deal to me."

Every shy person believes that shyness is a problem located exclusively within the self. But our work suggests that the solution to shyness lies outside the self. To break free of the prison of shyness, you must stop dwelling on your own insecurities and become more aware of the people around you.

Through our survey, we have identified a group of people we call the successfully shy. Essentially, they recognize that they are shy. They develop an understanding of the nature and dynamics of shyness, its impact on the body, on cognitive processes and on behavior. And they take action based on that self-awareness. The successfully shy overcome their social anxiety by letting go of their self-consciousness, that inward focus of attention on the things they can't do well (like tell a joke). They accept that they aren't great at small talk or that they get so nervous in social situations that they can't draw on what is inside their mind. Or that they are paying so much attention to their feelings that they don't pay full attention to the person they're talking to. In place of self-consciousness, they substitute self-awareness. Rather than becoming anxious about their silence in a conversation, they plan ahead of time

to have something to say, or rehearse asking questions. They arrive early at parties to feel comfortable in their new setting. By contrast, less successful shy people arrive late in an effort to blend in.

The fact is, these are the same kinds of strategies that non-shy people employ. Many of them develop a repertoire of opening gambits for conversation. When among others, they engage in social reconnaissance—they wait to gather information about speakers and a discussion before jumping in.

The successfully shy also take steps at the transpersonal level, getting involved in the lives of others. They start small, making sure their day-to-day exchanges involve contact with other people. When they pick up a newspaper, for instance, they don't just put their money on the counter. They focus on the seller, thanking him or her for the service. This creates a social environment favorable to positive interactions. On a larger scale, I encourage volunteering. Once the shy are more outwardly focused on the lives of other people, shyness no longer controls them.

The successfully shy don't change who they are. They change the way they think and the actions they make. There is nothing wrong with being shy. In fact, I have come to believe that what our society needs is not less shyness but a little more.

Bernardo Carducci, Ph.D., is the director of the Shyness Research Institute at Indiana University Southeast. His last article for PSYCHOLOGY TODAY, *also on shyness, appeared in the December 1995 issue.*

READ MORE ABOUT IT

Shyness: A Bold New Approach, Bernardo J. Carducci, Ph.D. (HarperCollins, 1999)

The Shy Child, Philip G. Zimbardo, Ph.D., Shirley L. Radl (ISHK Book Service, 1999)

What's in a face?

**Do facial expressions reflect inner feelings?
Or are they social devices for influencing others?**

BY BETH AZAR
Monitor staff

After 30 years of renewed interest in facial expression as a key clue to human emotions, frowns are appearing on critics' faces. The face, they say, isn't the mirror to emotions it's been held out to be.

The use of facial expression for measuring people's emotions has dominated psychology since the late 1960s when Paul Ekman, PhD, of the University of California, San Francisco and Carroll Izard, PhD, of the University of Delaware, reawakened the study of emotion by linking expressions to a group of basic emotions.

Many took that work to imply that facial expressions provided the key to people's feelings. But in recent years the psychology literature has been sprinkled with hotly worded attacks by detractors who claim that there is no one-to-one correspondence between facial expressions and emotions. In fact, they argue, there's no evidence to support a link between what appears on someone's face and how they feel inside.

But this conflict masks some major areas of agreement, says Joseph Campos, PhD, of the University of California at Berkeley. Indeed, he says, "there is profound agreement that the face, along with the voice, body posture and hand gestures, forecast to outside observers what people will do next."

The point of contention remains in whether the face also says something about a person's internal state. Some, such as Izard, say, "Absolutely." Detractors, such as Alan Fridlund, PhD, of the University of California, Santa Barbara, say an adamant "No." And others, including Campos and Ekman, land somewhere in the middle. The face surely can provide important information about emotion, but it is only one of many tools and should never be used as a "gold standard" of emotion as some researchers, particularly those studying children, have tended to do.

"The face is a component [of emotion]," says Campos. "But to make it the center of study of the human being experiencing an emotion is like saying the only thing you need to study in a car is the transmission. Not that the transmission is unimportant, but it's only part of an entire system."

WHERE IT ALL BEGAN

Based on findings that people label photos of prototypical facial expressions with words that represent the same basic emotions—a smile represents joy, a scowl represents anger—Ekman and Izard pioneered the idea that by carefully measuring facial expression, they could evaluate people's true emotions. In fact, since the 1970s, Ekman and his colleague Wallace Friesen, PhD, have dominated the field of emotion research with their theory that when an emotion occurs, a cascade of electrical impulses, emanating from emotion centers in the brain, trigger specific facial expressions and other physiological changes—such as increased or decreased heart rate or heightened blood pressure.

If the emotion comes on slowly, or is rather weak, the theory states, the impulse might not be strong enough to trigger the expression. This would explain in part why there can sometimes be emotion without expression,

> "The face is like a switch on a railroad track. It affects the trajectory of the social interaction the way the switch would affect the path of the train."
>
> *Alan Fridlund*
> *University of California, Santa Barbara*

they argue. In addition, cultural "display rules"—which determine when and whether people of certain cultures display emotional expressions—can derail this otherwise automatic process, the theory states. Facial expressions evolved in humans as signals to others about how they feel, says Ekman.

From *Monitor on Psychology,* January 2000, pp. 44-45. © 2000 by the American Psychological Association. Reprinted by permission.

"At times it may be uncomfortable or inconvenient for others to know how we feel," he says. "But in the long run, over the course of evolution, it was useful to us as signalers. So, when you see an angry look on my face, you know that I may be preparing to respond in an angry fashion, which means that I may attack or abruptly withdraw."

THE FACE IS LIKE A SWITCH

Although Fridlund strongly disagrees with Ekman in his writings, arguing that expressions carry no inherent meaning, the two basically agree that facial expressions forecast people's future actions. But instead of describing expressions from the point of view of the expresser, as Ekman tends to do, Fridlund thinks more in terms of people who perceive the expressions.

Expressions evolved to elicit behaviors from others, says Fridlund. So, a smile may encourage people to approach while a scowl may impel them to stay clear, and a pout may elicit words of sympathy and reassurance. And, he contends, expressions are inherently social. Even when people are alone they are holding an internal dialogue with another person, or imagining themselves in a social situation.

"The face is like a switch on a railroad track," says Fridlund. "It affects the trajectory of the social interaction the way the switch would affect the path of the train."

Thinking of facial expressions as tools for influencing social interactions provides an opportunity to begin predicting when certain facial expressions will occur and will allow more precise theories about social interactions, says Fridlund. Studies by him and others find that expressions occur most often during pivotal points in social interactions—during greetings, social crisis or times of appeasement, for example.

"At these pivotal points, where there's an approach, or proximity, or more intimacy, the face as well as the gestures form a kind of switching sta-

tion for the possibilities of social interactions," says Fridlund.

The University of Amsterdam's Nico Frijda, PhD, agrees that expressions are a means to influence others. They also, he believes, occur when people prepare to take some kind of action whether there are others present or not. For example, if you're scared and want to protect yourself, you frown and draw your brows in preparation—what Ekman would call a "fear" expression. But there is no one-to-one correspondence between the face and specific emotions, Frijda contends.

"There is some affinity between certain emotions and certain expressions," he says, "if only because some emotions imply a desire for vigorous action, and some facial expressions manifest just that."

NOT A 'GOLD STANDARD'

Herein lies the major point of contention within the facial expression community, says Berkeley's Campos.

"All sides agree that the face—and voice and posture, for that matter—forecast what a person will do next," he says. "But over and above that, is feeling involved?"

Although much work in the emotion literature relies on a link between facial expression and emotions, there's a paucity of evidence supporting it.

"There's some sense in which faces express emotion, but only in the sense that everything expresses emotion," says psychologist James Russell, PhD, of the University of British Columbia, a long-time critic of the expression-emotion link. "Music does, posture does, words do, tone of voice does, your behavior does. The real question is, 'Is there anything special about faces?' And there we really don't know much."

What's more likely, argues Russell, is that facial expressions tell others something about the overall character of a person's mood—whether it's positive or negative—and context then provides details about specific emotions.

Others, including Ekman and Campos, contend that the face can display information about emotions. But, they admit, it is by no means a "gold standard." The face is only one of many measures researchers can use to infer emotion. And those who only examine faces when trying to study emotion will jump to false conclusions.

"There is a link between facial expression and emotion," explains developmental psychologist Linda Camras, PhD, of DePaul University. "But it's not a one-to-one kind of relationship as many once thought. There are many situations where emotion is experienced, yet no prototypic facial expression is displayed. And there are times when a facial expression appears with no corresponding emotion."

In a classic set of experiments with infants, Camras found that some facial expressions can occur in the absence of the emotions they supposedly represent.

"An emotion has to be plausible [for the situation you're examining]," she says. "You can't do blind coding of facial expression and necessarily be on the right track, even for infants."

But to say, as Fridlund does, that there's no connection between some facial expressions and some emotions is simply wrong, says Ekman. When we look at people's expressions, he says, we don't receive direct information about their heart rate or other physiological changes that accompany emotions. We might even think, "He's going to whack me" rather than "He's angry," says Ekman.

"But these signals—facial expressions and physiological changes associated with internal emotions—can't exist independently," he contends.

FURTHER REFERENCE

Ekman, P., & Rosenberg, E. (1997). *What the Face Reveals.* New York: Oxford University Press.

Fridlund, A. (1994). *Human Facial Expression: An Evolutionary View.* San Diego, CA: Academic Press.

Russell, J., & Fernandez-Dols, J. M. (Eds.) (1997). *The Psychology of Facial Expression.* New York: Cambridge University Press.

How to Spot a Liar

With some careful observation—
and a little help from new software—anyone can
learn to be a lie detector

By JAMES GEARY/London
With reporting by Eric Silver/Jerusalem

"You can tell a lie but you will give yourself away. Your heart will race. Your skin will sweat . . . I will know. I am the lie detector." Thus began each episode of Lie Detector, a strange cross between a relationship counseling session and an episode of the Jerry Springer Show that ran on British daytime television last year. Against a backdrop of flashing computer screens and eerie blue light, participants—usually feuding couples but sometimes warring neighbors or aggrieved business partners—sat on a couch and were quizzed by the program's host. A frequent topic of discussion was one guest's suspicion that his or her partner had been unfaithful. The person suspected of infidelity denied it, of course, and the object of the show was to find out—through cross-examination and computer analysis—whether that person was telling the truth.

However much we may abhor it, deception comes naturally to all living things. Birds do it by feigning injury to lead hungry predators away from nesting young. Spider crabs do it by disguise: adorning themselves with strips of kelp and other debris, they pretend to be something they are not—and so escape their enemies. Nature amply rewards successful deceivers by allowing them to survive long enough to mate and reproduce. So it may come as no surprise to learn that human beings—who, according to psychologist Gerald Jellison of the University of South California, are lied to about 200 times a day, roughly one untruth every five minutes—often deceive for exactly the same reasons: to save their own skins or to get something they can't get by other means.

But knowing how to catch deceit can be just as important a survival skill as knowing how to tell a lie and get away with it. A person able to spot falsehood quickly is unlikely to be swindled by an unscrupulous business associate or hoodwinked by a devious spouse. Luckily, nature provides more than enough clues to trap dissemblers in their own tangled webs—if you know where to look. By closely observing facial expressions, body language and tone of voice, practically anyone can recognize the telltale signs of lying. Researchers are even programming computers—like those used on Lie Detector—to get at the truth by analyzing the same physical cues available to the naked eye and ear. "With the proper training, many people can learn to reliably detect lies," says Paul Ekman, professor of psychology at the University of California, San Francisco, who has spent the past 15 years studying the secret art of deception.

In order to know what kind of lies work best, successful liars need to accurately assess other people's emotional states. Ekman's research shows that this same emotional intelligence is essential for good lie detectors, too. The emotional state to watch out for is stress, the conflict most liars feel between the truth and what they actually say and do.

Even high-tech lie detectors don't detect lies as such; they merely detect the physical cues of emotions, which may or may not correspond to what the person being tested is saying. Polygraphs, for instance, measure respiration, heart rate and skin conductivity, which tend to increase when people are nervous—as they usually are when lying. Nervous people typically perspire, and the salts contained in perspiration conduct electricity. That's why a sudden leap in skin conductivity indicates nervousness—about getting caught, perhaps?—which might, in turn, suggest that someone is being economical with the truth. On the other hand, it might also mean that the lights in the television studio are too hot—which is one reason polygraph tests are inadmissible in court. "Good lie detectors don't rely on a single sign," Ekman says, "but interpret clusters of verbal and nonverbal clues that suggest someone might be lying."

Those clues are written all over the face. Because the musculature of the face is directly connected to the areas of the brain that process emotion, the countenance can be a window to the soul. Neurological studies even suggest that genuine emotions travel different pathways through the brain than insincere ones. If a patient paralyzed by stroke on one side of the face, for example, is asked to smile deliberately, only the mobile side of the mouth is raised. But tell that same person a funny joke, and the patient breaks into a full and spontaneous smile. Very few people—most notably, actors and politicians—are able to consciously control all of their facial expressions. Lies can often be caught when the liar's true feelings briefly leak through the mask of deception. "We don't think before we feel," Ekman says. "Expressions tend to show up on the face before we're even conscious of experiencing an emotion."

One of the most difficult facial expressions to fake—or conceal, if it is genuinely felt—is sadness. When someone is truly sad, the forehead wrinkles with grief and the inner corners of the eyebrows are pulled up. Fewer than 15% of the people Ekman tested were able to produce this eyebrow movement voluntarily. By contrast, the lowering of the eyebrows associated with an angry scowl can be replicated at will by almost everybody. "If someone claims they are sad and the inner corners of their eyebrows don't go up," Ekman says, "the sadness is probably false."

The smile, on the other hand, is one of the easiest facial expressions to counterfeit. It takes just two muscles—the zygomaticus major muscles that extend from the cheekbones to the corners of the lips—to produce a grin. But there's a catch. A genuine smile affects not only the corners of the lips but also the orbicularis oculi, the muscle around the eye that produces the distinctive "crow's-feet" associated with people who laugh a lot. A counterfeit grin can be unmasked if the lip corners go up, the eyes crinkle but the inner corners of the eyebrows are not lowered, a movement controlled by the orbicularis oculi that is difficult to fake. The absence of lowered eyebrows is one reason why false smiles look so strained and stiff.

Ekman and his colleagues have classified all the muscle movements—ranging from the thin, taut lips of fury to the arched eyebrows of surprise—that underlie the complete repertoire of human facial expressions. In addition to the nervous tics and jitters that can give liars away, Ekman discovered that fibbers often allow the truth to slip through in brief, unguarded facial expressions. Lasting no more than a quarter of a second, these fleeting glimpses of a person's true emotional state—or "microexpressions," as Ekman calls them—are reliable guides to veracity.

In a series of tests, Ekman interviewed and videotaped a group of male American college students about their opinions regarding capital punishment. Some participants were instructed to tell the truth—whether they were for or against the death penalty—and some were instructed to lie. Liars who successfully fooled the interviewer received $50. Ekman then studied the tapes to map the microexpressions of mendacity.

One student, for example, appeared calm and reasonable as he listed the reasons why the death penalty was wrong. But every time he expressed these opinions, he swiftly, almost imperceptibly, shook his head. But the movement is so subtle and quick many people don't even see it until it's pointed out to them. While his words explained the arguments against capital punishment, the quick, involuntary shudder of his head was saying loud and clear, "No, I don't believe this!" He was, in fact, lying, having been for many years a firm supporter of the death penalty.

Another student also said that he was against the death penalty. But during the interview, he spoke very slowly, paused often, and rarely looked the interrogator in the eye, instead fixing his gaze on some vague point on the floor. Speech that is too slow (or too fast), frequent hesitations, lack of direct eye contact: these are all classic symptoms of lying. But this man was telling the truth. He paused and hesitated because he was shy. After all, even honest and normally composed individuals can become flustered if they believe others suspect them of lying. His lack of eye contact could be explained by the fact that he came from Asia, where an averted gaze is often a sign of deference and respect, not deception. This scenario highlights Ekman's admonition that before branding someone a liar, you must first know that person's normal behavior patterns and discount other explanations, such as cultural differences.

Ekman has used this tape to test hundreds of subjects. His conclusion: most people are lousy lie detectors, with few individuals able to spot duplicity more than 50% of the time. But Ekman's most recent study, published last year in Psychological Science, found that four groups of people did significantly better than chance: members of the U.S. Central Intelligence Agency, other U.S. federal law enforcement officers, a handful of Los Angeles County sheriffs and a group of clinical psychologists. Reassuringly, perhaps, the federal officials performed best, accurately detecting liars 73% of the time. What makes these groups so good at lie catching? According to Ekman, it's training, experience and motivation. The jobs—and in some cases, the lives—of everyone in these groups depend on their ability to pick up deceit.

Ekman has used his findings to assist law enforcement agents—including members of the U.S. Secret Service and Federal Bureau of Investigation, Britain's Scotland Yard and the Israeli police force—in criminal investigations and antiterrorist activities. He refuses to work with politicians. "It is unlikely that judging deception from demeanor alone will ever be admissible in court," Ekman says. "But the research shows that it's possible for some people to make highly accurate judgements about lying without any special aids, such as computers."

But for those who still prefer a bit of technological assistance, there's the Verdicator—a device that, according to its 27-year-old inventor Amir Liberman, enables anyone equipped with a personal computer and a phone or microphone to catch a liar. A person's tone of voice can be just as revealing as the expression on his face. A low tone, for example, can suggest a person is lying or is stressed, while a higher pitch can mean excitement. Liberman claims the Verdicator, a $2,500 piece of software produced by Integritek Technologies in Petah Tikvah near Tel Aviv, is between 85% and 95% accurate

THE LYIN' KING

Four signs that may indicate deception

1. AN EMBLEM is a gesture with a specific meaning, like shrugging the shoulders to say, "I don't know." An emblem may be a sign of deceit if only part of the gesture is performed (a one-shoulder shrug, for example) or if it is performed in a concealed manner.

2. MANIPULATORS are repetitive touching motions like scratching the nose, tapping the foot or twisting the hair. They tend to increase when people are nervous, and may be an attempt to conceal incriminating facial expressions.

3. AN ILLUSTRATOR is a movement that emphasizes speech. Illustrators increase with emotion, so too few may indicate false feelings while too many may be an attempt to distract attention from signs of deceit on the face.

4. MICROEXPRESSIONS flash across the face in less than a quarter of a second—a frown, for example, that is quickly covered up by a grin. Though fleeting, they can reveal subtle clues about the true feelings that a person may wish to repress or conceal.

"With proper training, many people can learn to reliably detect lies."

"It would be an impossible world if no one lied."

James Geary/London
With reporting by Eric Silver/Jerusalem.

in determining whether the person on the other end of the line is lying, an accuracy rate better than that for traditional polygraphs. "Our software knows how to size you up," Liberman boasts.

The Verdicator delivers its results by analyzing voice fluctuations that are usually inaudible to the human ear. When a person is under stress, anxiety may cause muscle tension and reduce blood flow to the vocal cords, producing a distinctive pattern of sound waves. Liberman has catalogued these patterns and programmed the Verdicator to distinguish among tones that indicate excitement, cognitive stress—the difference between what you think and what you say—and outright deceit. Once linked to a communications device and computer, the Verdicator monitors the subtle vocal tremors of your conversational partner and displays an assessment of that person's veracity on the screen. "The system can tell how nervous you are," Liberman explains. "It builds a

psychological profile of what you feel and compares it to patterns associated with deception." And the Verdicator has one great advantage over the polygraph: the suspect doesn't need to know he's being tested. To be accurate, though, the Verdicator must pick up changes—which might indicate deceit—in a person's normal voice.

During the Monica Lewinsky scandal, Liberman demonstrated the system on President Clinton's famous disclaimer, "I did not have sexual relations with that woman." After analyzing an audio tape of the statement 100 times, the Verdicator showed that Clinton "was telling the truth," Liberman says, "but he had very high levels of cognitive stress, or 'guilt knowledge.' He didn't have sexual relations, but he did have something else."

Integritek will not name the law enforcement agencies, banks or financial institutions that are using the Verdicator. But company president Naaman Boury says that last year more than 500 Verdicators were sold in

North and South America, Australia, Asia and Europe. The Japanese firm Atlus is marketing a consumer version of the Verdicator in Asia. "We get the best results—close to 95% accuracy—in Japan," Liberman reports. "The Japanese feel very uncomfortable when lying. We get the poorest results—nearer 85% accuracy—in Russia, where people seldom seem to say what they really feel."

In moderation, lying is a normal—even necessary—part of life. "It would be an impossible world if no one lied," Ekman says. But by the same token, it would be an intolerable world if we could never tell when someone was lying. For those lies that are morally wrong and potentially harmful, would-be lie detectors can learn a lot from looking and listening very carefully. Cheating partners, snake oil salesmen and scheming politicians, beware! The truth is out there.

James Geary/London
With reporting by Eric Silver/Jerusalem

Revealing Personal Secrets

Anita E. Kelly[1]

Department of Psychology, University of Notre Dame, Notre Dame, Indiana

Abstract
Both the health benefits and the potential drawbacks of revealing personal secrets (i.e., those that directly involve the secret keeper) are reviewed. Making the decision to reveal personal secrets to others involves a trade-off. On the one hand, secret keepers can feel better by revealing their secrets and gaining new insights into them. On the other hand, secret keepers can avoid looking bad before important audiences (such as their bosses or therapists) by not revealing their secrets. Making a wise decision to reveal a personal secret hinges on finding an appropriate confidant—someone who is discreet, who is perceived by the secret keeper to be nonjudgmental, and who is able to offer new insights into the secret.

Keywords
revealing secrets; new insights; confidants

Psychologists and laypersons have long believed that keeping personal secrets is stressful and that unburdening oneself of such secrets offers emotional relief and physiological benefits. Supporting this notion is recent experimental research that has demonstrated the health benefits of revealing personal secrets (i.e., ones that directly involve the secret keeper). These findings lead to several key questions: Why do these health benefits occur? When does revealing personal secrets to various confidants backfire? And, finally, when should someone reveal his or her personal secrets?

SECRECY

Secrecy involves actively hiding private information from others. The most painful or traumatic personal experiences are often concealed, and most secrets are likely to involve negative or stigmatizing information that pertains to the secret keepers themselves. For example, people may keep secret the fact that they have AIDS, are alcoholic, or have been raped. Secrecy has also been called self-concealment and active inhibition of disclosure.

HEALTH BENEFITS OF REVEALING SECRETS

The belief that secrecy is problematic is supported by studies showing that, on average, people who tend to conceal personal information have more physical problems, such as headaches, nausea, and back pains, and are more anxious, shy, and depressed than people who do not tend to conceal personal information. Recent research has also shown that gay men who tend to conceal their sexual orientation from others are at a greater risk for cancers and infectious diseases than those who do not conceal their orientation.

Moreover, research has shown that talking or writing about private traumatic experiences is associated with health benefits, such as improved immunological functioning and fewer visits to the doctor. For example, a survey of spouses of suicide and accidental-death victims demonstrated that participants who had talked about the loss of their spouses with family and friends suffered fewer health problems the year after the loss than participants who did not speak with others about their loss (Pennebaker & O'Heeron, 1984). These correlations remained

From *Current Directions in Psychological Science*, August 1999, pp. 105-109. © 1999 by Anita E. Kelly and the American Psychological Society. Reprinted by permission of Blackwell Publishers.

even in an analysis that statistically adjusted for the number of friends these individuals had before and after the loss of the spouse.

Particularly compelling evidence concerning the benefits of revealing secrets has emerged from a series of in-the-field and laboratory experiments. One experiment showed that advanced-breast-cancer patients who were randomly assigned to a group that was designed to encourage them to talk about their emotions survived twice as long as patients assigned to a routine oncological-care group (Spiegel, Bloom, Kraemer, & Gottheil, 1989). In another experiment, medical students were randomly assigned to write about either private traumatic events or control topics for four consecutive days and then were vaccinated against hepatitis B (Petrie, Booth, Pennebaker, Davison, & Thomas, 1995). The group that wrote about traumatic events had significantly higher antibody levels against hepatitis B at the 4- and 6-month follow-ups than did the control group, suggesting that emotional expression of traumatic experiences can lead to improved immune functioning.

WHAT IS IT ABOUT REVEALING SECRETS THAT IS BENEFICIAL?

It is believed that revealing secrets offers these health benefits because the revealer gains new insights into the trauma and no longer has to expend cognitive and emotional resources actively hiding the trauma (Pennebaker, 1997). It has also been suggested that gaining catharsis (i.e., expressing pent-up emotions behaviorally) may play an important role in reducing one's level of emotional arousal surrounding a troubling event (Polivy, 1998), even though some studies have raise the questions of whether catharsis actually purges or provokes emotions (Polivy, 1998).

Because of the controversy surrounding the benefits of catharsis,

my colleagues and I recently conducted an experiment that directly compared the effect of gaining catharsis with the effects of gaining new insights into one's troubling secrets (Kelly, Klusas, von Weiss, & Kenny, 1999, Study 2). Undergraduates ($N = 85$) were randomly assigned to one of three groups, which differed as to whether they were asked (a) to try to gain new insights through writing about their secrets, (b) to try to gain catharsis by writing about their secrets, or (c) to write about their previous day. The results revealed that the new-insights group felt significantly better about their secrets after their writing than did the other groups, and thus the findings support the idea that the key to recovery from troubling secrets is gaining new insights. Correlational analyses of the content of the writing showed that participants' coming to terms with their secrets mediated the relation between their gaining new insights and feeling better about their secrets. In other words, it was only through coming to terms with their secrets that participants seemed to benefit from gaining new insights into them. These findings are consistent with the results from a series of writing-about-trauma studies which showed that when participants increased their use of words associated with insightful and causal thinking, they tended to experience improved physical health (Pennebaker, Mayne, & Francis, 1997, Study 1).

The reason why gaining new insights is likely to be curative is that people may be able to find closure on the secrets and avoid what has been termed the Zeigarnik effect, wherein people actively seek to attain a goal when they have failed to attain the goal or failed to disengage from it. Zeigarnik (1927) showed that people continue to think about and remember interrupted tasks more than finished ones, suggesting that they may have a need for completion or resolution of events. Revealing a secret with the explicit intention of gaining a new perspec-

tive on it may help people feel a sense of resolution about the secret.

SELF-PRESENTATION AND THE ROLE OF THE CONFIDANT

The findings from the experiments described so far clearly suggest that it is healthy to reveal one's secrets. However, almost all of the experiments conducted to date have involved revealing secrets in an anonymous setting, and the health benefits observed in those experiments may not generalize to circumstances in which people reveal unfavorable or stigmatizing information about themselves to important audiences (e.g., their coworkers or friends) in their everyday interactions. In such circumstances, the revealers may perceive that that they are being rejected by and alienated from the listeners.

Supporting this concern are the results from a 9-year longitudinal study of initially healthy, HIV-positive gay men who were sensitive to social rejection. Those who tended to conceal their sexual orientation from others experienced a slower progression of HIV-related symptoms than did those who tended to reveal their sexual orientation to others (Cole, Kemeny, & Taylor, 1997). These results qualify these same researchers' finding, referred to earlier, that gay men who tended to conceal their sexual orientation were at a greater risk for cancers and infectious diseases.

The essence of the problem with revealing personal, undesirable information is that revealers may come to see themselves in undesirable ways if others know their stigmatizing secrets. A number of experiments from the self-presentation literature have demonstrated that describing oneself as having undesirable qualities, such as being depressed or introverted, to various audiences leads to negative shifts in one's self-beliefs and behaviors (e.g., Schlenker, Dlugolecki, & Doherty, 1994; Tice, 1992). Moreover, a recent in-the-field study showed that among a sample of therapy outpatients who had received an average of 11 therapy sessions, the clients (40.5%) who reported that they were keeping a relevant secret from their counselors actually had a greater reduction in their symptomatology than did those who were not keeping a relevant secret (Kelly, 1998). These results were obtained after adjusting for clients' social-desirability scores (i.e., scores indicating their tendency to try to "look good" to other people) and their tendency to keep secrets in general. It is possible that clients hid negative aspects of themselves in an effort to provide desirable views of themselves for their therapists.

Another problem associated with revealing one's secrets is that confidants often cannot be trusted to keep the secrets or to protect one's identity. For example, in a study of college students' self-reports, the students indicated that when someone disclosed an emotional event to them, they in turn revealed the emotional disclosure to other people in 66% to 78% of the cases—despite the fact that these students were intimates of the original revealers in 85% of the cases (Christophe & Rime, 1997). Moreover, original disclosures that were of a high emotional intensity were more likely to be shared with others and were told to more people (specifically, to more than two people, on average) than disclosures that were low or moderate in emotional intensity. In addition, another study showed that in 78% of the cases in which the original event was disclosed to others, the name of the original revealer was explicitly mentioned. Christophe and Rime recommended that if people do not want others to learn about their emotional experiences, then they should avoid sharing the experiences with others altogether. It is important to note, however, that these researchers did not specifically ask the confidants if they had been sworn to secrecy.

In sum, two sets of findings qualify the conclusion that revealing se-

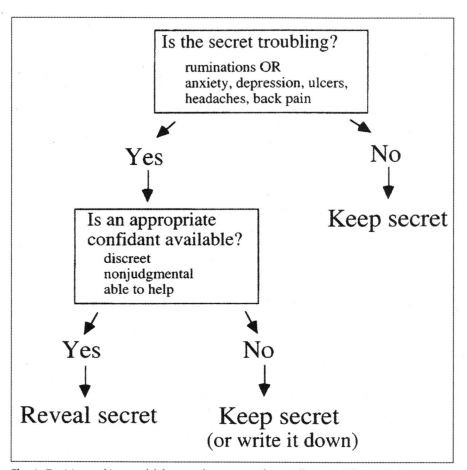

Fig. 1. Decision-making model for revealing secrets (from Kelly & McKillop, 1996).

crets leads to health benefits. First, the findings from the self-presentation literature suggest that revealing undesirable personal information to important audiences can have negative implications for one's self-image. Second, studies have shown that confidants often cannot be trusted to keep a secret or to protect the revealer's identity; therefore, revealing secrets may damage one's reputation.

WHEN TO REVEAL SECRETS

The findings just discussed, taken together, call attention to the trade-offs involved in revealing personal secrets. Revealing secrets can help a person feel better if he or she gains new insights into them, and yet not revealing secrets may help a person look good before important audiences (such as one's boss and thera-

pist). A way to avoid the negative side of revealing personal secrets is to carefully select a confidant. There is empirical support for the idea that if a troubled secret keeper has a confidant who can be trusted not to reveal a secret, is perceived by the secret keeper to be nonjudgmental, and is able to offer the secret helper new insights into the secret, then the secret keeper should reveal the secret to that person (see the model in Fig. 1; Kelly & McKillop, 1996). At the same time, however, because there are risks to one's identity associated with revealing secrets to others, people should reveal their personal secrets only if keeping the secrets seems to be troubling. Specifically, if a secret keeper is experiencing the symptoms that have been found to be associated with self-concealment, such as depression, ulcers, and headaches, then he or she should consider the possibility that the symptoms are the result of the secret keeping and should reveal the secret to an appropriate confidant. The rationale for taking such a risk is that even if the secret is not actually causing the symptoms, the secret helper is still unlikely to be harmed as a result of having revealed personal information to a discreet, nonjudgmental, and insightful confidant.

A limitation to the model for when to reveal secrets is the finding (Kelly, 1998), discussed earlier, that even with trained therapists who presumably fit all of the positive qualities of confidants, clients who were keeping a relevant secret experienced greater symptom reduction than those who were not keeping one. The seeming contradiction between this finding and the model can be resolved by the fact that the model emphasizes the revealer's perception of the confidant as nonjudgmental. It is likely that, at times, clients may imagine, or even accurately perceive, that their therapists are judgmental, particularly when the clients have committed unusually heinous acts, such as savagely beating their children. In such instances, the clients' decision to avoid revealing some of the details of their secrets to their therapists may not be problematic. It is possible that the clients may instead benefit from either discussing the themes of their secrets (e.g., experiencing uncontrollable anger) with the therapists or, as the model suggests, privately writing about the secrets in an effort to gain new insights into them.

CONCLUSION

Even though there is some exciting experimental evidence that revealing one's secrets leads to health benefits, these findings must be viewed with caution because the experiments have involved anonymous revealing of secrets and the findings may not generalize to everyday interactions with confidants. Researchers have not paid sufficient attention to the role of the confidant, and there is some preliminary evidence pointing to the possibility that revealing secrets, even to one's therapist, might backfire. Future research will need to examine the trade-offs between revealing and not revealing secrets to confidants who offer varying degrees of support. There is also a need for research assessing how a person's perceptions of such support can affect his or her self-images.

Recommended Reading

Derlega, V. J., Metts, S., Petronio, S., & Margulis, S. T. (1993). *Self-disclosure*. Newbury Park, CA: Sage.
Kelly, A. E., & McKillop, K. J. (1996). (See References)
Lane, J. D., & Wegner, D. M. (1995). The cognitive consequences of secrecy. *Journal of Personality and Social Psychology, 69,* 237–253.
Pennebaker, J. W. (1995). *Emotion, disclosure, and health*. Washington, DC: American Psychological Association.
Pennebaker, J. W. (1997). (See References)

Acknowledgments—I thank Thomas V. Merluzzi for his thoughtful feedback on a draft of this article.

Notes

1. Address correspondence to Anita E. Kelly, Department of Psychology, University of Notre Dame, Notre Dame, IN 46556; e-mail: kelly.79@nd.edu.

References

Christophe, V., & Rime, B. (1997). Exposure to the social sharing of emotion: Emotional impact, listener responses and secondary social sharing. *European Journal of Social Psychology, 27,* 37–54.
Cole, S. W., Kemeny, M. E., & Taylor, S. E. (1997). Social identity and physical health: Accelerated HIV progression in rejection-sensitive gay men. *Journal of Personality and Social Psychology, 72,* 320–335.
Kelly, A. E. (1998). Clients' secret keeping in outpatient therapy. *Journal of Counseling Psychology, 45,* 50–57.
Kelly, A. E., Klusas, J., von Weiss, R., & Kenny, C. (1999). *What is it about revealing secrets that leads to health benefits?* Unpublished manuscript, University of Notre Dame, Notre Dame, IN.
Kelly, A. E., & McKillop, K. J. (1996). Consequences of revealing personal secrets. *Psychological Bulletin, 120,* 450–465.
Pennebaker, J. W. (1997). *Opening up: The healing power of expressing emotions*. New York: Guilford Press.
Pennebaker, J. W., Mayne, T. J., & Francis, M. E. (1997). Linguistic predictors of adaptive bereavement. *Journal of Personality and Social Psychology, 72,* 863–871.
Pennebaker, J. W., & O'Heeron, R. C. (1984). Confiding in others and illness rate among spouses of suicide and accidental-death victims. *Journal of Abnormal Psychology, 93,* 473–476.
Petrie, K. J., Booth, R. J., Pennebaker, J. W., Davison, K. P., & Thomas, M. G. (1995). Disclosure of trauma and immune response to a hepatitis B vaccination program. *Journal of Consulting and Clinical Psychology, 63,* 787–792.
Policy, J. (1998). The effects of behavioral inhibition: Integrating internal cues, cognition, behavior, and affect. *Psychological Inquiry, 9,* 181–204.
Schlenker, B. R., Dlugolecki, D. W., & Doherty, K. (1994). The impact of self-presentations on self-appraisals and behavior: The power of public commitment. *Personality and Social Psychology Bulletin, 20,* 20–33.
Spiegel, D., Bloom, J. H., Kraemer, H. C., & Gottheil, E. (1989). Effects of psychosocial treatment of patients with metastatic breast cancer. *Lancet, 2,* 888–891.
Tice, D. M. (1992). Self-concept change and self-presentation: The looking glass self is also a magnifying glass. *Journal of Personality and Social Psychology, 63,* 435–451.
Zeigarnik, B. (1927). Uber das behalten von erledigten und unerledigten handlungen. *Psychologische Forschung, 9,* 1–85.

Discover the *Power* of Forgiveness

It's the hottest new medically proven lifesaver. Here's how you can use it

by Ellen Michaud

"I've done something very wrong." Carefully closing the door behind her, my friend Robin walked into my office and sat down. "I've come to apologize," she admitted, awkwardly smoothing her skirt.

Startled, I sat back in my chair. At 45, Robin was an ambitious woman who went after what she wanted. Apologies were not her style.

I looked over the top of my glasses at her. "You better tell me what you've done," I said. And for the next 5 minutes, she did. She told me how, from the day three years ago when the two of us had been promoted to senior positions within the company, she had privately bad-mouthed my work to our boss. Jealous of my success, she'd even encouraged our childless-by-choice boss to think that, as a working mother, I wouldn't be able to give the job the kind of time it required.

Robin took a deep breath and looked out the window behind my desk. "I don't like who I've become," she said quietly. "I'm trying to change."

She looked directly at me. "Can you ever forgive me?"

What's in It for Me?

Forgive her? Why would I forgive someone who had deliberately and knowingly betrayed me?

When I put the question to forgiveness researcher Robert Enright, PhD, a professor of educational psychology at the University of Wisconsin at Madison, he gave me the unvarnished facts: Unless I forgive the woman who tried to ruin my life, I could end up ruining it myself.

If I stop trusting people "because they always stab me in the back," I could miss out on some valuable and enriching friendships.

While my anger and resentment were perfectly natural—it's the way humans respond to injustice, says Dr. Enright—I ran the risk of letting my experience with Robin darken my attitude. My bitterness toward her could become a negative view of life that would affect how I think about everyone. For example, if I stop trusting people "because they always stab me in the back," I could miss out on some valuable and enriching friendships. And that would make me vulnerable to chronic anxiety, serious depression, general distrust, poor self-esteem, and a pervading sense of hopelessness.

What's more, those negative feelings can also trigger a cascade of stress hormones that accelerate the heart rate, shut down the immune system, and encourage blood clotting, which can lead to heart attacks and stroke, adds Richard Fitzgibbons, MD, a psychiatrist in suburban Philadelphia. In fact, **studies show that hanging on to anger and resentment increases your chance of a heart attack fivefold. It also increases your risk of cancer, high blood pressure, high cholesterol, and a host of chronic illnesses.**

Forgiveness, on the other hand, short-circuits that process entirely, says Dr. Fitzgibbons. It fosters healthful changes in both your attitude and your body, boosting your self-esteem and feelings of hope, as it lowers your blood pressure and heart rate. It can even help you sleep better.

What Forgiving Is . . . and Isn't

That's not to say forgiveness is easy. If your spouse cheats on you or your best friend betrays a confidence, forgiving them may take time—and it probably won't come easily. For most of us, "forgiveness is an intellectual decision you make to give up your anger and feelings for revenge," says Dr. Fitzgibbons.

Hidden Sources of ANGER

Sometimes we bury our anger so deeply that we no longer recognize its source. But it's easier to forgive when you can remember who did what to whom. For most people, the deepest disappointment in childhood and adolescence is with their fathers. "Their fathers simply haven't been there for them when they needed them. If you're in that particular boat, pay attention to the feelings you have for your dad," suggests Richard Fitzgibbons, MD, a psychiatrist in private practice near Philadelphia.

Here are other sources of hidden anger that Dr. Fitzgibbons says might be likely to affect you:

• anger with your children for not being sensitive to your needs

• anger with your spouse for ways in which he has disappointed you

• anger with an employer or a spouse's employer—particularly if one or the other of you has recently been downsized

---

But knowing what forgiveness is, and isn't, may help ease you into it. For example, forgiving someone who's done you wrong is not condoning what she did nor absolving her of guilt. It doesn't mean you've gone all soft and fuzzy toward her or that you're going to trust her or make yourself vulnerable in any way. If you decide to trust her at a later date, that's fine, says Dr. Fitzgibbons. But it's not necessary to trust, or even like, the other person again, in order to heal or maintain a healthy life. And forgiving is not forgetting: It *is* letting go of anger and hurt and moving on.

What *Doesn't* Work

"There are three ways to handle anger when someone hurts you," explains Dr. Fitzgibbons. "Deny it, express it, or forgive the person who caused it."

Denial doesn't work. That's just burying your anger, and anger rarely stays buried. What's more, studies show that denial leads to all sorts of mental illnesses, such as depression, which in turn can increase your risk of physical illnesses such as heart disease.

Expressing anger, while it seems helpful, can actually be equally harmful, according to Dr. Fitzgibbons, who first proposed using forgiveness as a therapeutic technique more than a decade ago. The problem is, most of us have tried the denial tactic at some point in our lives. But with so much buried anger, when we do finally express it, we risk detonating a hidden arsenal of deadly explosives that could ruin friendships, wreck marriages, and even harm our children.

According to *Prevention* advisor Redford B. Williams, MD, the director of the Behavioral Medicine Research Center at Duke University Medical Center in Durham, NC, the most important thing is to decide whether your anger requires action or not. "True anger is justifiable, and you'll need to act on it. Express it by assertion rather than blowing up." At other times you may be angry about something small or something that can't be changed. Either way, he adds, you can practice forgiveness as a way of getting out from under the anger.

How Forgiveness Can Heal You

Forgiveness heals by removing certain amounts of excess anger within a person each time they forgive someone, says Dr. Fitzgibbons. It also decreases the need for revenge and the need to make someone else change, explains Dr. Williams.

And there's now scientific support: Dr. Enright measured study participants' emotional states before and after they forgave those who had hurt them. He discovered that those who forgave eliminated feelings of anxiety and depression and boosted their

QUIZ:
How Forgiving Are You?

The Enright Forgiveness Inventory is a scientific test that measures how much you've forgiven someone for a particular offense. It's too long to be reproduced here, but Robert Enright, PhD, the psychologist who developed it, has come up with this shortened form especially for *Prevention*'s readers.

To see whether or not you've truly forgiven someone who's hurt you, think about a specific person and what he or she has done, says Dr. Enright. If there are a number of injustices, center on the most recent. Then respond to a, b, and c following each of the three statements by circling the number next to the answer that represents how you feel about the person who has hurt you.

SD = STRONGLY DISAGREE / D = DISAGREE
A = AGREE / SA = STRONGLY AGREE

1. The best description of my feelings is that I ...
a. resent him or her (SD–4, D–3, A–2, SA–1)
b. dislike him or her (SD–4, D–3, A–2, SA–1)
c. love him or her (SD–1, D–2, A–3, SA–4)

2. When I think about the person, I ...
a. wish him or her well (SD–1, D–2, A–3, SA–4)
b. think kindly about him or her (SD–1, D–2, A–3, SA–4)
c. do not respect the person at all (SD–4, D–3, A–2, SA–1)

3. If given the opportunity, I would ...
a. return his or her phone call (SD–1, D–2, A–3, SA–4)
b. put the person down (SD–4, D–3, A–2, SA–1)
c. try to be helpful (SD–1, D–2, A–3, SA–4)

SCORING

Total your points and compare them to the scoring below:

9–12 points: You're not forgiving the person and perhaps you're still angry.

13–20 points: You're not forgiving, but moving in the direction of forgiveness.

21–26 points: You're in transition to forgiveness.

27–36 points: You're forgiving.

self-esteem and sense of hope. Other researchers have found that forgiving results in better sleep, increased feelings of love, an enhanced ability to trust, and an end to the physical symptoms and illness caused by anger. It even lessens the impact of mental illness such as depression.

How to Forgive Those Who Trespass against You

Now that we know that forgiveness heals, how do we use it? The process looks surprisingly simple—but it may be one of the toughest things you ever do. Here's what Drs. Fitzgibbons and Enright suggest:

Acknowledge your anger—all of it. Think about how you were hurt, your response, and how you feel right now, says Dr. Enright. Just because you're not boiling mad doesn't mean you're not angry. Anger frequently disguises itself as depleted energy, a preoccupation with what happened, impatience with other people, and a tendency to look at the world in a negative way. (See box, "Hidden Sources of Anger.") If you're not sure at whom your anger is directed, or if you suspect that much of it has gotten buried under a veneer of "making nice," then every morning when you get up just say, "I want to forgive the people who disappointed me and caused me to feel sad or lonely." After a while, the source of your anger will emerge. You may be angrier than ever when you realize who it is and what they've done, adds Dr. Fitzgibbons. But that's the time to follow the next recommendation.

Decide to forgive. Some people decide to forgive because, like me, their religious beliefs demand that they turn the other cheek, embrace their enemy, and go on. Others decide to forgive because their anger is causing them so much emotional pain that they'll try anything to relieve it. Still others simply recognize that if anger is dictating how they feel, then their entire life is being controlled by the person who hurt them.

If none of those things are motivating you, you need to "go through the motions" in your head until you can truly feel forgiveness in your heart. Get up every morning and say to yourself, "I want to forgive so-and-so for what he or she has done," says Dr. Fitzgibbons. If it helps, stand in front of an empty chair, pretend the person who hurt you is sitting there, and say, "I forgive you."

Do no evil. Resolve not to act negatively against the person who hurt you, says Dr. Enright. You don't have to do anything *good* on her behalf—just don't do anything bad. For example, if the wrongdoer's name comes up in conversation, don't give in to the temptation to do some serious "dissing." That's the time to obey the old chestnut, "If you can't say something nice, don't say anything at all."

Consider the source. Is there anything in the background of the offender that could explain her behavior? If there is, don't let it sidetrack you into feeling sorry for her, says Dr. Enright. It's no excuse. But it will help you to forgive and move on if you can see some reason for her actions.

When my friend Robin was 16, for instance, both her parents died and she was left on her own to care for both herself and a younger sister. They had no money and no relatives to look out for them. But Robin kept the family together, put food on the table, and even got both herself and her sister full scholarships to prestigious universities.

I respect that. And although knowing it doesn't make what Robin did to me right, it does help me understand her need to get all the marbles she can in any game she plays.

Put yourself in the other person's shoes. This is empathy. Think about what was going on in the life of whoever hurt you when she did it, says Dr. Enright. Maybe she hit a rough stretch and needed to strike out—and you got in the way. Robin, for example, had married a guy who couldn't seem to keep a job. Did that make her feel like she was all alone and responsible for her family's financial security again? I didn't know, but just thinking about it, I could feel my anger toward Robin begin to soften.

Give yourself some time. Forgiving with both head and heart isn't something you can do overnight, says Dr. Fitzgibbons. "Some people think, 'Well, if I make the decision to forgive . . . bingo! There goes my anger and it's over.' Unfortunately, it takes weeks, months, sometimes years to get over being disappointed and angry," he explains. "It's like draining an abscess. And when you decide to forgive, you can drain only a certain amount of anger from the heart and the unconscious at a time."

Consider reconciliation. Forgiveness doesn't always lead to reconciliation, says Dr. Fitzgibbons. In some cases, you need to keep hurtful people at arm's length so they can't continue hurting you. But if you know the person is clearly not going to hurt you again or if she seems truly sorry, then reconciliation becomes possible.

It's up to you.

Ellen Michaud is a contributing editor at Prevention. *She forgave Robin.*

Welcome to the Love Lab

Words can heal an ailing relationship—or seal its negative fate.

By John Gottman, Ph.D. and Sybil Carrere, Ph.D.

The way a couple argues can tell you a lot about the future of their relationship. In fact, just three minutes of fighting can indicate whether the pair will flourish with time or end in ruin.

The 10-year study that led to this discovery was one of many we've conducted over the years. John Gottman began his groundbreaking research on married couples 28 years ago. Since then, his University of Washington laboratory—dubbed the "Love Lab"—has focused on determining exactly what makes marriages thrive or fail. With the help of a remarkable team and hundreds of couples, we can now predict a relationship's outcome with 88% to 94% accuracy.

To do this, we watch couples during spats and analyze partners' communication patterns and physiology, as well as their oral descriptions of their relationship histories. We then follow the pairs over time to see whether their patterns and descriptions lead to happy outcomes or breakups. We have learned that some negative emotions used in arguments are more toxic than others: Criticism, contempt, defensiveness and stonewalling (withdrawing from a discussion, most frequently seen among men) are all particularly corrosive. On the other hand, we have repeatedly found that happy couples use five times more positive behaviors in their arguments than negative behaviors. One way they do this is by using humor to break the tension in an argument. This is a kind of a "repair" effort to mend conflict. We find that happy couples also use expressions of affection for their partner and acknowledge their partner's point of view ("I'm sorry I hurt your feelings") in order to keep quarrels from getting too heated.

We have learned much from our couples over the last 11 years that we try to bring to our own marriages. Two things: One is the importance of building and maintaining a friendship in your marriage so that you give your partner the benefit of the doubt when times are tough. This takes constant work. The second thing is that you have a choice every time you say something to your partner. You can say something that will either nurture the relationship or tear it down. You may win a particular fight with your spouse, but you could lose the marriage in the long run.

In this article, we show just how we diagnose the health of a marriage. Using three examples of dialogue from real couples discussing their problems, we will illustrate how reading between the lines of people's arguments can predict where some marriages have gone wrong—and why others have stayed strong. Welcome to the "Love Lab!"

Susan, 45, and Bob, 47, have been married for 23 years.

Bob: Um, communication. The question is . . .

Susan: How we disagree.

B: On communication?

S: You don't see a need for it.

B: Oh yeah.

S: You just said you kept to yourself.

B: Well, yeah, I just. . . . I dunno. Idle chitchat, I guess.

Defensiveness; Tension

S: You what?

B: Idle chitchat, I guess, if that is what you refer to as communication.

S: What do you mean, chitchat?

B: General run-of-the-mill bull.

S: There's nonverbal communication if you're tuned in.

B: (Nods head)

S: Like that man said in that canoeing class, as they went over the rapids, that they were still communicating.

B: That's true. What do you think we need to talk about more then? Huh?

S: Well, I think when there's a problem, or I'm trying to tell you something, sometimes I shouldn't have to say anything. You can know when I'm in a hurry or tired.

B: I just take communication as being, uh, should we sit down and discuss things more fully.

S: We don't sit down and discuss anything unless it's a problem, or if somebody gets mad. You know lots of families have what they call, which is kinda silly, but a weekly meeting or some time when they just sit down and talk about everything that has been going on there all week, what they like and don't like.

B: We used to have those at home.

S: That's a little far-fetched, maybe, but I'm just saying.

B: I know. I just . . .

S: It makes sense.

B: . . . you know what major problem we have at work is communication.

S: It's a problem everywhere.

B: Yeah. Yeah.

S: People don't say what they mean.

B: Or assume that people know what they mean or want.

S: Well, how many times have I asked you what's wrong, and you say nothing. And then a month later you say what was wrong and I couldn't have guessed it in a million years.

B: I don't know why that is. Why, you know, you can ask almost anybody at work what's bothering them.

S: But you never ask me what's wrong.

B: Maybe I know.

Expressing Hidden Life Dream: Wants Husband To take Active Interest

S: No, I don't think you do.

B: Maybe I just enjoy the quietness of it. I don't know.

S: Well, seriously, I think that as long as we've been married that you don't know very much about me at all.

B: No, I think it's true, about both of us maybe.

GOTTMAN SAYS: This couple rates quite low in marital satisfaction. They are also emotionally disengaged, with high depression in addition to marital distress. The marriage has generally low conflict, but also low positivity (shared romance, humor, affection)—the best marker of emotional disengagement. Our findings suggest that, in general, emotionally disengaged couples divorce later in life than those who have a "hotter," more explosive pattern of unhappiness, although this couple did not break up.

This couple is also in a state of gridlocked conflict. Susan and Bob keep coming close to resolving their issue, which is that Bob would rather keep to himself than communicate. But they don't—they keep recycling it over and over again. Emotional disengagement is often a later stage of continued gridlock. After a while, a "hot" couple begins polarizing their positions, digging in and becoming more stubborn, vilifying one another, then trying to isolate the problem. Unfortunately, most gridlocked conflict cannot be permanently enclaved, and negotiations to fix a problem reach a stalemate.

The reason gridlocked conflicts don't get resolved is because there is an underlying life dream within each person that isn't being fulfilled. Susan's dream is expressed when she says, "You never ask me what's wrong." Bob responds that "maybe I just enjoy the quietness"—that he prefers emotional distance to fighting—but she sadly replies that he doesn't know her at all. They are lacking in what we call "love maps," which spouses construct by being interested in each other and tracking each other's stresses, hopes, dreams, concerns, etc. Her latent wish for love maps keeps them from agreeing to the weekly meeting plan.

This couple is still married, but unhappily so.

Valerie, 24, and Mark, 25, have a young baby. They have recently moved, and both have new jobs.

Valerie: (Laughter) We don't go that long without talking.

Mark: I know, I just start going stir-crazy.

Despite Initial Humor, The Problem Surfaces

V: The problem . . .

M: Huh?

V: . . . is, you told me that when you took the job as manager at Commonwealth that you'd come home in the afternoons and spend some time with us.

M: That's right, but I did not say that it would start in the first week when I'm trying to do two different jobs. I gotta get myself replaced. Right now, I'm not just a manager.

V: It's been three weeks.

M: Well, I just don't go out on the street and say "Hey you. Want to sell insurance?" It's not that easy. There's two people in the program. One of them is probably gonna be hired within the next couple weeks. But in the meantime it's tough. It's just the way it's gotta be.

V: I realize that.

M: Okay.

V: But.

M: At midnight when you get off work and you're all keyed up, I'm all worn out. I haven't been stimulated for two hours.

V: I realize that. That doesn't bother me that much, you going to sleep at night.

M: I'll just be starting to go to sleep and you'll go "Are you listening to me?" I'll be trying to stay awake . . .

V: I'm laughing about it usually. I'm not upset about it.

M: I don't know by then. I'm half out.

V: But now with me having a car, you'll be able to go to sleep early and get up with Stephanie a little bit. That's one of my big problems. I'm not getting any sleep. I don't get to sleep until two.

M: I've been getting up with her.

V: You've been real good about that.

M: Okay.

V: I guess I just wish that you didn't have to go in early.

M: Yeah, we don't get a whole lot of time together.

V: When I have the car, I can get out and get stuff then. I feel like I'm stuck at home and here you are . . .

M: I'll be able to meet you for lunch and stuff. I guess that wasn't any big problem.

V: It is a problem. It seems like we talk about it every day.

M: Yeah, we do.

V: That's about the only thing we really complain about.

M: Yeah. The last couple nights I tried to take you out to the lake and look at the stars and stuff, so . . .

V: I know.

M: We just need to get used to our schedules.

V: That first week I was so, I was real upset cause it seemed like all I did was stay home with Stephanie all morning till three and just work all evening. I wasn't doing anything. It didn't seem like we had family gatherings every weekend. We never had time to go out, just the two of us.

M: I got a little surprise for ya next weekend.

Criticism; Conflict Renewed

V: Yeah, it's always next weekend. It's never this weekend.

M: Eight weekends in a row.

V: I just went from not working at all and being home. We've both been through major job changes and all.

M: And I can't breathe.

V: But we're getting used to it and I feel so much better about going to work at three (o'clock), three-thirty now than I did that first week.

M: Um.

V: I just wish I had more time to do what I wanted to do. I, it's just being . . .

M: I'll, I'll be able to stay . . .

V: . . . a wife and mother.

M: . . . to stay at home during the days a little bit more or I'll have to go in early but then I can take a couple of hours off in the afternoons.

Retaliation with Anger

V: Do you have to go in early every day?

M: I'm going to go in early every day.

V: Why?

M: 'Cause there are things I need to do every morning.

V: I think you just like going in to your office.

M: You don't know a thing about it then. Randy was in there early every day, tell me why?

V: Yeah, but he was home at a decent hour too.

M: He stays out late.

V: Eight to eight or eight to nine every day.

M: Every day.

V: Now, then, I don't want you taking that job. You forget it.

M: No.

GOTTMAN SAYS: This couple also has low levels of marital satisfaction. Unlike the previous couple, they have the "hot," corrosive kind of marital conflict characterized by what I call the "Four Horsemen of the Apocalypse": criticism, contempt, defensiveness and stonewalling. This type of conflict tends to lead to early divorce. However, also unlike the previous couple, there is still a lot of strength in their relationship. Their friendship is intact. There is humor and affection, and they are confident that they can resolve their conflict.

Though the couple begins their discussion very well, by laughing, Valerie soon expresses anger because Mark's new job is demanding so much of his time. She then repairs this with humor and more affection. This shows that there is still quite a bit of strength in this marriage. The respite is only temporary; Valerie raises the family issue again. But Mark agrees affectionately, showing another strength: He makes her problems "their" problems.

They are doing very well discussing the problem until Valerie's angry line about going in early every day. This leads to a pattern of her anger and his defensiveness in response. So there is still a lot of strength in their interaction, but something is keeping him from fully understanding how hard it is for her to have him gone so much. Something is deteriorating in this relationship and it's exemplified by her ultimatums and his resistance.

When we were doing this research, we didn't intervene to help couples, and this one, unfortunately, divorced after seven years of marriage. Now I think we can prevent this type of marital meltdown. The secrets are in keeping fathers involved with their babies so they make the same kind of philosophical transformation in meaning that their wives are probably making; in teaching couples what to expect during this transition to parenthood; and in helping them with the inevitable marital conflict, sleepless irritability and depression that often follow a new baby.

Wilma, 31, and Harris, 35, have been married 11 years.

Wilma: The communication problem. Tell me your feelings. (Both laughing)

Harris: A lot of times I don't know. I've always been quiet.

W: Is it just because you have nothing to talk about, or is it because you don't want to talk about it?

H: A lot of times I don't know.

W: Okay. Example: when we went to Lake Bariessa. I mean, I can understand that you couldn't find your way around and everything, that was fine. But it still doesn't hurt to open your lips, you know?

H: I was kind of burned out that day . . .

W: Well, you suggested we go . . .

H: I was trying to take you out somewhere, then I was trying to figure out my money in the bank and I end up coming short . . .

W: You did all that driving up there . . .

H: Yeah. And I was trying to figure out my bank account and how I was going to, you know, have the gas money for the week.

W: But, like, when we got there, you didn't want to talk. We got off the truck, we got set up and you ate your sandwich. Your little bologna sandwich. (Both laughing)

H: Yeah. I was starving. (Laughing)

W: I didn't know you were. And then it was like, you still didn't want to talk, so Dominique and me started playing tennis.

H: It was almost time to go then and I had to drive back. I didn't want to check it out.

W: Yeah. I thought it was such a nice drive.

H: I didn't know it was going to be that far.

W: And I really appreciate that.

H: Thank you very much.

W: You're welcome. I don't mind you talking about bills all the time, but we can only pay what we can pay, so why worry?

H: 'Cause that's how I am.

W: You shouldn't do that.

Playful Acceptance of Differences

H: Well, I can't help it. I'm always trying to be preventive.

W: Okay, "Preventive." (Laughter)

H: I can't help it. I have learned from my mistakes. Have you ever heard of people worried about bills?

W: I've heard of those people. I'm one of those people.

H: And I'm one of those people, whether you know it or not.

W: The thing is, I just pay what I can. You can't give everybody money at the same time when you don't have it to give.

H: The only thing I can do is have life insurance for me and you. I paid the kids'. Now I can't pay ours.

W: So you haven't paid the insurance in a month and a half?

H: I paid the kids, but I haven't been able to pay ours.

W: You see, you don't say anything, so I've been thinking that everything is okay.

H: Yeah, I gathered that. (Laughter)

W: (Laughter) Honestly. We need to figure out how we can pay that before it's due. I mean, the same thing with the phone bill.

H: But you haven't been trying to keep that down. Yappity yappity yap!

W: Well, we'll try to figure it out. We'll both of us try to take something out.

H: Right. That's what I'd like.

W: All right. Work with me baby. And now maybe you'll start talking more. See, now you're sitting up here talking about this. And like that day at the park. We could have talked about that. It was a nice relaxing moment to discuss things.

H: I don't know what happened then. When I got there, I was blown out.

W: If you sit and talk with me like this . . .

H: When do we have a chance to sit down?

W: On weekends.

H: I don't think we have enough time on weekends to sit down.

W: See, that's why I said we need to take a day for ourselves. Momma would keep Dominique for a day. We've got to start focusing on ourselves more.

H: Mmm-hmm.

W: Just every now and then so we can do something for ourselves, even if it isn't anything more than taking in a movie.

H: Yeah.

W: Or go have dinner. When was the last time we had dinner in a restaurant?

H: That would be nice. Or go to a movie. How do you do it? First you go have dinner, then you go to a movie. (Laughter)

W: Or if you go to a movie early enough, you can go have dinner afterwards.

H: Right.

W: Right.

GOTTMAN SAYS: Wilma and Harris have a long-term, stable and happy marriage.

They easily discuss two long-standing marital issues: the fact that he doesn't talk very much and she wants him to, and their financial differences. These issues are never going to change fundamentally. Our research has revealed that 69% of couples experience "perpetual problems"—issues with no resolution that couples struggle with for many years. Our data now lead us to believe that whenever you marry someone, your personality differences ensure that you and your partner will grapple with these issues forever. Marriages are only successful to the degree that the problems you have are ones you can cope with.

For most perpetual conflicts in marriages, what matters is not conflict resolution, but the attitudes that surround discussion of the conflict. Wilma and Harris both basically accept that there will always be differences between them, and they essentially accept one another as they are. Still, it is their ability to exchange viewpoints, making each other feel comfortable and supported all the while, that keeps them from getting gridlocked.

This couple, which is typical of our long-term couples, are real pros at being married and at using positive affect—like humor and gentle teasing—to de-escalate conflict. This is likely a sign that they are keeping their arousal levels low. Notice the wide array of strategies used to alleviate potential tension, such as expressing appreciation, softening complaints, responding nondefensively, backing down and using humor. The two of them do this together.

What these middle-aged spouses do is exactly what newlyweds who wind up stable and happy do, and this process moves them toward some semblance of problem-solving. What this master couple has effectively accomplished is to actualize the great marital paradox: that people can only change if they don't feel they have to.

Harris and Wilma make it look easy, just like a high-wire act makes it look easy. They are "athletes" at marriage, and that is one reason we study long-term marriages. There is a marital magic in what they do. The only function of my research is to make this marital magic clear so therapists can teach it to other couples.

John Gottman, Ph.D., is William Mifflin Professor of Psychology at the University of Washington in Seattle. Sybil Carrere, Ph.D., is a research scientist at the University of Washington in Seattle.

READ MORE ABOUT IT

The Seven Principles for Making Marriage Work, John Gottman, Ph.D. (Crown, 1999)

The Marriage Clinic, John Gottman, Ph.D. (W. W. Norton, 1999)

PRESCRIPTION FOR PASSION

Jealousy ignites rage, shame, even life-threatening violence. But it is just as necessary as love. In fact, it preserves and protects that fragile emotion. Consider it a kind of old-fashioned mate insurance, an evolutionary glue that holds modern couples together.

BY DAVID M. BUSS, PH.D.

Every human alive is an evolutionary success story. If any of our ancestors had failed to survive an ice age, drought, predator or plague, the previously inviolate chain of descent would have been irreparably broken, and we would not be alive to tell the tale. Each of us owes our existence to thousands of generations of successful ancestors. As their descendants, we have inherited the passions that led to their success—passions that drive us, often blindly, through a lifelong journey in the struggle for survival, the pursuit of position and the search for relationships.

These passions have many sides. They inspire us to achieve life's goals. They impel us to satisfy our desire for sex, our yearning for prestige and our quest for love. But passions also have a darker, more sinister side. The same passions that inspire us to love can lead to the disastrous choice of a mate, the desperation of unrequited obsession or the terror of stalking. Jealousy can keep a couple committed or drive a man to savagely beat his wife.

Jealousy's Two Faces

Jealousy poses a paradox. Consider that in a sample of 651 university students who were actively dating, more than 33% reported that jealousy posed a significant problem in their current relationship. The problems ranged from loss of self-esteem to verbal abuse, from rage-ridden arguments to the terror of being stalked. But the irony of jealousy, which can shatter the most harmonious relationships, is that it flows from deep and abiding love. The paradox was reflected in O.J. Simpson's statement: "Let's say I committed this crime [the slaying of ex-wife Nicole Brown Simpson]. Even if I did, it would have to have been because I loved her very much, right?"

Consider these findings: 46% of a community sample said jealousy was an inevitable consequence of true love. St. Augustine noted this link when he declared, "He that is not jealous is not in love." Shakespeare's tormented Othello "dotes, yet doubts, suspects, yet strongly loves." Women and men typically interpret a partner's jealousy as a sign of the depth of their love; a partner's absence of jealousy as a lack of love. The psychologist Eugene Mathes of Western Illinois University asked a sample of unmarried but romantically involved men and women to complete a jealousy test. Seven years later, he contacted the participants again and asked them about the current status of their relationship. Roughly 25% had married, while 75% had broken up. The jealousy scores from seven years earlier for those who married averaged 168, whereas the scores for those who broke up registered significantly lower at 142. These results must be interpreted cautiously; it's just one study with a small sample. But it points to the idea that jealousy might be inexorably linked with long-term love. In fact, it may be integral to it.

Evolution of an Alarm

Jealousy is an adaptive emotion, forged over millions of years, symbiotic with long-term love. It evolved as a primary defense against threats of

Reprinted from *Psychology Today,* May/June 2000, pp. 54-61. Excerpted from *Dangerous Passion: Why Jealousy Is as Necessary as Love and Sex,* by David M. Buss. © 2000 by David M. Buss, by permission of The Free Press, a division of Simon & Schuster, Inc.

infidelity and abandonment. Coevolution tells us that reciprocal changes occur sequentially in interacting species or between the sexes in one species. As a result, women have become excellent detectors of deception, as indicated by their superiority in decoding nonverbal signals. Men, in turn, can be notoriously skilled at deceiving women.

Jealousy is activated when one perceives signs of defection—a strange scent, a sudden change in sexual behavior, a suspicious absence. It gets triggered when a partner holds eye contact with someone else for a split second too long, or when a rival stands too close to your loved one or is suddenly fascinated by the minutia of his or her life. These signals alert us to the possibility of infidelity, since they have been statistically linked with relationship loss over the long course of human evolutionary history.

Margaret Mead called jealousy 'a festering spot in every personality . . . '

Obviously, episodes of extreme irrational or pathological jealousy can destroy an otherwise solid marriage. In most instances, however, it's not the experience of jealousy per se that's the problem. Rather, it's the real threat of defection by a partner interested in a real rival. In 1931, Margaret Mead disparaged jealousy as "undesirable, a festering spot in every personality so afflicted, an ineffective negativistic attitude which is more likely to lose than to gain any goal." Her view has been shared by many, from advocates of polyamory, a modern form of open marriage, to religious treatises. But properly used, jealousy can enrich relationships, spark passion and amplify commitment. The total absence of jealousy, rather than its presence, is a more ominous sign for romantic partners, for it portends emotional bankruptcy.

This was certainly true for one wife, who, noting her husband's lack of jealousy, grew to feel unloved and began acting out. She raged at him, harassing him on the telephone at work, causing him great embarrassment. When the husband sought help from a

therapist, he was advised to act the part of the jealous husband. Having learned over many years how a jealous person behaves, he was able to perform the role so skillfully and subtly that his wife of 21 years didn't realize he was role-playing. While he had seldom called home in the past, he now called his wife frequently to check on her, to see whether she was home and to ask exactly what she was doing. He made suspicious and critical remarks about any new clothes she wore, and expressed displeasure when she showed the slightest interest in another man. The result was dramatic. The wife, flattered by her husband's attentiveness and newfound interest, stopped her jealous behavior completely. She became pleasant and loving toward her husband and expressed remorse over her earlier behavior. At an eight-month follow-up, she was still behaving more lovingly toward her husband, but as a precaution he still played the jealous one from time to time.

Evoking Jealousy

Once jealousy evolved in the human repertoire, it became fair game for partners to exploit for their own purposes. Eliciting jealousy intentionally emerged as an assessment device to gauge the strength of a mate's commitment. Both sexes do it, but not equally. In one study, 31% of women, but only 17% of men, reported that they had intentionally elicited jealousy in their romantic partner. Women and men also employ different tactics. In our study of newlyweds, we found that women more than men report flirting with others in front of a partner, showing interest in others, going out with others and talking to another man at a party, all to make their partner jealous or angry.

William Tooke, Ph.D., and his colleagues at the State University of New York at Plattsburgh have found strong sex differences in several clusters of acts designed to induce jealousy. First, women intentionally socialize with other people. One woman said that she purposefully neglected to invite her partner along when she went out with friends. Another said she made a point of talking with members of the opposite sex when she and her boyfriend went out to a bar. A third indicated that she made sure to casually mention to her boyfriend how much fun she had when she was out partying without him.

The second jealousy-inducing strategy centered on intentionally ignoring

a partner. One woman reported acting distant and uninterested in her partner to make him think she didn't care about him that much. Another said she deliberately failed to answer her phone when she knew her boyfriend was calling so he would think she was out with someone else. Yet another told her boyfriend she did not have time to see him, even though it was the weekend.

The third mode of strategic jealousy induction was especially effective at pushing men's jealousy buttons—direct flirtation with other men. One woman reported dancing closely and seductively with someone her partner didn't like while he stood on the sidelines. Several reported going out to bars with members of the opposite sex and coming back to the boyfriend a bit intoxicated. Others reported that they dressed in especially sexy outfits while going out without their boyfriends, a sure method of fanning a man's jealous flames.

A more subtle and ingenious tactic for evoking jealousy involves merely smiling at other men while out with a partner. Antonia Abbey, Ph.D., of Wayne State University, discovered a fascinating difference in how men and women interpret a woman's smiles. When women smile, men often erroneously read into it sexual interest, mistaking friendliness for romantic intent. Martie Haselton, Ph.D., of the University of Texas at Austin, and I have labeled men's sexual inference as "adaptive bias" in mind reading because it's part of men's unconscious strategy of casual sex. By inferring sexual interest from a woman's smile, men are more likely to make sexual overtures.

So when a woman smiles at another man while at a party with her partner, she deftly exploits the evolved psychology of two different men. The smile causes its target to think she's sexually interested in him, so he makes advances. Simultaneously, it evokes her partner's jealousy, so he gets angry both about the rival and about his perception that she's encouraging the other man. The upshot might be a confrontation between the two rivals or a lovers' quarrel. But who can blame a woman just for being friendly? No other method for strategically inducing jealousy is as effective, for it makes two men dance to a woman's tune with merely a well-timed glance.

Who Needs Jealousy?

Why do women walk such a dangerous tightrope, trifling with a mechanism

By evoking jealousy, a woman is telling her partner she could leave for greener mating pastures.

known to unleash male violence? Gregory White, Ph.D., of Southern Oregon University, conducted an in-depth study of 150 heterosexual couples in California to find out. He first asked each of the 300 participants whether they had ever intentionally tried to make their partner jealous and why. Only a few women reported that they induced jealousy to punish their partner. Eight percent reported doing it to bolster their self-esteem. Ten percent admitted doing it to act out feelings of revenge on a partner for a previous wrong. Increasing a partner's commitment, however, was cited by 38% of women. By evoking jealousy, a woman causes her partner to believe that she has attractive alternatives available, so that if he does not display greater commitment she might depart for greener mating pastures. Women who successfully use this tactic are more likely to keep the commitment of their mates. Fully 40% of women, the largest group, reported using jealousy to test the strength of the bond. By evoking jealousy, a woman gains valuable information about the depth and consistency of her partner's commitment.

Women reap this benefit most when the need to test the bond is especially strong: Women whose partners have been away for a while, those whose partners experience a sudden surge in status, and women who feel they might be perceived as less desirable than their partner, all need vital appraisals of a man's commitment.

For both sexes, the key to understanding who needs jealousy is determining who has the most to lose. White asked all 300 participants to rate whether they were more, equally or less involved in the relationship than their partner. Relative involvement is a powerful clue as to which partner is more desirable on the mating market, according to the principle of least interest—the less interested partner has the upper hand on the

scale of desirability. Although 61% of the couples were well matched in their level of involvement, 39% showed a mismatch. Does this index of relative involvement predict who will deploy the jealousy-induction strategy? The effect for men was modes: 15% of those who were less involved intentionally induced jealousy; 17% of those equally involved did, as did 22% of the men more involved. So there is a slight tendency for the less desirable men to attempt to evoke more jealousy.

The results for women were more dramatic. Whereas only 28% of the women who were less involved reported intentionally inspiring jealousy, fully 50% of the women who were more involved than their partner reported doing so. Since women who fall below their partners in overall desirability confront commitment problems more poignantly than other women, they induce jealousy to correct the imbalance.

Strategically inducing jealousy serves several key functions for women. It can bolster self-esteem because of the attention it attracts from other men. It can increase a partner's commitment by making him realize how desirable she really is. And it can test the strength of the bond: If he reacts to her flirtations with emotional indifference, she knows he lacks commitment; if he gets jealous, she knows he's in love. Evoking jealousy, although it inflicts a cost on the partner, provides valuable information that's difficult to secure otherwise. And it often works.

Virgil Sheets, Ph.D., and his colleagues at Indiana State University confirmed that one of the most common reactions in men whose jealousy is aroused is to increase the attention they pay to their partners. After becoming jealous, men report that they are more likely to "try to keep track of what my partner is doing," "do something special for my partner" and "try to show my partner more attention."

Although evoking jealousy can serve a useful function, it must be used with skill and intelligence to avoid unleashing unintended consequences.

Jealousy can spark or rekindle sexual passion.

Igniting Sexual Passion

Jealousy can also spark or rekindle sexual passion in a relationship. Consider the case of Ben and Stacy, a couple attending an intensive five-day jealousy workshop conducted by the Israeli psychologist Ayala Pines, Ph.D. Ben, 15 years older than Stacy, had been married before, but had been divorced for five years when he first got involved with Stacy.

Although Stacy had had a few romantic relationships, she was still a virgin when they met. Ben was flattered at the attentions of a woman as young and attractive as Stacy, but soon became bored with their sex life, and yearned for sex with other women. This unleashed intense jealousy in Stacy, which brought them into the workshop to solve what Ben described as "her problem." He saw no reason that he should not sleep with other women. During the early days of the workshop, Ben brought up Stacy's insecurity and jealousy, indicated his disapproval and proceeded to flirt with the other women in the group. During one session, Stacy was berated by the group for being so jealous. Tears streamed down her cheeks and others in the group responded with hugs and affection. The most attractive man in the group was especially supportive. He continued to comfort her, even after the session ended and Ben and the others had left the room. Hugging turned to kissing and eventually they had passionate sex right on the floor.

When Ben discovered the infidelity, he was furious, saying, "You hurt me more than any woman has done, and I trusted you to protect my feelings." Over the next two days the therapy group focused on Ben's jealousy. But when asked by the therapist whether any good had come of the event, he replied, "When we made love afterward, it was the most passionate sex we had ever had. It was unbelievably intense and exciting." Stacy agreed.

Ben's jealousy revived the sexual passion in their relationship. Why? Astute readers already have clues to the most probable explanations: The other man's attention reaffirmed Stacy's attractiveness in Ben's eyes. When it penetrates men's minds that other desirable men are interested in their partner, they perceive their partner as more sexually radiant.

There is also an evolutionary reason that Ben's jealousy reignited his passion for Stacy. A man whose partner has just been inseminated by another man is most at risk for genetic cuckoldry. By having sex with Stacy immediately following her infidelity, he reduced the odds that she would become pregnant with another man's child, although he obviously didn't think about it in those terms. The passionate nature of the sex implies that she had an orgasm, which causes the woman to retain more sperm. Increased sperm retention, in ancestral times, would have meant an increased likelihood of conception. Ben was merely a modern player in an ancient ritual in which men competed with one another in the battle for successful fertilization.

Emotional Wisdom

In my studies, I have discovered that some signs of jealousy are accurately interpreted as acts of love. When a man drops by unexpectedly to see what his partner is doing, this mode of jealous vigilance functions to preserve the safe haven of exclusivity while simultaneously communicating love. When a woman loses sleep thinking about her partner and wondering whether he's with someone else, it in-dicates simultaneously the depth of her love and the intensity of her jealousy. When a man tells his friends he is madly in love with a woman, it serves the dual purpose of conveying love and warning potential rivals to keep their hands off.

It is unlikely that love, with its tremendous psychological investment, could have evolved without a defense to shield it from the constant threat of rivals and the possibility of betrayal from a partner.

Jealousy evolved to fill that void, motivating vigilance as the first line of defense, and violence as the last. In its extreme forms, this vital shield has been called delusional, morbid and pathological, a symptom of neurosis and a syndrome of psychosis. Therapists try to expunge it from patients and individuals try to suppress it in themselves.

The experience of jealousy can be psychologically painful. But it alerts us to real threats from real rivals. It tells us when a partner's sexual indifference might not merely mean he or she is distracted by work. It causes us to remember subtle signals that, when properly assembled, portend a real defection.

Evolution has equipped all of us with a rich menu of emotions, including jealousy, envy, fear, rage, joy, humiliation, passion and love. The knowledge that comes with a deeper understanding of our dangerous passions will not eliminate conflicts between lovers, between rivals or between lovers who become rivals. But it may, in some small measure, give us the emotional wisdom to deal with them.

This article is from Dangerous Passion *by David Buss, Ph.D. (Free Press, 2000). He is a professor of psychology at the University of Texas at Austin.*

READ MORE ABOUT IT

The Red Queen: Sex and the Evolution of Human Nature, Matt Ridley (Penguin, 1995)
Romantic Jealousy: Causes, Symptoms, Cures, Ayala M. Pines, Ph.D. (Routledge, 1998)

Coping with CROWDING

A persistent and popular view holds that high population density inevitably leads to violence. This myth, which is based on rat research, applies neither to us nor to other primates

by Frans B. M. de Waal, Filippo Aureli and Peter G. Judge

FRANS B. M. DE WAAL, FILIPPO AURELI and PETER G. JUDGE share a research interest in the social relationships and behavioral strategies of nonhuman primates. Their work on aspects of this topic will appear in Natural Conflict Resolution, *to be published by the University of California Press. De Waal, author of* Chimpanzee Politics *and* Good Natured, *worked for many years at the Arnhem zoo in the Netherlands before coming to the U.S., where he is now director of the Living Links Center at the Yerkes Regional Primate Research Center in Atlanta and professor of psychology at Emory University. Aureli is a senior lecturer in biological and earth sciences at Liverpool John Moores University in England. Judge is an assistant professor at Bloomsburg University in Pennsylvania and a research associate at Yerkes.*

In 1962 this magazine published a seminal paper by experimental psychologist John B. Calhoun entitled "Population Density and Social Pathology." The article opened dramatically with an observation by the late-18th-century English demographer Thomas Malthus that human population growth is automatically followed by increased vice and misery. Calhoun went on to note that although we know overpopulation causes disease and food shortage, we understand virtually nothing about its behavioral impact.

This reflection had inspired Calhoun to conduct a nightmarish experiment. He placed an expanding rat population in a crammed room and observed that the rats soon set about killing, sexually assaulting and, eventually, cannibalizing one another. Much of this activity happened among the occupants of a central feeding section. Despite the presence of food elsewhere in the room, the rats were irresistibly drawn to the social stimulation—even though many of them could not reach the central food dispensers. This pathological togetherness, as Calhoun described it, as well as the attendant chaos and behavioral deviancy, led him to coin the phrase "behavioral sink."

In no time, popularizers were comparing politically motivated street riots to rat packs, inner cities to behavioral sinks and urban areas to zoos. Warning that society was heading for either anarchy or dictatorship, Robert Ardrey, an American science journalist, remarked in 1970 on the voluntary nature of human crowding: "Just as Calhoun's rats freely chose to eat in the middle pens, we freely enter the city." Calhoun's views soon became a central tenet of the voluminous literature on aggression.

In extrapolating from rodents to people, however, these thinkers and writers were making a gigantic leap of faith. A look at human populations suggests why such a simple extrapolation is so problematic. Compare, for instance, per capita murder rates with the number of people per square kilometer in different nations—as we did, using data from the United Nation's *1996 Demographic Yearbook*. If things were straightforward, the two ought to vary in tandem. Instead there is no statistically meaningful relation.

But, one could argue, perhaps such a relation is obscured by variation in national income level, political organization or some other variable. Apparently not, at least for income. We divided the nations into three categories—free-market, former East Block and Third World—and did the analysis again. This time we did find one significant correlation, but it was in the other direction: it showed more violent crime in the least crowded countries of the former East Block. A similar trend existed for free-market nations, among which the U.S.

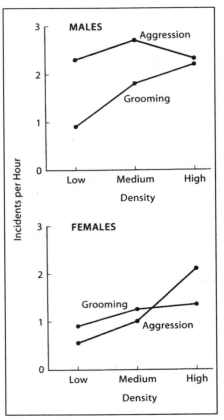

RHESUS MONKEYS from three different settings show different rates of grooming—that is, of calming one another. The monkeys seem to adapt to crowded conditions by grooming more frequently. Among the males, grooming of each other and of females was more common when they lived in crowded conditions than when they lived in more spacious quarters. Among female non-kin, aggression was common and increased further with crowding but was accompanied by increased grooming, which served to reduce conflicts.

BRYAN CHRISTIE

SOURCE: Peter G. Judge and Frans B. M. de Waal

had by far the highest homicide rate despite its low overall population density. The Netherlands had a population density 13 times as high, but its homicide rate was eight times lower.

Knowing that crime is generally more common in urban areas than it is in the countryside, we factored in the proportion of each nation's population that lives in large cities and controlled for it. But this correction did nothing to bring about a positive correlation between population density and homicide. Perhaps because of the overriding effects of history and culture, the link between available space and human aggression—if it exists at all—is decidedly not clear-cut.

Even if we look at small-scale human experiments, we find no supporting evidence. Crowding of children and college students, for instance, sometimes produced irritation and mild aggression, but in general, people seemed adept at avoiding conflict. Andrew S. Baum and his co-workers in the psychiatry depart-

ment at the Uniformed Services University found that dormitory residents who shared facilities with many people spent less time socializing and kept the doors to their rooms closed more often than did students who had more space. Baum concluded that the effects of crowding are not nearly as overwhelming as originally presumed. Published in the 1980s, these and other findings began to undermine, at least in the scientific community, the idea that people and rats react in the same ways to being packed together. In modern society, people commonly assemble in large masses—during their daily commute to work or during holiday-season shopping expeditions—and most of the time they control their behavior extraordinarily well.

Calhoun's model, we must conclude, does not generally apply to human behavior. Is this because our culture and intelligence makes us unique, or is the management of crowding part of an older heritage? To answer this question, we turn to the primates.

PRIMATES ARE NOT RATS

Primate research initially appeared to support the harrowing scenario that had been presented for rats. In the 1960s scientists reported that city-dwelling monkeys in India were more aggressive than were those living in forests. Others claimed that monkeys in zoos were excessively violent. Those monkeys were apparently ruled by terrifying bullies who dominated a social hierarchy that was considered an artifact of captivity—in other words, in the wild, peace and egalitarianism prevailed. Borrowing from the hyperbole of popularizers, one study of crowding in small captive groups of baboons even went so far as to report a "ghetto riot."

As research progressed, however, conflicting evidence accumulated. Higher population density seemed to increase aggression occasionally—but the opposite was also true. One report, for instance, described intense fighting and killing when a group of macaques were released into a corral 73 times *larger* than their previous quarters had been. Then, after two and a half years in the corral, a similar increase in aggression occurred when the monkeys were crowded back into a small pen.

Whereas the macaque study manipulated population density through environmental change, other early research did so by adding new monkeys to existing groups. Given the xenophobic nature of monkeys, these tests mainly measured their hostile attitude toward strangers, which is quite different from the effect of density. The better controlled the studies became, the less clear-cut the picture turned out to be. Increased population density led to increased aggression in only 11 of the

17 best-designed studies of the past few decades.

In the meantime, the view of wild primates was changing. They were no longer the purely peaceful, egalitarian creatures people had presumed them to be. In the 1970s field-workers began reporting sporadic but lethal violence in a wide range of species—from macaques to chimpanzees—as well as strict and well-defined hierarchies that remained stable for decades. This view of an often anxiety-filled existence was confirmed when researchers found high levels of the stress hormone cortisol in the blood of wild monkeys [see "Stress in the Wild," by Robert M. Sapolsky; SCIENTIFIC AMERICAN, JANUARY 1990.

As the view of primates became more complex, and as the rat scenario

was weakened by counterexamples, researchers began to wonder whether primates had developed a means to reduce conflict in crowded situations. We saw the first hint of this possibility in a study of the world's largest zoo colony of chimpanzees in Arnhem, the Netherlands. The apes lived on a spacious, forested island in the summer but were packed together in a heated building during the winter. Despite a 20-fold reduction in space, aggression increased only slightly. In fact, the effect of crowding was not entirely negative: friendly grooming and greetings, such as kissing and submissive bowing, increased as well.

We wondered if this conciliatory behavior mitigated tension and proposed a way to test this possibility. Without ig-

FRANS B. M. DE WAAL

CHIMPANZEES IN THE WILD have hostile territorial relations with other groups, and in captivity they are bothered by the presence of noisy neighboring chimps. By examining apes under three conditions—those living in a crowded space and able to hear their neighbors, those living in a crowded space without such worrisome sounds, and those living in isolated large compounds *(photograph below)*—we were able to measure the association between aggression, space and stress. Aggression *(photograph at left)* remained the same, but stress varied with neighbors' noise. Chimpanzees in small spaces exposed to vocalizations from other groups showed the highest levels of the stress hormone cortisol.

FRANS B. M. DE WAAL

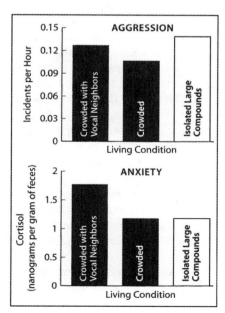

BRYAN CHRISTIE

SOURCE: Filippo Aureli and Frans B. M. de Waal

noring the fact that crowding increases the potential for conflict, we predicted that primates employ counterstrategies—including avoiding potential aggressors and offering appeasement or reassuring body contact. Because some of the skills involved are probably acquired, the most effective coping responses would be expected in animals who have experienced high density for a long time. Perhaps they develop a different "social culture" in the same way that people in different places have varying standards of privacy and interpersonal comfort zones. For example, studies show that white North Americans and the British keep greater distances from others during conversations than Latin Americans and Arabs do.

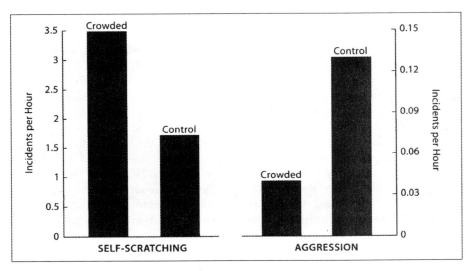

BRYAN CHRISTIE

SOURCE: Filippo Aureli and Frans B. M. de Waal

During brief periods of crowding, people often limit social interaction—a way of avoiding any conflict. Chimpanzees do the same, reducing their aggressive interactions. This doesn't mean that crowded situations do not induce anxiety. Chimpanzees packed together tend to scratch themselves more often—a sign of stress.

COPING CULTURE

We set about finding several populations of monkeys that were of the same species but that had been living in different conditions to see if their behavior varied in discernible ways. We collected detailed data on 122 individual rhesus monkeys at three different sites in the U.S.: in relatively cramped outdoor pens at the Wisconsin primate center in Madison, in large open corrals at the Yerkes primate center in Atlanta and on Morgan Island off the coast of South Carolina. These last monkeys had approximately 2,000 times more space per individual than the highest-density groups. All three groups had lived together for many years, often for generations, and included individuals of both sexes. All the groups had also been in human care, receiving food and veterinary treatment, making them comparable in that regard as well.

Rhesus society typically consists of a number of subgroups, known as matrilines, of related females and their offspring. Females remain together for life, whereas males leave their natal group at puberty. Rhesus monkeys make a sharp distinction between kin and non-kin: by far the most friendly contact, such as grooming, takes place within the matrilines. Females of one matriline also fiercely support one another in fights against other matrilines. Because of

their strict hierarchy and pugnacious temperament, rhesus seemed to be ideal subjects. We figured that if this aggressive primate showed coping responses, our hypothesis would have withstood its most rigorous test.

Our first finding was, surprisingly, that density did not affect male aggressiveness. Adult males increasingly engaged in friendly contact under crowded conditions. They groomed females more, and likewise the females groomed the males more frequently. (Grooming is a calming behavior. In another study, we demonstrated that a monkey's heart rate slows down when it is being groomed.) Females also bared their teeth more often to the males—the rhesus way of communicating low status and appeasing potentially aggressive dominant monkeys.

Females showed a different response with other females, however. Within their own matrilines they fought more but did not change the already high level of friendly interaction. In their dealings with other matrilines, they also showed more aggression—but here it was coupled with more grooming and submissive grinning.

These findings make sense in light of the differences between kin and non-kin

relationships. Related females—such as sisters and mothers and daughters—are so strongly bonded that their relationships are unlikely to be disrupted by antagonism. Rhesus monkeys are used to managing intrafamilial conflict, cycling through fights and reconciliations, followed by comforting contact. Crowding does little to change this, except that they may have to repair frayed family ties more often. Between matrilines, on the other hand, crowding poses a serious challenge. Normally, friendly contact between matrilines is rare and antagonism common. But reduced escape opportunities make the risk of escalated conflict greater in a confined space. And our data indicated that female rhesus monkeys make a concerted effort at improving these potentially volatile relationships.

EMOTIONS IN CHECK

In a second project, we turned our attention to chimpanzees. As our closest animal relatives, chimpanzees resemble us in appearance, psychology and cognition. Their social organization is also humanlike, with well-developed male bonding—which is rare in nature—reciprocal exchange and a long dependency of offspring on the mother. In the wild, male chimpanzees are extremely territorial, sometimes invading neighboring territories and killing enemy males. In captivity such encounters are, of course, prevented.

We collected data on more than 100 chimpanzees in various groups at the Yerkes primate center. Although some groups had only a tenth the space of others, cramped quarters had no measurable impact on aggression. In contrast to the monkeys, chimpanzees maintained their grooming and appeasement behavior— no matter the situation. If crowding did induce social tensions, our chimpanzees seemed to control them directly.

We usually do not think of animals as holding in their emotions, but chimpanzees may be different. These apes are known for deceptive behavior—for instance, they will hide hostile intentions behind a friendly face until an adversary has come within reach. In our study, emotional control was reflected in the way chimpanzees responded to the vocalizations of neighboring groups. Such noises commonly provoke hooting and charging displays, which in wild chimpanzees serve to ward off territorial intrusion.

In a confined space, however, excited reactions trigger turmoil within the group. We found that chimpanzees in the most crowded situations had a three times *lower* tendency to react to neighbors' vocalizations than chimpanzees with more space did. Chimpanzees may be smart enough to suppress responses to external stimuli if those tend to get them into trouble. Indeed, field-workers report that chimpanzee males on territorial patrol suppress all noise if being detected by their neighbors is to their disadvantage.

The inhibition of natural responses is not without cost. We know that continuous stress has the potential to suppress the immune system and therefore has important implications for health and longevity. We developed two noninvasive techniques to measure stress in our chimpanzees. One was to record the rate of self-scratching. Just as with college students who scratch their heads when faced with a tough exam question, self-scratching indicates anxiety in other primates. Our second technique was to collect fecal samples and analyze them for cortisol. Both measures showed that groups of chimpanzees who had little space and heard neighbors' vocalizations experienced more stress. Space by itself was not a negative factor, because in the absence of noisy neighbors, chimpanzees in small spaces showed the same stress level as those with a good deal of space.

So even though chimpanzees fail to show a rise in aggression when crowded, this does not necessarily mean that they are happy and relaxed. They may be working hard to maintain the peace. Given a choice, they would prefer more room. Every spring, when the chimpanzees at the Arnhem zoo hear the door to their outdoor island being opened for the first time, they fill the building with a chorus of ecstasy. They then rush outside to engage in a pandemonium in which all of the apes, young and old, embrace and kiss and thump one another excitedly on the back.

The picture is even more complex if we also consider short periods of acute crowding. This is a daily experience in human society, whether we find ourselves on a city bus or in a movie theater. During acute crowding, rhesus monkeys show a rise in mild aggression, such as threats, but not violence. Threats serve to keep others at a distance, forestalling unwanted contact. The monkeys also avoid one another and limit active social engagement, as if they are trying to stay out of trouble by lying low.

Chimpanzees take this withdrawal tactic one step further: they are actually less aggressive when briefly crowded. Again, this reflects greater emotional restraint. Their reaction is reminiscent of people on an elevator, who reduce frictions by minimizing large body movements, eye contact and loud verbalizations. We speak of the elevator effect, therefore, as a way in which both people and other primates handle the risks of temporary closeness.

Our research leads us to conclude that we come from a long lineage of social animals capable of flexibly adjusting to all kinds of conditions, including unnatural ones such as crowded pens and city streets. The adjustment may not be without cost, but it is certainly preferable to the frightening alternative predicted on the basis of rodent studies.

We should add, though, that even the behavioral sink of Calhoun's rats may not have been entirely the product of crowding. Food competition seemed to play a role as well. This possibility contains a serious warning for our own species in an ever more populous world: the doomsayers who predict that crowding will inevitably rip the social fabric may have the wrong variable in mind. We have a natural, underappreciated talent to deal with crowding, but crowding combined with scarcity of resources is something else.

Further Information

THE HIDDEN DIMENSION. E. T. Hall. Doubleday, 1966.

CROWDING. A. Baum in *Handbook of Environmental Psychology*, Vol. 1. Edited by D. Stokols and I. Altman. Wiley, 1987.

THE MYTH OF A SIMPLE RELATION BETWEEN SPACE AND AGGRESSION IN CAPTIVE PRIMATES. F. B. M. de Waal in *Zoo Biology* supplement, Vol. 1, pages 141–148; 1989.

INHIBITION OF SOCIAL BEHAVIOR IN CHIMPANZEES UNDER HIGH-DENSITY CONDITIONS. F. Aureli and F. B. M. de Waal in *American Journal of Primatology*, Vol. 41, No. 3, pages 213–228; March 1997.

RHESUS MONKEY BEHAVIOUR UNDER DIVERSE POPULATION DENSITIES: COPING WITH LONG-TERM CROWDING. P. G. Judge and F. B. M. de Waal in *Animal Behaviour*, Vol. 54, no. 3, pages 643–662; September 1997.

Unit 5

Key Points to Consider

❖ Is America becoming a teen-centered society? If you believe the answer is yes, why do you think this is happening? What role does the media play? Do you think this social change is a positive or negative one?

❖ Susan Faludi maintains that the American man has been betrayed. What does she mean by this? What are your personal feelings about this betrayal? If you believe there has been betrayal, what caused it? Do you think someone of the opposite sex would agree with you? Can anything be done to clarify the role of men and of masculinity in our society? Explain.

❖ What is the definition of prejudice? Do you, yourself, hold any biases? From where does prejudice originate? What is it that perpetuates the "isms" (racism, sexism, ageism, and other prejudices)? Do you think some of this is automatic, as suggested by cognitive psychologists? What can we do, if anything, to eliminate or overcome racism, sexism, ageism and sexual harassment?

❖ What is a cult? Why do people join cults? Would you ever join a cult? What are the advantages to members of cults? What recruiting techniques do cults use? What tragedies seem to follow cults? What would you say to a friend contemplating joining a cult?

❖ Do Americans work more today than ever before? Can you provide any anecdotes or statistics to support your answer? If you answered yes, why are Americans working harder? While hard work is a cherished American value, why might continuous work be deleterious to us? Why are boundaries blurring between free time and work? Do you think work should take precedence over family and leisure time? What can we do to cope better with the demands of work?

❖ What is workaholism? Why does it cause stress? What is the Type A personality? Can friends and family members really help us cope better with stress? When friends do provide us moral and emotional support, what is this called?

 **Links** | **www.dushkin.com/online/**

22. **AFF Cult Group Information**
    http://www.csj.org/index.html
23. **Explanations of Criminal Behavior**
    http://www.uaa.alaska.edu/just/just110/crime2.html
24. **National Clearinghouse for Alcohol and Drug Information**
    http://www.health.org
25. **Schools Health Education Unit (SHEU)**
    http://www.ex.ac.uk/~dregis/sheu.html

These sites are annotated on pages 4 and 5.

The passing of each decade brings changes to society. Some historians have suggested that changes are occurring more rapidly than in the past. In other words, history appears to take less time to occur. How has American society changed historically? The inventory is long. Technological advances can be found everywhere. Not long ago, few people knew what "user-friendly" and zip drive signified. Today these terms are readily identified with the rapidly changing computer industry. Twenty years ago, Americans felt fortunate to own a 13-inch television that received three local stations. Now people feel deprived if they cannot select from 200 different worldwide channels on their big, rear-screen sets. Today we can e-mail a message to the other side of the world faster than we can propel a missile to the same place.

In the Middle Ages, Londoners worried about the bubonic plague. Before vaccines were available, people feared polio and other diseases. Today much concern is focused on the transmission and cure of AIDS, the discovery of more carcinogenic substances, and the greenhouse effect. In terms of mental health, psychologists see few hysterics, the type of patient seen by Sigmund Freud in the 1800s. Psychosomatic ulcers and alcohol and drug addiction are more common today. In other words, lifestyle, more than disease, is killing Americans. Similarly, issues concerning the changing American family continue to grab headlines.

Nearly every popular magazine carries a story or two bemoaning the passing of the traditional, nuclear family and the decline in "family values." And as if these spontaneous or unplanned changes are not enough to cope with, some individuals are intentionally trying to change the world. Witness the continuing dramatic changes in Eastern Europe and the Middle East, for example.

This list of societal transformations, while not exhaustive, reflects society's continual demand for adaptation by each of its members. However, it is not just society at large that places stress on us. Smaller units within society, such as our work group, demand constant adaptation by individuals. Work groups expand and contract with every economic fluctuation. Even when group size remains stable, new members come and go as turnover takes place; hence, changes in the dynamics of the group occur in response to the new personalities. Each of these changes, welcome or not, probably places less strain on society as a whole and more stress on the individual, who then needs to adjust or cope with the change.

This unit addresses the interplay between the individual and society (or culture) in producing the problems each creates for the other.

The first few essays feature ideas about societal problems such as the "teening" of American childhood, fuzzy gender roles, and racism. In the unit's first article, "The Teening of America," Kay Hymowitz expresses her opinion that children are growing up too fast. In other words, 8-year-olds often look and act more like 15-year-olds or at least aspire to being an adolescent before their time. Hymowitz clearly blames the media for this social change.

The feminist movement has also created continuing changes in American society. In the next article, author Susan Faludi, who first wrote about the feminist movement, excerpts her new book on masculinity. Faludi contends that American men have no idea today what their role should be and how the ideal man should behave.

Racism is discussed by Annie Murphy Paul, in "Where Bias Begins: The Truth About Stereotypes." Social psychologists disagree with cognitive psychologists about the causes of prejudice and stereotyping. Cognitive psychologists assert that stereotypes are automatic thought processes over which we probably and unfortunately have little control. Social psychologists believe that prejudice is learned and can be overcome by new ways of thinking.

The following article in this unit offers a sensible and scientific approach to a topic that occasionally appears in the media—cults. Most people find cults abhorrent, but others gladly join. Why they join and the kinds of influences that cults have on their members are investigated in this essay.

Finally, the tendency to be all work and no play places us under immense stress. Mark Hunter, in "Work, Work, Work, Work," discusses how the boundaries between work and home and work and leisure have blurred. We seem to be working all the time, a tendency which Hunter says is unhealthy. Fortunately, Hunter also shares tips for coping with this increased pressure to work endless hours.

Individuals who work, work, work often face a great deal of stress. Stress is a modern American plague that affects our physical and psychological states. Benedict Carey suggests, in "Don't Face Stress Alone," that social support (help from and talking with friends) is highly effective in managing stress. In so doing, Carey also furnishes the reader with helpful information about the Type A or workaholic personality.

THE TEENING OF CHILDHOOD

BY KAY S. HYMOWITZ

A KID'S GOTTA do what a kid's gotta do!" raps a cocksure tyke on a 1998 television ad for the cable children's network Nickelodeon. She is surrounded by a large group of hip-hop-dancing young children in baggy pants who appear to be between the ages of three and eight. In another 1998 ad, this one appearing in magazines for the Gap, a boy of about eight in a T-shirt and hooded sweatshirt, his meticulously disheveled hair falling into his eyes and spilling onto his shoulders, winks ostentatiously at us. Is he neglected (he certainly hasn't had a haircut recently) or is he just street-smart? His mannered wink assures us it's the latter. Like the kids in the Nickelodeon ad, he is hip, aware, and edgy, more the way we used to think of teenagers. Forget about what Freud called latency, a period of sexual quiescence and naïveté; forget about what every parent encounters on a daily basis—artlessness, shyness, giggling jokes, cluelessness. These media kids have it all figured out, and they know how to project the look that says they do.

The media's darling is a child who barely needs childhood. In the movies, in magazines, and most of all on television, children see image upon irresistible image of themselves as competent sophisticates wise to the ways of the world. And maybe that's a good thing too, since their parents and teachers appear as weaklings, narcissists, and dolts. That winking 8-year-old in the Gap ad tells the story of his generation. A gesture once reserved for adults to signal to gullible children that a joke was on its way now belongs to the child. This child gets it; it's the adults who don't.

There are plenty of signs that the media's deconstruction of childhood has been a rousing success. The enthusiastic celebration of hipness and attitude has helped to socialize a tough, "sophisticated" consumer child who can assert himself in opposition to the tastes and conservatism of his parents. The market aimed at children has skyrocketed in recent years, and many new products, particularly those targeting the 8- to 12-year-olds whom marketers call tweens, appeal to their sense of teen fashion and image consciousness. Moreover, kids have gained influence at home. In part, this is undoubtedly because of demographic changes that have "liberated" children from parental supervision. But let's give the media their due. James McNeal, who has studied childhood consumerism for many decades, proclaims the United States a "filiarchy," a bountiful kingdom ruled by children.

Lacking a protected childhood, today's media children come immediately into the noisy presence of the media carnival barkers. Doubtless, they learn a lot from them, but their sophistication is misleading. It has no relation to a genuine worldliness, and understanding of human hypocrisy or life's illusions. It is built on an untimely ability to read the glossy surfaces of our material world, its symbols of hipness, its image-driven brands and production values. Deprived of the concealed space in which to nurture a full and independent individuality, the media child unthinkingly embraces the dominant cultural gestures of ironic detachment and emotional coolness. This is a new kind of sophistication, one that speaks of a child's diminished expectations and conformity rather than worldliness and self-knowledge.

Nowadays when people mourn the media's harmful impact on children, they often compare the current state of affairs to the Brigadoon of the 1950s. Even those who condemn the patriarchal complacency of shows like *Father Knows Best* or *Ozzie and Harriet* would probably concede that in the fifties parents did not have to fret over rock lyrics like *Come on bitch . . . lick up the dick* or T-shirts saying KILL YOUR PARENTS. These were the days when everyone, including those in the media, seemed to revere the protected and long-lived childhood that had been the middle-class ideal since the early 19th century.

But the reality of fifties media was actually more ambiguous than the conventional wisdom suggests. The fifties saw the rise of television, a medium that quickly opened advertisers' and manufacturers' eyes to the possibility of promoting in children fantasies of pleasure-filled freedom from parental control, which in turn fertilized the fields for liberationist ideas that came along in the next decade. American parents had long struggled to find a balance between their children's personal drives and self-expression and the demands of common life, but television had something else in mind. It was fifties television that launched the media's two-pronged attack on

From *American Educator*, Spring 2000, pp. 20-25. Reprinted with permission of the author and *American Educator*, the quarterly journal of the American Federation of Teachers.

the pre-conditions of traditional childhood, one aimed directly at empowering children, the other aimed at undermining the parents who were trying to civilize them. By the end of the decade, the blueprint for today's media approach to children was in place.

The first prong of attack was directed specifically at parents—or, more precisely, at Dad. Despite the assertions of those who see in *Father Knows Best* and *Ozzie and Harriet* evidence that the fifties were a patriarchal stronghold, these shows represent not the triumph of the old-fashioned family but its feeble swan song.[1] Dad, with his stodgy ways and stern commandments, had been having a hard time of it since he first stumbled onto television. An episode of *The Goldbergs*, the first television sitcom and a remake of a popular radio show featuring a Jewish immigrant family, illustrates his problem: Rosalie, the Goldbergs' 14-year-old daughter, threatens to cut her hair and wear lipstick. The accent-laden Mr. Goldberg tires to stop her, but he is reduced to impotent blustering: "I am the father in the home, or am I? If I am, I want to know!" It is the wise wife who knows best in this house; she acts as an intermediary between this old-world patriarch and the young country he seems unable to understand. "The world is different now," she soothes.[2] If this episode dramatizes the transgenerational tension inevitable in a rapidly changing immigrant country, it also demonstrates how television tended to resolve that tension at Dad's blushing expense. The man of the fifties television house was more likely to resemble the cartoon character Dagwood Bumstead ("a joke which his children thoroughly understand" according to one critic)[3] than Robert Young of *Father Knows Best*. During the early 1950s, articles began to appear decrying TV's "male boob" with titles like "What Is TV Doing to MEN?" and "Who Remembers Papa?" (an allusion to another early series called *I Remember Mama*).[4] Even *Ozzie and Harriet* was not *Ozzie and Harriet*. Ozzie, or Pop, as he was called by his children, was the Americanized and suburbanized papa who had been left behind in city tenements. Smiling blandly as he, apparently jobless, wandered around in his cardigan sweater, Ozzie was the dizzy male, a portrait of grinning ineffectuality. It is now coincidence that *Ozzie and Harriet* was the first sitcom to showcase the talents of a child character, when Ricky Nelson began his career as a teen idol. With parents like these, kids are bound to take over.

Still, the assumption that the first years of television were happy days for the traditional family has some truth to it. During the early fifties, television was widely touted as about the best thing that had ever happened to the family—surely one of the more interesting ironies of recent social history. Ads for the strange new appliance displayed a beaming mom and dad and their big-eyed kids gathered together around the glowing screen. It was dubbed the "electronic hearth." Even intellectuals were on board; early sociological studies supported the notion that television was family-friendly. Only teenagers resisted its lure. They continued to go to the movies with their friends, just as they had since the 1920s; TV-watching, they said, was family stuff, not an especially strong recommendation in their eyes.

IN ORDER to turn television into the children's oxygen machine that it has become, television manufacturers and broadcasters during the late forties and early fifties had to be careful to ingratiate themselves with the adults who actually had to purchase the strange new contraption. Families never had more than one television in the house, and it was nearly always in the living room, where everyone could watch it. Insofar as the networks sought to entice children to watch their shows, they had to do so by convincing Mom that television was good for them. It was probably for these reasons that for a few short years children's television was more varied and of higher quality than it would be for a long time afterward. There was little to offend, but that doesn't mean it was bland. In an effort to find the best formula to attract parents, broadcasters not only showed the familiar cowboy and superhero adventure series but also experimented with circus and science programs, variety shows, dramas, and other relatively highbrow fare, for example, Leonard Bernstein's *Young People's Concerts*. Ads were sparse. Since the networks had designed the earliest children's shows as a lure to sell televisions to parents, they were not thinking of TV as a means of selling candy and toys to kids; almost half of those shows had no advertising at all and were subsidized by the networks. At any rate, in those days neither parents nor manufacturers really thought of children as having a significant role in influencing the purchase of anything beyond, perhaps, cereal, an occasional cupcake, or maybe a holiday gift.

This is not to say that no one had ever thought of advertising to children before. Ads targeting youngsters had long appeared in magazines and comic strips. Thirties radio shows like *Little Orphan Annie* and *Buck Rogers in the Twenty-Fifth Century* gave cereal manufacturers and the producers of the ever-popular Ovaltine a direct line to millions of children. But as advertisers and network people were gradually figuring out, when it came to transporting messages directly to children, radio was a horse and buggy compared to the supersonic jet known as television, and this fact changed everything. By 1957, American children were watching TV an average of an hour and a half each day. And as television became a bigger part of children's lives, its role as family hearth faded. By the mid-fifties, as television was becoming a domestic necessity, manufacturers began to promise specialized entertainment. Want to avoid those family fights over whether to watch the football game or Disneyland? the ads queried. You need a *second* TV set. This meant that children became a segregated audience in front of the second screen, and advertisers were now faced with the irresistible opportunity to sell things to them. Before television, advertisers had no choice but to tread lightly around children and to view parents as judgmental guardians over the child's buying and spending. Their limited appeals to kids had to be more than balanced by promises to parents, however spurious, of health and happiness for their children.

That balance changed once television had a firm foothold in American homes and advertisers could begin their second prong of attack on childhood. With glued-to-the-tube children now segregated from adults, broadcasters soon went about pleasing kids without thinking too much about parents. The first industry outside of the tried-and-true snacks and cereals to capitalize on this opportunity was, predictably, toys.[5] By the mid-fifties, forward-looking toy manufacturers couldn't help but notice that Walt Disney was making a small fortune selling Mickey Mouse ears and Davy Crockett coonskin hats to the viewers of his *Disneyland* and *The Mickey Mouse Club*. Ruth and Eliot Handler, the legendary owner-founders of Mattel Toys, were the first to follow up. They risked their company's entire net worth on television ads during *The Mickey Mouse Club* for a toy called "the burp gun"; with 90 percent of the nation's kids watching, the gamble paid off bigger than anyone could have ever dreamed.

It's important to realize, in these days of stadium-sized toy warehouses, that until the advent of television, toys were nobody's idea of big business. There simply was not that big a market out there. Parents themselves purchased toys only as holiday or birthday presents, and they chose them simply by going to a specialty or department store and asking advice from a salesperson. Depression-traumatized grandparents, if they were still alive, were unlikely to arrive for Sunday dinner bearing Baby Alive dolls or Nerf baseball bats and balls. And except for their friends, children had no access to information about new products. At any rate, they didn't expect to own all that many toys. It's no wonder toy manufacturers had never shown much interest in advertising; in 1955 the "toy king" Lous Marx had sold fifty million dollars' worth of toys and had spent the grand total of $312 on advertising.

The burp gun ad signaled the beginning of a new era, a turning point in American childhood and a decisive battle in the filiarchal revolution. Toy sales almost tripled between 1950 and 1970. Mattel was now a boom company with sales rising from $6 million in 1955 to $49 million in 1961.[6] Other toy manufacturers who followed Mattel onto television also watched their profits climb.

But the burp gun ad was also a watershed moment, because it laid the groundwork for today's giant business of what Nickelodeon calls "kid kulture," a phenomenon that has helped to alter the dynamic between adults and children. Television transformed toys from a modest holiday gift enterprise mediated by parents into an ever-present, big-stakes entertainment industry enjoyed by kids. Wholesalers became less interested in marketing particular toys to adults than in the manufacturer's plans for promotional campaigns to seduce children. In short, the toy salesman had pushed open the front door, had crept into the den while Mom and Dad weren't looking, and had whispered to Dick and Jane, without asking their parents' permission, of all the happiness and pleasure they could have in exchange for several dollars of the family's hard-earned money.

That the burp gun had advanced more power to children became more apparent by 1959, when Mattel began to advertise a doll named Barbie. Barbie gave a hint as to just how far business was ready to take the filiarchal revolution that had been set in motion by the wonders of television. Regardless of the promotional revolution it had unleashed, the burp gun was a familiar sort of toy, a quirky accessory to the battlefield games always enjoyed by boys. But Barbie was something new. Unlike the baby dolls that encouraged little girls to imitate Mommy, Barbie was a swinger, a kind of Playboy for little girls. She had her own Playboy Mansion, called Barbie's Dream House, and she had lots of sexy clothes, a car, and a boyfriend. The original doll had pouty lips—she was redesigned for a more open California look in the sixties—and she was sold in a leopard skin bathing suit and sunglasses, an accessory whose glamour continues to have iconic status in the children's market. In fact, though it isn't widely known, Barbie was copied from a German doll named Lili, who was in turn modeled on a cartoon prostitute. Sold in bars and tobacco shops, Lili was a favorite of German men, who were suckers for her tight (removable) sweater and short (removable) miniskirt.

Barbie has become so familiar that she is seen as just another citizen of the toy chest, but it's not exaggeration to say that she is one of the heroes in the media's second prong of attack on childhood. She proved not only that toy manufacturers were willing to sell directly to children, bypassing parents entirely, but that they were willing to do so by undermining the forced and difficult-to-sustain latency of American childhood. According to marketing research, mothers without exception *hated* Barbie. They believed she was too grown-up for their 4-to-12-year-old daughters, the toy's target market. The complaint heard commonly today—that by introducing the cult of the perfect body Barbie promotes obsessive body consciousness in girls, often resulting in eating disorders—is actually only a small part of a much larger picture. Barbie symbolized the moment when the media and the businesses it promoted dropped all pretense of concern about maintaining childhood. They announced, first, that they were going to flaunt for children the very freedom, consumer pleasure, and sex that parents had long been trying to delay in their lives. And, second, they were going to do this by initiating youngsters into the cult of the teenager. If this formula sounds familiar, it's because it remains dominant today. Barbie began the media's teening of childhood; today's media images and stories are simply commentary.

ADS TARGETING children make perfect companion pieces to stories of family rot and children savvy enough to roll their eyes amusingly through all the misery. In ads today, the child's image frequently appears in extreme close-up—the child as giant. Appealing to children's fantasies of omnipotent, materialistic freedom, advertisers portray an anarchic world of misrule in which the pleasure-seeking child reigns supreme.[7] Spot, the red dot on the logo of containers of 7 Up, comes to life, escapes from the refrigerator, and tears through the house causing riotous havoc.[8] A Pepsi ad shows screaming teens and preteens gorging themselves with cake, pouring Pepsi over their heads, and jumping on the bed with an electric guitar. "Be young, have fun, drink Pepsi," says the voice-over.[9] Adult characters—even adult voice-overs and on-camera spokespeople—have been banished in favor of adolescent voices in the surfer-dude mode.[10] Any old folks left standing should prepare to be mocked. Perceived as carping, droning old-timers who would deny the insiders their pleasure or fun, adults are the butts of the child-world joke. They are, as the *New York Times'* Charles McGrath noted after surveying Saturday morning cartoons, "either idiots, like the crazed geek who does comic spots in 'Disney's 1 Saturday Morning,' or meanies, like the crochety, incompetent teachers and principals on the cartoons 'Recess' and 'Pepper Ann.' "[11] Teachers are, of course, citizens of the adult geekville as well: In one typical snack food ad, kids break out of the halls of their school or behind the back of dimwitted teachers droning on at the chalkboard.[12]

The misleading notion that children are autonomous figures free from adult influence is on striking display in ads like these. Children liberated from parents and teachers are only released into new forms of control. "Children will not be liberated," wrote one sage professor. "They will be dominated."[13] Nineteenth-century moralists saw in the home a haven from the increasingly harsh and inhuman marketplace. The advantage of hindsight allows us to see how this arrangement benefited children. The private home and its parental guardians could exercise their influence on children relatively unchallenged by commercial forces. Our own children, on the other hand, are creatures—one is tempted to say slaves—of the marketplace almost immediately.

The same advertisers who celebrate children's independence from the stodgy adult world and all its rules set out to educate children in its own strict regulations. They instruct children in the difference between what's in and what's out, what's hip and what's nerdy—or, to quote the inimitable Beavis and Butthead, "what's cool and what sucks." Giving new meaning to the phrase *hard sell*, today's ads demonstrate for children the tough posture of the sophisticated child who is savvy to the current styles and fashions. In a contest held by Polaroid for its Cool Cam promotion, the winning entry, from a Manassas, Virginia, girl, depicted a fish looking out a fishbowl at the kids in the house and sneering, "The only thing cool about these nerds is that they have a Cool Cam." Polaroid marketed the camera with a pair of sunglasses, the perennial childhood signifier of sophistication.

It should be clear by now that the pose the media has in mind for children—cool, tough, and sophisticated independence—is that of the teenager. The media's efforts to encourage children to identify with the independent and impulsive consumer teen—efforts that began tentatively, as we say, with Barbie—have now gone into overdrive. Teenagers are everywhere in children's media today. Superheroes like Mighty Morphin Power Rangers and Teenage Mutant Ninja Turtles are teenagers. Dolls based on the TV character Blossom; her suggestively named friend, Six; and her brother, Joey, portray teenagers, as do the dolls based on the TV series *Beverly Hills, 90210,* not to mention the ever-popular Barbie herself. Even the young children dressed in baggy pants who sing *A kid's gotta do what a kid's gotta do* for Nickelodeon are, for all intents and purposes, teenagers.

By populating kid's imaginative world with teenagers, the media simultaneously flatters children's fantasies of sophistication and teaches them what form those fantasies should take. Thus, the media's "liberation" of children from adults also has the mischievous effect of binding them more closely to the peer group. In turn, the peer group polices its members' dress and behavior according to the rules set by this unrecognized authority. In no time at all, children intuit that teens epitomize the freedom, sexiness, and discretionary income—not to mention independence—valued in our society. Teens do not need their mommies to tell them what to wear or eat or how to spend their money, nor do they have sober responsibilities to restrain them from impulse buying.

These days, the invitation to become one of the teen in-crowd arrives so early that its recipients are still sucking their thumbs and stroking their blankies. During the preschool lineup on Nickelodeon one morning, there was a special Nickelodeon video for a song entitled "I Need Mo' Allowance." In this video the camera focuses on a mock heavy metal rock band consisting of three teenaged boys in baggie pants and buzz cuts who rasp a chorus that includes lines like *Mo' allowance to buy CDs!* A dollar sign flashes repeatedly on the screen. This video was followed by an ad for a videotape of *George of the Jungle.* "This George rides around in a limo, baby and looks great in Armani," jeers the dude announcer. "It's not your parents' *George of the Jungle!*" Change the channel to *Sesame Street,* and although the only ads you'll get are for the letter *H* or the number *3,* you may still see an imitation MTV video with a group of longhaired, bopping, stomping muppets singing *I'm so cool, cool, cool!* That few 3-year-olds know the first thing about Armani, limos, or even cool is irrelevant; it's time they learned.

Many companies today have "coolhunters" or "street teams," that is, itinerant researchers who hang out in clubs, malls, and parks and look for trends in adolescent styles in clothes, music, and slang to be used in educating younger consumer trainees. Advertisers can then broadcast for children an aesthetic to emblazon their peer group identity. Even ads for the most naive, childlike products are packed with the symbols of contemporary cool. The Ken doll, introduced in 1993, has hair tinted with blond streaks and wears an earring and a thick gold chain around his neck. The rock and roll which accompanies many of these ads is the pulsing call to generational independence now played for even the youngest tot. The Honey Comb Bear (in sunglasses) raps the virtues of his eponymous cereal. The 1998 Rugrats movie is accompanied by musicians like Elvis Costello and Patti Smith. With a name like Kool-Aid, how could the drink manufacturer continue its traditional appeal to parents and capture today's child sophisticate as well? The new Mr. Kool Aid raps his name onto children's brains.

As math or geography students, American children may be mediocre, but as consumers they are world-class. They learn at prodigiously young ages to obey the detailed sumptuary laws of the teen material world, a world in which status emanates out of the cut of a pair of jeans or the stitching of a sneaker. M/E Marketing Research found that kids make brand decisions by the age of four.[14] *Marketing to and Through Kids* recounts numerous stories of kids under 10 unwilling to war jeans or sneakers without a status label. One executive at Converse claims that dealers inform him that children as young as two are "telling their parents what they want on their feet." Another marketing executive at Nike notes, "The big shift we've been seeing is away from unbranded to more sophisticated branded athletic shoes at younger and younger ages." At Nike the percentage of profit attributable to young children grew from nothing to 14 percent by the early nineties.[15]

Nowhere has the success of media education been more dramatically apparent than among 8-to-12-year-old "tweens." The rise of the tween has been sudden and intense. In 1987 James McNeal, perhaps the best-known scholar of the children's market, reported that children in this age group had an income of $4.7 billion. In 1992 in an article in *American Demographics* he revised that figure up to $9 billion, *an increase of almost 100 percent in five years.*[16] While children spent almost all their money on candy in the 1960s, they now spend two-thirds of their cash on toys, clothes, movies, and games they buy themselves.[17]

The teening of those we used to call preadolescents shows up in almost everything kids wear and do. In 1989 the Girl Scouts of America introduced a new MTV-style ad with rap music in order to, in the words of the organization's media specialist, "get away from the uniformed, goody-goody image and show that the Girl Scouts are a fun, mature, cool place to be."[18] Danny Goldberg, the chief executive officer of Mercury Records, concedes that teenagers have been vital to the music industry since the early days of Sinatra. "But now the teenage years seem to start at eight or nine in terms of

entertainment tastes," he says. "The emotions are kicking in earlier."[19] A prime example is Hanson, a rock-and-roll group whose three members achieved stardom when they were between the ages of 11 and 17. Movie producers and directors are finding it increasingly difficult to interest children this age in the usual children's fare. Tweens go to *Scream,* a horror film about a serial killer, or *Object of My Affection,* a film about a young woman who falls in love with a homosexual man.[20] After the girl-driven success of *Titanic,* Buffy Shutt, president of marketing at Universal Pictures, marveled, "They're amazing consumers."[21] Mattel surely agrees, as evidenced by their Barbie ad. "You, girls, can do anything." Clothing retailers are scrambling for part of the tween action. All over the country companies like Limited Too, Gap Kids, Abercrombie and Fitch, and Gymboree have opened stores for 6-to-12-year-olds and are selling the tween look—which at this moment means bell bottoms, ankle-length skirts or miniskirts, platform shoes, and tank tops.[22] Advertisers know that kids can spot their generational signature in a nanosecond—the hard rock and roll, the surfer-dude voices, the baggy pants and bare midriffs shot by tilted cameras in vibrant hues and extreme close-ups—and they oblige by offering these images on TV, the Internet, in store displays, and in the growing number of kid magazines.[23]

The seduction of children with dreams of teen sophistication and tough independence, which began with Barbie and intensified markedly in the last decade, appears to have had the desired effect: It has undermined childhood by turning children into teen consumers. This new breed of children won't go to children's moves and they won't play with toys. One of the stranger ironies of the rise of the tween is that toy manufacturers, who with the introduction of Barbie began the direct hard sell to children and were the first to push the teening of American childhood, have been hoist with their own petard. The 1998–99 Toy Industry Factbook of the Toy Manufacturer's Association says that the industry used to think of kids between birth and 14 as their demographic audience, but with the emergence of tweens they have had to shrink that audience to birth to 10.[24] Even seven- and eight-year-olds are scorning Barbie.[25]

Who needs a doll when you can live the life of the teen vamp yourself? Cosmetic companies are finding a bonanza among this age group. Lines aimed at tweens include nail polish, hair mascara, lotions, and lip products like lipstick, lip gloss, "lip lix." Sweet Georgia Brown is a cosmetic line for tweens that includes body paints and scented body oils with come-hither names like Vanilla Vibe or Follow Me Boy. The Cincinnati design firm Libby Peszyk Kattiman has introduced a line of bikini underwear for girls. There are even fitness clubs and personal trainers for tweens in Los Angeles and New York.[26]

Marketers point at broad demographic trends to explain these changes in the child market, and they are at least partially correct. Changes in the family have given children more power over shopping decisions. For the simple reason that fewer adults are around most of the time, children in single-parent homes tend to take more responsibility for obtaining food and clothes. Market researchers have found that these kids become independent consumers earlier than those in two-parent homes.[27] Children of working mothers also tend to do more of the family shopping when at around age eight or nine they can begin to get to the store by themselves. Though candy, toy, and cereal manufacturers had long been well aware of the money potential of tween cravings, by the mid-eighties, even though their absolute numbers were falling, tweens began to catch the eye of a new range of businesses, and ads and marketing magazines started to tout the potential of this new niche. The reason was simple: Market research revealed that more and more children in this age group were shopping for their own clothes, shoes, accessories, and drug-store items—indeed, they were even shopping for the family groceries. Just as marketers had once targeted housewives, now they were aiming at kids.[28] Jeans manufacturer Jordache was one of the first companies to spot the trend. "My customers are kids who can walk into a store with either their own money or their mothers'," the company's director of advertising explained at the time. "The dependent days of tugging on Mom or Dad's sleeve are over." Now as the number of children is rising again, their appeal is even more irresistible. Packaged Facts, a division of the worldwide research firm Find/SVP, has said that the potential purchasing power of today's kids "is the greatest of any age or demographic group in our nation's history."[29]

And there is another reason for the increasing power of children as consumers: By the time they are tweens, American children have simply learned to expect a lot of stuff.[30] Many of them have been born to older mothers; the number of first babies born to women over 30 has quadrupled since 1970, and the number born to women over 40 doubled in the six years between 1984 and 1990. Older mothers are more likely to have established careers and to be in the kind of financial position that allows them to shower their kids with toys and expensive clothes.[31] Also, grandparents are living longer and more comfortably, and they often arrive with an armload of toys, sports equipment, and fancy dresses. (The products of the children's clothes company Osh Kosh B'Gosh are known in the trade as "granny bait.") Divorce has also helped to inflate the child market: Many American children divide their time between parents, multiplying by two the number of soccer balls and Big Bird toothbrushes they must own. But as we have seen before, impersonal social forces have found support in human decisions. Important as they are, demographics by themselves can't explain 10-year-olds who have given up dolls for mascara and body oil. The teening of childhood has been a consummation the media devoutly wished—and planned.

The media has given tweens a group identity with its own language, music, and fashion. It has done this by flattering their sense of being hip and aware almost-teens rather than out-of-it little kids dependent on their parents. On discovering the rising number of child customers, Jordache Jeans did not simply run ads for kids; they ran ads showing kids saying things like "Have you ever seen your parents naked?" and "I hate my mother. She's prettier than me." When Bonne Bell cosmetics discovered the rising sales potential of younger shoppers, they did not merely introduce a tween line, which some parents might think bad enough; they introduced it with the kind of in-your-face language that used to send children to bed without dinner: "We know how to be cool. We have our own ideas. And make our own decisions. Watch out for us." Sassaby's "Watch your mouth, young lady" is a smirking allusion to old-fashioned childhood that is meant to sell a line of lip "huggers" and "gloss overs."

There is little reason to think that children have found the freedom and individuality that liberationists assumed they would find now that they have been liberated from old-fashioned childhood and its adult guards. The rise of the child consumer and the child market itself is compelling evidence that children will always seek out some authority for rules about how to dress, talk, and act. Today's school-age children, freed from adult guidance, turn to their friends, who in turn rely on a glamorous and flattering media for the relevant cultural messages. Recent studies have found that children are forming cliques at younger ages than in previous years and that those cliques have strict rules about dress, behavior, and leisure. By the fifth or sixth grade, according to *Peer Power: Preadolescent Culture and Identity*, girls are gaining status "from their success at grooming, clothes, and other appearance-related variables."[32] Teachers and principals also see an increasing number of 10- and 11-year-olds who have given up toys for hair mousse and name-brand jeans and who heckle those who do not. What matters to this new breed of child is, according to Bruce Friend, vice president of worldwide research and planning at Nickelodeon, "being part of the in-crowd" and "being the first to know what's cool."[33] These "free" children "are extremely fad conscious"; moreover, according to *American Demographics,* tweens' attraction to fads has "no saturation points."[34] Look for the tween consumer to become even more powerful.

A diminished home life and an ever more powerful media constitute a double blow against the conditions under which individuality flourishes. Whereas in the past eccentric or bookish children might have had the privacy of their home to escape the pressures of their media-crazed peers, today such refuge has gone the way of after-school milk and cookies. And if you think that at least such children have been freed of the pressure of yesterday's domineering fathers and frustrated mothers, you might want to reconsider. As Hannah Arandt once noted, "The authority of a group, even a child group, is always considerably stronger and more tyrannical than the severest authority of an individual person can ever be." The opportunity for an individual to rebel when bound to a group is "practically nil"; few adults can do it.[35] The truth is, yesterday's parent-controlled childhood protected children not only from sex, from work, and from adult decisions but also from the dominance of peers and from the market, with all its pressures to achieve, its push for status, its false lures, its passing fads.

But in the anticultural filiarchy which is replacing traditional childhood, adults no longer see their job as protecting children from the market. In fact, it is not that the child's hurried entrance into the market means that parents are increasingly failing to socialize children. It's the other way around. Children are viewed by manufacturers as the "opinion leaders in the household," according to a vice president at Keebler.[36] Manufacturers believe that children are exercising influence over family purchases never before remotely associated with the young. Holiday Inn and Delta Airlines have established marketing programs aimed at children, and Sport Illustrated for Kids publishes ads from American Airlines, IBM, and car manufacturers.[37]

While simply turning off the TV would help, at this point television is only one part of the picture. Kids learn of their sophisticated independence from retail displays and promotions, from magazines and direct mailings. With their captive audience, schools, too, have become an advertiser's promised land: Kids see ads in classrooms, on book order forms, on Channel One, on the Internet, on school buses, and now even in textbooks. Book order forms distributed in schools throughout the country from the putatively educational firm Scholastic look like cartoons and provide children with the opportunity to order stickers, autograph books, fan biographies, and books based on popular movies and television shows. Practically every Fortune 500 company has a school project, according to the New York Times, and many administrators expect that in the near future we will be seeing signs like CHEERLEADERS BROUGHT TO YOU BY REEBOK in school gyms.[38] "It isn't enough just to advertise on television," Carol Herman, a senior vice president of Grey Advertising, explains. "You've got to reach the kids throughout their day—in school, as they're shopping at the mall . . . or at the movies. You've got to become part of the fabric of their lives."[39]

The scorched earth policy in the name of the filiarchy requires that ever younger children be treated as potential customers, once again in the guise of education. When Sesame Street arrived on the airwaves in 1969, no one imagined that preschoolers could be a significant market segment. In fact, the improbability of preschool purchasing power was the reason Sesame Street had to appear on public television in the first place; no one wanted to put a lot of money into creating and broadcasting a program for kids who had no purchasing power. How shortsighted that was! By 1994 Children's Television Workshop was bringing in $120 million a year largely on the strength of its over 5,000 licensed products. The list includes not just educational items like books and audiotapes but bubble bath, pajamas, underwear, and Chef Boyardee Sesame Street pasta. Toy manufacturers gradually caught on to the power of the littlest people, especially where their education was concerned. The number of preschool toys exploded in the decades after Sesame Street was introduced, and many of them were stamped with a seal of approval from some expert or other—or with the image of Ernie or Big Bird, which in the minds of many amounted to the same thing.

And now Teletubbies has arrived to help carve out the pre-preschool market and to give power to the littlest people. Teletubbies was designed for one- and two-year-olds, and though no one has ever explained how it could possibly be educational for babies to watch television, it is clear that when toddlers see pictures of the four vividly hued plush and easily identified characters (with television screens on their stomachs) on bottles or bibs, they will cry for them and PBS will rake it in. In anticipation of opening up this new market segment, the media went into overdrive. Pictures of the characters appeared in ads in trade and consumer magazines and were plastered on buses in New York City and on a giant billboard in Times Square. The show was a topic on Letterman, Today, and Nightline. "If this isn't the most important toy at Christmas this year, then something desperately wrong will have happened," gloated Kenn Viselman, whose Itsy Bitsy Entertainment Company has the rights to Teletubbies products. "This show had more advance press than Titanic." Wondered one critic, "Where does it end: A TV in the amniotic sac?" But marketers were thrilled; according to the president of another licensing company, before now "the one-to-two-year-old niche hasn't been filled very well."[40] The one-to-two-year-old niche? McNeal has said that children become aware of the market as early as two months of age.[41] There is no more unmistakable sign of the end of childhood as Americans have known it.

REFERENCES

1. The history presented in this article is take from Lynn Spigel, Make Room for TV: Television and the Family Ideal in Post-war America (Chicago: University of Chicago Press, 1992); Gerard Jones, Honey, I'm Home: Sitcoms: Selling the American Dream (New York: Grove Weidenfeld, 1992); William Melody, Children's Television: The Economics of Exploitation (New Haven, Conn.: Yale University Press, 1973); Cy Schneider, Children's Television: The Art, the Business and How It Works (Chicago: NTC Business Books, 1987). Mark Crispin Miller, "Deride and Conquer," in Watching Television, ed. Todd Gitlin (New York: Pantheon Books, 1986), traces the "long decline of Dad" (pp. 196ff.) and the triumph of the ironic tone.
2. Quoted in Jones, p. 42.
3. Arthur Asa Berger, The Comic-Stripped American: What Dick Tracy, Blondie, Daddy Warbucks and Charlie Brown Tell Us About Ourselves (New York: Walker, 1973), p. 103.
4. Spigel, p. 60.

5. The history of toy advertising and Barbie comes from Schneider, pp. 18–26; G. Wayne Miller, *Toy Wars: The Epic Struggle Between G.I. Joe, Barbie, and the Companies That Make Them* (New York: Random House, 1998), p. 67; Gary Cross, *Kids' Stuff: Toys and the Changing World of American Childhood* (Cambridge: Harvard University Press, 1997), chap. 6.
6. Cross, pp. 165–166.
7. Ellen Seiter, *Sold Separately: Parents and Children in the Consumer Culture* (New Brunswick, N.J.: Rutgers University Press, 1993), notes this same theme (in chap. 4), and several of my examples come from there. Seiter, like other academics today writing in the Ariès tradition, believes Kid Kulture can "express a resistance to the middle-class culture of parenting . . . that may be very healthy indeed," (p. 232). In other words, she finds ads genuinely subversive.
8. Example from Selina S. Guber and Jon Berry, *Marketing to and Through Kids* (New York: McGraw-Hill, 1993), p. 133.
9. Patricia Winters, "Pepsi Harkens Back to Youth," *Advertising Age,* January 25, 1993. p. 3.
10. Seiter (p. 130) quotes research, comparing boys' toy ads from the fifties and those of today which finds that the adult male voice-over or on-camera spokesman has almost entirely disappeared.
11. Charles McGrath, "Giving Saturday Morning Some Slack," *New York Times Magazine*, November 9, 1997, p. 54.
12. Seiter, p. 121.
13. John E. Coons, "Intellectual Liberty and the Schools," *Notre Dame Journal of Law, Ethics, and Public Policy*, vol. 1, 1985, p. 503.
14. "News/Trends—Kidpower," *Fortune*, March 30, 1987, pp. 9–10.
15. Guber and Berry, pp. 27, 78.
16. James McNeal, "Growing Up in the Market, *American Demographics*, October 1992, p. 47.
17. Figure cited in Lisa Bannon, "As Children Become More Sophisticated, Marketers Think Older," *Wall Street Journal*, October 13, 1998, p. A1. McNeal says that aggregate spending on or for children between ages four and twelve doubled every decade in the 1960s, 1970s, and 1980s. In the 1990s the children's market picked up more steam: between 1990 and 1997, it had already tripled.
18. Jane Weaver, "Girl Scout Campaign: Shedding Old Image for Media Cool," *Adweek*, September 11, 1989, p. 11.
19. Quoted in Bernard Weinraub, "Who's Lining Up at Box Office? Lots and Lots of Girls," *New York Times*, Arts Section, February 23, 1998, p. 1.
20. Bannon, p. A8; Michele Willens, "Young and in a Niche That Movies Neglect," *New York Times*, Arts and Leisure Section, June 14, 1998, pp. 13–14.
21. Quoted in Weinraub, p. 4.
22. Bannon, pp. A1, 8.
23. The number of magazines for children almost doubled between 1986 and 1991. S.K. List, "The Right Place to Find Children," *American Demographics*, February 1992, pp. 44–47.
24. Toy Industry Factbook at www.toy-tma.com/PUBLICATIONS/factbook98/economics.html.
25. Bannon, p. A1.
26. Laura Klepacki, "Courting the 'Tweenie' Boppers," *WWD*, February 27, 1998, p. 10; Becky Ebenkamp, "Packaging: Sara Lee Repackages Youthful Underwear to Better Draw Juniors," *Brandweek*, January 5, 1998, p. 36.
27. James McNeal and Chyon-Hwa Yeh, "Born to Shop," *American Demographics*, June 1993, p. 37.
28. Carrier Telegardin, "Growing Up Southern: The Kids Take Over," *Atlanta Journal-Constitution*, June 7, 1993, p. E1. According to Telegardin, "America's new housewife [is] the housekid."
29. Quoted in Toy Industry Factbook. See also "Generation Y," *Business Week*, February 15, 1999, pp. 80–88, for how this generation is changing the marketplace.
30. The psychologist Marilyn Bradford found that preschoolers ask for an average of 3.4 toys for Christmas and receive 11.6. Cited in Gary Cross, "Too Many Toys," *New York Times*, November 24, 1995, p. 35.
31. Lisa Gubernick and Marla Matzer, "Babies as Dolls," *Forbes*, February 27, 1995, p. 78.
32. Patricia A. Adler and Peter Adler, *Peer Power: Preadolescent Culture and Identity* (New Brunswick, N.J.: Rutgers University Press, 1998), p. 55. Tellingly, by 1991 shoes and clothing were the fastest-growing categories among children up to age twelve and accounted for 13 percent of their spending, up from an unmeasurably small amount in 1988, according to Susan Antilla, " 'I Want' Now Gets," *New York Times*, April 4 1993, p. 17. See also Carol Pogash, "The Clothing Boom in the Land of the Little People," *Los Angeles Times*, August 29, 1995, p. 22.
33. Interview by the author, July 1998.
34. Judith Waldrop, "The Tween Scene," *American Demographics*, September 1992, p. 4.
35. Hannah Arendt, "Crisis in Education," *Partisan Review*, Fall 1958, p. 500.
36. Quoted in Guber and Berry, p. 84. See also Claire Collins, "Fighting the Holiday Advertising Blitz," *New York Times*, December 1, 1994, p. C4; Matt Murray, "Hey Kids! Marketers Want Your Help!" *Wall Street Journal*, May 6, 1997, pp. B1, 8; Antilla, p. 17; Steven A. Holmes, "Shoppers! Deciding? Just Ask Your Child," *New York Times*, Week in Review, January 8, 1995, p. 4; Becky Ebenkamp, Mike Beirne, and Christine Bittar, "Products for the Sophisticated Little Nipper," *Brandweek*, February 22, 1999. pp. 1, 53.
37. See Don Oldenberg, "Consummate Consumer: Children's Business: America's 90 Billion Plus Youth Market," *Washington Post*, July 6, 1995, p. C5.
38. Deborah Stead, "Classrooms and Commercialism," *New York Times*, Education Life, January 5, 1997, p. 30.
39. Quoted in Michael F. Jacobson and Laurie Ann Mazur, *Marketing Madness: A Survival Guide for a Consumer Society* (New York: Westview Press, 1995), p. 21. See also Carrie Goerne, "Marketers Try to Get More Creative at Reaching Teens," *Marketing News*, August 5, 1991, pp. 2, 6; Judann Dagnoli, "Consumer's Union Hits Kids Advertising," *Advertising Age*, July 23, 1990, p. 4.
40. Quoted in Lawrie Mifflin, "Critics Assail PBS over Plan for Toys Aimed at Toddlers," *New York Times*, April 20, 1998, p. A17.
41. Quoted in Oldenberg, p. C5. Mary Ellen Podmolik, "Kids' Clothing Boom," *Chicago Sun Times*, Financial Section, August 21, 1994, p. 1, quotes McNeal to the effect that 10 percent of a two-year-old's vocabulary is made up of brand names.

Kay S. Hymowitz is a senior fellow at the Manhattan Institute, a contributing editor at City Journal, *and an affiliate scholar at the Institute for American Values. This article is adapted from her recent book,* Ready or Not. *Copyright © 1999 by Kay S. Hymowitz. Reprinted by permission of The Free Press, an imprint of Simon & Schuster, Inc.*

The Betrayal Of The American Man

BOOK EXCERPT: Her groundbreaking 'Backlash' looked at the 'undeclared war on women.' Now in 'Stiffed,' the author explores the unseen war on men—the pressure to be masculine in a culture that no longer honors traditional codes of manhood.

By Susan Faludi

When I listen to the sons born after World War II, born to the fathers who won that war, I sometimes find myself in a reverie. I imagine a boy, in bed pretending to sleep, waiting for his father. The door opens, and the hall light streams in, casting a cutout shadow man across the bedroom floor. A minute later, the boy, wearing his coonskin cap and clutching his flashlight, races after his father along the shadowy upper hallway, down the stairs and out the screen door. The man and the boy kneel on the scratchy wool of the father's old navy peacoat, and the father snaps off the boy's flashlight. The father directs the boy's vision to a faraway glimmer. Its name is Echo. The boy looks up, knowing that the satellite his father is pointing out is more than just an object; it is a paternal gift rocketing him into his future, a miraculous inheritance encased in the transit of an artificial star, infinitesimally tiny, impossibly bright.

I knew this boy. Like everyone else who grew up in the late 1950s and early 1960s, I knew dozens of him. He was Bobby on the corner, who roamed the neighborhood with his cap gun and holster, terrorizing girls and household pets. He was Frankie, who blew off part of his pinkie while trying to ignite a miniature rocket in the schoolyard. Even if he wasn't brought out into the back-

> **The veterans of World War II**
> **were eager to embrace a manly ideal that revolved**
> **around providing rather than dominating. Ultimately, society**
> **double-crossed them.**

yard and shown a satellite glinting in the sky, he was introduced to the same promise and the same vision, and by such a father. Many of these fathers were veterans of World War II or Korea, but their bloody paths to virility were not ones they sought to pass on, or usually even discuss. This was to be the era of manhood after victory, when the pilgrimage to masculinity would be guided not by the god of war Mars, but by the dream of a pioneering trip to the planet Mars. The satellite; here was a visible patrimony, a visual marker of vaulting technological power and progress to be claimed in the future by every baby-boom boy. The men of the fathers' generation had "won" the world and now they were giving it to their sons.

Four decades later, as the nation wobbled toward the millennium, its pulse-takers all seemed to agree that a domestic apocalypse was underway: American manhood was under siege. Newspaper editors, legislators, preachers, marketers, no matter where they perched on the political spectrum, had a contribution to make to the chronicles of the "masculinity crisis." Right-wing talk-radio hosts and left-wing men's-movement spokesmen found themselves uncomfortably on common ground. MEN ON TRIAL, the headlines cried, THE TROUBLE WITH BOYS. Journalists—myself included—raced to report on one young-male hot spot after another: Tailhook, the Citadel, the Spur Posse, South Central gangsters, militiamen

Reprinted from *Newsweek,* September 13, 1999, pp. 48-58. Excerpted from *Stiffed: The Betrayal of the American Man,* © 1999 by Susan Faludi. Reprinted by permission of William Morrow/HarperCollins Publishers, Inc.

blowing up federal buildings and abortion clinics, schoolyard shooters across the country.

In the meantime, the media's softer lifestyle outlets happily turned their attention to male-crisis lite: the retreat to cigar clubs and lap-dancing emporiums, the boom in male cosmetic surgery and the abuse of steroids, the brisk sales of Viagra. Social scientists pontificated on "endangered" young black men in the inner cities, Ritalin-addicted white "bad boys" in the suburbs, "deadbeat dads" everywhere and, less frequently, the anguish of downsized male workers. Social psychologists issued reports on a troubling rise in male-distress signals—from depressive disorders to suicides to certain criminal behaviors.

Pollsters investigated the electoral habits of a new voting bloc they called "the Angry White Male." Marketers hastened to turn the crisis into entertainment and profits from TV shows like "The Man Show" to T shirts that proclaimed DESTROY ALL GIRLS or WIFE BEATER. And by the hundreds of thousands, men without portfolio confirmed the male-crisis diagnosis, convening in Washington for both the black Nation of Islam-led Million Man March and a largely white, evangelical-led Promise Keepers rally entitled, hopefully, "Stand in the Gap."

If so many concurred in the existence of a male crisis, consensus collapsed as soon as anyone asked the question Why. Everyone proposed a favorite whipping boy or, more often, whipping girl, and blame-seekers on all sides went after their selected culprits with righteous and bitter relish. Feminist mothers, indulgent liberals, videogame makers or testosterone itself all came under attack.

At Ground Zero of the Masculinity Crisis

THE SEARCH FOR AN ANSWER to that question took me on a six-year odyssey, with stops along the way at a shuttered shipyard in Long Beach, a suburban living room where a Promise Keepers group met, a Cleveland football stadium where fans grieved the loss of their team, a Florida horse farm where a Vietnam vet finally found peace, a grassy field in Waco where militiamen searched for an enemy and a slick magazine office where young male editors contended with a commodified manhood. But I began investigating this crisis where you might expect a feminist journalist to begin: at the weekly meetings of a domestic-violence group. Wednesday evenings in a beige stucco building a few blocks from the freeway in Long Beach, Calif., I attended a gathering of men under court order to repent the commission of an act that stands as the emblematic masculine sin of our age. What did I expect to divine about the broader male condition by monitoring a weekly counseling session for batterers? That men are by nature brutes? Or, more optimistically, that the efforts of such a group might point to methods of "curing" such beastliness?

Either way, I can see now that I was operating from an assumption both underexamined and dubious: that the male crisis in America was caused by something men were doing unrelated to something being done to them. I had my own favorite whipping boy, suspecting that the crisis of masculinity was caused by masculinity on the rampage. If male violence was the quintessential expression of masculinity run amok, then a domestic-violence therapy group must be at the very heart of this particular darkness.

I wasn't alone in such circular reasoning. I was besieged with suggestions along similar lines from journalists, feminists, antifemin-

In the new economy, work moved from vital production and job security to paper pushing and massive layoffs

The Broken Promise

On the surface, said Richard Foster, who came to McDonnell Douglas in the late '60s to work in the NASA space lab, life as an aerospace man seemed to offer the ultimate in masculine freedom. "It was idyllic," he told me. "All these little green lawns and houses all in a row. You could drive the freeways and plan your life out." But as time went on, he came to feel that it had all been planned without him, that he was expected to take the initiative in a game in which he was not even a player. "You began to feel so isolated," he said. Like the rest of the managers, he "belonged" to the company in only the most tenuous way. In the end, he would become a casualty of various corporate "cost-reduction" programs five times, his salary plunging from $80,000 to $28,000 to zero. Which was why he was sitting in a vinyl banquette in a chain restaurant in the shadow of McDonnell Douglas's blueglass tower in the middle of the afternoon, talking to me. "The next thing you know," he said, "you're standing outside, looking in. And you begin to ask, as a man, what is my role? What is it, really, that I do?"

About 11 miles up the road, a starkly different kind of leave-taking was unfolding at the Long Beach Naval Shipyard, one of the military bases slated for closure in 1995. If McDonnell Douglas had been the emblematic postwar corporation—full of functionaries whose jobs were unclear, even to themselves—the shipyard represented a particular vintage of American masculinity, monumental in its pooled effort, indefatigable in its industry and built on a sense of useful productivity. Ike Burr, one of the first black men to break into upper management, was a shipfitter who climbed steadily to project superintendent. "Everything you ever dreamed of is here," Burr said. Unlike the McDonnell Douglas men, he wasn't referring to his dream house in the suburbs. He was talking about the work itself. "The shipyard is like a world within itself. Most items are one-of-a-type items, done once and not to be repeated. There's satisfaction in it, because you start and complete something. You *see* what you've created. The world of custom-made is finished—except here." After the shipyard's closing was announced, Burr postponed his official signing-out. He had found a temporary job at another military installation and was always "too busy" to get back to Long Beach to turn in his badge. But one morning he arrived to pay his last respects. He dressed sharply for the occasion: double-breasted gray suit, paisley tie and matching pocket hankie, even a hint of cologne. The morning management meeting was underway and he had been asked to stop by. He offered a few pointers, and then the shipyard commander gave an impromptu speech—about how Burr was the kind of guy "you could rely on to get the job done." Then he handed Burr a homemade plaque with a lengthy inscription.

Burr tucked it under his arm, embarrassed by the attention. "I better go get the signing-out business over," he said, his voice bumping over choppy seas. He headed out to make the rounds and get his termination physical. By late afternoon, Ike Burr had arrived at a small office, to sign a form surrendering the code word that gave him access to the yard. Though he burst out laughing as he signed, his words belied the laughter. "I have nothing in my possession," he said. "I have lost everything."   S.F.

GHETTO STAR

In a South-Central gang, Kody Scott finally felt useful as a man. But the biggest part of the 'work' was promoting the gangster image.

Glamour in the 'Hood

My father's generation was the last responsible generation," said Sanyika Shakur (now Kody Scott's legally adopted name) as he welcomed me in August 1997 to his girlfriend's two-bedroom house in California's San Fernando Valley. Four years had passed since the publication of Shakur's best-selling memoir, "Monster: The Autobiography of an L.A. Gang Member," written while he was serving a four-year sentence for robbery at Pelican Bay State Prison. The book's cover photo of the pumped-up, bare-chested author clutching a semiautomatic MAC-10, combined with the much-advertised news of his six-figure advance, turned the former member of the Eight-Tray Gangsters (a Crips set in South-Central L.A.) into what he rightly called a "ghetto star."

Shakur had just been released from jail three days earlier, after a year's sentence for a parole violation, his second such since the publication of what was supposed to be his transformational autobiography. He had fled after his first violation, and the police eventually found him on a neighborhood porch, receiving a long line of autograph seekers. The dictates of a celebrity culture demanded a manhood forged by being glamorous, not responsible.

As a young man, he had still hoped that he could demonstrate a workmanlike "usefulness" within his gang set. "You put in work and you feel needed in a gang. People would call on me because they needed me. You feel useful, and you're useful in your capacity as a man. You know, 'Don't send me no boys. Send me a man!' " But he was beginning to see his former life in a different light. What he once perceived as "work" now seemed more like PR. "What the work was," he said, "was anything you did in *promotion* for the gang." He found it amusing how the media viewed gangs as clannish and occult. "We're not a secret society. Our whole thing is writing on walls, tattoos on necks, maintaining visibility. Getting media coverage is the s—t! If the media knows about you, damn, that's the top. We don't recognize ourselves unless we're recognized on the news."

Kody Scott's image-enhancement strategies were not homegrown. "I got all these ideas from watching movies and

> **Getting a rep:**
> 'If the media knows about you, damn, that's the top,' says Scott

watching television. I was really just out there acting from what I saw on TV." And he wasn't referring to "Superfly" or "Shaft." "Growing up, I didn't see one blaxploitation movie. Not one." His inspiration came from shows like "Mission: Impossible" and "Rat Patrol" and films like "The Godfather." "I would study the guys in those movies," he recalled, "how they moved, how they stood, the way they dressed, that whole winning way of dressing. Their tactics became my tactics. I went from watching "Rat Patrol' to being in it." His prime model was Arthur Penn's 1967 movie "Bonnie and Clyde." "I watched how in 'Bonnie and Clyde' they'd walk in and say their whole names. They were getting their reps. I took that and applied it to my situation." Cinematic gangsterism was his objective, and it didn't seem like much of a reach. "It's like there's a thin line in this country now between criminality and celebrity. Someone has to be the star of the 'hood. Someone has to do the advertising for the 'hood. And it's like agencies that pick a good-looking guy model. So it became, 'Monster Kody! Let's push him out there!' " He grinned as he said this, an aw-shucks smile that was, doubtless, part of his "campaign."

S.F.

---

ists and other willing advisers. Women's rights advocates mailed me news clips about male office stalkers and computer harassers. That I was not ensconced in the courtroom for O. J. Simpson's murder trial struck many of my volunteer helpers as an appalling lapse of judgment. "The perfect case study of an American man who thinks he's entitled to just control everything and everybody," one of them suggested.

But then, I had already been attending the domestic-violence group for several months—the very group O. J. Simpson was, by coincidence, supposed to have attended but avoided with the promise that he would speak by phone to a psychiatrist—and it was already apparent to me that these men's crises did not stem from a preening sense of entitlement and control. Each new member in the group, called Alternatives to Violence, would be asked to describe what he had done

to a woman, a request that was met invariably with the disclaimer "I was out of control." The counselors would then expend much energy showing him how he had, in fact, been in control the entire time. He had chosen his fists, not a knife; he had hit her in the stomach, not the face. No doubt the moment of physical contact for these men had grown out of a desire for supreme control fueled by a need to dominate. I cannot conceive of a circumstance that would exonerate such violence. By making the abusive spouse take responsibility for his actions, the counselors were pursuing a worthy goal. But the logic behind the violence still remained elusive.

A serviceman who had turned to night-club-bouncer jobs and pastry catering after his military base shut down seemed to confirm the counselors' position one evening shortly before his "graduation" from the group. "I denied it before," he said of the

night he pummeled his girlfriend. "I thought I'd blacked out. But looking back at that night, I didn't black out. I was feeling good. I was in power, I was strong, I was in control. I felt like a man." But what struck me most strongly was what he said next: that moment of control had been the only one in his recent life. "That feeling of power," he said, "didn't last long. Only until they put the cuffs on. Then I was feeling again like I was no man at all."

He was typical in this regard. The men I got to know in the group had, without exception, lost their compass in the world. They had lost or were losing jobs, homes, cars, families. They had been labeled outlaws but felt like castoffs. There was something almost absurd about these men struggling, week after week, to recognize themselves as dominators when they were so clearly dominated, done in by the world.

Underlying all the disagreement over what is confusing and unnerving to men runs a constant line of thinking that blinds us—whatever our political beliefs—to the nature of the male predicament. Ask feminists to diagnose men's problems and you will often get a very clear explanation: men are in crisis because women are properly challenging male dominance. Ask antifeminists and you will get a diagnosis that is, in one respect, similar. Men are troubled, many conservative pundits say, because women have gone far beyond their demands for equal treatment and now are trying to take power away from men.

Both the feminist and antifeminist views are rooted in a peculiarly modern American perception that to be a man means you are at the controls at all times. The popular feminist joke that men are to blame for everything is the flip side of the "family values" reactionary expectation that men should be in charge of everything.

The man controlling his environment is today the prevailing American image of masculinity. He is to be in the driver's seat, the king of the road, forever charging down the open highway, along that masculine Möbius strip that cycles endlessly through a numbing stream of movies, TV shows, novels, advertisements and pop tunes. He's a man because he won't be stopped. He'll fight attempts to tamp him down; if he has to, he'll use his gun. But we forget the true Daniel Boone frontiersmanship was only incidentally violent, and was based on creating, out of wilderness, a communal context to which a man could moor himself through work and family.

Modern debates about how men are exercising or abusing their control and power neglect to raise whether a lack of mooring, a lack of context, is causing men's anguish. If men are the masters of their fate, what do they do about the unspoken sense that they are being mastered, in the marketplace and at home, by forces that seem to be sweeping away the soil beneath their feet? If men are mythologized as the ones who make things happen, then how can they begin to analyze what is happening to them?

More than a quarter century ago, women began to free themselves from the box in which they were trapped by feeling their way along its contours, figuring out how it was shaped and how it shaped them. Women were able to take action, paradoxically, by understanding how they were acted upon. Men feel the contours of a box, too, but they are told that box is of their own manufacture, designed to their specifications. Who are they to complain? For men to say they feel boxed in is regarded not as laudable political protest but as childish whining. How dare the kings complain about their castles?

What happened to so disturb the sons of the World War II GIs? The prevailing narrative that the sons inherited—fashioned from the battlefronts of Europe and the Pacific, laid out in countless newspapers, newsreels

and movies—was a tale of successful fatherhood and masculine transformation: boys whose Depression-era fathers could neither provide for them nor guide them into manhood were placed under the benevolent wing of a vast male-run orphanage called the army and sent into battle. There, firm but kindly senior officers acting as surrogate fathers watched over them as they were tempered into men in the heat of a heroic struggle against malevolent enemies. The boys, molded into men, would return to find wives, form their families and take their places as adults in the community of a nation taking its place as a grown-up power in the world.

This was the story America told itself in dozens of war movies in which tough but tenderhearted commanding officers prepared their appreciative "boys" to assume their responsibilities in male society. It was the theme behind the 1949 film "Sands of Iwo Jima," with John Wayne as Sergeant Stryker, a stern papa molding his wet-behind-the-ears charges into a capable fraternity. "Before I'm through with you, you're gonna move like one man and think like one man," he tells them. "If I can't teach you one way, I'll teach you another, but I'm gonna get the job done." And he gets the job done, fathering a whole squad of youngsters into communal adulthood.

The veterans of World War II were eager to embrace a masculine ideal that revolved around providing rather than dominating. Their most important experiences had centered on the support they had given one another in the war, and it was this that they wished to replicate. As artilleryman Win Stracke told oral historian Studs Terkel in "The Good War," he came home bearing this most cherished memory: "You had 15 guys who for the first time in their lives could help each other without cutting each other's throat or trying to put down somebody else through a boss or whatever. I had realized it was the absence of competition and all those phony standards that created the thing I loved about the army."

The fathers who would sire the baby-boom generation would try to pass that experience of manhood on intact to their sons. The grunts who went overseas and liberated the world came home to the expectation that they would liberate the country by quiet industry and caretaking. The vets threw themselves into their federally funded educations,

and later their defense-funded corporate and production-line jobs, and their domestic lives in Veterans Administration-financed tract homes. They hoped their dedication would be in the service of a higher national aim.

For their children, the period of soaring expectations that followed the war was truly the era of the boy. It was the culture of "Father Knows Best" and "Leave It to Beaver," of Pop Warner rituals and Westinghouse science scholarships, of BB guns and rocket clubs, of football practice and lettered jackets, of magazine ads where "Dad" seemed always to be beaming down at his scampy, cowboy-suited younger son or proudly handing his older son the keys to a brand-new convertible. It was a world where, regardless of the truth that lay behind each garden gate, popular culture led us to believe that fathers were spending every leisure moment in roughhouse play and model-air-plane construction with their beloved boys.

In the aspiring middle-class suburb where I came of age, there was no mistaking the belief in the boy's pre-eminence; it was evident in the solicitous attentions of parents and schoolteachers, in the centrality of Cub Scouts and Little League, in the community life that revolved around boys' championships and boys' scores—as if these outposts of tract-home America had been built mainly as exhibition rings for junior-male achievement, which perhaps they had.

The speech that inaugurated the shiny new era of the 1960s was the youthful John F. Kennedy's address to the Democratic National Convention, a month before the launch of Echo. The words would become, along with his Inaugural oration, a haunting refrain in adolescent male consciousness. What Kennedy implicitly presented was a new rite of passage for an untested male generation. "The New Frontier of which I speak is not a set of promises," he told them. "It is a set of challenges." Kennedy understood that it was not enough for the fathers to win the world for their sons; the sons had to feel they had won it for themselves. If the fathers had their Nazis and "Nips," then Kennedy would see to it that the sons had an enemy, too. He promised as much on Inauguration Day in 1961, when he spoke vaguely but unremittingly of communism's threat, of a country that would be defined by its readiness to "pay any price" and "oppose any

---

The 'New Frontier' of space

turned out to be a void no man could conquer, let alone colonize. The astronaut was no Daniel Boone, just a flattened image for TV viewers to watch.

GONE TO SOLDIERS EVERY ONE

Michael Bernhardt went to Vietnam to honor his sense of justice. But the war destroyed his idea of manhood.

The Dogs of War

As far back as Michael Bernhardt could remember watching World War II movies, he could remember wanting to serve. The summers of his boyhood in the backyards of Long Island were one long idyll of war play on an imagined European front. "We had leaders," he said. "We attacked things with dirt bombs. We thought war was where we'd all go in together like D-Day and be part of this big coordinated army that would *do* something. And then you'd come back and have war stories to tell."

At his father's urging, Bernhardt headed off to college. But his mind was still on a military career. He joined not only Army ROTC but a special elite unit run by the Green Berets. Then in 1967, in the middle of his sophomore year, he dropped out and enlisted in the Army. He had only the haziest sense of what was going on in Vietnam: "It appeared to be about a small country that was having communism shoved down its throat, while we were trying, at least *ostensibly,* to give people a chance to do what they wanted to do. If I didn't go, somebody'd have to go in my place, which went against everything I'd grown up with."

Bernhardt ended up in Vietnam with Charlie Company, on the ground as a horrified witness to the My Lai massacre. He was the first soldier to break the silence and talk in public about what had happened in the face of the Army's cover-up. That decision caused great tension with the father he loved. "He believed that dissent and opposition to the government were uncalled for," said Bernhardt. "He never doubted authority. Nor did I. Up until Vietnam, it never occurred to me that I'd be opposed to the authorities, not in a million years."

After Bernhardt left the Army, he found himself sinking into another quagmire, the collapsing American economy of the 1970s. He bounced around Florida, working on a land surveyor's crew, then at a sign shop that made billboards for Sheraton and Kmart. He lived in a trailer, parked in a vacationer's lot on the Gulf of Mexico. But it wasn't really the recession that threw his peacetime life into disarray. Vietnam had changed forever his idea of a code of masculinity. "For years, I had been asking myself, did I do the right stuff? And I had thought that you just added it all up and you could say, This is my manliness score. You get points for going through the service, and bonus points for extra military stuff, and points for a job and a marriage and kids. But it didn't add up. There were all these people walking around with a high score who weren't much of a man in my estimation." Finally, he stopped keeping score, went back to college and got a degree in biology. He married and bought 10 acres of land in the Florida panhandle where he and his wife keep horses and a dozen stray dogs and cats. "In Charlie Company, cowardice and courage was all turned around. If you showed any sign of caring, it was seen as a sign of weakness. If you were the least bit concerned about the civilians, you were considered pathetic, definitely not a man." Now he's turned that experience around once more. "If you can define your manhood in terms of caring," he said, "then maybe we can come back from all that."

S.F.

---

foe." The fight was the thing, the only thing, if America was to retain its masculinity.

The drumrolls promised a dawning era of superpower manhood to the boy born on the New Frontier, a masculine honor and pride in exchange for his loyalty. Ultimately, the boy was double-crossed. The fix was in from the start: corporate and cold-war America's promise to continue the World War II GI's wartime experience of belonging, of meaningful engagement in a mission, was never authentic. "The New Frontier" of space turned out to be a void that no man could conquer, let along colonize. The astronaut was no Daniel Boone; he was just a flattened image for TV viewers to watch—and eventually, to be bored by. Instead of sending its sons to Normandy, the government dispatched them to Vietnam, where the enemy was unclear and the mission remained a tragic mystery. The

massive managerial bureaucracies of postwar "white collar" employment, especially the defense contractors fat on government largesse, produced "organization men" who often didn't even know what they were managing—and who suspected they weren't really needed at all. What these corporations offered was a secure job, not a vital role—and not even that secure. The postwar fathers' submission to the national-security state would, after a prosperous period of historically brief duration, be rewarded with pink slips, with massive downsizing, union-breaking and outsourcing. The boy who had been told he was going to be the master of the universe and all that was in it found himself master of nothing.

As early as 1957, the boy's diminished future was foreshadowed in a classic sci-fi film. In "The Incredible Shrinking Man," Scott Carey has a good job, a suburban home, a pleasure boat, a pretty wife. And yet, after he passes through a mist of atomic radiation while on a boating vacation in the Pacific, something happens. As he tells his wife in horror, "I'm getting smaller, Lou, every day."

As Carey quite literally shrinks, the promises made to him are broken one by one. The employer who was to give him lifetime economic security fires him. He is left with only feminine defenses, to hide in a doll house, to fight a giant spider with a sewing pin. And it turns out that the very source of his diminishment is implicitly an atomic test by his own government. His only hope is to turn himself into a celebrated freak and sell his story to the media. "I'm a big man!" Carey says with bitter sarcasm. "I'm famous! One more joke for the world to laugh at."

The more Carey shrinks, the more he strikes out at those around him. "Every day I became more tyrannical," he comments, "more monstrous in my domination of my wife." It's a line that would ring a bell for any visitor to the Alternatives to Violence group and for any observer of the current male scene. As the male role has diminished amid a sea of betrayed promises, many men have been driven to more domineering and some even "monstrous" displays in their frantic quest for a meaningful showdown.

The Ornamental Culture

IF FEW MEN WOULD DO WHAT Shawn Nelson did one evening in the spring of 1995, many could relate. A former serviceman whose career in an army tank unit had gone nowhere, a plumber who had lost his job, a former husband whose wife had left him, the 35-year-old Nelson broke into the National Guard armory, commandeered an M-60 army tank and drove it through the streets of San Diego, flattening fire hydrants, crushing 40 cars, downing enough utility poles to cut off electricity to 5,000 people. He was at war with the domestic world that he once thought he was meant to build and defend. He was going to drive that tank he had been meant to command if it killed him. And it did. The police shot Shawn Nelson to death through the turret hatch.

If a man could not get the infrastructure to work for him, he could at least tear it down. If the nation would not provide an enemy to fight, he could go to war at home. If there was to be no brotherhood, he would take his stand alone. A handful of men would attempt to gun down enemies they imagined they saw in family court, employee parking lots, McDonald's restaurants, a Colorado schoolhouse and, most notoriously, a federal office building in Oklahoma. A far greater number would move their destruction of the elusive enemy to the fantasy realm to a clear-cut and controllable world of action movies and video combat, televised athletic tournaments and pay-per-view ultimate-fighting bouts.

But none of it would satisfy, because the world and the fight had changed.

A few glamorous men understood intuitively that in the coming media and entertainment age the team of men at work would be replaced by the individual man on display. Elevated onto the new pedestal of mass media and entertainment, they were unreachable. Like the astronauts who were their forebears, the new celebrated men—media stars, moussed models, telegenic baby moguls—existed in a realm from which all lines to their brothers had been cut. Where we once lived in a society in which men participated by being useful in public life, we now are surrounded by a culture that encourages people to play almost no functional public roles, only decorative or consumer ones.

Ornamental culture has proved the ultimate expression of the century, sweeping away institutions in which men felt some sense of belonging and replacing them with visual spectacles that they can only watch and that benefit global commercial forces they cannot fathom. Celebrity culture's effects on men go far beyond the obvious showcasing of action heroes and rock musicians. The ordinary man is no fool: he knows he can't be Arnold Schwarzenegger. Nonetheless, the culture re-shapes his most basic sense of manhood by telling him that masculinity is something to drape over the body, not draw from inner resources; that it is personal, not societal; that manhood is displayed, not demonstrated. The internal qualities once said to embody manhood—surefootedness, inner strength, confidence of purpose—are merchandised to men to enhance their manliness. What passes for the essence of masculinity is being extracted and bottled and sold back to men. Literally, in the case of Viagra.

As old measures of masculinity faded, the swaggering boys of the Spur Posse made a game of sexual conquest

Who's Keeping Score

The Spur Posse burst out of the orderly suburb of Lakewood, Calif., as America's dreaded nightmare—teenage boys run amok, a microcosm of a misogynistic and violent male culture. In March 1993 police arrested nine Spurs, ages 15 to 19, on suspicion of nearly 20 counts of sexual crimes. In the end, prosecutors concluded that the sex was consensual and all but one count were dropped. But for a time that spring, it was difficult to flip the channels without running into one Spur or another, strutting and bragging their way through the TV talk shows. "You gotta get your image out there," explained Billy Shehan, then 19, a Spur who was not among those arrested but who, despite honor grades and a promising future, felt compelled to hit the media circuit. "It all about building that image on a worldwide basis." Tirelessly, the Spurs repeated the details of their sex-for-points intramural contest, in which each time you had sex with a girl you racked up a point. And for four years running, the winner was Billy Shehan—with a final score of 67.

The media-paid trip that Billy took to New York City with two fellow Spurs started out with many promises. "First they said to us, 'New York! For free!' " Billy recalled. " 'We'll give you $1,000, and you'll have limos every day, and elegant meals, and elegant this and elegant that.' " On the ride from the airport to the hotel, Billy felt like a long-exiled prince come to claim his kingdom. "Here I was in this limo in this giant-ass city, and it was like I owned the taxis and the cars, I owned the buildings and all the girls in the windows in the buildings. I felt like I could do whatever I wanted. I had instant exposure."

For the next week and a half, the shows vied for the Spurs' attention. "For 11 days, these guys were our best friends," Billy said of the TV producers. "They showered admiration on us." One night, Billy said, a senior staffer from "Night Talk With Jane Whitney" took them in a limo to a strip bar, a club in Queens called Goldfingers. "The Maury Povich Show" wooed the boys by sending them our for the evening with four young women from the program's staff. Afterward, the Spurs took a cab to Times Square. "Everything was a fantasy," Billy recalled, "like I was in Mauryland. Like the whole city was a talk show." Billy had his tape recorder out, and he was talking into it as he walked. Suddenly, two hands reached out from the darkness and yanked him between two buildings. "He was holding something against me that felt like a gun," Billy said. The man ripped the tape recorder out of his hands, extracted his wallet and fled. Billy lay in his hotel room all night listening to his heart pound. The next morning he phoned the staff of "The Maury Povich Show" and demanded that they reimburse him for the robbery. When they declined, he refused to go on the program. "I felt they owed me something."

Billy did, however, make an appearance on "Night Talk With Jane Whitney," where he would be much vilified for his boast about scoring his 67th point that week with a girl he lured back to his hotel room. And then he'd return home, poorer and without taped memories. "For a while when I got back," Billy said, "everybody recognized me because of the shows. But now . . ." His voice trailed off. "Uh, you know something sort of funny?" he said. "I didn't get that [final sex] point. The producer said, 'Act like you got a point on the show.' So I did." He gave a short, bitter laugh. "I even wrote a song about it later. 'Everyone thought I was a 67, when I was just a 66.' "

S.F.

The culture that '90s men are stranded in was birthed by their fathers' generation—by men who, weary of Depression and wartime deprivation, embraced the new commercialized American dream. What gets left out of the contemporary nostalgia of baby-boom men for their World War II fathers—evidenced in the huge appetite for the film "Saving Private Ryan" and books like Tom Brokaw's "The Greatest Generation"—is what those fathers did after the war. When "Dateline NBC" produced a documentary based on Brokaw's book, celebrating the World War II "tougher than tough" heroes, especially relative to their pampered sons, the troubling subtext was how devastatingly unfathered those sons were, how inadequately they'd been prepared for manhood by their "heroic" fathers.

The men I came to know in the course of researching this book talked about their father's failures in the most private and personal terms, pointing inevitably to the small daily letdowns: "My father didn't teach me how to throw a ball" or "My father was always at work." That their fathers had emotionally or even literally abandoned the family circle was painful enough. But these men suspected, in some way hard to grasp, that their fathers had deserted them in the public realm, too. "My father never taught me how to be a man" was the refrain I heard over and over again. Down the generations, the father wasn't simply a good sport who bought his son a car for graduation. He was a human bridge connecting the boy to an adult life of public engagement and responsibility.

The guiding standards of the fathers, the approving paternal eye, has nearly vanished in this barren new landscape, to be replaced by the market-share standards of a commercial culture, the ogling, ever-restless eye of the camera. By the end of the century, every outlet of the consumer world—magazines, ads, movies, sports, music videos—would deliver the message that manhood had become a performance game to be won in the marketplace, not the workplace, and that male anger was now part of the show. An ornamental culture encouraged young men to see surliness, hostility and violence as expressions of glamour. Whether in Maxim magazine or in Brut's new "Neanderthal" ads, boorishness became a way for men to showcase themselves without being feminized before a potentially girlish mirror. But if celebrity masculinity enshrined the pose of the "bad boy," his rebellion was largely cosmetic. There was nowhere for him to take a grievance because there was no society to take it to. In a celebrity culture, earnestness about social and political change was replaced by a pose of "irony" that was really just a sullen and helpless paralysis.

In a culture of ornament, manhood is defined by appearance, by youth and attractiveness, by money and aggression, by posture and swagger and "props," by the curled lip and flexed biceps, by the glamour of the cover boy and by the market-bartered "individuality" that sets one astronaut or athlete or gangster above another. These are the same traits that have long been designated as the essence of feminine vanity—the objectification and mirror-gazing that women have denounced as trivializing and humiliating qualities imposed on them by a misogynist culture. No wonder men are in such agony. At the close of the century, men find themselves in an unfamiliar world where male worth is measured only by participation in a celebrity-driven consumer culture and awarded by lady luck.

The more I consider what men have lost—a useful role in public life, a way of earning a decent living, respectful treatment in the culture—the more it seems that men are falling into a status oddly similar to that of women at midcentury. The '50s housewife, stripped of her connections to a wider world and invited to fill the void with shopping and the ornamental display of her ultrafemininity, could be said to have morphed into the '90s man, stripped of his connections to a wider world and invited to fill the void with consumption and a gym-bred display of his ultramasculinity. The empty compensations of a "feminine mystique" are transforming into the empty compensations of a masculine mystique, with a gentlemen's cigar club no more satisfying than a ladies' bake-off.

But women have rebelled against this mystique. Of all the bedeviling questions my travels and research raised, none struck me more than this: why don't contemporary men rise up in protest against their betrayal? If they have experienced so many of the same injuries as women, the same humiliations, why don't they challenge the culture as women did? Why can't men seem to act?

The stock answers don't suffice. Men aren't simply refusing to "give up the reins of power," as some feminists have argued. The reins have already slipped from most of their hands. Nor are men merely chary of expressing pain and neediness, particularly in an era where emoting is the coin of the commercial real. While the pressures on men to imagine themselves in control of their emotions are impediments to male revolt, a

propaganda to prop up the myth of male superiority, the argument went. Men, not the marketplace, many women believed, were the root problem and so, as one feminist activist put it in 1969, "the task of the women's liberation movement is to collectively combat male domination in the home, in bed, on the job." And indeed, there were virulent, sexist attitudes to confront. But the 1970s model of confrontation could get feminism only halfway to its goal.

The women who engaged in the feminist campaigns of the '70s were able to take advantage of a ready-made model for revolt. Ironically, it was a male strategy. Feminists had a clearly defined oppressive enemy: the "patriarchy." They had a real frontier to conquer: all those patriarchal institutions, both the old ones that still rebuffed women, like the U.S. Congress or U.S. Steel, and the new ones that tried to remold women, like Madison Avenue or the glamour and media-pimp kingdoms of Bert Parks and Hugh Hefner. Feminists also had their own army of "brothers": sisterhood. Each GI Jane who participated in this struggle felt useful. Whether she was working in a women's-health clinic or tossing her bottles of Clairol in a "freedom trash can," she was part of a greater glory, the advancement of her entire sex. Many women whose lives were touched by feminism felt in some way that they had reclaimed an essential usefulness; together, they had charged the barricades that kept each of them from a fruitful, thriving life.

The male paradigm of confrontation, in which an enemy could be identified, contested and defeated, proved useful to activists in the civil-rights movement, the antiwar movement, the gay-rights movement. It was, in fact, the fundamental organizing principle of virtually every concerted countercultural

---

What is left out of the nostalgia
of baby-boom men for their heroic World War II fathers is how devastatingly unfathered and unprepared for manhood some of those sons were

---

more fundamental obstacle overshadows them. If men have feared to tread where women have rushed in, then maybe women have had it easier in one very simple regard: women could frame their struggle as a battle against men.

For the many women who embraced feminism in one way or another in the 1970s, that consumer culture was not some intangible force; they saw it as a cudgel wielded by men against women. The mass culture's portfolio of sexist images was

campaign of the last half century. Yet it could launch no "men's movement." Herein lies the critical paradox, and the source of male inaction: the model women have used to revolt is the exact one men not only can't use but are trapped in.

Men have no clearly defined enemy who is oppressing them. How can men be oppressed when the culture has already identified them as the oppressors, and when even they see themselves that way? As one man wrote plaintively to Promise Keepers, "I'm like a kite with a broken string, but I'm also holding the tail." Men have invented antagonists to make their problems visible, but with the passage of time, these culprits—scheming feminists, affirmative-action proponents, job-grabbing illegal aliens—have come to seem increasingly unconvincing as explanations for their situation. Nor do men have a clear frontier on which to challenge their intangible enemies. What new realms should they be gaining—the media, entertainment and image-making institutions of corporate America? But these are institutions already run by men; how can men invade their own territory? Is technological progress the frontier? Why then does it seem to be pushing men into obsolescence, socially and occupationally? And if the American man crushes the machine, whose machine has he vanquished?

The male paradigm of confrontation has proved worthless to men. Yet maybe that's not so unfortunate. The usefulness of that model has reached a point of exhaustion anyway. The women's movement and the other social movements have discovered its limits. Their most obvious enemies have been sent into retreat, yet the problems persist. While women are still outnumbered in the executive suites, many have risen in the ranks and some have achieved authoritative positions often only to perpetuate the same transgressions as their male predecessors. Women in power in the media, advertising and Hollywood have for the most part continued to generate the same sorts of demeaning images as their male counterparts. Blaming a cabal of men has taken feminism about as far as it can go. That's why women have a great deal at stake in the liberation of the one population uniquely poised to discover and employ a new paradigm—men.

Beyond the Politics of Confrontation

THERE ARE SIGNS THAT MEN ARE seeking such a breakthrough. When the Million Man March and Promise Keepers attracted record numbers of men, pundits scratched their heads—why would so many men want to attend events that offered no battle plan, no culprit to confront? No wonder critics who were having trouble placing the gatherings in the usual frame of political conflict found it easier to focus their attentions on the reactionary and hate-mongering attitudes of the "leaders" of these movements, concluding that the real "agenda" must be the anti-Semitism of the Nation of Islam's Louis Farrakhan or the homophobia and sexism of Promise Keepers founder Bill McCartney. But maybe the men who attended these mass gatherings weren't looking for answers that involved an enemy. As Farrakhan's speech, chock-full of conspiracy theories and numerological codes, dragged on, men in droves hastened for the exits. "What was really fantastic about the day was just being together with all these men, and thinking about what I might do differently," George Henderson, a 48-year-old social worker, told me as he headed out early. The amassing of huge numbers of men was a summoning of courage for the unmapped journey ahead.

American men have generally responded well as caretakers in times of crisis, whether that be in wars, depressions or natural disasters. The pre-eminent contemporary example of such a male mobilization also comes on the heels of a crisis: gay men's response to AIDS. Virtually overnight, just as the Depression-era Civilian Conservation Corps

built dams and parks and salvaged farmland, so have gay men built a network of clinics, legal and psychological services, fund-raising and political-action brigades, meals on wheels, even laundry assistance. The courage of these caregivers has generated, even in this homophobic nation, a wellspring of admiration and respect. They had a job to do and they did it.

Social responsibility is not the special province of masculinity; it's the lifelong work of all citizens in a community where people are knit together by meaningful and mutual concerns. But if husbanding a society is not the exclusive calling of "husbands," all the better for men's future. Because as men struggle to free themselves from their crisis, their task is not, in the end, to figure out how to be masculine—rather, their masculinity lies in figuring out how to be human. The men who worked at the Long Beach Naval Shipyard, where I spent many months, didn't go there and learn their crafts as riggers, welders and boilermakers to be masculine; they were seeking something worthwhile to do. Their sense of their own manhood flowed out of their utility in a society, not the other way around.

And so with the mystery of men's non-rebellion comes the glimmer of an opening, a chance for men to forge a rebellion commensurate with women's and, in the course of it, to create a new paradigm for human progress that will open doors for both sexes. That was, and continues to be, feminism's dream, to create a freer, more humane world. It will remain a dream without the strength and courage of men who are today faced with a historic opportunity: to learn to wage a battle against no enemy, to own a frontier of human liberty, to act in the service of a brotherhood that includes us all.

WHERE BIAS BEGINS:
THE TRUTH ABOUT STEREOTYPES

Psychologists once believed that only bigoted people used stereotypes. Now the study of unconscious bias is revealing the unsettling truth: We all use stereotypes, all the time, without knowing it. We have met the enemy of equality, and the enemy is us.

By Annie Murphy Paul

Mahzarin Banaji doesn't fit anybody's idea of a racist. A psychology professor at Yale University, she studies stereotypes for a living. And as a woman and a member of a minority ethnic group, she has felt firsthand the sting of discrimination. Yet when she took one of her own tests of unconscious bias, "I showed very strong prejudices," she says. "It was truly a disconcerting experience." And an illuminating one. When Banaji was in graduate school in the early 1980s, theories about stereotypes were concerned only with their explicit expression: outright and unabashed racism, sexism, anti-Semitism. But in the years since, a new approach to stereotypes has shattered that simple notion. The bias Banaji and her colleagues are studying is something far more subtle, and more insidious: what's known as automatic or implicit stereotyping, which, they find, we do all the time without knowing it. Though out-and-out bigotry may be on the decline, says Banaji, "if anything, stereotyping is a bigger problem than we ever imagined."

Previously researchers who studied stereotyping had simply asked people to record their feelings about minority groups and had used their answers as an index of their attitudes. Psychologists now understand that these conscious replies are only half the story. How progressive a person seems to be on the surface bears little or no relation to how prejudiced he or she is on an unconscious level—so that a bleeding-heart liberal might harbor just as many biases as a neo-Nazi skinhead.

As surprising as these findings are, they confirmed the hunches of many students of human behavior. "Twenty years ago, we hypothesized that there were people who said they were not prejudiced but who really did have unconscious negative stereotypes and beliefs," says psychologist Jack Dovidio, Ph.D., of Colgate University. "It was like theorizing about the existence of a virus, and then one day seeing it under a microscope."

The test that exposed Banaji's hidden biases—and that this writer took as well, with equally dismaying results—is typical of the ones used by automatic stereotype researchers. It presents the subject with a series of positive or negative adjectives, each paired with a characteristically "white" or "black" name. As the name and word appear together on a computer screen, the person taking the test presses a key, indicating whether the word is good or bad. Meanwhile, the computer records the speed of each response.

A glance at subjects' response times reveals a startling phenomenon: Most people who participate in the experiment—even some African-Americans—respond more quickly when a positive word is paired with a white name or a negative word with a black name. Because our minds are more accustomed to making these associations, says Banaji, they process them more rapidly. Though the words and names aren't subliminal, they are presented so quickly that a subject's ability to make deliberate choices is diminished—allowing his or her underlying assumptions to show through. The same technique can be used to measure stereotypes about many different social groups, such as homosexuals, women, and the elderly.

THE UNCONSCIOUS COMES INTO FOCUS

From these tiny differences in reaction speed—a matter of a few hundred milliseconds—the study of automatic stereotyping was born. Its immediate ancestor was the cognitive revolution of the 1970s, an explosion of psychological research into the way people think. After decades dominated by the study of observable behavior, scientists wanted a closer look at the more mysterious operation of the human brain. And the development of computers—which enabled scientists to display infor-

LIKE THE CULTURE, OUR MINDS ARE SPLIT ON THE SUBJECTS OF RACE, GENDER, SEXUAL ORIENTATION.

mationvery quickly and to measure minute discrepancies in reaction time—permitted a peek into the unconscious.

At the same time, the study of cognition was also illuminating the nature of stereotypes themselves. Research done after World War II—mostly by European émigrés struggling to understand how the Holocaust had happened—concluded that stereotypes were used only by a particular type of person: rigid, repressed, authoritarian. Borrowing from the psychoanalytic perspective then in vogue, these theorists suggested that biased behavior emerged out of internal conflicts caused by inadequate parenting.

The cognitive approach refused to let the rest of us off the hook. It made the simple but profound point that we all use categories—of people, places, things—to make sense of the world around us. "Our ability to categorize and evaluate is an important part of human intelligence," says Banaji. "Without it, we couldn't survive." But stereotypes are too much of a good thing. In the course of stereotyping, a useful category—say women—becomes freighted with additional associations, usually negative. "Stereotypes are categories that have gone too far," says John Bargh, Ph.D., of New York University. "When we use stereotypes, we take in the gender, the age, the color of the skin of the person before us, and our minds respond with messages that say hostile, stupid, slow, weak. Those qualities aren't out there in the environment. They don't reflect reality."

Bargh thinks that stereotypes may emerge from what social psychologists call in-group/out-group dynamics. Humans, like other species, need to feel that they are part of a group, and as villages, clans, and other traditional groupings have broken down, our identities have attached themselves to more ambiguous classifications, such as race and class. We want to feel good about the group we belong to—and one way of doing so is to denigrate all those who aren't in it. And while we tend to see members of our own group as individuals, we view those in out-groups as an undifferentiated—stereotyped—mass. The categories we use have changed, but it seems that stereotyping itself is bred in the bone.

Though a small minority of scientists argues that stereotypes are usually accurate and can be relied upon without reservations, most disagree—and vehemently. "Even if there is a kernel of truth in the stereotype, you're still applying a generalization about a group to an individual, which is always incorrect," says Bargh. Accuracy aside, some believe that the use of stereotypes is simply unjust. "In a democratic society people should be judged as individuals and not as members of a group," Banaji argues. "Stereotyping flies in the face of that ideal."

PREDISPOSED TO PREJUDICE

The problem, as Banaji's own research shows, is that people can't seem to help it. A recent experiment provides a good illustration. Banaji and her colleague, Anthony Greenwald, Ph.D., showed people a list of names—some famous, some not. The next day the subjects returned to the lab and were shown a second list, which mixed names from the first list with new ones. Asked to identify which were famous, they picked out the Margaret Meads and the Miles Davises—but they also chose some of the names on the first list, which retained a lingering familiarity that they mistook for fame. (Psychologists call this the "famous overnight-effect.") By a margin of two-to-one, these suddenly "famous" people were male.

Participants weren't aware that they were preferring male names to female names, Banaji stresses. They were simply drawing on an unconscious stereotype of men as more important and influential than women. Something similar happened when she showed subjects a list of people who might be criminals: without knowing they were doing so, participants picked out an overwhelming number of African-American names. Banaji calls this kind of stereotyping *implicit,* because people know they are making a judgment—but just aren't aware of the basis upon which they are making it.

Even further below awareness is something that psychologists call automatic processing, in which stereotypes are triggered by the slightest interaction or en-

counter. An experiment conducted by Bargh required a group of white participants to perform a tedious computer task. While performing the task, some of the participants were subliminally exposed to pictures of African-Americans with neutral expressions. When the subjects were then asked to do the task over again, the ones who had been exposed to the faces reacted with more hostility to the request—because, Bargh believes, they were responding in kind to the hostility which is part of the African-American stereotype. Bargh calls this the "immediate hostile reaction," which he believes can have a real effect on race relations. When African-Americans accurately perceive the hostile expressions that their white counterparts are unaware of, they may respond with hostility of their own—thereby perpetuating the stereotype.

Of course, we aren't completely under the sway of our unconscious. Scientists think that the automatic activation of a stereotype is immediately followed by a conscious check on unacceptable thoughts—at least in people who think that they are not prejudiced. This internal censor successfully restrains overtly biased responses. But there's still the danger of leakage, which often shows up in nonverbal behavior: our expressions, our stance, how far away we stand, how much eye contact we make.

The gap between what we say and what we do can lead African-Americans and whites to come away with very different impressions of the same encounter, says Jack Dovidio. "If I'm a white person talking to an African-American, I'm probably monitoring my conscious beliefs very carefully and making sure everything I say agrees with all the positive things I want to express," he says. "And I usually believe I'm pretty successful because I hear the right words coming out of my mouth." The listener who is paying attention to non-verbal behavior, however, may be getting quite the opposite message. An African-American student of Dovidio's recently told him that when she was growing up, her mother had taught her to observe how white people moved to gauge their true feelings toward

THE CATEGORIES WE USE HAVE CHANGED, BUT STEREOTYPING ITSELF SEEMS TO BE BRED IN THE BONE.

> WE HAVE TO CHANGE HOW WE THINK WE CAN INFLUENCE
> PEOPLE'S BEHAVIORS. IT WOULD BE NAIVE TO THINK THAT
> EXHORTATION IS ENOUGH.

blacks. "Her mother was a very astute amateur psychologist—and about 20 years ahead of me," he remarks.

WHERE DOES BIAS BEGIN?

So where exactly do these stealth stereotypes come from? Though automatic-stereotype researchers often refer to the unconscious, they don't mean the Freudian notion of a seething mass of thoughts and desires, only some of which are deemed presentable enough to be admitted to the conscious mind. In fact, the cognitive model holds that information flows in exactly the opposite direction: connections made often enough in the conscious mind eventually become unconscious. Says Bargh: "If conscious choice and decision making are not needed, they go away. Ideas recede from consciousness into the unconscious over time."

Much of what enters our consciousness, of course, comes from the culture around us. And like the culture, it seems that our minds are split on the subjects of race, gender, class, sexual orientation. "We not only mirror the ambivalence we see in society, but also mirror it in precisely the same way," says Dovidio. Our society talks out loud about justice, equality, and egalitarianism, and most Americans accept these values as their own. At the same time, such equality exists only as an ideal, and that fact is not lost on our unconscious. Images of women as sex objects, footage of African-American criminals on the six o'clock news,—"this is knowledge we cannot escape," explains Banaji. "We didn't choose to know it, but it still affects our behavior."

We learn the subtext of our culture's messages early. By five years of age, says Margo Monteith, Ph.D., many children have definite and entrenched stereotypes about blacks, women, and other social groups. Adds Monteith, professor of psychology at the University of Kentucky: "Children don't have a choice about accepting or rejecting these conceptions, since they're acquired well before they have the cognitive abilities or experiences to form their own beliefs." And no matter how progressive the parents, they must compete with all the forces that would promote and perpetuate these stereotypes: peer pressure, mass media, the actual balance of power in society. In fact, prejudice may be as much

a result as a cause of this imbalance. We create stereotypes—African-Americans are lazy, women are emotional—to explain why things are the way they are. As Dovidio notes, "Stereotypes don't have to be true to serve a purpose."

WHY CAN'T WE ALL GET ALONG?

The idea of unconscious bias does clear up some nettlesome contradictions. "It accounts for a lot of people's ambivalence toward others who are different, a lot of their inconsistencies in behavior," says Dovidio. "It helps explain how good people can do bad things." But it also prompts some uncomfortable realizations. Because our conscious and unconscious beliefs may be very different—and because behavior often follows the lead of the latter—"good intentions aren't enough," as John Bargh puts it. In fact, he believes that they count for very little. "I don't think free will exists," he says, bluntly—because what feels like the exercise of free will may be only the application of unconscious assumptions.

Not only may we be unable to control our biased responses, we may not even be aware that we have them. "We have to rely on our memories and our awareness of what we're doing to have a connection to reality," says Bargh. "But when it comes to automatic processing, those cues can be deceptive." Likewise, we can't always be sure how biased others are. "We all have this belief that the important thing about prejudice is the external expression of it," says Banaji. "That's going to be hard to give up."

One thing is certain: We can't claim that we've eradicated prejudice just because its outright expression has waned. What's more, the strategies that were so effective in reducing that sort of bias won't work on unconscious beliefs. "What this research is saying is that we are going to have to change dramatically the way we think we can influence people's behaviors," says Banaji. "It would be naive to think that exhortation is enough." Exhortation, education, political protest—all of these hammer away at our conscious beliefs while leaving the bedrock below untouched. Banaji notes, however, that one traditional remedy for discrimination—affirmative action—may still be effective since it bypasses our unconsciously compromised judgment.

But some stereotype researchers think that the solution to automatic stereotyping lies in the process itself. Through practice, they say people can weaken the mental links that connect minorities to negative stereotypes and strengthen the ones that connect them to positive conscious beliefs. Margo Monteith explains how it might work. "Suppose you're at a party and someone tells a racist joke—and you laugh," she says. "Then you realize that you shouldn't have laughed at the joke. You feel guilty and become focused on your thought processes. Also, all sorts of cues become associated with laughing at the racist joke: the person who told the joke, the act of telling jokes, being at a party drinking." The next time you encounter these cues, "a warning signal of sorts should go off—'wait, didn't you mess up in this situation before?'—and your responses will be slowed and executed with greater restraint."

That slight pause in the processing of a stereotype gives conscious, unprejudiced beliefs a chance to take over. With time, the tendency to prevent automatic stereotyping may itself become automatic. Monteith's research suggests that, given enough motivation, people may be able to teach themselves to inhibit prejudice so well that even their tests of implicit bias come clean.

The success of this process of "de-automatization" comes with a few caveats, however. First, even its proponents concede that it works only for people disturbed by the discrepancy between their conscious and unconscious beliefs, since unapologetic racists or sexists have no motivation to change. Second, some studies have shown that attempts to suppress stereotypes may actually cause them to return later, stronger than ever. And finally, the results that Monteith and other researchers have achieved in the laboratory may not stick in the real world, where people must struggle to maintain their commitment to equality under less-than-ideal conditions.

Challenging though that task might be, it is not as daunting as the alternative researchers suggest: changing society itself. Bargh, who likens de-automatization to closing the barn door once the horses have escaped, says that "it's clear that the way to get rid of stereotypes is by the roots, by where they come from in the first place." The study of culture may someday tell us where the seeds of prejudice originated; for now the study of the unconscious shows us just how deeply they're planted.

THE LURE OF THE CULT

Out where religion and junk culture meet, some weird new offspring are rising

By RICHARD LACAYO

O**N SATURDAY, MARCH 22, AROUND** the time that the disciples of Heaven's Gate were just beginning their quiet and meticulous self-extinction, a small cottage in the French Canadian village of St.-Casimir exploded into flames. Inside the burning house were five people, all disciples of the Order of the Solar Temple. Since 1994, 74 members of that group have gone to their death in Canada, Switzerland and France. In St.-Casimir the dead were Didier Quèze, 39, a baker, his wife Chantale Goupillot, 41, her mother and two others of the faithful. At the last minute the Quèze children, teenagers named Tom, Fanie and Julien opted out. After taking sedatives offered by the adults, they closeted themselves in a garden shed to await their parents' death. Police later found them, stunned but alive.

For two days and nights before the blast, the grownups had pursued a remarkable will to die. Over and over they fiddled with three tanks of propane that were hooked to an electric burner and a timing device. As many as four times, they swallowed sedatives, then arranged themselves in a cross around a queen-size bed, only to rise in bleary frustration when the detonator fizzled. Finally, they blew themselves to kingdom come. For them that would be the star Sirius, in the constellation Canis Major, nine light-years from Quebec. According to the doctrines of the Solar Temple, they will reign there forever, weightless and serene.

Quite a mess. But no longer perhaps a complete surprise. Eighteen years after

Jonestown, suicide cults have entered the category of horrors that no longer qualify as shocks. Like plane crashes and terrorist attacks, they course roughly for a while along the nervous system, then settle into that part of the brain reserved for bad but familiar news. As the bodies are tagged and the families contacted, we know what the experts will say before they say it. That in times of upheaval and uncertainty, people seek out leaders with power and charisma. That the established churches are too fainthearted to satisfy the wilder kinds of spiritual hunger. That the self-denial and regimentation of cult life will soften up anyone for the kill.

The body count at Rancho Santa Fe is a reminder that this conventional wisdom falls short. These are the waning years of the 20th century, and out on the margins of spiritual life there's a strange phosphorescence. As predicted, the approach of the year 2000 is coaxing all the crazies out of the woodwork. They bring with them a twitchy hybrid of spirituality and pop obsession. Part Christian, part Asian mystic, part Gnostic, part *X-Files*, it mixes immemorial longings with the latest in trivial sentiments. When it all dissolves in overheated computer chat and harmless New Age vaporings, who cares? But sometimes it matters, for both the faithful and the people who care about them. Sometimes it makes death a consummation devoutly, all too devoutly, to be desired.

So the worst legacy of Heaven's Gate may yet be this: that 39 people sacrificed themselves to the new millennial kitsch. That's the cultural by-product in which spiri-

tual yearnings are captured in New Age gibberish, then edged with the glamour of sci-fi and the consolations of a toddler's bedtime. In the Heaven's Gate cosmology, where talk about the end of the world alternates with tips for shrugging off your fleshly container, the cosmic and the lethal, the enraptured and the childish come together. Is it any surprise then that it led to an infantile apocalypse, one part applesauce, one part phenobarbital? Look at the Heaven's Gate Website. Even as it warns about the end of the world, you find a drawing of a space creature imagined through insipid pop dust-jacket conventions: aerodynamic cranium, big doe eyes, beatific smile. We have seen the Beast of the Apocalypse. It's Bambi in a tunic.

By now, psychologists have arrived at a wonderfully elastic profile of the people who attach themselves to these intellectual chain gangs: just about anybody. Applicants require only an unsatisfied spiritual longing, a condition apt to strike anyone at some point in life. Social status is no indicator of susceptibility and no defense against it. For instance, while many of the dead at Jonestown were poor, the Solar Temple favors the carriage trade. Its disciples have included the wife and son of the founder of the Vuarnet sunglass company. The Branch Davidians at Waco came from many walks of life. And at Rancho Santa Fe they were paragons of the entrepreneurial class, so well organized they died in shifts.

The U.S. was founded by religious dissenters. It remains to this day a nation where faith of whatever kind is a force to be reck-

From *Time*, April 7, 1997, pp. 45-46. © 1997 by Time Inc. Magazine Company. Reprinted by permission.

oned with. But a free proliferation of raptures is upon us, with doctrines that mix the sacred and the tacky. The approach of the year 2000 has swelled the ranks of the fearful and credulous. On the Internet, cults multiply in service to Ashtar and Sananda, deities with names you could find at a perfume counter, or to extraterrestrials—the Zeta Reticuli, the Draconian Reptoids—who sound like softball teams at the *Star Wars* cantina. Carl Raschke, a cult specialist at the University of Denver, predicts "an explosion of bizarre and dangerous" cults. "Millennial fever will be on a lot of minds."

As so often in religious thinking, the sky figures importantly in the New Apocalypse. For centuries the stars have been where the meditations of religion, science and the occult all converged. Now enter Comet Hale-Bopp. In an otherwise orderly and predictable cosmos, where the movement of stars was charted confidently by Egyptians and Druids, the appearance of a comet, an astronomical oddity, has long been an opportunity for panic. When Halley's comet returned in 1910, an Oklahoma religious sect, the Select Followers, had to be stopped by the police from sacrificing a virgin. In the case of Hale-Bopp, for months the theory that it might be a shield for an approaching UFO has roiled the excitable on talk radio and in Internet chat rooms like—what else?—*alt.conspiracy.*

ASTRONOMICAL CHARTS MAY ALSO have helped determine the timing of the Heaven's Gate suicides. They apparently began on the weekend of March 22–23, around the time that Hale-Bopp got ready to make its closest approach to Earth. That weekend also witnessed a full moon and, in parts of the U.S., a lunar eclipse. For good measure it included Palm Sunday, the beginning of the Christian Holy Week. Shrouds placed on the corpses were purple, the color of Passiontide, or, for New Agers, the color of those who have passed to a higher plane.

The Heaven's Gate philosophy added its astronomical trappings to a core of weirdly adulterated Christianity. Then came a whiff of Gnosticism, the old heresy that regarded the body as a burden from which the fretful soul longs to be freed. From the time of St. Paul, some elements of Christianity have indulged an impulse to subjugate the body. But like Judaism and Islam, it ultimately teaches

reverence for life and rejects suicide as a shortcut to heaven.

The modern era of cultism dates to the 1970s, when the free inquiry of the previous decade led quite a few exhausted seekers into

JONESTOWN, 1978

At the Peoples Temple, more than 900 cult members died because Jim Jones decided it was time

intellectual surrender. Out from the rubble of the countercultures came such groups as the Children of God and the Divine Light Mission, est and the Church of Scientology, the robotic political followers of Lyndon LaRouche and the Unification Church of the Rev. Sun Myung Moon. On Nov. 18, 1978, the cultism of the '70s arrived at its dark crescendo in Jonestown, Guyana, where more than 900 members of Jim Jones' Peoples Temple died at his order, most by suicide.

Since then two developments have fostered the spread of cultism. One is the end of communism. Whatever the disasters of Marxism, at least it provided an outlet for utopian longings. Now that universalist impulses have one less way to expend themselves, religious enthusiasms of whatever character take on a fresh appeal. And even Russia, with a rich tradition of fevered spirituality and the new upheavals of capitalism, is dealing with modern cults.

Imported sects like the Unification Church have seen an opening there. Homegrown groups have also sprung up. One surrounds a would-be messiah named Vissarion. With his flowing dark hair, wispy beard and a sing-song voice full of aphorisms, he has managed to attract about 5,000 followers to his City of the Sun. Naturally it's in Siberia, near the isolated town of Minusinsk. According to reports in the Russian press, Vissarion is a former traffic cop who was fired for drinking. In his public appearances, he speaks of "the coming end" and instructs believers that suicide is not a sin. Russian authorities are worried that he may urge his followers on a final binge. In the former Soviet lands, law enforcement has handled cults in the old Russian way, with truncheons and bars. Some have been banned. Last year

a court in Kiev gave prison terms to leaders of the White Brotherhood, including its would-be messiah, Marina Tsvigun.

The second recent development in cultism is strictly free market and technological. For the quick recruitment of new congregations, the Internet is a magical opportunity. It's persuasive, far reaching and clandestine. And for better and worse, it frees the imagination from the everyday world. "I think that the online context can remove people from a proper understanding of reality and of the proper tests for truth," says Douglas Groothuis, a theologian and author of *The Soul in Cyberspace.* "How do you verify peoples' identity? How do you connect 'online' with real life?"

"The Internet allows different belief systems to meet and mate," adds Stephen O'Leary, author of *Arguing the Apocalypse,* which examines end-of-the-world religions. "What you get is this millennial stew, a mixture of many different belief systems." Which is the very way that the latest kinds of cultism have flourished. As it happens, that's also the way free thought develops generally. Real ideas sometimes rise from the muck, which is why free societies willingly put up with so much muck.

In Gustave Flaubert's story *A Simple Heart,* an old French woman pines for a beloved nephew, a sailor who has disappeared in Cuba. Later she acquires a parrot. Because it comes from the Americas, it reminds her of him. When the parrot dies, she has it stuffed and set in her room among her items of religious veneration. On her deathbed, she has a vision of heaven. The clouds part to reveal an enormous parrot.

The lessons there for Heaven's Gate? The religious impulse sometimes thrived on false sentiment, emotional need and cultural fluff. In its search for meaning, the mind is apt to go down some wrong paths and to mistake its own reflection for the face of God. Much of the time, those errors are nothing more than episodes of the human comedy. Occasionally they become something worse. This is what happened at Rancho Santa Fe, where foolish notions hardened into fatal certainties. In the arrival of Comet Hale-Bopp, the cult members saw a signal that their lives would end soon. There are many things about which they were badly mistaken. But on that one intuition, they made sure they were tragically correct.   **—Reported by Andrew Meier/Moscow, Richard N. Ostling/New York and Andrew Purvis/Toronto**

Work Work Work **Work!**

It's taking over our lives—invading our homes, haunting our holidays, showing up for dinner. **Should we care?**

by Mark Hunter

YOU'VE HEARD THE JOKE BY NOW, BUT IT RINGS SO true that it bears retelling: A guy reads a headline saying "Clinton creates 8 million jobs," and he cracks wearily, "Yeah, and I got three of 'em."

That gag may be the epitaph of the 1990s. In a very real sense, all of us—not just the 13 percent of us working two or three part-time jobs to survive—have three jobs. There's the work we do for a living, the work we do for ourselves (in many cases, to make sure we still can make a living tomorrow), plus the combination of housework and caregiving. Researchers differ on how much time we put into each of these categories, but most agree on one crucial point: The total keeps growing. As my brother Richard, a vice president of the Gartner Group, a high-tech advisory company, puts it: "It's like trying to fit a size 12 into a size eight shoe."

By far the biggest chunk of our time still goes to the work we do for a living. A survey of some 3,000 employees nationwide by the Families and Work Institute (FWI), a New York nonprofit organization that addresses work and family issues, discovered that over the past two decades, the average time spent at a full-time job has risen from 43.6 to 47.1 hours per week. Over a year, that comes to about four extra weeks—the same figure that Juliet B. Schor arrived at in her controversial 1991 study, *The Overworked American*, one of the first books to document what she called "the decline of leisure."

This fact hit home for me when I returned to the U.S. in 1996 after a decade abroad. I began to notice that not one of the other seven people in my office left their desks at lunchtime, the way folks used to. Throw in that traditional half-hour lunch break, and that's another two-and-a-half hours every week that many people give to work—or about three more weeks per year. Likewise, the Bureau of Labor Statistics reports that since 1985 paid vacation time has declined, and so has the average time that workers take off sick. Not surprisingly, more than one third of the people in the FWI survey said that they "often or very often feel used up at the end of the workday." It's true that some researchers, like John Robinson, a sociology professor at the University of Maryland, argue that it's mainly the well-off among us who are working more, as a matter of choice, and that on average our leisure time has increased. But that's not what I see all around me.

Simultaneously, the old line between work life and private life is vanishing. In trying to understand why employees often refused to take advantage of maternity leave and flex-time, sociologist Arlie Hochschild, author of *The Time Bind*, discovered, to her amazement, that "work has become a form of 'home' and home has become 'work.'" She reports that many people now see their jobs as "a more appreciative, personal sort of social world" compared with their homes, where in the age of divorce and double careers, "the emotional demands have become more baffling and complex." When I interviewed 40 men about their work-life tradeoffs, every one of them said that it was easier to be a success on the job than in his personal relationships. Is it just a coincidence that hit TV shows like *Taxi* or *Murphy Brown* substituted the workplace "family" for the domestic setting of *The Brady Bunch?*

Work has penetrated the home in another potent way, notes market researcher Judith Langer, who has interviewed several hundred people on this subject over the past ten years: "People feel that what they're required to do at work has spilled over into the rest of their lives—reading, keeping up with trends in their fields, keeping up with e-mail and voice mail. We had a guy come into a focus group carrying all the publications that had hit his desk that day and complain, 'Monday weighs 20 pounds.'"

Personal technology has turned what once were hobbies into jobs: When my brother goes home from the office, he fires up his PC and checks the online orders for his self-produced harmonica records. And when the

From *Modern Maturity*, May/June 1999, pp. 35-41, 49. © 1999 by Mark Hunter. Reprinted by permission.

The distinction between work and leisure no longer exists

one third of Americans with managerial or professional jobs leave home, work follows them on a cell phone, pager, or modem. This past winter I received numerous business-related e-mail messages from an executive who was on a hiking trip deep in the mountains of Utah. (Emergency rescue crews have reported finding stranded hikers in the wilderness who had filled their backpacks with a portable computer, but forgotten to bring enough food and water.) The next time a cell phone rings in a restaurant at dinner-time, notice how many people automatically reach for theirs, because it might be a business call. In the 1960s and 1970s, stress experts called this kind of thing "multiphasic behavior," otherwise known as doing several tasks at once. Nowadays we call it efficiency.

Ironically, the Baby Boomers, who came of age shouting their contempt for the man in the gray flannel suit, have done more than any other generation to erase the line between work and private life. Among the first to spot this paradox was Alvin Toffler in his 1980 futurist manifesto, *The Third Wave*. While most observers took those in the hippie movement for a bunch of unwashed, lazy bums, Toffler realized that they were really the prototype of a new kind of worker, the "prosumer"—people who, like frontier farmers, produce a share of what they consume, from home medicine to clothing (my fiancee creates a wardrobe every two years) to home-baked bread, instead of buying it all in the marketplace. "Once we recognize that much of our so-called leisure time is in fact spent producing goods and services for our own use," he noted, "then the old distinction between work and leisure falls apart."

Just as they turned the home into a workplace, Boomers redefined the ideal workplace as a playground. At the end of the 1970s, pollster Daniel Yankelovich found that this "New Breed" of Americans believed that work should be first and foremost a means to self-fulfillment—unlike their parents, who were taught by the Depression that any job that pays a secure wage was worth keeping. When Catalyst, a New York nonprofit organization that seeks to advance women in business, surveyed more than 800 members of two-career couples about what mattered most to them on the job, at the top of the list were emotional benefits such as supportive management, being able to work on their own, and having control over their product.

Our careers now start earlier and end later, reversing a trend that reached its peak after World War II, when child labor virtually disappeared and retirement became a right. These days, so many teenagers have jobs—and

as a result are cutting back on sleep, meals, and homework—that the National Research Council has called for strict new limits on the hours they're allowed to work. At the same time, the number of people 55 and older who still are in the labor force has increased by 6 million since 1950, and most of that increase is women. The Department of Labor projects that this number is going to grow by another 6 million by the year 2006.

None of this was supposed to happen. Only a generation ago, the conventional wisdom among economists was that America was turning into an "affluent society," in which ever more efficient technology would produce an abundance of wealth that we could enjoy with less and less labor. Science-fiction novelists like Kurt Vonnegut imagined a society in which a tiny elite ran the show, while everyone else sat around bored. In their vision, work would no longer be a burden, but a privilege for the happy few.

There are a lot of reasons why things didn't turn out quite that way. One is the Vietnam War, which heated the American economy to the boiling point just as the oil shocks of the 1970s arrived—a combination that led to double-digit inflation and sapped the value of wages. Then successive waves of recession, mergers, and downsizing crashed through the American economy during the '80s. With few exceptions, one of the surest ways to raise a company's stock price—and along with it the value of its executives' stock options—was to fire a piece of its workforce. (Fortunately, downsizing appears to be losing steam, as Wall Street begins to suspect it as a desperate attempt to make a company's bottom line look good in the short term.) Gradually, overtime pay replaced wage increases as the main way to stay ahead of the bills.

The Baby Boom played a role here, too. With so many Boomers competing for jobs, they became cheap for employers: "For the first time in recent American history," marvels Landon Y. Jones in *Great Expectations: America and the Baby Boom Generation*, "the relative earnings of college graduates *declined*." In order to maintain or, in many cases to surpass, the lifestyles of their parents—more Baby Boomers now own homes and, on average, bigger homes than Americans did in the 1950s—they have gone deeply into debt. About one fourth of the average family's income now goes to pay various creditors, more than in any previous generation.

Just as the feminist revolution was urging women to do something with their lives besides raise kids and clean house, it became difficult for the average family to make ends meet without two incomes. Today, in nearly four out of five couples—compared with one out of five in 1950—both partners are in the labor force, with women working nearly as many hours for pay as men. One positive result is that since the late 1970s men have taken over a steadily growing (though still smaller) share of the childcare and household chores—nearly two hours' worth per day—that used to be considered women's work.

Yet even visionary feminists like Dorothy Dinnerstein, who predicted this shift in her landmark 1976 book, *The Mermaid and the Minotaur,* did not foresee that it would also have a negative impact on our intimate lives. The Internet site BabyCenter recently polled roughly 2,000 of its new-mother visitors on whether they did or would return to work after their child was born. Two out of three survey participants said that they would go back to work within six months, but only one out of six said that she found the move "satisfying"; twice as many called it "wrenching." Men are also feeling the pinch. "I have absolutely no time for myself or my friends," a married male executive and father complained to a Catalyst researcher. "Not enough time for us as a couple, and even the extended family say they don't see us enough."

> # Work is focusing us to constantly learn new ways of working

In previous decades, surveys showed that the biggest source of problems for married couples was money; now, when both partners are asked what is the biggest challenge they face, the majority of two-career couples answer "too little time." Not surprisingly, a growing number of leading-edge companies now offer working couples flexible schedules, expanded parental leave, and other benefits that allow their employees to reconcile their jobs with their personal lives.

Paradoxically, the same technology that was supposed to make us all wealthy loafers has contributed to the work-life squeeze. Computers and the changes they wrought have eliminated entire categories of jobs—when was the last time, for example, you talked to a human operator, instead of an automated phone tree, when you called a big company? In his book *The End of Work,* Jeremy Rifkin warned that this trend would end by puffing nearly all of us out of a job—a neat Doomsday inversion of the old "affluent society" prophecy. But many economists argue that new jobs will be created by new technology, just as they always have been. Perhaps, but the pressures to adapt to these rapid technological changes are greater than ever.

Computers have even changed the rhythm of our work, giving us more of a say in how the job is done because technology-savvy frontline personnel become responsible for decisions that managers used to make, as they constantly feed information up and down the line. The same applies to managers, whose desktop PCs, equipped with software that does everything from keeping appointments to formatting business letters and writing contracts, have largely replaced personal secretaries.

We get more control—which happens to be one of the key measures of job satisfaction—but in return we end up giving more of ourselves to the job.

Beyond requiring us to put in longer hours for fear of losing our jobs, work is changing us in positive ways. In particular, it is literally forcing us to expand beyond the limits of what we previously thought we could accomplish, to constantly learn new ways of working. A lifelong career now means lifelong retraining. As the Radcliffe Public Policy Institute in Cambridge, Massachusetts, reports, "The qualities that once nearly guaranteed lifelong employment—hard work, reliability, loyalty, mastery of a discrete set of skills—are often no longer enough." That message has come through loud and clear. About one out of 12 Americans moonlights from his or her principal job in order to learn new skills or weave a "safety net" in case that job is lost. And American universities, starved for students only a few years ago as the Baby Boom grew up and out of the classrooms, have found a burgeoning new market in older workers. Census data show that by 1996 an incredible 468,000 college students were age 50 and older—an increase of 43 percent since 1990.

I don't have to look far to see that trend at work. My brother's wife earned her degree as a geriatric nurse in her late 40s, and it's now her part-time career. My mother, who runs her own public-relations agency, is working toward a degree as an English-language teacher, which will become her post-"retirement" career. And I'm riding that same train. This year I began teaching myself to write code for the Internet, just like my friend Randy, a former magazine editor who spent years of evenings learning to make Web pages in order to support his family. Why? Because by the year 2006 there will be fewer jobs for journalists, according to the Department of Labor. Like everyone else, I've got a choice between moving up—or out.

And there's real excitement in acquiring fresh skills—including the joy of proving wrong the adage that old dogs can't learn new tricks. But many older workers are not getting a chance to share in that excitement: They are being shunted aside from the retraining they will need to stay in the labor market at a moment when they are the fastest-growing share of the labor force. And the point at which a worker on the rise becomes a worker who's consigned to history is coming earlier in people's careers, usually around age 44, according to the Bureau of Labor Statistics. This situation persists at a time when a 77-year-old astronaut named John Glenn just went back into space—and while the minimum age for receiving Social Security benefits is rising.

Perhaps more managers should look at the hard science on this question. In a survey of the available research, Paula Rayman, director of the Radcliffe Public Policy Institute notes that there are "at least 20 studies showing that vocabulary, general information, and judgment either rise or never fall before age 60." Despite

six survival tips

THE RULES OF THE GAME MAY HAVE CHANGED, BUT midcareer and older workers still hold a number of aces—among them experience, wisdom, and adaptability. Here's some expert advice on how to play your cards and strengthen your hand for the future, gleaned from John Thompson, head of IMCOR, an interim executive placement firm in Stamford, Connecticut; Peter Cappelli, professor of management at The Wharton School in Philadelphia and author of *The New Deal at Work* (Harvard Business School Press 1999); and management gurus N. Fredric Crandall and Marc J. Wallace, authors of *Work and Rewards in the Virtual Workplace* (AMACOM, 1998)

LEARN WHILE YOU EARN If your company will pay for you to attend college-level courses to up-grade your skills, great. If not, take them anyway. Anything computer-related is a good bet. Microsoft offers training programs via organizations such as AARP.

FLEX YOUR MUSCLES By offering to work hours that younger workers may shun because of family and other commitments, you set yourself apart, especially in the eyes of employers in service industries who need 24-hour or seven-a-day week staffing. Employers such as the Home Shopping Network now rely on mature workers to fill a variety of positions.

CAST A WIDE NET The World Wide Web has radically changed the employment scene. A growing selection of jobs are being posted there, and so are résumés. Take a look at the Working Options section on AARP's Web site at www.aarp.org/working_options/home.html for career guidance and links to resources, including America's Job Bank.

BECOME AN MVP Do something to make yourself invaluable. For example, consider becoming a mentor to a young, up-and-coming manager who may need just the kind of guidance an experienced hand can offer. Another option: Seek out projects that matter to your boss and allow you to showcase your talents.

TEST THE WATERS Temporary workers are the fastest-growing segment of the labor force, for good reason. Companies faced with budget-cutting pressures are loathe to add full-time, permanent workers who drive up salary and benefit costs. It gives you an opportunity to try out an alternate career to see if it really fits. And temporary work often is the pathway to a permanent gig.

BE A COMEBACK KID Even if you're planning to retire or cut back from full-time work, don't forget job possibilities with your current employer. GE's information unit in Rockville, Maryland, offers a Golden Opportunity program that lets retirees work up to 1,000 hours a year, and many firms in Southern California use retirees to help with special engineering projects.

—*Tim Smart*

these results, they found that managers "consistently made different hiring, promotion, training, and discipline decisions based *solely* [my emphasis] on the age of the workers."

A recent survey of 405 human-resources professionals found that only 29 percent of them make an active effort to attract and/or retain older workers. Among those employers who have made such efforts, establishing opportunities for advancement, skills training, and part-time work arrangements are the most common. Overall, older employees are rated highly for loyalty and dedication, commitment to doing quality work, reliability in a crisis, solid work performance, and experience. This has given rise to a new phenomenon, in which downsized older workers are coming back to the workplace as consultants, temps. or contingent workers hired to work on specific projects.

Many who possess, skills that are high in demand, like computer experts or financial advisers are finding fresh opportunities: Brokerage firms, for example, have discovered that their clients enjoy having investment counselors whose life experience is written on their faces.

Other countries are grappling with this issue as well. The Danish government, for example now offers salaried one-year training programs to unemployed workers over age 50. The German government has made it more costly for companies to downsize. And the French government is experimenting with ways to reduce the hours people spend on the job, to spread the work around. For Americans, however, the likely solution will depend on the ability of older workers to take control of their careers as never before, to think of themselves as independent contractors—units of one, so to speak—and, to do whatever they can to enhance their value. At a time when work has become, all-encompassing for many of us, it remains an eminently desirable endeavor. And although much is uncertain about the future, one thing is clear: Work will be part of it.

Mark Hunter is the author of five books, including The Passions of Men: Work and Love in the Age of Stress *(Putnam, 1988). He lives in Paris.*

It's no news that stress can make you sick. But recent research says the solution isn't working less or playing more. It's having someone to confide in.

DON'T FACE STRESS ALONE

By Benedict Carey

THE CURE FOR EXCESSIVE STRESS SHOULD be excessive cash. A fat pile of Microsoft common that provides for limo service and trips to the Seychelles and nannies and someone to vacuum those tumbleweed pet hairs that breed in every corner of the house. Better still, a house that cleans itself. That way we'd have time to read Emerson, learn to play some baroque stringed instrument, and sample Eastern gurus like finger food, accumulating vast reserves of inner peace and healing energy. . . .

We're fooling ourselves. Even stinking rich, most of us would often feel rushed, harassed, afraid that the maid's boyfriend had designs on our Swedish stereo components. We'd lose sleep, lose our tempers, and continue to wonder whether stress was killing us. Not because money doesn't buy

Almost half of Americans say they'd rather be alone when they're stressed. Only 18 percent would call a friend.

tranquility; it buys plenty. But because what we call stress is more than the sum of our chores and responsibilities and financial troubles. It's also a state of mind, a way of interpreting the world, a pattern of behavior.

Think of the people you know. There are those who are so consumed with work that they practically sleep with their cell phones, who go wild when they just have to wait in line at the checkout. And then there are those who breeze through the day as pleased as park rangers—despite having deadlines and kids and a broken-down car and charity work and scowling Aunt Agnes living in the spare bedroom. Back in the 1960s cardiologists Ray Rosenman and Meyer Friedman labeled these polar opposites Type A and Type B. They described Type As as "joyless strivers," people who go through life feeling harried, hostile, and combative. Type Bs, by contrast, are unhurried, even tempered, emotionally secure. In person Type As may be twitchy, prone to interrupt, resentful of conversational diversions. Type Bs are as placid as giraffes, well mannered, affectionately patient. In a landmark 1971 study Rosenman and Friedman found that Type As were about twice as likely to develop coronary artery disease as Type Bs. This was the first evidence of a phenomenon that we now take for granted: People consumed by stress often live short lives.

Often. But not always. Some Type As live long and prosper. Some Type Bs succumb to heart attacks before they turn 50. Rosenman and Friedman's theory represented a giant step in tracing a link between disease and personality. But it only partly explained why stress sometimes damages the heart. So the search has been under way to discover a more specific connection between personality and illness. In the past decade findings in fields as seemingly unrelated as sociology and immunology have begun to converge on a surprising answer. Of course it matters if your life is a high-wire act of clamoring demands and pressing deadlines. And yes, it does make a difference whether you're angry or retiring, effusive or shy, belligerent or thoughtful. But what really matters appears to be something much simpler: whether you have someone in your life who's emotionally on call, who's willing to sit up late and hear your complaints.

HUMAN EMOTIONS ARE a messy affair, fleeting, contradictory, and as hard to define as human beings themselves. So it's no wonder researchers have found themselves groping around the dim and convoluted catacombs of personality, trying to locate the core of the trouble with Type As. Some suspect the real villain may be a specific trait such as hostility, cynicism, or self-centeredness. And indeed, all of these characteristics are prevalent in many people who develop coronary disease. But none has proved terribly useful for predicting who will get sick. The search has been a little like being fitted for glasses: Lens two looks clearer than lens one at first, but then you're not so sure. Still, something's there, all right, and several studies conducted in the late eighties and early nineties have finally brought its ghostly shape into focus.

"If you look across all of these studies for a pattern," says psychologist Margaret Chesney, who has spent the past 20 years doing precisely that, "you see that the hostility questionnaires and the Type A interview and all the other measures—they're all picking up the same thing. It's this person who's often suspicious; who sees people as being in their way; who, when they meet someone new, asks, 'What do you do? Where did you go to school?'—not to make a connection but to assess the competition."

More details emerged in 1989 when psychologists Jerry Suls and Choi Wan of the State University of New York at Albany reviewed the Type A research to look for a common thread. They concentrated on stud-

and fear associated with the garden-variety neurotic. These are the sort of people who need counseling but consider therapists overpriced palm-readers. "The picture we're getting is of someone who has deep problems but doesn't admit them," says Suls. "So there are a couple of possibilities here. Either they're in denial. Or they really don't have rich inner lives. They never really think about these things."

They aren't Oprah Winfrey fans, in short. They're happy enough talking about work, fashion, sports—anything but the mushy personal stuff. "If you confront them with that," says Suls, "they get angry. They blow up." As one researcher puts it, "They never let their guard down. If you come close, they wonder, What is this person after?" Spare me the advice, Sigmund, can't you see I'm busy?

This evidence, admittedly raw, is still the subject of much debate, but it has even the most authoritative, skeptical, hard-line figures in the field talking like late-night radio shrinks. Just listen to founding father Rosenman, who has guarded the Type A franchise like a hawk, staring down dozens of psychologists whose work he deemed soft or flawed. "After 40 years of observing and treating thousands of patients, and doing all of the studies, I believe that what's underneath the inappropriate competitiveness of Type As is a deep-seated insecurity. I never would have said that before, but I keep coming back to it. It's different from anxiety in the usual sense, because Type As are not people who retreat. They constantly compete because it helps them suppress the insecurity they're afraid others will sense.

"If I felt this way, how would I cover it up? I'd distract myself, go faster and faster, and win over everybody else. I'd look at everyone as a threat, because they might expose me."

Avoiding exposure inevitably means avoiding close relationships. The person

The people most vulnerable to stress are those who are emotionally isolated. They might have the biggest Rolodex, but they're alone.

ies whose authors had performed general psychological profiles as well as Type A assessments. As a rule, general psych profiles ask directly about fears, insecurities, childhood traumas, and so on, while the Type A diagnosis focuses on how pressured a person feels and how pleasantly he or she answers aggressive questions.

Suls and Wan had suspected that Type A behavior would be associated with emotional distress. But they found something strange. The Type As did show strains of insecurity and emotional isolation—but none of the anxiety

Rosenman is describing has friends, sure, but no genuine confidants, no one who's allowed so much as a whiff of frailty. That's why many researchers now believe that the symptom most common among those vulnerable to stress is emotional isolation. As Chesney puts it, "These people might have the biggest Rolodex, but they're alone. They're busy looking for more connections, charming more people. When they feel isolated they get busy. It's a defense mechanism."

According to Jonathan Schedler, a research psychologist affiliated with Harvard

They Touched a Nation

THANKS TO PUBLIC FIGURES who spoke out about their illnesses, we have all grown more comfortable in the past decade confronting health problems that were long shrouded in lonely silence.
—*Rita Rubin*

MUHAMMAD ALI

It was the most arresting moment of the 1996 Olympics in Atlanta: the former boxer, arm trembling, face frozen, raising the torch to light the ceremonial flame. Calls flooded the National Parkinson's Foundation, which adopted a torch as its symbol.

ANNETTE FUNICELLO

In 1992, when the onetime Mickey Mouse Club girl publicly revealed her diagnosis, we all suddenly knew at least one person with MS: Annette. "She is everyone's extended family member," says Arney Rosenblat of the National Multiple Sclerosis Society.

LINDA ELLERBEE

Months after the journalist underwent a double mastectomy, she produced an emotionally charged special on breast cancer. "I can be fair and honest," she says of the disease. "But objective I cannot be."

RONALD REAGAN

Ever-folksy, the former president announced he had Alzheimer's disease in a handwritten letter addressed to "my fellow Americans" in 1994. He called his gesture "an opening of our hearts."

WILLIAM STYRON

The novelist told of his depression in the New York Times and later in *Darkness Visible: A Memoir of Madness.* "The overwhelming reaction made me feel that inadvertently I had helped unlock a closet from which many souls were eager to come out."

CHRISTOPHER REEVE

"You only have two choices," says the actor whose 1995 fall from a horse left him permanently paralyzed and who has raised millions for spinal injury research. "Either you vegetate and look out the window or activate and try to effect change."

GREG LOUGANIS

Mortified that he'd hid his HIV-positive status when his head wound bloodied the Olympic pool in 1988, the diver finally told his story during an interview with Barbara Walters in 1995.

ball: from "slow down, spend more time with your family, and don't sweat the little things" to "control your anger, read more poetry, and verbalize affection." Hardly the sort of wisdom that transforms lives.

If these interventions have anything in common, though, it is the presence of other people. This makes sense if you think of stress the way most doctors do, as a hormonal response to pressure. The body perceives a threat, mental or physical, and releases hormones that hike blood pressure and suppress immune response. According to the theory, some of us (the hostile, the troubled, the Type As) have a higher risk of heart disease or cancer because we secrete more of these hormones more frequently than the average joe. This stress response isn't easy to moderate, but one of the few things that seems to help is contact with a supportive person. In several lab experiments, for instance, psychologists have shown that having a friend in the room calms the cardiovascular response to distressing tasks such as public speaking. It's the secret of group therapy: We relax around our own. The simple grace of company can keep us healthy.

Humans are, after all, social by nature. So perhaps it makes sense that the healthiest among us might be the ones who find solace in companionship, who can defuse building pressure by opening up our hearts to someone else. As the late biologist and writer Lewis Thomas observed, human beings have survived by being useful to one another. We are as indispensable to each other as hummingbirds are to hibiscus.

And by finding ways to help each other out, the latest research hints, we forge the emotional connections that could very well sustain us. Thomas understood this. In a *New York Times* interview in 1993, just two weeks before his death, the reporter asked him, "Is there an art to dying?"

"There's an art to living," Thomas replied. "One of the very important things that has to be learned around the time dying becomes a real prospect is to recognize those occasions when we have been useful in the world. With the same sharp insight that we all have for acknowledging our failures, we ought to recognize when we have been useful, and sometimes uniquely useful. All of us have had such times in our lives, but we don't pay much attention to them. Yet the thing we're really good at as a species is usefulness. If we paid more attention to this biological attribute, we'd get a satisfaction that cannot be attained from goods or knowledge."

Benedict Carey has been a staff writer at the magazine since 1988.

University, the tests researchers use to identify hostile personalities essentially measure something he calls interpersonal warmth. "It has to do with whether you see the people in your life as benevolent or malevolent, whether they offer nourishment or frustration," he says. "The fact is, humans are emotionally frail. We need real support from other people, and those who don't acknowledge it are going to feel besieged."

These notions could easily collapse into sentimentality. Yet scientific evidence for the physical benefits of social support is coming in from all sides. At Ohio State University, for example, immunologist Ron Glaser and psychologist Janice Kiecolt-Glaser have found that the biggest slump in immunity during exam periods occurs in medical students who report being lonely. Analyzing data from the Tecumseh Community Health Study, sociologist James House calculated

that social isolation was as big a risk factor for illness and death as smoking was. And these were just the warm-up acts. In 1989 David Spiegel of Stanford Medical School measured the effect of weekly group therapy on women being treated for breast cancer. As expected, those who met in groups experienced less pain than those who didn't. But that wasn't all. The women in counseling survived an average of 37 months—nearly twice as long as those without the group support. Other researchers, including Friedman, have also lengthened some heart patients' lives through group therapy.

The reason remains anyone's guess. Perhaps, as Spiegel has suggested, being in a group makes patients more likely to take their medications, perform prescribed exercise, and so on. Patients may also benefit from advice offered in therapy, which can range from the commonsensical to the corn-

Unit 6

Unit Selections

43. **What You Can Change & What You Cannot Change,** Martin E. P. Seligman
44. **Think Like a Shrink,** Emanuel H. Rosen
45. **Bad Choices: Why We Make Them, How to Stop,** Mary Ann Chapman
46. **Chronic Anxiety: How to Stop Living on the Edge,** *Harvard Health Letter*
47. **The Science of Women & Sex,** John Leland
48. **Mind Over Medicine,** Howard Brody

Key Points to Consider

❖ According to "What You Can Change and What You Cannot Change," what does Martin Seligman suggest can be changed by self-determination? What can be changed only by means of professional assistance? Is the self-approach better than professional help? Which problems seem immune to change?

❖ Can most individuals successfully cope with everyday difficulties? When do you believe professional intervention is necessary? Can most of us effectively change on our own, so that professional help is not necessary? Discuss.

❖ What types of therapy are available? Does one form seem better than another? Which type of therapy might suit you best and why? What ingredients do you think make therapy effective? Do you think therapy is more art than science? Why?

❖ How can you think like a shrink? What guidelines do therapists use to assess and monitor the mental health of their clients? How might these guidelines be equally useful for you? Why is there a gap between modern psychiatry and the popular culture? What is educational psychotherapy?

❖ What is self-defeating behavior? Can you provide some examples? Why do people make bad choices? How can we reverse some of our self-destructiveness or negative behaviors? Do you think some of these behaviors are more difficult to change than others?

❖ What is anxiety? What is an anxiety disorder? Why are some people chronically anxious? What are the symptoms of anxiety disorder? With what other disorders does anxiety co-exist? How can we recognize and treat these disorders?

❖ Why is female sexual dysfunction receiving so much attention in the literature? What is female sexual dysfunction? Can you name and describe some of these dysfunctions? Can women who have experienced them learn to enjoy and normalize their sexual relationships?

❖ What is a borderline personality? Do you know anyone with this syndrome? Do you think women are more prone to borderline disorder than men? Why? What can we do to help people with borderline personalities? If you were living with someone with a border personality disorder, what could you do to cope?

❖ Is stress necessarily negative? Under what situations might stress be positive? Does stress serve an adaptive function? How so?

❖ What is the mind/body issue? Why are psychologists interested in this issue? Can the mind hold power over the body? What is the placebo effect? Is there any evidence that placebos work? Can believing in something change our health trajectory?

 **Links** # www.dushkin.com/online/

These sites are annotated on pages 4 and 5.

On each college and university campus a handful of students experience overwhelming stress and life-shattering crises. One student learns that her mother, living in a distant city, has terminal cancer. Another receives the sad news that his parents are divorcing. A sorority blackballs a young woman who was determined to become their sister; she commits suicide. The sorority sisters now experience guilt.

Fortunately, almost every campus houses a counseling center for students; some universities also offer assistance to employees. At the counseling service, trained professionals are able to offer aid and therapy to troubled members of the campus community.

Many individuals are able to adapt to life's vagaries, even to life's disasters. Other individuals flounder. They simply do not know how to adjust to change. These individuals sometimes seek temporary professional assistance from a therapist or counselor. For these professionals, the difficulty may be how and when to intervene. Fortunately, very few individuals require long-term care.

There are as many definitions of maladjustment as there are mental health professionals. Some practitioners define mental illness as "whatever society cannot tolerate." Others define it in terms of statistics: "If a majority do not behave that way, then the behavior signals maladjustment." Some professionals suggest that an inadequate self-concept is the cause of maladjustment while others cite a lack of contact with reality. A few psychologists claim that to call one individual ill suggests that the rest are healthy by contrast, when, in fact, there may be few real distinctions among people.

Maladjustment is difficult to define and to treat. For each definition, a theorist develops a treatment strategy. Psychoanalysts press clients to recall their dreams, their childhood, and their intrapsychic conflicts in order to analyze the contents of the unconscious. Humanists encourage clients to explore all of the facets of their lives in order to become less defensive. Behaviorists are usually concerned with observable and therefore treatable symptoms or behaviors. For behaviorists, no underlying causes are postulated to be the roots of adjustment problems. Other therapists, namely psychiatrists who are physicians by training, may utilize these therapies and add drugs and psychosurgery.

This brief list of interventions raises further questions. For instance, is one form of therapy more effective, less expensive, or longer lasting than another? Is one diagnosis better treated by a particular form of therapy? Who should make the diagnosis? If two experts disagree on the diagnosis and treatment, how do we decide which one is correct? Should psychologists be allowed to prescribe psychoactive drugs? These questions continue to be debated.

Some psychologists question whether professional intervention is necessary at all. In one well-publicized but highly criticized study, researcher Hans Eysenck was able to show that spontaneous remission rates were as high as therapeutic "cure" rates. You, yourself, may be wondering whether professional help is always necessary. Can people be their own healers? Is support from friends as productive as professional treatment?

The first readings offer general information to individuals who are having difficulty adjusting and coping. Specifically, the articles pertain to the process of change as induced by treatments such as psychotherapy. Psychologist Martin Seligman, in "What You Can Change and What You Cannot Change," discusses what can be realistically managed in terms of self-improvement. Once an individual knows which behaviors cannot change, Seligman believes the individual will stop being so hard on him- or herself.

In "Think Like A Shrink," Emanuel Rosen, writing for *Psychology Today,* reveals how psychotherapists assess and help individuals with coping problems or with troubling problems of daily life. The guidelines that Rosen lays out can help even the nonprofessional bring about better mental health for themselves and others.

The following section offers a review of situations in which people find themselves and which have the potential to cause coping problems. The essay "Bad Choices: Why We Make Them, How to Stop," by Mary Ann Chapman, asserts that our own destructive behaviors are regulated by the immediate rewards we think we will receive rather than by the long-term destructive consequences. Once we learn how to manage the short-term effects, we can overcome self-destructiveness.

Anxiety is a common issue of everyday life. In the article "Chronic Anxiety: How to Stop Living on the Edge," the issue of long-term anxiety is discussed. Anxiety disorders in general are then described. These disorders often co-exist with depression. Methods for treating anxiety are also revealed.

Another common disorder is sexual dysfunction. Both men and women can suffer from various sexual dysfunctions. However, the next article deals only with dysfunction in women. New drugs for men, such as Viagra, have helped quell some of the cases of male sexual dysfunction. What the various disorders in women are and what researchers have discovered about them is the focus of this informative article.

In "Mind Over Medicine" we end this anthology on a positive note and examine an interesting concept from psychology, one that is receiving more and more attention—the placebo effect. The placebo effect is where we can convince ourselves that we want to feel better and thus we do.

What You Can Change & What You Cannot Change

There are things we can change about ourselves and things we cannot. Concentrate your energy on what is possible—too much time has been wasted.

Martin E. P. Seligman, Ph.D.

This is the age of psychotherapy and the age of self-improvement. Millions are struggling to change: We diet, we jog, we meditate. We adopt new modes of thought to counteract our depressions. We practice relaxation to curtail stress. We exercise to expand our memory and to quadruple our reading speed. We adopt draconian regimens to give up smoking. We raise our little boys and girls to androgyny. We come out of the closet and we try to become heterosexual. We seek to lose our taste for alcohol. We seek more meaning in life. We try to extend our life span.

Sometimes it works. But distressingly often, self-improvement and psychotherapy fail. The cost is enormous. We think we are worthless. We feel guilty and ashamed. We believe we have no willpower and that we are failures. We give up trying to change.

On the other hand, this is not only the age of self-improvement and therapy, but also the age of biological psychiatry. The human genome will be nearly mapped be-

fore the millennium is over. The brain systems underlying sex, hearing, memory, left-handedness, and sadness are now known. Psychoactive drugs quiet our fears, relieve our blues, bring us bliss, dampen our mania, and dissolve our delusions more effectively than we can on our own.

Our very personality—our intelligence and musical talent, even our religiousness, our conscience (or its absence), our politics, and our exuberance—turns out to be more the product of our genes than almost anyone would have believed a decade ago. The underlying message of the age of biological psychiatry is that our biology frequently makes changing, in spite of all our efforts, impossible.

But the view that all is genetic and biochemical and therefore unchangeable is also very often wrong. Many people surpass their IQs, fail to "respond" to drugs, make sweeping changes in their lives, live on when their cancer is "terminal," or defy the hormones and brain circuitry that "dictate" lust, femininity, or memory loss.

The ideologies of biological psychiatry and self-improvement are obviously colliding. Nevertheless, a resolution is apparent. There are some things about ourselves that can be changed, others that cannot, and some that can be changed only with extreme difficulty.

What can we succeed in changing about ourselves? What can we not? When can we overcome our biology? And when is our biology our destiny?

I want to provide an understanding of what you can and what you can't change about yourself so that you can concentrate your limited time and energy on what is possible. So much time has been wasted. So much needless frustration has been endured. So much of therapy, so much of child rearing, so much of self-improving, and even some of the great social movements in our century have come to nothing because they tried to change the unchangeable. Too often we have wrongly thought we were weak-willed failures, when the changes we wanted to make in ourselves

From *Psychology Today*, May/June 1994, pp. 34–41, 70, 72–74, 84. Excerpted from *What You Can Change & What You Can't* by Martin E. P. Seligman. © 1993 by Martin E. P. Seligman. Reprinted by permission of Alfred A. Knopf, Inc.

So much child rearing, therapy, and self-improvement have come to nothing.

were just not possible. But all this effort was necessary: Because there have been so many failures, we are now able to see the boundaries of the unchangeable; this in turn allows us to see clearly for the first time the boundaries of what *is* changeable.

With this knowledge, we can use our precious time to make the many rewarding changes that are possible. We can live with less self-reproach and less remorse. We can live with greater confidence. This knowledge is a new understanding of who we are and where we are going.

CATASTROPHIC THINKING: PANIC

S. J. Rachman, one of the world's leading clinical researchers and one of the founders of behavior therapy, was on the phone. He was proposing that I be the "discussant" at a conference about panic disorder sponsored by the National Institute of Mental Health (NIMH).

"Why even bother, Jack?" I responded. "Everyone knows that panic is biological and that the only thing that works is drugs."

"Don't refuse so quickly, Marty. There is a breakthrough you haven't yet heard about."

Breakthrough was a word I had never heard Jack use before.

"What's the breakthrough?" I asked.

"If you come, you can find out."

So I went.

I had known about and seen panic patients for many years, and had read the literature with mounting excitement during the 1980s. I knew that panic disorder is a frightening condition that consists of recurrent attacks, each much worse than anything experienced before. Without prior warning, you feel as if you are going to die. Here is a typical case history:

The first time Celia had a panic attack, she was working at McDonald's. It was two days before her 20th birthday. As she was handing a customer a Big Mac, she had the worst experience of her life. The earth seemed to open up beneath her. Her heart began to pound, she felt she was smothering, and she was sure she was going to have a heart attack and die. After about 20 minutes of terror, the panic subsided. Trembling, she got in her car, raced home and barely left the house for the next three months.

Since then, Celia has had about three attacks a month. She does not know when they are coming. She always thinks she is going to die.

Panic attacks are not subtle, and you need no quiz to find out if you or someone you love has them. As many as five percent of American adults probably do. The defining feature of the disorder is simple: recurrent awful attacks of panic that come out of the blue, last for a few minutes, and then subside. The attacks consist of chest pains, sweating, nausea, dizziness, choking, smothering, or trembling. They are accompanied by feelings of overwhelming dread and thoughts that you are having a heart attack, that you are losing control, or that you are going crazy.

THE BIOLOGY OF PANIC

There are four questions that bear on whether a mental problem is primarily "biological" as opposed to "psychological":

- Can it be induced biologically?
- Is it genetically heritable?
- Are specific brain functions involved?
- Does a drug relieve it?

Inducing panic. Panic attacks can be created by a biological agent. For example, patients who have a history of panic attacks are hooked up to an intravenous line. Sodium lactate, a chemical that normally produces rapid, shallow breathing and heart palpitations, is slowly infused into their bloodstream. Within a few minutes, about 60 to 90 percent of these patients have a panic attack. Normal controls—subjects with no history of panic—rarely have attacks when infused with lactate.

Genetics of panic. There may be some heritability of panic. If one of two identical twins has panic attacks, 31 percent of the cotwins also have them. But if one of two fraternal twins has panic attacks, none of the cotwins are so afflicted.

Panic and the brain. The brains of people with panic disorders look somewhat unusual upon close scrutiny. Their neurochemistry shows abnormalities in the system that turns on, then dampens, fear. In addition, the PET scan (positron-emission tomography), a technique that looks at how much blood and oxygen different parts of the brain use, shows that patients who panic from the infusion of lactate have

We are now able to see the boundaries of the unchangeable.

What Can We Change?

When we survey all the problems, personality types, patterns of behavior, and the weak influence of childhood on adult life, we see a puzzling array of how much change occurs. From the things that are easiest to those that are the most difficult, this rough array emerges:

Panic	Curable
Specific Phobias	Almost Curable
Sexual Dysfunctions	Marked Relief
Social Phobia	Moderate Relief
Agoraphobia	Moderate Relief
Depression	Moderate Relief
Sex Role Change	Moderate Relief
Obsessive-Compulsive Disorder	Moderate Mild Relief
Sexual Preferences	Moderate Mild Change
Anger	Mild Moderate Relief
Everyday Anxiety	Mild Moderate Relief
Alcoholism	Mild Relief
Overweight	Temporary Change
Posttraumatic Stress Disorder (PTSD)	Marginal Relief
Sexual Orientation	Probably Unchangeable
Sexual Identity	Unchangeable

higher blood flow and oxygen use in relevant parts of their brain than patients who don't panic.

Drugs. Two kinds of drugs relieve panic: tricyclic antidepressants and the anti-anxiety drug Xanax, and both work better than placebos. Panic attacks are dampened, and sometimes even eliminated. General anxiety and depression also decrease.

Since these four questions had already been answered "yes" when Jack Rachman called, I thought the issue had already been settled. Panic disorder was simply a biological illness, a disease of the body that could be relieved only by drugs.

A few months later I was in Bethesda, Maryland, listening once again to the same four lines of biological evidence. An inconspicuous figure in a brown suit sat hunched over the table. At the first break, Jack introduced me to him—David Clark, a young psychologist from Oxford. Soon after, Clark began his address.

"Consider, if you will, an alternative theory, a cognitive theory." He reminded all of us that almost all panickers believe that they are going to die during an attack. Most commonly, they believe that they are having heart attacks. Perhaps, Clark suggested, this is more than just a mere symptom. Perhaps it is the root cause. Panic may simply be the *catastrophic misinterpretation of bodily sensations.*

For example, when you panic, your heart starts to race. You notice this, and you see it as a possible heart attack. This makes you very anxious, which means that your heart pounds more. You now notice that your heart is *really* pounding. You are now *sure* it's a heart attack. This terrifies you, and you break into a sweat, feel nauseated, short of breath—all symptoms of terror, but for you, they're confirmation of a heart attack. A full-blown panic attack is under way, and at the root of it is your misinterpretation of the symptoms of anxiety as symptoms of impending death.

I was listening closely now as Clark argued that an obvious sign of a disorder, easily dismissed as a symptom, is the disorder itself. If he was right, this was a historic occasion. All Clark had done so far, however, was to show that the four lines of evidence for a biological view of panic could fit equally well with a misinterpretation view. But Clark soon told us about a series of experiments he and his colleague Paul Salkovskis had done at Oxford.

First, they compared panic patients with patients who had other anxiety disorders and with normals. All the subjects read the following sentences aloud, but the last word was presented blurred. For example:

dying
If I had palpitations, I could be
excited

choking
If I were breathless, I could be
unfit

When the sentences were about bodily sensations, the panic patients, but no one else, saw the catastrophic endings fastest. This showed that panic patients possess the habit of thinking Clark had postulated.

Next, Clark and his colleagues asked if activating this habit with words would induce panic. All the subjects read a series of word pairs aloud. When panic patients

---

Self-Analysis Questionnaire

Is your life dominated by anxiety? Read each statement and then mark the appropriate number to indicate how you generally feel. There are no right or wrong answers.

1. I am a steady person.

Almost never	Sometimes	Often	Almost always
4	3	2	1

2. I am satisfied with myself.

Almost never	Sometimes	Often	Almost always
4	3	2	1

3. I feel nervous and restless.

Almost never	Sometimes	Often	Almost always
1	2	3	4

4. I wish I could be as happy as others seem to be.

Almost never	Sometimes	Often	Almost always
1	2	3	4

5. I feel like a failure.

Almost never	Sometimes	Often	Almost always
1	2	3	4

6. I get in a state of tension and turmoil as I think over my recent concerns and interests.

Almost never	Sometimes	Often	Almost always
1	2	3	4

7. I feel secure.

Almost never	Sometimes	Often	Almost always
4	3	2	1

8. I have self-confidence.

Almost never	Sometimes	Often	Almost always
4	3	2	1

9. I feel inadequate.

Almost never	Sometimes	Often	Almost always
1	2	3	4

10. I worry too much over something that does not matter.

Almost never	Sometimes	Often	Almost always
1	2	3	4

To score, simply add up the numbers under your answers. Notice that some of the rows of numbers go up and others go down. The higher your total, the more the trait of anxiety dominates your life. If your score was:

10–11, you are in the lowest 10 percent of anxiety.

13–14, you are in the lowest quarter.

16–17, your anxiety level is about average.

19–20, your anxiety level is around the 75th percentile.

22–24 (and you are male) your anxiety level is around the 90th percentile.

24–26 (and you are female) your anxiety level is around the 90th percentile.

25 (and you are male) your anxiety level is at the 95th percentile.

27 (and you are female) your anxiety level is at the 95th percentile.

Should you try to change your anxiety level? Here are my rules of thumb:

- If your score is at the 90th percentile or above, you can probably improve the quality of your life by lowering your general anxiety level—regardless of paralysis and irrationality.
- If your score is at the 75th percentile or above, and you feel that anxiety is either paralyzing you or that it is unfounded, you should probably try to lower your general anxiety level.
- If your score is 18 or above, and you feel that anxiety is unfounded and paralyzing, you should probably try to lower your general anxiety level.

got to "breathlessness-suffocation" and "palpitations-dying," 75 percent suffered a full-blown panic attack right there in the laboratory. No normal people had panic attacks, no recovered panic patients (I'll tell you more in a moment about how they got better) had attacks, and only 17 percent of other anxious patients had attacks.

The final thing Clark told us was the "breakthrough" that Rachman had promised.

Issues of the soul can barely be changed by psychotherapy or drugs.

"We have developed and tested a rather novel therapy for panic," Clark continued in his understated, disarming way. He explained that if catastrophic misinterpretations of bodily sensation are the cause of a panic attack, then changing the tendency to misinterpret should cure the disorder. His new therapy was straightforward and brief:

Patients are told that panic results when they mistake normal symptoms of mounting anxiety for symptoms of heart attack, going crazy, or dying. Anxiety itself, they are informed, produces shortness of breath, chest pain, and sweating. Once they misinterpret these normal bodily sensations as an imminent heart attack, their symptoms become even more pronounced because the misinterpretation changes their anxiety into terror. A vicious circle culminates in a full-blown panic attack.

Patients are taught to reinterpret the symptoms realistically as mere anxiety symptoms. Then they are given practice right in the office, breathing rapidly into a paper bag. This causes a buildup of carbon dioxide and shortness of breath, mimicking the sensations that provoke a panic attack. The therapist points out that the symptoms the patient is experiencing—shortness of breath and heart racing—are harmless, simply the result of overbreathing, not a sign of a heart attack. The patient learns to interpret the symptoms correctly.

"This simple therapy appears to be a cure," Clark told us. "Ninety to 100 percent of the patients are panic free at the end of therapy. One year later, only one person had had another panic attack."

This, indeed, was a breakthrough: a simple, brief psychotherapy with no side effects showing a 90-percent cure rate of a disorder that a decade ago was thought to be incurable. In a controlled study of 64 patients comparing cognitive therapy to drugs to relaxation to no treatment, Clark and his colleagues found that cognitive

therapy is markedly better than drugs or relaxation, both of which are better than nothing. Such a high cure rate is unprecedented.

How does cognitive therapy for panic compare with drugs? It is more effective and less dangerous. Both the antidepressants and Xanax produce marked reduction in panic in most patients, but drugs must be taken forever; once the drug is stopped, panic rebounds to where it was before therapy began for perhaps half the patients. The drugs also sometimes have severe side effects, including drowsiness, lethargy, pregnancy complications, and addictions.

After this bombshell, my own "discussion" was an anticlimax. I did make one point that Clark took to heart. "Creating a cognitive therapy that works, even one that works as well as this apparently does, is not enough to show that the *cause* of panic is cognitive." I was niggling. "The biological theory doesn't deny that some other therapy might work well on panic. It merely claims that panic is caused at the bottom by some biochemical problem."

Two years later, Clark carried out a crucial experiment that tested the biological theory against the cognitive theory. He gave the usual lactate infusion to 10 panic patients, and nine of them panicked. He did the same thing with another 10 patients, but added special instructions to allay the misinterpretation of the sensations. He simply told them: "Lactate is a natural bodily substance that produces sensations similar to exercise or alcohol. It is normal to experience intense sensations during infusion, but these do not indicate an adverse reaction." Only three out of the 10 panicked. This confirmed the theory crucially.

Anxiety scans your life for imperfections. When it finds one, it won't let go.

The therapy works very well, as it did for Celia, whose story has a happy ending. She first tried Xanax, which reduced the intensity and the frequency of her panic attacks. But she was too drowsy to work and she was still having about one attack every six weeks. She was then referred to Audrey, a cognitive therapist who explained that Celia was misinterpreting her heart racing and shortness of breath as symptoms of a heart attack, that they were actually just symptoms of mounting anxiety, nothing more harmful. Audrey taught Celia progressive relaxation, and then she demonstrated

the harmlessness of Celia's symptoms of overbreathing. Celia then relaxed in the presence of the symptoms and found that they gradually subsided. After several more practice sessions, therapy terminated. Celia has gone two years without another panic attack.

EVERYDAY ANXIETY

Attend to your tongue—right now. What is it doing? Mine is swishing around near my lower right molars. It has just found a minute fragment of last night's popcorn (debris from *Terminator* 2). Like a dog at a bone, it is worrying the firmly wedged flake.

Attend to your hand—right now. What's it up to? My left hand is boring in on an itch it discovered under my earlobe.

Your tongue and your hands have, for the most part, a life of their own. You can bring them under voluntary control by consciously calling them out of their "default" mode to carry out your commands: "Pick up the phone" or "Stop picking that pimple." But most of the time they are on their own. They are seeking out small imperfections. They scan your entire mouth and skin surface, probing for anything going wrong. They are marvelous, nonstop grooming devices. They, not the more fashionable immune system, are your first line of defense against invaders.

Anxiety is your mental tongue. Its default mode is to search for what may be about to go wrong. It continually, and without your conscious consent, scans your life—yes, even when you are asleep, in dreams and nightmares. It reviews your work, your love, your play—until it finds an imperfection. When it finds one, it worries it. It tries to pull it out from its hiding place, where it is wedged inconspicuously under some rock. It will not let go. If the imperfection is threatening enough, anxiety calls your attention to it by making you uncomfortable. If you do not act, it yells more insistently—disturbing your sleep and your appetite.

You can reduce daily, mild anxiety. You can numb it with alcohol, Valium, or marijuana. You can take the edge off with meditation or progressive relaxation. You can beat it down by becoming more conscious of the automatic thoughts of danger that trigger anxiety and then disputing them effectively.

But do not overlook what your anxiety is trying to do for you. In return for the pain it brings, it prevents larger ordeals by making you aware of their possibility and goading you into planning for and forestalling them. It may even help you avoid them altogether. Think of your anxiety as the "low oil" light flashing on the dashboard of your car. Disconnect it and you will be less distracted and more comfortable for a while. But this may cost you a burned-up engine. Our *dysphoria,* or bad feeling, should, some of the time, be tolerated, attended to, even cherished.

GUIDELINES FOR WHEN TO TRY TO CHANGE ANXIETY

Some of our everyday anxiety, depression, and anger go beyond their useful function. Most adaptive traits fall along a normal spectrum of distribution, and the capacity for internal bad weather for everyone some of the time means that some of us may have terrible weather all of the time. In general, when the hurt is pointless and recurrent—when, for example, anxiety insists we formulate a plan but no plan will work—it is time to take action to relieve the hurt. There are three hallmarks indicating that anxiety has become a burden that wants relieving:

First, is it *irrational?*

We must calibrate our bad weather inside against the real weather outside. Is what you are anxious about out of proportion to the reality of the danger? Here are some examples that may help you answer this question. All of the following are not irrational:

- A fire fighter trying to smother a raging oil well burning in Kuwait repeatedly wakes up at four in the morning because of flaming terror dreams.
- A mother of three smells perfume on her husband's shirts and, consumed by jealousy, broods about his infidelity, reviewing the list of possible women over and over.
- A student who had failed two of his midterm exams finds, as finals approach, that he can't get to sleep for worrying. He has diarrhea most of the time.

The only good thing that can be said about such fears is that they are well-founded.

In contrast, all of the following are irrational, out of proportion to the danger:

- An elderly man, having been in a fender bender, broods about travel and will no longer take cars, trains, or airplanes.
- An eight-year-old child, his parents having been through an ugly divorce, wets his bed at night. He is haunted with visions of his bedroom ceiling collapsing on him.
- A housewife who has an MBA and who accumulated a decade of experience as a financial vice president before her twins were born is sure her job search

will be fruitless. She delays preparing her résumés for a month.

The second hallmark of anxiety out of control is *paralysis.* Anxiety intends action: Plan, rehearse, look into shadows for lurking dangers, change your life. When anxiety becomes strong, it is unproductive; no problem-solving occurs. And when anxiety is extreme, it paralyzes you. Has your anxiety crossed this line? Some examples:

- A woman finds herself housebound because she fears that if she goes out, she will be bitten by a cat.
- A salesman broods about the next customer hanging up on him and makes no more cold calls.
- A writer, afraid of the next rejection slip, stops writing.

'Dieting below your natural weight is a necessary condition for bulimia. Returning to your natural weight will cure it.'

The final hallmark is *intensity.* Is your life dominated by anxiety? Dr. Charles Spielberger, one of the world's foremost testers of emotion, has developed well-validated scales for calibrating how severe anxiety is. To find out how anxious *you* are, use the self-analysis questionnaire.

LOWERING YOUR EVERYDAY ANXIETY

Everyday anxiety level is not a category to which psychologists have devoted a great deal of attention. Enough research has been done, however, for me to recommend two techniques that quite reliably lower everyday anxiety levels. Both techniques are cumulative, rather than one-shot fixes. They require 20 to 40 minutes a day of your valuable time.

The first is *progressive relaxation,* done once or, better, twice a day for at least 10 minutes. In this technique, you tighten and then turn off each of the major muscle groups of your body until you are wholly flaccid. It is not easy to be highly anxious when your body feels like Jell-O. More formally, relaxation engages a response system that competes with anxious arousal.

The second technique is regular *meditation.* Transcendental meditation™ is one

useful, widely available version of this. You can ignore the cosmology in which it is packaged if you wish, and treat it simply as the beneficial technique it is. Twice a day for 20 minutes, in a quiet setting, you close your eyes and repeat a *mantra* (a syllable whose "sonic properties are known") to yourself. Meditation works by blocking thoughts that produce anxiety. It complements relaxation, which blocks the motor components of anxiety but leaves the anxious thoughts untouched.

Done regularly, meditation usually induces a peaceful state of mind. Anxiety at other times of the day wanes, and hyperarousal from bad events is dampened. Done religiously, TM probably works better than relaxation alone.

There's also a quick fix. The minor tranquilizers—Valium, Dalmane, Librium, and their cousins—relieve everyday anxiety. So does alcohol. The advantage of all these is that they work within minutes and require no discipline to use. Their disadvantages outweigh their advantages, however. The minor tranquilizers make you fuzzy and somewhat uncoordinated as they work (a not uncommon side effect is an automobile accident). Tranquilizers soon lose their effect when taken regularly, and they are habit-forming—probably addictive. Alcohol, in addition, produces gross cognitive and motor disability in lockstep with its anxiety relief. Taken regularly over long periods, deadly damage to liver and brain ensue.

If you crave quick and temporary relief from acute anxiety, either alcohol or minor tranquilizers, taken in small amounts and only occasionally, will do the job. They are, however, a distant second-best to progressive relaxation and meditation, which are each worth trying before you seek out psychotherapy or in conjunction with therapy. Unlike tranquilizers and alcohol, neither of these techniques is likely to do you any harm.

Weigh your everyday anxiety. If it is not intense, or if it is moderate and not irrational or paralyzing, act now to reduce it. In spite of its deep evolutionary roots, intense everyday anxiety is often changeable. Meditation and progressive relaxation practiced regularly can change it forever.

DIETING: A WAIST IS A TERRIBLE THING TO MIND

I have been watching my weight and restricting my intake—except for an occasional binge like this—since I was 20. I weighed about 175 pounds then, maybe 15 pounds over my official "ideal" weight. I weigh 199 pounds now, 30 years later, about 25 pounds over the ideal. I have tried about a dozen regimes—fasting, the Beverly Hills Diet, no carbohydrates, Metrecal for lunch, 1,200 calories a day, low fat, no lunch, no starches, skipping every other dinner. I lost 10 or 15 pounds on each in about a month. The pounds always came back, though, and I have gained a net of about a pound a year—inexorably.

This is the most consistent failure in my life. It's also a failure I can't just put out of mind. I have spent the last few years reading the scientific literature, not the parade of best-selling diet books or the flood of women's magazine articles on the latest way to slim down. The scientific findings look clear to me, but there is not yet a consensus. I am going to go out on a limb, because I see so many signs all pointing in one direction. What I have concluded will, I believe, soon be the consensus of the scientists. The conclusions surprise me. They will probably surprise you, too, and they may change your life.

Here is what the picture looks like to me:

- Dieting doesn't work.
- Dieting may make overweight worse, not better.
- Dieting may be bad for health.
- Dieting may cause eating disorders—including bulimia and anorexia.

ARE YOU OVERWEIGHT?

Are you above the ideal weight for your sex, height, and age? If so, you are "overweight." What does this really mean? Ideal weight is arrived at simply. Four million people, now dead, who were insured by the major American life-insurance companies, were once weighed and had their height measured. At what weight on average do people of a given height turn out to live longest? That weight is called ideal. Anything wrong with that?

You bet. The real use of a weight table, and the reason your doctor takes it seriously, is that an ideal weight implies that, on average, if you slim down to yours, you will live longer. This is the crucial claim. Lighter people indeed live longer, on average, than heavier people, but how much longer is hotly debated.

But the crucial claim is unsound because weight (at any given height) has a normal distribution, *normal* both in a statistical sense and in the biological sense. In the biological sense, couch potatoes who overeat and never exercise can legitimately be called overweight, but the buxom, "heavy-boned" slow people deemed overweight by the ideal table are at their natural and healthiest weight. If you are a 155-pound woman and 64 inches in height, for example, you are "overweight" by around 15 pounds. This means nothing more than that the average 140-pound, 64-inch-tall woman lives somewhat longer than the average 155-pound woman of your height. It

does not follow that if you slim down to 125 pounds, *you* will stand any better chance of living longer.

In spite of the insouciance with which dieting advice is dispensed, no one has properly investigated the question of whether slimming down to "ideal" weight produces longer life. The proper study would compare the longevity of people who are at their ideal weight without dieting to people who achieve their ideal weight by dieting. Without this study the common medical advice to diet down to your ideal weight is simply unfounded.

This is not a quibble; there is evidence that dieting damages your health and that this damage may shorten your life.

MYTHS OF OVERWEIGHT

The advice to diet down to your ideal weight to live longer is one myth of overweight. Here are some others:

- *Overweight people overeat.* Wrong. Nineteen out of 20 studies show that obese people consume no more calories each day than nonobese people. Telling a fat person that if she would change her eating habits and eat "normally" she would lose weight is a lie. To lose weight and stay there, she will need to eat excruciatingly less than a normal person, probably for the rest of her life.
- *Overweight people have an overweight personality.* Wrong. Extensive research on personality and fatness has proved little. Obese people do not differ in any major personality style from nonobese people.
- *Physical inactivity is a major cause of obesity.* Probably not. Fat people are indeed less active than thin people, but the inactivity is probably caused more by the fatness than the other way around.
- *Overweight shows a lack of willpower.* This is the granddaddy of all the myths. Fatness is seen as shameful because we hold people responsible for their weight. Being overweight equates with being a weak-willed slob. We believe this primarily because we have seen people decide to lose weight and do so in a matter of weeks.

But almost everyone returns to the old weight after shedding pounds. Your body has a natural weight that it defends vigorously against dieting. The more diets tried, the harder the body works to defeat the next diet. Weight is in large part genetic. All this gives the lie to the "weak-willed" interpretations of overweight. More accurately, dieting is the conscious will of the

individual against a more vigilant opponent: the species' biological defense against starvation. The body can't tell the difference between self-imposed starvation and actual famine, so it defends its weight by refusing to release fat, by lowering its metabolism, and by demanding food. The harder the creature tries not to eat, the more vigorous the defenses become.

BULIMIA AND NATURAL WEIGHT

A concept that makes sense of your body's vigorous defense against weight loss is *natural weight*. When your body screams "I'm hungry," makes you lethargic, stores fat, craves sweets and renders them more delicious than ever, and makes you obsessed with food, what it is defending is your natural weight. It is signaling that you have dropped into a range it will not accept. Natural weight prevents you from gaining too much weight or losing too much. When you eat too much for too long, the opposite defenses are activated and make long-term weight gain difficult.

There is also a strong genetic contribution to your natural weight. Identical twins reared apart weigh almost the same throughout their lives. When identical twins are overfed, they gain weight and add fat in lockstep and in the same places. The fatness or thinness of adopted children resembles their biological parents—particularly their mother—very closely but does not at all resemble their adoptive parents. This suggests that you have a genetically given natural weight that your body wants to maintain.

The idea of natural weight may help cure the new disorder that is sweeping young America. Hundreds of thousands of young women have contracted it. It consists of bouts of binge eating and purging alternating with days of undereating. These young women are usually normal in weight or a bit on the thin side, but they are terrified of becoming fat. So they diet. They exercise. They take laxatives by the cup. They gorge. Then they vomit and take more laxatives. This malady is called *bulimia nervosa* (bulimia, for short).

Therapists are puzzled by bulimia, its causes, and treatment. Debate rages about whether it is an equivalent of depression, or an expression of a thwarted desire for control, or a symbolic rejection of the feminine role. Almost every psychotherapy has been tried. Antidepressants and other drugs have been administered with some effect but little success has been reported.

I don't think that bulimia is mysterious, and I think that it will be curable. I believe that bulimia is caused by dieting. The bulimic goes on a diet, and her body attempts to defend its natural weight. With repeated dieting, this defense becomes more vigorous. Her body is in massive revolt—insistently demanding food, storing fat, craving sweets, and lowering metabolism. Periodically, these biological defenses will overcome her extraordinary willpower (and extraordinary it must be to even approach an ideal weight, say, 20 pounds lighter than her natural weight). She will then binge. Horrified by what this will do to her figure, she vomits and takes laxatives to purge calories. Thus, bulimia is a natural consequence of self-starvation to lose weight in the midst of abundant food.

The therapist's task is to get the patient to stop dieting and become comfortable with her natural weight. He should first convince the patient that her binge eating is caused by her body's reaction to her diet. Then he must confront her with a question: Which is more important, staying thin or getting rid of bulimia? By stopping the diet, he will tell her, she can get rid of the uncontrollable binge-purge cycle. Her body will now settle at her natural weight, and she need not worry that she will balloon beyond that point. For some patients, therapy will end there because they would rather be bulimic than "loathsomely fat." For these patients, the central issue—ideal weight versus natural weight—can now at least become the focus of therapy. For others, defying the social and sexual pressure to be thin will be possible, dieting will be abandoned, weight will be gained, and bulimia should end quickly.

These are the central moves of the cognitive-behavioral treatment of bulimia. There are more than a dozen outcome studies of this approach, and the results are good. There is about 60 percent reduction in binging and purging (about the same as with antidepressant drugs). But unlike drugs, there is little relapse after treatment. Attitudes toward weight and shape relax, and dieting withers.

Of course, the dieting theory cannot fully explain bulimia. Many people who diet don't become bulimic; some can avoid it because their natural weight is close to their ideal weight, and therefore the diet they adopt does not starve them. In addition, bulimics are often depressed, since binging-purging leads to self-loathing. Depression may worsen bulimia by making it easier to give in to temptation. Further, dieting may just be another symptom of bulimia, not a cause. Other factors aside, I can speculate that dieting below your natural weight is a necessary condition for bulimia, and that returning to your natural weight and accepting that weight will cure bulimia.

OVERWEIGHT VS. DIETING: THE HEALTH DAMAGE

Being heavy carries some health risk. There is no definite answer to how much,

because there is a swamp of inconsistent findings. But even if you could just wish pounds away, never to return, it is not certain you should. Being somewhat above your "ideal" weight may actually be your healthiest natural condition, best for your particular constitution and your particular metabolism. Of course you can diet, but the odds are overwhelming that most of the weight will return, and that you will have to diet again and again. From a health and mortality perspective, should you? *There is, probably, a serious health risk from losing weight and regaining it.*

In one study, more than five thousand men and women from Framingham, Massachusetts, were observed for 32 years. People whose weight fluctuated over the years had 30 to 100 percent greater risk of death from heart disease than people whose weight was stable. When corrected for smoking, exercise, cholesterol level, and blood pressure, the findings became more convincing, suggesting that weight fluctuation (the primary cause of which is presumably dieting) may itself increase the risk of heart disease.

If this result is replicated, and if dieting is shown to be the primary cause of weight cycling, it will convince me that you should not diet to reduce your risk of heart disease.

DEPRESSION AND DIETING

Depression is yet another cost of dieting, because two root causes of depression are failure and helplessness. Dieting sets you up for failure. Because the goal of slimming down to your ideal weight pits your fallible willpower against untiring biological defenses, you will often fail. At first you will lose weight and feel pretty good about it. Any depression you had about your figure will disappear. Ultimately, however, you will probably not reach your goal; and then you will be dismayed as the pounds return. Every time you look in the mirror or vacillate over a white chocolate mousse, you will be reminded of your failure, which in turn brings depression.

On the other hand, if you are one of the fortunate few who can keep the weight from coming back, you will probably have to stay on an unsatisfying low-calorie diet for the rest of your life. A side effect of prolonged malnutrition is depression. Either way you are more vulnerable to it.

If you scan the list of cultures that have a thin ideal for women, you will be struck by something fascinating. All thin-ideal cultures also have eating disorders. They also have roughly twice as much depression in women as in men. (Women diet twice as much as men. The best estimate is that 13 percent of adult men and 25 percent of adult women are now on a diet.) The cultures without the thin ideal have no eating disor-

ders, and the amount of depression in women and men in these cultures is the same. This suggests that around the world, the thin ideal and dieting not only cause eating disorders, but they may also cause women to be more depressed than men.

THE BOTTOM LINE

I have been dieting off and on for 30 years because I want to be more attractive, healthier, and more in control. How do these goals stack up against the facts?

Attractiveness. If your attractiveness is a high-enough priority to convince you to diet, keep three drawbacks in mind. First, the attractiveness you gain will be temporary. All the weight you lose and maybe more will likely come back in a few years. This will depress you. Then you will have to lose it again and it will be harder the second time. Or you will have to resign yourself to being less attractive. Second, when women choose the silhouette figure they want to achieve, it turns out to be thinner than the silhouette that men label most attractive. Third, you may well become bulimic particularly if your natural weight is substantially more than your ideal weight. On balance, if short-term attractiveness is your overriding goal, diet. But be prepared for the costs.

Health. No one has ever shown that losing weight will increase my longevity. On balance, the health goal does not warrant dieting.

Control. For many people, getting to an ideal weight and staying there is just as biologically impossible as going with much less sleep. This fact tells me not to diet, and defuses my feeling of shame. My bottom line is clear: I am not going to diet anymore.

DEPTH AND CHANGE: THE THEORY

Clearly, we have not yet developed drugs or psychotherapies that can change all the problems, personality types, and patterns of behavior in adult life. But I believe that success and failure stems from something other than inadequate treatment. Rather, it stems from the depth of the problem.

We all have experience of psychological states of different depths. For example, if you ask someone, out of the blue, to answer quickly, "Who are you?" they will usually tell you—roughly in this order—their name, their sex, their profession, whether they have children, and their religion or race. Underlying this is a continuum of depth from surface to soul—with all manner of psychic material in between.

I believe that issues of the soul can barely be changed by psychotherapy or by drugs. Problems and behavior patterns somewhere between soul and surface can be changed somewhat. Surface problems can be changed easily, even cured. What is changeable, by therapy or drugs, I speculate, varies with the depth of the problem.

My theory says that it does not matter *when* problems, habits, and personality are acquired; their depth derives only from their biology, their evidence, and their power. Some childhood traits, for example, are deep and unchangeable but not because they were learned early and therefore have a privileged place.

Rather, those traits that resist change do so either because they are evolutionarily prepared or because they acquire great power by virtue of becoming the framework around which later learning crystallizes. In this way, the theory of depth carries the optimistic message that we are not prisoners of our past.

When you have understood this message, you will never look at your life in the same way again. Right now there are a number of things that you do not like about yourself and that you want to change: your short fuse, your waistline, your shyness, your drinking, your glumness. You have decided to change, but you do not know what you should work on first. Formerly you would have probably selected the one that hurts the most. Now you will also ask yourself which attempt is most likely to repay your efforts and which is most likely to lead to further frustration. Now you know your shyness and your anger are much more likely to change than your drinking, which you now know is more likely to change than your waistline.

Some of what does change is under your control, and some is not. You can best prepare yourself to change by learning as much as you can about what you can change and how to make those changes. Like all true education, learning about change is not easy; harder yet is surrendering some of our hopes. It is certainly not my purpose to destroy your optimism about change. But it is also not my purpose to assure everybody they can change in every way. My purpose is to instill a new, warranted optimism about the parts of your life you can change and so help you focus your limited time, money, and effort on making actual what is truly within your reach.

Life is a long period of change. What you have been able to change and what has resisted your highest resolve might seem chaotic to you: for some of what you are never changes no matter how hard you try, and other aspects change readily. My hope is that this essay has been the beginning of wisdom about the difference.

Yes, you too can see through the defenses people hide behind. To guide you, just consult the handy primer below. Put together by psychiatrist Emanuel H. Rosen, it distills years of Freudian analytical training into a few simple principles that make sense of our psyches.

THINK LIKE A SHRINK

I have always thought it horribly unfortunate that there is such a tremendous gap between psychiatry and popular culture. Psychiatrists are regularly vilified in entertainment, media, and common thought, and our patients are regularly stigmatized. Indeed, I've yet to see a single movie that accurately portrays what we do. From *Silence of the Lambs* to *The Prince of Tides,* we shrinks have a reputation as crazy unbalanced people who can read people's minds. Even the hit comedy *The Santa Clause* made us out to be bimbos.

To some degree, we've gotten just what we deserve. We've allowed ourselves to become, in the public mind at least, mere pill-pushers and to have our uncommon sense dismissed as having zero significance when, in fact, it applies to every moment of every person's life. It is our failure to educate our patients and the general public about the deeper principles of human functioning that have left us so isolated from our communities.

Most patients come to psychiatrists because they recognize that, to some degree, their perceptions contain some distortions. These are usually defensive. For example, a 40-year-old woman may begin her first session with a psychiatrist complaining of a "biological depression" and demanding Prozac. By the end of the hour, however, she may acknowledge that her husband's 10-year refusal to have sex may have as much to do with her unhappy mood.

In my practice, I've engaged in a kind of educational psychotherapy, explaining simply to patients what they are doing and why they are doing it. The result has been not only remarkably effective but catalytic in speeding up the process of psychotherapy The same approach can help the general pub-

> **W**e all play to a hidden audience—Mom and Dad—inside our heads. Especially to Mom, whose nurturing is vital to our self-esteem—though it's not politically correct to say so.

lic delve beneath social images and better understand the deeper struggles of the people around them, and of themselves as well.

Ideas and principles can be introduced directly without the jargon psychiatrists normally hide behind in professional discussions. Doing this in a compassionate and empathic way could lead to a broadening of the vocabulary of the general public and bring about a wider acceptance of certain basic psychological truths.

The core of what we do as psychotherapists is strip away people's protective strategies. If you understand these defensive strategies and the core issues people tend to defend themselves against, you can see through people and, to a lesser extent, yourself.

Here, then, are some general principles to help you think like a shrink. Master them and you will—in some cases dramatically—increase your understanding of the world around you. You *can* see through people. *You* can read their minds.

1.

If you want to know how emotionally healthy someone is, look only at their intimate relationships.

Good-looking, athletic, charismatic, confident, rich, or intelligent people are not always emotionally healthy. For example, chronologically they may be adults, but emotionally, they may be two-year-olds. You will not really be able to make any kind of accurate, in-depth assessment of people until you learn to distinguish their superficial physical qualities from meaningful emotional ones. There are at least three key things you want to know:

• Most importantly how long-lived and committed are their current intimate relationships?

• Secondly, how much negative conflict do they experience in their work environments and how long have they held their current jobs?

• Finally what was their childhood experience like in their family of origin? Or, in plain English, did they get along with their family?

2.

How you feel about yourself (your self-esteem) is significantly determined by how nurturing your mother, father, and siblings were to you when you were growing up—especially your mother, though it is not politically correct to say so.

It is not that mothers are to blame for all of a patient's problems. It is simply that stable healthy mothering is a strong buffer against a tremendous amount of pathology.

3.

How you relate to intimate people is always based on how you related to your family when you were growing up.

Basically, we all keep our families with us forever. We keep them in our heads. For the rest of our lives, we will have tendencies to either take on the roles of our childhood selves or those of our parents. Examine carefully your relationships with your family. It will tell you a lot about who you are.

4.

We all play to a hidden audience—Mom and Dad—inside our heads.

You often see people do strange things in their interpersonal interactions. "Where did *that* come from," you often ask. It came from a hidden screenplay that was written in that person's head.

Ostensibly he's reacting to you, but in his head, he's reacting to his mother. In fact, the less he remembers of his childhood, the more he is going to act out with you. This leads nicely to. . . .

5.

People who say they "don't remember" their childhood are usually emotionally troubled.

Physically healthy individuals who can't recall their youth have frequently endured some painful experiences that their minds are blocking out. As a result, they really don't know who they are. They have what we psychiatrists call a diminished sense of identity.

6.

Victims like to be aggressors sometimes, and aggressors are often reconstituted victims.

People actually may become more actively aggressive when they feel forced into a passive position.

7.

Yes, Virginia, there is an "unconscious" or "non-conscious" mind, and it basically determines your life, everything from what job you choose to whom you marry.

All the feelings that you had about yourself, your parents, and family are buried in this "unconscious mind." Also buried here are some very deep fears which will be touched on below

The more aware you are of your unconscious mind, the more freedom you will have.

8.

Sex is critical, no matter what anyone says.

Sex has become passé as an important explanatory factor of human behavior. Nowadays, it is more politically correct to emphasize the role of feelings, thoughts, and emotions than the role of sex. Nonetheless, sexual functioning and sexual history *do* tell you a tremendous amount about what people are really like.

9.

Whenever you have two men, or two women, in a room, you have homosexual tension.

It is a core truth that all people have both heterosexual and homosexual drives. What varies is how you deal with those drives. Just because you have a homosexual impulse or idea has absolutely nothing to do with your sexual orientation. You are defined by your sexual *behavior*, not your sexual *impulses*.

The people in our society who are most against homosexuality are the people who are most uncomfortable with their own homosexual impulses. These impulses are banished from their conscious awareness.

10.

Yes, children do want to be sexual with the opposite sex parent at some point in their young lives, often between the ages of four and six.

Just about everyone is grossed out at the thought of their parents having sex. This is because there is a significant resistance against one's own memory of sexual feelings towards one's parents.

It does not mean, however, that you have to remember your sexual impulses towards a parent to be emotionally healthy. In fact, one of the most common issues an adult has to deal with is the incomplete repression of this core conflict.

11.

There is indeed such a thing as castration anxiety.

In fact, it's the most frightening core fear that people have. It's probably not only evolutionary adaptive, but emotionally important.

12.

Women do not have nearly as much penis envy as men do.

Men are all deep down very preoccupied with their penis. Concerns usually revolve around how big it is, how long, how thick, and how deep it goes.

This is an important issue that will likely never be researched because it makes everyone way too uncomfortable to talk about. There is more mythology on this subject than the Greeks ever wrote.

13.

The Oedipus complex is what keeps psychiatrists in business.

Though lay people tend to think only of the complex's sexual aspects, it really boils down to competition. It's commonly about being bigger, richer, more powerful, a winner or a loser. The feelings surrounding it are universal—and intense.

Getting through the various stages of psychological development—oral, anal, and Oedipal—can be summarized as teaching you three key things:

- To feel stable and secure, to depend on people reasonably
- To feel in control
- To feel able to compete successfully and to feel like a man or a woman.

14.

People are basically the same underneath it all; that is, they all want to satisfy similar deeper needs and quell identical underlying fears.

In general, people all seem to want money, power, and admiration. They want sexual gratification. They want to, as the Bible notes of Judah and Israel, "sit under their vine and fig tree and have none make them afraid." They want to feel secure. They want to feel loved.

Related to this principle: money and intelligence do not protect you. It is only emotional health that keeps you on an even keel; your feelings about yourself and your intimate stable relationships are the only ballast that matters in life.

> **M**en have much more penis envy than do women. They're all very preoccupied with their penis—how big it is, how long, how thick, and how deep it goes.

> **O**ur best defense is a good offense. When people act in an egotistical fashion, their underlying feeling is that they are "dick-less" or impotent.

15.

People often act exactly the opposite of the way they feel, especially when they are unhealthy.

Or: the best defense is a good offense. When people act egotistical, their underlying feeling is that they are "dick-less" or impotent.

16.

More on defenses . . .

Here is human nature in a nutshell. My favorite line from the movie *The Big Chill* is voiced by the character played by Jeff Goldblum. "Where would you be, where would any of us be, without a good rationalization? Try to live without a rationalization; I bet you couldn't do it."

We distort reality both outside and in our minds in order to survive. Distortions of our inner world are common. *Regression*, one of the most intriguing defenses, can be particularly illuminating to acknowledge; it means acting like a kid to avoid the real world.

"Outside" distortions can get us in very serious trouble.

Denial can be fatal whether it involves alcohol abuse or a herd of charging elephants.

Devaluing, or, in simple terms, throwing the baby out with the bath water, comes in handy when we want to insult somebody. But it can be detrimental—for example, causing us to miss a lecturer's important points because we consider the teacher to be a "total jerk."

Idealizing, or putting people on a pedestal, can be hurtful—say when you realize your ex-Navy Seal stockbroker has been churning your brokerage account.

Projecting feelings onto others is a common defensive distortion. Guilt is a painful feeling, so sometimes we may see other people as angry at us rather than feel guilty ourselves. "I know that you are angry that I forgot your birthday" you say. "Don't deny it."

Finally *splitting* our view of the world into good guys and bad guys is a distortion, even if it makes for a great western.

17.

To be successful in the highly competitive American business marketplace requires a personality ethos that will destroy your intimate relationships.

At this point, you are probably experiencing some confusion. After all, I've been saying that it is unhealthy to be striving continuously to compensate for feelings of inferiority or impotency Yet most people know that it is in fact the strivers who achieve enormous power and success in the world around them.

In order to be emotionally healthy, however, it is necessary for these "winners" to leave their work personalities at the door of their homes and become their natural selves once they cross the threshold. It is absolutely essential that the driven, rushed, acquisitive capitalist ethos not enter into the realm of intimate relationships.

CEOs of corporations and doctors are particularly at risk for this type of contamination of their family life. People who have the best of both worlds—career and relationships—are those who realize that success in the workplace does not make up for lack of success at home.

18.

How well people deal with death is usually identical to how well they have dealt with life.

19.

How people relate to you in everyday life can tell you a lot about their deeper issues, even in a very short time.

You can tell a tremendous amount about somebody's emotional stability and character by the way they say goodbye to you. People who cling or drag out good-byes often have deep-seated issues with separation. Of course, we all have issues with separation; it's a matter of degree. Those of us from loving stable backgrounds carry around a warm fuzzy teddy bear of sorts that helps us cope with saying good-bye and being alone. Without this security blanket of loving memories, being alone or saying good-bye can be hell.

A stranger who tells you his entire life's story on the first interview even if you are a psychiatrist, is also probably emotionally unhealthy because there is no boundary between that person and you—and there should be. After all, you are a stranger to that person.

20.

Listen with your third ear.

One of my mentors at Duke University Medical Center once defined the "third ear" as follows: "While you're listening to what a patient is saying, with your third ear listen to why they are saying it." Psychiatrists listen in a unique way. A family practitioner examines your ears with an otoscope. A psychiatrist examines your feelings with himself as the tool.

When you are interacting with another person, if you notice yourself feeling a certain way the odds are that your companion is somehow intending you to feel that way. You have to be emotionally stable to accurately use yourself as the examining tool.

When you become adept at identifying what you are feeling, the next step is to

> **S**trangers who blurt out their entire life story at a first meeting, even if it's with a psychiatrist, are likely to be troubled. They have no "boundary"—and they should.

determine why. There are usually two reasons. Number one, it may be because you are resonating with what the person is feeling. A second possibility is that you are being subtly provoked to play a complementary emotional role in a scene that has an often hidden script.

The process of using one's own heart as a "scope" is hard work. The fancy term for this process is "counter-transference."

21.

Behind every fear, there is a wish.

Wishes that are often consciously unacceptable can be expressed more easily as "fears." Related to this principle is the maxim: "Beware unsolicited denials." A common example is the seemingly spontaneous statement, "1 don't really care at all about money!" Hold on to your wallet.

BAD Choices

WHY WE MAKE THEM
HOW TO STOP

If cigarettes, gambling, those last 10 pounds, that credit card habit and the one drink too many are standing in between you and your goals, this new formula may finally make the difference. And the good news is, it's all in your hands.

By Mary Ann Chapman, Ph.D.

As the police car pealed out behind Lynn with its lights blinking in her rearview mirror, she remembered with dread that second glass of wine she drank just before leaving the party. Her heart raced as she considered the implications of getting a DWI ticket. She had been preparing to leave the party and knew she had to drive home, so why did she indulge?

Most of the bad choices we make in our lives involve an immediate reward—in Lynn's case, the taste and feel of the extra glass of wine. Like Lynn, we often choose to live now even though we're likely to end up paying the price later. This carpe-diem philosophy becomes even more powerful when the punishment is not a sure thing. In Lynn's case, the probability of her being pulled over by the police was not very high. If she had expected them to stop her, she might have reached for a ginger ale.

Our day-to-day bad choices have alarming results. For example, one-third of Americans are overweight, costing the U.S. government $100 billion each year in treatment of related illnesses.

We're also steeped in debt:

The Consumer Federation of America calculates that 60 million households carry an average credit card balance of $7,000, for a total national credit card debt topping $455 billion. Our failure to make sacrifices now for rewards later is particularly devastating when it comes to following prescribed medical regimens. Studies have found that only half of us take antidepressants, antihypertensives, asthma medications and tuberculosis drugs as prescribed. Such lack of compliance is the major cause of hospital admissions in people who have previously had heart failure, and it's entirely preventable.

Our desire to take the path of least resistance is so strong that we continue our sometimes destructive behavior even though we know, as in the cases of smoking and overeating, it literally may kill us. But we don't need to be slaves to instant gratification. Consider the ways we already suffer in the present for reward in the future: We get tetanus shots to protect against lockjaw and use condoms to reduce the risk of sexually transmitted diseases; we have money taken out of our paychecks for retirement, and parents routinely make sacrifices for their children's future. The key to breaking a bad habit and adopting a good one is making changes in our daily life that will minimize the influence of the now and remind us of the later. It sounds difficult, but new tricks make it possible.

A look at the animal kingdom reveals clues as to how this is done. Working in a laboratory with pigeons, Howard Rachlin, Ph.D., of the State University of New York at Stony Brook, found that when birds were given a simple choice between immediate and delayed reward, they chose the immediate reward 95% of the time. This was true even though the delayed reward (food) was twice the size of the immediate one.

Then researchers made the task more complicated, giving birds the chance to choose between 1) the same immediate and delayed options as in the first part of the study, or 2) a no-option condition in which they were only allowed access to the delayed reward. This situation is analogous to the choice between going to a gym where you have the option of relaxing in the sauna or hopping on the stationary bicycle, and going to a gym that has only exercise equipment—giving you no option but to exercise once you get there.

As the researchers increased the amount of time birds had to wait after selecting between the two alternatives, the birds in-

PT's Good-Choice Guide

	BEHAVIOR	NOW	LATER	STRATEGIES FOR CHANGE
BAD CHOICES	Overeating	Food tastes good, is comforting	You get fat, unhealthy; suffer lowered self-esteem	Only snack when sitting at the table—never in front of the TV; keep inspiring picture or story on the fridge or cupboard; calculate how long it would take to burn off the calories of what you're about to eat
	Eating fast food	Quick; easy; tastes good	Too much fat; not nutritious; not healthful	Identify health-food places close to home; locate low fat/calorie menu items
	Anger	Temporary relief	Problems interacting with others	Apologize immediately for getting angry; reward yourself for situations in which you avoid anger
	Constant complaining	Sympathy from others	Viewed negatively; social repercussions	Tell friends to change topics when you start complaining
	Smoking	Pleasure from cigarette	Lung cancer; possible death	Confine smoking to one designated area (preferably one you don't like); keep a day calendar in your cigarette cupboard and rip off a day for every cigarette pack you open to symbolize days off your life
	Gambling	Occasionally win money	Lose money over the long term	Donate all winnings (preferably to a cause you dislike); keep track of losses, place them prominently; consider ways you could have spent the money you lost
GOOD CHOICES	Healthful eating	Extra effort; taste not as good	Good health; reduced chance of many diseases	Reduce effort by buying preprepared healthful foods or by preparing them over the weekend; dine with a friend who shares an interest in healthy eating
	Saving money	Less money to spend now	Avoid interest charges on loans or credit cards; can afford larger or more meaningful items	Have automatic deductions taken out of your paycheck
	Using condoms	Some say less pleasurable sex	Prevent AIDS, sexually transmitted diseases, pregnancy	Always keep condoms handy; use other techniques to enhance sex; donate money to AIDS causes
	Going to the dentist	Painful, scary	Avoid further pain of root canals, existing cavities	Find a friendly dentist; schedule appointments at the same time as a friend; give yourself a small reward each time you go
	Exercising	Extra effort; give up relaxation time	Improved circulation; reduced risk of disease; weight loss; increased energy; greater self-esteem	Move near a gym; buy weights or a bike; after a workout, write down how good you feel and read it next time you are in a slump
	Overcoming shyness	Disruption of "safe" pattern of behavior	More friends and social activities	Start by prolonging a conversation someone starts with you and make it a habit

creasingly chose the second option, to have only the delayed reward available. In this way, the researchers effectively altered the birds' environment to minimize the value of the immediate choice.

BREAKING A BAD HABIT

We can apply the same logic to help us break our bad habits: We need to 1) minimize or avoid the immediate reward, and 2) make the long-term negative consequence seem more immediate.

My friend John, for example, relies too much on his credit card. When the lunch bill comes, he charges the total tab and pockets his colleagues' cash. You may not know John, but I bet you know that he doesn't rush to the bank and deposit that money.

John needs to avoid the immediate positive effect of using his credit card. The most logical step would be to leave it at home—except that he might need it for travel or emergencies. John's best bet would be to do a little preplanning: He could stop by the bank after work to make sure he had enough money for the next day's lunch. Or he could locate an ATM near the restaurant to make it more convenient—and therefore more likely—for him to withdraw cash.

As a reminder of that big scary negative at the end of the month, John could paste his latest credit card bill near his computer, on the refrigerator or someplace he will see it every day. He might also tape the amount he owes to the face of the credit card. These nearly effortless gestures will make it hard for John to readily ignore his problem and help him bridge the gap between now and later.

STARTING A GOOD HABIT

You might be eager to start eating healthy meals, getting regular exercise or making new friends. Most likely, the going will be tough at first, but the potential long-term benefits are well worth it. Once again, the idea is to minimize the immediate—a nega-

tive this time—and bridge the distance to the future, the good stuff.

For the past couple of months, I have been trying to get myself to drink a small glass of soy milk every day. Each week I buy a carton of soy milk and after two weeks, I dump it down the drain. I have convinced myself that I need to drink soy milk for the protein and the long-term health benefits. But somehow, the immediate negative of drinking the milk (and even thinking about drinking the milk!) has been seemingly impossible to overcome.

What would help lessen the yuck of soy milk? I tried drinking it in my favorite special cup. That helped a little, but not enough. My new strategy is to mix half a cup of soy milk with regular milk. Every day I drink the soy milk I put an X on my calendar for that day, which makes me feel accomplished and helps me associate drinking the soy milk with a positive consequence. And to make the long-term benefits more immediately apparent, I tore out magazine articles that tout the health benefits of soy and taped them to my refrigerator.

WHEN OLD HABITS DIE HARD

It's never very easy to change, but for some people, it is exceptionally difficult. Twenty-two-year-old Jimmy is a good example. Jimmy's arms are bruised and scarred from his heroin habit. For him, the immense immediate pleasure of heroin far outweighs the long-term consequences of his habit: tuberculosis, lack of money and the inability to hold down a job.

You might not think you have anything in common with Jimmy—or a compulsive gambler or a kleptomaniac. But researchers are beginning to recognize that all of these behavioral patterns involve, to varying extents, maximizing immediate consequences despite huge negative long-term ones.

To find out if some people are more prone to favor the here and now than others, the University of Missouri's Alan Strathman, Ph.D., and his colleagues con-

ducted surveys in Missouri and California. They asked survey participants how much they agreed with statements such as "I consider how things might be in the future and try to influence those things with my day-to-day behavior," and "Convenience is a big factor in the decisions I make or the actions I take." Strathman found that individuals did indeed have varying degrees of what he calls "future orientation"—preference for delayed consequences—and that this orientation remains stable over time. The individual differences were reflected in general health concerns and in environmentally friendly behaviors such as recycling.

The good news is that the behavioral change strategies can work just as well for people who tend to favor the here and now. They don't require special genes or exceptional chemistry. They are very simple and that's their beauty. Time and again, they have been used successfully to help people overcome problems from obesity to sulking to failing grades. These simple strategies are effective because behaviors are mostly learned and, therefore, can be unlearned. They can take us off autopilot and introduce ideas (namely, long-term consequences) that we normally wouldn't consider. Even if we have focused on the short-term all our lives, these strategies can help us maximize our chances of success.

Mary Ann Chapman earned her Ph.D. in experimental psychology from Washington State University in 1994. She is a scientific communications writer in southern California.

FURTHER READING

Self-Help Without the Hype, R. Epstein (Performance Management Publications, 1997)

Self-Directed Behavior: Self-Modification for Personal Adjustment (seventh edition), D.L. Watson and R.G. Tharp (Books/Cole, 1996)

Managing Everyday Problems, T.A. Brigham (Guilford Press, 1988)

Chronic Anxiety:

How to Stop Living on the Edge

Feeling nervous is a normal response to stressful situations. Sweaty palms, a racing heart, and butterflies in the stomach are felt by everyone from seasoned performers stepping into the spotlight to the person addressing a group for the first time. These sensations are caused by a rush of stress hormones, such as norepinephrine and cortisol, which prepare the body and mind to rise to a challenge.

Chronic anxiety, however, is very different from the healthy feelings of nervousness that make a speaker effective or enable a sprinter to win a race. Indeed, anxiety disorders are, by definition, psychiatric illnesses that are not useful for normal functioning. Instead of calling a person to action, chronic anxiety can damage relationships, reduce productivity, and make someone terrified of everyday experiences.

Anxiety illnesses are among the most common disorders, affecting more than 23 million Americans (about 1 in 9). Fortunately, sufferers often get substantial relief from various forms of talk therapy, medication, or both. But the majority of people with anxiety disorders do not seek help because they may not recognize their symptoms as a psychiatric problem or may fear being stigmatized with a "mental illness."

There is strong evidence that anxiety conditions run in families. And recent findings suggest that a genetic predisposition to anxiety, when triggered by certain life experiences (such as early losses or trauma), may alter a person's brain chemistry, causing an illness to surface.

> **Although anxiety disorders are common, many people do not seek help because they don't realize that treatments are available.**

The most common of these conditions and, surprisingly, the least understood is *generalized anxiety disorder* (GAD). Believed to affect about 10 million Americans, it is characterized by unrelenting, exaggerated worry and tension; it can keep people from socializing, traveling, getting a better job, or pursuing a sport or avocation. GAD affects people of both sexes and all ages but is diagnosed more often in adult women, possibly because of hormonal differences or because women seek mental health treatment more frequently than men, whose rate of anxiety may be underestimated. Some mental health experts believe that men manifest anxiety (as well as depression) differently from women: they drink more alcohol, smoke more, and are more prone to aggressive behavior.

The psychiatric diagnosis of GAD is chronic, exaggerated worry and tension that has lasted for more than 6 months, although most people with the disorder can trace it back to childhood or adolescence. They may worry excessively about health, money, family, or work, even when there is no sign of difficulty. And they have trouble relaxing and often have insomnia. Many live from day to day with distressing physical symptoms such as trembling, sweating, muscle tension, or headaches, which tend to worsen when they face even mild stress.

Excerpted from *The Harvard Health Letter,* July 1998, pp. 1-3. © 1998 by the President and Fellows of Harvard College. Reprinted by permission.

GAD frequently coexists with depression, and certain antidepressants seem to work quite well for people with GAD. Many of these medications regulate levels of brain chemicals such as serotonin and norepinephrine, but scientists do not have a complete understanding of the biology of anxiety or depression or why they often go hand in hand.

A March 1998 symposium in Boston, cosponsored by the National Institute of Mental Health and the Anxiety Disorders Association of America, was among the first dedicated to the interplay between fear and anxiety and the workings of the brain. Some scientists are focusing on a brain structure called the *amygdala,* which regulates fear, memory, and emotion. When a person is exposed to a fearful event, the amygdala coordinates the brain's physical responses, such as increased heart rate and blood pressure. And preliminary research suggests that the release of the stress hormones norepinephrine and cortisol may act in a way that greatly increases memory of the fearful or traumatic event, allowing it to remain vivid for years. (For more on stress hormones, see *Harvard Health Letter,* April 1998.)

Because basic research has uncovered chemical and hormonal differences in how males and females respond to fear and anxiety, investigators are studying the role that estrogen and cyclical hormonal changes may play in women with anxiety disorders.

Late-life anxiety

Although studies indicate that the prevalence of major depression and certain anxiety disorders declines in the over-65 population, depression affects about 1 in 7 in this group. But there are no hard data on how many of them are troubled by chronic anxiety. Researchers, however, believe that GAD is the most common form of anxiety in older people. They estimate that up to two thirds of older individuals with depression have GAD, and the same amount with GAD have depression. (For more on late-life depression, see *Harvard Health Letter,* March 1995.)

Doctors may have difficulty diagnosing anxiety disorders in older people because some of the characteristics of anxiety, such as blood pressure elevations or a racing heart, may be attributable to a physical illness. Indeed, anxiety may be overlooked when a potentially serious medical condition captures a doctor's attention.

Getting well

There are two main roads to treating GAD: talk therapy and medication. Some mental health professionals place great value on *cognitive-behavioral therapy* (CBT); instead of focusing on deep-seated childhood feelings, the therapist helps the patient look realistically at the exaggerated or pessimistic beliefs that flood the mind. Eventually, the

Finding Help

The following national organizations can provide referrals for mental health professionals and/or support groups in your area.

American Psychiatric Association
Phone: (202) 682-6220
Internet: http://www.psych.org

American Psychological Association
Phone: (202) 336-5800
Internet: http://www.helping.apa.org

Anxiety Disorders Association of America
Phone: (301) 231-9350
Internet: http://www.adaa.org

National Alliance for the Mentally Ill
Phone: (800) 950-NAMI
Internet: http://www.nami.org

person learns to think rationally about his or her fears, and anxiety is reduced.

However, other mental health experts say that although CBT may have an excellent short-term effect, it is not necessarily a lifetime one. Many psychotherapists believe that the only way to help someone reduce chronic anxiety for good is to work with the patient over time so he or she can talk about and process traumatic or fearful events, which may have occurred years earlier. Indeed, many people experience a substantial reduction in anxious thoughts when they explore childhood fears or secrets with a supportive and knowledgeable psychiatrist, psychologist, or social worker.

Useful medications

Some types of drugs, such as *benzodiazepines* (mild tranquilizers) are taken every day or on an as-needed basis when stress or worry becomes overwhelming; others, such as antidepressants, must be taken daily, sometimes indefinitely. It is best to combine some form of talk therapy with medication, but many people do not feel the need or they lack the financial resources to do both.

Historically, anxiety has been treated with benzodiazepines. These include diazepam (Valium), alprazolam (Xanax), and lorazepam (Ativan). Although many people who consider taking one of these medications or who are currently on one worry that they are addictive, this is usually not the case, particularly if the person has never abused drugs or alcohol in the past. Some individuals may develop a physical dependence on them, which means that they should reduce their dose slowly when going off the medication. Doctors rarely prescribe benzodiazepines for people with addictive tendencies.

Although the medications are generally well tolerated by people who do not abuse them, they can be a problem in older people, because early side effects include drowsiness, impaired reflexes and motor skills, and confusion. Older individuals are more prone to falls and car accidents during the first few weeks of taking a benzodiazepine.

Antidepressants are being used more frequently to treat GAD. They do not generally have the side effects of benzodiazepines and are considered safer and more effective for long-term use. Numerous investigations have shown that the *selective-serotonin reuptake inhibitors* (SSRIs), sold as Prozac, Paxil, and Zoloft, newer antidepressants such as nefazodone (Serzone), and the older tricyclic antidepressants (imipramine, for example) can

significantly reduce symptoms of GAD. A drug called buspirone (BuSpar), which is not an antidepressant but is designed specifically for anxiety, is useful for some people.

The first step in getting help is to see your primary care physician, who can refer you to a mental health professional if you want to explore talk therapy. Another way to find a good counselor is to ask friends or family who have worked with one they liked.

Either your primary care doctor or a psychiatrist can prescribe medication. However, primary care physicians generally do not have time to engage in lengthy or ongoing discussions, so you may prefer to see a mental health professional. Whether you've lived with chronic anxiety for 6 months or 60 years, GAD can be treated. You can get the help you need by asking for it.

The Science of
Women & Sex

INSPIRED BY VIAGRA, researchers are rushing to unlock the mysteries of female desire. The answers are turning out to be much more complex than anyone expected.

BY JOHN LELAND

FOR ELLEN, A 45-YEAR-OLD COLLEGE professor in rural Maryland, the music of the bedroom has never been as harmonious as it is in magazines. She cannot reach orgasm with her husband, and has only tepid interest in sex. "Frankly, it's the one fly in the ointment of our marriage," she says. Sexual couples counseling didn't help; her gynecologist, "immanently unhelpful," told her nothing could be done.

How do we define sexual dysfunction in women?

It's both a mind and body thing, and many women have a problem at some point in their lives. Doctors say sexual woes rise to the level of dysfunction only when they are persistent and—most important—cause personal distress.

Then she heard about a Baltimore urologist named Toby Chai who was conducting a small trial of Viagra among women with sexual complaints. She'd read of the miraculous results in men and thought this might finally dispel the "iceberg" intruding on her marital life. "It's not something we talk about every day, but it's always there." Returning home with six pills—three placebo, three Viagra—Ellen became a pilgrim in the increasingly frenzied search to unlock the mysteries of female desire.

Women's sexuality, Sigmund Freud opined, is the "dark continent" of the soul: an uncharted netherworld receding behind folds of flesh and muscle. Among the Big Ideas of the last century, few were as asinine as Freud's on sex and women, most notably his theory of penis envy. Yet in the decades that followed, science has continued to put forward as much ignorance as bliss. Until the late '20s, doctors manually stimulated women as a treatment for "pelvic disorder"; the vibrator, originally coal-fired, caught on as a way to shorten office visits.

In the 1950s and '60s, Alfred Kinsey and the team of Masters and Johnson began exploring female sexuality through the prism of its male counterpart. "We are still in a culture which has defined sexuality, sexual pleasure and [sexual goals] in male terms," says Dr. John Bancroft, current head of the Kinsey Institute. "Then we apply the same paradigm to women. That is a mistake." The male paradigm is simple: erection and release. Women's satisfactions and drives are more complex, organized as much around the health of the relationship as the majesty that is orgasm.

How does loss of testosterone affect women?

Women produce testosterone in their adrenal glands and ovaries. Around the time of menopause, the amount produced declines, which may lead to a loss of desire, as well as fatigue and thinning hair.

Add science to this simple insight and it becomes a program for revolution. Sparked by the stunning success of Viagra, and the prospect that it might be duplicated with women, a new era of sexual experimentation is now taking shape—this time not in the bedroom, but in the laboratory. "It's such a Wild West frontier of new discovery," says Dr. Irwin Goldstein, the media-friendly Boston urologist and pioneer in research on men and women. (Like many doctors interviewed for this article, Goldstein is a paid consultant and gets research money from one or more of the drug companies, but does not own stock in any.)

As many as four in 10 American women experience some form of sexual dissatisfaction, a figure likely to grow as the 41 million women of the baby boom, for whom unencumbered sex seemed a birthright, make the passage through menopause. The shadow cast by dysfunction can spread far beyond the bedroom, darkening a woman's entire sense of well-being. "It was probably in some ways more devastating than breast cancer," says a 55-year-old college professor who lost her ability to become aroused after hysterectomy. "This huge piece of who I am had just gone." Drug companies, research clinicians and traditional therapists are all leaping into the fray. Their work, still in its embryonic stages, is already starting to yield a radical new understanding of anatomy, dysfunction—and even the evolutionary meaning of orgasm.

A dozen drug manufacturers, including Pfizer, the maker of Viagra, are rushing headlong into research and development, mostly on drugs originally intended to treat impotence in men. Both male and female genitals have smooth muscle tissue that engorges with blood during arousal. Researchers hope Viagra will relax this tissue in the clitoris, as it does in the penis, allowing the vessels in the organ to swell with blood. The early prognosis, though, is less than thrilling. In the most comprehensive female trial of Viagra to date, released this week, the drug proved no more effective than a placebo. Nonetheless, Cheryl Bourque, an analyst at Decision Resources, projects that by 2008, the market for treatments for women, including testosterone and estrogen (sidebar), could hit $1.7 billion. Drugs conceived specifically for women, still perhaps decades away, could make this figure seem minuscule.

The Risks of **Estrogen**

AFTER MENOPAUSE, changes in women's bodies can make sex painful. But new studies raise doubts about hormone therapy. BY SHARON BEGLEY

HOW MUCH RISK WILL A WOMAN ACCEPT IN RETURN FOR GOOD SEX? Many women approaching or past menopause view estrogen-replacement therapy (ERT) as a foundation of youth in a pill. By pumping up blood concentrations of estrogen to near-youthful levels, ERT vanquishes the hot flashes and night sweats responsible for libido-killing insomnia and irritability. It also prevents the thinning and drying out of vaginal tissue that comes with plummeting estrogen levels, notes Dr. Margery Gass, an Ob-Gyn at the University of Cincinnati College of Medicine. After menopause, thinner, less flexible vaginal tissue can make sex so painful that the body recoils even when the heart is willing. Virtually any form of estrogen—the pill Premarin, a patch, vaginal creams or vaginal rings kept in place for three months— "improves vaginal tissues," says Gass.

Because estrogen alone stimulates the uterine lining and increases the risk of endometrial cancer, women with an intact uterus are advised to pair estrogen with progestin—which blocks this effect—in a regimen called hormone-replacement therapy (HRT). Estrogen alone has long had a dark side: it is associated with an increased risk of breast cancer. Now, in one of those you-can't-win cases, it appears that progestin may increase the risk of breast cancer even more than estrogen alone, says Dr. Ronald Ross of the University of Southern California. Scientists now think that estrogen-progestin increases the risk of breast cancer 53 percent compared with not taking hormones; estrogen by itself raises the risk 34 percent. The longer a woman takes HRT, the greater her risk.

The standard retort to concerns about breast cancer has been, "Sure, but estrogen reduces the risk of osteoporosis." That remains pretty much unquestioned: estrogen decreases the amount of bone that is resorbed in the constant process of skeletal building and demolishing. But estrogen's killer app is supposed to be preventing heart disease. It lowers bad LDL cholesterol and raises good HDL. (Creams and rings are not effective because their estrogen is absorbed directly by the bloodstream, bypassing the liver, where cholesterol levels are adjusted.) That heart benefit was supposed to swamp the risk of breast cancer, especially since heart disease kills nine times as many American women every year as does breast cancer. But results of the newest, best-designed studies are dismaying. They find that HRT provides no heart benefits to women with existing cardiovascular disease; it may actually increase their risk of heart attacks. And it may not protect healthy women from developing heart disease: in April, researchers at the Women's Health Initiative, run by the National Institutes of Health, warned that HRT seems to raise the risk of heart attacks and stroke in healthy women, at least initially. "Women with heart disease should not take estrogen with the expectation that it will help their heart," says Dr. David Herrington of Wake Forest University. Not even great sex can fix a broken Heart.

*Why do we know
so little about
sex and older women?*

In the past, women (and men) simply accepted dysfunction as a natural part of aging. After the spectacular success of Viagra, researchers began focusing on ways to help women remain sexually active.

Jennifer Berman is one of the few female urologists working on the cutting edge of this research. At the Women's Sexual Health Clinic in

Boston not long ago, Berman received a 54-year-old woman who, since menopause and a mastectomy, suffered vaginal dryness and pain

It's Really Not Just a Headache, Honey

As researchers learn more about the causes and types of female sexual dysfunction, they're uncovering new ways to help. There's no female equivalent to Viagra yet, but women have new reason to hope.

DYSFUNCTION TYPES

■ **Desire:** A lack of libido can have both physical and psychological roots. Stress and depression (as well as some medications) are major causes.

■ **Arousal:** Critical to sexual response, it may be expressed as a lack of subjective excitement or genital lubrication

■ **Lack of orgasm:** It's a more common problem than previously believed: a substantial number of women have never experienced the sensation

■ **Pain:** This condition can occur at any age, but it is especially troublesome after menopause, when natural lubricants dry up

DYSFUNCTION CAUSES

■ **Psychological:** These range from depression and past sexual abuse to unsatisfactory relationships and a bad body image

■ **Physical:** Factors include vaginal atrophy at menopause, nerve damage, diabetes, heart disease, smoking and obesity

TREATMENT OPTIONS

Researchers are looking at a wide range of medications and devices, most still in the experimental stage. For many women, the most effective treatment may combine drugs, hormones and counseling.

Viagra: The pill was no better than a placebo in women with a wide range of symptoms. New trials will target post-menopausal women.

Prostaglandin E-1 cream: Still in early clinical trials, this 'vasodilator' dilates

WHO SUFFERS

Problems* with physical intimacy affect more women than men and vary by age, education, race and marital status. The reasons are still unclear.

Sexual dysfunction

Women	Low sexual desire	22%
	Arousal problems	14
	Pain during intercourse	7
Men	Premature ejaculation	21%
	Erectile dysfunction	5
	Low sexual desire	5

*PROBLEMS THAT HAVE OCCURRED OVER THE LAST 12 MONTHS.

Health factors
These may contribute to sexual dysfunction

■ Poor health
■ Emotional problems or stress
■ Urinary-tract symptoms
■ A history of STDs

Low interest in sex

By age	Women	Men
18–29	32%	14%
30–39	32	13
40–49	30	15
50–59	27	17

By race	Women
White	29%
Black	44
Hispanic	30
Other	42

Painful intercourse

By age	Women
18–29	21%
30–39	15
40–49	13
50–59	8

By marital status	
Married	14%
Never married	17
Divorced, widowed, separated	16

Absence of orgasm

By age	Women	Men
18–29	26%	7%
30–39	28	7
40–49	22	9
50–59	23	9

High-school education

Less than	34%
Graduate	29

College

Some	24
Graduate	18

arteries, increasing blood flow to genital tissues.

Alprostadil cream: Another version of prostaglandin E-1 and still under study, this compound is being tested for improved arousal and lubrication

Dr. K's Dream Cream: Sold 'off label' by Dr. Jed Kaminetsky, this combination of vasodilators may increase genital engorgement and arousal

Clitoral device: Approved earlier this month by the FDA, this prescription device creates a 'genital suction' over the clitoris in order to increase blood flow and sensation

Testosterone patch: Women whose hormone levels have declined apply the patch (still in clinical trials) to their abdomen to increase libido

Natural aids are popular, but not subject to FDA oversight

For arousal L-arginine an amino acid
        Yohimbe   made from the bark of a tree

For libido DHEA   helps fuel testosterone production

SOURCES: THE JOURNAL OF THE AMERICAN MEDICAL ASSOCIATION, NEWSWEEK REPORTING.

during intercourse, and lost all interest in sex. "I feel like I'm less than a woman," the woman says. Berman wanted to test the flow of blood to the woman's genitals. Supplied with a pair of 3-D glasses and a vibrator, the woman watched an erotic videotape while an ultrasound probe resembling an electronic tampon

monitored her blood flow—an attempt to tease out the physical component of dysfunction. Berman and her sister, Laura, a sex therapist, have become the telegenic faces of female sexual dysfunction, a two-headed Oprah for the erotically aggrieved. Together they tag-team the mind and body, a synergy many

doctors believe will provide the best relief for female sexual dysfunction. For women, more so than for men, simply "medicalizing" the problem is too reductive. While many Viagra-enhanced men are happy just to get erections, fixing women's blood flow will cure little if libido-killing stresses still assail the relationship, the home life and the woman's self-esteem. Women presenting identical complaints might require a drug, a weekend retreat or a sex toy, or some combination of the three.

Even so, medical advances promise important keys. Anatomists are finding that we haven't even mapped the basic body parts. In a conference room at Boston University, Trudy Van Houten stops an unsuspecting medical student. *The clitoris,* she challenges the young woman, a fourth-year med student: *how big is it?* The woman looks momentarily stunned. *Would you say it's one centimeter or 10?* By the fourth year of medical school, students should know the gross details of the body, but this seemingly simple question has the woman in a pickle. "It can't be as big as 10," she tries. Oh, but it is, it is. "It's here, it's here, it's here, it's here," says Van Houten, tracing a finger across an anatomical drawing. "Wow," says the student. "Thank you."

The new research borders on the macabre: Goldstein talks of "harvesting" clitorises, labia and vaginas from cadavers, surgery patients or animals to study the microprocesses of sexual response; Cindy Meston, a psychologist at the University of Texas at Austin, has reported that stimulating the same branch of the nervous system that shuts down sexual arousal in men seems to facilitate it in women. Researchers like Van Houten are only now starting to map the myriad nerves that spider through the pelvic region, hoping ultimately to spare hysterectomy patients from nerve damage, as surgeons do when they remove men's prostate glands.

As they learn about the body, scientists are also rethinking the types and roots of dysfunction. They have identified four sexual woes: a low sex drive or aversion to sex, difficulty becoming aroused, inability to reach orgasm and pain during sex. Healthy women might experience any of these on occasion. They rise to the level of dysfunction only when they are persistent or recurring, and—most important—when they cause personal distress. Root causes can be physical (diabetes, obesity or other strain on the circulatory system), emotional (stress, fatigue or depression) or an interplay between the two. A cruel irony is that many drugs used to fight de-

Do female orgasms serve any biological function?

Evolutionary biologists haven't yet figured that one out, and it's a controversial subject. One possible theory: orgasms in women have no function and are just a development vestige, like male nipples.

pression also dampen libido. For women now in middle age, the biggest threat to their sexual satisfaction may be social: after the age of 60 half of all women are without a partner.

Real help for many women is still far off. In his frenzied office at the New York Center for Human Sexuality, Dr. Ridwan Shabsigh proudly shows off a color photograph of dense, tangled tubes. His lab team, he explains, injected a hardening resin into the bloodstream of a live rat, then dissolved the rodent in acid, leaving only the solidified resin where the blood vessels used to be.

The image, created with an electron microscope, describes the vascular system of a rat vagina. "This is big," he said—one giant leap for science, one bad date for Queen Rat.

Shabsigh's team of head and body doctors uses an updated theoretical framework for female sexual response. In the 1970s, the influential psychiatrist Helen Singer Kaplan sorted women's responses into three successive phases—desire to arousal to orgasm—a one-way arrow pointing straight to nirvana. The arrow model, says Shabsigh, ignores the more reciprocal play between the various states of pleasure. "We think of female sexual function not as a line but as a circle" joining the four points of desire, arousal, orgasm and satisfaction. Turbulence or interruption at any point affects the weather at all the others. In other words, today's frustration about orgasm dampens next week's libido.

Though libido is the most common complaint, most of the drugs currently being tested target arousal. Many doctors think this will limit the pills' future impact. But for women like Ellen, the Maryland professor, this is splitting sexual hairs. The quiet disconnect of her marital bed, she says, caused emotional stress for both her and her husband. She was hoping Viagra would jumpstart her libido, but she wanted an orgasm, as well. "It'd be nice to have your cake and eat it, too," she says. Unfortunately, the pills did not work for her. "I haven't given up," she says.

Many of the drugs in development—VasoFem, Alista, FemProx—act a lot like Viagra, and this week's discouraging trial results are a potential wet blanket for the industry. "We're definitely continuing our research," says Heather Van Ness, a Pfizer rep. "We feel this [area] is significantly more complicated than

For women, the relationship and the context of sexuality can be even more critical to satisfaction than the majesty that is orgasm.

Freud thought dysfunction was all in a woman's head. Now, high-tech tests reveal the role of physical causes.

erectile dysfunction." One researcher in the Viagra trials, Dr. Rosemary Basson, says the study may have incorporated too broad a range of ages and complaints to be definitive. Viagra may work for some conditions but not others. A more targeted study, limited to post-menopausal women, is now gearing up in the United States. Also being tested is a "dopamine agonist" called apomorphine, recently recommended for approval for use in men, which sends electrical impulses from the hypothalamus to the genitals to trigger increased blood flow.

Drugs, however, aren't the only potential stairway to heaven. Earlier this month the FDA approved an apparatus called EROS-CTD, a clitoral suction device the size of a computer mouse that draws blood to the organ. The device is available by prescription only and costs about $360. The best part of participating in the EROS trials, says a 35-year-old at-home mother in St. Paul, Minn., "is that we get one for free."

Hormone therapy is also promising, but can be a wild ride. Testosterone, for reasons no one quite understands, is involved in the sex drive of both men and women. In their 30s and 40s, most women experience a 15 percent drop in testosterone levels. Removal of the ovaries, often a part of hysterectomy, reduces production to near zero. At the University of California, San Francisco, Dr. Louann Brizendine has been experimenting with testosterone replacement therapy, in both oral form and patches. This is the

tricky end of the erotic medicine cabinet: side effects include increased risk of heart disease and liver damage, and long-term consequences are unknown. Also, the surges of biochemical desire can leave patients reeling. One woman unwittingly doubled her dosage and had to excuse herself every few hours just to seek relief.

As biologists expand their grasp of amatory nitty and gritty, the thorniest riddle may be more global: why, from an evolutionary point of view, do women have orgasms? Unlike the male O, women's climax does not appear to be necessary for reproduction. The traditional answer, phrased by anthropologist Don Symons in 1979, is that female orgasm is a relic of Darwinian sloppiness, like male nipples: evolution had no good motive specifically to cut one gender out of the fun. If you think this argument has passed unchallenged, you haven't breathed the air on campus lately. Proclaiming orgasmic empowerment, anthropologists speculated that the sweet paroxysm kept women supine after sex, facilitating insemination—a dubious argument, since nature did not design most women to climax reliably through intercourse, especially in the missionary position. The evolutionary biologist Sarah Blaffer Hrdy proposed that this skittishness was itself an evolutionary adaptation: our unsatisfied ancestresses would seek remedy from multiple partners—in turn tapping each for protection and resources, and counting on confusion about paternity to

multiply the generosity. Or maybe orgasm allows women to influence which mate will father their children. British biologists Robin Baker and Mark Bellis, who went so far as to attach micro video cameras to the ends of men's penises, found that women retained more of their partners' ejaculate if they reached orgasm as well. In an only-in-America study at the University of New Mexico, researchers Randy Thornhill and Steven Gangestad found that, other things being equal, women were more likely to climax when their partners' bodies were symmetrical, a marker of desirable genes. "It's all consistent with female choice," says Thornhill. Since competing explanations arise, you are free to accept this as gospel or just another reminder that the mysteries of sex won't be solved overnight.

The new science of sex, though, is not wholly academic. Revolutions in the lab will likely rearrange the bedroom, perhaps even the surrounding communities, in ways unforeseeable. As Jared Diamond describes in his book "Guns, Germs and Steel," new technologies often create societies' needs for them, rather than the other way around. Invention, in other words, can be the mother of necessity. Right now we are just approaching the cusp of that maternity. The dark continent is growing brighter and more electric with each turn of the circle.

With CLAUDIA KALB *and*
NADINE JOSEPH

MindoverMedicine

Diseases and disorders are hardly ever "all in your head," but often, the power to heal is. Howard Brody, M.D., Ph.D., reveals how we can tap into our "inner pharmacy" to stay healthy and recover more rapidly from illness

By Howard Brody, M.D., Ph.D.

We begin and end with a mystery—a mystery of healing. So it seems appropriate to lead off with a riddle: What do the following people have in common?

Albert consults his physician about a bothersome cold. Because the condition is viral, his doctor knows antibiotics won't help. But Albert—a bit of a hypochondriac—is sure the cold is turning into pneumonia, although it shows no medical signs of doing so, and he pleads for antibiotics. His physician writes him a prescription for what he says is a potent antibiotic. In reality, it is a simple sugar pill—100% medically ineffective. Yet once Albert begins taking the "antibiotic," his cold disappears almost overnight.

Beatrice, who strongly believes in herbal remedies, purchases a new and much-touted organic food supplement at a health food store. After taking it for several weeks, she feels considerably more energized—despite the lack of any recognized scientific evidence that the supplement can physiologically affect the body.

Charles develops cancer and undergoes the standard surgery and chemotherapy. As he believes strongly in the healing powers of the mind, he also begins practicing meditation, thinking positive thoughts and forgiving all the people against whom he harbored grudges. He also stops blaming himself for contracting the disease, realizing it was a bad break but hardly his fault. Not only does he feel better and enjoy life more, he also remains in remission after several years.

Just what is it that Albert, Beatrice and Charles have in common? At first glance, you'd probably say, "Nothing at all." Not me. I'd suggest, by contrast, that it's that mysterious phenomenon of the mind working in tandem with the body to enhance healing: the placebo response. What I mean by that phrase is that when a certain set of circumstances are present, ill persons seem to improve greatly in what at first seems an inexplicable way.

The placebo response occurs when we receive certain types of messages or signals from the environment around us. These messages work in some fashion, at some level, to alter the meaning of our state of health or illness. What does the body do with these messages? The best way to summarize what science has taught us about the placebo response is to visualize an "inner pharmacy," which we all possess.

Our bodies are capable of producing many substances which can heal a wide variety of illnesses, and make us feel generally healthier and more energized. When the body simply secretes these substances on its own, we have what is often termed "spontaneous healing." Some of the time, our bodies seem slow to react, and a message from outside can serve as a wake-up call to our inner pharmacy. The placebo response can thus be seen as the reaction of our inner pharmacies to that wake-up call—the message of new meaning.

One of the most often-repeated stories about the placebo response is a case reported by a colleague to Dr. Bruno Klopfer and published by Klopfer in 1957. As a single incident, it must be interpreted with skepticism; but the facts are so intriguing, it's difficult to discount. Klopfer's colleague was the personal physician of a patient, known as "Mr. Wright," who was suffering from cancer of the lymph system and had developed large tumors throughout his body that could easily be felt by his doctors.

At the time, a group of physicians was studying a new chemical formula called krebiozen, which was being widely touted by the media as a miracle cure for cancer—although the medical establishment was less convinced. Wright's cancer was so far advanced that the physicians gave him the drug only as a compassionate exception—not because they expected any response. What happened next truly seemed like a miracle. Wright gained weight, looked and felt better, and his tumors shrank so drastically, they could hardly be detected.

Wright's improvement continued until newspapers began reporting krebiozen was not the great advance they had thought. After reading the negative coverage,

Wright became discouraged, immediately began to lose weight, and his tumors grew once more.

Assuming that the power of suggestion had been largely responsible for Wright's response to the medication, the physicians decided to tell him that the first batches of krebiozen had not been at full potency. The lab had corrected the problem, they assured him, and the new, stronger batch of the drug would soon be on its way. They continued to encourage Wright's hopes, finally announcing that the big day was here—the new batch of the drug had arrived. They then proceeded to give Wright injections just as before—using sterile water.

Wright showed the same dramatic improvements that had occurred with the krebiozen. His remission lasted until, for a second time, the newspapers undermined the physicians—stating unequivocally, "AMA reports that krebiozen is worthless against cancer." Mr. Wright once again began to sink, his tumors grew massive, and shortly thereafter, he died.

THE FLIP SIDE OF THE COIN

What happens when a sick person like Mr. Wright attaches a negative rather than a positive meaning to the attempt at treatment? This negative mindset can be so strong, it's been given its own name: the nocebo response.

One of the more compelling case reports of the nocebo response was recorded by renowned cardiologist Dr. Bernard Lown.

Early in his career, Dr. Lown was working under a very distinguished senior cardiologist, who in turn was taking care of a woman, Mrs. S., with a non-life-threatening heart valve condition called tricuspid stenosis. She also suffered from a mild degree of congestive heart failure, which was successfully controlled with medication. At the time of the precipitating event, Mrs. S. was in the hospital to have some tests done, and was in her usual stable condition.

One day, the senior cardiologist came into her room, accompanied by a bevy of residents, interns and medical students. The group talked among themselves—excluding her from their conversation. Before turning on their heels and filing out of the room, the senior physician announced, "This woman has TS"—employing an abbreviation for tricuspid stenosis.

Dr. Lown came back shortly thereafter and was stunned to find Mrs. S. anxious, frightened and breathing very rapidly. Her lungs, which had been perfectly clear, now displayed the most crackling noises in the lower portions which portended worsening of the congestive heart failure. When Lown asked Mrs. S. what was the matter, she replied, "That doctor said I was going to die for sure."

Lown protested that his senior couldn't possibly have made such a statement. "I heard him," Mrs. S. replied

After a heart patient thought she heard doctors say she would die—she did—later that same day, despite the total lack of evidence that anything had changed in her heart condition.

firmly. "He said I had TS. I know that means 'terminal situation.' You doctors never tell us the truth straight out. But I know what he meant."

Despite Lown's attempts to clear up the misunderstanding, Mrs. S. continued to slide into progressively worse heart failure, despite the total lack of objective evidence that anything fundamental had changed in her underlying heart condition. She passed away later that same day.

Historically, medicine first discovered the effect of symbolic significance on health by seeing improvement in patients who were given bread pills, sugar pills or other dummy medicines that could exert only a symbolic power. Today, we need not be limited by that history. We realize that virtually every time a healer administers a treatment to a person with an illness, or every time an individual treats herself for an illness with some healing substance or process, he or she receives messages from the environment that may trigger a placebo response.

By defining our terms in such a way that the placebo response does not depend in any way on administering placebos, we have cleared the path for completely ethical, nondeceptive communications between the healer and the patient.

In terms of deception, physicians had assumed for centuries that if sugar pills worked, they could work only because the patient did not know what they really were. No one could conceive of handing a patient sugar pills, saying, "This is a bottle of sugar pills," and still see the patient get better.

Two psychiatrists, Lee Park and Lino Covi, decided in the early 1960s to study truth-telling in the use of placebos. They were doing research on psychiatric patients who suffered from what at the time was generally termed "neurosis." The patients had quite a number of different bodily symptoms which were thought to be part of their condition, and Park and Covi were using a detailed symptom checklist to keep track of total symptoms over time. The authors used the symptom checklist scores to determine which treatment or set of treatments worked best at reducing symptoms. Some studies had

Some study subjects taking placebos were so convinced that the pills contained "real" medication that they reported experiencing a number of side effects.

involved placebo control groups, and as expected, a number of patients got noticeably better while taking placebos. In those studies, no subject knew whether he was receiving a placebo or the study drug.

Now Park and Covi enrolled a group of 15 new patients in trials with neither an "active" drug group nor psychotherapy, as they had done in the past. Instead, after the patients went through the symptom checklist process, they were given a bottle of pills. The experimenters told them frankly, "These are sugar pills, which contain no active medicine." Then they added that despite that fact, many patients had gotten better after taking one of the pills three times a day for a week. A checkup visit was to be held at the end of that week.

When 14 of the 15 subjects returned a week later, the new symptom checklists showed that 13 of those 14 had significantly reduced symptoms. From their conversations with the subjects, Park and Covi learned, first of all, that not all their subjects had believed them about what was being prescribed. In fact, the 14 subjects could be divided into three roughly equivalent groups. The first group took the scientists at their word and assumed they were taking sugar pills. The second group decided you simply couldn't trust psychiatry researchers and believed the pills were really some kind of tranquilizer—and that they'd been lied to, possibly to make the study more accurate or because there would be less chance of their getting hooked on the drug. The third group was merely unsure of what they had received.

Park and Covi then asked the "certain-placebo" subjects how they could account for their having gotten better. Despite the limited size of the group, their answers give us some of the most important clues about what physicians must do to trigger a placebo response in their patients. About half of these subjects said that they got better because they took the placebo, while the other half claimed they improved because somehow they had drawn upon their own innate abilities to cope.

One woman reported that every time she took one of the placebos, she reminded herself that she really could do something to better her own condition. Some other subjects also testified that they appreciated the fact that they were not getting an "active" drug, and so were spared the likely side effects and risks of addiction.

By contrast, the "certain-real drug" group explained that, because they thought they were getting an active drug, they saw their symptoms improving. The improvement served to reinforce their views that the pills were genuine medicine. Some people even reported a number of side effects they had felt throughout the week.

By the mid-1960s, most physicians believed that the placebo response hinged on patients' expectations of a cure. But few physicians imagined that their own expectations could be equally powerful when disclosed to the patient.

That's what Dr. E. H. Uhlenhuth and his colleagues at the Johns Hopkins University Department of Psychiatry had to deal with when they sat down to analyze the data from a double-blind randomized study of two tranquilizers compared to placebo for psychiatric clinic patients with anxiety. These tranquilizers are generally viewed as effective for anxiety symptoms, and so the investigators naturally expected to show in their study that they did better than the placebo. When their data did not show this, they knew that something must have gone wrong. It occurred to them to analyze the data according to which of the two psychiatrists the patients had seen when they were being given their capsules.

The psychiatrists were supposed to treat all patients identically, and they claimed to have done so. But if you considered only the half of the patients who had seen psychiatrist A, there was no difference between either of the tranquilizers and the placebo. If you considered only those patients seeing psychiatrist B, however, one of the drugs was better than placebo. When the data were combined, the lack of effect on the A side obscured the effect on the B side so that overall there was no statistical difference between the medication and the control groups.

It turned out that Dr. A was a younger physician who seemed rather noncommittal to patients, and in his own mind doubted that any of the drugs actually made a difference. Dr. B, by contrast, was older and appeared more fatherly to the patients; his own thinking was that one of the drugs, meprobamate, was definitely superior to placebo, though he was not so convinced about the other "active" drug.

Neither A nor B was consciously aware of having transmitted his personal views to any of the experimental subjects. We can only speculate what sorts of signals A and B could have transmitted to their patients' inner pharmacies. Whatever it was, the experimental results were virtually identical to the unexpressed expectations of the two physicians.

As you can see from these research findings, there seems to be a consistent thread of "mind over matter"— the ability of the body to undergo a healing change because the mind expects it to happen. In the case of the Uhlenhuth experiment, the expectancy lay perhaps more in the mind of the physician than in that of the patient, but it still worked. One case report showed a small child to be affected by the healing expectations of the parent. In an older study, patients improved more on placebos than on tranquilizers when the medicine was administered by nurses who strongly disapproved of giving "drugs" to these patients.

One patient became 100% convinced that his two-colored capsules would not work unless he swallowed them green-end first.

Other bits of data that seem to support the expectancy theory are findings about which placebos work most effectively, and for what conditions. Many investigators have found that capsules work better than drugs taken by mouth, and that injections that sting work better than painless injections. Surgery can be an especially powerful placebo stimulus. Placebos taken four times a day seem to be more effective than placebos taken twice a day. When placebo (or drugs, for that matter) are in the form of colored capsules or coated tablets, blue, green and purple ones seem to work especially well as sedatives and sleeping pills, while red, yellow and orange seem to work best as stimulants or energy-boosters. All of these effects seem to go along with the natural expectancy of the average person. One patient, unlike the average person, became 100% convinced that his two-colored capsules would not work unless he swallowed them green-end first. Needless to say, what he expected ended up happening.

Psychologists add depth to the expectancy theory by tying it to an evolutionary view of human behavior. According to this view, the body's reaction to a message from the outside world will be a combination of two factors: the "bottom-up" processing of the incoming information, in which the higher centers of the brain analyze the new information in detail; and a "top-down" response, in which the brain quickly scans its existing inventory of behavior patterns for something that seems to match the overall pattern of the new information. The bottom-up process may take a long time, so the human body is hard-wired to respond to some situations from the top-down reaction—a sort of "shoot first, ask questions later" mode. The top-down process is most likely to be triggered in situations where the mind-body unity regards itself as being in significant danger, and where the extra time required for a full bottom-up analysis might be too risky.

For example, you see something in the grass at your feet that might be a snake. The top-down reaction is basically, "Snake!", which produces a rapid jump backward, as well as stress responses such as faster heart rate, increased blood pressure and higher muscle tone. The bottom-up reaction is, "Let's look at this more carefully. It's long and thin and brown, so it could be a snake. But it's not moving, and it's pretty straight. . . . Maybe it's actually a stick. Let me reach down carefully and touch it—yup, it's a stick." The evolutionary part of the theory proposes that for most of its history, the human race had a much better survival chance if the top-down response was the first to kick in. So natural selection favored our minds' developing and retaining a number of top-down response patterns.

The placebo response might be just such a top-down reaction. Since illness is a threat to the organism, the brain may well have stored in its memory files certain pathways of healing: signals that can be sent to the inner pharmacy to stimulate the release of healing chemicals. If a message is then received that resembles in its outward form something that the person expects to be associated with healing, that might be enough to trigger one of the stored top-down reaction pathways, leading to a release from the inner pharmacy, followed by bodily healing. That can occur even if a more careful analysis would have shown that the message was a fraud—that the pill was a sugar pill and not a chemically powerful substance.

Science has yet to discover a single pathway—a term scientists use to describe a series of causes and effects—that accounts for the placebo response. Our inner pharmacies, it would seem, have quite an array of different biochemical substances on their shelves. There are at least three known mind-body healing pathways.

Endorphins: We have a strong suspicion that at least some placebo pain relief, and perhaps the effects placebos have on anxiety and shortness of breath, occur because placebos stimulate the release of endorphins, a morphine-like drug produced by the body.

Stress/Relaxation Response: Many diseases, including hypertension, memory loss and chronic fatigue syndrome, are associated with elevated levels of stress hormones, such as cortisol. Placebos may trigger the body's lowering of these stress hormones in a transaction known as the "relaxation response." Strong social support plays an important role in heightening this response, much as a support group relaxes and fortifies its members.

Psychoneuroimmune Pathways: While this area of research is relatively new, my impression is that it has proven, beyond a reasonable doubt, that mental and emotional changes can alter the immune system, influencing the manufacture and function of immune cells. It stands to reason, then, that a person's emotional state or behavior may be linked to disease. In this pathway, placebos positively influence a person's emotional state or behavior, and thereby boost his or her immune system.

You can use all of these various pathways to invoke the placebo response—and take charge of your own health. Some key elements for stimulating your own inner pharmacy are: constructing a meaningful "story" about the condition you may be suffering from, being open to alternative and traditional medicine, finding a physician with whom you can form a healing partnership, and maintaining positive social connections.

At this point, it's easy to be optimistic. I've seen the processes we've discussed work, as have countless physicians and scientists. These means of healing don't often produce results as dramatic as, say, the faith healings at Lourdes. No, the paralyzed may not throw down their crutches and walk away unaided. Nonetheless, the processes are effective at the level where most good medicine functions: People suffer less from the symptoms of their illness, discover they can do more despite their illness, and realize that, even with illness, their lives are meaningful.

When all this happens, I know that I am in the presence of healing. Just how and why it happens may remain a mystery. That it happens is as certain as anything can be in the practice of medicine.

Excerpted from The Placebo Response *by Howard Brody, M.D., Ph.D., with permission from HarperCollins (June 2000). Brody is Director of the Center for Ethics and Humanities in the Life Sciences at Michigan State University.*

READ MORE ABOUT IT

The Placebo Effect, Anne Harrington, Ed. (Harvard University Press, 1999)
The Power of Hope: A Doctor's Perspective, Howard M. Shapiro, M.D. (Yale University Press, 1998)

SWEET SABOTAGE How Sugar Pills Compromise Drug Trials

By Joseph Arpaia, M.D.

The placebo effect can work wonders for your body, but its powerful influence renders drug trials misleading and unreliable. How can a simple sugar pill sabotage a test of powerful medication?

The problem arises in "double-blind" studies—the gold standard for testing new medications—in which neither researchers nor subjects know who is getting the medication and who is getting placebo. While the "double-blind system is supposed to guard against the bias that the placebo effect can cause, it fails miserably. Noticeable sensations from the medication easily distinguish the drug takers from placebo takers, effectively removing the blindfold and allowing bias to shine through.

Reports began surfacing in the 1950s that the double-blind design was not as scientifically objective as originally assumed. In 1993, Seymour Fisher, Ph.D., and Roger P. Greenberg, Ph.D., raised radical questions about the methodology when their investigation of previous reviews of antidepressant literature, as one sample of drug trials, turned up only the most modest evidence of the drugs' therapeutic power. They were surprised to find that even the most positive research reviews indicated that 30% to 40% of antidepressant studies showed that there was no significant difference in response to drug versus placebo.

Patients learn to discriminate between drug and placebo largely from bodily sensations and symptoms—or lack thereof. Studies suggest that 70% to 80% of study subjects correctly guess which pill they're taking. And since the more open to bias a drug trial is, the greater the apparent superiority of the drug over placebo, the result is an industry-sanctioned drug test that systematically overestimates the power of drugs, especially those with noticeable side effects!

Imagine that a new antidepressant that is being tested causes side effects such as insomnia, dizziness, weight gain and sexual dysfunction (which many do), and that it doesn't actually relieve depression. Participants in a "double-blind" study who experience those marked symptoms will most likely conclude that they are taking "real" medication, rather than placebo, since no sugar pill would produce such side effects. Just knowing they are taking "real" medication produces a powerful healing effect, which makes the drug being tested look extremely beneficial. The placebo effect is so powerful that it could even make a medication that produces a mild depression appear to be an effective antidepressant—as long as the drug produces noticeable side effects. Conversely, if another antidepressant—one that actually has a small beneficial effect—does not cause marked side effects, drug trial participants might conclude that they're not getting any medicine. In that case, the placebo effect would not kick in, and the drug would not seem as beneficial as the one with side effects.

In this way, the double-blind study may actually select for drugs that are toxic—and potentially less effective—over their gentler, more subtle cousins. This carries an immense personal and economic cost.

Last year, the *Journal of the American Medical Association* reported that adverse drug effects may be the fourth leading cause of death in hospitalized patients, killing 100,000 people a year. The fact is, we are more likely to die from a medication than from most diseases.

Such faulty testing techniques have yielded a new batch of antidepressants, so-called selective serotonin reuptake inhibitors (SSRIs), that can end up making people more depressed and even suicidal, according to a report in the May 1998 *Clinical Psychiatry News.* Worse, Internal Food & Drug Administration documents show that these drugs can also cause hypomania/mania—a severe psychotic disorder involving

(continued)

extreme overactivity, insomnia, racing thoughts, frantic outbursts, paranoia and suicide—in 1% of users. That means 1,000 of every million Americans taking one of the newer antidepressants will likely develop manic reactions. The figures could be even more disastrous, since FDA drug trials excluded patients already at risk of psychotic mania. The drugs' manic effect is even more pronounced in children. In *Reclaiming Our Children*, psychiatrist Peter R. Breggin, M.D., cites research indicating a 6% rate of mania and an even higher rate of behavioral problems—including violence—in children taking these antidepressants.

The problem is not limited to antidepressants: It affects every medication, including those for pain, digestion and blood pressure, anti-inflammatory drugs and others. The drug Rezulin, used to treat diabetes, was recently recalled because it was causing liver failure. The anti-heartburn drug Propulsid was pulled from the shelves because it was causing cardiac arrest, and 80 people had died from taking it.

After the double-blind design botches drug trials, thanks to the placebo effect, aggressive marketing of the resulting FDA-approved medications creates a one-two punch. With glossy, full-page magazine ads touting the sweeping promises of happier days, it is easy to understand how a drug like Prozac, for example, gained its popularity, though studies have shown that most of its benefit can be attributed to the placebo effect. In fact, an article in the *British Journal of Psychiatry* in 1998 pointed out that in seven out of nine studies reviewed, subjects taking an antidepressant did no better than those taking a substance that was not an antidepressant, but that had similar noxious side effects. This phenomenon has been called the "active placebo" effect, in which side effects convince all subjects that they are getting "strong" or "real" medicine, heightening their positive response to the pills. The research team, led by Joanna Moncrieff of the Institute of Psychiatry in London, concluded, "The effects of antidepressants may be smaller than generally believed, with placebo accounting for more of the clinical improvement . . . than is known to be the case."

The studies pharmaceutical companies claim "prove effectiveness," therefore, actually prove nothing. The drug companies have been so stymied by their inability to show that psychiatric drugs are better than placebo that they recently held a conference that focused on how to get around the placebo effect. This past May, in Chicago, eight major pharmaceutical companies joined several research institutes and the Johns Hopkins School of Medicine to explore ways of improving clinical trial design and conduct for successful drug development. It was a researcher from Eli Lilly Laboratories who led the featured panel discussion on "minimizing the placebo response."

The medical profession is not off the hook, either. Current thinking holds that every condition requires one or more pills to treat it. But doctors would do well to realize that many of the drugs they prescribe today

The way we test drugs may select for ones that are toxic, and perhaps less effective, over their gentler cousins.

are no more effective than the drugs of 30 years ago.

Being a physician means offering knowledge and hope, not just drugs. Doctors must remember that the most powerful therapeutic intervention is the patient's own internal healing response, which they can stimulate by educating, motivating and encouraging the patient to engage in healthy patterns of behavior—something that is nearly impossible to do in today's seven-minute office visit.

We would do well to place our faith instead in our own internal healing abilities. That would reduce our dependence on marginally effective drugs, reign in growing health care costs, and prevent thousands of people from dying unnecessarily of side effects.

Joseph Arpaia, M.D., is a psychiatrist and medical director of the Cascades Wellness Center. He also teaches in the psychology department at the University of Oregon. For more information, visit www.creatingsynergy.com.

This glossary of psychology terms is included to provide you with a convenient and ready reference as you encounter general terms in your study of psychology and personal growth and behavior that are unfamiliar or require a review. It is not intended to be comprehensive, but taken together with the many definitions included in the articles themselves, it should prove to be quite useful.

abnormal behavior Behavior that contributes to maladaptiveness; is considered deviant by the culture; or that leads to personal psychological distress.

absolute threshold The minimum amount of physical energy required to produce a sensation.

accommodation Process in cognitive development; involves altering or reorganizing the mental picture to make room for a new experience or idea.

acculturation The process of becoming part of a new cultural environment.

acetylcholine A neurotransmitter involved in memory.

achievement drive The need to attain self-esteem, success, or status. Society's expectations strongly influence the achievement motive.

achievement style The way people behave in achievement situations; achievement styles include the direct, instrumental, and relational styles.

acquired immune deficiency syndrome (AIDS) A fatal disease of the immune system.

acquisition In conditioning, forming associations in first learning a task.

actor-observer bias Tendency to attribute the behavior of other people to internal causes and our own behavior to external causes.

acupuncture Oriental practice involving the insertion of needles into the body to control pain.

adaptation The process of responding to changes in the environment by altering responses to keep a person's behavior appropriate to environmental demands.

adjustment How we react to stress; some change that we make in response to the demands placed upon us.

adrenal glands Endocrine glands involved in stress and energy regulation.

adrenaline A hormone produced by the adrenal glands that is involved in physiological arousal; adrenaline is also called epinephrine.

affective flattening Individuals with schizophrenia who do not exhibit any emotional arousal.

aggression Behavior intended to harm another member of the same species.

agoraphobia Anxiety disorder in which an individual is excessively afraid of places or situations from which it would be difficult or embarrassing to escape.

alarm reaction The first stage of Hans Selye's general adaptation syndrome. The alarm reaction is the immediate response to stress; adrenaline is released and digestion slows. The alarm reaction prepares the body for an emergency.

all-or-none law The principle that states that a neuron only fires when a stimulus is above a certain minimum strength (threshold), and when it fires, it does so at full strength.

alogia Individuals with schizophrenia that show a reduction in speech.

alpha Brain-wave activity that indicates that a person is relaxed and resting quietly; 8–12 Hz.

altered state of consciousness (ASC) A state of consciousness in which there is a redirection of attention, a change in the aspects of the world that occupy a person's thoughts, and a change in the stimuli to which a person responds.

ambivalent attachment Type of infant-parent attachment in which the infant seeks contact but resists once the contact is made.

amphetamine A strong stimulant; increases arousal of the central nervous system.

amygdala A part of the limbic system involved in fear, aggression, and other social behaviors.

anal stage Psychosexual stage during which, according to Sigmund Freud, the child experiences the first restrictions on his or her impulses.

analytical psychology The personality theory of Carl Jung.

anorexia nervosa Eating disorder in which an individual becomes severely underweight because of self-imposed restrictions on eating.

antisocial personality disorder Personality disorder in which individuals who engage in antisocial behavior experience no guilt or anxiety about their actions; sometimes called sociopathy or psychopathy.

anxiety disorder Fairly long-lasting disruption of a person's ability to deal with stress; often accompanied by feelings of fear and apprehension.

applied psychology The area of psychology that is most immediately concerned with helping to solve practical problems; includes clinical and counseling psychology as well as industrial, environmental, and legal psychology.

approach-approach conflict When we are attracted to two equally desirable goals that are incompatible.

approach-avoidance conflict When we are faced with a single goal that has positive and negative aspects.

aptitude test Any test designed to predict what a person with the proper training can accomplish in the future.

archetypes In Carl Jung's personality theory, unconscious universal ideas shared by all humans.

arousal theory Theory that focuses on the energy (arousal) aspect of motivation; it states that we are motivated to initiate behaviors that help to regulate overall arousal level.

asocial phase Phase in attachment development in which the neonate does not distinguish people from objects.

assertiveness training Training that helps individuals stand up for their rights while not denying rights of other people.

assimilation Process in cognitive development; occurs when something new is taken into the child's mental picture.

associationism A theory of learning suggesting that once two stimuli are presented together, one of them will remind a person of the other. Ideas are learned by association with sensory experiences and are not innate.

attachment Process in which the individual shows behaviors that promote proximity with a specific object or person.

attention Process of focusing on particular stimuli in the environment.

attention deficit disorder Hyperactivity; inability to concentrate.

attitude Learned disposition that actively guides us toward specific behaviors; attitudes consist of feelings, beliefs, and behavioral tendencies.

attribution The cognitive process of determining the motives of someone's behavior, and whether they are internal or external.

autism A personality disorder in which a child does not respond socially to people.

autokinetic effect Perception of movement of a stationary spot of light in a darkened room.

autonomic nervous system The part of the peripheral nervous system that carries messages from the central nervous system to the endocrine glands, the smooth muscles controlling the heart, and the primarily involuntary muscles controlling internal processes; includes the sympathetic and parasympathetic nervous systems.

aversion therapy A counterconditioning therapy in which unwanted responses are paired with unpleasant consequences.

avoidance conditioning Learning situation in which a subject avoids a stimulus by learning to respond appropriately before the stimulus begins.

avoidant attachment Type of infant-parent attachment in which the infant avoids the parent.

avolition Individuals with schizophrenia who lack motivation to follow through on an activity.

backward conditioning A procedure in classical conditioning in which the US is presented and terminated before the termination of the CS; very ineffective procedure.

basic research Research conducted to obtain information for its own sake.

behavior Anything you do or think, including various bodily reactions. Behavior includes physical and mental responses.

behavior genetics How genes influence behavior.

behavior modification Another term for behavior therapy; the modification of behavior through psychological techniques; often the application of conditioning principles to alter behavior.

behaviorism The school of thought founded by John Watson; it studied only observable behavior.

belongingness and love needs Third level of motives in Maslow's hierarchy; includes love and affection, friends, and social contact.

biological motives Motives that have a definite physiological basis and are biologically necessary for survival of the individual or species.

biological response system Systems of the body that are important in behavioral responding; includes the senses, muscles, endocrine system, and the nervous system.

biological therapy Treatment of behavior problems through biological techniques; major biological therapies include drug therapy, psychosurgery, and electroconvulsive therapy.

bipolar disorder Mood disorder characterized by extreme mood swings from sad depression to joyful mania; sometimes called manic-depression.

blinding technique In an experiment, a control for bias in which the assignment of a subject to the experimental or control group is unknown to the subject or experimenter or both (a double-blind experiment).

body dysmorphic disorder Somatoform disorder characterized by a preoccupation with an imaginary defect in the physical appearance of a physically healthy person.

body language Communication through position and movement of the body.

bottom-up processing The psychoanalytic process of understanding communication by listening to words, then interpreting phrases, and finally understanding ideas.

brief psychodynamic therapy A therapy developed for individuals with strong egos to resolve a core conflict.

bulimia nervosa Eating disorder in which an individual eats large amounts of calorie-rich food in a short time and then purges the food by vomiting or using laxatives.

bystander effect Phenomenon in an emergency situation in which a person is more likely to help when alone than when in a group of people.

California Psychological Inventory (CPI) An objective personality test used to study normal populations.

Cannon-Bard theory of emotion Theory of emotion that states that the emotional feeling and the physiological arousal occur at the same time.

cardinal traits In Gordon Allport's personality theory, the traits of an individual that are so dominant that they are expressed in everything the person does; few people possess cardinal traits.

catatonic schizophrenia A type of schizophrenia that is characterized by periods of complete immobility and the apparent absence of will to move or speak.

causal attribution Process of determining whether a person's behavior is due to internal or external motives.

central nervous system The part of the human nervous system that interprets and stores messages from the sense organs, decides what behavior to exhibit, and sends appropriate messages to the muscles and glands; includes the brain and spinal cord.

central tendency In statistics, measures of central tendency give a number that represents the entire group or sample.

central traits In Gordon Allport's personality theory, the traits of an individual that form the core of the personality; they are developed through experience.

cerebellum The part of the hindbrain that is involved in balance and muscle coordination.

cerebral cortex The outermost layer of the cerebrum of the brain where higher mental functions occur. The cerebral cortex is divided into sections, or lobes, which control various activities.

cerebrum (cerebral hemisphere) Largest part of the forebrain involved in cognitive functions; the cerebrum consists of two hemispheres connected by the corpus callosum.

chromosome Bodies in the cell nucleus that contain the genes.

chunking Process of combining stimuli in order to increase memory capacity.

classical conditioning The form of learning in which a stimulus is associated with another stimulus that causes a particular response. Sometimes called Pavlovian conditioning or respondent conditioning.

clinical psychology Subfield in which psychologists assess psychological problems and treat people with behavior problems using psychological techniques (called psychotherapy).

cognition Mental processes, such as perception, attention, memory, language, thinking, and problem solving; cognition involves the acquisition, storage, retrieval, and utilization of knowledge.

cognitive behavior therapy A form of behavior therapy that identifies self-defeating attitudes and thoughts in a subject, and then helps the subject to replace these with positive, supportive thoughts.

cognitive development Changes over time in mental processes such as thinking, memory, language, and problem solving.

cognitive dissonance Leon Festinger's theory of attitude change that states that, when people hold two psychologically inconsistent ideas, they experience tension that forces them to reconcile the conflicting ideas.

cognitive expectancy The condition in which an individual learns that certain behaviors lead to particular goals; cognitive expectancy motivates the individual to exhibit goal-directed behaviors.

cognitive learning Type of learning that theorizes that the learner utilizes cognitive structures in memory to make decisions about behaviors.

cognitive psychology The area of psychology that includes the study of mental activities involved in perception, memory, language, thought, and problem solving.

cognitive restructuring The modification of the client's thoughts and perceptions that are contributing to his or her maladjustments.

cognitive therapy Therapy developed by Aaron Beck in which an individual's negative, self-defeating thoughts are restructured in a positive way.

cognitive-motivational-relational theory of emotion A theory of emotion proposed by Richard Lazarus that includes cognitive appraisal, motivational goals, and relationships between an individual and the environment.

collective unconscious Carl Jung's representation of the thoughts shared by all humans.

collectivistic cultures Cultures in which the greatest emphasis is on the loyalty of each individual to the group.

comparative psychology Subfield in which experimental psychologists study and compare the behavior of different species of animals.

compulsions Rituals performed excessively such as checking doors or washing hands to reduce anxiety.

concept formation (concept learning) The development of the ability to respond to common features of categories of objects or events.

concrete operations period Stage in cognitive development; from 7 to 11 years, the time in which the child's ability to solve problems with reasoning greatly increases.

conditioned response (CR) The response or behavior that occurs when the conditioned stimulus is presented (after the CS has been associated with the US).

conditioned stimulus (CS) An originally neutral stimulus that is associated with an unconditioned stimulus and takes on the latter's capability of eliciting a particular reaction.

conditioned taste aversion (CTA) An aversion to particular tastes associated with stomach distress; usually considered a unique form of classical conditioning because of the extremely long interstimulus intervals involved.

conditioning A term applied to two types of learning (classical and operant). Conditioning refers to the scientific aspect of the type of learning.

conflict Situation that occurs when we experience incompatible demands or desires; the outcome when one individual or group perceives that another individual or group has caused or will cause harm.

conformity Type of social influence in which an individual changes his or her behavior to fit social norms or expectations.

connectionism Recent approach to problem solving; the development of neural connections allows us to think and solve problems.

conscientiousness The dimension in the five-factor personality theory that includes traits such as practical, cautious, serious, reliable, careful, and ambitious; also called dependability.

conscious Being aware of experiencing sensations, thoughts, and feelings at any given point in time.

conscious mind In Sigmund Freud's psychoanalytic theory of personality, the part of personality that we are aware of in everyday life.

consciousness The processing of information at various levels of awareness; state in which a person is aware of sensations, thoughts, and feelings.

consensus In causal attribution, the extent to which other people react as the subject does in a particular situation.

conservation The ability to recognize that something stays the same even if it takes on a different form; Piaget tested conservation of mass, number, length, and volume.

consistency In causal attribution, the extent to which the subject always behaves in the same way in a situation.

consolidation The biological neural process of making memories permanent; possibly short-term memory is electrically coded and long-term memory is chemically coded.

contingency model A theory that specific types of situations need particular types of leaders.

continuum of preparedness Martin Seligman's proposal that animals are biologically prepared to learn certain responses more readily than they are prepared to learn others.

control group Subjects in an experiment who do not receive the independent variable; the control group determines the effectiveness of the independent variable.

conventional morality Level II in Lawrence Kohlberg's theory, in which moral reasoning is based on conformity and social standards.

convergence Binocular depth cue in which we detect distance by interpreting the kinesthetic sensations produced by the muscles of the eyeballs.

conversion disorder Somatoform disorder in which a person displays obvious disturbance in the nervous system without a physical basis for the problem.

correlation Statistical technique to determine the degree of relationship that exists between two variables.

counterconditioning A behavior therapy in which an unwanted response is replaced by conditioning a new response that is incompatible with it.

creativity A process of coming up with new or unusual responses to familiar circumstances.

critical period hypothesis Period of time during development in which particular learning or experiences normally occur; if learning does not occur, the individual has a difficult time learning it later.

culture-bound The idea that a test's usefulness is limited to the culture in which it was written and utilized.

cumulative response curve Graphed curve that results when responses for a subject are added to one another over time; if subjects respond once every 5 minutes, they will have a cumulative response curve value of 12 after an hour.

curiosity motive Motive that causes the individual to seek out a certain amount of novelty.

cyclothymia disorder A moderately severe problem with numerous periods of hypomanic episodes and depressive symptoms.

death instinct (also called Thanatos) Freud's term for an instinct that is destructive to the individual or species; aggression is a major expression of death instinct.

decay Theory of forgetting in which sensory impressions leave memory traces that fade away with time.

defense mechanisms Psychological techniques to help protect ourselves from stress and anxiety, to resolve conflicts, and to preserve our self-esteem.

delayed conditioning A procedure in classical conditioning in which the presentation of the CS precedes the onset of the US and the termination of the CS is delayed until the US is presented; most effective procedure.

delusion The holding of obviously false beliefs; for example, imagining someone is trying to kill you.

dependent variable In psychology, the behavior or response that is measured; it is dependent on the independent variable.

depersonalization disorder Dissociative disorder in which the individual escapes from his or her own personality by believing that he or she does not exist or that his or her environment is not real.

depolarization Any change in which the internal electrical charge becomes more positive.

depression A temporary emotional state that normal individuals experience or a persistent state that may be considered a psychological disorder. Characterized by sadness and low self-esteem.

descriptive statistics Techniques that help summarize large amounts of data information.

developmental psychology Study of physical and mental growth and behavioral changes in individuals from conception to death.

Diagnostic and Statistic Manual of Mental Disorders (DSM) Published by the American Psychiatric Association in 1952, and revised in 1968, 1980, 1987, and 1994, this manual was provided to develop a set of diagnoses of abnormal behavior patterns.

diffusion of responsibility Finding that groups tend to inhibit helping behavior; responsibility is shared equally by members of the group so that no one individual feels a strong commitment.

disorganized schizophrenia A type of schizophrenia that is characterized by a severe personality disintegration; the individual often displays bizarre behavior.

displacement Defense mechanism by which the individual directs his or her aggression or hostility toward a person or object other than the one it should be directed toward; in Freud's dream theory, the process of reassigning emotional feelings from one object to another one.

dissociative disorder Psychological disorder that involves a disturbance in the memory, consciousness, or identity of an individual; types include multiple personality disorder, depersonalization disorder, psychogenic amnesia, and psychogenic fugue.

dissociative fugue Individuals who have lost their memory, relocated to a new geographical area, and started a new life as someone else.

dissociative identity disorder (multiple personality disorder) Dissociative disorder in which several personalities are present in the same individual.

distinctiveness In causal attribution, the extent to which the subject reacts the same way in other situations.

Down syndrome Form of mental retardation caused by having three number 21 chromosomes (trisomy 21).

dream analysis Psychoanalytic technique in which a patient's dreams are reviewed and analyzed to discover true feelings.

drive Motivational concept used to describe the internal forces that push an organism toward a goal; sometimes identified as psychological arousal arising from a physiological need.

dyssomnia Sleep disorder in which the chief symptom is a disturbance in the amount and quality of sleep; they include insomnia and hypersomnia.

dysthymic disorder Mood disorder in which the person suffers moderate depression much of the time for at least two years.

ego Sigmund Freud's term for an individual's sense of reality.

egocentric Seeing the world only from your perspective.

eidetic imagery Photographic memory; ability to recall great detail accurately after briefly viewing something.

Electra complex The Freudian idea that the young girl feels inferior to boys because she lacks a penis.

electroconvulsive therapy (ECT) A type of biological therapy in which electricity is applied to the brain in order to relieve severe depression.

emotion A response to a stimulus that involves physiological arousal, subjective feeling, cognitive interpretation, and overt behavior.

empiricism The view that behavior is learned through experience.

encoding The process of putting information into the memory system.

encounter group As in a sensitivity training group, a therapy where people become aware of themselves in meeting others.

endorphins Several neuropeptides that function as neurotransmitters. The opiate-like endorphins are involved in pain, reinforcement, and memory.

engineering psychology Area of psychology that is concerned with how work is performed, design of equipment, and work environment; also called human factors psychology.

engram The physical memory trace or neural circuit that holds memory; also called memory trace.

episodic memory Highest memory system; includes information about personal experiences.

Eros Sigmund Freud's term for an instinct that helps the individual or species survive; also called life instinct.

esteem needs Fourth level of motives in Abraham Maslow's hierarchy; includes high evaluation of oneself, self-respect, self-esteem, and respect of others.

eustress Stress that results from pleasant and satisfying experiences; earning a high grade or achieving success produces eustress.

excitement phase First phase in the human sexual response cycle; the beginning of sexual arousal.

experimental group Subjects in an experiment who receive the independent variable.

experimental psychology Subfield in which psychologists research the fundamental causes of behavior. Many experimental psychologists conduct experiments in basic research.

experimenter bias Source of potential error in an experiment from the action or expectancy of the experimenter; might influence the experimental results in ways that mask the true outcome.

external locus of control In Julian Rotter's personality theory, the perception that reinforcement is independent of a person's behavior.

extraversion The dimension in the five-factor personality theory that includes traits such as sociability, talkativeness, boldness, fun-lovingness, adventurousness, and assertiveness; also called surgency. The personality concept of Carl Jung in which the personal energy of the individual is directed externally.

factor analysis A statistical procedure used to determine the relationship among variables.

false memories Memories believed to be real, but the events never occurred.

fast mapping A process by which children can utilize a word after a single exposure.

fetal alcohol syndrome (FAS) Condition in which defects in the newborn child are caused by the mother's excessive alcohol intake.

five-factor model of personality tracts A trait theory of personality that includes the factors of extraversion, agreeableness, conscientiousness, emotional stability, and openness.

fixed action pattern (FAP) Unlearned, inherited, stereotyped behaviors that are shown by all members of a species; term used in ethology.

fixed interval (FI) schedule Schedule of reinforcement where the subject receives reinforcement for a correct response given after a specified time interval.

fixed ratio (FR) schedule Schedule of reinforcement in which the subject is reinforced after a certain number of responses.

flashbulb memory Memory of an event that is so important that significant details are vividly remembered for life.

forgetting In memory, not being able to retrieve the original learning. The part of the original learning that cannot be retrieved is said to be forgotten.

formal operations period Period in cognitive development; at 11 years, the adolescent begins abstract thinking and reasoning. This period continues throughout the rest of life.

free association Psychoanalytic technique in which the patient says everything that comes to mind.

free recall A verbal learning procedure in which the order of presentation of the stimuli is varied and the subject can learn the items in any order.

frequency theory of hearing Theory of hearing that states that the frequency of vibrations at the basilar membrane determines the frequency of firing of neurons carrying impulses to the brain.

frustration A cause of stress that results from the blocking of a person's goal-oriented behavior.

frustration-drive theory of aggression Theory of aggression that states that it is caused by frustration.

functionalism School of thought that studied the functional value of consciousness and behavior.

fundamental attribution error Attribution bias in which people overestimate the role of internal disposition and underestimate the role of external situation.

gate-control theory of pain Theory of pain that proposes that there is a gate that allows pain impulses to travel from the spinal cord to the brain.

gender-identity disorder (GID) Incongruence between assigned sex and gender identity.

gender-identity/role Term that incorporates gender identity (the private perception of one's sex) and gender role (the public expression of one's gender identity).

gene The basic unit of heredity; the gene is composed of deoxyribonucleic acid (DNA).

general adaptation syndrome (GAS) Hans Selye's theory of how the body responds to stress over time. GAS includes alarm reaction, resistance, and exhaustion.

generalized anxiety disorder Anxiety disorder in which the individual lives in a state of constant severe tension, continuous fear, and apprehension.

genetics The study of heredity; genetics is the science of discovering how traits are passed along generations.

genotype The complete set of genes inherited by an individual from his or her parents.

Gestalt psychology A school of thought that studied whole or complete perceptions.

Gestalt therapy Insight therapy designed to help people become more aware of themselves in the here and now and to take responsibility for their own actions.

grandiose delusion Distortion of reality; one's belief that he or she is extremely important or powerful.

group therapy Treatment of several patients at the same time.

groupthink When group members are so committed to, and optimistic about, the group that they feel it is invulnerable; they become so concerned with maintaining consensus that criticism is muted.

growth The normal quantitative changes that occur in the physical and psychological aspects of a healthy child with the passage of time.

GSR (galvanic skin response) A measure of autonomic nervous system activity; a slight electric current is passed over the skin, and the more nervous a subject is, the easier the current will flow.

hallucinations A sensory impression reported when no external stimulus exists to justify the report; often hallucinations are a symptom of mental illness.

hallucinogens Psychedelic drugs that result in hallucinations at high doses, and other effects on behavior and perception in mild doses.

halo effect The finding that once we form a general impression of someone, we tend to interpret additional information about the person in a consistent manner.

haptic Relating to or based on the sense of touch. Also, a predilection for the sense of touch.

Hawthorne effect The finding that behavior can be influenced just by participation in a research study.

health psychology Field of psychology that studies psychological influences on people's health, including how they stay healthy, why they become ill, and how their behavior relates to their state of health.

heuristic Problem-solving strategy; a person tests solutions most likely to be correct.

hierarchy of needs Abraham Maslow's list of motives in humans, arranged from the biological to the uniquely human.

higher order conditioning Learning to make associations with stimuli that have been learned previously.

hippocampus Brain structure in the limbic system that is important in learning and memory.

homeostasis The state of equilibrium that maintains a balance in the internal body environment.

hormones Chemicals produced by the endocrine glands that regulate activity of certain bodily processes.

humanistic psychology Psychological school of thought that believes that people are unique beings who cannot be broken down into parts.

hyperphagia Disorder in which the individual continues to eat until he or she is obese; can be caused by damage to ventromedial hypothalamus.

hypersomnia Sleep disorder in which an individual falls asleep at inappropriate times; narcolepsy is a form of hypersomnia.

hypnosis Altered state of consciousness characterized by heightened suggestibility.

hypochondriasis Somatoform disorder in which the individual is obsessed with fears of having a serious medical disease.

hypothalamus Part of the brain's limbic system; involved in motivational behaviors, including eating, drinking, and sex.

hypothesis In the scientific method, an educated guess or prediction about future observable events.

iconic memory Visual information that is encoded into the sensory memory store.

id Sigmund Freud's representation of the basic instinctual drives; the id always seeks pleasure.

identification The process in which children adopt the attitudes, values, and behaviors of their parents.

identity diffusion In Marcia's adolescent identity theory, the status of individuals who have failed to make a commitment to values and roles.

illusion An incorrect perception that occurs when sensation is distorted.

imitation The copying of another's behavior; learned through the process of observation.

impression formation Developing an evaluation of another person from your perceptions; first, or initial, impressions are often very important.

imprinting A form of early learning in which birds follow a moving stimulus (often the mother); may be similar to attachment in mammals.

independent variable The condition in an experiment that is controlled and manipulated by the experimenter; it is a stimulus that will cause a response.

indiscriminate attachment phase Stage of attachment in which babies prefer humans to nonhumans, but do not discriminate among individual people.

individuation Carl Jung's concept of the process leading to the unification of all parts of the personality.

inferential statistics Techniques that help researchers make generalizations about a finding based on a limited number of subjects.

inferiority complex Adler's personality concept that states that because children are dependent on adults and cannot meet the standards set for themselves they feel inferior.

inhibition Restraint of an impulse, desire, activity, or drive.

insight A sudden grasping of the means necessary to achieve a goal; important in the Gestalt approach to problem solving.

insight therapy Therapy based on the assumption that behavior is abnormal because people do not adequately understand the motivation causing their behavior.

instinct Highly stereotyped behavior common to all members of a species that often appears in virtually complete form in the absence of any obvious opportunities to learn it.

instrumental conditioning Operant conditioning.

intelligence Capacity to learn and behave adaptively.

intelligence quotient (IQ) An index of a person's performance on an intelligence test relative to others in the culture; ratio of a person's mental age to chronological age.

interference Theory of forgetting in which information that was learned before (proactive interference) or after (retroactive interference) causes the learner to be unable to remember the material of interest.

internal locus of control In Rotter's personality theory, the perception that reinforcement is contingent upon behavior.

interstimulus interval Time interval between two stimuli; in classical conditioning, it is the elapsed time between the CS and the US.

intrinsic motivation Motivation inside the individual; we do something because we receive satisfaction from it.

introspection Method in which a subject gives a self-report of his or her immediate experience.

introversion The personality concept of Carl Jung in which the personal energy of the individual is directed inward; characterized by introspection, seriousness, inhibition, and restraint.

James-Lange theory of emotion Theory of emotion that states that the physiological arousal and behavior come before the subjective experience of an emotion.

just noticeable difference (JND) Difference threshold: minimum amount of energy required to produce a difference in sensation.

kinesthesis The sense of bodily movement.

labeling of arousal Experiments suggest that an individual experiencing physical arousal that cannot be explained will interpret these feelings in terms of the situation she or he is in and will use environmental and contextual cues.

language acquisition device (LAD) Hypothesized biological structure that accounts for the relative ease of acquiring language, according to Noam Chomsky.

latent dream content In Sigmund Freud's dream theory, the true thoughts in the unconsciousness; the true meaning of the dream.

latent learning Learning that occurs when an individual acquires knowledge of something but does not show it until motivated to do so.

law of effect Edward Thorndike's law that if a response produces satisfaction it will be repeated; reinforcement.

learned helplessness Condition in which a person learns that his or her behavior has no effect on his or her environment; when an individual gives up and stops trying.

learned social motives Social motives that are learned; include achievement and affiliation.

learning The relatively permanent change in behavior or behavioral ability of an individual that occurs as a result of experience.

learning styles The preferences students have for learning; theories of learning styles include personality differences, styles of information processing, and instructional preferences.

life instinct (also called Eros) Sigmund Freud's term for an instinct that helps the individual or species survive; sex is the major expression of life instinct.

life structure In Daniel Levinson's theory of adult personality development, the underlying pattern of an individual's life at any particular time; seasonal cycles include preadulthood, early adulthood, middle adulthood, and late adulthood.

linguistic relativity hypothesis Proposal that the perception of reality differs according to the language of the observer.

locus of control Julian Rotter's theory in which a person's beliefs about reinforcement are classified as internal or external.

long-term memory The permanent memory where rehearsed information is stored.

love An emotion characterized by knowing, liking, and becoming intimate with someone.

low-ball procedure The compliance technique of presenting an attractive proposal to someone and then switching it to a more unattractive proposal.

magic number 7 The finding that most people can remember about seven items of information for a short time (in short-term memory).

magnetic resonance imaging (MRI) A method of studying brain activity using magnetic field imaging.

major depressive disorder Severe mood disorder in which a person experiences one or more major depressive episodes; sometimes referred to simply as depression.

maladjustment Condition that occurs when a person utilizes inappropriate abilities to respond to demands placed upon him or her.

manic depressive reaction A form of mental illness marked by alternations of extreme phases of elation (manic phase) and depression.

manifest dream content In Sigmund Freud's dream theory, what a person remembers about a dream upon waking; a disguised representation of the unconscious wishes.

massed practice Learning as much material as possible in long continuous stretches.

maturation The genetically controlled process of growth that results in orderly changes in behavior.

mean The arithmetic average, in which the sum of scores is divided by the number of scores.

median The middle score in a group of scores that are arranged from lowest to highest.

meditation The practice of some form of relaxed concentration while ignoring other sensory stimuli.

memory The process of storing information so that it can be retrieved and used later.

memory attributes The critical features of an event that are used when the experience is encoded or retrieved.

mental age The age level on which a person is capable of performing; used in determining intelligence.

mental set Condition in which a person's thinking becomes so standardized that he or she approaches new problems in fixed ways.

Minnesota Multiphasic Personality Inventory (MMPI-2) An objective personality test that was originally devised to identify personality disorders.

mnemonic technique Method of improving memory by combining and relating chunks of information.

modeling A process of learning by imitation in a therapeutic situation.

mood disorder Psychological disorder in which a person experiences a severe disruption in mood or emotional balance.

moral development Development of individuals as they adopt their society's standards of right and wrong; development of awareness of ethical behavior.

motivated forgetting (repression) Theory that suggests that people want to forget unpleasant events.

motivation The forces that initiate and direct behavior, and the variables that determine the intensity and persistence of the behavior.

motivator needs In Federick Herzberg's theory, the factors that lead to job satisfaction; they include responsibility, the nature of the work, advancement, and recognition.

motive Anything that arouses the individual and directs his or her behavior toward some goal. Three categories of motives include biological, stimulus, and learned social.

Müller-Lyer illusion A well-known illusion, in which two horizontal lines have end lines either going in or out; the line with the end lines going in appears longer.

multiple approach-avoidance conflict Conflict that occurs when an individual has two or more goals, both of which have positive and negative aspects.

multiple attachment phase Later attachment stage in which the baby begins to form attachments to people other than the primary caretaker.

multiple intelligences Howard Gardner's theory that there exists several different kinds of intelligence.

Myers-Briggs Type Indicator (MBTI) Objective personality test based on Carl Jung's type theory.

narcotic analgesics Drugs that have an effect on the body similar to morphine; these relieve pain and suppress coughing.

naturalistic observation Research method in which behavior of people or animals in their normal environment is accurately recorded.

Necker cube A visual illusion. The Necker cube is a drawing of a cube designed so that it is difficult to determine which side is toward you.

negative reinforcement Removing something unpleasant to increase the probability that the preceding behavior will be repeated.

NEO Personality Inventory (NEO-PI) An objective personality test developed by Paul Costa Jr. and Robert McCrae to measure the five major factors in personality; consists of 181 questions.

neodissociation theory Idea that consciousness can be split into several streams of thought that are partially independent of each other.

neuron A specialized cell that functions to conduct messages throughout the body.

neurosis A Freudian term that was used to describe abnormal behavior caused by anxiety; it has been eliminated from *DSM-IV*.

neutral stimulus A stimulus that does not cause the response of interest; the individual may show some response to the stimulus but not the associated behavior.

norm A sample of scores representative of a population.

normal curve When scores of a large number of random cases are plotted on a graph, they often fall into a bell-shaped curve; as many cases on the curve are above the mean as below it.

observational learning In social learning theory, learning by observing someone else behave; people observe and imitate in learning socialization.

obsessions Fears that involve the inability to control impulses.

obsessive compulsive disorder Anxiety disorder in which the individual has repetitive thoughts (obsessions) that lead to constant urges (compulsions) to engage in meaningless rituals.

object permanence The ability to realize that objects continue to exist even if we can no longer see them.

Oedipus complex The Freudian idea that the young boy has sexual feelings for his mother and is jealous of his father and must identify with his father to resolve the conflict.

olfaction The smell sense.

openness The dimension in the five-factor personality theory that includes traits such as imagination, creativity, perception, knowledge, artistic ability, curiosity, and analytical ability; also called culture or intellect.

operant conditioning Form of learning in which behavior followed by reinforcement (satisfaction) increases in frequency.

opponent-process theory Theory that when one emotion is experienced, the other is suppressed.

optimum level of arousal Motivation theory that states that the individual will seek a level of arousal that is comfortable.

organic mental disorders Psychological disorders that involve physical damage to the nervous system; can be caused by disease or by an accident.

organizational psychology Area of industrial psychology that focuses on worker attitudes and motivation; derived primarily from personality and social psychology.

orgasm The climax of intense sexual excitement; release from building sexual tension, usually accompanied by ejaculation in men.

paired-associate learning A verbal learning procedure in which the subject is presented with a series of pairs of items to be remembered.

panic disorder Anxiety disorder characterized by the occurrence of specific periods of intense fear.

paranoid schizophrenia A type of schizophrenia in which the individual often has delusions of grandeur and persecution, thinking that someone is out to get him or her.

partial reinforcement Any schedule of reinforcement in which reinforcement follows only some of the correct responses.

partial reinforcement effect The finding that partial reinforcement produces a response that takes longer to extinguish than continuous reinforcement.

pattern recognition Memory process in which information attended to is compared with information already permanently stored in memory.

Pavlovian conditioning A bond or association between a neutral stimulus and a response; this type of learning is called classical conditioning.

perception The active process in which the sensory information that is carried through the nervous system to the brain is organized and interpreted; the interpretation of sensation.

persecutory delusion A delusion in which the individual has a distortion of reality; the belief that other people are out to get one.

person perception The process of using the information we gather in forming impressions of people to make evaluations of others.

personal unconscious Carl Jung's representation of the individual's repressed thoughts and memories.

personality disorder Psychological disorder in which there are problems in the basic personality structure of the individual.

phantom-limb pain Phenomenon in which people who have lost an arm or leg feel pain in the missing limb.

phobias Acute excessive fears of specific situations or objects that have no convincing basis in reality.

physiological needs First level of motives in Abraham Maslow's hierarchy; includes the biological needs of hunger, thirst, sex, exercise, and rest.

placebo An inert or inactive substance given to control subjects to test for bias effects.

plateau phase Second phase in the human sexual response cycle, during which the physiological arousal becomes more intense.

pleasure principle In Freudian theory, the idea that the instinctual drives of the id unconsciously and impulsively seek immediate pleasure.

positive reinforcement Presenting a subject something pleasant to increase the probability that the preceding behavior will be repeated.

postconventional morality Level III in Lawrence Kohlberg's theory, in which moral reasoning is based on personal standards and beliefs; highest level of moral thinking.

posttraumatic stress disorder (PTSD) Condition that can occur when a person experiences a severely distressing event; characterized by constant memories of the event, avoidance of anything associated with it, and general arousal.

Prägnanz (law of) Gestalt psychology law that states that people have a tendency to group stimuli according to rules, and that people do this whenever possible.

preconscious mind In Sigmund Freud's psychoanalytic theory of personality, the part of personality that contains information that we have learned but that we are not thinking about at the present time.

preconventional morality Level I of Lawrence Kohlberg's theory, in which moral reasoning is largely due to the expectation of rewards and punishments.

prejudice An unjustified fixed, usually negative, way of thinking about a person or object.

Premack principle Principle that states that, of any two responses, the one that is more likely to occur can be used to reinforce the response that is less likely to occur.

preoperational thought period Period in cognitive development; from two to seven years, the period during which the child learns to represent the environment with objects and symbols.

primacy effect Phenomenon where items are remembered because they come at the beginning of a list.

primary appraisal Activity of determining whether a new stimulus event is positive, neutral, or negative; first step in appraisal of stress.

primary narcissism A Freudian term that refers to the oral phase before the ego has developed; the individual constantly seeks pleasure.

primary reinforcement Reinforcement that is effective without having been associated with other reinforcers; sometimes called unconditioned reinforcement.

probability (p) In inferential statistics, the likelihood that the difference between the experimental and control groups is due to the independent variable.

procedural memory The most basic type of long-term memory; involves the formation of associations between stimuli and responses.

projection Defense mechanism in which a person attributes his or her unacceptable characteristics or motives to others rather than himself or herself.

projective personality test A personality test that presents ambiguous stimuli to which subjects are expected to respond with projections of their own personality.

proximity Closeness in time and space. In perception, it is the Gestalt perceptual principle in which stimuli next to one another are included together.

psyche According to Carl Jung, the thoughts and feelings (conscious and unconscious) of an individual.

psychoactive drug A drug that produces changes in behavior and cognition through modification of conscious awareness.

psychoanalysis The school of thought founded by Sigmund Freud that stressed unconscious motivation. In therapy, a patient's unconscious motivation is intensively explored in order to bring repressed conflicts up to consciousness; psychoanalysis usually takes a long time to accomplish.

psychobiology (also called biological psychology or physiological psychology) The subfield of experimental psychology concerned with the influence of heredity and the biological response systems on behavior.

psychogenic amnesia A dissociative disorder in which an individual loses his or her sense of identity.

psychogenic fugue A dissociative disorder in which an individual loses his or her sense of identity and goes to a new geographic location, forgetting all of the unpleasant emotions connected with the old life.

psychographics A technique used in consumer psychology to identify the attitudes of buyers and their preferences for particular products.

psycholinguistics The psychological study of how people convert the sounds of a language into meaningful symbols that can be used to communicate with others.

psychological dependence Situation in which a person craves a drug even though it is not biologically needed by the body.

psychological disorder A diagnosis of abnormal behavior; syndrome of abnormal adjustment, classified in *DSM*.

psychological types Carl Jung's term for different personality profiles; Jung combined two attitudes and four functions to produce eight psychological types.

psychopharmacology Study of effects of psychoactive drugs on behavior.

psychophysics An area of psychology in which researchers compare the physical energy of a stimulus with the sensation reported.

psychosexual stages Sigmund Freud's theoretical stages in personality development.

psychosomatic disorders A variety of body reactions that are closely related to psychological events.

psychotherapy Treatment of behavioral disorders through psychological techniques; major psychotherapies include insight therapy, behavior therapy, and group therapy.

psychotic disorders The more severe categories of abnormal behavior.

puberty Sexual maturation; the time at which the individual is able to perform sexually and to reproduce.

punishment Any event that decreases the likelihood that the behavior preceding it will be repeated.

quantitative trait loci (QTLs) Genes that collectively contribute to a trait for high intelligence.

rational-emotive therapy A cognitive behavior modification technique in which a person is taught to identify irrational, self-defeating beliefs and then to overcome them.

reaction formation Defense mechanism in which a person masks an unconsciously distressing or unacceptable trait by assuming an opposite attitude or behavior pattern.

reality principle In Freudian theory, the idea that the drives of the ego try to find socially acceptable ways to gratify the id.

reciprocal determinism The concept proposed by Albert Bandura that the behavior, the individual, and the situation interact and influence each other.

reciprocal inhibition Concept of Joseph Wolpe that states that it is possible to break the bond between anxiety-provoking stimuli and responses manifesting anxiety by facing those stimuli in a state antagonistic to anxiety.

reflex An automatic movement that occurs in direct response to a stimulus.

regression Defense mechanism in which a person retreats to an earlier, more immature form of behavior.

reinforcement Any event that increases the probability that the behavior that precedes it will be repeated; also called a reinforcer; similar to a reward.

reinforcement therapy A behavior therapy in which reinforcement is used to modify behavior. Techniques in reinforcement therapy include shaping, extinction, and token economy.

releaser (sign stimulus) Specific environmental cues that stimulate a stereotyped behavior to occur; releasers cause fixed action patterns.

repression Defense mechanism in which painful memories and unacceptable thoughts and motives are conveniently forgotten so that they will not have to be dealt with.

residual schizophrenia Type of schizophrenia in which the individual currently does not have symptoms but has had a schizophrenic episode in the past.

resistance Psychoanalytic term used when a patient avoids a painful area of conflict.

resolution phase The last phase in the human sexual response cycle; the time after orgasm that the body gradually returns to the unaroused state.

Restricted Environmental Stimulation Technique (REST) Research technique in which environmental stimuli available to an individual are reduced drastically; formerly called sensory deprivation.

retroactive interference Interference caused by information learned after the material of interest.

retrograde amnesia Forgetting information recently learned because of a disruptive stimulus such as an electric shock.

reversible figure In perception, a situation in which the figure and ground seem to reverse themselves; an illusion in which objects alternate as the main figure.

risky-shift The tendency for groups to make riskier decisions than individuals.

Rorschach Inkblot Test A projective personality test in which subjects are asked to discuss what they see in cards containing blots of ink.

safety needs Second level of motives in Abraham Maslow's hierarchy; includes security, stability, dependency, protection, freedom from fear and anxiety, and the need for structure and order.

Schachter-Singer theory of emotion Theory of emotion that states that we interpret our arousal according to our environment and label our emotions accordingly.

scheme A unit of knowledge that the person possesses; used in Jean Piaget's cognitive development theory.

schizophrenia Severe psychotic disorder that is characterized by disruptions in thinking, perception, and emotion.

scientific method An attitude and procedure that scientists use to conduct research. The steps include stating the problem, forming the hypothesis, collecting the information, evaluating the information, and drawing conclusions.

secondary appraisal In appraisal of stress, this is the evaluation that an individual's abilities and resources are sufficient to meet the demands of a stressful event.

secondary reinforcement Reinforcement that is effective only after it has been associated with a primary reinforcer; also called conditioned reinforcement.

secondary traits In Gordon Allport's personality theory, the less important situation-specific traits that help round out personality; they include attitudes, skills, and behavior patterns.

secure attachment Type of infant-parent attachment in which the infant actively seeks contact with the parent.

self-actualization A humanistic term describing the state in which all of an individual's capacities are developed fully. Fifth and highest level of motives in Abraham Maslow's hierarchy; this level, the realization of one's potential, is rarely reached.

self-efficacy An individual's sense of self-worth and success in adjusting to the world.

self-evaluation maintenance model (SEM) Tesser's theory of how we maintain a positive self-image despite the success of others close to us.

self-handicapping strategy A strategy that people use to prepare for failure; people behave in ways that produce obstacles to success so that when they do fail they can place the blame on the obstacle.

self-serving bias An attribution bias in which an individual attributes success to his or her own behavior but failure to external environmental causes.

semantic memory Type of long-term memory that can use cognitive activities, such as everyday knowledge.

sensation The passive process in which stimuli are received by sense receptors and transformed into neural impulses that can be carried through the nervous system; first stage in becoming aware of environment.

sensitivity training group (T-group) Therapy group that has the goal of making participants more aware of themselves and their ideas.

sensorimotor period Period in cognitive development; first two years, during which the infant learns to coordinate sensory experiences with motor activities.

sensory adaptation Tendency of the sense organs to adjust to continuous stimulation by reducing their functioning; a stimulus that once caused sensation and no longer does.

sensory deprivation Situation in which normal environmental sensory stimuli available to an individual are reduced drastically; also called REST (Restricted Environmental Stimulation Technique).

serial learning A verbal learning procedure in which the stimuli are always presented in the same order, and the subject has to learn them in the order in which they are presented.

sex roles The set of behaviors and attitudes that are determined to be appropriate for one sex or the other in a society.

shaping In operant conditioning, the gradual process of reinforcing behaviors that get closer to some final desired behavior. Shaping is also called successive approximation.

signal detection theory Research approach in which the subject's behavior in detecting a threshold is treated as a form of decision making.

similarity Gestalt principle in which similar stimuli are perceived as a unit.

simple phobia Excessive irrational fear that does not fall into other specific categories, such as fear of dogs, insects, snakes, or closed-in places.

simultaneous conditioning A procedure in classical conditioning in which the CS and US are presented at exactly the same time.

Sixteen Personality Factor Questionnaire (16PF) Raymond Cattell's personality test to measure source traits.

Skinner box B. F. Skinner's animal cage with a lever that triggers reinforcement for a subject.

sleep terror disorder (pavor nocturnus) Nonrapid-eye-movement (NREM) sleep disorder in which the person (usually a child) wakes up screaming and terrified, but cannot recall why.

sleepwalking (somnambulism) NREM sleep disorder in which the person walks in his or her sleep.

social cognition The process of understanding other people and ourselves by forming and utilizing information about the social world.

social cognitive theory Albert Bandura's approach to personality that proposes that individuals use observation, imitation, and cognition to develop personality.

social comparison Theory proposed by Leon Festinger that we tend to compare our behavior to others to ensure that we are conforming.

social exchange theory Theory of interpersonal relationships that states that people evaluate the costs and rewards of their relationships and act accordingly.

social facilitation Phenomenon in which the presence of others increases dominant behavior patterns in an individual; Richard Zajonc's theory states that the presence of others enhances the emission of the dominant response of the individual.

social influence Influence designed to change the attitudes or behavior of other people; includes conformity, compliance, and obedience.

social learning theory An approach to social psychology that emphasizes observation and modeling; states that reinforcement is involved in motivation rather than in learning, and proposes that aggression is a form of learned behavior.

social phobia Excessive irrational fear and embarrassment when interacting with other people. Social phobias may include fear of assertive behavior, fear of making mistakes, or fear of public speaking.

social psychology The study of how an individual's behavior, thoughts, and feelings are influenced by other people.

sociobiology Study of the genetic basis of social behavior.

sociocultural Emphasizes the importance of culture, gender, and ethnicity in how we think, feel, and act.

somatic nervous system The part of the peripheral nervous system that carries messages from the sense organs and relays information that directs the voluntary movements of the skeletal muscles.

somatization disorder Somatoform disorder in which a person has medical complaints without physical cause.

somatoform disorders Psychological disorders characterized by physical symptoms for which there are no obvious physical causes.

specific attachment phase Stage at about six months of age, in which the baby becomes attached to a specific person.

split-brain research Popular name for Roger Sperry's research on the syndrome of hemisphere deconnection; research on individuals with the corpus callosum severed. Normal functioning breaks down in split-brain subjects when different information is presented to each hemisphere.

SQ5R A technique to improve learning and memory. Components include survey, question, read, record, recite, review, and reflect.

stage of exhaustion Third stage in Hans Selye's general adaptation syndrome. As the body continues to resist stress, it depletes its energy resources and the person becomes exhausted.

stage of resistance Second stage in Hans Selye's general adaptation syndrome. When stress is prolonged, the body builds some resistance to the effects of stress.

standardization The process of obtaining a representative sample of scores in the population so that a particular score can be interpreted correctly.

Stanford-Binet Intelligence Scale An intelligence test first revised by Lewis Terman at Stanford University in 1916; still a popular test used today.

state-dependent learning Situation in which what is learned in one state can only be remembered when the person is in that state of mind.

statistically significant In inferential statistics, a finding that the independent variable did influence greatly the outcome of the experimental and control group.

stereotype An exaggerated and rigid mental image of a particular class of persons or objects.

stimulus A unit of the environment that causes a response in an individual; a physical or chemical agent acting on an appropriate sense receptor.

stimulus discrimination Responding to relevant stimuli.

stimulus generalization Responding to stimuli similar to the stimulus that had caused the response.

stimulus motives Motivating factors that are internal and unlearned, but do not appear to have a physiological basis; stimulus motives cause an individual to seek out sensory stimulation through interaction with the environment.

stimulus trace The perceptual persistence of a stimulus after it is no longer present.

strange situation procedure A measure of attachment developed by Mary Ainsworth that consists of eight phases during which the infant is increasingly stressed.

stress Anything that produces demands on us to adjust and threatens our well-being.

Strong Interest Inventory An objective personality test that compares people's personalities to groups that achieve success in certain occupations.

structuralism First school of thought in psychology; studied conscious experience to discover the structure of the mind.

subject bias Source of potential error in an experiment from the action or expectancy of a subject; a subject might influence the experimental results in ways that mask the true outcome.

subjective organization Long-term memory procedures in which the individual provides a personal method of organizing information to be memorized.

sublimation Defense mechanism; a person redirects his or her socially undesirable urges into socially acceptable behavior.

successive approximation Shaping; in operant conditioning, the gradual process of reinforcing behaviors that get closer to some final desired behavior.

sudden infant death syndrome (SIDS) Situation in which a seemingly healthy infant dies suddenly in its sleep; also called crib death.

superego Sigmund Freud's representation of conscience.

surface traits In Raymond Cattell's personality theory, the observable characteristics of a person's behavior and personality.

symbolization In Sigmund Freud's dream theory, the process of converting the latent content of a dream into manifest symbols.

systematic desensitization Application of counterconditioning, in which the individual overcomes anxiety by learning to relax in the presence of stimuli that had once made him or her unbearably nervous.

task-oriented coping Adjustment responses in which the person evaluates a stressful situation objectively and then formulates a plan with which to solve the problem.

test of significance An inferential statistical technique used to determine whether the difference in scores between the experimental and control groups is really due to the effects of the independent variable or to random chance. If the probability of an outcome is extremely low, we say that outcome is significant.

Thanatos Sigmund Freud's term for a destructive instinct such as aggression; also called death instinct.

Thematic Apperception Test (TAT) Projective personality test in which subjects are shown pictures of people in everyday settings; subjects must make up a story about the people portrayed.

theory of social impact Latané's theory of social behavior; it states that each member of a group shares the responsibility equally.

Theory X Douglas McGregor's theory that states that the worker dislikes work and must be forced to do it.

Theory Y Douglas McGregor's theory that states that work is natural and can be a source of satisfaction, and, when it is, the worker can be highly committed and motivated.

therapy In psychology, the treatment of behavior problems; two major types of therapy include psychotherapy and biological therapy.

time and motion studies In engineering psychology, studies that analyze the time it takes to perform an action and the movements that go into the action.

tip-of-the-tongue phenomenon A phenomenon in which the closer a person comes to recalling something, the more accurately he or she can remember details, such as the number of syllables or letters.

token economy A behavior therapy in which desired behaviors are reinforced immediately with tokens that can be exchanged at a later time for desired rewards, such as food or recreational privileges.

trace conditioning A procedure in classical conditioning in which the CS is a discrete event that is presented and terminated before the US is presented.

trait A distinctive and stable attribute in people.

trait anxiety Anxiety that is long-lasting; a relatively stable personality characteristic.

transference Psychoanalytic term used when a patient projects his feelings onto the therapist.

transsexualism A condition in which a person feels trapped in the body of the wrong sex.

trial and error learning Trying various behaviors in a situation until the solution is found.

triangular theory of love Robert Sternberg's theory that states that love consists of intimacy, passion, and decision/commitment.

triarchic theory of intelligence Robert Sternberg's theory of intelligence that states that it consists of three parts: componential, experiential, and contextual subtheories.

Type-A behavior Behavior shown by a particular type of individual; a personality pattern of behavior that can lead to stress and heart disease.

unconditional positive regard Part of Carl Rogers's personality theory; occurs when we accept someone regardless of what he or she does or says.

unconditioned response (UR) An automatic reaction elicited by a stimulus.

unconditioned stimulus (US) Any stimulus that elicits an automatic or reflexive reaction in an individual; it does not have to be learned in the present situation.

unconscious mind In Sigmund Freud's psychoanalytic theory of personality, the part of personality that is unavailable to us; Freud suggests that instincts and unpleasant memories are stored in the unconscious mind.

undifferentiated schizophrenia Type of schizophrenia that does not fit into any particular category, or fits into more than one category.

validity The degree to which you actually measure what you intend to measure.

variability In statistics, variability measures the range of the scores.

variable interval (VI) schedule Schedule of reinforcement in which the subject is reinforced for the first response given after a certain time interval, with the interval being different for each trial.

variable ratio (VR) schedule Schedule of reinforcement in which the subject is given reinforcement after a varying number of responses; the number of responses required for reinforcement is different for every trial.

vestibular sense Sense that helps keep our balance.

visuo-spatial sketch pad Responsible for visual images involved in geographical orientation and spatial task.

vulnerability-stress model Theory of schizophrenia that states that some people have a biological tendency to develop schizophrenia if they are stressed enough by their environment.

Weber's Law Ernst Weber's law that states that the difference threshold depends on the ratio of the intensity of one stimulus to another rather than on an absolute difference.

Wechsler Adult Intelligence Scale (WAIS) An intelligence test for adults, first published by David Wechsler in 1955; it contains verbal and performance subscales.

Wechsler Intelligence Scale for Children (WISC-III) Similar to the Wechsler Adult Intelligence Scale, except that it is designed for children ages 6 through 16, and helps diag-nose certain childhood disorders, such as dyslexia and other learning disabilities.

Wechsler Preschool and Primary Scale of Intelligence (WPPSI-R) Designed for children between the ages of 4 and 7; helps diagnose certain childhood disorders, such as dyslexia and other learning disabilities.

withdrawal Unpleasant physical reactions that a drug-dependent user experiences when he or she stops taking the drug.

within-subject experiment An experimental design in which each subject is given all treatments, including the control condition; subjects serve in both experimental and control groups.

working memory The memory store, with a capacity of about 7 items and enduring for up to 30 seconds, that handles current information.

Yerkes-Dodson Law Popular idea that performance is best when arousal is at a medium level.

Sources for the Glossary:
The majority of terms in this glossary are from *Psychology: A ConnecText*, 4th Edition, Terry F. Pettijohn. © 1999 McGraw-Hill/Dushkin, Guilford, CT 06437. The remaining terms were developed by the *Annual Editions* staff.

Test Your Knowledge Form

We encourage you to photocopy and use this page as a tool to assess how the articles in **Annual Editions** expand on the information in your textbook. By reflecting on the articles you will gain enhanced text information. You can also access this useful form on a product's book support Web site at **http://www.dushkin.com/online/.**

NAME: _____ DATE: _____

TITLE AND NUMBER OF ARTICLE: _____

BRIEFLY STATE THE MAIN IDEA OF THIS ARTICLE: _____

LIST THREE IMPORTANT FACTS THAT THE AUTHOR USES TO SUPPORT THE MAIN IDEA:

_____

WHAT INFORMATION OR IDEAS DISCUSSED IN THIS ARTICLE ARE ALSO DISCUSSED IN YOUR TEXTBOOK OR OTHER READINGS THAT YOU HAVE DONE? LIST THE TEXTBOOK CHAPTERS AND PAGE NUMBERS:

_____

LIST ANY EXAMPLES OF BIAS OR FAULTY REASONING THAT YOU FOUND IN THE ARTICLE:

_____

LIST ANY NEW TERMS/CONCEPTS THAT WERE DISCUSSED IN THE ARTICLE, AND WRITE A SHORT DEFINITION:

_____

ANNUAL EDITIONS revisions depend on two major opinion sources: one is our Advisory Board, listed in the front of this volume, which works with us in scanning the thousands of articles published in the public press each year; the other is you—the person actually using the book. Please help us and the users of the next edition by completing the prepaid article rating form on this page and returning it to us. Thank you for your help!

ANNUAL EDITIONS: Personal Growth and Behavior 01/02

ARTICLE RATING FORM

Here is an opportunity for you to have direct input into the next revision of this volume. We would like you to rate each of the 48 articles listed below, using the following scale:

1. **Excellent: should definitely be retained**
2. **Above average: should probably be retained**
3. **Below average: should probably be deleted**
4. **Poor: should definitely be deleted**

Your ratings will play a vital part in the next revision. So please mail this prepaid form to us just as soon as you complete it. Thanks for your help!

We Want Your Advice

RATING

ARTICLE

1. A Dance to the Music of the Century: Changing Fashions in 20th–Century Psychiatry
2. The Last Interview of Abraham Maslow
3. Psychoanalyst: Sigmund Freud
4. Private Lives: Discipline and Knowing Where to Draw the Line
5. The Stability of Personality: Observations and Evaluations
6. How Culture Molds Habits of Thought
7. Human Nature: Born or Made?
8. The Gender Blur
9. The Personality Genes
10. Decoding the Human Body
11. Autism Is Likely to Be Linked to Several Genes
12. The Future of the Brain
13. The Biology of Joy
14. The Tick-Tock of the Biological Clock
15. The Gold Medal Mind
16. Faith & Healing
17. The Seven Stages of Man
18. Fetal Psychology
19. Four Things You Need to Know About Raising Baby
20. Why Children Turn Out the Way They Do
21. Invincible Kids
22. A World of Their Own
23. How Well Do You Know Your Kid?

RATING

ARTICLE

24. The Road Ahead: A Boomer's Guide to Happiness
25. Live to 100? No Thanks
26. Start the Conversation
27. Friendships and Adaptation Across the Life Span
28. Emotional Intelligence: Do You Have It?
29. Shyness: The New Solution
30. What's in a Face?
31. How to Spot a Liar
32. Revealing Personal Secrets
33. Discover the Power of Forgiveness
34. Welcome to the Love Lab
35. Prescription for Passion
36. Coping With Crowding
37. The Teening of Childhood
38. The Betrayal of the American Man
39. Where Bias Begins: The Truth About Stereotypes
40. The Lure of the Cult
41. Work, Work, Work, Work!
42. Don't Face Stress Alone
43. What You Can Change & What You Cannot Change
44. Think Like a Shrink
45. Bad Choices: Why We Make Them, How to Stop
46. Chronic Anxiety: How to Stop Living on the Edge
47. The Science of Women & Sex
48. Mind Over Medicine

(Continued on next page)

ABOUT YOU

Name _____   Date _____

Are you a teacher? ☐ A student? ☐

Your school's name _____

Department _____

Address _____   City _____   State _____ Zip _____

School telephone # _____

YOUR COMMENTS ARE IMPORTANT TO US !

Please fill in the following information:
For which course did you use this book?
_____

Did you use a text with this *ANNUAL EDITION*? ☐ yes ☐ no
What was the title of the text?
_____

What are your general reactions to the *Annual Editions* concept?
_____

Have you read any particular articles recently that you think should be included in the next edition?
_____

Are there any articles you feel should be replaced in the next edition? Why?
_____

Are there any World Wide Web sites you feel should be included in the next edition? Please annotate.
_____

May we contact you for editorial input? ☐ yes ☐ no
May we quote your comments? ☐ yes ☐ no

To our honored ancestors,
Who first used these words
And preserved them
To our care. . .

"To you [who follow] . . . we throw
The torch; be yours to hold it high."

John McCrae

Credits

Art Director: Dennis McCarthy

Co-authors: Mary Colgan McNamara
               Dorothy M. Colgan
               Betsy Johnson
               Laura Nanni

Design and Production: Mary Fran Zidron

Editor: Dennis McCarthy

Illustration: Bryan Hendrix

This **WordBook** was electronically produced using Apple Macintosh
equipment, Quark XPress, Adobe Illustrator and Adobe Photoshop
software. The typefaces used are from the Garamond, Mead and Stone
families. The cover stock is 10 pt. Francote and the text stock is
50# Spectra Offset Georgia Pacific.

Contents

In a Word Icons

Chameleon Letters . .

are letters in any word part that change or drop out when they combine with another word part, mainly for pronunciation. The most common examples in **WordBook I** involve prefixes that change their final letter when attaching to a root. For example, AD changes to AT when combining with roots starting with T. Hence, AD + TRACT = ATTRACT. D is considered the **chameleon letter** because it is the one that changes. Prefixes ending in consonants change most often. See Page 24.

Intensives . . .

are prefixes that heighten the meaning of the root to which they attach. See page 25.

Memory Jogger . . .

the little brain with jogging shoes, is used as a printing bullet in important summary material. Far more than clever and enjoyable cartoons, every illustration in this series serves as a mnemonic **(memory jogger)** at some level, a visual image of the word's derivation. On occasion they contain subtle puns and other forms of wordplay. Moreover, each root in the series is introduced by a mnemonic image of the entire word family.

TeacherTips . . .

give clarification and expansion of ideas to study leaders, be they teachers, parents, or older students. Collectively, they serve as a readily accessible manual-within-the-text, something that the most inquisitive students can profit from as well.

SideSpinners . . .

allow Webster, the spinning spider, to take fascinating little detours into words with unusual or interesting stories.

Dictionary . . .

appears whenever students might need to consult some reference book beyond this **WordBook**.

Psst!

is the multi-purpose icon that gives specific suggestions, reminders, cautions, foreshadowings. It functions almost as a mentor at a student's elbow who can whisper timely help into his or her ear.

WebStretchers . . .

provide enrichment, challenge, optional extra-credit sections for eager and excited students. The material is considerably harder and not meant as required classwork. In fact, we urge teachers not to hold students rigorously accountable for any material in this **WordBook**. Let it soak in gradually and give its cumulative rewards after students have learned to take delight in words.

Interdisciplinary . . .

signals material that relates to other curriculum areas. We want students to know that these words are not exclusive to a vocabulary text or class but can aid them in all aspects of their studies and their lives.

Interaction Level . . .

offers a suggested level of student response to material. Three levels are possible: think, indicated by the thought bubble, speak, by the word bubble, and write/do, by the stubby pencil. The arrow points to the **interaction level** anticipated by the authors. Individual teachers, of course, may choose another **interaction level** when more suitable to a particular class or situation. Where student response level is clear, as for instance when response lines are provided for writing, this icon is usually not used.

Quizzicals . . .

bring each root to a whimsical conclusion. Our motto: **Instead of a quiz, a quizzical** reinforces our hope that students learn this material through love rather than fear, through humor and playfulness rather than brain-antagonistic attempts at memorization, especially for the TEST at the end of a lesson.

pandemonium apteryx arabesque
mosaic whereabouts
oolong hiatus somersault
existential cyclops paraphernalia
gnu catamaran
gesticulate portfolio
hurlyburly shenanigans
morpheme affinity
defunct doldrums
pseudonym
apogee espalier
zephyr gargantuan
oboe prolyx rapier
samara ruminate

Do you have any idea

how many words there are

in the English language

Hi! I'm Wordsworth Worm and I'm here to help you get your Word's Worth out of every word you meet.

So, to start with, just how many English words are there anyway? At last count, 700,000 and growing! Most vocabulary programs present about 500 to 600 new words a year. At that rate, it would take nearly one thousand, four hundred years of sheer memorization to learn them all. That memorization method makes for a very overburdened brain. A sad brain. A bewildered brain.

Instead I'm going to show you what brains do best: **Patterns**. That's it. Just that simple.

Brains love patterns the way eyes love color and stomachs love food. They see patterns that are already there and make new ones. All the time. Brains find patterns of space, sound, silence, patterns of number, color, and motion. From these patterns, the human brain creates wonders of math, music, physics, art . . .

 Look around your classroom right now or out the window. What kind of patterns can you see, hear, touch? Talk with your teacher and classmates about those patterns.

Language, of course, is one of the most advanced, complicated, and important patterns within the brain. Think for a moment of the kinds of patterns words have – patterns of sound like rhymes and tongue twisters, patterns of spelling like I before E except after C.

In this book, you'll learn special kinds of word patterns, **patterns of meaning**. Words can be related to each other because they share the same meaning parts. You could say that words sharing meaning parts belong to the same word family.

Maybe you've never thought about it before, but words are a lot like people. Most of them live in families. Very few live alone. Words even have ancestors! In fact, that's the reason for this book.

Families are made special and different from other families by the things they have in common. Family members often share the same values, memories, special traditions, even physical characteristics, such as height, hair color or freckles.

Many families have a crest or coat of arms to show the family history and heritage. Whatever kind of family you have, you share some of your history with them.

 In the outline, design a crest for your family. Draw several pictures representing what makes your family special or what you like best about your family. Later you may wish to tell your friends what your crest says about your family and its history.

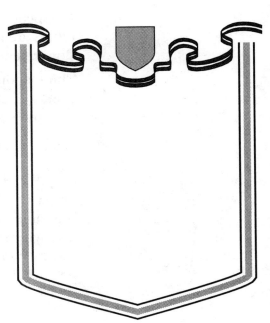

Word families have things in common too. Words may sound or look alike, share meaning parts, or be descended from the same ancestor.

Words are like people in other ways. Did you know that new words are being born every day? Stop and think for a moment about words that didn't exist when your great-grandparents were children. Did they make their oatmeal in a microwave? Did they watch cartoons on television?

Microwave and television are new words that represent twentieth century inventions. Can you name two other words that didn't exist sixty or more years ago?

_____   _____

Think about what might cause new words to be born and where this could be happening. What is the newest English word that you and your friends know?

_____

Where do you think you'd be most likely to find brand new words: in the newspaper, a magazine, a dictionary, or an encyclopedia? Why?

Like people, words die too. Some become unfashionable; others are replaced by better words. Words often die slowly, generally from lack of use.

Think about these four words: **trousers, slacks, pants, jeans.** Each represents an item of clothing that has two legs and covers you from your hips to your ankles.

Which word sounds the most outdated? _____

Which sounds the newest? _____

Other words such as **breeches** and **hiphuggers** describe the same piece of clothing. Breeches were worn long ago, whereas hiphuggers have only been around since the sixties. One word may soon die and the other was born recently.

Can you or your teachers and parents think of any words that have died? Where might you find these words?
Discuss your thoughts with a classmate or friend.

TeacherTip

Some children may never have seen a family tree. You may want to show an example from an encyclopedia or history book or draw a simple one on the board.

Words resemble families in one more important way. Have you ever seen a family tree? It is a written account of all members of a certain family, starting with the founders and branching out as children are born, marry, and have children of their own.

Words can be grouped together in the same way. The founder or ancestor of a word family is a meaning part, and it branches out to include related words. Rather than build word families on trees, we're going to build them on webs.

For that, you'll have to meet my friend **WEBSTER**. She is a spinner, a weaver of words.

She finds word families by looking at meaning parts like **ROOTS, PREFIXES** and **SUFFIXES**. **ROOTS** are the main meaning parts of words. **PREFIXES** are meaning parts attached to the beginnings of words. **SUFFIXES** are meaning parts added at the end of words. **ROOTS, PREFIXES** and **SUFFIXES** are the smallest possible meaning pieces in any language, but they are called by a whopper name: **MORPHEMES**.

DID YOU KNOW THAT WEBSTER ONCE MEANT WEAVER OF CLOTH?

Webster and I call them **MORPHS** for short.

When she finds words that share morphs, she weaves them into webs. Many of her webs pattern dozens of words. Some of the bigger webs pattern hundreds of words. Just imagine how much happier that makes your brain than the one-at-a-time memorization method!

MORPHS: THE SMALLEST POSSIBLE MEANING PIECES IN A LANGUAGE

Weaving Your First WordWeb

Ready to experiment with a WordWeb? See what Webster is riding? A unicycle. Chances are you've never ridden one. Most likely, though, you've ridden some other member of the **CYCLE** family. Because these words are so familiar, Webster wants to start with a web for the **CYCLE** family. Look at the next page. Notice she spins the word **CYCLE** into the center of her web. On one web strand she spins the word **UNICYCLE.** Now it is your turn. Help her expand the web by looking at these pictures.

Write the names of these three cycles on the web strands Webster has woven for you on the next page.

Now you have the beginning of your first WordWeb. Not really that hard, is it?

TeacherTip

In this entire series, **WebStretchers** serve as optional enrichment and challenge sections for you to approach as suitable for your students.

WebStretcher: What would an **OCTOCYCLE** look like? Who might ride it? What could you call a **CYCLE** with five wheels? Think of more than one name if you can.

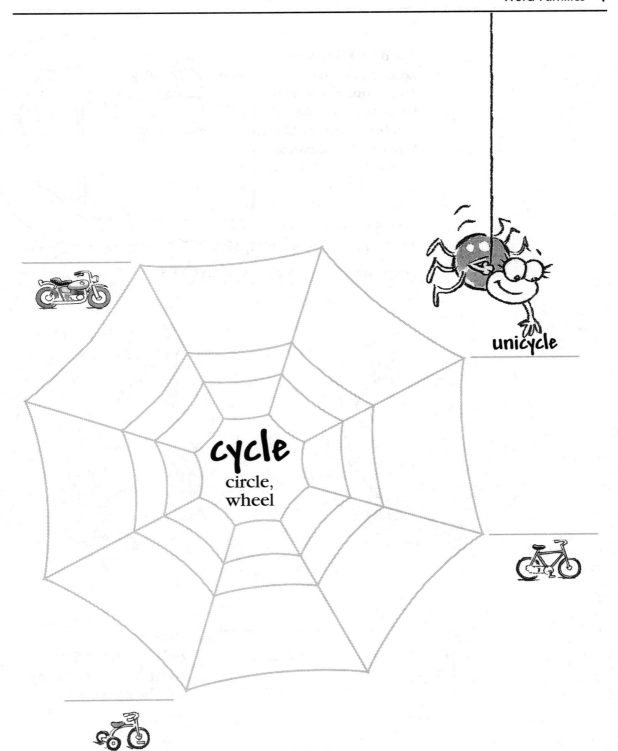

unicycle

cycle
circle,
wheel

The **CYCLE** web is
far from complete.
To continue we need
to think about the
family name, **CYCLE.**
What does it mean all
by itself?

Write your ideas about
the meaning of **cycle** on my sign.

Then study these pictures of **CYCLES.**

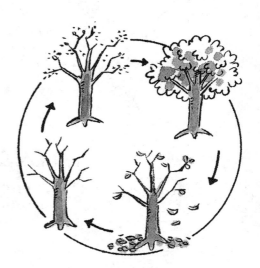

_____

_____

_____

_____

_____

_____

_____

What makes each one a
cycle? What do these
cycles have in common
with the **cycles** you can
ride?

Expanding Your First WordWeb

Now that you understand that the **CYCLE** family name means **CIRCLE** or **WHEEL**, Webster has a few new words to add to the web.

recycle   cyclops   cyclone   encyclopedia

Think about the way the word **RECYCLE** is made. **RE + CYCLE.** You already know what **CYCLE** means. What do you think the prefix **RE** in the word **RECYCLE** most likely means? Circle one.

a. above   c. again

b. never   d. a musical note.

 Check your answer by writing your dictionary's definition of **RECYCLE** on my sign.

RECYCLE

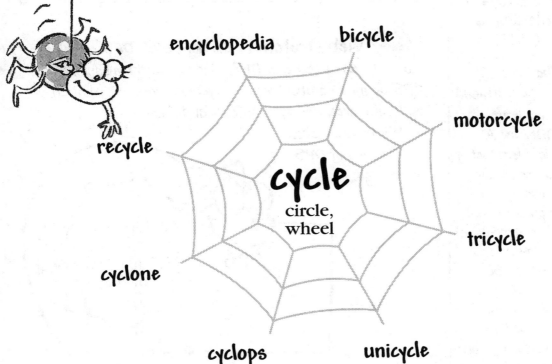

encyclopedia   bicycle

motorcycle

recycle

cycle
circle,
wheel

tricycle

cyclone

cyclops   unicycle

SideSpinner

*You also see the word **ENCYCLOPEDIA** on the **CYCLE** WordWeb. It has three main parts: **EN** = in, **CYCLO** = circle, wheel, **PEDIA** = education of children.*

(PSST!) ***What kind of doctor is a pediatrician?***

*How do we get from **EDUCATION IN A CIRCLE** to a large set of reference books usually found in a library? In Greek this phrase meant general (all-encompassing) education. In English it has come to describe the set of books in which a summary of all known **education** is held, the knowledge believed to turn **children into** well-**rounded** adults.*

Now our web words get a bit harder. Consider **CYCLONE** and **CYCLOPS**. Think about how and why each one belongs to the **CYCLE** family.

Choose one of these two words and write or draw your explanation below.

WebStretcher: *The word **CYCLOPS** contains two roots, **CYCL(E)** and **OPS**. Figure out the meaning of **OPS** by thinking about what a **Cyclops** looks like, what an **optician** makes, and what an **optical** illusion is. Write your ideas about the meaning of **OPS** on my sign.*

OPS

Uni Family WordWeb

Words can belong to more than one family. **UNICYCLE, BICYCLE, TRICYCLE** all belong to the **CYCLE** family. Because of its prefix, each one also belongs to a second, different family.

 Can you figure out the meaning of the prefixes?

UNI = _____ BI = _____ TRI = _____

What helped you figure out these meanings?

Help Webster weave the **uni** web. The first answer is filled in for you. Read the other clues and choose the answers from the words given. Write the answer on the web strand near the clue.

Here are the words:

unicorn	**uniform**
unify	**unique**
unison	**universe**

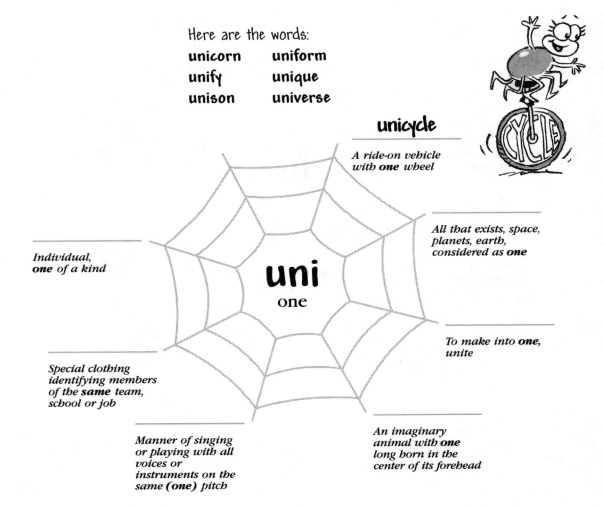

unicycle

*A ride-on vehicle with **one** wheel*

*All that exists, space, planets, earth, considered as **one***

*Individual, **one** of a kind*

uni
one

*To make into **one**, unite*

*Special clothing identifying members of the **same** team, school or job*

*Manner of singing or playing with all voices or instruments on the same (**one**) pitch*

*An imaginary animal with **one** long horn in the center of its forehead*

Bi Family WordWeb

To complete the **BI** web, follow the same procedure as you used for the **UNI** web. This time, since you have no wordlist, you need to think of the words yourself just by reading the descriptions.

A few of these may stump you, so don't forget to rely on your trusty dictionary.

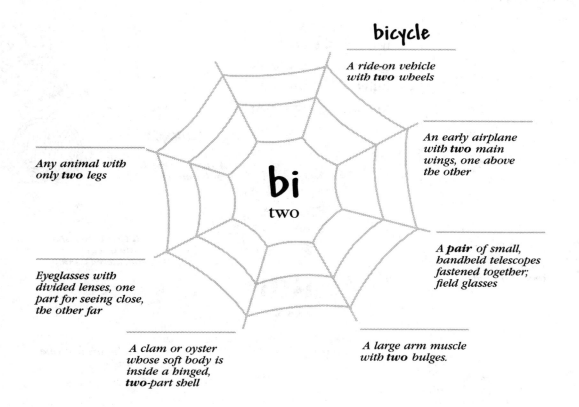

bicycle

*A ride-on vehicle with **two** wheels*

*An early airplane with **two** main wings, one above the other*

*Any animal with only **two** legs*

A pair of small, handheld telescopes fastened together; field glasses

bi
two

Eyeglasses with divided lenses, one part for seeing close, the other far

*A clam or oyster whose soft body is inside a hinged, **two**-part shell*

*A large arm muscle with **two** bulges.*

Tri Family WordWeb

TeacherTip

This **Psst!** is key. As students become 'morph-conscious', they will inevitably make beginners' mistakes. 100% accuracy is not nearly as important as their growing ability to understand a word through a knowledge of its morphs. Adults will need a certain mellowness, as well, to hunch, be wrong, and hunch again. The morph method is, above all, a process: unlimited trial, frequent errors at first, enduring rewards.

 WebStretcher: Using the space below, design your own **TRI** web. Find four or more words in your dictionary. Write your clues. Then share your web with others.

(PSST!) **Not every word beginning with the letters TRI belongs on this web. Why not? For example, why would you not choose words like trick and trip? What do you have to look for when choosing your words for this web?**

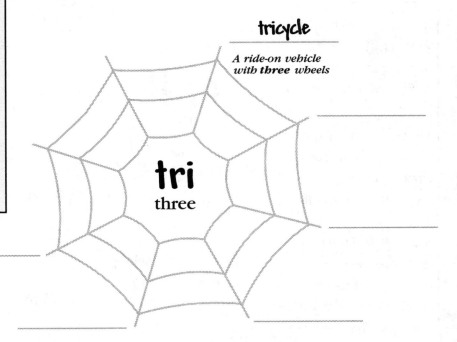

tricycle

A ride-on vehicle with three wheels

tri
three

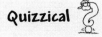 **Quizzical** You've probably all seen **triplets**, used **biceps** to do a tough job, but have you ever tasted fresh **unicorn** on the cob?

TeacherTip

This page shows where the 'morph method' can take students. It is included here as a foreshadowing meant to excite teacher and student alike. If it seems overwhelming, glance at it quickly and pass on.

Those students who love a challenge may want to hunt in a dictionary that gives good etymologies (word origins) for the meaning of the morphs of the new words on this megaweb.

***Biopsy** is very tricky. Based on the morphs students already know, they could intelligently hunch that it would translate **bi (two) + ops (eye) + y**. It doesn't. Its first morph is **bio (life)**. **Bio** joins with **ops**. The two **O**s become one. **Bio (life) + ops (eye) + y (the act of)** = **biopsy** – the **act of** using the **eye** to examine tissue from a **living** organism.*

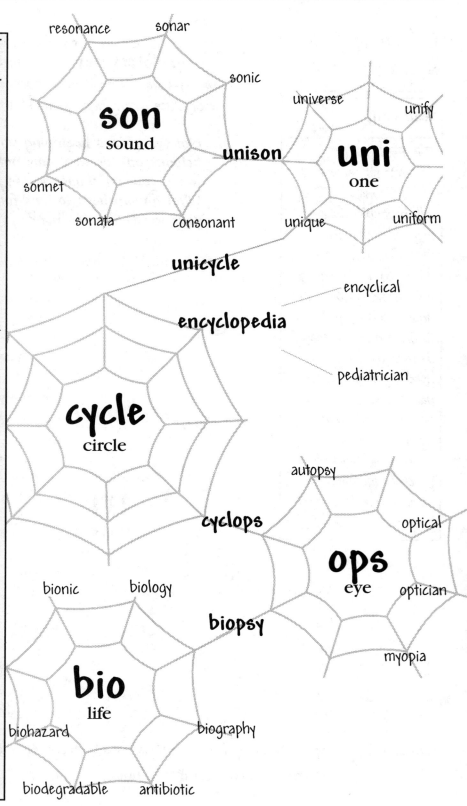

Meet the Morphs

You can never get your total Word's Worth out of any word without knowing more about the morphs. First of all, remember what morphs are?

MORPHS: THE SMALLEST POSSIBLE MEANING PIECES IN A LANGUAGE

Right! The smallest possible pieces in any language that have meaning. The pieces Webster uses to weave her webs. The three most important morphs for her – and for us – are PREFIXES, ROOTS AND SUFFIXES.

ROOTS, as you may remember, are the main morphs in words. They give the basic idea or meaning to words. You might even say words grow from ROOTS.

ROOTS can be words by themselves without PREFIXES or SUFFIXES, but PREFIXES and SUFFIXES cannot stand alone. They need to attach themselves to ROOTS in order to become words.

Adding Attachments

To really understand PREFIXES and SUFFIXES, you need to think a bit about what an attachment, any attachment, can do. Machines, for example, have all kinds of attachments.

Think about machines in your home. Describe one that has an attachment. What does the attachment do? What does the attachment add to the machine? Be specific.

_____

_____

_____

People form attachments too. Babies and young children become attached to blankets or favorite toys, a special grandparent, aunt or uncle. Teens are often attached to their friends (and their CD collections)! Teens and adults can be attached to an idea, a goal, a lifework. Like me, Wordsworth. I'm a bit attached to words. I can't imagine my life without them.

Think about some attachment you have or had to a person, place, thing or goal. What difference has this attachment made in your life? How has it changed you? Briefly write or draw your reflections.

Just the way attachments change people and machines, so they change words. Since **PREFIXES** attach to the beginning of words, we'll start with them.

On the Front End

Want to see how **PREFIXES** attach to **ROOTS** and change their meanings? Let's take some easy **ROOTS** like **fair, happy, true.**

Attach the prefix **UN** to each of these **ROOTS**. What happens? When **UN** is attached to a **ROOT**, I noticed that

PREFIXES ATTACH TO THE FRONT OF A ROOT AND CHANGE ITS MEANING.

_____

_____

UN, you might say, is not at all an uncommon **PREFIX**, but at times it might be slightly **un**popular!

Popular or not, **UN** does teach us the first important point to remember about **PREFIXES**. They attach to the front of **ROOTS** and change their meaning in some way.

TeacherTip

Examples of quantitative **PREFIXES** abound. They will be handled much more extensively in a subsequent **WordBook** in this series. A sample group includes: penta, deca, ambi, demi, multi, macro, micro, mega, mono, prim, proto, bin, olig, pan, poly, semi, tele... Enthusiastic students may want to start their collections now!

There's a big difference, after all, between lucky and unlucky, healthy and unhealthy. As a **PREFIX**, **UN** changes a word into its opposite.

Most **PREFIXES** don't change a **ROOT** as completely as **UN** does. Remember, for example, some of the **PREFIXES** you already met. When Webster rode into our book, she came on a unicycle. In the word **unicycle**, the **PREFIX UNI** attaches to the **ROOT CYCLE** and tells how many wheels it has – one. A **bi**cycle has two wheels, a **tri**cycle, three.

 UNI, **BI** and **TRI** are just a few of the many **PREFIXES** that show number, quantity, size or distance. Be on the lookout for others, especially in your math and science lessons.

In this **WordBook**, Webster and I want to focus mainly on another group of **PREFIXES**. We call them **directional PREFIXES** and you'll soon see why.

Webster can really help us with these. In her spare time, she's quite an athlete. With as many legs as she has, it's quite easy to master many different kicks. Cheerleaders, eat your hearts out!

Truth is, she can send a ball in almost any direction she chooses. Her athletic ability will help explain directional **PREFIXES**. First you need to imagine all the different directions a person (or a very talented spider) might throw or kick a ball – **to, toward, down, away, out of, in, into, over, under, against, through, across, around, back and forth,** to mention a few. There is at least one **PREFIX**, sometimes more, in the English language to describe each of these directions.

Let's see how these directional prefixes work.

Look at the picture for **AD.** In what direction is Webster kicking the ball? Right toward the ROOT. That's because **AD** means TO or TOWARD.

What happens when Webster adds **AD** to a ROOT? Think about the ROOT **JOIN,** which means CONNECT. If we say: Webster's workshop **ADJOINS** her garage, that means the workshop CONNECTS TO the garage.

AD + JOIN = CONNECT TO.

Notice that we put the PREFIX meaning TO after the ROOT'S meaning CONNECT.

 Sometimes, as in this example, saying the prefix after the root makes more sense in English. Try this method if saying the prefix first doesn't make sense.

The ROOT **OPT** means CHOOSE or SELECT. When people **ad + opt (adopt)** a child, they CHOOSE to bring that child TOWARD their family. They welcome the child INTO the family.

The ROOT **HERE** means STICK. If your gum **ad + here (adheres)** to your mother's new shoe, it will STICK TO it, and you'll be in a STICKY situation, won't you?

Hoot! Hoot!
AD gives a boot
Toward the **ROOT!**

TeacherTip

In their original languages, these **PREFIXES** were often prepositions. In English, they became the first part of the **ROOT** instead. So what would have been BREATHE OUT, for example, becomes the English word EXHALE (out + breathe), a blend of the **PREFIX** EX (out, out of) and the **ROOT** HALE (breathe). Similarly, DIRECT TOWARD becomes ADDRESS (toward + direct). CARRY BACK becomes REPORT (back + carry).

PREFIXES become much clearer to students if they are regularly challenged to understand the connection between **PREFIX** meaning and **ROOT** meaning. They should always be asking themselves: How does this **PREFIX** add to or change the meaning of the **ROOT?** Be prepared for the fact that in some words the relationship will be much clearer than in others. Words are altogether as individual and unpredictable as the people who use them.

Webster and I have worked through one **PREFIX** as an example. Now it's your turn. For each new **PREFIX**, study the picture and the crazy cheer. Watch what direction Webster is kicking the ball.

Use your understanding of the meaning of the **PREFIX** and the **ROOT** to write a definition for each word. Check your definition with the dictionary and add to it if necessary. Then write a sentence using the new word.

COM

What are Webster and Wordsworth doing with the ball?

_____

COM (with, together) + **PUTE** (think, figure) = **COMPUTE**

My definition

_____

My sentence

_____

We call on **COM**
To hold things **together**,
The **PREFIX with** glue
For all kinds of weather.

DE

What direction is Webster kicking the ball?

_____

DE (down, away) + **SCEND** (climb) = **DESCEND**

My definition

_____

My sentence

_____

Hey! Hey!
DE boots **away!**
DE takes the **ROOTS**
Down and **away.**
Rather **de**-basing,
Wouldn't you say?

EX

What direction is Webster kicking the ball?

_____

EX (out, out of) + **IT** (go) = **EXIT**

My definition

_____

My sentence

_____

Give a shout!
EX boots **out!**
Let's hear it for **EX**
And what it's about.
EX takes away.
EX takes **out.**

IN

What direction is Webster kicking the ball?

_____

IN (in, into, on, upon) + **HALE** (breathe) = **INHALE**

My definition

_____

My sentence

_____

Go!
Fight!
Win!
IN boots **in!**

RE

What direction is Webster kicking the ball?

_____

RE (back, again) + **TURN** (turn) = **RETURN**

My definition

_____

My sentence

_____

RE is a copycat.
No doubt about that.
Anything done once,
RE goes **back**
And does **again**
It doesn't matter
What, where, or when.

Dive away from thunder!
SUB boots **under**.
SUB comes **up from under**,
From **beneath** or **below**,
So it emerges,
A useful **PREFIX** to know.

SUB

What direction is Webster kicking the ball?

_____

SUB (under, up from under, beneath, below) +
MERGE (place, plunge) = SUBMERGE

My definition

_____

My sentence

_____

TRANS

What direction is Webster kicking the ball?

_____

TRANS (across, over) + FUSE (pour) = TRANSFUSE

My definition

_____

My sentence

_____

The **PREFIX TRANS**,
Quite a rover,
Moves the **ROOT**
Across and **over**.

Good ol' Webster could go on kicking for a long time yet! There are dozens of **PREFIXES** left. We're afraid, though, that you might get **exhausted** before she does!

 See the word **exhausted?** It means **ex** (OUT) + **haust** (DRAIN). If you're **exhausted,** all your energy is **DRAINED OUT** of you.

We don't want that to happen so we're stopping now! The eight **PREFIXES** she's already done are the most common ones in this WordBook. Besides, we have a few other things to show you about **PREFIXES**.

Chameleon Letters

In the exercises you just completed, the **directional PREFIXES** were easy to find. Sometimes it's not so easy. Have you ever heard of chameleons? Do you know what they do?

Chameleons are nature's camouflage artists. If they crawl onto a green leaf, their skin color turns green. If they sleep on an old log, their skin becomes brown. They blend into their background.

PREFIXES act a bit like chameleons at times. They don't change color, of course! They change spelling. **PREFIXES** sometimes change their last letter to fit or match the first letter of the **ROOT**. Why? To blend better into words. To make words easier to pronounce.

Webster and I call the letter that changes a **CHAMELEON LETTER**. Every time we use one in this book, we put this little icon of a chameleon in the margin to alert you: Be on the lookout for a chameleon letter.

Let's take a look at how chameleon letters work. The letter **D** in the **PREFIX AD** is one of the most common chameleons. That letter has ten different ways to disguise itself! Watch that crafty **D** at work.

Account

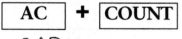

If **AD** joins a root beginning with **C**, such as **count**, the chameleon letter **D** changes to a **C**. Presto! Chango! We have the word **account**.

So **ad + count = account.** In the same way, **ad + fix = affix, ad + point = appoint**, and so on.

D is a chameleon letter!

You try one: **ad + prove =**

_____

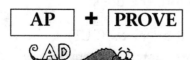

D is a chameleon letter!

Let's look at another **PREFIX, COM.** **M** is the chameleon. Watch how it connects with different roots:

com + lect = collect, com + nect = connect.

M is a chameleon letter!

Try one yourself: **com + rect =** _____ .

Webster and I don't want to confuse you with too much information about these crazy chameleon letters. They will get much easier to spot as you work your way through our **WordBook**. Every time a CHAMELEON LETTER appears, you'll see our friend Longfellow, the chameleon, in the margin and you'll know what to expect.

Prefixes as Intensives

For such little morphs, PREFIXES are certainly important! There's one last thing Webster and I want you to know about PREFIXES. It doesn't happen often, but any PREFIX can function as an INTENSIVE. What does that mean? If the weather forecaster predicts intense cold, it will be really, really cold. If a light is intense, it shines very, very brightly, almost too brightly.

When a PREFIX is used as an INTENSIVE, it makes the meaning of the root more intense. The PREFIX becomes like a highlighter and helps you underline or emphasize the meaning of the ROOT. As an INTENSIVE, any PREFIX can be 'translated' by the words COMPLETELY, THOROUGHLY, or REALLY.

Despoil

DE thoroughly, completely	+	SPOIL damage, harm

In the word **DESPOIL,** for example, the PREFIX DE is an INTENSIVE. The ROOT SPOIL means DAMAGE or HARM. The PREFIX heightens that meaning. **Despoil** means to rob, plunder, or pillage, in other words, to DAMAGE COMPLETELY.

Combustion

COM thoroughly, completely	+	BUST burn	+	ION

In the word **COMBUSTION,** the PREFIX COM functions as an INTENSIVE. The ROOT BUST means BURN. The PREFIX adds the idea of BURNING up COMPLETELY and quickly, almost violently. **Combustion** can be used to describe REALLY BURNING feelings of anger or upset.

Webster and I have never figured out why **PREFIXES** become **INTENSIVES** in some words and not others. There are so many quirky things about language. Don't worry about it, though. We'll be sure to let you know when you meet an **INTENSIVE** in this **WordBook**. You'll see the **INTENSIVE** icon, a flame, burning brightly.

Prefix Summary

It's about time we finish up what we have to say about **PREFIXES**.

There are four main points to remember.

PREFIXES attach to the front of roots.

Some **PREFIXES** show direction.

The last letter in some **PREFIXES** changes to make it easier to pronounce. We call these letters **CHAMELEON LETTERS**.

Most **PREFIXES** will be used as **INTENSIVES** once in awhile.

Morph-O-Meter

I'm amazed at my own patience! We've been together for 26 pages already and all that time I've been dying to show you my most exciting invention ever, the **MORPH-O-METER**.

Bringing Up the Rear

SUFFIXES OFTEN CHANGE A WORD'S PART OF SPEECH.

Before I can, we need to take a quick look at the one morph left, **SUFFIXES**.

SUFFIXES are the cabooses of the word train. They finish a word off in a way that shows the word's part of speech, such as noun, adjective, or verb. In fact, that's the single most important point about **SUFFIXES**.   They usually change a word's part of speech rather than its meaning. They offer a quick and easy way to increase your vocabulary.

That's because if you know the meaning of a word without a **SUFFIX**, you usually know the meaning of the word with the **SUFFIX** added. Let's try some examples.

If you know the verb **celebrate** means to have a good time, then you know that the noun **celebration** refers to any event where people have a good time, like a birthday party, a Bar Mitzvah, a wedding.

If you know **content** means happy, then you know that a person filled with **contentment** is filled with

_____.

When a teacher is calm even though his students are acting wild, he can be described as **patient.** That means he has a lot of _____ with his students.

If you know **rely** means to trust, then a **reliable** person (circle one):

    a. is always late

    b. is someone you can count on

    c. can't keep a secret

    d. sneaks around

If you know **create** means to make, which of the following people might not be considered very **creative?** Circle one.

    a. someone who writes music

    b. someone who designs clothes

    c. a cook who follows a cookbook

    d. a cook who makes up unique recipes

I hope you amaze yourself as much as you amaze me! You've already met several very common SUFFIXES – **-ion, -ment, -ent, -ence, -able,** and **-ive.** Not terribly hard, are they? You see that they rely on the ROOT for their meaning.

People-Making Suffixes

Guess what. SUFFIXES become even easier as you get to know them better. That's why we've decided to show you just one more group of SUFFIXES. This new group of SUFFIXES changes things, ideas, subjects or actions into people. These SUFFIXES are usually easy to spot.

Thing: a guitar. **Person:** guitarist.

What is the suffix? ＿＿＿＿＿＿＿

Subject: science. **Person:** scientist.

What is the suffix? ＿＿＿＿＿＿＿

Action: reserve. **Person:** reservist.

What is the suffix? ＿＿＿＿＿＿＿

IST as a **SUFFIX** lets you know the performer of an action.

Identify these **IST** people.

Someone who rides a bike _____

Someone who paints or draws _____

Someone who studies biology _____

The **SUFFIXES ER** and **OR** also create people. A skater, a catcher, a director all perform the action contained in their name.

Can you identify these people?

A person who performs in plays or movies _____

A person who does tap and jazz _____

ER and **OR** can also create things: accelerator, transistor, receiver.

Look around your classroom and see if you can find one or two more **er** or **or** objects.

-**EE**, -**EER**, -**ESS**, -**EY**, -**IE**, -**Y** are all **SUFFIXES** that identify people, animals or things. Just think of the many examples in common use: employee, absentee, balladeer, mutineer, actress, lioness, attorney, goalie, sweetie, dolly, doggy.

Poof! You're a thing!

As we've said already, the best way to learn about other **SUFFIXES** is probably to see them in action. Webster will weave many of them into her webs as we meet new word families.

For now, the three most important things to remember about **SUFFIXES** are:

- Suffixes attach to the end of words.

- Suffixes often change parts of speech.

- When you know a word without a suffix, you usually know (or can figure out) the word with a suffix added.

TeacherTip

The **M-O-M** is structured to register the four basic patterns of word-weaving:

1. **Root = Word**

2. **Prefix Morph + Root Morph = Word**

3. **Root Morph + Suffix Morph = Word**

4. **Prefix Morph + Root Morph + Suffix Morph = Word.**

Words may have two or more **prefixes, roots** and/or **suffixes.** That does not alter the basic pattern. Words with two roots are often compound words. The more practice students get with these patterns, the easier 'decoding' word meanings will become for them.

As you go along, you will realize more and more clearly that morphs do not always coincide with syllables. The ability of students to break words into morphs is much more significant to their overall education than is syllabification.

Many quick, intriguing games can be developed challenging students to 'translate' English words into their meaning parts. As a teacher, make it a habit to ask questions that encourage students to think along these lines, such as: What morphs (meaning parts) make up this word? What do these parts mean by themselves? How do they help you understand the meaning of the whole word? What does the word mean when all the morph meanings are added together?

Such exercises can be a great help with specialized vocabulary in other subjects within the curriculum as well. All classrooms and homes need one good dictionary that gives etymologies in a way that's accessible to the age and ability of the learner. With such a dictionary, see what students can do, for example, with triangle, circumference, geology, seismograph, thermometer, scientist, alliteration, symbolism, etc.

Whenever any word seems particularly difficult, have students check to see if it can be broken into smaller meaning chunks or traced back to a word picture that might serve as a memory aid. If you have trouble remembering that the word **RECALCITRANT,** for example, means STUBBORN, perhaps the word's picture can help. The Latin word **CALX** means HEEL. A **RECALCITRANT** (RE = AGAIN + CALX) person digs in his HEELS over and over AGAIN.

Develop a classroom dictionary of all the words the class 'translates' in this way. It will form an invaluable resource for a lifetime of continued growth with words.

Meet the Morph-O-Meter

At last, my big moment has arrived! I can unveil my pride and joy, the **MORPH-O-METER**. Now that you know a bit about **PREFIXES**, **ROOTS** and **SUFFIXES**, you're ready to learn how breaking words into their smaller pieces (morphs) helps you understand them better.

That's where my **MORPH-O-METER** comes into the picture. How does it work? Easy. You know those dollar-changing machines? Put in a dollar. Get back a dollar's worth of change. That's my model for the **M-O-M**. (That's its nickname.) Put in a word. Get back that word's worth of **MORPHEMES**.

You see that the **M-O-M** has three windows. The left window tells how many **PREFIXES** a word has. The middle window tells how many **ROOTS** a word has. The right window tells how many **SUFFIXES** a word has.

Let's try some words from our first lesson, **Word Families,** and see what my machine does with them. We may as well start with the word **cycle.** Presto! See what my machine did with it? That word has only one **MORPH**, a **ROOT**. It has no **PREFIX** or **SUFFIX**.

Now let's feed the machine some more words from our first lesson, **Word Families.** Watch each one carefully.

unicycle

cyclist

bicyclist

cyclone

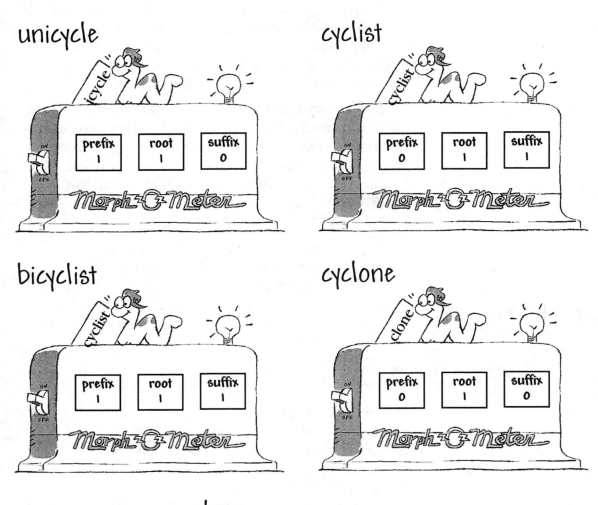

cyclops

Before we continue, I want to make sure you can read the M-O-M with no trouble. Look carefully at all the MORPH-O-READINGS on page 32 and see if you can answer these questions.

What are the two words made up of one or more **ROOTS** and nothing more?

_____

_____

What word contains only a **ROOT** and a **SUFFIX?** _____

What is the **SUFFIX?** _____

What is the only word that contains one each, a **PREFIX,** a **ROOT** and a **SUFFIX?** _____

What is the **PREFIX?** _____

What is the **ROOT?** _____

What is the **SUFFIX?** _____

Morph Mix 'n Match

Do you think by now you could operate my machine yourself?
I've got a treasure chest of **MORPHS** for you to use.

Prefixes	Roots	Suffixes
dis	help	ful
pre	count	able
re	sent	er
	play	

The idea of this game is to see how many real words you can make with these
MORPHS. Try to weave at least two words to fit each **M-0-M** reading. How do you
do that? In the box above, look for **MORPHS** that stand alone. Where do they
belong? Next see if you can mix and match any **PREFIXES** with **ROOTS** to make
words. Try to join **ROOTS** and **SUFFIXES** to make other words. Then try to match
PREFIXES, ROOTS and **SUFFIXES**. Webster and I have done one example of each
M-0-M to get you started. Write your words under the **MORPH-O-METER** where
they belong on this or the following page.

1. __count__

2. _____

3. _____

1. __replay__

2. _____

3. _____

| prefix 0 | root 1 | suffix 1 |

Morph-O-Meter

1. _____**helpful**_____

2. _____

3. _____

| prefix 1 | root 1 | suffix 1 |

Morph-O-Meter

1. _____**dissenter**_____

2. _____

3. _____

WebStretcher: *Have a treasure hunt of your own. Find easy, everyday words to put into the* **MORPH-O-METER** *and test your friends. Look at newspaper headlines, billboards, magazines, textbook material, even cartoons, to find your words. Try to find two words for each of these word-weaving patterns.*

Use these roots

count   fine   help   play   prove   sent   test   work

and any prefix or suffix already mentioned in our **WordBook**.

prefix + root = word

_____   _____

root + suffix = word

_____   _____

prefix + root + suffix = word

_____   _____

Build your own **MORPH-O-METER** *out of a cardboard box or other material. Make it a bit like a cash register so you can store all the words your machine has read and divided into* **MORPHS**.

Above all, become a wordhound. Find MORPHS everywhere. Sniff them out and translate them into word meanings.

Webster and I have heard that knowing 30 good MORPHS unlocks the meaning of 10,000 English words and knowing 50 leads you to 100,000 words.

Why not be the student who proves that theory right?

We've written this WordBook and the ones that follow to help you do just that. From here on, each WordWeb focuses on one specific ROOT and the words that belong in its family. That way you learn clusters of words rather than isolated words. That way you get your Word's Worth, someday maybe even 100,000 words' worth!

Now we're ready to begin our ROOT WordWebs. Each time we introduce a new ROOT, Webster and I try to imagine why people created it. What did they need to talk about or explain the very first time that word was ever used?

Meet the Press

Early humans led active lives, full of hard work and movement. They had to hunt, gather food, make clothing, escape harsh weather, find shelter and protect themselves. Everyday words give hints about some of that activity – lots of pushing, pulling, carrying, dragging. Our new root **PRESS** is one good example. **Press** means to SQUEEZE, PUSH TOGETHER or STRIKE.

(PSST!) *Think of an iron to remember that press means push together or squeeze.*

suppress   compress

repress   decompress

press
squeeze,
push together,
strike

oppress   depress

impress   express

Think about how often it is necessary to **press** something. Even typing out these words involves **pressing** keys or buttons, just as touch-tone telephones, calculators and doorbells do. More examples may occur to you as you study our new web.

The central member of the **PRESS** family, of course, is **press.** The first thing Webster and I notice is that **press** is not just a root, a small part of a larger word. It is also a word by itself, just like CYCLE.

Press can be used as a verb or a noun. As a verb, **press** means to PUSH or SQUEEZE, even to flatten, as in the case of **pressing** clothes with an iron.

As a noun, **press** usually describes a pressure or PUSH. It can also mean a printing **press.** People who report news for newspapers, magazines, television or radio are known as the media or members of the **press.**

Identify **press** as either a verb or a noun in the sentences that follow. Place a **V** on the line for verb, an **N** for noun.

_____ To speak to a service representative, please **press** two on your touch-tone telephone.

_____ The **press** has been known to exaggerate stories in order to attract public attention.

_____ Would you please **press** this dress for me since I am running quite late for a very important date?

Write two of your own sentences using the word **press** once as a noun and once as a verb.

_____

_____

_____

_____

Now that we have looked at **press** as a word in itself, we can turn our attention to the web. Webster spins **press** into the center. Next she weaves eight different prefixes onto **press.**

What word-weaving pattern is Webster using for this web? Circle one.

a. prefix + root

b. prefix + root + suffix

c. root + suffix

d. root + root

Compress

COM	**+**	**PRESS**
together, with		push together, squeeze

Compress means to SQUEEZE TOGETHER or make smaller by applying some type of pressure.

If a car runs over your lunch bag, your peanut butter sandwich will undoubtedly be **compressed.**

One of these words would not describe your sandwich. Circle it.

a. flattened

b. leveled

c. expanded

d. smashed

As a noun, a **compress** is a pad of cloth applied to some part of the body to create PRESSURE or reduce inflammation. You might apply a **compress** to a sprained ankle beginning to swell.

Decompress

DE	+	**COM**	+	**PRESS**
not		together, with		push together, squeeze

TeacherTip

DECOMPRESS adds a second prefix.
M-O-M = 2 + 1 + 0.
The prefix DE sometimes reverses the action of the word to which it attaches just the way the prefix UN would.

Decompress involves removing pressure from something already **compressed.** Look at the illustrations of the jack-in-the-box.

 How is the **pressure** removed from poor Jack?

Decompress also involves lessening the pressure of air on or in something, such as a balloon or a tire.

Depress

DE	+	**PRESS**
down, away		push together, squeeze

To **depress** is to make sad or gloomy or cause someone to feel **DOWN** or have low spirits.

Seeing all the homeless animals at the Humane Society **depresses** me.

It also means to **PUSH** down, as in **depressing** the "O" button on a telephone to reach an operator.

Which of the following events might cause a person to become **depressed?** Circle one.

   a. surfing the waves

   b. relaxing on the beach

   c. snorkeling in the ocean

   d. breaking a leg just before you go to the beach

Express

EX + PRESS
EX out, out of	**+**	PRESS push together, squeeze

Express means to put into words or show feelings or opinions by look, voice or action. You PUSH your thoughts or feelings OUT OF yourself. A frown **expresses** displeasure. A scream **expresses** alarm. A nod **expresses** agreement.

How do you **express** yourself in the following situations?

Meeting a new classmate

_____

_____

When disappointed by a friend

_____

_____

Winning an award

_____

_____

Impress

IM + PRESS
IM in, into, on, upon	**+**	PRESS push together, squeeze

N is a chameleon letter!

To **impress** is to PUSH a thought or feeling INTO the mind of a person or group of people.

The coach attempted to **impress** upon the players how important it is to wear safety equipment to avoid injury.

Some people spend lots of time and money in an effort to **impress** others. Such **impressions** may be positive or negative.

Susan spent the entire afternoon baking a fancy cake to **impress** her dinner guests.

I'M IMPRESSED!

If you want to **impress** your track coach, you might (circle one):

a. buy the most expensive track shoes you can find

b. practice hard and have a positive attitude

c. drink lots of water

d. stay focused and ignore suggestions for improvement

Oppress

OP	+	PRESS
against		push together, squeeze

B is a chameleon letter!

Oppress means to PUSH AGAINST, rule harshly or keep down by unjust or cruel treatment. An **oppressed** person is weighed down or burdened in some way.

THIS HEAT IS OPPRESSIVE!

TeacherTip

OB is one of the most difficult prefixes to 'pin down,' since it can mean so many contradictory things, such as **toward** and **against**. Students need to learn to recognize its many forms -- **OP** in **oppress**, for example -- without worrying too much about how to translate it exactly in individual words. In the early books in this series, Wordsworth will always give the translation that best fits the word being studied.

Based on historical information, which of the following leaders would be considered **oppressive?** Write a sentence about each person explaining what kind of leader he or she was.

a. **Abraham Lincoln**

_____

b. **Mother Teresa**

_____

c. **Martin Luther King, Jr.**

_____

d. **King Henry VIII**

_____

Repress

RE back, again	**+**	**PRESS** push together, squeeze

To **repress** is to PUSH BACK a feeling or action by an act of willpower.

When driving, Ethan fought constantly to **repress** the painful memories of the accident that killed his best friend.

When people are **repressed,** they have been PUSHED down over and over AGAIN by others or by difficult circumstances.

BE STILL, MY HEART!

DON'T REPRESS YOUR EMOTIONS!

Which of the following people would most likely be **repressed?** Circle one.

  a. prisoners of war

  b. children running in a park

  c. a rock star performing on stage

  d. a batter who just hit a grand slam

Suppress

SUP below, under	**+**	**PRESS** push together, squeeze

Suppress means to PUSH UNDER, put an end to or stop by force. It often refers to keeping in, holding back, or subduing something, like news, a rebellion or an urge to cough.

B is a chameleon letter!

 Have you ever **suppressed** the truth to protect a friend?

If you were trying to **suppress** your anger, would you (circle one):

  a. let it all out

  b. take it out only on your family

  c. take it out only on strangers

  d. stay under control

NEW! NOHAX COUGH SUPPRESSANT

IT REALLY WORKS!

LINK 'N LEARN

Draw a line from each word in Column I to its best synonym(s) in Column II.

PRESS (as a root)	make sad, discourage
COMPRESS	make smaller
DEPRESS	stop by force, crush, conceal
EXPRESS	treat cruelly, rule harshly
IMPRESS	push, squeeze, strike
OPPRESS	affect thoughts and feelings, mark firmly
REPRESS	speak out, put into words
SUPPRESS	force out of one's mind

TeacherTip

REPRESS and **SUPPRESS** are usually given as synonyms for each other. The small shade of difference involves personal will and external force. **REPRESS** more often describes something one does to oneself and has more psychological implications. **SUPPRESS** usually includes outside, often abusive, authority. As the **RE** suggests, **REPRESS** is an act that continues over time. **SUPPRESS** often happens in response to a crisis in the here and now.

Choose one word from this list to fill in each blank. Each word is used only once.

compress   depression   expression   impress   repress

Into the Wild Blue Yonder

Conrad Cool set out to _____ his friends by showing them what an accomplished scuba diver he had become. While showing off in the deep blue sea, he swam into a large, jagged coral reef and was knocked unconscious. Fortunately, his buddies rescued poor Conrad, and when he regained consciousness, he found himself with a cold _____ on his forehead to relieve swelling. Conrad tried desperately to _____ his anger and embarrassment, but it was obvious from his pained _____ that he had sadly sunk into the depths of a deep blue _____.

Press Part Two

Webster and I are **impressed!** You already know eight prefix morph + root morph words in the **PRESS** family.

So what does Webster do? She gets busy weaving her next web. You probably won't have a bit of trouble handling some more of her **pressing** matters. The words in this **expressive** family present quite an **impressive** list. Try not to let the number of words **depress** you. After all, they are all related.

What's more, you will recognize the word patterns. Look carefully at the new web.

How are most of the words made? Right you are!
The **prefix morph + root morph + suffix morph** pattern. Two words on the web don't fit that pattern because they don't have prefixes. Can you find them?

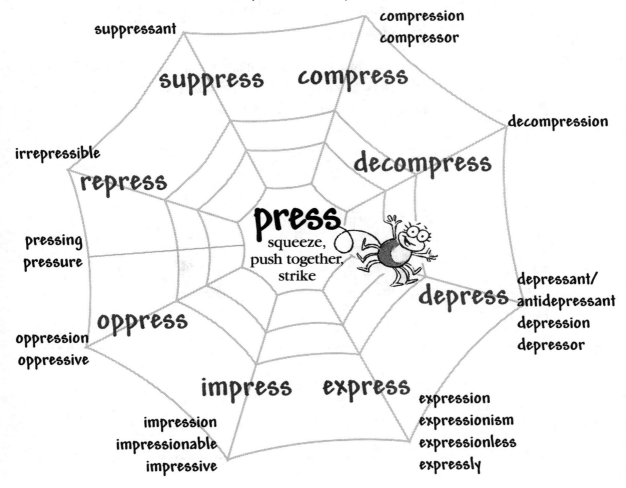

suppressant

compression
compressor

suppress   compress

decompression

irrepressible

decompress

repress

press
squeeze,
push together,
strike

pressing
pressure

depressant/
antidepressant
depression
depressor

depress

oppress

oppression
oppressive

impress   express

impression
impressionable
impressive

expression
expressionism
expressionless
expressly

Compression

Compression is the act of SQUEEZING or PUSHING something TOGETHER through the use of some form of **pressure.**

Decompression

Decompression is the process of removing **pressure** in some way; it's just the opposite of **compression.**

You may have heard of a **decompression** chamber, a device used to help anyone who has spent long periods of time in a high air **pressure** environment, such as deep under water, to return to normal **pressure.** This is especially useful for scuba divers who surface from deep-sea dives too quickly and experience the pain of **decompression** sickness or 'the bends.'

 If you wanted to let the air out of a balloon, would this involve **compression** or **decompression** of air pressure? (A very tough question!)

Look carefully at the illustrations for these two words. Tell a little story about the jack-in-the-box, using the words **compression** and **decompression.**

_____

_____

_____

_____

Compressor

Compressor is a person or thing that **compresses** or **presses TOGETHER**. It usually refers to a machine used to **compress** gases.

Depressor

Using the definition for **compressor** as your guide, write a definition for the word **depressor**.

_____

_____

What do you think a tongue **depressor** does? Who might use one?

_____

_____

Depression

Depression can refer to physical **pressing DOWN**, such as **depressions** in the snow caused by tires, boots or skis.

Depression also describes a person emotionally **pressed DOWN, depressed.** Many common phrases, such as "**DOWN** in the dumps" or "full of gloom and doom," describe this kind of **depression**.

Give at least two examples of words or phrases used to describe someone who is **NOT** in a state of **depression**. You may want to ask an adult for some suggestions.

_____

_____

_____

 You may also see the word **Depression** in your Social Studies book. During periods of economic **depression**, people are **pressed DOWN** because prices are high and jobs are hard to get.

Does anyone in your family have memories of the Great **Depression** of the 1930s? If so, ask them what life was like back then.

Expression

Expression literally means a **pressing** OUT and often relates to putting an idea or thought into words.

Joel's **expression** of 'true love' for Isabel wasn't enough to keep her from marrying Carlos.

Expression also describes common or popular phrases such as "bad hair day" or "on cloud nine."

Expression can mean showing your feelings by look, voice or action.

A scowl is an **expression** of displeasure.

In the sentences that follow, identify which definition is appropriate for the word **expression.**

  a. **statement**
  b. **commonly used phrase**
  c. **feelings shown by looks**

"Get a grip" is a popular **expression.**   _____

Socrates and Plato are well known for their **expression** of philosophical ideas.   _____

The children had happy **expressions** on their faces as they left the movie theater.   _____

Expressionless

Expressionless means without **expression,** especially in reference to a look that shows no feeling. Many times people choose to hide their feelings for various reasons. Poker players are known for their **expressionless** looks, called a "poker face." They don't want other players to know if they have a terrific hand or a pitiful one.

TeacherTip

*LESS is the only suffix that changes a word into its opposite the way the prefix **UN** does. Call attention to the addition of a second suffix in the words **expressionless** and **expressionism**.*

Many times a convicted criminal will remain **expressionless** as the jail sentence is read by the judge. Why might a criminal choose not to show **expression?**

Can you think of another situation where a person might choose to be **expressionless** and why?

_____

_____

_____

Expressionism

Expressionism describes a movement in art, drama and literature that began during the early 1900s. Free **expression** of the artist, often by distorting nature or reality, makes **expressionistic** works unique.

 Remember UNIQUE from the UNI family?

TeacherTip

*If possible, show students examples of **expressionism** and have a brief discussion of some well-known artists who were part of this movement.*

EXPRESSIONISM

WebStretcher: *Do a bit of research on* **Expressionism** *and* **Impressionism.** *Bring some examples of either kind of art to class or create your own sample.*

Expressly

Expressly has two main meanings.

1. definitely; clearly

That chocolate cake is for the bake sale, and you are **expressly** forbidden to eat it.

2. on purpose, specially, specifically

You really need to thank Uncle Otto, since he baked those cookies **expressly** for you.

Impression

Impression is an effect, a feeling or an imprint made ON a person based on an experience.

I met your sister only once, but I got the **impression** she is very intelligent.

Impression is also commonly used to describe a mark made by **pressing** or stamping.

Dr. Stiffupperlip, my orthodontist, made plaster **impressions** of my zigzag teeth.

Think of someone you have recently met. What was your first **impression** of that person? Have you since changed your opinion?

Impressive

When you've been favorably **impressed** by something or someone, that thing or person can be called **impressive.**

The new kid on our tennis team sure has an **impressive** serve!

Impressionable

Impressionable means ABLE to be **impressed** or easily influenced.

 PSST! Notice the addition of a second suffix to this word. How would it look in the Morph-O-Meter?

Would you say that adults or children are more **impressionable?** Give at least one reason for your answer.

_____

_____

Oppression

When a group of people has been **oppressed (PUSHED DOWN)** by a cruel leader, an unjust system of government, or even an uncaring society, they are victims of **oppression.**

Many dictators practice **oppression** of the poor in order to gain control of a country.

Oppressive

When a situation is **oppressive,** it is hard to bear, burdensome, cruel or unjust. **Oppressive** situations can be caused by other people or by circumstances such as lack of food or water or extreme weather.

After four days of **oppressive** rain, the whole family suffered from 'cabin fever'.

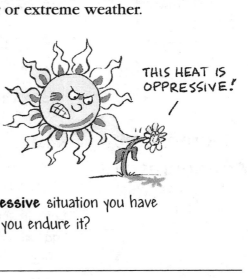

THIS HEAT IS OPPRESSIVE!

What is the most **oppressive** situation you have experienced? How did you endure it?

_____

_____

_____

_____

SideSpinner

Even though **reprimand** *may not look exactly like other members of the* **PRESS** *family, it is. It combines and shortens two words.*
   REPRESS + COMMAND = REPRIMAND.
It means to scold or rebuke harshly, especially in a formal or official way. Imagine a person in authority (an official) giving an order **(command)** *to punish someone and you have a picture of the word* **reprimand.**

Irrepressible

Suppressant

Depressant
Antidepressant

Irrepressible means difficult to control, **repress** or hold **BACK**; uncontrollable.

The Gigglealot twins fell into **irrepressible** laughter, almost ruining their oral report on **depression**.

Identify at least two other behaviors that might be **irrepressible**.

_____   _____

Suppressant is the name given to something such as a medicine or drug made to reduce **(suppress)** the seriousness of a problem rather than cure or solve it.

If you take a cough **suppressant,** you can expect (circle one):

a. **no relief**

b. **to get rid of the cough completely**

c. **that your cough may be less severe**

d. **a cherry flavored syrup**

Now that you know a little bit about a **suppressant** drug, what do you think a **depressant** drug might do for the body? How about an **antidepressant?**

Look in your dictionary, and write down the definition of a **depressant** and an **antidepressant.**

Do a Morph-O-Meter reading on the word **antidepressant.**

Press + Suffix Words

Pressing

Use your knowledge of the meanings of **press** to answer the following question.

If Ms. Ditheraday, your teacher, is called away on **pressing** business, would these be particularly important or unimportant matters?

Circle the best synonym for **pressing** as it is used in this sentence.

    a. steaming   b. printed   c. urgent   d. newsworthy

Pressure

TeacherTip

In WordWeb Two, no attempt is made to include every possible word. Some very easy words and some very hard ones have been omitted. Encourage students to add words to webs as they find them.

Pressure describes the weight or force of a situation on a person.

The **pressure** of Tuesday's project deadline forced many of the students to cancel their plans for the weekend.

When people are under **pressure,** for whatever reason, it can cause them to feel strained or "stressed out."

Many parents worry about their children dealing with peer **pressure.** Write your description of peer **pressure.** Why are parents sometimes concerned about it?

_____

_____

WebStretcher: You may be familiar with many of the **PRESS** relatives listed below. A number of them are associated with the printed or spoken word, the media. Look at the list and identify which words are very familiar and attempt to define them. Look in the dictionary for help with those less familiar. Be sure to think about why these words belong in this family.

expressive	impressionist	press conference
expresso (espresso)	press agent	press release
expressway	pressbox	printing press

Try to use at least four of these words in silly sentences or in a clever story of your own.

STORY REVIEW

 In the passage that follows, substitute one of these words from the **PRESS** family for the word or words in each underlined area.

expressionless	oppressive	pressing
expressly	press	pressure
impressionable	press conference	suppress
irrepressible	pressed	

Long Live the King!

The president of Presley Inc. invited members of the _____ to attend
                                                                    media

a special _____ organized _____ to stop the
              media meeting   *specifically*

_____ rash of rumors concerning an Elvis sighting. Many suspected
  uncontrollable

these rumors had been started as a prank to fool _____ Elvis fans.
                                                           easily influenced

The _____ heat in the packed room transformed the normally
       hard to bear, overwhelming

excitable reporters into _____ zombies. At last the president arrived.
                              poker-faced

Would he _____ all hope that the King was still alive? Because of the
              subdue, crush

_____ nature of the problem, the president seemed to be under a
      urgent

tremendous amount of _____, but at least he showed up in a freshly
                            stress; strain

_____ suit!
      ironed

Quizzical Can you guess what **vintners** press?

Getting In Shape

Never underestimate Webster's energy! Barely finished with her **press**ing matters, she's already busy **forming** the **FORM** family onto a web.

How can I, Wordsworth, make sure you get your Word's Worth out of this web? Start by imagining a potter with a lump of clay, fashioning or **forming** it into a beautiful work of art. In the process, this piece of clay takes on various shapes until the artist arrives at a finished product.

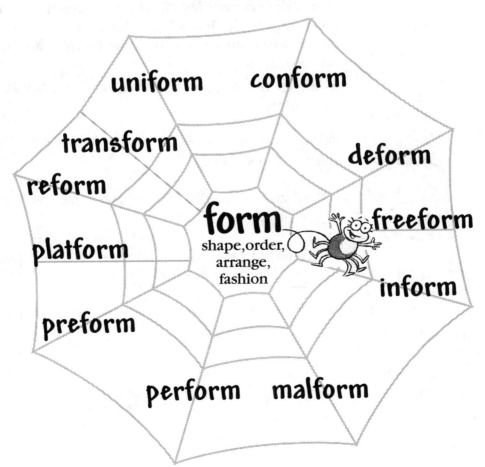

uniform

conform

transform

deform

reform

platform

form
shape, order,
arrange,
fashion

freeform

inform

preform

perform

malform

Likewise, many words in the English language come from a simple **form** and take on new looks and meanings. Our new root **FORM** offers helpful examples.

Like the word, the root **form** means to SHAPE, FASHION, ARRANGE or ORDER.

 Think of a formation of geese to help you remember that form means shape, fashion, arrange or order.

You are probably quite familiar with many **form** words. Are you able to think of a few? While studying the **FORM** web, ask yourself how these words relate to SHAPING, FASHIONING, ARRANGING, or ORDERING.

This web starts, as you see, with **form**. Like **press, form** can be used as either a noun or a verb. As a noun, **form** means the external SHAPE and structure of an object. It does not refer to things like color or material. A square blue wooden puzzle has the same **form** as a square green cardboard one.

As a verb, **form** means to FASHION or give SHAPE to something.

Identify which sentence below uses **form** as a noun **(N)** and which as a verb **(V)**.

1. Those claymation artists surely **form** some crazy-looking characters. _____

2. That melted candy bar has taken on quite an unusual **form**. _____

If you were asked to **form** your own crazy-looking character to set on your bedroom shelf, you might (circle one):

a. buy a bendable rubber doll

b. type up a descriptive paragraph of a kooky individual

c. make a collage of famously fit athletes

d. get out the modeling clay

The **form** of your crazy character might be (circle one):

a. wood or cardboard

b. purple and green with orange polka dots

c. oblong with triangular ears and square eyes

d. all of the above

Conform

CON together, with	**+**	**FORM** shape, arrange, order

To **conform** to something involves going along WITH its SHAPE, FASHION, or FORM. You SHAPE your feelings or choices to match someone else's. You agree. You may **conform** to the latest styles or to the expectations of a group of friends.

 Can you think of other instances where you find yourself **conforming?** Discuss some of the possible consequences that you might face if you make a decision not to **conform**. Is it sometimes important not to **conform?**

If you are a **conformist,** you will probably (circle one):

a. become a great artist

b. break numerous laws

c. keep up with the latest customs and styles

d. be able to bend and shape your body in various ways

Deform

DE +	FORM
away, down	shape, arrange, order

Deform means to take AWAY from the natural **form** or beauty of something. The original **form** may be disfigured or misshapen.

A well-known baseball player, Jim Abbott, has a **deformed** arm.

Despite such an obstacle, he has become an accomplished pitcher. You may have seen him pitch for the Yankees or the Angels.

If your friend exclaims that one of her french fries is **deformed**, she means that it is (circle one):

a. **cold and soggy**

b. **abnormally shaped**

c. **unusually straight and uniform looking**

d. **greasy and gross**

Freeform

FREE +	FORM
loose, unrestricted	shape, arrange, order

Freeform describes a flowing form or structure that may be irregular or out of the ordinary. Although **freeform** often pertains to an object such as a vase or particular work of art, it may also include things such as styles of dance, writing, painting, drawing, etc.

If your assignment in art class is to create a **freeform** pottery bowl, it would most likely be (circle one):

a. **extremely heavy and durable**

b. **hand-painted with stenciled designs**

c. **made from a ceramic mold**

d. **one-of-a-kind and uniquely shaped**

 How might a **freeform** dance differ from a structured dance? Would a **freeform** sculpture of a person be realistic? Why?

Inform

IN	**+**	**FORM**
in, into, within		shape, arrange, order

You stay **informed** to have ORDER IN your life, to ARRANGE your schedule accordingly.

 Give an example of a time when not being **informed** caused disORDER IN your life.

To **inform** means to pass on directly to a person facts or knowledge of some kind. If you **inform** your parents about a birthday party you wish to attend, you get the details IN ORDER and communicate them. That way you and your parents can ARRANGE transportation, gift buying, etc.

You rely on people everyday to stay **informed.** Name two groups of people whose job it is to **inform** others.

_____

_____

Which of the following might NOT be a good source to use if you were interested in staying **informed** on current events? Circle it.

a. comic books   c. sports magazines

b. newspapers   d. the Weather Channel

Malform

MAL	+	FORM
bad or badly, poor or poorly		shape, arrange, order

Something that is **malformed** is BADLY or POORLY SHAPED or distorted.

A **malformed** tennis ball would possibly be (circle one):

a. perfectly round

b. a good ball to use in a match

c. lopsided and ragged

d. a good ball to use for practice

Draw your own version of what a **malformed** ball of any kind might look like.

 WebStretcher:

Remember that many words, like unicycle, bicycle and tricycle, belong to more than one family. A fascinating web can be woven from the **mal** family. Create a web of five or more words for **mal**. Give clues and see if your friends can guess the words. Be on the alert because not every word beginning with **mal** belongs on this web. Why not?

mal
bad or badly, poor or poorly

Don't miss **mal**aria as an interesting story. What do its two morphs mean? What does their meaning tell you about what people used to think caused this disease? What really causes it?

Perform

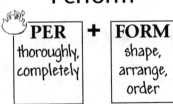

PER thoroughly, completely	**FORM** shape, arrange, order

The first clue about this word is that **per** is an INTENSIVE prefix. It means **forming COMPLETELY.** Think about that. If you give something COMPLETE **form,** you usually act it out in some way. You do something. You give what you know **form** outside of your mind.

 If necessary, check page 25 to review the meaning of an INTENSIVE.

Perform emphasizes accomplishing or doing something, usually in a skillful manner. You may **perform** well as an actor, a musician, an athlete or a student. There is no end to the various ways that you may **perform** well!

 Think of some of the things that you **perform** with skill.

An example of people who **perform** their duties especially well might be (circle one):

    a. inept idlers

    b. bungling burglars

    c. messy maids

    d. proficient pilots

Explain why you chose this answer.

Platform

PLAT	**+**	**FORM**
flat, broad		shape, arrange, order

MY PLATFORM IS MALFORMED!

A **platform** is usually a raised FLAT or level surface where speakers stand to address audiences.

 (PSST!) *Think of a plate to remember that plat means flat.*

It also describes all the plans and promises politicians make before they are elected. These promises are probably called **platforms** because politicians usually stand on **platforms** to announce them.

If you were running for class president, would you prefer to deliver your speech from a stage or from an orchestra pit? Why?

Have you ever heard of **platform** shoes? Explain how they fit into the meaning of **platform**.

The prefix **plat** doesn't have a large family. However, it does have some fun and funny family members.

Fill in the missing words.

A **plat**itude is a **flat**, dull remark.

A **plat**eau is a **flat** _____ .

A **plat**ypus has **flat**, webbed _____ and a **flat, broad** _____ .

Preform

PRE	**+**	**FORM**
before, beforehand, in advance		shape, arrange, order

Preform pertains to SHAPING or **forming** IN ADVANCE or BEFOREHAND.

 If you were planning to grill hamburgers for a party, would you save time by purchasing bulk hamburger or **preformed** hamburger patties? Why?

Reform

RE again, anew, once more	**+**	**FORM** shape, arrange, order

Reform is literally to FORM AGAIN or take a new SHAPE. Most commonly it means to make better or improve something by removing its imperfections or faults. Many people are interested in **reforming** laws or even entire governments.

Name some things that you would like to **reform.**

In attempting to **reform** a dog's unruly behavior, which of the following might be the best choice? Circle it.

a. **enroll the dog in obedience classes**

b. **buy the dog a nice collar**

c. **get a cat**

d. **take the dog to a good groomer**

REFORM SCHOOL

Transform

TRANS across, over	**+**	**FORM** shape, arrange, order

Transform refers to a change in **form** or appearance. It suggests a change in the look, SHAPE or nature of a person or thing, not always for the better.

Fairy tales often include characters that are **transformed** in some way. The wolf in Little Red Riding Hood appeared to be a kindly grandmother. Try to think of other examples of characters being **transformed** in fairy tales, stories, movies or TV shows.

Which of the following would NOT cause a person to be **transformed?** Circle one.

a. **having plastic surgery**

b. **losing a lot of weight**

c. **having split personalities**

d. **keeping the same hairstyle**

Uniform

UNI	+	FORM
one, single		shape, arrange, order

 Remember UNIFORM from the UNI web?

A **uniform** is a **form** that is always the same, all alike and not changing or varying. You are probably most familiar with **uniform** as clothing or a type of dress worn by a group. If you wear a **uniform** at school or as part of a team, your clothing itself **forms** you into ONE group.

 Can you give some other examples of items that are **uniform** in some way?

When a salesperson in the sporting goods department informs you that all the soccer balls in stock are **uniform** in size, this means (circle one):

a. some of the balls are much smaller than others

b. all of the balls are exactly the same

c. only one color is available

d. only one size is available

UNIFORM

LINK 'N LEARN

 Draw a line from each word in Column I to its best synonym(s) in Column II.

FORM (as a root)	shape beforehand
CONFORM	disfigure
DEFORM	change
INFORM	do, carry out, act
PERFORM	shape, arrange, order
PREFORM	tell, give facts
REFORM	agree, go along with, follow
TRANSFORM	improve, renew

 TeacherTip

For this review, we have included only the web words with directional prefixes since the mastery of these prefixes in their multiple forms and meanings is key to so many more difficult words.

Form
Part Two

Remember WordWeb Two does not contain every possible word. Can you add others?

Now that you've been **transformed** by some **FORM** words, you are quite well-**informed** and will probably **conform** to this new lesson rather easily. Get ready to **perform** new tasks as you gather **information** about the SHAPE, FASHION, and ARRANGEMENT of more members of the **form** family.

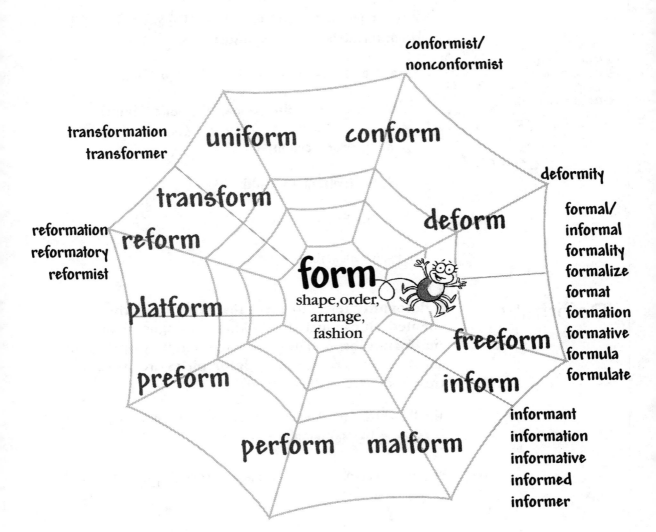

Conformist

Conformists are people who easily follow customs, rules or styles of a group. They stick with the FASHION of the day. **Nonconformists** do just the opposite. They choose not to obey or comply.

 Would a rebel in a group be considered a **conformist** or a **nonconformist?** Why? Is it possible to be both a **conformist** and a **nonconformist?** Give examples of when you are a **conformist.** When might you be a **nonconformist?**

Based on your understanding of these two terms, decide whether the people or types of people listed below are most likely **conformists** or **non-conformists.**

THAT NONCONFORMIST IS DEFORMING OUR FORMATION!

a. Dennis Rodman of the Chicago Bulls

b. the pope of the Roman Catholic Church

c. a career criminal

d. a disobedient child

e. an Eagle Scout

 Explain your answers.

Deformity

A **deformity** refers to a part that is not properly **formed.** It can include any kind of disfigurement or **malformation** usually considered unsightly or ugly. In some societies people with **deformities** are cruelly treated or shunned.

The Hunchback of Notre Dame was despised and feared because of his **deformity.**

 Would a piece of candy that has a **deformity** be safe to eat? Why or why not?

Inform Words

Remember that **inform** means to pass facts or knowledge on to another person. The facts are ORDERED or ARRANGED to make clear communication possible. Keep this definition in mind while attempting the exercises below.

Would an **informant** be helpful to police investigating a crime? Explain your answer.

_____

_____

_____

Knowledge, facts or news of any kind is commonly called _____. Choose a web word from page 65 for your answer.

Imagine that you are planning your very first snow skiing vacation. Who would you expect to be most well-**informed** on the subject? Circle one.

a. a travel agent specializing in cruises

b. your best friend who is an avid water-skier

c. a ski instructor from the area you wish to visit

d. your grandparents who have friends in Colorado

Which two words from the web on page 65 are good synonyms for tattletale?

_____

_____

SideSpinner

There are several words in our language that have been created by combining portions of words to make a new word. An example that you may be familiar with is: brocciflower (broccoli and cauliflower). The **form** family has one of these words also. An **infomercial** combines two common words, **information** and commercial. Longer than a regular commercial, an **infomercial** gives education and instruction about a product and its use. Can you think of other such words? Try your hand at making up some combinations of your own to create completely new words. Test your creations out on a friend. Why not make a list of your group's creations.

Reformation
Reformatory
Reformist

REFORM SCHOOL

Reformists are persons interested in improving, correcting or ending a certain practice. Their main goal is a change for the better. In order to accomplish it, thoughts, ideas or practices must be ARRANGED AGAIN in a different and hopefully better FASHION.

Young people who need to make a serious change for the better are sometimes sent to a **reformatory.**

 What might be the main goals of a **reformatory** or a **reform** school?

Reformation describes the change that takes place.

If Tom Sawyer's frustrated aunt decided to send him to a **reformatory,** she would hope that he would experience a **reformation.**

 When used with a capital R, the term **Reformation** refers to a significant historical movement in Europe during the 16th century. What started out as a plan to **reform** the Roman Catholic Church ended up as the **forming** of the Protestant churches in Western Europe.

Transformation
Transformer

In the classic Grimm's fairy tale *Cinderella,* many magical changes occur. The story focuses much attention upon how Cinderella is **transformed.**

Complete each sentence with either **transformation** or **transformer.**

When Cinderella's fairy godmother appears with her magic wand, she plays the role of the _____ in the tale.

Cinderella's change from a servant girl in rags to a beautiful princess elegantly adorned for the ball is an example of a

_____.

In the world of electricity, a **transformer** is a device that changes electric current into higher or lower voltage. Such devices are often used for electric trains, portable CD players, electric keyboards and numerous children's toys. They lower the voltage required in an effort to make these items safer. The electrical energy coming out of an ordinary household outlet is changed or altered through the use of a **transformer**.

WebStretcher: *Among the words on the web on page 65 that follow the* **prefix + root + suffix = word pattern,** *you will notice words with identical suffixes or endings.*

For example the words **informer** *and* **transformer** *both end in* **er.** *Review what you learned about the suffix* **er** *on page 29. How does the suffix change the words* **inform** *and* **transform?**

Think of two or three other easy verbs like work and swim to which you could add an **er.** *(Sometimes, as in swimmer, the last consonant needs to be repeated.)*

_____

_____

_____

Would the words **weather** *and* **feather** *be examples of* **er** *suffix words? Why or why not?*

Form + Suffix Words

Formal/ Informal

Formal implies careful attention to set **forms** and procedures according to certain customs or rules. Tuxedos and evening gowns are examples of **formal** attire.

 What are examples of **formal** clothing? **Informal** clothing? Which do you prefer?

Where would you expect to hear a fair amount of **formal** language? Circle one.

a. a locker room

b. a courtroom

c. a rock concert

d. at home

WELL, YOU'RE IN HIGH FORM!

FORMAL   INFORMAL

Which of the following is an example of a **formal** greeting? Circle it.

a. Hi there, folks!

b. Good evening, ladies and gentlemen.

c. Nice to see ya!

d. How's it going?

Give your own example of a **formal** goodbye.

_____

_____

TeacherTip

*Emphasize the different meanings of the prefix **IN**. In informal, in means **not**. **Informal** is the opposite of **formal**. In informant, in means **in** or **into**. An **informant** puts **information** into the minds or hands of someone else. When students meet a new word that begins with the prefix **in**, the question they need to ask is: Does the **in** in this word mean **in** or **not?** Students gain power over language by learning the right questions to ask of words.*

Formality

A **formality** is any procedure required by custom or rule, outward **form** or ceremony. Bowing in the presence of royalty is considered a **formality,** as is shaking hands before the start of a boxing match or at the end of a tennis match. **Formalities** are used in **formal** settings or on **formal** occasions.

Give at least one example of a **formality** that is part of your culture and one that is part of another culture anywhere in the world.

My culture

_____

_____

_____

Another culture

_____

_____

_____

Formalize

FORMAL

To **formalize** is to make **formal** or give a definite **form** to something, to ARRANGE all the details. If you **formalize** your plans to go to a movie, you make the plan definite by establishing where, when and with whom you will see a selected film.

What might you need to do to **formalize** an invitation to a party?

Format

Format has come to mean the design or ARRANGEMENT of things but especially the ARRANGEMENT of a book or magazine.

The **format** for a weekly television sitcom usually includes (circle one):

a. all new actors for each episode

b. a tragic ending

c. no commercials

d. a new story for each episode

List two or three common things included in many book or magazine **formats.**

_____

_____

Formation

Formation most commonly emphasizes the way in which something is **formed.** It specifically pertains to ARRANGEMENT or structure.

The geese flew in a perfect V-**formation.**

Where might you see some interesting **formations?** Circle one.

a. a cloudy sky

b. a military base

c. a football game

d. all of the above

THAT NONCONFORMIST IS DEFORMING OUR FORMATION!

 Explain your answer.

Formative

Formative refers to development, **forming** or molding.

During a child's **formative** years, which of the following is especially significant? Circle one.

a. becoming a Republican

b. receiving proper nutrition and exercise

c. wearing stylish clothes

d. lifting weights

Formula

Formula has numerous useful meanings. Originally, it referred to a set **form** of words. It has also come to refer to a rule for doing something; a recipe or prescription; a mixture; an expression of a chemical compound using chemical symbols (e.g., H_2O); or a definite plan or method.

DID YOU FOLLOW THE FORMULA?

The use of **formulas** is very critical in our world today.

 Think of some reasons why **formulas** are so important. What might happen if **formulas** are not used or followed? Do you ever use **formulas?** Why are formulas even necessary?

Formulate

Formulate means to state definitely or systematically. It involves careful arrangement of ideas, such as **formulating** a plan.

In the military world, it is very important to **formulate** specific guidelines for soldiers to follow.

 Why is this so important? Think of other places where **formulating** ideas and plans is critical for smooth operations.

WebStretcher: *Based on your knowledge of the root* **FORM** *and any help you need from your trusty dictionary, give your own definition of the following words:*

multiform

_____

_____

cruciform

_____

_____

cuneiform

_____

_____

formless

_____

_____

After reading the silly student poem that follows, write one of your own, using any of the words that have been studied in the **FORM** family. Try hard to make clear in your poem the meaning of the word you choose.

Formless from Gormless

There once was an alien formless
Who came from the planet of Gormless.
His shape never stayed
When soccer he played
And as a result he was scoreless!

STORY REVIEW

 In the passage that follows, substitute one of these words from the **FORM** family for the word or words in each underlined area.

deformities	informed	transformed
formations	platform	uniform
formulate	reform	

All Cracked Up

Proudly dressed in his dignified _____, Humpty Dumpty sat on a
clothing worn by a group

dangerously narrow _____. Dreamily he gazed up at the slow-moving
raised, flat surface

cloud _____ floating by. Within seconds a most terrible tragedy
arrangements

_____ him into quite a different egg!
changed in form

The authorities regretfully _____ his family that poor Mr. Dumpty had
passed on facts

suffered serious _____. Not even the king's finest horses and men
disfigurements

could _____ a plan to _____ him. The family never
prepare, arrange   *shape again*

quite understood what the horses could have done anyway.

Guess what! A free page just for your thoughts and doodles . . .

Porter, Please

The human person served as the first beast of burden. Long before animals became domesticated, throughout the hunting and gathering days of prehistory, your earliest ancestors followed the weather and the seasons from place to place, CARRYING their belongings with them. Does that give you a picture of how naturally CARRY words found their way into language?

No wonder, then, that there are so many ways in English to say CARRY. One large word family involves the root **PORT**. **PORT** words explain how persons, things, messages are CARRIED from one place **(port)** to another. The way persons CARRY (conduct) themselves is also part of the **PORT** family.

(PSST!) *Think of a porter to remember that port means CARRY.*

Then relax and let these next two lessons CARRY you to a deeper understanding of **PORT** words.

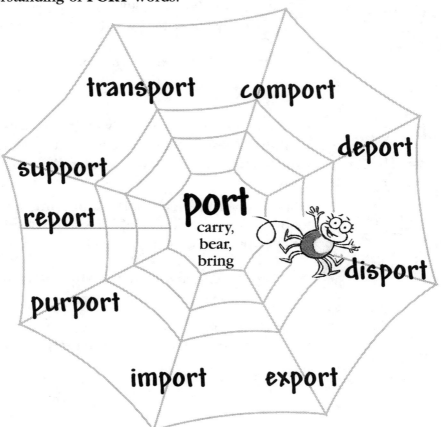

Like **press** and **form, port** is both a root and a word. As a word in itself, **port** means harbor, a place where boats can load and unload. Cargo is CARRIED into and out of boats. The boats CARRY the goods from one place to another. Wherever you see the word **port,** be on the lookout for something being CARRIED.

Comport

COM	+	PORT
together, with		carry, bear, bring

To **comport** yourself properly is to CARRY yourself WITH dignity, to get your act TOGETHER, to behave in an appropriate manner.

Sometimes persons are expected to **comport** themselves with reverence and respect, other times with assurance, authority, humor, lightheartedness, etc.

 Can you name such occasions? It is wise to **comport** yourself properly at all times. Why?

If you were being interviewed, would you try to **comport** yourself with (circle all correct choices):

    a. ease   b. respect   c. aloofness   d. humility

Deport

DE	+	PORT
from, away		carry, bear, bring

People in any country illegally might be **deported** (CARRIED AWAY) legally. A government has the right to expel **(deport)** those who threaten the welfare of its citizens.

Might a government consider **deporting** any of the following – foreign criminals, spies, stowaways, persons without proper permits and papers?

 Give any reasons you can think of why a government might consider allowing such people to remain.

Deport can also be used as a synonym for **comport,** the way people behave or CARRY themselves.

On their **report** cards, your grandparents and great grandparents received regular grades in **deportment,** what today you call conduct grades. Why not ask some older person you know if they ever received **deportment** grades. Maybe you'll hear a great memory from that person's childhood.

Disport

DIS	+	PORT
away		carry, bear, bring

You may live your entire life without ever seeing or hearing the word **disport** actually used. It means to let yourself be CARRIED AWAY, to amuse yourself in a carefree way, to have fun.

Yet one of the most common words in English is a shortened form of **disport.** Can you guess what that word is?

 No newspaper would be quite complete without this section and many people read it first when the paper comes.

Of course, the word is **sport** and still means an activity that CARRIES people AWAY from their jobs and worries and lets them have fun "at the old ball game."

Good **sports** CARRY themselves properly and don't get CARRIED AWAY with anger and frustration, even when they lose.

 Who is the best **sport** you know?

Export

EX out, out of	**+**	**PORT** carry, bear, bring

This **port** word is easy to understand just by looking at its morphs. Something gets taken OUT OF one country and CARRIED in some way to another, often to be sold.

As you know, the harbor from which something is **exported** by water is called a **port** and the receiving harbor is also a **port**. Goods CARRIED by air go in and OUT OF air**ports**.

Many harbor cities have the word **port** in their name, such as **Port**land, New**port**, Shreve**port**, Daven**port**. Can you name others? Can you think of a country with **port** in its name?

Can you name several things your country **exports?** Why does a country **export?**

EXPORTS   IMPORTS

Import

IM in, into	**+**	**PORT** carry, bear, bring

N is a chameleon letter!

Import, as you can see from its morphs, is the direct opposite of **export**. Goods brought INTO any country from outside are **imported** goods. Labels sewn INTO your clothes may tell whether they are **imported**. Perhaps you have ridden in an automobile that is an **import**.

Does your country **import** any of these items – tulip bulbs, coffee, oil, tin? What else does your country **import?** Why do countries **import** things? Is an item made in California and sent to New York an **import?** Explain your answer.

Import as a noun means to be of worth, influence or significance.

The message sent to the gallows proved of great **import** to the prisoner whose life was spared.

Purport

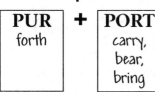

PUR forth	+	PORT carry, bear, bring

Purport means to CARRY FORTH in the sense of an intention or a scheme of some kind.

He **purported** to mow the grass before he left on his skateboard.

Often the word is used for a false claim or intention. (If that's the case in the previous example, the grass is still growing!)

They **purported** interest in their classmate but really only wanted a cheap ride to the party.

As a noun, **purport** means the essential meaning or main idea of something, such as the **purport** of a newspaper editorial or a political speech.

When Mr. Roundabout lectures, it's often impossible to catch the **purport** of his message.

Report

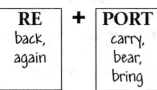

RE back, again	+	PORT carry, bear, bring

From the morphs of **report,** you know that something such as a message or news item is CARRIED BACK and delivered to others. If you **report** for the media, you CARRY the news to the public AGAIN and AGAIN. Such a **report** might be spoken or written.

If your home is robbed, you **report** (CARRY the news) to the police. If you have a job, you **report** (CARRY yourself BACK) to work. Any time people are asked to check BACK in with a certain person or at a set time or place, **report** can be used.

The students on the field trip were told to **report** back to the bus at three.

Below are several crossword clues about things **reported** in newspapers, on radio and tv. Fill in the missing letters.

W ___ ___ ___ ___ ___ ___   Clue: Check the skies.

T ___ ___ ___ ___ ___ ___   Clue: Check the streets.

S ___ ___ ___ ___   M ___ ___ ___ ___ ___   (Two words)
                                                     Clue: Check your wallet.

Support

SUP	**+**	**PORT**
under, up from under		carry, bear, bring

B is a chameleon letter!

The morphs in **support** create a picture of someone or something CARRIED or held UP FROM UNDERneath, the way a bridge would be **supported** by its pylons. People wear leg or back braces for **support**, to help them CARRY themselves without pain. You might offer moral **support** to some group or individual, which means you agree with their cause or goal and encourage them.

Monetary **support** means you are assisting (circle the answer):

   a. for the moment   **c. for one month**

   b. with money   **d. with promises**

We depend on many persons and institutions as we go through life. Describe what kinds of **support** could come from family and friends, schools, places of worship and government.

Transport

TRANS	+	PORT
over, across		carry, bear, bring

Persons and things CARRIED OVER or ACROSS a long distance are said to be **transported,** hauled from place to place. **Imports** and **exports,** of course, have to be **transported** in some way. Troops are **transported** by land, air and water.

Emotions can **transport** a person's feelings to a higher degree, usually of joy ("on cloud nine," "head in the clouds").

Can you think of an ad or commercial that claims some product can **transport** you to a new or different way of feeling? Do you think these claims really work?

Study the entire **PORT** WordWeb once more. Place some form of a **PORT** word in each blank. Use words only once.

A late-breaking news story _____ that if the athlete could not _____ himself properly, the scholarship committee could no longer _____ him.

The products that country buys are of better quality than the things it _____.

The realization that they would not be _____ because they found their passports _____ them into a state of excited relief.

PORTER, PLEASE TRANSPORT MY PORTMANTEAU THROUGH THAT PORTAL.

AND WATCH OUT FOR THE PORTCULLIS!

SideSpinner

The word **RAPPORT** fits in this family, too. It's an interesting com- bination of two prefixes, each with a chameleon letter, and the root. **RE + AD + PORT = RAPPORT.**
The letter **E** in **RE** drops out. The letter **D** in **AD** morphs to **P.** The blending makes the strong and lovely English word **RAPPORT.**
Rapport means "TO CARRY TOWARD OVER AND OVER AGAIN." **Rapport** describes a relationship in which there is under- standing, respect, and often affection on both sides. Mutual feelings are carried **TOWARD** the other by each per- son in the relationship.

Her clients rated her highly as a babysitter because of her **rapport** with children.

E is a chameleon letter!

D is a chameleon letter!

WebStretcher: Explain how the words **airport**, **carport** and **passport** belong to the **PORT** family.

LINK 'N LEARN

Draw a line from each word in Column I to its best synonym(s) in Column II.

PORT (as a root)	banish
COMPORT	inform, announce
DEPORT	carry, bear, bring
DISPORT	behave
EXPORT	receive goods
IMPORT	encourage
PURPORT	claim, intend
REPORT	haul; cause strong feelings
SUPPORT	play, amuse
TRANSPORT	ship goods

Port
Part Two

I'm pleased to **report** that you haven't quite finished with the **PORT** family yet. Many **important** new words remain for you to learn. Be a good **sport!** Webster and I will **support** your efforts. Don't forget to add to the web words that Webster didn't include.

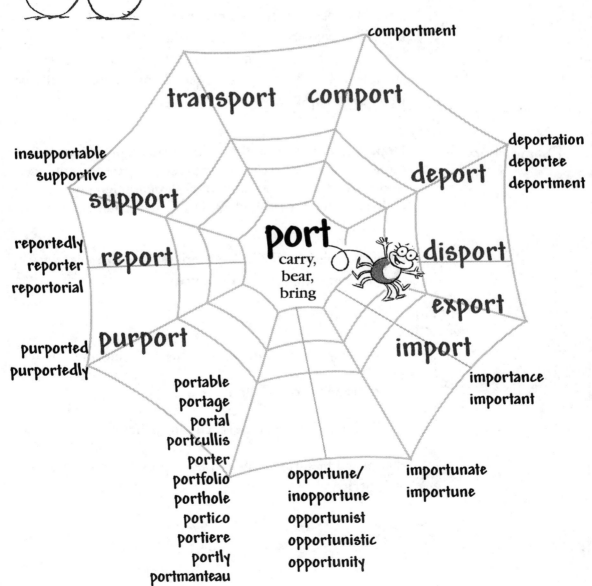

comportment

transport   comport

deportation
deportee
deport   deportment

insupportable
supportive

support

port
carry,
bear,
bring

disport

reportedly
reporter   report
reportorial

export

purported   purport
purportedly

import

importance
important

portable
portage
portal
portcullis
porter
portfolio
porthole
portico
portiere
portly
portmanteau

opportune/
inopportune
opportunist
opportunistic
opportunity

importunate
importune

Comportment
Deportment

The suffix **MENT** changes the verbs **comport** and **deport** into nouns, **comportment** and **deportment**. As you know, both verbs can mean "to CARRY oneself." **Comportment** and **deportment** too, are synonyms and mean how a person behaves, good or bad manners.

The **deportment** of the sixth grade class during their winter field trip earned them another one in the spring.

 Think of some book you have read recently. Give an example of both good and bad **deportment** by the characters in the story. How did the **comportment** of these characters affect the story? Does your **comportment** affect your life in some way?

Deportee

Deportee comes from the other meaning of **deport**, to force to leave a country. A **deportee** is a person sentenced to **deportation** or banishment FROM a foreign country. An exile is a person banished FROM his own country for some reason.

All of the following EXCEPT one are reasons **deportees** might have for not wanting to be **deported**. Circle it.

I'M BEING DEPORTED.

a. need to keep a job

b. desire to reunite with family in homeland

c. freedom of religion

d. fear of political persecution at home

 What would be a reason that a young person might not want to be deported?

Important
Importance

Important and **importance** are two common words in this family. Both mean BEARING or CARRYING great value, meaning, influence or power in a person's life.

 Can you name a person, a thing and an activity that have **importance** in your life? How does what you consider **important** tell **important** things about you as a person?

Importune
Importunate

Importune and **importunate** are two less familiar words in this family. They mean to annoy or pester, to bother others with constant demands.

Mr. Wilson considers Dennis the Menace a very **importunate** boy.

  Think of some **importunate** TV character. What makes this person so annoying?

In the word **IMPORTANT**, IM = IN. Something **important** CARRIES its value INside itself.

In the word **IMPORTUNATE**, IM = NOT. An **importunate** person is NOT a **port** of refuge for the person being annoyed.

TeacherTip

Review the two meanings of the prefix **IN** in the words **INFORMANT** and **INFORMAL**, page 70. The prefix **IM** has the same two meanings: **IN** and **NOT**. In the word **IMPRISON**, for example, **IM** means **IN**. In the word **IMPATIENT**, **IM** means **NOT**. Make sure students understand this difference in easy words so they can handle it in more difficult words like the ones in this lesson.

IT'S IMPORTANT TO CARRY A MAP!

DEAD END

Opportunity
Opportune
Opportunistic

TeacherTip

*Note that even though there is no verb **OPPORT**, several significant nouns and adjectives exist. It might be challenging to ask students to invent a meaning for the imaginary word **OPPORT** after you have studied this small section of the lesson.*

THIS IS A GREAT OPPORTUNITY!

I HOPE HE'S NOT BEING OPPORTUNISTIC!

FOR SALE

Everyone gets an **opportunity** now and then. Perhaps you've never wondered, though, where the word gets its meaning. The familiar saying in English "When my ship comes in" means "When good luck comes my way." That is exactly what the morphs in **OPPORTUNITY** mean. In this word **OB** means "at" and **PORT** means "harbor," literally  B is a chameleon letter! the time when my ship comes into **port**, a long awaited moment, a time for rejoicing. An **opportunity** provides a lucky break, just the time or chance you've been wanting.

Opportune is a close relative of **opportunity**. It means just the right time for something to happen.

Everyone agreed that the week after exams was the most **opportune** time for the party.

Suppose, though, that you were invited to the party, really wanted to go, but had already promised to babysit. For you the party came at an **inopportune** time.

In the last sentence, **INOPPORTUNE** means (circle the two most accurate answers):

a. **exactly the right time**

b. **exactly the wrong time**

c. **an unfortunate time**

d. **an important time**

Opportunistic people (**opportunists**) are those who use every **opportunity** for selfish reasons without thinking of others. Such a person might offer lecture notes to a classmate who had been ill only in exchange for candy.

 Either by yourself or in small groups, write a 5 to 7 sentence story using at least four **opportune** words. If there is time, act out your story for the class.

Purported
Purportedly
Reportedly

Purported is a synonym for assumed or supposed.

Mr. T. Rex is the **purported** author of that quote on dinosaur disappearance.

Purportedly and **reportedly** are closely related in meaning. Something **purportedly** said or heard can often be misleading or completely false, the result of rumor and gossip. Something **reportedly** said should arise from facts and proper investigation.

Which word is more closely related to hearsay?

_____

Which word describes the work of the tabloids?

_____

Which word describes information likely to be accurate?

_____

Reporter
Reportorial

A **reporter** writes or broadcasts the news, CARRIES it to the public, often in a style or manner described as **reportorial.**

Choose some event that has happened recently, either in your life or in world news, and write a short article about it in a **reportorial** style.

_____

_____

_____

_____

_____

Supportive

Make your own **Morph-O-Meter** reading of the word **supportive**.

SUP (a chameleon form of **SUB**) is a prefix meaning _____ _____ .

PORT is a root meaning _____ .

IVE is a suffix meaning likely to.

Study the morphs. Circle the closest synonym for **supportive**:

a. overbearing   c. helpful

b. likable   d. underpaid

Complete the following sentences with information that makes them true.

A **supportive** person often

_____

Supportive evidence might help a jury

_____

Insupportable

Insupportable can describe conditions very difficult to BEAR, statements that cannot be proven or an offensive attitude.

Supportive and **insupportable** each fit in one blank in the following sentence. Place each word where it belongs.

With all our banners and noisemakers, we had hoped to be

_____

of our team but, when the sleet and hail started, we found the whole situation _____ .

Port + Suffix Words

Portable
Portage
Porter
Portly

Some **PORT** + words develop by adding a simple suffix. The suffix **ER** usually indicates a person, the doer of an action.

What does a **porter** do?

_____

_____

_____

_____

PORTER, PLEASE TRANSPORT MY PORTMANTEAU THROUGH THAT PORTAL.

AND WATCH OUT FOR THE PORTCULLIS!

The suffix **ABLE** means what it says "able to."

Something **portable** is able to be _____.

The suffix **AGE** has multiple meanings, including "the act of." **Portage** is the ACT OF CARRYING boats and supplies over land from one body of water to another.

 Look carefully at the illustration of this word. Who is being **portaged**, Webster or Wordsworth? Who seems to be employed by a **portaging** company?

The suffix **LY** can mean "like." **Portly** means CARRYING a certain amount of physical weight LIKE a person of some **importance**. A **portly** person, although large and heavy, usually CARRIES himself with a certain dignity.

Portal
Portcullis
Portico
Portiere

Remember that **port** as a word means harbor? It can also mean gate, another kind of passageway through which things can be CARRIED. There are four **port +** words that describe different kinds of gates or doorways.

Portal is the most generic of these four words. It can refer to any gate, doorway or entrance. However, it often describes the entrance to a splendid building or one where important activities take place. A library, for example, might be considered a **portal** of knowledge, a courtroom, a **portal** of justice.

A **portico** is a porch or covered walkway or entryway often across the front of a building. The roof of fancier **porticoes** can be supported by columns.

A **portcullis** is a heavy iron grating like the ones lowered to protect the entry of a castle or fortified town. Its morphs have an interesting translation:

port (GATE) + cullis (SLIDING) = portcullis.

A **portiere** is a curtain of cloth or beads hung in a doorway to form a partition from one room to another.

Which one might you be afraid to cross? Which one would you like at the entrance to your bedroom?

Draw your own version of each of these passageways and ask a classmate to identify them.

PORTER, PLEASE TRANSPORT MY PORTMANTEAU THROUGH THAT PORTAL.

AND WATCH OUT FOR THE PORTCULLIS!

Port + Root Words

Portfolio
Porthole
Portmanteau

Some **port** words are compound, words that have more than one root.

A **portfolio** is a flat carrying case for items like business documents, manuscripts or photographs. Its morphs **port (CARRY) + folio (SHEET OF PAPER)** describe a briefcase. **Portfolio** can also refer to the things CARRIED in the case, like a stock **portfolio** or an artist's collection of paintings and sketches.

MY PORTFOLIO SHOULD BE PORTABLE BUT IT'S TOO PORTLY TO TRANSPORT!

 Does your school use **portfolio** assessment? If so, how does this form of student evaluation fit in with the definition of **portfolio?**

The word **portmanteau** describes a case larger than a **portfolio.** Once again, its morphs give us all the information we need to understand it: **port (CARRY) + manteau (CLOAK, MANTLE).** They show that a **portmanteau** is a traveling suitcase that opens into two flat compartments in which you might CARRY both paper and clothing.

The word **porthole** refers to a window on the side of a ship and also to an opening in the walls of a fort. People in forts used **portholes** as lookout places for defense.

Choose one word from this list to fill in each blank. Each word is used only once.

portage   **portal**   **portfolio**   **portico**   **portly**

The _____ gentleman, with _____ in hand, walked through the open _____ onto the _____ where he discussed with the waiting group of campers the best way to _____ in the north woods.

WebStretcher: *Those of you who love language as much as I do can really learn something complicated and interesting here. The* **PORT** *family contains two other words that look quite different from their relatives. That's because they begin and end with chameleon letters.*

P is a chameleon letter!   T is a chameleon letter!

In these two words, the **P** at the beginning of **PORT** becomes an **F, Fl** or **FJ.** The **T** at the end becomes a **D.** We end up with **ford** and **fjord.**

A **ford** describes a shallow place in a river across which people and goods can be **CARRIED.** What is the relationship between **portaging** supplies and **fording** supplies? Redraw the **portage** picture to illustrate **fording** instead. What changes must be made to the picture?

A **fjord** (alternate spelling **fiord**) is a long narrow inlet of the sea between steep cliffs. Because it is so narrow, a **fjord** may offer the only place for **CARRYING** things or people across the sea. What countries are known for their **fjords?**

Quizzical Does an eskimo need a **portico?**

STORY REVIEW

 In the passage that follows, substitute one of these words from the **PORT** family for the word or words in each underlined area.

comportment	opportune	porthole	reports
importance	portable	portly	supportive
imported	porter	purportedly	transporting
insupportable	portfolio	rapport	

Time to Face the Music

Portia Davenport bought a _____ CD player _____

easily carried *supposedly*

_____ from Tuneport, the electronics capital of the world. She carried

brought into a country

it around in a special _____ and constantly bragged about its

briefcase

_____ to her. Her usually _____ friends found her

worth, value *helpful*

bragging _____.

unbearable

Since Portia's obnoxious _____ was causing her to lose friends, she

behavior

decided to stop _____ her CD player to school. Now she happily

carrying, hauling

_____ that her _____ with her friends is greatly

tells the news *relationship*

improved. This could not have happened at a more _____ time! The

fortunate

CD player no longer works after being dropped through a _____ by a

a window on the side of a ship

_____ and very apologetic _____.

large, dignified *person who carries luggage*

Guess what! A free page just for your thoughts and doodles . . .

Tractors . . . What a Drag!

Like carrying, PULLING and DRAGGING have always played a big part in human life. As early as possible, humans trained animals to do the heaviest work. Gradually, machines began to do the work of animals.

PSST! **How and why do you think the word horsepower was born?**

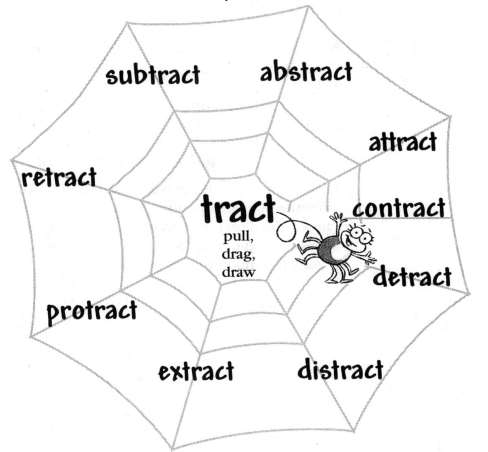

subtract

abstract

retract

attract

tract
pull,
drag,
draw

contract

detract

protract

extract

distract

In the late 1800s, **tractors** began to replace farm animals to PULL plows. These days, **tractors** are complicated pieces of machinery used not only in agriculture but also in many areas of construction. Modern **tractors** are capable of PULLING much more than plows.

Our new root, **TRACT,** means to PULL, DRAG or DRAW.

 Think of a TRACTOR to remember that TRACT means PULL.

See how many new words you can PULL from this root.

Like press, form, and port, **tract** is both a root and a word. As a word in itself, **tract** has several different meanings, all referring to PULLING, DRAGGING, DRAWING in some way. The most common use refers to a **tract** of land or water, a section DRAWN OUT of a larger area.

The sailors feared that particular **tract** of the Pacific Ocean where many ships had sunk.

 Which word is not an appropriate synonym for **tract** in the following sentence? Circle it.

The county planning commission selected a(n) **tract** of land along the river for a public park.

    a. parcel   **b. stadium**   **c. area**   **d. portion**

Another important use of **tract** refers to different systems within the body that perform specific functions. For example, the digestive **tract** is the collection of organs DRAWN throughout the body that digests food and converts it to nutrients the body needs.

Abstract

AB(S)	**+**	TRACT
away from		pull, drag, draw

S is a chameleon letter!

Attract

AT	**+**	TRACT
to, toward		pull, drag, draw

D is a chameleon letter!

To **abstract** something is to PULL or DRAW it AWAY, to remove it, sometimes without permission. Key ideas or examples can be **abstracted** from a larger work. In this use, **abstract** means to summarize or DRAW a meaningful piece or thought AWAY FROM the whole.

The poet **abstracted** several poems from his portfolio to send to the publisher.

 Remember PORTFOLIO from the PORT lesson?

 Some people like to read complete books or articles. Others prefer a shorter form **abstracted** from the whole. Short forms of a longer work are called **abstracts** or abridgments. Give one advantage of each kind of reading.

To be **attracted** to something is to be DRAWN TOWARD it. To **attract** is to cause interest, attention, even admiration. What types of people are you **attracted** to and why? Think of your best friends and what first **attracted** you to them.

Are your friends smart, funny, athletic or maybe extra friendly? Your friends probably share many qualities that you find **attract**ive in other people. Have you ever heard someone say: "You can **attract** more flies with honey than with vinegar!" What do you think it means?

Contract

CON together, with	**+**	TRACT pull, drag, draw

M is a chameleon letter!

As a verb, the word **contract** has several different meanings. When people contract with one another, they PULL TOGETHER and form some type of agreement. People can **contract** WITH other people simply by making a promise.

 Can you think of instances where you have **contracted** with a family member, a teacher or others?

When the event is more important, the **contractual** process can become more formal.

(PSST!) *Remember FORMAL from the FORM lesson?*

We **contracted** with Acme Roofing Company to replace the leaky roof on our home.

Some important events in life even require legal documents called **contracts.** They will be explained in **Tract Part Two.**

People can also **contract** an illness. In this case **contract** means to "get" something that you are PULLED down WITH.

I **contracted** a bad case of the flu over the weekend.

Objects and even muscles can **contract** too. By shrinking, they are DRAWN TOGETHER and reduced in size.

When Cindy touched the caterpillar with a twig, its body **contracted** into a small ball.

In the examples above, the word **contracted** has been used in different ways. Match the appropriate synonym to the meaning of **contracted** in each sentence.

a. shriveled   b. formed an agreement   c. acquired

We **contracted** with Acme Roofing _____

I **contracted** a bad case of the flu _____

The caterpillar's body **contracted** _____

CONTRACT

Detract

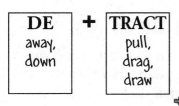

DE	**+**	**TRACT**
away, down		pull, drag, draw

To **detract** is to DRAG DOWN, DRAW or PULL AWAY from the value or beauty of something. Often, to **detract** from something is to reduce it in quality, value or importance. What kind of weather might **detract** from a vacation at the beach?

Can you think of other things that can happen to **detract** from a perfect vacation?

Imagine that you own an antique store selling valuable pieces of furniture, glassware and jewelry. All of them will be worth more if they are in mint condition.

List several things that could **detract** from the value of each of the following items and cause you to lower your asking price.

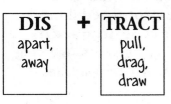

THAT BILLBOARD DETRACTS FROM THE SCENERY!

a. A mahogany roll-top desk _____

b. A porcelain doll _____

c. A diamond engagement ring _____

All of your answers would be referred to as **detractions,** things that lessen the value or quality of other things.

Distract

DIS	**+**	**TRACT**
apart, away		pull, drag, draw

YOU SEEM DISTRACTED.

To be **distracted** is to be PULLED AWAY from something you are focused on or find interesting. When you are reading a book and the phone rings or the dog barks, you are being **distracted.** The phone and the dog are called **distractions,** whatever it is that's causing you to be **distracted.**

People can be emotionally **distracted** too. If you are feeling unsettled by troubling thoughts, PULLED in different directions by a problem, or even very excited about an upcoming event, you are experiencing emotional **distraction.**

The new parents were **distracted** from enjoying the party by concerns about their young babysitter.

If you are at the doctor's office with your three-year old sister and she is about to get a shot, what might you do to **distract** her?

Extract

EX	**+**	TRACT
out, out of		pull, drag, draw

To **extract** something is to PULL or DRAW it OUT, often using force or effort.

Oil wells **extract** petroleum from deep under the earth.

To **extract** sometimes means to obtain something despite resistance. If you've ever been to the dentist's office to have a tooth **extracted,** you know that they rarely come out easily! The process of removing something by **extracting** it is known as **extraction.** When you PULL a splinter OUT OF your finger or weeds from your garden, you have **extracted** them. You can also **extract** information for a school report from the Internet or the truth from a young child.

Have you ever heard of an ingredient used in cookies and cakes called vanilla **extract**? Try to find out where it comes from and why it is used in baking.

At the end of the school year most kids clean out their backpacks. What types of things do you **extract** from the bottom of your backpack at the end of the year?

Protract

PRO	**+**	TRACT
forth		pull, drag, draw

I HAVE A PROTRACTED ILLNESS. IT JUST DRAGS ON AND ON!

To **protract** is to DRAG FORTH (DRAW out) a process. When something is **protracted,** it is delayed or DRAWN out much longer than expected. Many everyday occurrences can become **protracted** for a variety of reasons. A quick phone call may be **protracted** if the doorbell rings. Your soccer season can be **protracted** because of too many rainy weekends. A business meeting will be **protracted** if there are frequent interruptions or many areas of disagreement.

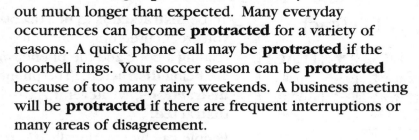

If you are engaged to be married and your engagement becomes **protracted,** would you be disappointed? What circumstances might cause a couple to **protract** their engagement?

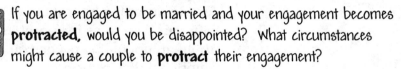

Retract

RE back	**+**	TRACT pull, drag, draw

To **retract** is to DRAW or PULL BACK. This word is often used when people change their minds about something they have said or something they believe in. When they **retract** their statement or belief, they publicly DRAW it BACK or disavow it. Offers and promises can be **retracted** too. A father might **retract** a promise to take his daughter fishing if the weather looks stormy.

 If you offer to babysit for a neighbor, can you think of reasons you might have to **retract** your offer?

Two of these factors might cause a politician to **retract** a statement about her country's policy on immigration. Circle them.

RETRACT

a. **She strongly believed in her statement.**

b. **The facts she presented are true.**

c. **The statement was based on inaccurate information.**

d. **Some immigrant groups were offended by her remarks.**

Subtract

SUB under, up from under	**+**	TRACT pull, drag, draw

To **subtract** is to DRAW one amount out from UNDER another amount. To subtract is to deduct or take away from something.

As punishment for not doing the dishes last night, my mom is **subtracting** a dollar from my allowance this week!

LINK 'N LEARN

Draw a line from each word in Column I to its best synonym(s) in Column II.

Column I	Column II
TRACT (as a root)	agree, shrivel
ABSTRACT	prolong
ATTRACT	pull, draw, drag
CONTRACT	divert, unsettle
DETRACT	summarize
DISTRACT	reduce
EXTRACT	diminish, damage
PROTRACT	remove
RETRACT	cancel
SUBTRACT	charm, entice

Tract
Part Two

Our new web contains key words **abstracted** from the **TRACT** family to further your understanding of this root. Don't let these new words PULL you down. Be sure to DRAW from what you have already learned about this family in the previous lesson!

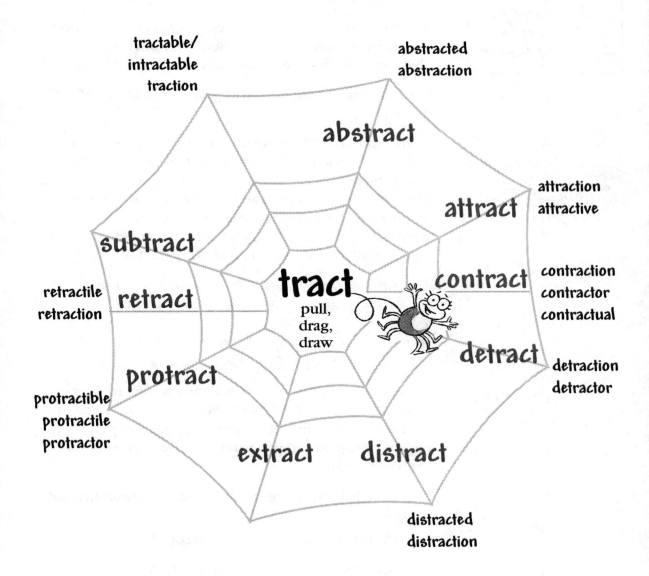

tractable/
intractable
traction

abstracted
abstraction

abstract

attraction
attractive

attract

subtract

tract
pull,
drag,
draw

contraction
contractor
contractual

contract

retractile
retraction

retract

detract

detraction
detractor

protract

protractible
protractile
protractor

extract

distract

distracted
distraction

Abstraction

The word **abstract** can be used to describe anything that DRAWS AWAY FROM reality. **Abstract** ideas, also called **abstractions,** are not represented by physical objects (things that can be seen or touched) but by emotions and thoughts.

Three of the following six words represent abstract ideas. Circle them.

Telephone	Faith	Alligator
Building	Honesty	Pain

Abstract can also mean "difficult to understand" or even "impersonal, showing no emotion." In both meanings **abstract** DRAWS AWAY FROM understanding and feeling.

Death is an **abstraction** for most young children, something that occurs only on TV.

Some modern art is **abstract.** It doesn't focus on the subject as it really is. A picture of an apple, for example, would be considered **abstract** if it didn't look very much like a real apple. A portrait of a person that looks just like the person would be considered realistic, not **abstract.** Technically, a stick figure of a person drawn by a preschooler could be called **abstract** art! Why?

If possible, ask an art teacher to show you some famous examples of **abstract** and non-**abstract** (realistic) art.

Would a scenic photograph of the Grand Canyon be considered **abstract?** Give reasons for your answer.

Abstracted

An **abstracted** person is preoccupied, off in another world, DRAWN AWAY FROM the here and now. If one of your friends becomes abstracted during an important history lesson, would you want to borrow his notes to study for the test?

One of the following words is NOT a synonym for **abstracted.** Circle it.

a. absent-minded   c. focused

b. unaware   d. clueless

Attractive

The previous lesson noted that certain qualities in your friends make them **attractive** to you. **Attractive** means having the power to **attract,** to DRAW other people TOWARD you. It means much more than just how you look or how popular you are.

Attractive people are appealing for many different reasons. Can you name some?

Things can be **attractive** too. You might dream of owning an **attractive** new car or an **attractive** piece of real estate on the beach. You'd surely hope to buy it at an **attractive** price if you could!

Attraction

An **attraction** has the ability to DRAW people TOWARD it and usually charm them in the process.

Disneyworld, Kennedy Space Center and Daytona Beach are popular central Florida tourist **attractions**.

You might sometimes hear the phrase 'main **attraction**' used to describe the central focus of an object or event.

The food fight that broke out at table three was the main **attraction** in the school cafeteria today.

What type of ride would you design as the main **attraction** if you owned your own theme park?

Contraction

A **contract** is an agreement formed when two or more parties DRAW TOGETHER. The agreement may be verbal (spoken), but more often it is written down, signed by the people involved and enforceable by law. Many of life's major decisions or transactions are supported by a **contract.**

Circle all of the following activities that might require a formal, written, legally binding **contract.**

a. forming a business partnership

b. offering to mow your neighbor's lawn

c. borrowing books from the library

d. getting married or divorced

e. buying a new home

f. inviting a friend to sleep over

A **contraction** is the PULLING TOGETHER of two words to form a single word, such as I'm from "I am" and won't from "will not." As you see, some letters are eliminated and some sounds combined. Be on the lookout for other examples of word **contractions.**

As any athlete knows, muscle **contraction** occurs when a muscle PULLS TOGETHER or cramps. Labor pains, caused by muscles cramping during the birth of a child, are called **contractions.**

Contractor

A **contractor** is a person who agrees to provide materials or services under the terms of a **contract,** frequently in the construction business.

Mr. I. M. Leakey, the **contractor** hired to install our town's new outdoor swimming pool, did a really poor job. The pool can't even hold water!

Think of some home improvement projects you'd like to hire a **contractor** (preferably a capable one) to perform around your house. (Sorry. **Contractors** don't usually clean bedrooms!)

Contractual

A **contractual** obligation is any duty that must be performed under the terms of a **contract.**

Do you think making the monthly payment on your car loan is a **contractual** obligation?

Detraction

You learned in the previous chapter that a **detraction** DRAWS AWAY the value of something. **Detractions** can also cause a reduction in quality.

Could having a bad cold be a **detraction** from doing your best at a track meet?

Detraction is also used to describe a negative comment made about a person's character. In this case, the **detraction** PULLS AWAY from that person's reputation.

THAT BILLBOARD DETRACTS FROM THE SCENERY!

I consider your remark a vicious **detraction** designed to ruin my chances of winning the class presidency!

Libel and slander are serious forms of **detraction.**

Detractor

A **detractor** is a critic, someone likely to voice negative opinions (**detractions,** criticisms) about another person.

The school principal was beloved by students and parents alike, her **detractors** very few.

Celebrities and public figures may have many admirers, but most have many **detractors** too.

 Batman and his sidekick Robin receive hero's treatment in Gotham City. Yet even heroes are not without **detractors!** Can you name some **detractors** of the dynamic duo?

Distracted

To describe a person as **distracted** can indicate something more serious than diverted attention.

Lucy felt **distracted** over the loss of her beloved pet canary.

In this example Lucy is very distressed. Her emotions are PULLED AWAY in grief.

Distraction

You can sometimes help a **distracted** person by providing a **distraction,** something to DRAW attention AWAY from what is troubling to something amusing or fun.

A sleepover with a friend would be a great **distraction** for Lucy right now.

 If one of your friends lost a pet, what type of **distractions** might you suggest to keep them from feeling **distracted?**

 Make sure to notice the two uses of distracted.

Protractile
Protractible

Protractile and **protractible** (the words are interchangeable) are ways of describing something which can be extended or DRAWN FORTH. Some animals have **protractile** body parts. Shark's teeth are one example. During an attack, a shark's teeth DRAW FORWARD from the mouth to enable it to fully capture its prey.

Large pieces of machinery sometimes have **protractile** parts. The wheels on airplanes are **protractible.** They are DRAWN FORTH from the body of the plane before landing.

Can you think of other animals or machines that have **protractile** parts? What are they?

Protractor

A **protractor** is a mathematical instrument used to draw or measure angles. Typically, **protractors** are used with compasses to produce geometrical figures.

Does your math book have any problems that require **protractors?**

Retractile

Retractile objects can be DRAWN BACK IN. A shark's teeth and an airplane's wheels have been given as examples of **protractile** objects.

Would these also be **retractile?** Would you expect most things that are protractile to be **retractile** and vice versa?

Retraction

A **retraction** is the act of DRAWING or taking BACK a previously issued promise or statement. A **retraction** can be a formal process in which a previously issued statement is **retracted** "for the record."

During his State of the Union address, the President issued a **retraction** of his campaign promise not to raise income taxes.

If your teacher had promised not to give homework over the weekend, how would a **retraction** of that promise make you feel?

RETRACT

Tract + Suffix Words

Traction

Traction, another useful word from the **tract** family, has several different meanings.

Traction refers to being DRAWN or PULLED, particularly the PULLING of a vehicle or a load over a surface (road) by motor power. Tractors are one of many vehicles that operate using **traction.** Traction also refers to a quality known as "adhesive friction", the ability of a tire to grab onto the surface of a road without slipping.

Each of the following factors will either increase (**I**) or decrease (**D**) a tire's **traction** on the road surface. Guess the effect each factor will have and mark it either **I** or **D**. Ask an experienced driver if you have guessed right.

a. **The tires are new.** _____

b. **There is ice on the road.** _____

c. **The road is wet.** _____

d. **The road is freshly paved.** _____

When a person suffers a break of a major bone, doctors sometimes use **traction** to help the bone heal. This process involves mechanically PULLING the area surrounding the bone to relieve pressure and to help it set properly. Comic strips sometimes show pictures of a person in **traction.** Be on the lookout to see if you can find one.

Tractable/ Intractable

An easily managed or controlled person is said to be **tractable.** A **tractable** person can be DRAWN or led to obedient behavior. By contrast, an **intractable** person is difficult to manage, not easily controlled, and very stubborn.

I'M TRYING TO EXTRACT YOU BUT YOU'RE INTRACTABLE!

SideSpinner

*Humans are funny animals! Webster and I have both noticed how often you give a human failing to an animal. **Intractable** is a good example of what we're saying. It means stubborn, right? Just think of how many synonyms for **intractable** mention an animal. We can think of pigheaded, bullheaded, mulish and dogged. Why not start a class list of all kinds of phrases that mention animals.*

Would you prefer to train a dog that is **tractable** or **intractable?**

WebStretcher: *Two of these words are synonyms for **tractable** and two are synonyms for **intractable**:*

obstinate   **amenable**   **submissive**   **incompliant**

Group them under the appropriate word.

TRACTABLE   INTRACTABLE

_____   _____

_____   _____

*Are the synonyms for the word **tractable** antonyms for the word **intractable** and vice versa?*

See if you can do a Morph-O-Meter reading for two of the new words listed above.

STORY REVIEW

In the passage that follows, substitute one of these words from the **TRACT** family for the word or words in each underlined area.

attract	detract	extract	retract
contract	distracted	intractable	
contractor	distraction	protracted	

Real Estate Woes

When the Millers put their house up for sale last summer, they hoped it would

_____ a buyer. They worried that the house under construction next
lure

door might be a _____ for potential buyers. It wasn't long, however,
disturbance, bother

before their realtor found a buyer who presented them with a _____
written agreement

to purchase the house. Alas! The home inspection revealed that a family of rats had

built a nest in the attic. Naturally the Millers were _____ to hear the
emotionally upset

news. It would be necessary to _____ them before the sale could go
remove

through. Luckily for the Millers, the buyers really loved the house and even the rats

couldn't _____ from their desire to buy the home. They promised
take away

not to _____ their offer, as long as any damage to the attic was
pull back

repaired. Unfortunately, it took quite a while for the _____ to get rid
builder

of the _____ pests and the selling process was _____.
stubborn prolonged

Guess what! A free page just for your thoughts and doodles . . .

Are You Being Served?

Early humans had great need of each other for **PROTECTION** against all forms of threat and danger. They **served** each other in many ways, **WATCHING OVER, PROTECTING** and **KEEPING** each other from harm.

(PSST!) **Think of** service **to help you remember that** serve **means HELP, WATCH OVER, KEEP, PROTECT.**

Many of these different meanings will **serve** you as you come to understand the **SERVE** family.

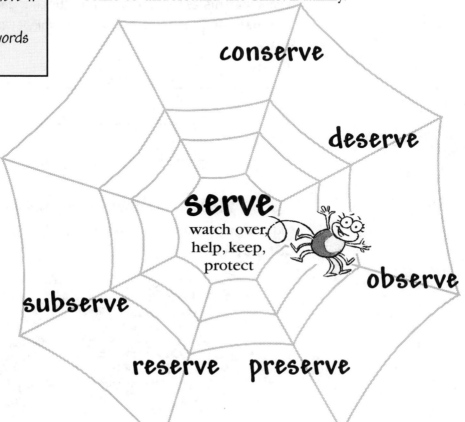

conserve

deserve

serve
watch over, help, keep, protect

observe

subserve

reserve   preserve

Like press, form, port and tract, **serve** is both a word and a root. As a word in itself, **serve** has several different meanings. When you **serve,** you HELP, WATCH out for, PROTECT someone or something. You can work for or **serve** another person, a place like a school or business, even a country. You can **serve** a tennis ball. You can **serve** time. (We hope not!) **Serve** has a lot to offer.

To KEEP or PROTECT with care so as not to waste is to **conserve.** People can **conserve** time, energy, natural resources and national treasures.

Conserve

CON	+	SERVE
with		watch over, help, keep, protect

 Many people today are particularly concerned with **conserving** natural resources like fresh water and rainforests. Why are they important to **conserve?** Can you think of two other natural resources that are important to **conserve?**

If your parents asked you to help reduce the family electric bill by **conserving** electricity, name three things you could do to HELP.

_____

_____

_____

WebStretcher: How do the words annihilation, endangered species, and extinction relate to the meaning of CONSERVE?

Deserve

DE	**+**	**SERVE**
thoroughly, completely		watch over, help, keep, protect

Teacher Tip

This word uses the prefix **DE** as an intensive. If necessary, have students check page 25 to review what an **INTENSIVE** prefix does.

The ancient word **deserve** meant to devote oneself totally to the **service** of someone else. Over time, **deserve** came to mean earning praise through **service**. Today, when you **deserve** something, you have earned it with your actions (not necessarily **service**) and you don't always receive praise.

I ATE MY DINNER. I DESERVE DESSERT!

Draw a line between the words in Column A and Column B that make the most sense in the sentence:

Column A **If you . . .**	Column B **you deserve . . .**
Misbehave	Trust
Are trying your best	Punishment
Always tell the truth	Criticism
Do sloppy work	Encouragement

Complete the blank spaces with your own examples.

_____ _____

_____ _____

Observe

OB	**+**	**SERVE**
over		watch over, help, keep, protect

To **observe** involves WATCHING OVER something, HOLDING your attention on it. Quite simply, if you **observe** it, you see it!

Observe can also mean KEEPING WATCH OVER what is valued and cherished. People **observe (KEEP)** the laws and **observe (HOLD)** celebrations on holidays.

I THINK WE'RE BEING OBSERVED.

Write the letter of the appropriate synonym for **observe** on the line after the sentence.

a. follow   **b. notice**   **c. look**

On our sight-seeing tour around Amsterdam, we **observed** that many people were riding bicycles. _____

Although he hated leaving the party early, Justin chose to **observe** the curfew set by his parents. _____

If you **observe** closely, you might see a small hummingbird among the flowers.

_____

Preserve

PRE before	**+**	SERVE watch over, help, keep, protect

BEFORE things spoil or are ruined, steps must be taken to **preserve (KEEP)** them for the future.

<u>Food</u>, <u>wildlife</u>, and <u>historic sites</u> all need to be **preserved.**

Write each of these words or phrases in the blank where it belongs.

_____ is/are **preserved** by game wardens, hunting and fishing laws and regulations.

_____ is/are **preserved** by canning, freezing, or curing.

_____ is/are **preserved** by the law, park rangers, and concerned visitors.

PRESERVE OUR HERITAGE!

If you eat food that has not been properly **preserved**, what might happen?

As a concerned visitor to any local, state, or national park, what things could you do to help **preserve** its natural beauty?

Reserve

RE back	**+**	**SERVE** watch over, help, keep, protect

RESERVED
FOR
WEBSTER

To hold or **KEEP BACK** some of what you already have for future use is to **reserve** it.

My friend always **reserves** some of her birthday money for summer vacation.

You might also **reserve** something you want, like a ticket to a concert or a table at a restaurant.

Write the letter of the appropriate synonym for **reserve** on the line after the sentence.

a. claimed   **b. shy**   **c. protected**

Persons who hold back their feelings and thoughts are said to be **reserved**.   _____

Tables or seats held ahead of time are **reserved**.   _____

Notices appearing in books often say: "All rights **reserved**," meaning the contents are the property of the authors.   _____

Subserve

SUB under, up from under	**+**	**SERVE** watch over, help, keep, protect

---

TeacherTip

You may want to point out that the word **subserve** *is not used nearly as often as* **subservient**, *which will be studied in* **SERVE, Part Two**.

Proper diet, rest, and exercise **subserve** a person's well-being. They help reach the larger goal of overall physical and mental health.

As long as people are **KEPT UNDER** someone else's authority, they **subserve**. They assist and follow the orders of another but have no real authority of their own. Many words can be used to describe a person who **subserves** another: attendant, aide, assistant, right-hand man or woman, servant, slave.

MY SERVANT
IS VERY
SUBSERVIENT.

Some of these words apply to people who have chosen to **subserve** another and probably earn wages and respect for their work. Name them.

_____

_____

Some of these describe people who are forced to **subserve** another and who receive little or no respect or money for their work. Name them.

_____

_____

LINK 'N LEARN

Draw a line from each word in Column I to its best synonym(s) in Column II.

SERVE (as a root)   set aside

CONSERVE   merit, earn

DESERVE   protect from harm or waste

OBSERVE   keep for the future, protect from spoiling

PRESERVE   notice, see, celebrate

RESERVE   help, keep, watch over, protect

SUBSERVE   assist, obey

Serve Part Two

Have you **CONSERVED** enough energy to learn more interesting words from the **SERVE** family? Webster and I hope you have **PRESERVED** what you learned and are ready to **OBSERVE** some new words. You certainly **DESERVE** the chance to try! This lesson should HELP you KEEP a strong HOLD on the meaning of **SERVE** and its many uses in the English language.

conservation
conservationist
conservatism
conservative
conservatively
conservatory

conserve

deserving

deserve

subservient

subserve

serve
watch over
help, keep,
protect

observance
observant
observation
observatory
observer

observe

service
serviceable
servile
servitude

reserve

preserve

reservation
reservationist
reservoir

preservation
preservationist
preservatives

Conservation

Conservation is the act of **conserving, KEEPING** and **PROTECTING** for future generations, our planet's natural resources. Many people and groups are busy promoting and working toward **conservation.**

Listed below are three groups that practice **conservation.** Consult with an adult, an encyclopedia, or the Internet to find out a little about each one.

1. The Audubon Society

_____

_____

_____

2. The National Parks Service (Federal Government)

_____

_____

_____

3. Greenpeace

_____

_____

_____

_____

Conservationists

People who belong to **conservation** groups, support them financially, and care deeply about their work, are called **conservationists.**

Would you expect people who litter to call themselves **conservationists?** How about a person who recycles or buys recycled products?

CONSERVE OUR TREES!

Conservatory

A place where plants and flowers are KEPT and PROTECTED is called a **conservatory**. **Conservatories** are greenhouses (enclosed glass rooms) designed to display a variety of species while also **conserving** them.

A **conservatory** is also another name for a school of music, a place that PROTECTS the art of music by teaching and playing it.

I'M VERY CONSERVATIVE WITH MONEY.

Conservative

Conservative people like tradition and favor KEEPING things as they are or were in the past. **Conservative** people are slow to warm up to changes, are cautious and don't take unnecessary risks.

Conservatively

People who live **conservatively** usually follow all the laws, practice religion, watch closely over their children, and stick to a budget. You would expect most **conservative** people to avoid bad habits such as drinking too much and smoking.

Conservatism

Conservative people follow a philosophy of **conservatism**. They believe in respect for traditional institutions and dislike changes in the established order.

Show your understanding of the many forms of the word **conservative** by describing an outfit and a hairstyle that is **conservative**, and NOT **conservative**, by today's standards.

	Conservative	Not Conservative
clothing	_____	_____
	_____	_____
hairstyle	_____	_____
	_____	_____

All of the following words are antonyms for **conservative** except one. Circle it.

a. liberal   c. trendy   b. moderate   d. progressive

Deserving

I ATE MY DINNER. I DESERVE DESSERT!

A person described as **deserving** is worthy of something, usually but not always something good.

The class valedictorian was **deserving** of the many college scholarships awarded her.

In contrast, a juvenile delinquent could be **deserving** of the punishment handed down by a judge.

 Can you think of a time when you felt **deserving** of an honor or award but didn't get it? How did you feel? How did other people (adults or friends) react to your disappointment?

Observant

An **observant** person notices things and pays attention to detail. Teachers and mothers are sometimes described as "having eyes in the back of their heads" because they always seem to know when their children are up to something. Of course, they don't really have eyes in the back of their heads. They are just very **observant.**

Name several occupations, other than teacher, where being **observant** would be particularly important.

_____

_____

_____

_____

Observation

An **observation** is information gained by **observing.**

The psychiatrist recorded his **observations** of the patient's unusual behavior before making his diagnosis.

Frequently, **observations** involve **WATCHING** for some special purpose or study. When students perform experiments, they often record **observations** used to support or disprove the hypothesis.

A simple remark or comment can also be referred to as an **observation.**

Have you ever heard a sports reporter ask a coach to make some **observations** about why her team won or lost the game?

Make some **observations** about the weather outside today and use them to decide what activities you might choose for this type of day.

_____

_____

Observance

Observance refers to keeping or following laws, customs, rules or religious rituals.

In **observance** of local law, grocery stores can't sell liquor on Sundays.

Schools are closed in **observance** of certain holidays during the year. Can you name four of them?

_____   _____

_____   _____

Observatory

An **observatory** is a place or building designed for **observing.** Some are built in high areas to provide the best possible view. Most **observatories** are designed to study astronomy and contain powerful telescopes for the **observation** of stars, planets and other heavenly bodies.

Observer

I THINK WE'RE BEING OBSERVED.

A person who **observes** rather than participates is an **observer.** Suppose you show up at a neighborhood softball game and someone invites you to play. You might reply, "No thanks. I'm just an **observer** today!"

A casual **observer** is a person who just happens to be around and can offer **observations** or opinions.

As a casual **observer,** I would say the fight broke out between the two football teams because the wide receiver teased the defenders after scoring a touchdown.

Preservation

Preservation is the act of **preserving, KEEPING** something safe from harm or change.

The **preservation** of our city's scenic waterfront depends on strong support from the citizens and local businesses.

People involved in these activities are **preservationists.** Historical **preservationists** have been responsible for saving many old and beautiful homes, churches and buildings for the enjoyment of future generations.

Have you read about or visited any examples of historical **preservation?**

Preservatives

Preservation of food usually involves the use of **preservatives.** Natural **preservatives** include vinegar to preserve vegetables or salt for meat. Artificial or chemical **preservatives** are found in many of the convenience and snack foods we eat today.

Name two foods without **preservatives** and two that you suspect are full of **preservatives.**

_____   _____

_____   _____

Reservation

To **reserve** a table at a restaurant, a seat on a plane or a hotel room, you need a **reservation.** **Reservations** guarantee that something in demand like a table, seat or room will be **HELD** for you because you asked for it first. Restaurants, airlines, and hotels employ **reservationists** to **HELP** you.

Land **KEPT** for specific use by the government is also known as a **reservation.** An Indian **reservation,** land set aside for Native Americans, is the most common example.

When a person has doubts about a situation, is **HOLDING BACK** on complete approval, you might say she has **reservations.**

Amy's mother had **reservations** about letting Amy ride her bicycle to school alone.

 Can you think of something you wanted to do that your parents had **reservations** about? What were their **reservations?** Did you convince them or did their concerns win out?

Reservoir

A **reservoir** is a place where something is collected and stored (**KEPT**). The most common **reservoir** is a tank or pool used to **HOLD** large quantities of water for use by a business or local government.

Subservient

Subservient describes someone overly obedient and mindful of his place. A **subservient** attitude is meek and humble, never loud and demanding.

In some high schools, the freshmen students are expected to be **subservient** toward the upperclassmen.

Three of the following words are antonyms for subservient. Circle the synonym.

a. arrogant   c. subordinate

b. superior   d. haughty

Serve + Suffix Words

Servile

Another synonym for **subservient** is **servile**. **Servile** implies behavior expected of a servant or slave. A person with a **servile** attitude rarely has a high opinion of herself. Difficult or extremely unpleasant chores can be described as **servile.**

Listed below are four groups of people. The first person listed is someone who might act **subservient,** or **servile,** toward the second person. Which group doesn't fit? Circle it.

a. an army recruit / the Drill Sergeant

b. a new employee / the company President

c. an eager fan / a movie star

d. a teenager / his little sister

Servitude

Servitude describes the condition of slavery. Throughout history, individuals and entire populations have been forced into **servitude** by others. Even today, in some third world countries, **servitude** is a way of life for poor children and other unfortunate people.

Service

Service is another useful word related to the root **SERVE**. When you perform a **service** for someone, you are acting useful or HELPFUL to others. "May I be of **service**?" is another way of asking "Can I HELP you?"

To be "at your **service**" means you are available to HELP at a moment's notice. If a gas pump is "out of **service**," it isn't working and therefore isn't at all HELPFUL.

Serviceable

Something described as **serviceable** is quite useful and possibly has been for a long time.

This old car may not look like much, but it has certainly been **serviceable** over the years.

Serviceable can also be used to describe something that's good, but maybe not great.

The room at the Fireside Inn wasn't fancy, but it was **serviceable**.

Write the letter of the appropriate pair of synonyms on the line after each example.

a. durable, lasting   **b. practical, acceptable**

The **serviceable** old car   _____

The **serviceable** Inn room   _____

STORY REVIEW

In the passage that follows, substitute one of these words from the **SERVE** family for the word or words in each underlined area.

conservation	deserving	reservation	serviceable
conservationists	observed	reservationist	servile
conservative	observer	reserve	subservient
conservatively	preservationists	reservoir	
deserved	preserve	service	

It Happened One Night. . .

Last Friday night, Sally Servuwell, the _____ at the downtown
hotel clerk

Mayview Hotel, learned that she had made a dreadful mistake. She had accepted a

_____ from two local charities to use the hotel's main ballroom for a
guarantee of availability

fundraising event that evening.

The Ladies' Historical Society was a group of _____ dressed,
traditionally

high society, elderly women. The other group, Concerned Citizens for

_____, were free-spirited liberals. This group was definitely not
protecting resources

interested in sharing the ballroom with _____ old ladies. As one
not trendy

_____ noted, "Should be one whale of a party!"
bystander

Of course, both charities felt their cause was more _____ and their
worthy

fundraising event should not be cancelled. Neither group had any intention of

being _____ to the other and they began to argue loudly. The hotel
subordinate

manager was so upset about the situation that his attitude was positively

_____. He promised to do everything in his power to be of
slavelike

_____.
help

Unfortunately, the situation got worse when someone _____ that
saw

water was leaking from the ceiling of the ballroom. As it turned out, a pipe had

burst and the ballroom was not even _____! The dance floor was so
useful

full of water that it looked like a _____. In order to
water tank

_____ his hotel's reputation, the manager promised to
keep unspoiled

_____ the main ballroom for each group separately, at no cost, once
hold back

the room had been repaired. There were plenty of disappointed

_____ and _____
people who belong to conservation groups   people who belong to preservation groups

that evening. Some might feel that they got what they _____ for not
earned

attempting to cooperate with one another!

Quizzical Can a **serviette** do what a nap-kin?

Guess what! A free page just for your thoughts and doodles . . .

As I Live and Breathe

Webster and I sometimes wonder about the first human words ever spoken. What were they? Mumbles, grunts, shouts of alarm and danger? Coos, babbles, watery smiles as a baby began to see and grow?

However it started, your human language grew out of everyday experience and need. Common, useful objects surely received their names first. Your earliest ancestors named what they knew, what they saw, heard, felt, feared, did.

What could be more important to language than breath? The sound of each word starts on a breath and is carried to others on the force of that breath. It comes as no surprise, then, that many English words contain roots meaning TO BREATHE.

PSST! Breath can be used to mean energy, effort, vitality, life or lifeforce.

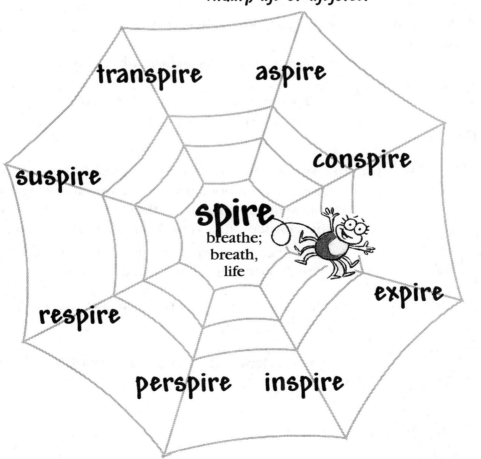

transpire

aspire

suspire

conspire

spire
breathe;
breath,
life

respire

expire

perspire   inspire

Aspire

A to, toward	**+**	**SPIRE** breathe; breath, life

D is a chameleon letter!

TeacherTip 🍎

Very rarely does the Chameleon Letter become invisible and drop out of a word entirely. **Aspire** is one such word. Ask students to hunch why it happens in this word.

Conspire

CON together, with	**+**	**SPIRE** breathe; breath, life

M is a chameleon letter!

SHHH!

CONSPIRE

To **aspire** to something means to give most of your **BREATH** (time, energy) to that thing, whatever it is. You dream about it, desire it strongly and work toward that goal.

Webster and I **aspire** to create a series of **WordBooks** that will **inspire** you with a love of language!

(PSST!) **Stay tuned!** Inspire **is coming up.**

If you **aspire** to sports fame, you will most likely (circle one):

a. **practice a lot**

b. **develop many hobbies**

c. **neglect your schoolwork**

d. **fill up on snacks before a big game**

 Give a reason for your answer, using some form of **aspire** in your explanation.

To **conspire** means to use your **BREATH** (energy) with others, often but not always in a harmful or illegal way. It has the sense of doing something in secret, the way you might whisper under your **BREATH** so others cannot hear.

A group planning a surprise party is an example of people who might **conspire** in a fun and friendly way.

An example of people who might **conspire** in a harmful way would be (circle one):

a. **sportscasters**   b. **pilots**   c. **terrorists**   d. **artists**

Expire

EX out, out of	**+**	**SPIRE** breathe; breath, life

S is a chameleon letter!

TeacherTip

*Here is a rare instance of a letter in the root itself changing (dropping out altogether) instead of the last letter of the prefix. The **S** in **SPIRE** gives way to the **X** in **EX***

When a living thing **BREATHES** out its last **BREATH** (is **OUT OF BREATH, LIFE**), it has **expired.**

Three of my grandmother's closest friends have **expired** during the past year. Naturally she is quite upset about it.

Many times, **expire** is used to signal the end or finish of something with a definite time frame. Magazine subscriptions, temporary jobs and club memberships are examples of things that have a predetermined life, the period of time they cover. They will all **expire** eventually.

My subscription to *Dinosaurs R Us* **expired** just as I was about to discover why T. Rex disappeared.

The word **expired** is used above in two different ways.

 Write the best synonym for each example on the line given. Choose from the following words:

went away   **lapsed**   **died**   **disappeared**

Grandmother Example _____

Magazine Example _____

Imagine that you have a coupon for a free ice cream sundae from your favorite ice cream shop. Printed at the bottom of the coupon are these words "**Expiration** Date: July 31st." If today is August 6th, has this coupon **expired?** Will you still get your free sundae?

MINE EXPIRED!

Inspire

IN	+	SPIRE
in, into		breathe; breath, life

To **inspire** is to **BREATHE INTO** someone the desire to do something. If you are **inspired,** you have been motivated by something or someone to take action. A beautiful sunset might **inspire** you to get your camera and take a picture. A year-end clearance sale could **inspire** you to purchase that new bike you've been wanting.

Draw a line between the words in Column A and the words in Column B that would make sense in the following sentence:

Column A might **inspire** you to **Column B**.

Column A	Column B
Gaining 15 pounds	Contribute to charity
A church sermon on giving	Practice free throws after school
Seeing a serious car accident	Go on a diet
Meeting a famous basketball player	Wear your seat belt

Complete the blank spaces with your own examples.

_____   _____

_____   _____

TeacherTip

Students may ask about words like **spire** *(of a building) and* **spiral**. *If they do, they are truly thinking deeply about language. Compliment them for their good detective work. Then explain briefly that neither word belongs directly in the* **breathe** *family.* **Spire** *comes from Old English and* **spiral** *from the Greek word meaning coil. We suspect that both relate to the feeling of drawing breath into the body to a peak and then breathing out. However, we have yet to find any confirmation of our suspicions.*

Perspire

PER through	**+**	SPIRE breathe; breath, life

PERSPIRE

To **perspire** is to BREATHE THROUGH the pores of your skin. **Perspiring** is your body's way of cooling off after hard work or strenuous exercise and usually happens when you are already BREATHING hard as a result of your efforts.

Most people **perspire** when they exercise, but sometimes people **perspire** when they are nervous, embarrassed or afraid.   When this happens, your body is working hard too, to deal with strong emotions. **Perspiring** is the way your body BREATHES THROUGH the difficulty.

Add a suffix morph to the word **perspire** to create a synonym for the noun sweat. _____

Then do a Morph-O-Meter reading on your new word.

| prefix | root | suffix |

Morph-O-Meter

Respire

RE again	**+**	SPIRE breathe; breath, life

To BREATHE or to BREATHE AGAIN is the exact meaning of the word **respire.**

We were all terrified when someone noticed the child sinking to the bottom of the pool, but he began to **respire** on his own just a few moments after being rescued.

The process of BREATHING in and out, inhaling and exhaling, is called **respiration.**

Respiration is used more frequently than **respire.**

ARTIFICIAL RESPIRATION

Suspire

SU	+	SPIRE
under, up from under		breathe; breath, life

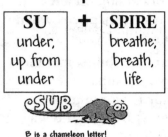

B is a chameleon letter!

Like **respire, suspire** is another way of saying TO BREATHE, although it, too, is not frequently used.

Suspire is actually used to mean "sigh," a way of releasing a heavy BREATH UP FROM UNDER your lungs. If something weighs on you heavy enough to cause a sigh, that BREATH comes FROM a place deep UNDER your skin.

Transpire

TRAN	+	SPIRE
over, across		breathe; breath, life

S is a chameleon letter!

Several hundred years ago, the word **transpire** was used mainly to describe information that had 'leaked out,' BREATHED ACROSS the gap between private and public information, come to be known by the public.

Today **transpire** is used in a more familiar way.

Although it was supposed to be a surprise, it **transpired** that Leslie figured out Friday's party was to celebrate her sixteenth birthday.

If you were to substitute the word happened for **transpired** in this sentence, it would still make sense. In this way, the word **transpire** has come to mean something that happens or occurs. The use of **transpire** in a sentence in place of happen tends to sound formal and stuffy.

 Would most people say, "What happened after I left Leslie's party?" or "What **transpired** after I left Leslie's party?"

TeacherTip

No root in this book has more chameleon letter irregularities than **spire**. *In* **suspire** *the B in SUB drops out entirely, exactly as D did in* **aspire**.

Note here that the S in **trans** *drops or blends with the S in* **spire**.

Although you might not use this word frequently, you will see it in literature. It might even be fun to slip it into one of your creative writing assignments! It **transpired** on a dark and stormy night...

LINK 'N LEARN

Draw a line from each word in Column I to its best synonym(s) in Column II.

Column I	Column II
SPIRE (as a root)	die, end
ASPIRE	dream, seek, pursue
CONSPIRE	encourage, motivate
EXPIRE	sweat
INSPIRE	sigh
PERSPIRE	plan secretly
RESPIRE	happen, become known
SUSPIRE	inhale and exhale
TRANSPIRE	breathe; breath, life

Guess what! A free page just for your thoughts and doodles . . .

Spire
Part Two

Settle down, catch your **BREATH**, and get ready to learn lots of new words from the **SPIRE** family! Hopefully you are still **INSPIRED** because there are plenty of useful words left to learn. This is one root that won't **EXPIRE** easily! If you **ASPIRE** to an impressive vocabulary, this is the root you simply must know!

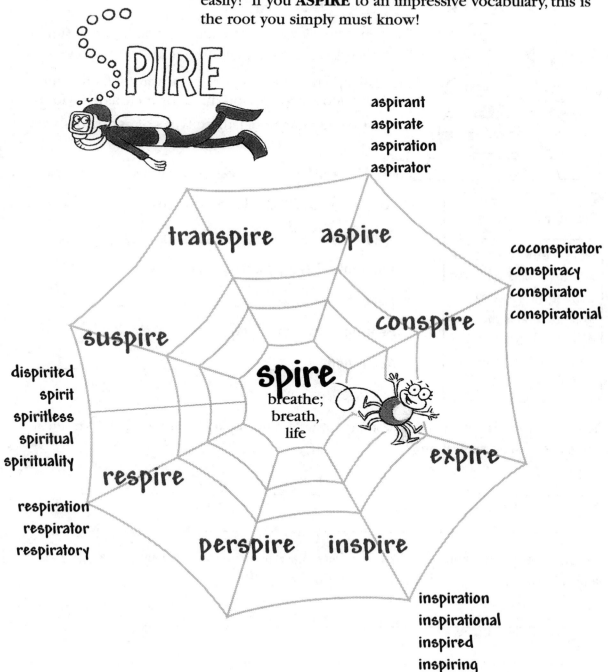

aspirant
aspirate
aspiration
aspirator

transpire

aspire

coconspirator
conspiracy
conspirator
conspiratorial

conspire

suspire

spire
breathe;
breath,
life

dispirited
spirit
spiritless
spiritual
spirituality

respiration
respirator
respiratory

respire

expire

perspire

inspire

inspiration
inspirational
inspired
inspiring

Aspirant
Aspiration

An **aspirant** is a person **aspiring** to something, usually an honor or sought-after position. Candidates for a job opening, beauty pageant contestants, or students applying for a scholarship are all **aspirants,** each **aspiring** to a different thing.

The principal reviewed the applications of all the **aspirants** for the National Honor Society and then made her selections.

An **aspiration** is the wish or goal toward which a person **aspires.** Most people work hard for their **aspirations.**

In the preceding material, three types of **aspirants** were mentioned.

On the line provided, list one possible **aspiration** of each **aspirant.**

Aspirant: Candidates for a job opening

Aspiration _____

Aspirant: Beauty pageant contestants

Aspiration _____

Aspirant: Students applying for a scholarship

Aspiration _____

TeacherTip

Note that with **spir,** *as with* **serv** *and* **cycl,** *the stem vowel* **e** *changes to other vowels in different forms of the word or as suffixes are added.*

You have probably already formed an idea of what your life will be like in the future. What are some of your **aspirations?**

_____

_____

Do other people (parents, guardians, teachers) have **aspirations** for your future? Are your **aspirations** the same as theirs or are they different? How?

_____

_____

Aspirate
Aspirator

Aspirate is another verb formed combining the prefix **AD (TO, TOWARD)** with the root **SPIRE (TO BREATHE)**. To this word, however, the suffix **ATE (TO MAKE, DO, FORM)** is added. Do a M-O-M reading for **aspirate**.

TeacherTip

Strictly speaking, as you can see from its structure, the word **coconspirator** is redundant: **co** (with) + **con** (with) + **spirator**.

The verb **aspirate** has a more physical meaning than the verb **aspire** and is directly related to **BREATHING**. To **aspirate** something is to **BREATHE** it in toward your lungs, to inhale it. If you **aspirate** a small piece of food while chewing, you will choke on it.

An **aspirator** is any machine used to suction fluids from the body during medical procedures. While working on your teeth, your dentist probably uses an **aspirator** to suction excess saliva from your mouth.

Conspirators
Conspiracy
Coconspirator

When people plot together to do something sneaky or wrong, they are called **conspirators**. The agreement or plan to perform the wrongdoing is called a **conspiracy** and involves the joining together of two or more people. One **conspirator** could refer to his 'partners in crime' as **coconspirators**.

If you and your classmates make a plan to set the class hamsters free so you won't have to take a test, are you **conspirators?** Suppose your buddies start to whisper among themselves and act nervous just before they open the cage. Do you think the teacher will suspect a **conspiracy?**

Conspiratorial

This kind of behavior could be called **conspiratorial,** typical of people who are **conspirators.** A **conspiratorial** smile is a guilty smile, one that a person might give when he is up to something.

 Many books and movies have plots that revolve around a **conspiracy** of some sort. Can you think of a book or movie that has **conspirators** in it? Who were they and what were they plotting to do? In your brief description, use several **conspiracy** words.

_____

_____

_____

_____

_____

_____

_____

Teacher Tip

Your students may already be familiar with the terms **protagonist** *(proto -- first + agon -- struggle + ist -- person who = main actor, contender) and* **antagonist** *(ant -- against + agon -- struggle + ist -- person who) in literature. You may wish to point out that* **conspirators** *are often considered the* **antagonists** *within a story. They plot against the main character. (For sheer interest,* **agony** *and all* **agogue** *words, such as* **demagogue, pedagogue** *and* **synagogue** *belong to this family. In the* **agogue** *words, the struggle is that of leadership, working or driving to accomplish a goal.)*

SHHH!

CONSPIRE

Inspiration

Do you know what it means to "have an **inspiration**"?
An **inspiration** is a great idea that suddenly occurs to
you, is **BREATHED** into you.

When people have **inspirations,** they are usually feeling
inspired, full of brilliant thoughts. Many important
inventions and significant works of
art or literature begin as
inspirations of their creators.
Very creative people are often
referred to as **inspired.** This
word implies that they are blessed
with their bright ideas from a higher
source.

Ordinary people have **inspirations**
too. You might have an **inspiration** to clean your room,
inspired by the sleepover planned for this weekend. A
programmer might have an **inspiration** about how to
work out a bug in a computer program she's creating.

Not only do people have **inspirations,** they can be an
inspiration. They give encouragement, guidance and
support. Famous athletes are frequently an **inspiration** to
those who play or follow their sport. Teachers, coaches,
friends and relatives can all be an **inspiration** to a young
person.

Think of two people, one famous and one not, who are an
inspiration to you. Write two or three sentences about each
person and what they do that **inspires** you.

Famous

_____

_____

_____

Not Famous

_____

_____

Inspirational
Inspired
Inspiring

Music, writing, or speaking intended to **inspire** people is **inspirational** or **inspiring.** If a politician gives an **inspiring** speech, you might be **inspired** to vote for him. An **inspirational** poem might be thoughtful, uplifting or beautiful and cause the reader to feel emotionally **inspired.** **Inspirational** music has a similar effect on the listener.

Which group would be most likely to perform **inspirational** music? Circle one.

   a. the Rolling Stones

   b. a polka band

   c. a church choir

   d. Miss Piggy and The Muppets

Respiration
Respirator

Respiration is the act of BREATHING. Sometimes, during medical emergencies such as a near drowning or a heart attack, a person will stop BREATHING. It is then necessary for someone to perform artificial **respiration** to save the victim's life. Artificial **respiration** is the life-saving technique of forcing air into and out of a person's lungs, until the lungs take over and begin to function again on their own.

Ambulance crews and hospitals use a machine called a **respirator** to perform artificial **respiration** during surgery or whenever a patient is having difficulty BREATHING.

Under which of the following circumstances would a person be least likely to need artificial **respiration** or the use of a **respirator?** Circle one.

   a. after watering a lawn

   b. after choking on food

   c. after being almost electrocuted

   d. during an operation

ARTIFICIAL RESPIRATION

Respiratory

The **respiratory** system refers to all the parts of the body used in the breathing process. The **respiratory** system of humans and most large animals includes the nose, throat, bronchial tubes and lungs. The **respiratory** system of fish and marine animals is obviously quite different from ours, since they are able to breathe underwater.

 What is **respiratory** failure? What might cause this? How could you treat it?

Spir + Words

Spirit
Spiritless
Dispirited

Most of the other important words in the **spire** family are variations of the word **spirit**. Your **spirit** is your soul, essence, BREATH, the part of you that is not your body.

Your **spirit** also determines what type of person you are and even what type of mood you might be in. A mean-**spirited** person is not pleasant to be around, whereas someone in good or high **spirits** is feeling upbeat. A person with low **spirits** is having a hard day and a **spiritless** person is downright depressed or **dispirited** (**dis** – APART + **spirit** = dispirit, AWAY FROM or APART FROM your **spirit**).

Greg was feeling **dispirited** about his performance on the English exam.

In this sentence, **dispirited** means (circle one):

a. unaffected   c. hopeful

b. encouraged   d. discouraged

The word **spirit** has several other meanings. **Spirits** are ghosts and otherworldly creatures such as angels, demons, fairies and elves. Some **spirits** are believed to be good and others evil.

Just as the **spirit** is the essence or soul of a person, **spirit** can also be the essence of a group of people. Ask anyone who plays team sports how important team **spirit** can be for their success.

Which of the following would not be a good way to show school **spirit?** Circle one.

a. attending school athletic events

b. skipping classes

c. wearing school colors

d. running for Student Council

Spiritual
Spirituality

Spiritual matters are those relating to the soul and to what a person considers sacred. They often involve a place of worship or religious beliefs. **Spiritual** people are those with a strong sense of belief in a world beyond the material one we touch and see. A **spiritual** discussion could involve discussing religious beliefs with another person.

WebStretcher: Study the history of **spirituals** in American music. Explain how the name of these powerful songs relates to the meaning of the root **spire.**

Pastors, ministers, rabbis and other religious leaders offer **spiritual** guidance to their congregations. They help people strengthen their **spirituality. Spirituality** is the commitment that people feel toward a higher being or life force, toward anything that is **spiritual** rather than material.

How might people seek to become more **spiritual,** to strengthen their **spirituality?** Circle one.

a. go on a shopping spree at the mall

b. play eighteen holes of golf

c. go gambling in Las Vegas

d. attend a temple, synagogue or church

Quizzical Could you **expire** in a quagmire?

WebStretcher: *Two instruments used by the medical profession to indicate certain aspects of breathing are* **spirometers** *and* **spirographs**. *The suffix* **meter** *means a MEASURING device. A* **spirometer** *MEASURES how much air the lungs can hold. The suffix* **graph** *indicates a device for WRITING, DRAWING or RECORDING results of some kind. A* **spirograph** *RECORDS the amount of air taken in per breath and the number of breaths per minute.*

Many instruments, not just in medicine, contain the suffix **meter** *or* **graph**. *Can you think of the device weather forecasters use to MEASURE atmospheric pressure? How about the device used to RECORD the intensity of earthquakes? What might you use to take your temperature? Can you think of still more kinds of* **meter** *and* **graph** *machines?*

STORY REVIEW

In the passage that follows, substitute one of these words from the **SPIRE** family for the word or words in each underlined area.

aspire	high-spirited	perspire
dispirited	inspiration	team spirit
expire		

A Matter of Breath and Death

The normally _____ gymnasts worried that they might
enthusiastic

_____ during their rigorous routines and ruin their new costumes.
sweat

Distressed at seeing them so _____ Spiro Breathmaster, their coach,
discouraged

consoled them, explaining that to _____ to success means not letting
dream of

yourself get overly worried about small matters like sweat. They used his words as

_____ to perform at their very best. _____ ran high! One
encouragement   *Good group feeling*

gymnast joked that they would wow the audience or _____ trying.
die

(That gymnast must have been studying the root **spire** to use such an educated expression!)

Guess what! A free page just for your thoughts and doodles . . .

Ferry Me Back

Stop and think about the kinds of things you CARRY every day . . . burdens, backpacks, secrets, sports equipment, memories, money, dreams. Which ones do you CARRY physically? Which ones mentally and emotionally?

CARRYING is a very important part of being human, as you saw in the **PORT** lessons. Words in the **FER** family also CARRY, often in a less physical, more mental and figurative sense.

(PSST!) **Think of a FERRY boat to remember that FER means CARRY.**

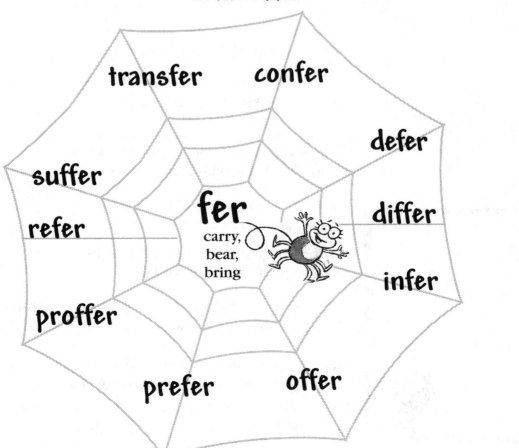

transfer

confer

defer

suffer

refer

fer
carry,
bear,
bring

differ

infer

proffer

prefer

offer

In our world of motorboats and jetskis, the lazy summer days when a **ferry** commonly *CARRIED* people and goods across bodies of water are almost gone.

Yet **FER** continues to *CARRY* a large number of words into the English language.

Confer

CON with, together	+	FER carry, bear, bring

M is a chameleon letter!

To **confer** involves *BRINGING* your ideas, opinions *TOGETHER* with someone else's. Students might **confer** *WITH* (talk to) a teacher or each other to complete a group project.

Business people **confer** (consult with each other) face-to-face, by phone, fax, E-mail, even video. Whole industries have grown up around **teleconferencing** and **videoconferencing**.

With whom and about what might the following people **confer**?

Someone about to graduate _____

_____

Someone planning a trip _____

_____

Someone who fears a friend is on drugs _____

_____

Someone searching for buried treasure _____

_____

Confer can also be used to mean *BRINGING* an honor or award *TOGETHER* with the recipient of that honor.

The principal **conferred** ribbons for perfect attendance on the students who earned them.

Confer might even involve *BRINGING* a certain feeling or atmosphere to an occasion.

The arrival of the principal in the noisy cafeteria **conferred** a feeling of relief on the stressed-out lunchroom aides.

Invent an award that you wish could be **conferred** on you today, ten years from now, or at the end of your life. On the scroll provided, draw and/or describe this award, making sure to emphasize why it would mean so much to you. Who would **confer** this award?

Defer

DE +	FER
down, away	carry, bear, bring

I'LL DEFER TO YOU!

Homework gets **deferred** a lot, that is, CARRIED AWAY and postponed until later, maybe even forgotten altogether! By **deferring** homework, students may BRING DOWN their grades. In college athletics, first year students are commonly redshirted while they are adjusting to campus life. That means their actual playing days are **deferred** for one year.

Another important meaning for **defer** involves CARRYING your opinions or ideas AWAY from the "top spot" in your own mind and giving way to the opinions or decisions of someone else.

An amateur detective might be wise to **defer** to Sherlock Holmes if they were working on a case together.

If payment on something you wish to buy, but can't afford, can be **deferred,** would you choose to buy it? Why or why not?

 WebStretcher: *The haunting and beautiful poem,* **A Dream Deferred,** *by Langston Hughes begins: "What happens to a dream* **deferred** *. . . ?" Describe what you understand by a dream* **deferred.** *Do you know anyone who has* **deferred** *a dream? Tell about this person and the dream. What do you think happens to such a dream?*

Differ

DIF +	FER
down, away, apart	carry, bear, bring

DIS
S is a chameleon letter!

If you **differ** from someone else, a friend or relative, you CARRY AWAY, separate out what makes you *you*. **Differences** emphasize the ways you are not alike, the many characteristics that set you APART and make you special. People can **differ** in physical ways: size, shape, color, height,

weight; emotional ways: preferences, reactions, feelings; mental ways: opinions, judgments, ideas, beliefs.

Fill in these blanks about yourself: I **differ** . . .

from my best friend in the way I

_____

from other members of my family because

_____

from the image people have of me, especially

_____

Infer

IN	**+**	**FER**
in, into		carry, bear, bring

To **infer** something means to CARRY or BRING enough evidence INTO view – at least mentally – to reach a reasonable conclusion.

From fast-moving, dark clouds, you could **infer** that a storm threatens.

From a collection of sawdust in the corner of the toolshed, you could **infer** that termites already had lunch.

Think of situations in which the following people might infer something and be mistaken:

| a teacher | a sportscaster |
| a teenager | a detective |

 Choose one situation and write a short paragraph about what happened. Use at least one form of the word **infer** somewhere in the paragraph.

I INFER THAT IT'S COLD OUT.

Offer

OF toward	**+**	FER carry, bear, bring

B is a chameleon letter!

To **offer** something, you **CARRY** it **TOWARD** another person. You can **offer** advice, your hand, a gift, an opinion, good wishes, season's greetings, a shoulder to cry on.

 The Greeks **offered** the Trojans a huge, hollow wooden horse. Scout around in a dictionary, encyclopedia or mythology book to see if the Trojans rejoiced to receive such an **offering**.

A common saying in English is "an **offer** you can't refuse." What does it mean?

_____

_____

You pass a car along the side of the street with a sign in the window: FOR SALE -- $3600 or BEST **OFFER**.
If the sellers accept a best **offer** bid, what will they most likely receive? Circle your answer.

a. **more than $3600**   d. **a car in trade**

b. **less than $3600**   e. **a Trojan horse**

c. **exactly $3600**

Prefer

PRE before, in front of	**+**	FER carry, bear, bring

I PREFER ICE CREAM TO ONIONS!

Some people **prefer** cats over dogs. They **CARRY** their feelings for cats **IN FRONT** or ahead of their feelings for dogs. They like them better and choose them as pets.

(Some people **prefer** cats and dogs to their brothers and sisters!)

Sometimes you can't even explain the things you **prefer.** Your choices seem to come from a time in your life **BEFORE** you became aware of having or making a choice.

 Conduct a little survey of your family, your classmates or your neighbors. Find out what news source they **prefer**, radio, TV, newspaper or magazines. Report your findings.

Proffer

| **PRO** forth, forward | **+** | **FER** carry, bear, bring |

Proffer is a synonym for **offer.** It is a polite, literary word most often describing an **offer** made in formal or solemn circumstances.

You **proffer** sympathy to loved ones at the time of a death.

You **proffer** regrets if you are unable to attend an important celebration.

Proffer is seldom used in spoken English. You may see it in written form occasionally.

 Could this be a word about to die?

Refer

| **RE** back, again | **+** | **FER** carry, bear, bring |

Refer indicates that you CARRY your concerns or questions BACK to a person or source that can help you in some way.

For a question about your health, you might **refer** your concerns to a doctor, a pharmacist or a medical manual.

In a sporting event, you might **refer** a question or dispute to a coach or a pro.

Refer also means to mention, to BRING to attention.

The newspaper article **referred** to the horrors of child labor in some of the world's poorest countries.

In this sentence, the words **referred to** most closely mean (circle your answer):

PLEASE BRING BACK MY DICTIONARY SO I CAN **REFER** TO IT.

a. condemned   c. didn't mention

b. tried to deny   d. brought to public notice

The new cafeteria rules **refer** only to the evening rush hours.

In this sentence the word **refer** means:

a. apply   c. defer

b. leave out   d. complain

Suffer

SUF	+	FER
under, up from under		carry, bear, bring

B is a chameleon letter!

People **suffer** what they feel deeply. That gives a clue about how the word relates to its morphs, CARRY and UNDER.

Suffering can be CARRIED deep UNDER the surface, quite different from pain that may pass.

Sometimes **suffering** is disguised UNDER an appearance of health and wellbeing and CARRIED in silence.

Teams, businesses, property can also be described as **suffering** – harm, losses, damage. **Suffer** even has several meanings that don't indicate physical pain or harm.

One of these meanings appears in both of the following sentences. Circle the word that can replace **suffer** in each sentence.

The varsity team **suffered** its third straight loss in as many games.

    a. avoided   b. experienced   c. deferred

Our teacher, Mr. Buzzsaw, does not **suffer** fools gladly.

    a. tolerate   b. replace   c. ignore

Circle the most accurate meaning of this sentence.

The Wednesday night gymnastics squad **suffers** by comparison with the more talented Saturday group.

  a. Some members of the Saturday squad think they are much better gymnasts than those in Wednesday's group.

  b. The talents of the Wednesday squad are sometimes overlooked because of the more talented Saturday group.

  c. The Wednesday squad had more injuries than the Saturday group.

Transfer

TRANS	**+**	FER
over, across		carry, bear, bring

Of all the words on this web, **transfer** is the one that stays closest to the original meaning of both prefix and root.

If you **transfer** something, you CARRY it ACROSS from one person, place or thing to another. You might **transfer** yourself, your family, your possessions, maybe even your love and loyalty.

Transfer and **transport** (from the **PORT** family) both mean to CARRY ACROSS. Yet they are not always used in the same way. Let your ear be your guide. Decide which word fits in each of the following sentences.

Shopping has never been easier! My bank now makes it possible electronically to _____ funds from my account directly to the store where I'm shopping.

Shopping _____ me to another world where I forget all about my worries for awhile.

My biggest worry right now is that next week I have to _____ to a new school in a new town. What will become of all my friends?

How will I ever _____ all my paraphernalia in my little suitcase?

To get to the new school, I won't have to _____ busses the way I do now.

LINK 'N LEARN

Draw a line from each word in Column I to its best synonym(s) in Column II.

FER (as a root)	choose, favor
CONFER	conclude, assume
DEFER	carry, bear, bring
DIFFER	give
INFER	give (formal, literary)
OFFER	set apart, separate
PREFER	consult, meet, award
PROFFER	hurt, endure, tolerate
REFER	move, change
SUFFER	mention, call attention
TRANSFER	postpone, give way

Guess what! A free page just for your thoughts and doodles . . .

Fer
Part Two

Now that you have been introduced to some of the words from the **FER** family, let's see just how much further this root can CARRY us. BEARING in mind your understanding of the root, ask yourself why the following words belong in this family.

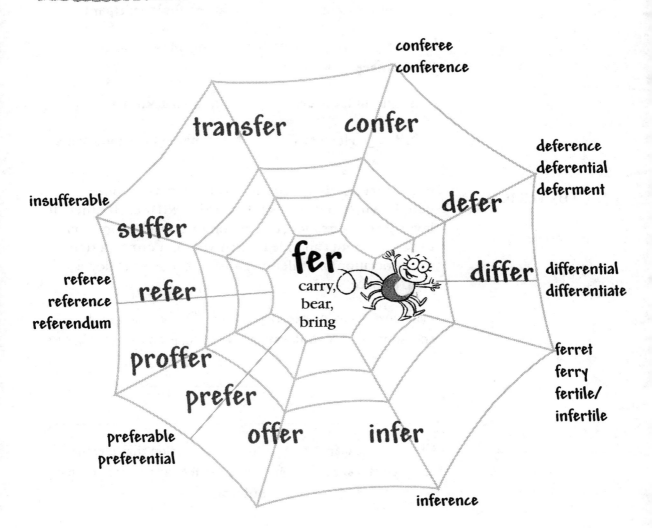

conferee
conference

transfer

confer

deference
deferential
deferment

defer

insufferable

suffer

fer
carry,
bear,
bring

differ

differential
differentiate

referee
reference
referendum

refer

ferret
ferry
fertile/
infertile

proffer

prefer

offer

infer

preferable
preferential

inference

Conferee

A **conferee** is a person who participates in a **conference** or a person upon whom an honor is **conferred.**

If you attend a conference with your parents and your teacher, identify the **conferees** at such a meeting.
Circle your answer.

    a. you   c. your parents

    b. your teacher   d. all of the participants

Imagine you are attending the Grammy Music Awards.
The **conferees** are:

    a. the announcers   c. the award winners

    b. the performers   d. the nominated musicians

Conference

A **conference** is a meeting involving two or more people who want or need to **confer WITH** each other. It involves conversation, discussion or consultation. You **CARRY** thoughts and ideas **WITH** you to a **conference.** An association of athletic teams is also often called a **conference.**

List some of the people in your life with whom you might choose to have a **conference.** What topics might you discuss?

_____

_____

Find a newspaper article in the sports section that identifies some **conference** of teams. What is the purpose of grouping teams together to form a **conference?**

_____

_____

Deference

Deference means showing respect for and courtesy to another person. It can also involve giving in to their wishes or ideas.

In a courtroom, everyone usually shows **deference** to the presiding judge.

 Why? Give at least one other example of someone to whom you show **deference** and explain why you think it is important to behave in such a way with this person.

Deferential

Deferential means being respectful, polite, CARRYING yourself in a courteous manner.

A clerk in a department store should be **deferential** to:

a. the manager   c. co-workers

b. the customers   d. all of the above

A manager in a department store should be **deferential** to:

a. the customers   c. other managers

b. the clerks   d. all of the above

Deferment

Deferment is a delay or postponement and often refers to a military postponement of service or reporting for duty.

If your older brother agreed to a **deferment** of a loan he had made to you, would you be pleased or displeased? Why? Give one example of something else on which you might hope to get a **deferment**.

Differential

Differential means showing a **difference,** having distinguishing or discriminating characteristics. This word has many scientific and mathematical uses, such as **differential** calculus or **differential** equations. Ask your math teacher.

There is even a gear in your car that makes it possible for one back wheel to turn faster than the other when going around a curve. Guess what it's called. The **differential,** of course. Ask a mechanic!

Differentiate

Differentiate is to make or show **differences.** Usually children don't like it if parents or teachers **differentiate** a lot in the way they treat each child in the family or the classroom. What **differentiates** one person from others can sometimes be a badge of honor. Can you think of any examples?

 Some people in the sports or entertainment worlds go to a lot of trouble to **differentiate** themselves from others. Can you name any? Why do you think they might do this?

Inference

TeacherTip

*This illustration contains a subtle pun: The penguin is **inferring** while being dressed **in fur.** Students may benefit from a short discussion of what a pun is, especially a visual one, and how the pun might help them remember the meaning of this difficult word.*

An **inference** is an educated guess that you make about something based on facts or something you've seen or heard.

What **inference** might you draw from hearing a siren and smelling smoke?

Your **inference** that I don't like baked beans is wrong. I am going to eat them when they cool down a bit.

 Think about an **inference** you made that turned out to be mistaken. What facts did you take into consideration? What facts did you overlook or not know at the time?

I INFER THAT IT'S COLD OUT.

Insufferable

I CAN'T BEAR IT!

Insufferable is best defined by a few synonyms such as: UNBEARABLE, intolerable, painful and agonizing.

(PSST!) *The prefix in used here means not.*

An **insufferable** headache would be very painful and hard to BEAR, as would a barking dog's **insufferable** noise in the middle of the night. In fact, the dog's **insufferable** barking would probably make an **insufferable** headache even more **insufferable!**

Now that you are familiar with some synonyms for **insufferable,** circle three antonyms.

a. detestable   b. acceptable   c. pleasant

d. outrageous   e. endurable   f. dreadful

Preferable

Preferable describes something desirable or favored.

Do you consider chocolate ice cream **preferable** to vanilla or do you prefer some of each?

Most people would agree that it is **preferable** to:

I PREFER ICE CREAM TO ONIONS!

a. know how to spend money

b. know how to save money

c. know how to earn money

d. all of the above

Preferential

Preferential means giving or receiving **preference,** being favored or chosen above others. If a coach gives **preferential** treatment to the divers on the swim team, is this an appropriate way to behave? Why or why not?

Can you think of any examples where **preferential** treatment would be appropriate?

Referee

A **referee** is a person who judges play in certain games and sports. A **referee** CARRIES out the rules of any sport. Without a **referee,** what might happen at a basketball game?

Reference

Reference has to do with CARRYING BACK or AGAIN. A dictionary as a **reference** book CARRIES you BACK to the meanings of words. When an employer asks a job applicant for **references,** these are statements given by others that CARRY information about the applicant's character and abilities. If an author makes **reference** to the famous dancer, Fred Astaire, in a book about the history of dance, this means that Fred Astaire is mentioned somewhere in the book.

PLEASE BRING BACK MY DICTIONARY SO I CAN **REFER** TO IT.

List at least two types of **reference** books in addition to a dictionary.

Why would an employer be interested in **references** before hiring someone?

Have you ever needed **references** for baby or pet sitting or some other job? Who would give **references** for you?

Referendum

Referendum involves bringing some matter to citizens for a direct vote. A proposal is CARRIED BACK to the voters who will make the final decision.

REFEREE, I DEMAND A REFERENDUM!

Our community held a **referendum** to decide if we would build a new park in the neighborhood.

Fer + Suffix Words

Ferret

Ferret as a noun refers to a weasellike mammal often trained to kill rats and drive rabbits from holes. As a verb, **ferret** means to hunt, search out or track down. So, when a **ferret** gets caught up in the business of **ferreting**, it is BEARING DOWN on or attempting to CARRY AWAY its prey.

Detectives often **ferret** out new evidence while investigating cases.

Have you ever **ferreted** out any useful or interesting information? Tell about your experience.

Ferry

Ferry is also a noun and a verb. In its noun form, it simply means a **ferryboat**. In verb form, it means to CARRY passengers, goods and vehicles in a boat across a body of water.

In the sentences that follow, **differentiate** between **ferry** used as a noun and **ferry** used as a verb. Place a **V** on the line for verb, an **N** for noun.

While traveling in Canada last summer, we decided to take a **ferry** across Lake Michigan. _____

To reach our destination, we **ferried** our car as well as ourselves across the river. _____

If you ever have a chance to travel by **ferry**, you really should take advantage of such an opportunity. _____

There is nothing like a **ferry** to carry you and your belongings across a wide open stretch of water! _____

Fertile

Fertile means able to BEAR seeds, fruit, young. It describes anything that is able to reproduce. Every group of living things must have **fertile** members to survive over time. **Fertile** is also used to describe land that has particularly rich soil for growing crops. Many times **fertile** is used to describe a person's mind as especially creative, inventive or resourceful. In each instance, the focus is on the ability to BEAR or to CARRY in a highly productive way.

 For years after the volcanic eruption, the surrounding land remained **infertile**. What effect might such land **infertility** have on the local people?

Circumference

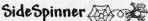

SideSpinner

Periphery is an exact etymological twin of **circumference**. **Circum** means AROUND in Latin, **peri** in Greek. In Greek FER, spelled **PHER**, also means to CARRY. Both mean a line AROUND a closed figure. **Periphery** also indicates the outer boundary. Someone living on the **periphery** of town lives on the outskirts.

Peripheral vision is what you see out of the corner of your eyes. An item of **peripheral** interest has very little importance. Computer **peripherals** are the gadgets that surround it, a mouse, a printer, etc.

Our final word stands alone in a way. It doesn't add a suffix to a word you already learned or to **FER** without a prefix. Yet it is a great word in the **FER** family.

Circumference is the boundary line of a circle or certain other surfaces. It specifically refers to the distance AROUND something and literally means to CARRY AROUND.

In math you may have measured the **circumference** of a circle.

In science you may have discussed the **circumference** of the earth.

The **circumference** of a baby's head is usually measured at birth.

 When shopping for a new pair of jeans, it is most helpful to know the **circumference** of what part of your body?

 Study the illustration for **circumference** carefully. Explain how the picture shows the meaning of the morphs **circum (AROUND) + fer (CARRY)**. How will this picture help you remember the meaning of **circumference**?

SideSpinner

ParaPHERnalia is one of those fun and whopper words with which you can amaze your friends and relatives. Today it means personal and professional belongings or equipment, such as a photographer's **paraphernalia**.

Sometimes it means just plain junk. But its story is priceless. In Greek, the word for a woman's dowry was **pherne**, what she **CARRIED** with her into a marriage. **Para** here means **beyond**, as it does in words like **para**dox and **para**normal. So **paraphernalia** started out its life meaning the things a woman **CARRIED** into her marriage in addition to **(beyond)** her dowry. What do you guess some of those things might have been?

WebStretcher: *Find the following words in your dictionary and explain why each one is a member of the* **FER** *family. Write your own definition for each word using* **CARRY** *or* **BEAR** *in the definition.*

aqui**fer** _____

_____

_____

coni**fer** _____

_____

_____

carboni**fer**ous _____

_____

_____

voci**fer**ous _____

_____

_____

Do you know anyone named Christo**pher**? The **pher** in his name is another spelling of **fer**, as you learned earlier in the SideSpinner on peri**pher**y. Look up the legend about how St. Christo**pher** got his name and what it means.

Likewise the woman's name **Bernice** comes from this root. Nike is the Greek goddess of victory. **Ber** is another form of **fer**. So **Bernice** means **BEARING** victory.

Quizzical Is a **ferret** feracious or ferocious and should I be precautious or precocious?

STORY REVIEW

In the passage that follows, substitute one of these words from the **FER** family for the word or words in each underlined area.

conference	fertile	preferential
deference	inference	referee
deferment	insufferable	referred
differentiate	preferred	suffer

United States vs. Petite Umpire

Just before the trial, the prosecuting attorney, former basketball center Ferdinand Fernandez,

requested a _____ with the judge, Ms. Carrie Littleperson. Judge Littleperson
        meeting

was widely known for _____ treatment of short people. Since the defendant
        partial

in this case happened to be a five-foot two-inch _____, Mr. Fernandez made
        judge of play in games or sports

the _____ that Ms. Littleperson could not be fair.
        assumption

Ms. Littleperson tried hard to make it clear to him that she would never

_____ between people based on size. Tall Mr. Fernandez was not at all
        treat differently

convinced by her arguments, so showing _____ to her proved to be an
        courteous submission

almost _____ task. He did, however, manage to _____ in
        unbearable   *carry under*

silence, which was definitely the _____ form of behavior.
        favored

Next, he pleaded unsuccessfully for a _____ of the trial. At the end of
        postponement

their meeting, Judge Littleperson _____ to Mr. Fernandez's
        made some mention of

_____ imagination as a reason for denying his request.
creative, inventive

On To **WordBook II**

Congratulations! You have travelled with Webster and me all the way through **WordBook I**. I'm already busy stirring up another cyclone of words that Webster can choose for her **WordWebs** in **WordBook II**. Can't wait to see you there . . .

actuary caricature tendinitis

morpheme systematize finesse

coagulum cargo

jurisprudence finial chariot

actuary axiom

precursor credenza

conjecture

morpheme proclivity

helix kinetic plesiosaurus

neurilemma wry

jester chiaroscuro

vertigo precursor

kinetic caricature

*The economic theory and
measurement of environmental benefits*

The economic theory and measurement of environmental benefits

Per-Olov Johansson

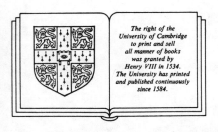

The right of the
University of Cambridge
to print and sell
all manner of books
was granted by
Henry VIII in 1534.
The University has printed
and published continuously
since 1584.

CAMBRIDGE UNIVERSITY PRESS

Cambridge
Port Chester *New York*
Melbourne *Sydney*

Published by the Press Syndicate of the University of Cambridge
The Pitt Building, Trumpington Street, Cambridge CB2 1RP
40 West 20th Street, New York, NY 10011-4211, USA
10 Stamford Road, Oakleigh, Melbourne 3166, Australia

© Cambridge University Press 1987

First published 1987
Reprinted 1991

Printed in Great Britain by
Athenaeum Press Ltd, Newcastle upon Tyne

British Library cataloguing in publication data

Johansson, Per-Olov
The economic theory and measurement of environmental benefits.
1. Environmental policy. 2. Human ecology — Economic aspects
I. Title
333.7'1   HC79.E5

Library of Congress cataloguing in publication data

Johansson, Per-Olov, 1949—
The economic theory and measurement of environmental benefits.
Bibliography.
Includes index.
1. Consumers' surplus. 2. Consumers' surplus — Econometric models.
3. Public goods. 4. Externalities (Economics)
I. Title
HB825.J64 1987   339.4   86-33364

ISBN 0 521 32877 2 hard covers
ISBN 0 521 34810 2 paperback

CE

Contents

v

Preface

A few years ago I applied for and obtained a position in the Department of Forest Economics at the Swedish University of Agricultural Sciences (SLU) in Umeå. In particular, my work was supposed to include evaluations of different uses of forest land. When the pressure to start undertaking research finally became irresistible, it was quite natural for me to begin by looking for surveys of available methods. I was especially interested in consumer surplus approaches to environmental problems.

It soon became apparent to me that there is a vast number of articles published within this field. In addition, a few books have recently been published which shed considerable light on the problems involved in deriving money measures of utility change. Unfortunately, these books are mainly concerned with goods that are traded in the market. Environmental economics, on the other hand, generally deals with goods and services that are not traded in the market. Moreover, time, discreteness, as well as uncertainty, are important complications in many applications of consumer surplus analysis to environmental issues.

For these reasons, I decided to collect available material on consumer surplus measures for different classes of private and public goods. In a few instances this has enabled me to derive new results, or, treating new cases that have escaped earlier investigators but nevertheless seemed worth pursuing. Throughout this book, I have aimed at presenting the theoretical properties of different consumer surplus measures as well as the practical methodologies available in calculating the measures.

I am grateful to Runar Brännlund, Bengt Kriström, Peter Lohmander, Leif Mattsson, Henry Ohlsson, Bo Ranneby, and Jon Strand for helpful discussions and comments upon parts of earlier versions of the manuscript. My special thanks must go to my friend, teacher, and colleague Karl Gustaf Löfgren who has the quite unusual quality of supporting others not only in times of success but also in times of adversity. His

ix

detailed comments on various versions of the manuscript have been of invaluable importance for the completion of this work. Alan Harkess and Chris Hudson made the manuscript readable by scrutinizing the language. I am also indebted to Solveig Edin, Barbro Gunnarsson, Marie Hammarstedt, and Cici Rüetschi for their incredible endurance and ability to decipher hieroglyphics. I also owe a great debt to the Multiple-Use Forestry Project at the SLU for providing me with research funds for all the arduous travelling around the world needed to pursue this topic. Finally, I wish to thank the Trade Union Institute for Economic Research, Stockholm, and its research staff for their hospitality and support during my extended stays there.

In spite of all the help that has been provided by outsiders, there are undoubtly errors, flaws, and 'Scandinavianisms' remaining. As a matter of good form, I remind the reader that they are the responsibility of the author.

P.O.J.

CHAPTER 1

Introduction

Scope of the study

The environment provides the economy with raw materials and energy. Ultimately these return to it as waste products. The environment also provides services directly to consumers, such as air to breath, water to drink, and recreational opportunities.

In many cases an environmental asset provides different but conflicting services. For example, a wilderness area can be left unspoiled and used for various recreational purposes *or* it can be commercially exploited by harvesting the trees. This is an example of a kind of land-use conflict that has become increasingly important during the last decade. In many countries, one would expect still more severe conflicts in the future between 'development' interests and 'conservation' interests. Similarly there is an increasing awareness of the fact that pollution, e.g. acid rain, reduces the benefits derived from recreational activities as well as the value of real estate. In addition, the health of human beings as well as the existence of some species may be threatened by various human activities. A well-known example of the latter is the blue whale stock whose growth has been insufficient to prevent the depletion of the animal almost to extinction. Besides the fact that a living stock of blue whales has a value in itself to most people, there is also the possibility that an extinction may imply the loss of some unique genetic material that may turn out to be useful in, for example, medicine sometime in the future.

Since choices concerning the environment's assets are inevitable, there must be a criterion on which selection among various, and usually conflicting, options can be made. This forces us to place some sort of value on the various service flows received and waste products returned.

Consumer surplus analysis is a very important part of the economic approach to this issue. There is a long tradition of work in this field by

1

economists. Unfortunately, there is also a long tradition of confusing and seemingly contradictory statements concerning the usefulness of the consumer surplus concept.

This study is an attempt to introduce students to some of the mysteries of consumer surplus analysis, or what Morey (1984) so strikingly calls confuser surplus. Even if the notion of 'Foggy Economics' comes to mind, recent research has undoubtly considerably increased the 'range of visibility'. The study's first goal is therefore to explain the circumstances in which a consumer surplus measure correctly ranks commodity bundles or projects. The study's second aim is to extend such measures so as to include the types of commodities which are important in environmental economics. Finally, the study attempts to present empirical approaches which can be used to calculate the consumer surplus measures of programmes that affect the environment.

The first part of this study derives consumer surplus measures to be used in a timeless world. Throughout, the emphasis is on the circumstances in which a money measure correctly ranks/measures the underlying utility change. Four major cases are to be considered: unrationed private goods, rationed private goods, public goods or 'bads' (externalities), and discrete choices. Reviews of practical methodologies are also included in order to calculate the consumer's surplus for these classes of goods. The second part of the book considers intertemporal issues. In particular, it derives consumer surplus measures, and presents practical methodologies, to be used when the consumer faces a risky rather than a perfectly certain future.

A brief review of the literature

The literature that deals with the theory and measurement of the *consumer's surplus* is both large and growing.[1] The concept of consumer surplus was first introduced by Dupuit (1844), who was concerned with the benefits and costs of constructing a bridge. Marshall (1920) introduced the concept to the English-speaking world. As a measure of consumer surplus, Marshall used the area under the demand curve less actual money expenditure on the good. At least this is a common interpretation.[2] Marshall's measure, like that of Dupuit, was an all-or-nothing measure: 'The excess of the price which he would be willing to pay rather than go without the thing, over that which he actually does pay is the economic measure of this surplus of satisfaction' (Marshall, 1920, p. 124). Later, Hicks, in a series of articles in 1940/1–1945/6, and Henderson (1940/1) demonstrated that consumer surplus could be interpreted in terms of amounts of money that must be given to/taken from a household.

An analysis of the welfare foundations of different consumer surplus measures and the conditions under which they coincide began with the work by Samuelson (1942) and Patinkin (1963). The debate centred around the interpretation of the *constancy of the marginal utility of income or money*; some kind of constancy assumption is needed for the area to the left of a demand curve to be proportional to the underlying change in utility. In recent years, much attention has been devoted to the more general question of how to evaluate consumer surpluses in the multiple price change case. Although the basic problem, which is known as the *path-dependency issue*, was introduced in 1938 by Hotelling, the main stream of papers on this issue have appeared in the 1970s and the 1980s. (See, however, Samuelson's (1950) historical survey of the integrability issue.) The basic problem is that the sum of the changes in consumer surpluses in general depends on the order in which prices are changed. However, conditions for path independency have been established, and these conditions turn out to be closely related to the aforementioned constancy of the marginal utility of income (see Burns, 1973; Harberger, 1971; Just *et al.*, 1982; McKenzie and Pearce, 1982; Morey, 1984; Silberberg, 1972; 1978; to mention just a few).

The previously mentioned literature is generally confined to situations in which the only constraint facing the consumer is the size of his budget. In many situations, however, one would expect individuals to face *quantity constraints*. For example, the government may impose price ceilings or floors which result in excess demand or supply in markets for goods and factors. Or the 'carrying capacity' of a natural area for recreation activity may be limited so that its use must be rationed.

The seminal work on utility maximization subject to quantity constraints is that of Tobin and Houthakker (1950/1). They examined a situation where constraints are just on the verge of binding at the examined point. More recently, the Tobin–Houthakker results have been generalized to situations where the rationing constraints are not optimal (see Howard, 1977; Mackay and Whitney, 1980; Neary and Roberts, 1980). There are also a few attempts to derive consumer's surpluses in quantity-constrained regimes (see, for example, Cornes and Albon, 1981; Just *et al.*, 1982; Randall and Stoll, 1980).

In the growing literature on the economics of the environment, the concepts of *public goods* and *externalities* are important. There are at least two basic characteristics that distinguish pure public goods from private goods. Firstly, the same unit of a public good can be consumed by many. Secondly, once a public good is provided for some individuals, it is impossible or at least very costly to exclude others from benefiting from it. A private good, on the other hand, once consumed by one individual cannot be consumed by others. Moreover, the buyer of the good is free to exclude other individuals from consuming it.

Discussions of externalities are often concerned with the case where one party affects the consumption or production possibilities of another. However, most important external effects concern a large number of individuals. For example, a dam may flood and destroy a valuable wilderness area which is used for hiking, fishing, hunting and bird watching, and hence affect many (groups of) individuals. Another example is pollution of the air and water. These examples also show that there is a close correspondence between public goods ('bads') and externalities. In fact, it is reasonable to view a public good or 'bad' as a special kind of externality in consumption. For further discussion on the definitions of public goods and external effects see McGuire and Aaron (1969), Musgrave (1959), Mäler (1974), Ng (1979), Samuelson (1954, 1955, 1969), and Strotz (1958). For recent surveys of the environment in economics and externalities, the reader is referred to Fisher and Peterson (1976) and Mishan (1971) respectively.

Since demand functions for public goods or 'bads' are not directly observable the central task is to overcome the *problem of preference revelation* for such goods. Different methods have been proposed in the literature. Of particular interest, in the present context, are methods which exploit the selfish interest of consumers to communicate, in the market, true signals about preferences for private goods, thereby simultaneously providing the information needed about public goods as well. By observing the effect on demand schedules for private goods one can in certain circumstances infer the value consumers place on changes in the levels of public goods or 'bads'.

There are important situations in which consumers face a *discrete* rather than a continuous set of *choices*. For example, a household cannot simultaneously visit two different recreation sites. Or quality changes, such as pollution or the development of new sites, may induce households to switch from trips to one area to another. In order to handle such discrete choice situations, the continuous choice models must be modified.

To my knowledge, no general discrete choice theory is available for use in deriving consumer surplus measures. A few authors, notably Mäler (1974) and Small and Rosen (1981), have rigorously derived surplus measures for particular classes of discrete choices. Mäler considers a good which must be purchased in a given quantity or not at all. Small and Rosen concentrate on the case when two goods are mutually exclusive, but also briefly discuss other kinds of discrete choice situations. A unified framework for formulating econometric models of such discrete/continuous choices has been formulated by Hanemann (1984a).

It is straightforward to extend single-period models to cover optimization for *T*-period horizons, at least provided the world is perfectly competitive. Such models have been used by, for example, Boadway and Bruce (1984) to derive overall or *lifetime consumer surplus measures*. However, such measures require huge amounts of information and may hence be difficult to calculate and estimate. Recently, Blackorby *et al.* (1984) have shown that the present value of *instantaneous consumer's surpluses* can be a sign-preserving measure of the overall utility change. These findings probably simplify calculations in many cases.

In many situations involving time, households operate under various forms of *uncertainty*. It is probably fair to say that the majority of effort in the consumer surplus field has been concentrated on analyses of situations in which prices are random but uncertainty is resolved before decisions are taken. In particular, a considerable theoretical literature has developed which focuses on the effects of stabilizing commodity prices. Most of these studies base their analysis on the concept of consumer surplus. The approach was first used by Waugh (1944) who showed that consumers facing exogenous random prices are better off than if these prices are stabilized at their arithmetic means. Later studies, e.g. Samuelson (1972) and Turnovsky *et al.* (1980), have shown that the Waugh result is not generally correct.

In a seminal paper Weisbrod (1964) argued that an individual who was unsure of whether he would visit, say, a national park would be willing to pay a sum in excess of his *expected consumer surplus* to ensure that the park would be available:

To see why, the reader need recognize the existence of people who anticipate purchasing the commodity (visiting the park) at some time in the future, but who, in fact, never will purchase (visit) it. Nevertheless, if these consumers behave as 'economic men' they will be willing to pay something for the option to consume the commodity in the future. This 'option value' should influence the decision of whether or not to close the park and turn it to an alternative use. (Weisbrod, 1964, p. 472)

This argument seemed both novel and intuitively appealing. Nevertheless, there has been much discussion about the precise definition of *option value*. There seem to be at least two different interpretations. The first interpretation links the definition to the idea of a *risk premium* arising from uncertainty as to the future value of the commodity (park) if it were preserved. This view has been advanced by Bishop (1982), Bohm (1975), Cicchetti and Freeman (1971), Freeman (1984a), Graham (1981), Plummer and Hartman (1985), and Schmalensee (1972), among others.

A second interpretation of option value focuses on the intertemporal aspects of the problem and the *irreversibility* of any decision to close the park and convert it to alternative uses. This concept, sometimes called the *quasi-option value*, was developed by Arrow and Fisher (1974) and Henry (1974). Recently Fisher and Hanemann (1983), Hanemann (1984b), and Mäler (1984) have analysed the relationship between the two different definitions of option value.

Plan of the study

The arrangement of chapters in this book is based on the above presentation of the consumer surplus issue for different classes of private and public goods. However, in pursuing the study of consumer surplus measures, we will need a few basic concepts such as the direct utility function, demand functions, the indirect utility function, the cost or expenditure function, and the compensation or money-metric function. These concepts will be defined in Chapter 2.

The basic topic of consumer surplus measures for unrationed goods is dealt with in Chapters 3 and 4. The emphasis is on path-independency conditions for consumer surplus measures with multiple price changes. Conditions under which there is an exact correspondence between the dollar gain reported by a money measure and the underlying utility change are clarified. The ordinal/cardinal properties of money measures of utility change are discussed, and the problem of aggregation across individuals is addressed. We also discuss the approaches that can be used to estimate consumer surpluses in real world situations.

Chapter 5 derives consumer surplus measures to be used in quantity-constrained situations. Path-independency conditions for ordinary or uncompensated as well as Hicksian or income compensated measures are derived. The chapter also offers an interpretation of the results in terms of virtual or market clearing prices.

The first part of Chapter 6 derives consumer surplus measures for public goods. It is a straightforward matter to interpret these measures in terms of external effects or public 'bads'. For this reason the second part of the chapter considers measures which can be calculated with market data. Chapter 7 contains a review of some of the methodologies that have actually been used to calculate consumer surpluses for non-priced commodities.

Chapter 8 shows how the methods can be modified to handle situations in which consumers face a discrete rather than a continuous set of choices. The chapter concentrates on a case intermediate to those dealt with by Mäler (1974) and Small and Rosen (1981), but the analysis is much inspired by the work of these authors. A household is assumed to have the option to visit a particular recreation site. This is the discrete part of the choice. However, if the household decides to visit the site it is free to choose the on-site time subject to budget and time constraints. Later, the option to choose among several different sites is introduced. Finally, we discuss the application of discrete choice models and present a recent attempt to estimate the value of a hunting permit from discrete, i.e. 'yes' and 'no', response data.

Chapter 9 extends the single-period model of Chapters 3 and 4 to cover optimization for *T*-period horizons. Overall as well as instantaneous consumer surplus measures are introduced. In some applications, e.g. fishing and hunting, the size of the stock of a natural resource is of importance. For this reason the second part of the chapter focuses on models with renewable natural resources. In particular, we introduce a model used by Hammack and Brown (1974) to analyse the optimal allocation of prairie wetlands in the north-central U.S. and southern Canada. The chapter also presents different frameworks which have been suggested for the aggregation of intergenerational welfares. Obviously this is an important issue since environmental programmes often affect not only the present but also future generations.

The assumption that agents face no uncertainty is relaxed in Chapter 10. The first section of the chapter is devoted to exploring some basic concepts, e.g. risk attitudes, cardinal properties of preferences and concavity/convexity of a function. Then the welfare measures are modified so as to be able to cope with cases of uncertainty where certain decisions must be made before prices are known. This is done in the context of simple two-commodity models as well as in the context of more complex intertemporal models. The chapter also illustrates the practical use of such models by presenting an empirical study involving discrete choices as well as uncertain prices.

Finally, in Chapter 11 the tools developed in the previous chapters are put together in an analysis of the total benefits of an environmental asset in a certain as well as in a risky world. The concepts of existence value, supply-side option value, access value, and quasi-option value are defined and illustrated. The chapter also presents the Brookshire *et al.* (1983) study, which is concerned with two wildlife populations, grizzly bear and bighorn sheep in Wyoming, whose future availability is uncertain. The chapter ends with brief discussions of the choice of money measure in situations involving risks and some possible directions for future research.

CHAPTER 2

Some basic concepts

In order to be able to derive consumer surplus measures a number of essential tools and definitions are required. Instead of waiting until those different concepts arise in the text before introducing them, this chapter presents the basic tools used in the subsequent chapters. For this reason, the chapter serves as a basic point of reference for the analysis in the remainder of this volume.

Section 1 considers the properties of the *direct utility function*. Equipped with this function, we then turn to the consumer's utility maximization problem. Necessary and sufficient conditions for utility maximization are stated in Section 2, while the *demand functions* for commodities are derived and examined in Section 3. The rest of the chapter is devoted to a presentation of the *indirect utility function*, the *expenditure function*, and the *compensation or money-metric function*. These concepts will turn out to be extremely useful in derivations of consumer surplus measures.

By necessity, the presentation of different concepts must be brief. The main sources used in this chapter are Barten and Böhm (1982), Deaton and Muellbauer (1983), Diewert (1982), Katzner (1970), and Varian (1978). The reader interested in more details, as well as heavier and more precise mathematical artillery, is referred to one or other of the books listed above.

1 The utility function

Let us assume that the consumer possesses a continuous and increasing[1] utility function $U = U(\mathbf{x})$, where $\mathbf{x} = (x_1, \ldots, x_n)$ is a vector, or bundle, of goods consumed. The existence of such a function is taken for granted, i.e. a set of axioms of choice, which represent sufficient conditions for the existence of the above utility function, is not presented. Instead, we will

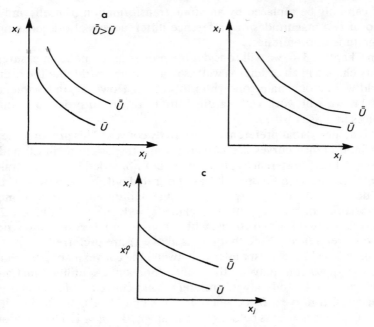

Figure 2.1 (a) Strictly convex preferences, (b) convex preferences, and (c) strictly convex preferences generating corner solutions

concentrate on a few properties of the utility function which are essential for the analysis to be carried out in the subsequent chapters.

First of all, it is important to note that the function $U(\mathbf{x})$ is not unique in an ordinal world. Any other function that produces the same ordering of commodity bundles must be just as good. If $U = U(\mathbf{x})$ is a utility function representing a preference ordering, any other increasing function or monotonic transformation of $U(\mathbf{x})$, say $F(\mathbf{x}) = f(U(\mathbf{x}))$ with $\partial f/\partial U > 0$, will represent exactly the same preferences. This is so since $f(U(\mathbf{x}^1)) \geqslant f(U(\mathbf{x}^2))$ if and only if $U(\mathbf{x}^1) \geqslant U(\mathbf{x}^2)$, where $\mathbf{x}^1$ and $\mathbf{x}^2$ are any two bundles in the consumption set X, which is taken to be the non-negative orthant of Euclidean n-space.[2] The purpose of the utility function is to order commodity bundles. The actual values taken by the function are not in themselves meaningful in an ordinal world.

A much more stringent requirement would be that the relative magnitude of the intervals between different levels of utility have some definite meaning. In order to meet this requirement, we would need to restrict $f(\ )$ to be a positive affine transformation, such as $G(\mathbf{x}) = a + bU(\mathbf{x})$ with the constant $b > 0$. A utility function is said to be (strongly) cardinal if it can only be replaced by an affine transformation of itself, and the ratio of two magnitudes of preference differences is also a meaningful magnitude of preference.

In Chapters 3–6, we will consider the properties of money measures of utility change in an ordinal as well as in a cardinal world, but the ordinal world will be our main concern in this book. However, in Chapters 10 and 11, we will work with cardinal utility theory in order to examine choices in a risky world.

It is assumed that preferences are strictly convex. This property means that indifference curves are curved toward the origin as illustrated in Figure 2.1a. If preferences are convex, but not strictly convex, straight line segments, as in Figure 2.1b, are not ruled out. Note, however, that we do not rule out the possibility that indifference surfaces might intersect one or more $x_j = 0$ hyperplanes $(j = 1, \ldots, n)$. In Figure 2.1c this is illustrated for two goods, with a non-essential[3] good j and strictly convex preferences. Note that points above x_i^0 are preferred to x_i^0.

There is a close correspondence between the convexity of preferences and the quasi-concavity of the utility function. A utility function is quasi-concave if, and only if, preferences are convex. A function is said to be quasi-concave if $U(\pi x^1 + (1-\pi)x^2) \geqslant \min \{U(x^1), U(x^2)\}$ for all x^1, $x^2 \in X$, where $\in$ means belongs to, and any $\pi, 0 \leqslant \pi \leqslant 1$. The function is strictly quasi-concave (and preferences strictly convex) if the strict inequality holds for $0 < \pi < 1$. It should be noted that quasi-concavity is a property which relates directly to the preference ordering. This property is preserved under increasing transformations, i.e. it is an ordinal property. (Concavity of a function, on the other hand, is a cardinal property (see Kannai, 1977).)

The above technical restrictions on the utility function may seem too strong. Indeed, some of the assumptions are not needed at all or can be weakened in certain analyses of consumer behaviour. However, in deriving money measures of utility change, the above set of assumptions will turn out to be convenient. In point of fact, we will frequently need an additional assumption, namely that the utility function is thrice continuously differentiable on the interior of X.

In the theory of demand, it is usually assumed that the utility function has well-defined first and second derivatives. This assumption eliminates kinks in the indifference curves. The assumption also (almost) ensures that the demand functions are differentiable. However, in consumer surplus analysis, one sometimes makes assumptions about the second derivatives of the demand functions and the 'marginal utility of income function'. Hence, we might as well assume that the utility function is thrice continuously differentiable. In point of fact, we will sometimes use the expression 'a smooth function'. This is taken to mean a function which has well-defined derivatives of all orders, i.e. first, second, third, fourth, and nth derivatives.

However, in most cases we will speak of a well-behaved utility function. The following definition is introduced.

Definition: A utility function $U(\mathbf{x})$ is said to be *well-behaved* if (i) it is continuous where finite on X, (ii) it is increasing (and $\partial U(\mathbf{x})/\partial x_i > 0$ for all i), (iii) it is strictly quasi-concave on X, and (iv) it generates at least twice continuously differentiable demand functions (on a set, say Ω_1, of strictly positive prices and income; this set will be discussed further in Section 3).

2 Utility maximization

Having established a convenient form of the representation of preferences, a start can now be made with the investigation of consumer behaviour. Let us assume that the consumer has an exogenous budget y, which is to be spent on some or all of n commodities. These can be bought in non-negative quantities at given, fixed, strictly positive prices p_i. Because of our assumption that the household is not satiated, the best choice lies on, rather than inside, the budget constraint.

The problem of utility maximization can then be written as

$$
\left.
\begin{aligned}
&\max\ U(\mathbf{x}) \\
&\text{s.t. } y - \mathbf{p}\mathbf{x}' = 0 \\
&\mathbf{x} \text{ is in } X
\end{aligned}
\right\}
\tag{2.1}
$$

where $\mathbf{x} = (x_1, \ldots, x_n)$ is a vector of commodities, $\mathbf{p} = (p_1, \ldots, p_n)$ is a vector of strictly positive prices ($\mathbf{p} \gg 0$), $y > 0$ is income, and a prime denotes a transposed vector. In order to simplify notation this prime is suppressed hereafter.

According to (2.1), the consumer is assumed to act as if he/she maximizes a well-behaved ordinal utility function subject to his budget constraint. The first-order conditions for an interior solution (i.e. $\mathbf{x} \gg 0$) to (2.1) are

$$
\left.
\begin{aligned}
&\frac{\partial U(\mathbf{x})}{\partial \mathbf{x}} - \lambda \mathbf{p} = 0 \\
&y - \mathbf{p}\mathbf{x} = 0
\end{aligned}
\right\}
\tag{2.2}
$$

where λ is the Lagrange multiplier of the budget constraint, and $\partial U(\mathbf{x})/\partial \mathbf{x}$ is a vector of order $n \times 1$ whose elements are given by $\partial U(\mathbf{x})/\partial x_i > 0$ for $i = 1, \ldots, n$.

The consumer wants to find the point on the budget plane that achieves

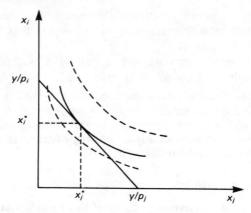

Figure 2.2 Preference maximization

highest satisfaction. Consider the two goods case in Figure 2.2. Here, the budget line is tanget to a smoothly convex indifference curve at a single point, and both goods are bought. This means that an interior solution requires that the marginal rate of substitution $(\partial U/\partial x_i)/(\partial U/\partial x_j)$ between goods must be equal to the price ratio p_i/p_j. This can be verified by rearranging the equations in (2.2).

Under strict quasi-concavity of the utility function, the necessary second-order condition for a relative maximum is satisfied. Geometrically, the second-order condition means that the set of all bundles $\mathbf{x}$ that are at least as good as $\mathbf{x}^*$ (the upper contour set) must lie above the budget hyperplane at $\mathbf{x}^*$, as in Figure 2.2 (see, for example, Varian, 1978).

3 *Demand functions*

The first-order conditions (2.2) can be solved for the n unknown variables x_i (and the Lagrange multiplier λ) in terms of prices and income

$$\mathbf{x} = \mathbf{x}(\mathbf{p}, y) \qquad (= [x_1(\mathbf{p}, y), \ldots\ldots\ldots, x_n(\mathbf{p}, y)]') \tag{2.3}$$

with the quantity demanded being a function of prices and income.

In this book, it will be generally assumed that the demand functions are twice continuously differentiable. This means that attention is restricted to a dense, open subset, denoted by Ω, of the set of strictly positive prices and incomes. This subset Ω contains all $\mathbf{p} \gg 0$, $y > 0$ for which the demand functions are twice continuously differentiable. However, corner solutions are not excluded, i.e. utility maximizing commodity bundles may lie on the boundary of the commodity space X. For example, the quasi-linear utility function $U = f(x_1, \ldots, x_{n-1}) + ax_n,$

where $a > 0$, which is frequently used in the subsequent chapters, may generate corner solutions.

This complication can be handled by partitioning Ω into subsets corresponding to interior solutions and corner solutions respectively. The demand functions have the appropriate properties on the interiors of these subsets. An example which will help to clarify these matters can be found in the appendix to Chapter 2. However, unless otherwise stated, we hereafter only consider a set, say Ω_I, of prices and incomes which generates both interior solutions ($\mathbf{x} \gg 0$) and twice continuously differentiable demand functions. Analyses involving corner solutions can be found in Chapters 6 and 8.

Several important properties of the demand functions can be deduced. Firstly, the demand for any commodity is a single-valued function of prices and income (on Ω_I). This follows from the strict convexity of preferences, i.e. indifference curves are curved towards the origin so that a single commodity combination corresponds to a given configuration of prices and income.

Secondly, the fact that the demand functions satisfy the budget constraint ($\mathbf{px} = y$), places a set of restrictions on the functions which is referred to as the adding-up restriction. For example, the sum of the income effects equals unity ($\mathbf{p}\partial\mathbf{x}/\partial y = 1$) (see, for example, Deaton and Muellbauer (1983) Chapter 3 for details).

Thirdly, demand functions are homogeneous of degree zero in prices and income. If all prices and income change in the same proportion, the quantities demanded remain unchanged. Intuitively, multiplying all prices and income by some positive number does not change the budget set and thus cannot affect the solution to the utility maximization problem. This can be checked by multiplying $\mathbf{p}$ and y in the first-order conditions (2.2) by a positive constant π. As a consequence, we can write the demand functions as $\mathbf{x}(\mathbf{p}, y) = \mathbf{x}(\pi\mathbf{p}, \pi y)$. Next, π is set equal to the (inverted) price of an arbitrarily selected commodity, say x_n, generally called the *numéraire*. This procedure illustrates that only relative prices, i.e. p_i/p_n, matter for a rational consumer. Alternatively, income is used as the *numéraire* ($\pi = 1/y$). Both these approaches are common in consumer surplus analysis, as we shall see in the next chapter.

It can also be shown that the change in demand for commodity i resulting from a change in the price of commodity j can be written as

$$\frac{\partial x_i}{\partial p_j} = \frac{\partial \bar{x}_i}{\partial p_j} - x_j \frac{\partial x_i}{\partial y} \quad \text{for all } i, j \tag{2.4}$$

The first term on the right-hand side describes the change in demand in response to the price change assuming that utility is kept constant. This is the (cross-) substitution effect. The second term on the right is known as the income effect, which states the rate at which the consumer's purchases of the commodity would change with changes in his income, prices remaining constant. The sum of the two terms gives the total effect on demand for good i of small changes in the jth price.

In general, the terms in (2.4) may be of either sign. If commodity i is a superior (inferior) good, the income effect is positive (negative). The signs of the cross-substitution effects are not known in general. However, as is demonstrated in Section 5, the substitution effect on the ith commodity resulting from a change in the jth price is equal to the substitution effect on the jth commodity resulting from a change in the ith price. Moreover, it is possible to show that the own-price substitution effect is negative if the utility function is strongly quasi-concave. For the moment, this concludes our examination of the properties of the demand functions, but we will return to these issues in Section 5.

4 *The indirect utility function*

An alternative approach, using the notion of an indirect utility function, has become an important tool of demand analysis. In particular, the indirect utility function arises in a variety of places in welfare economics. Apart from this, it also provides a simple technique for computing demand functions.

In order to obtain the indirect utility function, substitute the demand functions (2.3) into the direct utility function

$$U(\mathbf{x}(\mathbf{p},\, y)) = V(\mathbf{p},\, y) \tag{2.5}$$

Due to the assumed properties of the direct utility function and the demand functions, the indirect utility function is: (i) continuous, (ii) strictly quasi-convex, i.e. $-V(\mathbf{p},\, y)$ is strictly quasi-concave, (iii) homogeneous of degree zero in prices and income, (iv) decreasing in prices, (v) increasing in income, and (vi) thrice continuously differentiable in all arguments (on Ω_{I}).

We shall not attempt to provide proofs here. Detailed proofs can be found in Diewert (1982) and Varian (1978, Ch. 3). Most of the properties listed above, however, follow straightforwardly from our earlier discussion.

We now examine the differential properties of the indirect utility function. Differentiating (2.5) with respect to the ith price and invoking the envelope theorem yields

$$\frac{\partial V}{\partial p_i} = -\lambda x_i(\mathbf{p},\, y) < 0 \quad \text{for all } i \tag{2.6}$$

as is shown in the appendix to this chapter. Thus, the partial derivatives of the indirect utility function with respect to prices are the demand functions multiplied by $(-\lambda)$. In turn, it is easily demonstrated that λ, the Lagrange multiplier associated with the budget constraint, is the derivative of the indirect utility function with respect to income

$$\frac{\partial V}{\partial y} = \lambda(\mathbf{p}, y) \tag{2.7}$$

In the light of this result, it is not surprising that λ is frequently referred to as the marginal utility of income.

Dividing (2.6) by (2.7) one obtains the demand function for the ith good. This result, arrived at by Roy (1942), is known as Roy's identity. It suggests that a theory of demand may be constructed by making assumptions on the indirect utility function instead of on the direct utility function. Moreover, the second (and third) derivatives of the indirect utility function can be used to examine the properties of both the demand functions and $\lambda(\mathbf{p}, y)$, as well as the relationship between changes in utility and changes in x and λ.

It is important to describe two additional results. These relate to the properties of λ, which is used in subsequent chapters to transform unobservable utility changes to observable money measures. For this reason, the properties of the function $\lambda(\mathbf{p}, y)$ are of the vital importance to us.

In the previous section, it was shown that the demand functions for commodities are homogeneous of degree zero in prices and income. The 'marginal utility of income function' does not have this property. This may be illustrated by multiplying prices and income in the first-order conditions (2.2) by a positive scalar π to obtain

$$\frac{\partial U(\mathbf{x}(\mathbf{p}, y))}{\partial \mathbf{x}} = \lambda\mathbf{p} = \frac{\partial U(\mathbf{x}(\pi\mathbf{p}, \pi y))}{\partial \mathbf{x}} = \lambda^*\pi\mathbf{p} \tag{2.8}$$

where the derivatives are evaluated at the same x, since $\mathbf{x}(\mathbf{p}, y) = \mathbf{x}(\pi\mathbf{p}, \pi y)$ for $\pi > 0$. In order to preserve the equalities in (3.8), λ^* must be equal to λ/π. This finding implies that the marginal utility of income is homogeneous of degree minus one in prices and income. If prices and income double, λ must halve.

It is also important to note that λ is not invariant under increasing transformations of the utility function. To show this, we use the fact that the ordinal indirect utility function, as well as the direct utility function, is unique except for a monotonic transformation. Hence, $f[V(\mathbf{p}, y)] = f[U(\mathbf{x}(\mathbf{p}, y))]$. Differentiation with respect to income establishes that the new marginal utility of income is $(\partial f/\partial V)\lambda$. It is easily verified that the demand functions are left unchanged by such transformations since $\partial f/\partial V$ appears in both the numerator and the denominator when dividing (2.6) by (2.7) in order to obtain the demand function for the ith good.

5 *The expenditure function*

We now turn to an alternative approach which is based on the concept of an expenditure or cost function. Given an attainable utility level, $\bar{U}$ say, the expenditure function is the minimum amount of expenditure necessary to attain a utility level at least as high as $\bar{U}$ at given prices **p**.

Hence, the expenditure function is defined as

$$e(\mathbf{p},\ \bar{U}) = \min_{\mathbf{x}}\ \{\mathbf{px}|U(\mathbf{x})\geqslant\bar{U}\}$$
$$= \mathbf{px}(\mathbf{p},\ \bar{U}) \tag{2.9}$$

where a tilde denotes a compensated demand function. (See the appendix to this chapter for a derivation of these demand functions.)

If the utility function is well-behaved, then the expenditure function is: (i) jointly continuous in $(U,\ \mathbf{p})$, (ii) concave in prices, (iii) positively linearly homogeneous in prices, (iv) increasing in prices, (v) increasing in utility, and (vi) thrice continuously differentiable in all of its arguments (on Ω_I).

The partial derivatives of the cost function with respect to prices are the cost-minimizing demand functions, $\partial e/\partial p_i=\tilde{x}_i$ as is shown in the appendix to Chapter 2. These cost-minimizing demand functions are known as Hicksian or compensated demand functions. They tell us how demand is affected by prices when income is adjusted in such a way as to leave utility unchanged. Hence, the properties of these demand functions differ from the ordinary or Marshallian demand functions considered in the previous sections, where income remained fixed when prices were changed.

However, the utility maximization and expenditure minimization problems are 'dual' problems. Suppose the price–income vector is such that utility maximization produces the utility level $\bar{U}$. We can then reformulate the problem as one of selecting goods to minimize the expenditure or income necessary to attain $\bar{U}$ at the given price vector. Clearly, both problems generate the same optimal commodity bundle, i.e.

$$y=\mathbf{px}(\mathbf{p},\ y)=\mathbf{p\tilde{x}}(\mathbf{p},\ \bar{U})=e(\mathbf{p},\ \bar{U}) \tag{2.10}$$

Although we refrain from stating a formal proof, inspection of Figure 2.3 should convince the reader that $x_i=\tilde{x}_i$ for all i in optimum.

However, in general, a change in a price affects ordinary and compen-

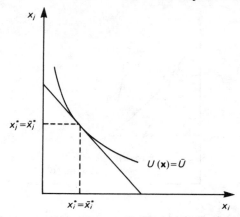

Figure 2.3 The utility maximizing bundle $\mathbf{x}^*$ is equal to the cost-minimizing bundle $\bar{\mathbf{x}}^*$

sated demands in different ways. Let us use (2.10) to write the compensated demand function for commodity i in terms of its ordinary demand function, i.e. $\bar{x}_i = x_i(\mathbf{p}, e(\mathbf{p}, \bar{U}))$. That is, if a price is changed, expenditure (income) is adjusted so as to leave utility unchanged. Differentiating this expression with respect to p_j yields

$$\frac{\partial \bar{x}_i}{\partial p_j} = \frac{\partial x_i}{\partial p_j} + \frac{\partial x_i}{\partial y} \bar{x}_j \qquad (2.11)$$

where $\bar{x}_j = \partial e / \partial p_j$. The first term on the right of (2.11) gives the change in ordinary demand with respect to changes in the jth price. The second term is an income effect.

From the Slutsky equation (2.11) it can be seen that the compensated demand functions have the property that a price change has a substitution effect, but not an income effect. Therefore, in general, the slope of a compensated demand curve is different from the slope of an ordinary demand curve. As is illustrated in Figure 2.4, the compensated demand curve is steeper than the ordinary demand curve in the case of a normal good. Only in the case of zero income effects do the curves coincide.

Next we illustrate a result which will turn out to have far-reaching consequences in the subsequent chapters. According to Young's theorem, the cross derivatives of a twice continuously differentiable function are symmetric. Applying this property to the expenditure function (2.9), it follows that $\partial \bar{x}_i / \partial p_j = \partial \bar{x}_j / \partial p_i$. Hence, Young's theorem implies that the cross-price derivatives of the Hicksian demands are symmetric. In the appendix to this chapter, it is demonstrated that Young's theorem does not imply that the cross-price derivatives of the

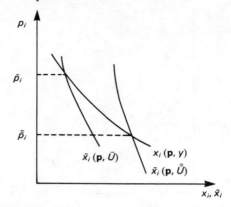

Figure 2.4 An ordinary demand function and compensated demand functions associated with utility levels $\bar{U}$ and $\bar{\bar{U}}$ respectively ($\bar{\bar{U}} > \bar{U}$)

ordinary or Marshallian demand functions are symmetric. It is the presence of income effects which causes the asymmetry. In point of fact, this asymmetry is the source of the problems which will confront us when deriving ordinary consumer surplus measures in the next chapter.

Finally, we indicate the properties of the behaviour functions with respect to monotonic transformations of the utility function. We have already argued that $x_i(\mathbf{p}, y) = \bar{x}_i(\mathbf{p}, \bar{U})$ for any $\bar{U}$, provided $y = e(\mathbf{p}, \bar{U})$, and that x_i is left unaffected by a monotonic transformation of the utility function. In order for the equality to be preserved, the compensated demand functions must also be unaffected by such a transformation. Intuitively, indifference surfaces are unaffected by the transformation; they are simply relabelled. Therefore, the minimum cost of reaching any given indifference surface (commodity bundle) remains unchanged.

On the other hand, $\partial e/\partial U$ or the marginal cost of utility is affected by the transformation. As is shown in the appendix, the marginal cost of utility is the reciprocal of the marginal utility of income, and we have already demonstrated that the marginal utility of income cannot remain unaffected by the considered transformation.

6 *The compensation function*

The expenditure function can be used to introduce a construction, the compensation function or money-metric function, which has received considerable attention in welfare economics. The fact that the expenditure function, is, by assumption, increasing in utility, enables us to make the following construction:

$$f(\mathbf{p}; \mathbf{p}^c, y) = e(\mathbf{p}, V(\mathbf{p}^c, y)) \tag{2.12}$$

where $\mathbf{p}$ is a vector of reference prices. This is the (indirect) compensation function.

If the utility level is fixed, say $V(\mathbf{p}^c, y) = \bar{U}$, (2.12) is an expenditure function. Hence, partial derivatives can be taken of $e(\ )$ with respect to prices $\mathbf{p}$ to obtain the Hicksian demand functions $\bar{x}(\mathbf{p}, \bar{U})$.

On the other hand, with respect to changes in utility, via $\mathbf{p}^c$ or y with $\mathbf{p}$ fixed, the compensation function behaves like a utility function since, by assumption, $\partial e/\partial U > 0$. In fact, for any fixed $\mathbf{p}$, the compensation function is, itself, a utility function, i.e. it is a monotonic transform of the (direct or) indirect utility function. In other words, the compensation function ranks commodity bundles in the same order as the utility function (and only the ranking, not the values a function takes, make sense in an ordinal world). The reader interested in a detailed analysis of the properties of compensation functions is referred to Weymark (1985).

Appendix

On the properties of the indirect utility function

In order to examine the partial derivative of the indirect utility function (2.5) with respect to the ith price we use the first-order conditions (2.2) to obtain

$$V_i = \frac{\partial V(\mathbf{p}, y)}{\partial p_i} = \sum_{j=1}^{n} \frac{\partial U}{\partial x_j} \frac{\partial x_j}{\partial p_i} = \Sigma \lambda p_j \frac{\partial x_j}{\partial p_i} \tag{A2.1}$$

Differentiating the budget constraint $y = \mathbf{p}\mathbf{x}$ with respect to p_i we obtain

$$0 = \Sigma p_j \frac{\partial x_j}{\partial p_i} + x_i \tag{A2.2}$$

Inserting (A2.2) into (A2.1) we find that

$$V_i = \frac{\partial V(\mathbf{p}, y)}{\partial p_i} = -\lambda x_i \quad \text{for all } i \tag{A2.3}$$

which is the expression stated in equation (2.6). Using the same approach as above, it is a straightforward matter to show that $\partial V/\partial y = \lambda$.

In Section 5, it was argued that the cross-price derivatives of the ordinary demand functions are not generally symmetrical. If the indirect utility function is twice continuously differentiable, then according to Young's theorem

$$V_{ij} = V_{ji} \quad \text{for all } i, j \tag{A2.4}$$

where $V_{ij} = \partial^2 V/\partial p_i \partial p_j = -\lambda \partial x_i/\partial p_j - x_i \partial \lambda/\partial p_j$ from (A2.3). Thus, $\partial x_i/\partial p_j \neq \partial x_j/\partial p_i$ unless $x_i \partial \lambda/\partial p_j = x_j \partial \lambda/\partial p_i$. This shows that the cross-price derivatives are not generally symmetrical.

The expenditure function

The first-order conditions of the expenditure minimization problem (2.9) can be written as

$$\left.\begin{aligned} \mathbf{p} - \frac{\mu \partial U}{\partial \bar{\mathbf{x}}} &= 0 \\[2ex] \bar{U} - U(\bar{\mathbf{x}}) &= 0 \end{aligned}\right\} \tag{A2.5}$$

where μ is the Lagrange multiplier associated with the constraint $\bar{U} - U(x) = 0$. Solving this system we obtain the compensated demand functions $\bar{\mathbf{x}} = \bar{\mathbf{x}}(\mathbf{p}, \bar{U})$.

Next, differentiating the expenditure function (2.9) with respect to p_i yields

$$\begin{aligned} \frac{\partial e}{\partial p_i} &= \sum_{j=1}^{n} p_j \frac{\partial \bar{x}_j}{\partial p_i} + \bar{x}_i \\[2ex] &= \frac{\mu \partial U}{\partial p_i} + \bar{x}_i = \bar{x}_i \quad \text{for all } i \end{aligned} \tag{A2.6}$$

i.e. the partial derivatives of the expenditure function with respect to prices are the Hicksian demand functions. In order to show that $\mu \partial U/\partial p_i = \Sigma p_j \partial \bar{x}_j/\partial p_i = 0$, use the first-order conditions (A2.5), and the fact that the utility level is fixed, i.e. $U(\mathbf{x}) = \bar{U}$.

Let us examine the effect on expenditure of changes in the utility level:

$$\frac{\partial e}{\partial U} = \Sigma p_i \frac{\partial \bar{x}_i}{\partial U} = \mu \Sigma \frac{\partial U}{\partial \bar{x}_i} \frac{\partial \bar{x}_i}{\partial U} = \mu \tag{A2.7}$$

where we interpret μ as the marginal cost of utility. In other words, μ is the reciprocal of the marginal utility λ of income. To demonstrate this, fix the utility level at an arbitrarily chosen level $\bar{U}$, say, and insert the corresponding expenditure function into the indirect utility function to obtain $\bar{U} = V(\mathbf{p}, e(\mathbf{p}, \bar{U}))$. Differentiating this expression with respect to U yields

$$1 = \frac{\partial V}{\partial y} \frac{\partial e}{\partial U} = \lambda \mu \tag{A2.8}$$

i.e. $\mu = 1/\lambda$.

Finally, if the expenditure function is twice continuously differentiable, then it holds that

$$\frac{\partial^2 e}{\partial p_i \partial p_j} = \frac{\partial \tilde{x}_i}{\partial p_j} = \frac{\partial \tilde{x}_j}{\partial p_i} = \frac{\partial^2 e}{\partial p_j \partial p_i} \tag{A2.9}$$

Thus, the cross-price derivatives of the compensated demands are symmetrical. Compare the discussion in Section 5; see Diamond and McFadden (1974) for a comprehensive discussion.

Corner solutions

In Section 3 we discussed the implications of corner solutions. The following example is adapted from Katzner (1970).
    The utility function is

$$U = (x_1 + 1)(x_2 + 1)x_3 \tag{A2.10}$$

From utility maximization we obtain (for x_1)

$$\left.\begin{array}{ll} x_1 = \dfrac{y - 2p_1 + p_2}{3p_3} & \text{on } \Omega^1 \\[2mm] x_1 = \dfrac{y - p_1}{2p_1} & \text{on } \Omega^2 \\[2mm] x_1 = 0 & \text{on } \Omega^3 \cup \Omega^4 \end{array}\right\} \tag{A2.11}$$

where

$$\Omega^1 = \{(\mathbf{p}, y) \mid y - 2p_1 + p_2 > 0, \; y - 2p_2 + p_1 > 0\}$$
$$\Omega^2 = \{(\mathbf{p}, y) \mid y - 2p_2 + p_1 \leq 0, \; y > p_1\}$$
$$\Omega^3 = \{(\mathbf{p}, y) \mid y - 2p_1 + p_2 \leq 0, \; y > p_2\}$$
$$\Omega^4 = \{(\mathbf{p}, y) \mid y \leq p_1, \; y \leq p_2\}$$

It is easily verified that the demand functions are everywhere continuous and the Slutsky equations have the appropriate properties on the interiors of Ω^i for $i = 1, \ldots, 4$.

CHAPTER 3

The concept of consumer surplus

This chapter, which is inspired by the analysis in Just *et al.* (1982), deals with the measurement of consumer surplus under multiple price changes. Section 1 considers the relationship between a change in utility and areas to the left of ordinary or Marshallian demand curves. In particular, it is shown that the sum of the changes in consumer surpluses in general depends on the order in which prices are changed. Conditions under which there is a unique or path-independent ordinary money measure are investigated in Section 2. Section 3 introduces two of the measures (the compensating and equivalent variations) suggested by Sir John R. Hicks. In order to appreciate the results, it is useful to illustrate them by means of a few straightforward examples. Section 4, which ends this chapter, introduces two simple preference functions which are used as a basis for deriving consumer surplus measures.

1 Money measures and areas under ordinary demand curves

Consider a household that derives satisfaction from consuming n different commodities. The household is assumed to act as if it maximizes a well-behaved utility function subject to its budget constraint. The indirect utility function of this household is written as $V(\mathbf{p}, y)$, where $\mathbf{p}$ is a vector of prices and y is income.

Taking partial derivatives of the indirect utility function with respect to p_i and y, and invoking the envelope theorem, it can be shown that

$$\left. \begin{aligned} V_i &= \frac{\partial V(\mathbf{p}, y)}{\partial p_i} = -x_i(\mathbf{p}, y)\, \lambda\,(\mathbf{p}, y) \quad \text{for all } i \\[2mm] V_y &= \frac{\partial V(\mathbf{p}, y)}{\partial y} = \lambda(\mathbf{p}, y) \end{aligned} \right\} \tag{3.1}$$

as was demonstrated in Chapter 2. Thus, by taking the partial derivative

22

of the indirect utility function with respect to the ith price, we can obtain the demand function for that good multiplied by the Lagrange multiplier λ. From the bottom line of (3.1) it is seen that λ gives the marginal utility of income. λ has been written as a function of prices and income to highlight the fact that λ is not a constant.

Armed with these expressions, we can examine the impact on utility of *infinitesimal* changes in prices and/or income. Totally differentiating the indirect utility function, using (3.1), we obtain

$$dV = \sum_{i=1}^{n} \frac{\partial V}{\partial p_i} \, dp_i + \frac{\partial V}{\partial y} \, dy$$

$$= -\lambda \Sigma x_i dp_i + \lambda dy \tag{3.2}$$

$$= -\lambda(\mathbf{x}d\mathbf{p} - dy)$$

where $d\mathbf{p} = (dp_1, \ldots, dp_n)'$.

This is a type of marginal cost-benefit rule, where the changes are assumed to be so small that the marginal utility of income can be treated as a constant (see, for example, Boadway, 1975). Therefore, the benefit/loss of a marginal change in a price can be obtained by simply observing the quantity x_i purchased. It should be recalled that $\partial V / \partial p_i = -\lambda x_i$, and λ can be set equal to one. If many, possibly all, prices and/or income are changed, the simple addition of these effects will yield the total impact on welfare. That is the essential meaning of the marginal welfare change criterion.

Consider now a *discrete* change in prices and income. The change in utility associated with a change in prices and income from $\mathbf{p}^0, y^0$ to $\mathbf{p}^1, y^1$ can be represented as a line integral

$$\triangle U = V(\mathbf{p}^1, y^1) - V(\mathbf{p}^0, y^0)$$

$$= \int_c \left(\sum_{i=1}^{n} V_i dp_i + V_y dy \right) \tag{3.3}$$

$$= -\int_c \lambda(\mathbf{p}, y)[\mathbf{x}(\mathbf{p}, y)d\mathbf{p} - dy]$$

where c is some path of prices and income between initial and final price–income vectors. Loosely speaking, the first term within brackets in the last line of (3.3) gives the sum of the areas under ordinary uncompensated or Marshallian demand curves for a change in prices from $\mathbf{p}^0$ to $\mathbf{p}^1$. The second term within brackets represents a change in lump-sum income. The marginal utility of income, λ, is there to convert the changes from dollars to units of utility. These concepts will be further discussed and interpreted below.

The exact welfare change measure (3.3) requires information on the

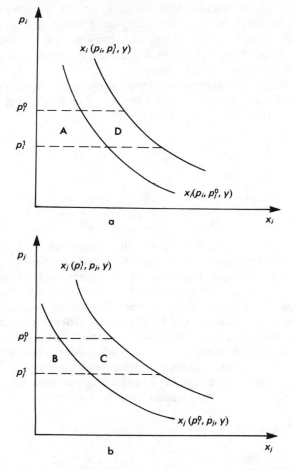

Figure 3.1 Consumer surpluses when two prices change (with all other prices and income fixed)

marginal utility of income, a variable which is, in general, unobservable. Economists have therefore tried to convert (3.3) to a money measure by eliminating λ from the expression. Then, we obtain

$$S = \int_c [\mathbf{x}(\mathbf{p}, y)d\mathbf{p} - dy] = y^1 - y^0 - \int_c [\mathbf{x}(\mathbf{p}, y)d\mathbf{p}] \qquad (3.4)$$

In words: a money measure S of utility change is obtained by adding to the change in income all the changes in consumer surpluses in the markets where prices change. Unfortunately, the order in which prices and income are changed may affect the magnitude as well as the sign of S.

The argument is illustrated in Figure 3.1. Assume p_i is lowered from p_i^0 to p_i^1 with all other prices and income fixed. The change in consumer surplus in the ith market is given by area A in Figure 3.1a. The change in p_i shifts the position of the demand curve in the jth market to the right (left) if goods i and j are complements (substitutes). However, if income and all prices but the ith price are fixed, the total change in consumer surplus is still given by area A in the figure. Recall that $\mathbf{x}d\mathbf{p} = x_i dp_i$ in (3.4) if $dp_j = 0$ for all $j \neq i$, implying that we need only bother about the ith market. Thus, the shift in the demand curve of the jth good in Figure 3.1b does not have any significance *per se* when calculating a money measure of the utility change associated with a change in the price of good i. This can also be verified by using Roy's identity discussed in Chapter 2.

Next, lower the price of the jth good. The change in consumer surplus in the market for this good must be evaluated given the fact that we have already reduced the price of the ith good. Thus, the relevant change in consumer surplus in the market for the jth good is equal to area B+C in Figure 3.1b. The money measure S of the utility change caused by the combined fall in p_i and p_j is equal to area A+B+C in the figure.

Assume that we instead lower p_j before p_i. The change in consumer surplus in the jth market is now measured to the left of the demand curve drawn for $p_i = p_i^0$, i.e. is equal to area B in Figure 3.1b. As the price of good j is lowered, the demand curve for the ith good may move leftward or rightward. In any case, the change in consumer surplus in market i must be evaluated to the left of the 'final' demand curve obtained for $p_j = p_j^1$, i.e. is equal to area A+D in Figure 3.1a.

In general, the considered paths of price adjustment impute different dollar gains or total consumer surpluses to the underlying unique change in utility, i.e. area A+B+C need not be equal to area B+A+D. In addition, it should be noted that these areas are obtained by considering just two out of possibly an infinite number of paths between initial and final prices since we could proceed by alternate, small changes in p_i and p_j. However, if the cross-price effects are equal ($\partial x_i / \partial p_j = \partial x_j / \partial p_i$), the change in total consumer surplus will not depend on which procedure or path we take, i.e. area A+B+C = area B+A+D in Figure 3.1. Intuitively, the shift in the demand curve for good i as the price of good j is changed is equal to the shift in the demand curve for good j as p_i is changed, implying that area D is equal to area C in the figure. As will be demonstrated below, a sufficient condition for the cross-price effects to be equal is that the marginal utility of income is constant with respect to those parameters (prices and/or income) which are changed. Nevertheless, if the path-independency conditions hold, the money measure depends only on the terminal values of the considered path, and not on the path itself.

2 Path-independency conditions and the constancy of the marginal utility of income

It remains to investigate under what conditions the line integral in (3.4) is independent of the path of adjustment. Consider a line integral

$$\int_{\bar{c}} \sum_{i=1}^{n} f_i (q_1, \ldots, q_n) dq_i \tag{3.5}$$

where $\bar{c}$ is some path between initial and final q-vectors, and assume that all f_i have continuous first derivatives in a (pathwise) simply-connected open set R of space. Accordingly, a set, for example a convex set, where any two points can be joined by a path lying in R, and any two paths in R with the same end points can be deformed into each other without moving the end points and without leaving R.

Then, the value of the line integral (3.5) is independent of the particular choice of path $\bar{c}$, as defined in the appendix to this chapter, in R and determined solely by the end points of $\bar{c}$ if and only if (iff) the mixed derivatives are symmetric, i.e.

$$\frac{\partial f_i}{\partial q_j} = \frac{\partial f_j}{\partial q_i} \quad \text{for all } i, j \tag{3.6}$$

It is important to notice that conditions (3.6) are necessary for, and almost suffice to ensure, path independency. They become sufficient if we add the assumption, stated above, concerning the geometrical properties of the region in space in which (3.5) is considered (see Courant and John, 1974, pp. 95–106). This assumption is assumed to hold throughout, thus we only refer to conditions (3.6) in the remainder of this volume.

Applying (3.6), it follows that the money measure

$$S = \int_c [-\mathbf{x}(\mathbf{p}, y) \cdot d\mathbf{p} + 1 \cdot dy] \tag{3.4a}$$

is path independent if it satisfies the conditions

$$\frac{\partial x_i}{\partial p_j} = \frac{\partial x_j}{\partial p_i} \quad \text{for all } i, j \tag{3.7'}$$

$$\partial x_i / \partial y = \partial(1) / \partial p_i = 0 \quad \text{for all } i, j \tag{3.7''}$$

All of these conditions cannot hold simultaneously. Zero income effects for all goods means that the budget constraint is violated. At most, demand for $n-1$ goods can be independent of the level of income y, implying that if y is changed, all additional income is spent on the nth good.

To further interpret these results and investigate their relationship to the marginal utility of income, it is useful to consider the path-independency conditions for equation (3.3)

$$\left.\begin{aligned} \frac{\partial(\lambda x_i)}{\partial p_j} &= \frac{\partial(\lambda x_j)}{\partial p_i} \\ \frac{\partial(\lambda x_i)}{\partial y} &= \frac{\partial \lambda}{\partial p_i} \end{aligned}\right\} \quad \text{for all } i, j \tag{3.8}$$

where $\partial(\lambda x_i)/\partial p_j = x_i \partial \lambda/\partial p_j + \lambda \partial x_i/\partial p_j = -V_{ij}$. Conditions (3.8) hold by construction since the integrand of (3.3), denoted by L here, is an exact, i.e. the total, differential of the indirect utility function. The latter condition is both necessary and sufficient for path independency since a line integral $\int L$, i.e. (3.3), taken over a path c in an open set R of space ($R \subseteq \Omega_I$) is independent of the particular choice of path and determined solely by the initial and final point of c iff L is the total differential of a function $f(p, y)$ in R, assuming x, λ, V_p and V_y are continuous functions of $\mathbf{p}$ and y in R (Courant and John, 1974, p. 97). Clearly, there exists a function, namely the indirect utility function $V(\mathbf{p}, y)$, for which $dV = L$. However, in many cases it may be difficult to ascertain whether a given differential is a total differential or not. In general it turns out to be easier to use the necessary and (almost) sufficient conditions (3.6). The reader should also recall the discussion of Young's theorem in Section 5 of Chapter 2. According to Young's theorem, the cross derivatives are symmetric, i.e. $V_{ij} = V_{ji}$, provided the indirect utility function is twice continuously differentiable. Using (3.1), the reader can easily verify that these symmetry conditions coincide with those stated in (3.8) (see also the appendix to this chapter).

If λ is independent of all prices and income, conditions (3.8) reduce to conditions (3.7). However, from (3.8) and the first-order conditions for utility maximization, it follows that λ cannot be independent of all prices and income. In Section 4 of Chapter 2, it was shown that if all prices and income double, λ must halve; λ is homogeneous of degree minus one in prices and income. This result implies that λ, at most, can be independent of all n prices but not of income, or independent of $n-1$ prices and income.

Equations (3.7) and (3.8) clarify the relationship between the money measure (3.4a) and the constancy of the marginal utility of income. Consider a change in all prices with income fixed (i.e. let income serve as the *numéraire*). If $\partial x_i/\partial p_j = \partial x_j/\partial p_i$ for all i, j, then $x_i \partial \lambda/\partial p_j = x_j \partial \lambda/\partial p_i$ from (3.8). Hence, path independency of the money measure (3.4a) does not imply that λ is constant with respect to all prices, but rather that λ changes at the same rate for each price change. Clearly, however, if $\partial \lambda/\partial p_i = 0$ for all i in (3.8), then the path independency conditions (3.7') must hold. This case, i.e. $\lambda = \lambda(y)$, represents the first interpretation of constancy of the marginal utility of income put forward by Samuelson (1942). Thus, if $\lambda = \lambda(y)$, the money measure (3.4a) gives an exact or at least a proportional measure of utility change, i.e. $S = \triangle U/\lambda$, when prices vary with income fixed.[1]

It has been demonstrated (see, for example, Silberberg, 1972) that conditions (3.7') require that the utility function is homothetic. A function is homothetic if all contours are radial scale replicas of each other. It is not required that the value of the function increases in the same proportion along these contours. However, there is a close connection between homotheticity and homogeneity. A utility function is said to be homothetic if $W(\mathbf{x})$ can be written as $f(U(\mathbf{x}))$ where f is a positive, finite, continuous and strictly monotonically increasing function of one variable with $f(0) = 0$, and U is a positively homogeneous function of n variables (Lau, 1969, p. 375). In the case of a homothetic utility function, the demand functions take the form $\mathbf{x} = g'(\mathbf{p})y$ with $g'(\mathbf{p})$ homogeneous of degree -1, as is shown in, for example, Lau (1969), which implies that the income elasticities are equal to one. This property means that the income expansion paths are straight lines emanating from the origin. The reader is invited to use the homothetic indirect utility function $V(\mathbf{p}, y) = -g(\mathbf{p}) + \ell n\, y$ to check (i) that such a function generates demand functions that have the above stated income elasticity property, and (ii) that the path independency conditions stated in (3.7') hold. The latter result is easily obtained by comparing the second derivatives of the indirect utility function and the cross-price derivatives of the demand functions. The reader is also referred to Section 4 where a simple example of a homothetic utility function can be found.

The assumption of homothetic utility functions is very restrictive. It should be stressed, however, that if only a subset of prices change, then conditions (3.7') need only be satisfied for that particular subset of prices, implying that the indirect utility function can be written as $V(\mathbf{p}, y) = f(\mathbf{p}) + g(\mathbf{p}^s, y)$, where $\mathbf{p}^s$ denotes the prices that remain fixed throughout the movement. Finally, if only a single price, say p_1 changes, the money measure can be written as

$$S_1 = -\int_{p_1^0}^{p_1^1} x_1\,(p_1, p_2^0, \ldots, y^0)dp_1 \tag{3.9}$$

Note that the area to the left of the demand curve between the initial and the final price is unique in the single-price-change case. If only one price is changed, holding all other prices and income constant throughout the movement, there can hardly be a path dependency problem, but, of course, the size of the area is determined by the levels of the fixed prices and income, since demand is a function of all prices and income.

Thus far, income has been assumed to be fixed. Consider now the case where income and $n-1$ prices are free to vary. The remaining good, say x_n, is used as *numéraire*. It is seen from (3.7) that the corresponding path independency conditions are

$$
\left.
\begin{array}{l}
\dfrac{\partial x_i}{\partial p_j} = \dfrac{\partial x_j}{\partial p_i} \\[2mm]
\dfrac{\partial x_i}{\partial y} = 0
\end{array}
\right\} \quad i, j = 1, \ldots, n-1 \tag{3.10}
$$

i.e. they require zero income effects for $n-1$ goods, implying a vertical income-consumption path; if income is changed, all additional income is spent on the nth good. In other words, $n-1$ demand functions must have the property that a price change has a substitution effect, but not an income effect (on the set Ω_I of prices and income). A necessary and sufficient condition for this to be the case is that the utility function is quasi-linear, i.e. takes the form $U=u(x_1, \ldots, x_{n-1}) + ax_n$, where $a>0$ is a constant. A detailed discussion of the properties of quasi-linear utility functions is found in Katzner (1970, Ch. 5). Also note that the second interpretation of the constancy of the marginal utility of income (money), discussed by Samuelson (1942), assumes that $\lambda=\lambda(p_n)$. It is seen from (3.8) that the path independency conditions (3.10) are implied by this constancy assumption.

It is easily checked that the following money measure satisfies conditions (3.10)

$$
\frac{\triangle U}{\lambda(p_n)} = S_b = -\sum_{i=1}^{n-1} \int_{p_i^0}^{p_i^1} x_i(\mathbf{p})dp_i + \triangle y \tag{3.11}
$$

This measure states: Add the changes in consumer surpluses in markets where prices change. The way in which prices are changed makes no difference, but the change in consumer surplus in a given market must be evaluated subject to all previously considered price changes. See Figure 3.2 and equation (3.24) for illustrations of the procedure.

If only a subset of prices and/or income is changed, the 'constancy' condition can be weakened. Hence the only requirement is that λ is independent of the prices (income) which are changed. This is a much

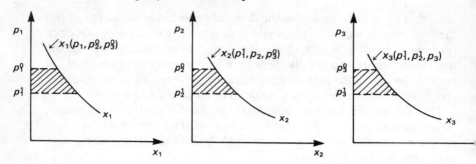

Figure 3.2 Illustration of consumer surpluses when three prices are lowered and the underlying utility function is quasi-linear; x_4 is the *numéraire* good whose price is set equal to unity

less restrictive assumption than the one employed in (3.11), at least if only a few prices are changed. Nevertheless, any constancy assumption imposes severe restrictions on the properties of the consumer's preference ordering.

3 *The compensating and equivalent variations*

If the path independency conditions (3.7) hold,[2] a unique measure of consumer surplus exists, i.e. a measure which depends only on the terminal values of the considered path, and not on the path itself. On the other hand, if the path independency conditions do not hold, there is possibly an infinite number of money measures S of a unique change in utility. In particular, this means that one can find paths such that $S<0$ even if $\triangle U>0$, and vice versa (compare Chipman and Moore, 1980).

The deficiencies of money measures based on ordinary demand functions have led economists to search for other and, hopefully, less restrictive money measures of utility change. A second reason is that many economists want to get rid of the cardinal interpretation of the utility function which seems to be implied by concepts like marginal utility of income or money (see, for example, Ng, 1979).

Although a great number of measures have been proposed in the literature, attention is focused here on the concepts of compensating and equivalent variation. The reader interested in other, less frequently used, measures is referred to McKenzie and Pearce (1982), McKenzie (1983), Ng (1979), and Stahl (1983a).

The concepts of compensating and equivalent variations were originally introduced by Sir John R. Hicks in a series of articles in the *Review of Economic Studies* (1940/1–1945/6). The compensating variation gives

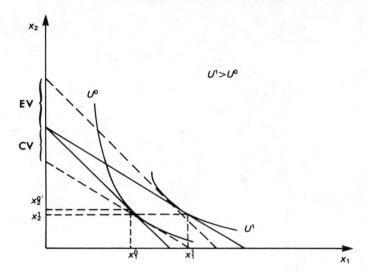

Figure 3.3 Compensating (CV) and equivalent (EV) variations when p_1 falls. Note: CV of a price fall is equal to $-$EV of the reversed price rise

the maximum (minimum) amount of money that can be taken from (must be given to) a household while leaving it just as well off as it was before a fall (rise) in prices. The equivalent variation gives the minimum (maximum) amount of money that must be given to (taken from) a household to make it as well off as it would have been after a fall (rise) in prices. These concepts are illustrated in Figure 3.3, where the price of the first good falls while the price of the second good remains fixed.

In order to derive concepts of compensating and equivalent variation, it is useful to introduce the expenditure function

$$e(\mathbf{p}, \bar{U}) = \min_{\mathbf{x}} \{\mathbf{px} | U(\mathbf{x}) \geqslant \bar{U}\} = \mathbf{p\tilde{x}}(\mathbf{p}, \bar{U}) \tag{3.12}$$

This function gives the minimal expenditure necessary to reach, at most, a pre-specified utility level $\bar{U}$. The compensated or Hicksian demand functions, denoted by a tilde, are obtained by taking the partial derivatives of the expenditure function with respect to prices. The Hicksian demand functions, like the Marshallian demand functions, are assumed to be twice continuously differentiable. A compensated demand function has the property that a change in the own price has a substitution effect, but not an income effect. Moreover, the cross-price effects, the matrix of substitution effects, are symmetric. For a discussion of these claims,

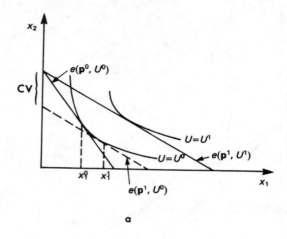

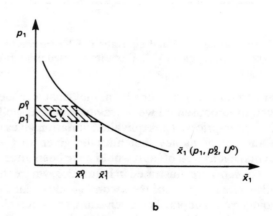

Figure 3.4 Compensating variations in income when only the price of one good changes: p_1 falls from p_1^0 to p_1^1

including necessary assumptions regarding the properties of the underlying direct utility function, the reader is referred to Section 5 of Chapter 2.

The compensating variation

Using the expenditure function, the compensating variation (CV) in income associated with a change in prices and income from $\mathbf{p}^0, y^0$ to $\mathbf{p}^1, y^1$ is written as

$$\text{CV} = y^1 - y^0 + e(\mathbf{p}^0, U^0) - e(\mathbf{p}^1, U^0)$$

$$= \triangle y - \int_c \tilde{\mathbf{x}}(\mathbf{p}, U^0) d\mathbf{p} \tag{3.13}$$

where c is some path between initial and final price–income vectors to be discussed below. Note that $y^0 = e(\mathbf{p}^0, U^0)$ and $y^1 = e(\mathbf{p}^1, U^1)$, where U^1 is the final utility level. These results are obtained from equation (2.10); see also Figure 3.4. The reader should observe that this definition of CV (and the one of EV below) gives the opposite sign from the definition used by some economists.

In interpreting (3.13) it is useful to consider the following sequence of changes in income–price space. Assume income changes from y^0 to y^1 with all prices fixed at $\mathbf{p}^0$. The corresponding compensating variation, i.e. the sum of money that must be taken from/given to the household to hold it at the initial utility level U^0, equals the actual change in income $\triangle y$; in the middle term of (3.13) $e(\mathbf{p}^0, U^0)$ and $e(\mathbf{p}^1, U^0)$ are equal and cancel when $\mathbf{p}^0 = \mathbf{p}^1$. Equivalently, the integral in (3.13) is equal to zero when $d\mathbf{p} = 0$.

Consider next a change in prices from $\mathbf{p}^0$ to $\mathbf{p}^1$ with income fixed at, say y^0. Then

$$\text{CV} = e(\mathbf{p}^0, U^0) - e(\mathbf{p}^1, U^0) = -\int_c \tilde{\mathbf{x}}(\mathbf{p}, U^0) d\mathbf{p} \tag{3.14}$$

Equation (3.14) gives the minimal expenditure necessary to reach the utility level U^0 when $\mathbf{p} = \mathbf{p}^0$ less the minimal expenditure required to reach U^0 when prices are changed to $\mathbf{p} = \mathbf{p}^1$. In Figure 3.4a, which depicts the single price change case, the two levels of expenditure are indicated by 'budget lines'. In order to arrive at the integral in (3.14) note that

$$\frac{\partial e(\mathbf{p}, U^0)}{\partial \mathbf{p}} = \tilde{\mathbf{x}}(\mathbf{p}, U^0) \tag{3.15}$$

for infinitesimal price changes as was discussed in Chapter 2. Integrating (3.15) over some path between $\mathbf{p}^0$ and $\mathbf{p}^1$ yields $-\text{CV}$; due to the order in which prices appear in (3.14), the order of integration must be reversed to arrive at (3.14). Hence, (3.14) gives the sum of areas to the left of compensated demand curves between $\mathbf{p}^0$ and $\mathbf{p}^1$. See Figure 3.4b for an illustration of the single price change case.

The choice of adjustment path c has not yet been discussed. Consider the condition for path independence of (3.13)

$$\frac{\partial \tilde{x}_i}{\partial p_j} = \frac{\partial \tilde{x}_j}{\partial p_i} \quad \text{for all } i, j \tag{3.16}$$

By construction, this condition is fulfilled for compensated demand functions; recall that the cross-price effects are symmetric. Hence, the

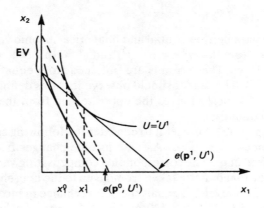

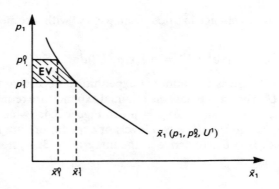

Figure 3.5 The equivalent variation in income when p_1 falls from p_1^0 to p_1^1

integrand of (3.13) is an exact differential and one may arbitrarily choose the order in which prices (and income) are changed. The area to the left of the compensated demand curve for a particular good between its initial and final price, however, must be evaluated subject to all previously considered price changes in other markets; recall Figures 3.1 and 3.2.

The equivalent variation

Equivalent variation (EV) is the amount of money that must be given to (taken from) the household at initial prices and income $\mathbf{p}^0$, y^0 to make the household as well off as it would be at final prices and income $\mathbf{p}^1$, y^1

$$EV = y^1 - y^0 + e(\mathbf{p}^0, U^1) - e(\mathbf{p}^1, U^1)$$

$$= \triangle y - \int_c \bar{\mathbf{x}}(\mathbf{p}, U^1)d\mathbf{p} \tag{3.17}$$

where U^1 is the fixed (final) utility level.

The equivalent variation is equal to the sum of the change in income plus all the changes in consumer surpluses in the markets where prices change. The changes in consumer surpluses are evaluated to the left of compensated demands, where the demand functions are evaluated at the final utility level. Since the path independency conditions hold (see 3.16), the order in which prices are changed makes no difference. Nevertheless the change in consumer surplus in the ith market must be evaluated conditional on all previously considered price changes in other markets. The single-price-change case is depicted in Figure 3.5.

We have shown that the CV and EV measures are path independent. It has also been demonstrated that in general this is not true for the ordinary consumer surplus measure. Unfortunately, these results are not sufficient as a basis on which to choose a money measure of utility change. For example, we have not shown that there is a money measure, if any, which ranks commodity bundles in the same order as the consumer would have done. Nor have we addressed the problem of a multihousehold economy. In real world applications, one often faces the problem that some consumers gain while others lose from a proposed project. Thus we need a rule for aggregating individual welfare changes. Even if we find more or less satisfactory theoretical solutions to these issues, there remains the problem of figuring out how to calculate consumer surplus changes.

However, before turning to a discussion of these important questions, two examples of the path independency results derived in this chapter are given.

4 *Two examples*

In order to appreciate the results derived in the previous sections, it is useful to illustrate them by a few examples. Consider first the utility function

$$U = \ell n \; x_1^\alpha x_2^{1-\alpha} = \alpha \ell n \; x_1 + (1-\alpha)\ell n \; x_2 \tag{3.18}$$

This homothetic function can be interpreted as a monotone transformation of a function, the Cobb–Douglas function, which is homogeneous of degree one.

Maximization of (3.18) subject to the usual budget constraint yields demand functions for goods and the 'marginal utility of income' function

$$
\left.\begin{aligned}
x_1 &= \frac{\alpha y}{p_1} \\
x_2 &= \frac{(1-\alpha)y}{p_2} \\
\lambda &= \frac{1}{y}
\end{aligned}\right\} \tag{3.19}
$$

Substituting the first two lines of (3.19) into (3.18), rearranging and suppressing constants yields an indirect utility function of the form

$$
V(p_1, p_2, y) = -\alpha \ell n\, p_1 - (1-\alpha)\ell n\, p_2 + \ell n\, y \tag{3.20}
$$

It can easily be checked that taking partial derivatives of (3.20) with respect to prices and income after a few calculations, yields (3.19).

The path independency conditions (3.7') require that $\partial x_1/\partial p_2 = \partial x_2/\partial p_1$. Obviously, this holds for the demand functions in (3.19). Hence, if p_1 and p_2 are changed, with income fixed, the order in which prices are changed makes no difference. It is also clear that the change in consumer surplus associated with a price change is proportional to the underlying utility change. This is because the marginal utility of income λ is independent of prices, i.e. $\lambda = 1/y$. Thus, the change in utility associated with a change in prices from $\mathbf{p}^0$ to $\mathbf{p}^1$ is

$$
\begin{aligned}
\triangle V &= -\lambda[\textstyle\int_a x_1 dp_1 + \int_b x_2 dp_2] \\
&= -(\tfrac{1}{y})\,[\textstyle\int_a \frac{\alpha y}{p_1}\, dp_1 + \int_b \frac{(1-\alpha)y}{p_2}\, dp_2] = \frac{1}{y}\, S
\end{aligned} \tag{3.21}
$$

where $a = (p_1^1, p_1^0)'$ and $b = (p_2^1, p_2^0)'$. Note that the sum of the terms within brackets gives the sum of changes in consumer surpluses evaluated to the left of ordinary demand curves. The practical method of evaluating an integral depends on finding a function with the function to be integrated as its derivative. Thus, the integrals in (3.21) can be evaluated in terms of the functions $\ell n\, p_i$. The reader, however, is recommended not to integrate over a range from $\mathbf{p}^i \to \infty$ to some finite price vector, since utility tends to infinity. We avoid such paths throughout this volume unless otherwise stated. See the appendix to Chapter 6 for a discussion concerning the convergence/divergence of integrals that are improper by virtue of an infinite limit of integration.

The proportionality between the money measure S and the change in utility in (3.21) vanishes if the utility function (3.18) is replaced by the (homothetic and homogeneous) Cobb–Douglas utility function, denoted by u. The reason being that $\lambda = \lambda(y)$ is replaced by $\lambda = \lambda(\mathbf{p})$; and in (3.21) all prices change while income is fixed. The indirect utility functions corresponding to U and u can be written as $V(\mathbf{p}, y) = \ell\mathrm{n}[y/h(\mathbf{p})]$ and $G(\mathbf{p}, y) = y/h(\mathbf{p})$, respectively. Taking partial derivatives with respect to y yields the stated properties of λ. Nevertheless, the two utility functions produce the same ordering of commodity bundles (price vectors), implying that $\mathrm{sgn}(\triangle U) = \mathrm{sgn}(\triangle u)$. Moreover, the demand functions and hence also S are unaffected by the considered monotonic transformation of the utility function. Hence, $\mathrm{sgn}(\triangle u) = \mathrm{sgn}(S) = \mathrm{sgn}(\triangle U)$. Compare equations (4.3) in Chapter 4.

Turning next to CV and EV measures, we first derive the expenditure function. This function can be obtained by minimizing expenditure subject to a pre-specified utility level. Alternatively, the indirect utility function (3.20) can be used and the level of utility fixed for example at $\bar{U}$. Income y can then be replaced by the expenditure function $e(p_1, p_2, \bar{U})$ to obtain

$$e(p_1, p_2, \bar{U}) = \exp \{\bar{U} + \alpha\ell\mathrm{n}\, p_1 + (1-\alpha)\ell\mathrm{n}\, p_2\} = y \qquad (3.22)$$

Taking partial derivatives with respect to prices and the utility level yields

$$\frac{\partial e}{\partial p_1} = \bar{x}_1 = \frac{\alpha}{p_1} \exp \{\bar{U} + \alpha\ell\mathrm{n}\, p_1 + (1-\alpha)\ell\mathrm{n}\, p_2\}$$

$$\frac{\partial e}{\partial p_2} = \bar{x}_2 = \frac{1-\alpha}{p_2} \exp \{\bar{U} + \alpha\ell\mathrm{n}\, p_1 + (1-\alpha)\ell\mathrm{n}\, p_2\} \left.\vphantom{\frac{\frac{a}{b}}{\frac{a}{b}}}\right\} \quad (3.23)$$

$$\frac{\partial e}{\partial U} = \Sigma p_i \bar{x}_i = \exp \{\bar{U} + \alpha\ell\mathrm{n}\, p_1 + (1-\alpha)\ell\mathrm{n}\, p_2\}$$

Using (3.23), the compensating variation of a change in prices from $\mathbf{p}^0$ to $\mathbf{p}^1$ can be written as

$$CV = - \int_a [\frac{\alpha}{p_1} \exp \{U^0 + \alpha\ell\mathrm{n}\, p_1 + (1-\alpha)\ell\mathrm{n}\, p_2^0\}]\, dp_1$$

$$- \int_b [\frac{1-\alpha}{p_2} \exp \{U^0 + \alpha\ell\mathrm{n}\, p_1^1 + (1-\alpha)\ell\mathrm{n}\, p_2\}]\, dp_2 \qquad (3.24)$$

Note that the compensating variation in the second market is evaluated subject to the price change in the first market. However, since the path independency condition holds, i.e. $\partial\bar{x}_i/\partial p_j = \partial\bar{x}_j/\partial p_i$ in (3.23), the order in which prices are changed makes no difference. For example, we could change p_2 before p_1. Then, p_2^0 is replaced by p_2^1 and p_1^1 by p_1^0 in (3.24). However, this does not affect the value of CV since this value is determined solely by the end points of the paths.

An EV measure is obtained by fixing utility at its final level, not at the initial level as in (3.24).

A second example of an interesting preference function is

$$U = \sum_{i=1}^{n-1} \beta_i \ell n \, x_i + \beta_n \, x_n \tag{3.25}$$

where the constants β will be suppressed in what follows. It can easily be verified that the demand functions corresponding to this quasi-linear utility function can be written as

$$\left. \begin{aligned} x_i &= \frac{p_n}{p_i} \\ x_n &= \frac{y}{p_n} - (n-1) \end{aligned} \right\} \tag{3.26}$$

where x_n is assumed to be positive. Moreover, since it can be shown that $\lambda = 1/p_n$, the utility function (3.25) corresponds to Samuelson's second interpretation of the constancy of the marginal utility of income.

In this case, ordinary and compensated demand functions coincide. Substituting (3.26) into (3.25) and replacing y by $e(p_1, p_2, \bar{U})$ we obtain the expenditure function

$$e(p_1, p_2, \bar{U}) = p_n \bar{U} + p_n \sum \ell n \, p_i \tag{3.27}$$

where constants are suppressed. Taking the partial derivative of (3.27) with respect to the price of the ith good yields the compensated demand for that good. It follows that $\bar{x}_i = p_n/p_i = x_i$ which establishes the claim.

Hence, given a utility function of the form specified in (3.25), all three consumer surplus measures considered coincide. This result is not obtained by a mere chance. It holds for all quasi-linear utility functions (defined below equation (3.10) in Section 2). On the other hand, a homothetic utility function, such as (3.18), does not generate measures of equal size, i.e. $S \neq CV \neq EV$. The marginal utility of income depends on income and the level of utility. Some inspection of equations (3.21) and (3.24) should make this clear. These claims will be discussed in Chapter 4.

Appendix

Definition of a path

By a path (a 'simple oriented arc' or a 'regular curve') $\bar{c} = (\mathbf{q}^b, \mathbf{q}^a)' = \mathbf{q}^{\widehat{a}} \mathbf{q}^b$ in R joining two points $\mathbf{q}^a = (q_1^a, \ldots, q_n^a)$ and

$\mathbf{q}^b = (q_1^b, \ldots, q_n^b)$, we mean n continuous functions $q_i = g_i(t)$ defined in the interval $0 \leqslant t \leqslant 1$ (say) such that the point $\mathbf{q}^t = (g_1(t), \ldots, g_n(t))$ lies in R for all t of the interval, different t in the interval correspond to different points $\mathbf{q}$, and coincides with $\mathbf{q}^a$ for $t = 0$ and $\mathbf{q}^b$ for $t = 1$. Ordering points according to either increasing or decreasing t converts a simple arc into an oriented simple arc (denoted by '$\frown$'). Finally, attention is restricted to paths or arcs that are continuously differentiable or at least sectionally smooth, e.g. simple polygonal arcs; the latter kind of arcs can always be approximated by smooth (differentiable) ones in R with the same end points. (see Courant and John, 1974, Ch. 1; Widder, 1961, Ch. 7).

Line integrals

Suppose $dV = V_\mathbf{p}d\mathbf{p} + V_y dy$ is the total differential of $V(\mathbf{p}, y)$. Consider the line integral

$$\int_c L = \int_c (V_\mathbf{p} \, d\mathbf{p} + V_y dy) = \int_c (\Sigma V_i dp_i + V_y dy) \tag{A3.1}$$

where $V_i = \partial V/\partial p_i$ for all i, $c = \widehat{AB}$ with $A = \mathbf{p}^0, y^0$, $B = \mathbf{p}^1, y^1$, and $c \in \Omega_I$. We take the set Ω_I, as defined in Chapter 2, as our domain. The line integral (A3.1) exists if all functions $V_\mathbf{p}$, V_y are continuous on c. This is clearly valid since $V \in C^3$, i.e. thrice continuously differentiable, in Ω_I by assumption (see Chapter 2).

Using the definition of a path given above, (A3.1) can also be written as

$$\int_c L = \int_0^1 (\Sigma V_i \frac{dp_i}{dt} + V_y \frac{dy}{dt}) dt \tag{A3.2}$$

where $p_i = g_i(t)$, $y = g_y(t)$, and we have used the fact that $(dp_i/dt)dt = (\partial g_i/\partial t)dt$, $(dy/dt)dt = (\partial g_y/\partial t)dt$.

By the chain rule of differentiation, we then have

$$\int_c L = \int_0^1 [\frac{dV(\mathbf{g}(t))}{dt}] dt = V|_0^1 = V(\mathbf{p}^1, y^1) - V(\mathbf{p}^0, y^0) \tag{A3.3}$$

where $\mathbf{g}(t) = (g_1(t), \ldots, g_n(t), g_y(t))$, and $p_i^s = g_i(s)$, $y^s = g_y(s)$ for $s = 0,1$. Since the final expression in (A3.3) does not depend on $g_i(t)$ or $g_y(t)$, the integral extended over c is independent of c. This result can be proved by invoking Theorem II below.

Moreover, line integrals are additive, implying that

$$\int_c L = \sum_{i=1}^n \int_{c_i} V_i dp_i + \int_{c_{n+1}} V_y dy \tag{A3.4}$$

where $c_i = p_i^0 \widehat{p_i^1}$ for all i, $c_{n+1} = \widehat{y^0 y^1}$, and $V_i = V_i(p_1^1, \ldots, p_{i-1}^1, p_i, p_{i+1}^0, \ldots, p_n^0, y^0)$, assuming that the prices are changed in order from initial to final values, and that each Riemann integral in the right-hand expression of (A3.4) exists.

The following definitions and theorems, which are proved in Fleming (1965), are useful.

Definition: A differential form of degree 1 (a 1-form)
$f = \Sigma f_i(\mathbf{p}, y)dp_i + f_y(\mathbf{p}, y)dy$ is *exact* if there is
a function $F(\mathbf{p}, y)$ such that $f = dF$.

Definition: A 1-form f of class C^1 which satisfies

$$\left.\begin{aligned}
\frac{\partial f_i}{\partial p_j} &= \frac{\partial f_j}{\partial p_i} \quad \left(= \frac{\partial^2 F}{\partial p_i \partial p_j} = \frac{\partial^2 F}{\partial p_j \partial p_i}\right) \\
\frac{\partial f_i}{\partial y} &= \frac{\partial f_y}{\partial p_i} \quad \left(= \frac{\partial^2 F}{\partial p_i \partial y} = \frac{\partial^2 F}{\partial y \partial p_i}\right)
\end{aligned}\right\} \quad \forall i, j$$

is called a *closed* 1-form.

Theorem I: If Ω_I is a simply-connected open subset of non-negative Euclidean $(n+1)$-space, then every closed 1-form with domain Ω_I is exact.

Theorem II: Let Ω_I be open, and f a continuous 1-form with domain Ω_I. The following statements are equivalent:
  (i) f is exact.
  (ii) If c_1 and c_2 are any two piecewise smooth curves lying in Ω_I, then $\int_{c_1} f = \int_{c_2} f$.

Corollary: If Ω_I is simply connected and f is of class C^1, then each of the statements (i) and (ii) of Theorem II is equivalent to the statement that f is closed.

CHAPTER 4

Topics in the theory of consumer surplus measures

This chapter is a natural sequel to Chapter 3 in that it is essentially a comparison of the three different consumer surplus measures presented there. We begin in Section 1 with an analysis of the conditions under which the different consumer surplus measures coincide. As the measures in general impute different dollar gains to a unique utility change, the question naturally arises as to whether any of the measures rank commodity bundles correctly, i.e. in the same way as the consumer would. The ordinal/cardinal properties of money measures of utility change are also briefly discussed. Section 2 is devoted to the problem of aggregation over individuals, and the chapter ends with a presentation of different techniques for determining consumer surpluses in empirical situations.

1 A comparison of different money measures of utility change

Three different money measures of utility change were introduced in Chapter 3. Unfortunately, these measures need not coincide. This was demonstrated by means of two examples in the final section of the chapter. What is the relationship between these measures?

There is a simple case in which the three considered measures (CV, EV and the ordinary consumer surplus measure S) coincide. If the utility function is quasi-linear, then demand for $n-1$ goods are independent of the level of income, implying that all additional income is spent on the nth good. Thus, the ordinary and compensated demand function for any good (but the nth) must coincide.[1] Consequently, $S=CV=EV$ and must equal the measure given by equation (3.11). If only a restricted number of prices are changed, the three measures still coincide provided the demands for those goods whose prices are changed are independent of the level of income.

41

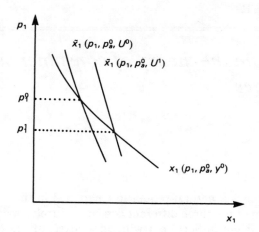

Figure 4.1 Ordinary and compensated demand curves

If income elasticities differ from zero, our money measures impute three different values to a unique utility change. Consider the case where income elasticities are positive over the entire adjustment path. Then, EV > CV for a fall in a single price since $\partial \bar{x}/\partial U > 0$ and $U^1 > U^0$; recall that CV is defined for $U = U^0$ and EV for $U = U^1$. This means that the EV is evaluated left of a curve which is situated outside that one used in evaluating the CV.[2] Moreover, since an ordinary demand curve connects the compensated demand curves, the consumer surplus evaluated to the left of the ordinary demand must exceed (fall short of) the corresponding compensating variation (equivalent variation), i.e. CV < S < EV (see Figure 4.1). Unfortunately, this result does not hold in the multiple price change case unless the path independency conditions (3.7′) hold for the goods whose prices are changed or the set of paths is restricted. This is shown in Dixit and Weller (1979) and Stahl (1983b; 1984) respectively. Also note that our definition of the money measures yields the opposite signs and hence the variation from the definition used by some economists.

Since $S \neq CV \neq EV$ in general, the question naturally arises as to whether all three measures rank commodity bundles correctly, i.e. in the same order as that chosen by the consumer. From equation (3.21) it can be seen that if the utility function is homothetic and income is fixed, then the ordinary money measure S ranks any number of bundles (price vectors) correctly. Recall that by subjecting a homothetic utility function to a suitable monotonic transformation, $S = \triangle U/\lambda$ is obtained. Obviously, S is a sign-preserving measure of utility change also in the case of a quasi-linear utility function, provided one price is fixed. If the utility function does not belong to one or other of these classes of functions or if all prices *and* income are free to vary (including the special case in which, say, income is not constant throughout the movement although the initial and final levels coincide), then there is no money measure S such that S is both unique and a sign-preserving measure of utility change. Recall that all of the path-independency conditions (3.7) cannot hold simultaneously, and that conditions (3.7′) hold iff the utility function is homothetic while conditions (3.10) hold iff the utility function is quasi-linear. (If only a few prices and/or income are changed, these conditions can be weakened, as was shown in Section 2 of Chapter 3.) An illustration of the failure of S to always provide a correct ranking of commodity bundles can be found in Just *et al.* (1982, Ch. 5).

Turning next to the CV and EV measures, these measures rank bundles correctly, provided one considers only two commodity bundles, the initial and final ones (corresponding to different prices and/or incomes). Matters are different in the more general case where there are two or more final bundles.

In order to illustrate these claims, it is useful to restate the CV and EV measures of Chapter 3 in the following way:

$$\left. \begin{aligned} CV &= e(\mathbf{p}^1, U^1) - e(\mathbf{p}^1, U^0) \\ EV &= e(\mathbf{p}^0, U^1) - e(\mathbf{p}^0, U^0) \end{aligned} \right\} \quad (4.1)$$

where the definitions given below equation (3.13) have been used to eliminate y^0 and y^1 from the measures, and a superscript 1(0) refers to final (initial) values. Since the expenditure function, by assumption, is increasing in utility, it follows that $U^1 \geq U^0$ implies that CV as well as EV have non-negative signs. This means that both measures rank any two commodity bundles in the same order as the underlying utility function. Note that this result holds also if all prices and income are changed since $\mathbf{p}$ in (4.1) refers to a vector of prices, not to a single price, and $y^1 \gtreqless y^0$.

By introducing a third price vector $\mathbf{p}^2$ corresponding to utility level U^2, it is straightforward to show that the EV measure ranks any three (any number of) bundles correctly. The EV measure uses $\mathbf{p}^0$ as base or reference prices in comparing the bundles, implying that bundles are ranked according to the utility they give to the consumer[3]. Thus, the EV measure will have the convenient properties of the compensation function introduced in Section 6 of Chapter 2. Recall that for fixed base prices, $\mathbf{p}^0$ say, the compensation function ranks commodity bundles in the same order as the underlying utility function.

The CV measure, on the other hand, evaluates changes at *final* prices. In the case of three bundles, we have to compare (4.1) and

$$\text{CV}_1 = e(\mathbf{p}^2, U^2) - e(\mathbf{p}^2, U^0) \tag{4.2}$$

Suppose that $U^1 = U^2$ so that the two final bundles refer to the same level of utility. Then, in order to correctly evaluate the change, the two CV measures in (4.1) and (4.2) must coincide. However, since the measures are based on two different (base) price vectors, we may end up with two different compensating variations for the unique change in utility. Hence, the CV measures may wrongly tell us that one change is preferred to the other. It has been shown (see Chipman and Moore, 1980; Hause, 1975) that only homothetic (with income fixed) and quasi-linear (with $p_n = 1$) utility functions ensure that the CV measure correctly ranks any number of commodity bundles or projects. The reader is also referred to the appendix to Chapter 6.

This result has led some economists, notably McKenzie (1983), McKenzie and Pearce (1982), and Morey (1984), to argue that the EV measure is the dollar measure of utility change. For the sake of completeness, however, the following should be noted. If there are two or more initial commodity bundles but only one final bundle, then it is straightforward to show that the bundles are ranked in the same order by both the CV measure and the consumer. This is not necessarily true for the EV measure. Hence, as pointed out by Ng (1979 p. 100), neither measure can be regarded as strictly superior to the other.

We now turn to the question of whether money measures of utility changes can be used to figure out *how much* a consumer prefers a project A over a project B. For example, if $\text{EV}_A = \$100$ and $\text{EV}_B = \$50$, does it follow that the consumer likes A twice as much as B?

In an *ordinal* world, we only require that our money measure ranks commodity bundles correctly, i.e. in the same order as that chosen by the consumer. This is equivalent to requiring that 'the money measure associated with a shift in the price–income vector has a positive sign if and only if the level of satisfaction increases'. In a restricted sense, there exist such money measures of utility change. For example, the EV measure has been shown to rank bundles correctly provided we restrict ourselves to a single initial commodity bundle or set of reference prices. We have also established conditions which ensure that the ordinary consumer surplus measure S and the CV measure respectively, rank bundles correctly.

In general, however, it is not true that $\triangle U = \lambda \text{EV}$ say, since λ is not constant with respect to changes in prices and/or income. It is important here to note that the path independency of the CV and EV measures is due to the symmetry of the cross-substitution effects and *not* to a constancy of the 'marginal utility of income'. Hence, one faces the above 'conversion' problem regardless of which money measure is used.

We have established conditions which ensure that the marginal utility of income (money) λ is independent of a subset of prices and/or income. The requirement is that the utility function is either homothetic or quasi-linear. For these classes of utility functions, it may seem meaningful to say that a certain project is twice as good as some other project. However, the marginal utility of income is *not* left unaffected by a monotone increasing transformation of the utility function. Let us consider the indirect utility function $V(\mathbf{p}, y)$. In an ordinal world, $G = f(V(\mathbf{p}, y))$, where $\partial f/\partial V > 0$, will serve equally well since the ordering is preserved. Taking the partial derivatives of V and G respectively with respect to the ith price yields

$$\left. \begin{array}{l} \dfrac{\partial V}{\partial p_i} = -\lambda x_i \\[2mm] \dfrac{\partial G}{\partial p_i} = \dfrac{\partial f}{\partial V} \dfrac{\partial V}{\partial p_i} = -\dfrac{\partial f}{\partial V} \lambda x_i \end{array} \right\} \quad \textit{for all} \quad i \qquad (4.3)$$

This shows that we cannot establish a linear relationship between the marginal money measure x_i and the change as measured by a utility index (and matters are not simpler in the discrete change case). Only the sign of the change in utility, i.e. the ranking of bundles, makes sense in an ordinal world. The transformation in (4.3) obviously preserves the signs of both the money measure and the utility change since $\partial f/\partial V > 0$. In point of fact, the money measure, but not the size of the 'utility change', is left unaffected by the considered transformation.[4]

To sum up, in an ordinal world we 'only' require that the money measure is a monotone increasing transformation (a sign-preserving transformation) of the utility function. The cardinal magnitude of differences, such as $EV_A = \$100$ while $EV_B = \$50$, reveal nothing about the intensity of preferences. Because an ordinalist's preferences do not have intensities, one can only infer that project A is preferred to project B.

We now turn to the question: What about a cardinal world? In such a world, the utility function $U(\mathbf{x})$ is unique except for an affine transformation $F(\mathbf{x}) = a + bU(\mathbf{x})$, where a and b are constants ($b > 0$). If λ is constant over the entire path considered, it now makes sense to say that the consumer likes A twice as much as B. If λ is not a constant, we can infer no more from our money measures than in an ordinal world. They tell us no more than that the consumer thinks project A is better than project B. Moreover, the conditions that are necessary for a money measure to yield a correct ranking are as restrictive in a cardinal as in an ordinal world (for further details, see Morey, 1984).

In closing, we turn to quite a different question, often raised by students, namely whether a consumer surplus measure can be infinitely large. With regard to a price fall, the compensating variation is bounded by y^0, while the equivalent variation may be infinite. In the case of price increases, the opposite result holds. A sufficient condition for a non-inferior good, say x_1, to have a finite uncompensated consumer's surplus is that the good is what Willig (1978) calls non-essential. The assumption of non-essentiality is both necessary and sufficient in order for the compensated surplus measures to always be finite. Non-essentiality of x_1 means that for any bundle $\mathbf{x} = x_1, \ldots, x_n$ where $x_1 > 0$ there exists a bundle $x_1' = 0, x_2', \ldots, x_n'$ such that $U(\mathbf{x}) = U(\mathbf{x}')$, i.e. any bundle including x_1 can be matched by a bundle excluding x_1. Geometrically, this is equivalent to all indifference surfaces intersecting the $x_1 = 0$ hyperplane. Unbounded measures may cause some problems in empirical investigations, e.g. when estimating the willingness to pay (EV) for having a natural resource preserved. We will return to this issue below; see also the appendix to Chapter 6.

2 *Aggregation over individuals*

Thus far, the chapter has dealt with the single consumer case. The aggregate demand for a commodity at any given price–income vector is the sum of the quantities demanded by the individual consumers. Thus, we must investigate under what conditions aggregate consumer surpluses, i.e. areas under ordinary and compensated market demand curves respectively, can be used to measure the gain or loss to the group as a whole.

Consider first the ordinary consumer surplus case. Areas to the left of ordinary market demands can be given a welfare interpretation if the (constant) *social* marginal utility of income is identical for all individuals. In order to show this, we introduce a Bergsonian welfare function of an H-household society. This function is written as

$$W = W(U^1(\mathbf{x}^1), \ldots, U^H(\mathbf{x}^H)) \tag{4.4}$$

This function, which relates the welfare of society or perhaps of a 'social planner' to the utility levels of the individuals, is usually assumed to have the following properties: (1) an increase in the utility level of any individual while all other individuals utility levels are kept constant increases social welfare; (2) if the utility of one individual is reduced, the utility of at least one other individual must then be increased for social welfare to be unchanged; and (3) the welfare weight of an individual depends on his/her utility level.

In order for a social welfare function to become a useful concept, full comparability of utility is often assumed. This means that the utility levels are expressed in units that can meaningfully be compared across individuals. It is thus not very useful to talk about a welfare function being defined over ordinal utilities. For example, consider the utilitarian welfare function which adds utilities, $W = \Sigma_h U^h$. If U^H is a utility index for the Hth consumer, any positive monotonic transformation, $f(U^H)$ say, of it is also a utility index. Nevertheless, the sum of utilities and hence the properties of the welfare function are changed by the transformation. Even an affine transformation, $a^H + b^H U^H$, applied to one of the utility functions, changes the properties of the welfare function. For this reason, one generally only allows transformations where both a and b are identical for all households (see Arrow, 1951; Bergson, 1938; Deaton and Muellbauer, 1983, Ch. 9; Just *et al.*, 1982, Ch. 3; Ng, 1982; Samuelson, 1947, Ch. 8, for discussion of the properties of social welfare functions).

We shall now use the social welfare function to examine the conditions under which an aggregate consumer surplus measure has any welfare significance. Assume that the welfare function is continuously differentiable. Thus differentiation of (4.4) and substitution of the indirect utility functions (3.2) yields

$$dW = \sum_{h=1}^{H} \frac{\partial W}{\partial V^h} \, dV^h = \Sigma \frac{\partial W}{\partial V^h} \lambda^h [-\mathbf{x}^h d\mathbf{p} + dy^h] \tag{4.5}$$

where $\partial W / \partial V^h > 0$ for all h gives the welfare weight of household h according to the 'social planner'.

According to the marginal welfare change measure (4.5), each individual is weighted by the product of the marginal welfare weight given to him/her and his/her marginal utility of income. If we want to consider discrete changes in prices and incomes, (4.5) must be integrated between initial and final price–income vectors.

Let us assume that the product of the welfare weight and the marginal utility of income is constant and equal across all individuals (implying that the welfare distribution is optimal as is demonstrated in the appendix to this chapter). The sum of changes in consumer surpluses, i.e. areas to the left of market demands, is then proportional to the change in social welfare; since $\partial W / \partial V \cdot \lambda$ is a constant, it can be factored out from the right-hand side of (4.5), if the expression is integrated between initial and final price vectors. This assumption, however, has the probably unreasonable implication that the welfare weight of a high-income household exceeds the welfare weight of a low-income group. This would be the case if λ is a strictly decreasing function of income.

Even if we consider the case in which all individuals have the same constant welfare weight and λ^h is constant for all individuals, one problem remains. In order that the sum of the changes in the consumers' surpluses be proportional to the change in social welfare, λ^h must not only be a constant but also identical for all individuals.

If the product of the welfare weight and the marginal utility of income varies across individuals, the sum of the consumer's surpluses and the change in social welfare need not then have the same sign. In order to be able to put a sign on the effect of a project on aggregate welfare, we must figure out the welfare weight given to each affected individual as well as his/her marginal utility of income. Of course, in addition we must calculate the change in each individual's consumer surplus. In the case of non-marginal changes, we also face the problem that neither $\partial W / \partial V^h$ nor λ^h needs to be constant.

The concepts of compensating and equivalent variation appear to be less restrictive in the above sense. Suppose the sum of changes in consumer surpluses evaluated to the left of compensated demands is positive in a multi-household society. Accordingly, the amount of money necessary to hold losers on their intitial or pre-project utility levels is less than the amount of money that can be extracted from the gainers of the project without leaving them worse off than without the project (the sum of CVs is positive). Furthermore the amount of money the gainers must be given to be persuaded to forgo the project exceeds the amount of money the losers are willing to pay to avoid the project (the sum of EVs is positive).

The sum of the consumers' surpluses represents what is left over after losers have been compensated. The project passes the Pareto test, i.e. no one is made worse off and the net surplus can be distributed so as to increase welfare of, for example, all individuals. It can be seen from (4.5) that if $dU^h = dV^h \geqslant 0$ for all h and $dV^h > 0$ for at least one h, then social welfare unambiguously increases. The argument assumes, however, that compensation is paid. If this is not the case some individuals may gain from the project while others lose. Hence one faces the same problem as when adding ordinary consumer surpluses over individuals. Accordingly, a social welfare function must be used to examine whether the weighted sum of gains and losses is positive or negative.

In Section 1 it was shown that the individual CV and EV measures usually differed in magnitude. Hence their aggregate counterparts may also differ. This means that one may end up in a situation where the costs of a project, such as the loss of producer's surplus, fall somewhere in between consumers aggregate CV and aggregate EV (both assumed to be positive so that consumers gain from the project). In such a case, no conclusive decision can be made regarding the desirability of the project.

Hence, according to one criterion, the project is desirable while the other criterion tells us that the project is not desirable.

In particular, this may be a serious problem in environmental economics. In order to illustrate this point let us assume that a decision is under way to close a national park and convert the land to other uses, such as mining or forestry. Accordingly, the visitors are questioned regarding their willingness to pay for having the park preserved. The maximum amount of money, the EV, that any user is willing to pay for this must be limited by his/her budget. Thus, this particular measure must be finite. On the other hand, the sum that must be given to a visitor to make him/her as well off without as with the park, the CV, may be infinitely large. If the cost of preserving the park falls somewhere in between the CV and the EV, no simple decision criterion is available.

A final remark is in order. The discussion in this section has not explicitly been based on the compensation criteria developed by Hicks (1939), Kaldor (1939), and Scitovsky (1941) (see Just *et al.*, 1982, Ch. 3 for definitions). However, the reader familiar with compensation criteria recognizes the close relationship between compensating and equivalent variations on the one hand and compensation criteria on the other hand. In fact, it has recently been demonstrated that if $\Sigma CV^h > 0$, then gainers can more than compensate losers (see Just *et al.*, 1982, Appendix D). The Just *et al.* (1982) result, if correct, resolves what has been known as the Boadway paradox in the literature. Boadway (1974) argued, in a general equilibrium context, that a positive aggregate compensating or equivalent variation does not indicate that gainers can more than compensate losers. The reader interested in this controversy is referred to Boadway (1974), Boadway and Bruce (1984), Just *et al.* (1982), Mishan (1976), and Smith and Stephen (1975).

3 *Estimation of consumer surplus*

It remains to briefly indicate what approaches can be used to estimate consumer surpluses in real world situations. The basic problem is that the Hicksian demand curves are unobservable. At best, Marshallian demand curves can be estimated directly. Several different approaches of the estimation of the compensating and equivalent variations have been suggested in the literature.

One of these approaches assumes that ordinary demand functions have been estimated. Then, if an expenditure function exists it must satisfy the following system of partial differential equations:

$$\frac{\partial e(\mathbf{p}, \bar{U})}{\partial p_i} = \tilde{x}_i(\mathbf{p}, \bar{U}) = x_i(\mathbf{p}, e(\mathbf{p}, \bar{U})) \quad \text{for all } i \qquad (4.6)$$

where $\bar{U}$ is the specified utility level, say initial or final. It must also satisfy the initial condition

$$e(\bar{\mathbf{p}}, \bar{U}) = \bar{\mathbf{p}}\mathbf{x}(\bar{\mathbf{p}}, \bar{y}) = \bar{\mathbf{p}}\bar{\mathbf{x}} = \bar{y} \qquad (4.7)$$

In principle, this system can be solved to obtain the expenditure function which in turn can be used to construct compensated demand functions (see Hurwics and Uzawa, 1971; Varian, 1978). Hausman (1981) and Bowden (1984) have used this approach to show that in some cases, it is a fairly straightforward matter to derive compensated demand curves from observed market demand curves. An example can be found in the appendix to this chapter.

A second approach assumes that a utility function, either direct or indirect, has been specified. This function can be used to derive a functional form for the ordinary demand functions. Once these are estimated, the estimated parameters are substituted into the utility function.

Advocates of this second approach do not need CV and EV measures since the direct or indirect utility function can be used to rank projects. Even advocates of the first approach may find money measures unnecessary. This is the case at least in relation to the solution of the integrability problem. The underlying utility function can then be derived and used in ranking projects. However, to date, only particular solutions have been worked out even in the minimally realistic case of price variation in two goods. For this reason it is useful to have some reasonably simple method which can be used to estimate CV and EV measures from market data.

It should be recalled that the Hicksian demand curves, contrary to the Marshallian curves, are unobservable. On the other hand, money measures based on Hicksian curves rank commodity bundles correctly (under the conditions stated in Section 1). This is not in general true for measures based on the Marshallian demand concept.

In order to illustrate the latter, it is useful to consider Harberger's (1971) approximate consumer surplus measure. This measure, in the form presented by Harberger, is

$$\frac{\triangle U}{\lambda + 0.5 \, \triangle\lambda} = \Sigma p_i \triangle x_i + 0.5 \, \Sigma \triangle p_i \triangle x_i + \frac{0.25 \, \triangle\lambda\Sigma\triangle p_i \triangle x_i}{\lambda + 0.5 \, \triangle\lambda} \qquad (4.8)$$

Harberger argues that the third term on the right can be ignored, because it is a third-order term. Since $\lambda + 0.5 \, \triangle\lambda$ is positive, the sum of the two right-hand side terms, calculated from market data, and $\triangle U$ will have the same sign.

However, it was shown in Chapter 2 that λ, contrary to the demand functions, is not invariant under a monotone increasing transformation of the utility function. By a suitable choice of the transformation, the third term in (4.8) becomes as small or as large as we wish to make it. For this reason, there is no simple relationship between areas under ordinary demand curves and the sign of the underlying utility change in (4.8). (See McKenzie, 1983, Ch. 6 for a detailed discussion of the properties of the Harberger measure; see also Zabalza, 1982.)

Let us now turn to methods which can be used to estimate CV and EV measures from market data. (A comprehensive survey of the literature on estimating a theoretically plausible demand system is given by Blackorby *et al.*, 1978, Ch. 8.) One such approximation procedure uses the familiar Slutsky equation. If we have an econometric estimate of the ordinary demand function $x_i(\mathbf{p}, y)$, we know the own-price derivative $\partial x_i/\partial p_i$ as well as the income derivative $\partial x_i/\partial y$. Since the substitution effect can be calculated from this information (see below), it is possible to obtain an estimate of the slope of the compensated demand. Thus, by estimating (possibly a system of) Marshallian demands, one obtains all the information needed to estimate CV and EV measures of price changes. This is the case at least if we are able to estimate ordinary demand functions for the individual consumer.

Unfortunately, matters are more complicated if only market (aggregate) data are available. In general, we cannot deduce the properties of the consumer's demand functions from market data. However, one can figure out the conditions under which the aggregate compensated demand function can be computed from an econometric estimate of the Marshallian market demand function. The procedure is exact if each consumer has the same marginal propensity to consume the good, i.e. if $\partial x_i^h/\partial y^h = \gamma^h$ is the same for everyone, and each household's share of aggregate income is fixed and constant with respect to changes in prices and incomes. Suppose then, that we have a point estimate of the slope of the aggregate uncompensated demand curve. Moreover, assume that the Slutsky decomposition can be made:

$$\partial \bar{X}_i/\partial p_i = \alpha_i = \beta_i + \gamma X_i \tag{4.9}$$

where $\beta_i = \partial X_i/\partial p_i$, and capital letters denote aggregates, i.e. $\Sigma_h \bar{x}_i^h$ etc. According to (4.9) the aggregate substitution effect of a change in the own price is equal to the total effect less the aggregate income effect of the price change. A second-order Taylor series expansion of the sum of the expenditure functions, with all prices except p_i fixed, and using (4.9) yields

$$\Sigma_h \triangle e^h \approx \Sigma_h \frac{\partial e^h}{\partial p_i} \triangle p_i + 0.5 \, \Sigma_h \frac{\partial^2 e^h}{\partial p_i^2} \triangle p_i \triangle p_i$$

$$= X_i \triangle p_i + 0.5 \alpha_i \triangle p_i \triangle p_i$$

$$= X_i \triangle p_i + 0.5(\beta_i + \gamma X_i) \triangle p_i \triangle p_i \tag{4.10}$$

where all derivatives are evaluated at initial values of prices and expenditures. Equation (4.10) states that a Slutsky decomposition can be used to calculate aggregate CV or EV measures of a discrete price change from aggregate market data, provided that the aforementioned aggregation conditions hold. This approach is an example of the so-called aggregation theory, which deals with the conditions that are necessary for market demands to correspond to a utility function and its solution.

In general, the conditions necessary for exact aggregation are quite restrictive. For example, we require that the indirect utility functions are quasi-homothetic,[5] i.e. of the Gorman polar form, and given by

$$V^h(\mathbf{p}, y^h) = \frac{y^h - a^h(\mathbf{p})}{b(\mathbf{p})} \quad \text{for all } h \tag{4.11}$$

where, although y and a are indexed by h, $b(\mathbf{p})$ is not. To see why, use Roy's identity to obtain the ordinary demand functions

$$x_i^h = \frac{\partial a^h}{\partial p_i} + (y^h - a^h) \frac{\partial b/\partial p_i}{b} \quad \text{for all } i \tag{4.12}$$

A check shows that the income effect is itself independent of income, $\partial x_i^h / \partial y^h = (\partial b / \partial p_i)/b$, and hence is the same for each consumer. Provided individuals maximize utility (and preferences are such as to satisfy the aggregation condition), average demands $X_i/H = \bar{x}_i = \bar{\alpha}_i(\mathbf{p}) + \gamma_i \bar{y}$, where a bar denotes an average, will automatically be consistent with utility maximization. Moreover, since the income effect is independent of income, the aggregate substitution effect needed in (4.10) is easily calculated.

If aggregation is to hold for global changes in prices but with a fixed distribution of income, then all individuals must have homothetic utility functions. If aggregation holds for all income distributions, then individuals must have identical homothetic utility functions. These are very stringent requirements, and they are generally violated by aggregate demand data.

Another approach, developed by Willig (1973; 1976), aims at determining error bounds when ordinary consumer surpluses are used as a proxy for the compensating or equivalent variations. Varian (1978, pp. 212–13) derives the following approximation of the Willig formulae:

$$\frac{CV - S_i}{S_i} \approx -\frac{S_i \eta}{2y^0} \tag{4.13}$$

where S_i is the ordinary consumer surplus, CV is the compensating variation, η is the income elasticity, and y^0 is initial income (expenditure). This expression gives the relative error when S_i is used instead of

CV. The error is likely to be small in practice as demonstrated by Willig (1973; 1976) and Just *et al.* (1982). The Willig approach can be generalized to the multiple price change case (see Just *et al.*, 1982, pp. 375–86 for details).

This approach may seem simple to apply in real world situations. However, it is important to note that (4.13) is derived for a single consumer. In a multi-household economy, the approach requires information about each and every consumer's income and income elasticity. One can then determine from market data upper and lower bounds for the sum of compensating and equivalent variations. If there are large variations in income and/or income elasticity of demand between consumers, the aggregate error may become quite large (see Just *et al.*, 1982, Appendix B for details; see also McKenzie, 1983; Stahl, 1984; Vartia, 1983, for discussion of the Willig approach).

A similar procedure has been suggested by Seade (1978). The procedure is designed to be relevant for systems exhibiting linear Engel curves, i.e. for utility functions of the Gorman polar form. It is possible to show (see McKenzie, 1983) that Seade's approximation of the EV measure can be written as

$$\text{EV} \approx -\frac{(\exp(\eta S_i/y)-1)y}{\eta} \tag{4.14}$$

Thus, if we have estimates of the ordinary consumer surplus change, income, and the income elasticity, we can calculate an approximation to the EV measure.

In common with the Willig method in (4.13), Seade's approximation procedure in (4.14) is likely to generate accurate approximations when only one price varies. However, once again, the measure is derived for a single consumer. In a multi-household economy, the approach requires information about each and every consumer's income and income elasticity.

It should also be recalled that the Seade approach assumes a particular form of utility function. Once the ordinary demand functions are estimated, the estimated parameters can be substituted into the utility function. This function can be used to rank any changes in prices and income. Thus, given that a particular form of the utility function is postulated, it may seem a bit unnecessary to worry about the properties of different money measures.

A technique for determining the equivalent variation has been developed by McKenzie (1983) and McKenzie and Pearce (1982). They write the EV measure in terms of a Taylor series expansion. This approach only requires information on the demand functions in a neighbourhood of the initial price–income configuration $\mathbf{p}^0$, y^0. On the other hand, it seems as if the McKenzie–Pearce approach, as was the case with the Willig approach, requires information on each individual's demand equations. If so, the approach is less useful in empirical investigations where, in general, only market demand equations can be estimated.

Finally, it is important to emphasize that the sum of the consumers' surpluses does not necessarily have the same sign as the change in welfare according to some social welfare function. This was discussed at some length in the previous section. In some cases, we may be able to derive the weights from the implicit trade-offs underlying actual decisions or from some other source. Otherwise, a disaggregation which identifies those who gain and those who lose from a particular project may be useful. At least, such a disaggregation gives the policy maker an opportunity to apply his/her own distributive weights to the material.

Appendix

Welfare maximization

In Section 2 of Chapter 4 it was claimed that the product of the welfare weight and the marginal utility of income is equal among individuals if the welfare distribution is optimal. In order to show this, we maximize the social welfare function

$$W = W(U^1(x_1^1, \ldots, x_n^1), \ldots, U^H(x_1^H, \ldots, x_n^H)) \tag{A4.1}$$

subject to an implicit aggregate production function of the economy

$$F(x_1, \ldots, x_n) = 0 \tag{A4.2}$$

where

$$x_i = \sum_{h=1}^{H} x_i^h \quad \text{for all } i$$

Using the first-order conditions for utility maximization, the first-order conditions for maximization of (A4.1) subject to (A4.2) are

$$\frac{\partial W}{\partial U^h} \frac{\partial U^h}{\partial x_i^h} = \frac{\partial W}{\partial U^h} \lambda^h p_i = \theta \frac{\partial F}{\partial x_i} \quad \text{for all } i, h \tag{A4.3}$$

where θ is the Lagrange multiplier associated with (A4.2).

Rearranging (A4.3), it can be seen that

$$\frac{\partial W}{\partial U^a} \lambda^a = \frac{\partial W}{\partial U^b} \lambda^b \tag{A4.4}$$

for any two households a, b. Thus, an interior solution (assuming the second-order conditions are satisfied) requires that the product of the welfare weight and the marginal utility of income is equal among households.

The integrability problem

The following example is adapted from Hausman (1981). Consider the non-stochastic demand function

$$x = \beta p + \lambda y + \delta \mathbf{z} \tag{A4.5}$$

where both p and y are deflated by the price of the other good, and $\mathbf{z}$ is a vector of socioeconomic characteristics.

Let us assume that we remain on a given indifference curve. As the price changes we will use the equation $V(p(t), y(t)) = \bar{U}$. Hence, in order to stay on the indifference curve we have along a path of price change

$$\frac{\partial V}{\partial p}\frac{dp}{dt} + \frac{\partial V}{\partial y}\frac{dy}{dt} = 0 \tag{A4.6}$$

From (A4.6) and Roy's identity, we obtain

$$\frac{dy(p)}{dp} = \beta p + \gamma y + \delta \mathbf{z} \tag{A4.7}$$

This ordinary differential equation can be solved to yield

$$y(p) = Ce^{\gamma p} - \frac{(\beta p + (\beta/\gamma) + \delta \mathbf{z})}{\gamma} \tag{A4.8}$$

where C is the constant of integration. Set $C = \bar{U}$. Solving (A4.8), we then find the indirect utility function

$$V(p, y) = C = e^{-\gamma p}\left[y + \frac{\beta p + (\beta/\gamma) + \delta \mathbf{z}}{\gamma}\right] \tag{A4.9}$$

If we have estimated the Marshallian demand function (A4.5), the parameter estimates can be substituted into (A4.9). The partial derivative of (A4.9) with respect to p can then be used to calculate the impact on welfare associated with a change in the price of x. Thus, it is not necessary to calculate CV or EV measures in this case; but the expenditure function follows simply from (A4.9) by interchanging the utility level with the income variable.

According to the second approach discussed in Section 3 of this chapter, the procedure is reversed. First, specify a utility function, for example of the form in (A4.9). Second, derive the demand equation(s), (A4.5) say.

CHAPTER 5

Consumer surplus measures in quantity-constrained regimes

In many situations individuals could be expected to face quantity constraints. Governments, for example, sometimes impose price ceilings or floors which result in excess demand or supply in markets for goods and factors. In other circumstances quotas are imposed. This is sometimes the case when drugs or chemicals are considered harmful and consumption is therefore restricted; possibly a total ban is imposed.

Quantity constraints are also of considerable importance in the analysis of recreation activities. For example, U.S. waterfowl hunters face three different quantity constraints or institutional limits. These are the maximum number of waterfowl that may be bagged in one day, the maximum number of days during which waterfowl may be shot, and the maximum number of birds a hunter may have in his possession (Hammack and Brown, 1974, p. 18). Similarly, the carrying capacity of a natural area for recreational activities may be limited so that the number of visitors must be restricted. In order to be useful in such situations, the consumer surplus measures, derived in the previous chapters, need to be modified.

The seminal work on utility maximization subject to quantity constraints is that of Tobin and Houthakker (1950/1). They examined a situation where constraints are just on the verge of binding at the examined point. More recently, the Tobin–Houthakker results have been generalized to situations where the rationing constraints are not optimal (see Howard, 1977; Mackay and Whitney, 1980; Neary and Roberts, 1980). There are also a few attempts to derive consumer's surpluses in quantity-constrained regimes (see, for example, Cornes and Albon, 1981; Just *et al.*, 1982; Randall and Stoll, 1980).

The major purpose of this chapter is to derive consumer surplus measures to be used in quantity-constrained situations. It is organized as follows: Section 1 presents the model of a consumer maximizing utility

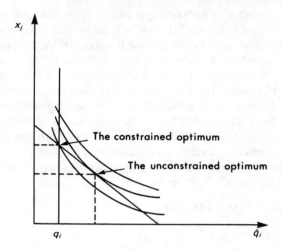

Figure 5.1 Utility maximization subject to both a budget constraint and a quantity constraint

subject to both a budget constraint and quantity constraints on the consumption of some goods. Section 2 derives a consumer surplus measure which is obtained as an area under an ordinary or uncompensated marginal willingness to pay curve and examines path independency conditions for such a measure. This measure and its relation to an area below an ordinary demand curve is illustrated by means of an example in Section 3. Section 4 derives concepts of compensating and equivalent variation (surplus) in quantity-constrained situations. Finally, Section 5 offers an interpretation of the results in terms of market clearing prices.

1 *Quantity-constrained utility maximization*

Consider a household which faces quantity constraints on its consumption of goods $\hat{q}_1, \ldots, \hat{q}_m$, but is unconstrained in its consumption of goods $x_1, \ldots, x_n$. The household's well-behaved utility function is written as[1]

$$U = U(\mathbf{x}, \hat{\mathbf{q}}) \tag{5.1}$$

The budget constraint is given by

$$\mathbf{px} + \mathbf{P}\hat{\mathbf{q}} - y = 0 \tag{5.2}$$

where $\mathbf{P} \gg 0$ is the vector of prices of rationed goods. Moreover, the household faces the quantity constraints

$$\mathbf{q} = \hat{\mathbf{q}} \tag{5.3}$$

where $\mathbf{q} \geqslant 0$ is a vector of imposed quantities. Only the under-consumption case, illustrated in Figure 5.1, in which the household is compelled to consume less of $\hat{\mathbf{q}}$ than it would choose if unconstrained, is considered. However, a 'feasible' $\mathbf{x}$ cannot always be found; for example, if $U = \hat{q}_1 - 1/x_1$, then utility is bounded above by q_1 (Neary and Roberts, 1980, p. 30). However, in this chapter it is assumed that a feasible $\mathbf{x}$ always exists. Moreover, as is indicated by the assumption regarding the properties of the direct utility function, attention is restricted to functions, which are appropriately differentiable or smooth (on a set Ω_{Iq} of strictly positive prices, quantity constraints and incomes).

The quantity-constrained indirect utility function associated with this maximization problem is written as

$$V(\mathbf{p}, y - \mathbf{Pq}, \mathbf{q}) = \max_{\mathbf{x}} \ \{U(\mathbf{x}, \mathbf{q}) | \mathbf{px} + \mathbf{Pq} - y = 0\}$$

$$= U(\mathbf{x}(\mathbf{p}, y - \mathbf{Pq}, \mathbf{q}), \mathbf{q}) \tag{5.4}$$

This function has the following properties, as is demonstrated in the appendix to this chapter

$$\left.\begin{aligned}
\frac{\partial V}{\partial \mathbf{p}} &= -\lambda \mathbf{x}(\mathbf{p}, y - \mathbf{Pq}, \mathbf{q}) \\[1em]
\frac{\partial V}{\partial y} &= \lambda(\mathbf{p}, y - \mathbf{Pq}, \mathbf{q}) \\[1em]
\frac{\partial V}{\partial \mathbf{P}} &= -\lambda \mathbf{q} \\[1em]
\frac{\partial V}{\partial \mathbf{q}} &= \frac{\partial U(\mathbf{x}(\cdot), \mathbf{q})}{\partial \mathbf{q}} - \lambda \mathbf{P}
\end{aligned}\right\} \tag{5.5}$$

The first line of (5.5) gives the ordinary or uncompensated demand functions for unrationed goods (multiplied by the marginal utility of income, λ, which in general depends on the same factors as demand for unrationed goods, as is seen from the second line). These demand functions have the following properties. As in the unrationed case considered in Chapter 2, a change in the price of an unrationed good has both a substitution effect and an income effect. A reduction in a quantity constraint also causes two distinct impacts. Firstly, it has an income effect, i.e. the household reduces its expenditures on (normal) unrationed goods in order to be able to consume more rationed goods. Secondly, the marginal utilities of unrationed goods are affected by a reduction in rationing. This impact is captured by the last argument in the demand functions. An increased price of rationed goods causes an income effect, but not a substitution effect. This is because the household is unwilling to reduce its consumption of a rationed good even if its price increases, provided the rationing is binding. This property is revealed by the third line of (5.5).

The final line of (5.5) gives the effect of a reduction in the severity of rationing on the household's utility level. The effect of a marginal change in q_i is equal to the difference between the marginal valuation of q_i and the market price of q_i (converted to units of utility through multiplication by the marginal utility of income). Clearly, this difference is positive as long as the household is compelled to consume less of q_i than it would if unconstrained; only at an unconstrained interior optimum, is an equality obtained, i.e. $\partial U/\partial \mathbf{q} = \lambda \mathbf{P}$. The reader interested in detailed examinations of the properties of the behaviour functions under rationing is referred to Benassy (1982), Cuddington *et al.* (1984) and Neary and Roberts (1980).

2 *Consumer's surplus under rationing*

Consider now a change in the vector $\mathbf{q}$ from $\mathbf{q}^0$ to $\mathbf{q}^1$, assuming that the constraints are binding over the entire path, and holding all prices and income fixed. The associated change in utility can be written as

$$\triangle U = V(\mathbf{p}, y - \mathbf{Pq}^1, \mathbf{q}^1) - V(\mathbf{p}, y - \mathbf{Pq}^0, \mathbf{q}^0)$$

$$= \int_c V_\mathbf{q}(\mathbf{p}, y - \mathbf{Pq}, \mathbf{q})d\mathbf{q} = \int_c [U_\mathbf{q}(\mathbf{x}(\mathbf{p}, y - \mathbf{Pq}, \mathbf{q}), \mathbf{q}) - \lambda \mathbf{P}]d\mathbf{q} \quad (5.6)$$

where a subscript $\mathbf{q}$ denotes a partial derivative with respect to $\mathbf{q}$, and c (in Ω_{Iq}) is some path between initial and final $\mathbf{q}$-vectors. Inspection of the arguments of $U_\mathbf{q}$ in the final expression shows that this derivative includes the effect of changed optimal demands for unrationed goods as $\mathbf{q}$ is changed. The integrand in (5.6) is an exact differential of the indirect utility function (5.4) with respect to $\mathbf{q}$, implying that (5.6) is path independent. Recall that the last equality of (5.6) is obtained from the final line of (5.5).

The change in utility as $\mathbf{q}$ is changed from $\mathbf{q}^0$ to $\mathbf{q}^1$ is evaluated by the sum of the changes in the areas under marginal valuation 'curves' for rationed goods less the change in expenditures on such goods; the latter terms are converted to units of utility through multiplication by λ.

A money measure is obtained by eliminating λ from the final expression in (5.6). This money measure is proportional to $\triangle U$ if the marginal utility of income is constant with respect to changes in the rations for goods. A sufficient condition for this to be the case is that λ only depends on the price of an unconstrained good, say x_n, which is taken as a *numéraire* (see the appendix to this chapter). This is Samuelson's second interpretation of the constancy of the marginal utility of income (money) discussed in Chapter 3. More importantly, this assumption ensures that

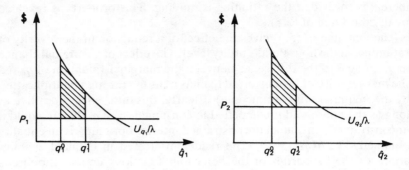

Figure 5.2 Change in 'consumer surplus' caused by a change in $\mathbf{q}$ from q_1^0, q_2^0 to q_1^1, q_2^1 (when only two goods are rationed) where

$$U_{q_1} = U_{q_1}(\mathbf{x}^a, q_1, q_2^0) \qquad\qquad U_{q_2} = U_{q_2}(\mathbf{x}^b, q_1^1, q_2)$$

$$\mathbf{x}^a = \mathbf{x}(\mathbf{p}, y - P_1 q_1 - P_2 q_2^0, q_1, q_2^0) \qquad \mathbf{x}^b = \mathbf{x}(\mathbf{p}, y - P_1 q_1^1 - P_2 q_2, q_1^1, q_2)$$

the money measure is path independent. If $\lambda = \lambda(p_n)$, the money measure of utility change becomes

$$\frac{\triangle U}{\lambda(p_n)} = S_{\mathbf{q}} = \int_c \left[\frac{U_{\mathbf{q}}}{\lambda(p_n)} - \mathbf{P}\right] d\mathbf{q} \tag{5.7}$$

which states: Use the change in the difference between the marginal willingness to pay for a rationed good and the market price of the good to evaluate a change in a quantity constraint. If several constraints are altered, the order in which rations are changed makes no difference, but the area under the marginal willingness to pay curve for a particular good must be evaluated subject to all previously considered changes in rations, as is illustrated in Figure 5.2. On the other hand, if the utility function is such that the money measure is path dependent, then one can find a path of integration such that $S_{\mathbf{q}} < 0$ even if $\triangle U > 0$ (compare Chapter 4). The reader interested in detailed path independency conditions is referred to the appendix to this chapter.

It is important to note that, in this chapter, prices remain fixed while rations are changed. This means that there is no 'windfall' gain (loss) from the original amount of expenditure on the good (i.e. following a changed price, i.e. $\triangle \mathbf{P} \cdot \mathbf{q}^0$). For this reason, one must be careful in interpreting the gain from a reduction in a quantity constraint in terms of an area under a demand curve. Empirical applications would be greatly simplified if one could use areas under ordinary demand curves to calculate changes in consumer's surplus under rationing. This is because market demand curves can often be estimated (identified) even under conditions of rationing (see, for example, White and Ziemer, 1983). The relationship between the money measure (5.7) and areas under ordinary demand curves is illustrated by means of an example in the subsequent section.

3 *An example*

In this section the transformed Cobb–Douglas model of Section 4 in Chapter 3 is used to illustrate the derivation of a quantity-constrained consumer surplus measure. In particular, we illustrate its relationship to an area under an ordinary demand curve. Suppose the household is rationed in the market for the first good. The household then maximizes

$$U = \alpha\ell n\, q_1 + (1-\alpha)\ell n\, x_2 \tag{5.8}$$

subject to the usual budget constraint. Straightforward calculations yield the indirect utility function

$$V(p_2, y - P_1 q_1, q_1) = \alpha\ell n\, q_1 + (1-\alpha)\ell n(y - P_1 q_1) - (1-\alpha)\ell n\, p_2 \tag{5.9}$$

Taking partial derivatives of (5.9), it is easily demonstrated that the properties of these derivatives resemble those of the derivatives in (5.5).

Next, the ordinary unrationed demand function $x_1 = \alpha y / p_1$, from Section 4 of Chapter 3, is examined to ascertain whether it can be used to obtain a money measure of utility change. In order to perform this investigation, invert the demand function for x_1 to obtain the demand price, and take the difference between the marginal willingness to pay $(\partial U/\partial q_1)/\lambda$, obtained by differentiating (5.8) and (5.9) with respect to q_1 and y respectively, and the demand price $p_1 = \alpha y / x_1$ for $q_1 = x_1$ to obtain

$$\left.\begin{aligned}\frac{(\partial U/\partial q_1)}{\lambda} - p_1 &= \frac{\alpha(y - P_1 q_1)}{(1-\alpha)q_1} - \frac{\alpha y}{x_1} \\[2mm] &= \frac{\alpha}{(1-\alpha)q_1}\,(p_1 q_1 - P_1 q_1)\end{aligned}\right\} \tag{5.10}$$

This expression has a non-negative sign since $P_1 \leqslant p_1$ by assumption. It should be recalled that P_1 is fixed below the 'market-clearing' level.

This result shows that the ordinary demand curve is not, in general, suitable for use in calculating a money measure of a changed ration level. The problem is caused by an 'income effect'. The marginal willingness to pay is derived from the assumption that the household pays P_1 per (additional) unit of the commodity. On the other hand, the use of the ordinary demand curve assumes that the household pays $p_1 \geq P_1$ for marginal units of the commodity. Hence the household must adjust (reduce) its consumption of other commodities over and above what is required if the price remains fixed at P_1. It can easily be checked that a utility function of the form $U = U(x_1, \ldots, x_{n-1}, \mathbf{q}) + x_n$ where x_n is the *numéraire* commodity, avoids this problem since demands are independent of income (see Section 4 of Chapter 3).

4 *Compensating and equivalent variations (surpluses) in quantity-constrained situations*

The investigation performed in the previous sections demonstrates that ordinary demand curves are of limited use under conditions of rationing. This section examines whether measures based on compensated demand functions are applicable. In addition to the concepts of compensating and equivalent variation, which were discussed at some length in the previous chapters, Hicks (1943) introduced so-called compensating and equivalent surplus measures. The latter measures refer to situations where the consumer is constrained to consume at the new (old) prices, the same quantity he would buy in absence of compensation. Obviously, these surplus concepts are of interest in quantity-constrained situations. However, the case dealt with in this chapter is more general since the consumer is constrained in some markets and unconstrained in others. For this reason, the compensated measures to be derived in this section will be denoted (quantity-constrained) compensated and equivalent variations.

In order to derive concepts of quantity-constrained compensating and equivalent variation, it is useful to specify the quantity-constrained expenditure function. This function, which by assumption is appropriately differentiable, denotes the minimum level of expenditure for any given prices, values of the quantity constraints, and level of utility

$$e(\mathbf{p}, \mathbf{P}, \mathbf{q}, \bar{U}) = \min_{\mathbf{x}} \{\mathbf{p}\mathbf{x} + \mathbf{P}\mathbf{q} \mid U(\mathbf{x}, \mathbf{q}) \geq \bar{U}\}$$

$$= \mathbf{p}\tilde{\mathbf{x}}(\mathbf{p}, \mathbf{q}, \bar{U}) + \mathbf{P}\mathbf{q} \tag{5.11}$$

Taking partial derivatives of (5.11) one obtains

$$\frac{\partial e}{\partial \mathbf{p}} = \tilde{\mathbf{x}}(\mathbf{p}, \mathbf{q}, \bar{U})$$

$$\left.\frac{\partial e}{\partial \mathbf{P}} = \mathbf{q} \phantom{\frac{\partial \tilde{\mathbf{x}}}{\partial \mathbf{q}}}\right\} \tag{5.12}$$

$$\frac{\partial e}{\partial \mathbf{q}} = \mathbf{P} + \mathbf{p}\frac{\partial \tilde{\mathbf{x}}}{\partial \mathbf{q}} = \mathbf{P} - \frac{U_{\mathbf{q}}(\tilde{\mathbf{x}}, \mathbf{q})}{\lambda}$$

In Chapter 2 it was shown that a change in a price has a substitution but not an income effect, on compensated demands. This is still true for changes in prices of unrationed goods. However, since $\mathbf{q}$ is fixed, a change in a P_i has no substitution effect, implying that the compensated demands for unrationed goods are left unchanged. This is also seen from the second line of (5.12). A change in a q_i, on the other hand, affects compensated unrationed demands in a complicated way, at least in the case of multiple quantity constraints. The reader is referred to Mackay and Whitney (1980) and Neary and Roberts (1980) for further details.

In order to interpret the effect of a change in a q_i on the level of expenditure, it should be noted that the right-hand side expression in the bottom line of (5.12) is obtained in the following way: Differentiate the utility function with utility held constant and insert the first-order conditions for cost minimization. This operation yields the expression in question, as is shown in the appendix to this chapter. Thus, $\partial e/\partial q_i$ in (5.12) is equal to the price of the rationed good less the compensated marginal willingness to pay for the good. Note that both $U_{\mathbf{q}}$ and λ are evaluated given the specified level of utility. It has been demonstrated, by for example, Mackay and Whitney (1980), that the Lagrange multiplier λ of the quantity-constrained maximized utility problem equals the inverse of the Lagrange multiplier, say μ, of the quantity-constrained cost minimized problem, provided λ and μ refer to the same level of utility (commodity bundle). This result is indeed confirmed by (5.12), where $1/\lambda = \mu$ appears in the right-hand side of the expression.

Using the bottom line of (5.12), the compensating variation associated with a change in quantity constraints from $\mathbf{q}^0$ to $\mathbf{q}^1$ can be written as

$$CV_{\mathbf{q}} = e(\mathbf{p}, \mathbf{P}, \mathbf{q}^0, U^0) - e(\mathbf{p}, \mathbf{P}, \mathbf{q}^1, U^0)$$

$$= \int_c \left[\frac{U_{\mathbf{q}}(\bar{\mathbf{x}}, \mathbf{q})}{\lambda} - \mathbf{P} \right] d\mathbf{q} \tag{5.13}$$

where prices and income are fixed, for simplicity, and utility is being held constant at the initial level.

If the household's utility is fixed at the final level, the equivalent variation associated with a move from $\mathbf{q}^0$ to $\mathbf{q}^1$ is defined as

$$EV_{\mathbf{q}} = e(\mathbf{p}, \mathbf{P}, \mathbf{q}^0, U^1) - e(\mathbf{p}, \mathbf{P}, \mathbf{q}^1, U^1)$$

$$= \int_c \left[\frac{U_{\mathbf{q}}(\bar{\mathbf{x}}, \mathbf{q})}{\lambda} - \mathbf{P} \right] d\mathbf{q} \tag{5.14}$$

where the unconstrained compensated demand functions $\bar{\mathbf{x}}$ and the marginal utility of income λ now are evaluated given $U = U^1$.

By construction, the integrands of (5.13) and (5.14) are exact differen-

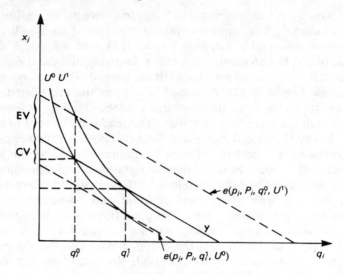

Figure 5.3 The compensating variation and the equivalent variation associated with a change in q_i from q_i^0 to q_i^1 where

$$y = e(p_j, P_i, q_i^0, U^0) = e(p_j, P_i, q_i^1, U^1)$$

tials of the constrained expenditure function with respect to $\mathbf{q}$. Hence, both money measures (5.13) and (5.14) are path independent, i.e. the order in which rations are changed makes no difference. This is shown in the appendix to this chapter. The CV measure gives the maximum (minimum) sum of money that must be taken from (given to) the household while leaving it just as well off as before the change in rations $\mathbf{q}$. The equivalent variation gives the minimum (maximum) sum of money that must be given to (taken from) the household to make it as well off as it would be with an increase (reduction) in $\mathbf{q}$. Using indifference curves, these measures can be illustrated as in Figure 5.3. Alternatively, both measures can be calculated as the change in the area under a compensated marginal willingness to pay curve for, say, good q_i between q_i^0 and q_i^1 less the change in expediture on the good. If several rations are changed, the curve for good q_i is evaluated subject to all previously considered changes in quantity constraints in other markets (see Figure 5.2). The aggregate or total $CV_{\mathbf{q}}$ and $EV_{\mathbf{q}}$ measures are obtained by adding the measures for the markets where rations are changed.

5 Some further results

It would be useful if the shadow prices U_q/λ could be related to hypothetical market prices such that an unconstrained consumer would choose, at these prices, the same commodity bundle as he chooses at prevailing market prices. In fact, such a virtual price approach has been developed by Neary and Roberts (1980); however, the first to use virtual prices was probably Rothbarth (1940/1), who used them in an analysis of the measurement of real income under rationing. The Neary–Roberts approach is more general than the approach used by Tobin and Houthakker (1950/1) since the quantity constraints can be fixed at arbitrary levels. The Tobin–Houthakker approach, on the other hand, assumes what Samuelson (1947) calls auxiliary constraints, i.e. constraints that are just on the verge of binding at the examined point.

The problem boils down to a question of specification of a virtual price vector $\hat{\mathbf{p}}$, $\hat{\mathbf{P}}$ which generates the demands $\mathbf{x}$, $\mathbf{q}$. It can be shown that $\hat{\mathbf{p}} = \mathbf{p}$, while $\hat{\mathbf{P}} \neq \mathbf{P}$ in general. Following Neary and Roberts (1980), the constrained expenditure function (5.11) is written as

$$e(\mathbf{p}, \mathbf{P}, \mathbf{q}, \bar{U}) = \mathbf{p}\bar{\mathbf{x}}(\mathbf{p}, \mathbf{q}, \bar{U}) + \mathbf{P}\mathbf{q}$$

$$= \mathbf{p}\bar{\mathbf{x}}(\mathbf{p}, \hat{\mathbf{P}}, \bar{U}) + \mathbf{P}\bar{\mathbf{q}}(\mathbf{p}, \hat{\mathbf{P}}, \bar{U})$$

$$= \hat{e}(\mathbf{p}, \hat{\mathbf{P}}, \bar{U}) + (\mathbf{P}-\hat{\mathbf{P}})\mathbf{q} \tag{5.15}$$

where $\mathbf{q} = \bar{\mathbf{q}}(\mathbf{p}, \hat{\mathbf{P}}, \bar{U}) = \partial\hat{e}/\partial\hat{\mathbf{P}}$, i.e. $\hat{\mathbf{P}}$ is such that the *quantity-unconstrained* compensated demands at prices $\hat{\mathbf{P}}$, $\mathbf{p}$ are equal to the quantity constraints $\mathbf{q}$, and $\hat{e}(.,.,.)$ gives the minimum expediture for the specified utility level, given virtual prices $\mathbf{p}$, $\hat{\mathbf{P}}$. In terms of Figure 5.1, the slope and position of the budget line are changed in such a way that the budget line becomes tangent to the indifference curve at the constrained optimum.

Taking the partial derivative of (5.15) with respect to $\mathbf{q}$ yields

$$\frac{\partial e(\mathbf{p}, \mathbf{P}, \mathbf{q}, \bar{U})}{\partial\mathbf{q}} = \frac{\partial\hat{e}}{\partial\hat{\mathbf{P}}}\frac{\partial\hat{\mathbf{P}}}{\partial\mathbf{q}} - \mathbf{q}\frac{\partial\hat{\mathbf{P}}}{\partial\mathbf{q}} + (\mathbf{P}-\hat{\mathbf{P}}) = \mathbf{P}-\hat{\mathbf{P}} \tag{5.16}$$

where $\partial\hat{e}/\partial\hat{\mathbf{P}} = \hat{\mathbf{q}}(\mathbf{p}, \hat{\mathbf{P}}, \bar{U}) = \mathbf{q}$. A comparison of equations (5.16) and (5.12) confirms what one would expect, namely that $\hat{\mathbf{P}} = U_q/\lambda$. The virtual price of any rationed good is thus equal to the compensated marginal willingness to pay for that good. This means that the gain to the consumer of a marginal reduction in a quantity constraint, say q_i, is equal to the vertical distance, measured at the imposed quantity, between the compensated demand function $\bar{q}_i(\mathbf{p}, \hat{\mathbf{P}}, \bar{U})$ and the ruling market price. This is an important result since it states that areas under the usual

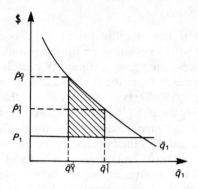

Figure 5.4 Calculating the CV or EV measures of a change in a rationed good. q_1, using the quantity-unconstrained compensated demand function where $\tilde{q}_1 = \tilde{q}_1(\mathbf{p}^0, \hat{P}_1, \bar{U})$

compensated demand curves have a distinct meaning even under conditions of rationing. In other words, the compensated demand functions derived in Chapter 3 can be used to calculate the CV and EV measures associated with a change in a quantity constraint.[2] The reader should note, however, that one must calculate an area under, not to the left of, the compensated demand curve when a ration is changed, as is shown in Figure 5.4.

The following holds for the unconstrained ordinary demand functions for $\mathbf{x}$ and $\hat{\mathbf{q}}$, respectively

$$\mathbf{x} = \mathbf{x}(\mathbf{p}, y\text{-}\mathbf{Pq}, \mathbf{q}) = \mathbf{x}(\mathbf{p}, \hat{\mathbf{P}}, \hat{y}) \tag{5.17'}$$

$$\hat{\mathbf{q}} = \hat{\mathbf{q}}(\mathbf{p}, \hat{\mathbf{P}}, \hat{y}) = \mathbf{q} \tag{5.17''}$$

where $\hat{y} = \hat{e}(\mathbf{p}, \hat{\mathbf{P}}, \bar{U}) = y + (\hat{\mathbf{P}} - \mathbf{P})\mathbf{q}$, i.e. the income which, at most, enables the consumer to reach utility level $\bar{U}$, given virtual prices $\mathbf{p}, \hat{\mathbf{P}}$. Unfortunately, (5.17″) does not imply that ordinary demand curves, if observed or estimated, can be used to calculate error bounds on the loss to the consumer of quantity constraints. The problem is that $\hat{y} > y$ as long as $\hat{\mathbf{P}} > \mathbf{P}$. This means that (5.17″) defines demand functions given that income continuously adjusts to 'clear' markets. Ordinary demand curves, on the other hand, are derived by varying the price of the good in question, holding income (and all other prices) constant. Hence, for normal goods, a 'demand' curve derived from (5.17″) falls outside the ordinary fixed income demand curve as long as $\hat{\mathbf{P}} > \mathbf{P}$ since, then, $\hat{y} > y$. Only for $\hat{\mathbf{P}} = \mathbf{P}$, $\hat{y} = y$ and the curves then coincide, unless we invoke the assumption of a constant marginal utility of income, i.e. $\lambda = \lambda(p_n)$. In the latter case, uncompensated and compensated demand functions coincide and the differences between different measures vanish. This is because the demand functions are then constant with respect to changes in income (utility).

These findings complicate applications of the Willig approach, presented in Chapter 4, for determining error bounds when the area under an ordinary demand curve is used as a proxy for compensating and equivalent variations. However, Just *et al.* (1982) and Randall and Stoll (1980) have adapted the Willig technique to situations in which quantities, rather than prices, are changed. The reader interested in details is referred to equation (7.9) in Chapter 7.

Two further results should be mentioned. Firstly, both the CV and the EV measures rank any two vectors of quantity constraints in the same order as the underlying utility function. In fact, the EV measure, but not necessarily the CV measure, can be used to compare any number of projects involving quantity constraints.[3] In order to illustrate, suppose the current price–quantity constraint–income vector is denoted by $\mathbf{A}$, and two projects or changes involving different vectors of quantity constraints are considered. Denote these by $\mathbf{B}$ and $\mathbf{C}$. Then, if $\mathbf{C}$ is preferred to $\mathbf{B}$ and $\mathbf{B}$ is preferred to $\mathbf{A}$, according to the consumer's well-behaved utility function, it holds that $EV_C > EV_B > 0$ while $0 < CV_C \gtreqless CV_B > 0$. Secondly, in the single ration change case, the relationship between the sizes of the three money measures considered resembles the one derived for the quantity-unconstrained measures in Chapter 4, i.e. $CV \leqslant S \leqslant EV$ for a good whose 'demand price' is a non-decreasing function of income ($\partial(V_q/\lambda)/\partial y \geqslant 0$). Unfortunately, no such simple relationship is generally available in the multiple ration change case.

With regard to the application of the models, it is important to note that there exists a large and growing body of literature on disequilibrium econometrics. Using such econometric techniques, the market demand curve can be identified and estimated even in situations in which effective excess supply or demand prevail (see Bowden, 1978; also Richard E. Quandt's 'Bibliography of rationing and disequilibrium models'). Once the demand curve has been estimated, it can be used to calculate changes in aggregate consumers surpluses; however, one must keep in mind the 'income adjustment' problem discussed above. Moreover, the underlying rationing scheme is of critical importance for the interpretation in terms of welfare effects. For example, one would expect different outcomes depending on whether we have an equal ration for each household or an all-or-nothing rationing rule. To my knowledge, however, no general theory of rationing schemes and their implications for applied welfare economics is available.

Appendix

The effective demand functions

In this appendix, the effective demand functions are derived. Firstly, equation (5.3) is substituted into equations (5.1) and (5.2). The maximization of (5.1) subject to (5.2) then yields the following first-order conditions for an interior solution

$$\left. \begin{array}{l} \dfrac{\partial U(\mathbf{x}, \mathbf{q})}{\partial \mathbf{x}} - \lambda \mathbf{p} = 0 \\[2mm] \mathbf{px} + \mathbf{Pq} - y = 0 \end{array} \right\} \qquad \text{(A5.1)}$$

where λ is the Lagrange multiplier of the budget constraint.

Next, (A5.1) is totally differentiated to obtain

$$\left. \begin{array}{l} U_{\mathbf{xx}} d\mathbf{x} - d\lambda \mathbf{p} = \lambda d\mathbf{p} - U_{\mathbf{xq}} d\mathbf{q} \\[2mm] \mathbf{p} d\mathbf{x} + 0 = dy - \mathbf{P} d\mathbf{q} - d\mathbf{Pq} - d\mathbf{px} \end{array} \right\} \qquad \text{(A5.2)}$$

where $U_{\mathbf{xx}}$ is an $n \times n$ matrix with elements $\partial^2 U / \partial x_i \partial x_j$, and $U_{\mathbf{xq}}$ is a $1 \times n$ vector with elements

$$U_{x_i \mathbf{q}} = \sum_{k=1}^{m} \partial^2 U / \partial x_i \partial q_k$$

Applying Cramer's rule to (A5.2) yields

$$dx_i = \frac{\lambda \sum\limits_{j=1}^{n} D_{ji} dp_j - \sum\limits_{j=1}^{n} D_{ji} U_{x_j \mathbf{q}} d\mathbf{q} + D_{n+1 i}(dy - \mathbf{P} d\mathbf{q} - d\mathbf{Pq} - d\mathbf{px})}{D}$$

$$d\lambda = \frac{\lambda \sum\limits_{j=1}^{n} D_{j(n+1)} dp_j - \sum\limits_{j=1}^{n} U_{x_j \mathbf{q}} d\mathbf{q} + D_{(n+1)(n+1)}(dy - \mathbf{P} d\mathbf{q} - d\mathbf{Pq} - d\mathbf{px})}{D}$$

$$\text{(A5.3)}$$

where D is the determinant of (A5.2) and D_{ij} is the cofactor of the ith row and jth column. In more compact form, the demand functions and λ can be written as

$$\left. \begin{array}{l} \mathbf{x} = \mathbf{x}(\mathbf{p}, y - \mathbf{Pq}, \mathbf{q}) \\[2mm] \lambda = \lambda(\mathbf{p}, y - \mathbf{Pq}, \mathbf{q}) \end{array} \right\} \qquad \text{(A5.4)}$$

In particular, note from (A5.3) that a change in a price of a rationed good only has an income effect on demand for unrationed goods and the marginal utility of income. A change in a ration level, on the other hand, is also seen to affect the marginal utilities of unrationed goods and hence demands. A sufficient condition for the removal of this latter effect is that the utility function is weakly separable in the sense that

$$U(\mathbf{x}, \hat{\mathbf{q}}) = u(\mathbf{x}) + v(\hat{\mathbf{q}}) \tag{A5.5}$$

since in this case the terms $U_{x,q}$ in (A5.3) disappear. For details see Cuddington *et al.* (1984, Appendix A).

If the utility function is of the form

$$U(\mathbf{x}, \hat{\mathbf{q}}) = u(x_1, \ldots, x_{n-1}, \hat{\mathbf{q}}) + ax_n \tag{A5.6}$$

then the marginal utility of income only depends on the price of the *numéraire* good x_n; a is a constant in (A5.6). This corresponds to Samuelson's second interpretation of the constancy of the marginal utility of income or money. Note that the kind of separability assumed in (A5.5) is not sufficient to eliminate the influence of $\hat{\mathbf{q}}$ on the marginal utility of income; $\hat{\mathbf{q}}$ still affects λ through the budget constraint.

Finally, substitution of (A5.4) into the utility function gives the quantity-constrained indirect utility function

$$U(\mathbf{x}(\mathbf{p}, y - \mathbf{Pq}, \mathbf{q}), \mathbf{q}) = V(\mathbf{p}, y - \mathbf{Pq}, \mathbf{q}) \tag{A5.7}$$

Differentiation of the left-hand expression of (A5.7) with respect to, say, p_i yields

$$\frac{\partial U}{\partial p_i} = \sum_{j=1}^{n} \frac{\partial U}{\partial x_j} \frac{\partial x_j}{\partial p_i}$$

$$= \sum_{j=1}^{n} \lambda p_j \frac{\partial x_j}{\partial p_i} \tag{A5.8}$$

where the final expression is obtained from the first-order conditions (A5.1). Differentiation of the budget constraint in (A5.1) with respect to p_i yields

$$x_i + \sum_{j=1}^{n} p_j \frac{\partial x_j}{\partial p_i} = 0 \tag{A5.9}$$

Substituting this expression into (A5.8) we obtain

$$\frac{\partial U}{\partial p_i} = -\lambda x_i(\mathbf{p}, y - \mathbf{Pq}, \mathbf{q}) = \frac{\partial V(\mathbf{p}, y - \mathbf{Pq}, \mathbf{q})}{\partial p_i} \tag{A5.10}$$

a result that confirms the first line of equations (5.5) in the text. The remaining partial derivatives of the quantity-constrained indirect utility function can then be simply derived.

Finally, we show how to derive $\partial e/\partial \mathbf{q} = \mathbf{P} - U_{\mathbf{q}}/\lambda$ in equations (5.12).

Suppose that the utility level is held constant; $U = \bar{U} = \bar{V}$. Then, inserting the expenditure function into the indirect utility function yields

$$\bar{V} = V(\mathbf{p}, e(\mathbf{p}, \mathbf{P}, \mathbf{q}, \bar{U}) - \mathbf{Pq}, \mathbf{q}) \tag{A5.11}$$

This expression gives the minimum expenditure or income necessary to reach the fixed utility level $\bar{U} = \bar{V}$ for any given prices and levels of quantity constraints. Equivalently, the maximal utility from an income equal to $e(\cdot)$ is $\bar{V}$. Differentiating (A5.11) with respect to $\mathbf{q}$, using the fact that utility remains constant, yields

$$\begin{aligned}
\frac{\partial \bar{V}}{\partial \mathbf{q}} = 0 &= \frac{\partial V}{\partial e}\frac{\partial e}{\partial \mathbf{q}} + \frac{\partial V}{\partial \mathbf{q}} \\
&= \lambda(\mathbf{P} + \mathbf{p}\frac{\partial \bar{\mathbf{x}}}{\partial \mathbf{q}}) + (U_{\mathbf{q}} - \lambda \mathbf{P}) \\
&= \lambda \mathbf{p}\frac{\partial \bar{\mathbf{x}}}{\partial \mathbf{q}} + U_{\mathbf{q}}
\end{aligned} \tag{A5.12}$$

Inserting the final expression into the last line of (5.12) we obtain

$$\frac{\partial e}{\partial \mathbf{q}} = \mathbf{P} - \frac{U_{\mathbf{q}}(\bar{\mathbf{x}}, \mathbf{q})}{\lambda} \tag{A5.13}$$

This is the right-hand expression in the bottom line of equation (5.12).

Path independency conditions

Let us consider the welfare change measure

$$\int_c [U_{\mathbf{q}}(\mathbf{x}(\mathbf{p}, y - \mathbf{Pq}, \mathbf{q}), \mathbf{q}) - \lambda \mathbf{P}]d\mathbf{q} \tag{A5.14}$$

This measure satisfies the path independency conditions

$$U_{q_i q_j} - \lambda_{q_j}P_i = U_{q_j q_i} - \lambda_{q_i}P_j \quad \text{for all } i, j \tag{A5.15}$$

where $U_{q_i q_j} = \partial U_{q_i}/\partial q_j = \partial^2 U/\partial q_i \partial q_j$ and $\lambda_{q_i} = \partial \lambda/\partial q_i$. These symmetry conditions can be obtained by differentiating each $\partial V/\partial q_i$ in (5.5) with respect to q_j.

The money measure

$$S_{\mathbf{q}} = \int_c [\frac{U_{\mathbf{q}}(\mathbf{x}(\mathbf{p}, y - \mathbf{Pq}, \mathbf{q}), \mathbf{q})}{\lambda} - \mathbf{P}]d\mathbf{q} \tag{A5.16}$$

is path independent if

$$U_{q_i q_j} - \frac{\lambda_{q_j}U_{q_i}}{\lambda} = U_{q_j q_i} - \frac{\lambda_{q_i}U_{q_j}}{\lambda} \quad \text{for all } i, j \tag{A5.17}$$

There is no reason to believe that these conditions hold in the general constrained case.

The corresponding path independency conditions for the compensated money measures hold by construction. This is because the cross-quantity derivatives of the expenditure function (5.11) in the main text are symmetric (from Young's theorem discussed in Chapter 2). Hence

$$\frac{\partial^2 e}{\partial q_i \partial q_j} = \frac{\tilde{U}_{q_i q_j} \cdot \tilde{\lambda} - \tilde{U}_{q_i} \partial \tilde{\lambda} / \partial q_j}{\tilde{\lambda}^2}$$

$$= \frac{\partial^2 e}{\partial q_j \partial q_i} \quad \text{for all } i, j \tag{A5.18}$$

where a tilde denotes a compensated function.

These are also the conditions for path independency of the measures (5.13) and (5.14).

CHAPTER 6

Public goods and externalities in consumption

In the growing body of literature on the economics of the environment, the concepts of public goods and externalities are important. There are at least two basic characteristics that distinguish pure public goods from private goods. Firstly, the same unit of a public good can be consumed by many. Secondly, once a public good is provided for some individuals, it is impossible or at least very costly to exclude others from benefiting from it. A private good, on the other hand, once consumed by one individual cannot be consumed by others. Moreover, the buyer of the good is free to exclude other individuals from consuming it.

Discussions of externalities are often concerned with the case where one party affects the consumption or production possibilities of another. However, most important external effects affect a large number of individuals. For example, a dam may flood and destroy a valuable wilderness area now used for hiking, fishing, hunting, and bird watching, and hence affect many (groups of) individuals. Another example is pollution of the air and water. These examples also show that there is a close correspondence between public goods ('bads') and externalities. In fact, it is reasonable to view a public good or 'bad' as a special kind of externality in consumption.[1]

The first part of this chapter, Sections 1–4, derives consumer surplus measures for public goods. The reinterpretation of these measures in terms of 'traditional' external effects is a straightforward matter. Accordingly we proceed in a different manner in Section 5. In many situations, it is reasonable to believe that, for example, pollution affects the *quality* of private goods, say the life of cars, and public goods, such as air quality. Similarly, the 'carrying capacity' of a natural area for recreation activity may be limited so that increased use of the area erodes the utility derived from the recreation experience. Section 5 derives measures which capture both the effects of such changes in quality attributes and permit an assessment in terms of market prices. In Chapter 7 other proposed methods which can be used to measure the willingness to pay for public goods/bads, are reported.

1 *A utility maximizing household consuming private and public goods*

Consider a household which consumes n private goods $x_1, \ldots, x_n$ and k public goods $z_1, \ldots, z_k$. The household's utility function

$$U = U(\mathbf{x}, \mathbf{z}) \tag{6.1}$$

is assumed to be well-behaved. The budget constraint is

$$\mathbf{px} - y = 0 \tag{6.2}$$

where $\mathbf{p} \geqslant 0$, and $y > 0$ is the fixed income of the household net of any lump sum taxes to finance the government's production of public goods. Hence, households do not have to pay directly for the consumption of public goods. In particular, in a multi-household economy there need not be any correspondence between the individual household's consumption of public goods and its contribution to the government's tax revenues.

The household maximizes its utility function (6.1) subject to the budget constraint (6.2). The first-order conditions for an interior solution are

$$\left.\begin{array}{c} \dfrac{\partial U(\mathbf{x}, \mathbf{z})}{\partial \mathbf{x}} - \lambda \mathbf{p} = 0 \\[3mm] \mathbf{px} - y = 0 \end{array}\right\} \tag{6.3}$$

where λ is the Lagrange multiplier of the budget constraint.

Solving the equations in (6.3) yields ordinary demand functions (and λ) as functions of prices $\mathbf{p}$, income y and the provision of public goods $\mathbf{z}$. Substitution of these functions into (6.1) gives the indirect utility function which is defined as

$$V(\mathbf{p}, y, \mathbf{z}) = \max_{\mathbf{x}} \{U(\mathbf{x}, \mathbf{z}) | \mathbf{px} - y = 0\}$$

$$= U(\mathbf{x}(\mathbf{p}, y, \mathbf{z}), \mathbf{z}) \tag{6.4}$$

As usual, all functions considered are assumed to be appropriately differentiable (on a set Ω_{Iz} of strictly positive prices, vectors $\mathbf{z}$ and incomes).

The demand functions for private goods in (6.4) have the usual properties described in Chapter 2 with respect to changes in prices and income. The level of provision of public goods affects the demands for private goods through the marginal utilities of such goods, i.e. $\partial^2 U/\partial x_i \partial z_j \neq 0$ in general. By differentiating (6.4) with respect to income, the reader can easily verify that the marginal utility of income, just like the demand for private goods, is a function of prices, the levels of provision of public goods, and income, in general.

The effect of a change in the provision of a public good on utility is obtained by differentiating (6.4) with respect to z_i

$$\frac{\partial V(\mathbf{p}, y, \mathbf{z})}{\partial z_i} = \lambda \mathbf{p} \frac{\partial \mathbf{x}}{\partial z_i} + \frac{\partial U}{\partial z_i} = \frac{\partial U(\mathbf{x}(\cdot), \mathbf{z})}{\partial z_i} \tag{6.5}$$

and is equal to the marginal valuation of the good in question. The optimal levels of consumption of individual private goods may also be affected by a change in z_i, but $\mathbf{p}\partial\mathbf{x}/\partial z_i$ is equal to zero when prices and income remain fixed. This is seen from the budget constraint.

2 *Public goods and uncompensated money measures of utility change*

A comparison of the equation in (6.5) of this chapter and the equations (5.5) in Chapter 5 reveals that the formal analysis of public goods almost parallels the analysis of rationed goods. The difference is that rationed goods were assumed to be priced in Chapter 5. Hence, there was a kind of income effect associated with changes in rations; without charging a price, this effect vanishes. If consumers have to pay a positive price, however low, for a fixed level of consumption of public goods, then the formal analysis of public goods parallels the analysis in Chapter 5. Or, to put it the other way round, if $\mathbf{P}$ is set equal to zero in Chapter 5, then the results hold also for unpriced public goods. This is the case at least at the individual level.

Nevertheless, since the analyses differ in the multi-household case, money measures will be derived. A characteristic that distinguishes public goods from private goods is non-rivalry, i.e. the same unit of a public good can be consumed by many, possibly all, individuals. Another reason for deriving money measures for public goods is the fact that most textbooks on welfare economics restrict the formal analysis to private goods. Hence, it is useful to also supply a formal treatment of public goods.

Proceeding in the same way as in the previous chapters, especially Chapter 5, we obtain the following individual utility change measure when $\mathbf{z}$ is changed from $\mathbf{z}^0$ to $\mathbf{z}^1$

$$\triangle U^h = V^h(\mathbf{p}, y^h, \mathbf{z}^1) - V^h(\mathbf{p}, y^h, \mathbf{z}^0)$$

$$= \int_c \frac{\partial V^h}{\partial \mathbf{z}} d\mathbf{z} = \int_c \frac{\partial U^h(x^h(\mathbf{p}, y, \mathbf{z}), \mathbf{z})}{\partial \mathbf{z}} d\mathbf{z} \tag{6.6}$$

where a superscript h refers to the hth household, and c is some path (in Ω_{Iz}) between initial and final $\mathbf{z}$-vectors. Summing over all H individuals yields

$$\Sigma_h \triangle U^h = \Sigma_h \int_c \frac{\partial U^h}{\partial \mathbf{z}} d\mathbf{z} \tag{6.7}$$

Accordingly, the effect of a change in the provision of public goods is equal to the sum of the individual marginal valuations of $\mathbf{z}$ between $\mathbf{z}^0$ and $\mathbf{z}^1$. If only a subset of individuals, say those living in a certain area, are affected, then (6.6) will be equal to zero for all other individuals living in the country under consideration.

Equation (6.7) must be interpreted with care; (6.7) gives the sum of the individuals valuation of the change in $\mathbf{z}$. From the discussion of aggregate welfare change measures in Section 2 of Chapter 4 it should be obvious that the change in society's welfare need not be equal to the unweighted sum of individual utility changes. A direct correspondence between the change in the society's welfare and the change reported by expression (6.7) holds only if the welfare weights are equal across all affected individuals over the entire path considered. This should be remembered when reading the remainder of this chapter.

Since, in general, utility functions are unobservable it is useful to convert (6.6) and (6.7) to money measures of utility change. This is done by dividing by λ^h, the marginal utility of income of the hth individual. A sufficient condition for λ^h to be constant with respect to changes in $\mathbf{z}$ is that the utility function is weakly separable in $\mathbf{z}$, i.e. there exists a monotone transformation such that $U = u(\mathbf{x}) + v(\mathbf{z})$. From the first-order conditions (6.3) for utility maximization it is seen that this property eliminates the influence of $\mathbf{z}$ on both demands for goods and the marginal utility of income. An alternative approach would be to assume that the utility function is quasi-linear with some private good, say the nth good, being the *numéraire* good. This assumption ensures that ordinary uncompensated measures and compensated measures coincide, since $\lambda^h = a/p_n$, where $a > 0$ is a constant, from the first-order conditions for utility maximization. As is demonstrated below, the aforementioned separability assumption does not ensure this property.

More importantly, the assumption that λ^h is constant with respect to changes in $\mathbf{z}$ for all h ensures that the money measure of utility change is path independent and can be written as

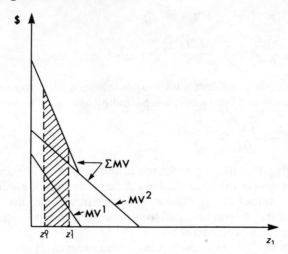

Figure 6.1 Individual and aggregate ordinary marginal willingness to pay curves for a public good; $MV^i = [\partial U^i(\mathbf{x}^i, \mathbf{z})/\partial z_1]/\lambda^i$

$$\Sigma_h \triangle U^h/\bar{\lambda}^h = S_\mathbf{z} = \Sigma_h \int_c \frac{\partial U^h(\mathbf{x}^h, \mathbf{z})/\partial \mathbf{z}}{\bar{\lambda}^h} d\mathbf{z} \qquad (6.8)$$

where $\bar{\lambda}^h$ is a constant.

This measure yields the sum of each individual's uncompensated marginal willingness to pay for a change in the vector $\mathbf{z}$ from $\mathbf{z}^0$ to $\mathbf{z}^1$. This is illustrated in Figure 6.1 for the single public good case. For the sake of simplicity, assume that only two individuals are affected. Their marginal valuations of the public good are vertically added since the consumption of a public good by one individual does not restrict the other individual(s) consumption of the good. The shaded area in the figure gives the aggregate willingness to pay for a change from z_1^0 to z_1^1. This area is proportional to the sum of changes in utility provided λ^h is constant over the considered path for each indvidual.

3 *Compensating and equivalent variations*

In empirical investigations, households are typically asked, for example, to make financial sacrifices in return for better air quality or are offered compensation in order to induce them to accept worse air quality. For this reason the concepts of compensating variation and equivalent variation are useful. In order to derive income compensated measures, the expenditure functions are defined as

$$e^h(\mathbf{p}, \mathbf{z}, \bar{U}^h) = \min_{\mathbf{x}^h} \{\mathbf{p}\mathbf{x}^h | U^h(\mathbf{x}^h, \mathbf{z}) \geq \bar{U}^h\} \quad \text{for all } h$$

$$= \mathbf{p}\bar{\mathbf{x}}^h(\mathbf{p}, \mathbf{z}, \bar{U}^h) \tag{6.9}$$

The expenditure function of the hth individual gives the minimum expenditure required to reach the specified utility level, given prices $\mathbf{p}$ and the provision of public goods $\mathbf{z}$.

The compensated demand functions for private goods in (6.9) have the usual properties with respect to changes in $\mathbf{p}$ and $\bar{U}^h$. An increase in $\mathbf{z}$ affects demands for private goods through the marginal utilities of such goods, in general. Moreover, since an increase in $\mathbf{z}$ increases utility, expenditure on private goods must fall in order to maintain the individual at the specified utility level. In general, the sign of the total effect of a change in a z_i on the demand for a private good is ambiguous. It should be noted, however, that the separability assumption discussed in Section 2 ensures that the effect on the marginal utilities of private goods vanishes. Then, if private goods are normal, an increase in $\mathbf{z}$ reduces demand for such goods. This is because income must be reduced in order for the individual to remain at the specified utility level.

Differentiating (6.9) with respect to $\mathbf{z}$ yields

$$\frac{\partial e^h}{\partial \mathbf{z}} = \mathbf{p}\partial\bar{\mathbf{x}}^h/\partial\mathbf{z} = -\mu^h\frac{\partial U^h(\bar{\mathbf{x}}^h, \mathbf{z})}{\partial \mathbf{z}} \tag{6.10}$$

i.e. the negative of the sum of marginal valuations of public goods multiplied by the marginal cost μ^h of utility. Expenditure on private goods must be reduced in order to restore the prespecified level of satisfaction since an increased provision of public goods increases utility. To obtain the final expression in (6.10), the utility function (6.1) is totally differentiated, the utility level is held constant and the usual first-order conditions for expenditure minimization are inserted, to obtain

$$dU^h = \frac{\partial U^h}{\partial\bar{\mathbf{x}}^h}d\bar{\mathbf{x}}^h + \frac{\partial U^h}{\partial\mathbf{z}}d\mathbf{z}$$

$$= \frac{1}{\mu^h}\mathbf{p}d\bar{\mathbf{x}}^h + \frac{\partial U^h}{\partial\mathbf{z}}d\mathbf{z} = 0 \tag{6.11}$$

where $\mu^h = \mu^h(\mathbf{p}, \mathbf{z}, \bar{U}^h)$ is the Lagrange multiplier of the cost minimization problem. Equation (6.11) explains the equality obtained in (6.10).

The aggregate compensating variation associated with discrete changes in the provision of public goods $\mathbf{z}$ can be defined as

$$\mathrm{CV}_\mathbf{z} = \Sigma_h[e^h(\mathbf{p}, \mathbf{z}^0, U^{h0}) - e^h(\mathbf{p}, \mathbf{z}^1, U^{h0})]$$

$$= \Sigma_h\int_c\frac{\partial e^h}{\partial\mathbf{z}}d\mathbf{z} = \Sigma_h\int_c(\mu^h\frac{\partial U^h(\bar{\mathbf{x}}^h, \mathbf{z})}{\partial\mathbf{z}})d\mathbf{z} \tag{6.12}$$

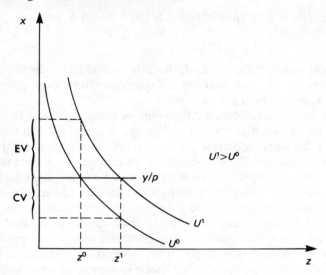

Figure 6.2 Compensated money measures associated with an increase in the provision of a public good z. Note that the equivalent variation associated with a decrease in z from z^1 to z^0 is equal to $-CV$ while the compensating variation is equal to $-EV$

where, for expositional simplicity, all prices and exogenous income are fixed. The change in z is now evaluated under compensated marginal willingness to pay curves. In order to interpret the CV_z measure, let us first consider the individual consumer. The compensating variation is the maximum amount of money that the individual is willing to pay to secure an increased provision of public goods. If the supply of z is reduced, then the CV_z measure gives the minimum compensation that must be given to the individual while leaving him as well off as before the reduction in z. See Figure 6.2 for a graphical illustration of these results. In order to obtain an aggregate measure, as in (6.12), the compensating variations for all affected individuals are added together. In the case of an equivalent variation measure, each individual remains at his final, as opposed to his initial, level of satisfaction. This measure represents the sum of the minimum (maximum) sum of money that must be given to (taken from) each individual to make him as well off as he would have been following an increase (decrease) in z.

The CV_z measure (like the EV_z measure) is path independent since the integrand in (6.12) is an exact differential of the expenditure function.[2] Hence, the order in which z_i and z_j are changed makes no difference, but

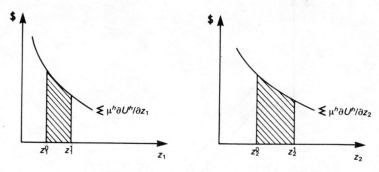

Figure 6.3 Evaluating a change in the levels of provision of two public goods, where

$\mu^h = \mu^h(\mathbf{a})$	$\mu^h = \mu^h = \mu^h(\mathbf{b})$
$\partial U^h/\partial z_1 = f^h(\bar{\mathbf{x}}^h(\mathbf{a}), z_1, z_2^0)$	$\partial U^h/\partial z_2 = f^h(\bar{\mathbf{x}}^h(\mathbf{b}), z_1^1, z_2)$
$\mathbf{a} = (\mathbf{p}, z_1, z_2^0, U^0)$	$\mathbf{b} = (\mathbf{p}, z_1^1, z_2, U^0)$

the individual's marginal willingness to pay curve for z_i must be evaluated subject to all previously considered changes in the provision of other public goods. This is illustrated in Figure 6.3. Moreover, it is a straight-forward matter to generalize the measures to capture changes in prices and exogenous income since the path independency conditions remain valid. General measures that capture changes in prices, the provision of public goods, and quantity constraints can be found in the appendix to this chapter and in Section 1 of Chapter 11.

4 *On the properties of money measures*

In general.the CV_z and EV_z measures impute different dollar values to a utility change. This is because the marginal willingness to pay for a public good depends on the utility level. Once again, however, a quasi-linear utility function ensures that $S_z = CV_z = EV_z$, i.e. that all money measures impute the same money gain to the utility change that follows from an increase in the provision of public goods. The reader should also note that the weak separability assumption discussed in Section 2 ensures that the ordinary money measure is proportional to $\triangle U$, since the marginal utility of income will be constant with respect to changes in $\mathbf{z}$. However, this is not the case for the compensated money measures of an increase in $\mathbf{z}$ since income must be reduced in order to maintain the individual at the specified utility level. Some inspection of the first-order

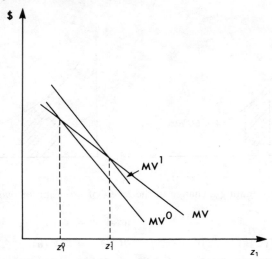

Figure 6.4 Aggregate marginal willingness to pay curves for a public good. The MV^0-curve (MV^1-curve) maintains each individual at his initial (final) utility level, while the MV-curve assumes that each individual is free to adjust his utility level

conditions (6.3) should convince the reader that λ ($= 1/\mu$) depends on income even when the utility function is weakly separable in public goods.

However, if public goods are 'normal', then $CV_z < S_z < EV_z$ in the case of a change in supply of a single public good. For a 'normal' public good, the marginal willingness to pay is an increasing function of income, i.e. $\partial(V_z/\lambda)\partial y > 0$. The result then follows by noting that the money measures refer to gradually higher utility (income) levels (see, for example, Hicks, 1946). In other words, when a public good is normal in the above sense, a marginal willingness to pay curve that refers to a higher utility level must lie above a curve that refers to a lower utility level. This is illustrated in Figure 6.4.

This has an important implication for applied research in the field. Let us assume that we have collected preference information by asking the consumers how much they are willing to pay for some change in the provision of a public good or an environmental service. If this measure is interpreted as a compensating variation and the good is normal, we know that the resulting amount of money would be smaller than if the consumers had been questioned regarding their equivalent variations (or, for that matter, ordinary willingness to pay).

These money measures are also unaffected if the utility function is subjected to a monotone increasing transformation $f(U(\mathbf{x},\mathbf{z}))$. Intuitively, indifference surfaces are unaffected by the transformation; they are simply relabelled. Therefore, the minimum cost or income necessary to reach any given indifference surface (commodity bundle) remains unchanged. This may be easily verified using (6.12). The new marginal cost of utility, μ^* say, can be seen to be equal to the initial one divided by $\partial f/\partial U$. Thus, this last derivative appears in both the numerator and the denominator of the money measure.

Nevertheless, by performing such a transform of the utility function, it can be easily verified that in terms of the example used in Chapter 4, where $EV_A^k = \$100$ and $EV_B^k = \$50$, we are unable to conclude that the consumer likes project A twice as much as project B. This is the case, at least in an ordinal world, where preferences lack intensities, i.e. only the ranking of bundles (projects) makes sense. In a cardinal world, the above relationship between A and B holds if and only if the marginal utility λ of income is constant over the entire path considered. In all other cases, the only inference that can be made from $EV_A^k = \$100$ and $EV_B^k = \$50$ is that the consumer prefers project A to project B.

It is also important to note that if we compare two (or more) final vectors of public goods, e.g. $\mathbf{z}^1$ and $\mathbf{z}^2$, the EV measure will rank these, and the initial vector $\mathbf{z}^0$, say, in the same order as the consumer. This is not necessarily true for the CV measure, as is demonstrated in the appendix to this chapter. The EV measure always selects the cheapest commodity bundle necessary to reach a particular (the final) utility level. Thus, if $\mathbf{z}^1$ is cheaper than $\mathbf{z}^2$, the former must correspond to a lower utility level. The CV measure, on the other hand, compares the cost of achieving the *initial* utility level when $\mathbf{z}$ is fixed at $\mathbf{z}^1$ and $\mathbf{z}^2$ respectively. Even if the two vectors should correspond to the same *final* utility level, the associated changes in costs need not coincide. Hence the inference from the CV measure that one vector is preferred to the other may be incorrect. Figure 6.2 can be used to give an idea of these results. For example, the CV of an increase in income from y to $y+EV$ with $\mathbf{z}=\mathbf{z}^0$ is equal to EV and exceeds the CV of an increase in $\mathbf{z}$ from $\mathbf{z}^0$ to $\mathbf{z}^1$ with income held fixed at y. The two EV measures, on the other hand, coincide and hence correctly indicate that the consumer is indifferent between the two considered changes.

From a practical point of view, these results are extremely important. If only a single z_i is changed, both the CV measure and the EV measure rank the change in the same order as the consumer would do. In fact, both measures are suitable for any *binary* comparison, i.e. for the comparison of any two vectors of public goods. However, if a study involves the comparison of more than two vectors, only the EV measure will necessarily rank the vectors correctly. In order to illustrate this point, assume that a decision to close one of two national parks is under way. The visitors are assumed to be indifferent with regard to which park is closed. Nevertheless, let us further assume that information is collected about the compensation that would have to be paid for the initial level of satisfaction to be maintained following the closure of either park. The resulting aggregate CV measures may provide an incorrect indication that visitors are more concerned about the preservation of one of the parks.[3] The two EV measures, on the other hand, will be of equal size and hence correctly indicate that the consumer is indifferent with regard to which park is closed. The reader who still needs to employ the CV measure may assume that the utility function is such that the ordinary money measure is path independent. This assumption ensures that the CV measure can be used to compare any number of z-vectors. The same kind of restriction on the utility function applies in the case of rationing.

Finally, it should also be noted that (uncompensated as well as compensated) consumer surplus measures may be infinite if the MV-curves in Figure 6.4 do not intersect the $-axis (see the appendix to this chapter for further details). It does not seem unlikely that certain environmental goods have infinite consumer surpluses in terms of the compensation required for utility to remain unchanged if the resource is destroyed. For example, advances in technology cannot augment the supply, and reduce the scarcity value, of the amenity resources of a natural environment. The value of its extractive resources on the other hand may be reduced by changes in technology and production of close substitutes (see Fisher and Peterson, 1976; also Knetsch and Sinden, 1984). Hence, the loss of a unique environment may be more irreversible than the extraction of a non-renewable resource since substitutes for the latter can be made available. This issue will be further discussed in Chapters 9 and 11.

5 *External effects, quality changes, and market data*

An external effect occurs when the utility of a consumer depends upon the consumption or production levels of other agents in the economy. As noted earlier in this chapter, Samuelsonian public goods represent a type of externality in consumption. For this reason, the consumer surplus measures derived in Sections 1–4 can be given quite broad interpretations. The measures can be used for an analysis of positive external effects and, with reversed signs, negative external effects. This is because an externality, like a public good, is usually modelled by including the externality as a separate argument in the utility functions of households.

Moreover, neither externalities nor public goods appear in the budget constraint of a household.

However, the measures derived in the previous sections are not directly observable from market data. This section, following Bradford and Hildebrandt (1977), Mäler (1971; 1974), Small and Rosen (1981), and Willig (1978), develops an approach which can be tested with market data. Suppose z_i represents the quality attributes of the private good x_i or is a public good which is complementary to x_i. Below we employ the stronger assumption that when $x_i = 0$ then the level of z_i makes no difference, i.e. $\partial U(x_1, \ldots, 0, \ldots, x_n, z)/\partial z_i = 0$. Next assume that x_i is non-essential. Formally, for any commodity bundle x, $z \geqslant 0$ there exists x', z such that $U(x, z) = U(x'_1, \ldots, 0, \ldots, x'_n, z)$, i.e. any bundle including x_i can be matched by some other bundle which excludes x_i.

Willig (1978) has shown that when $x_i = 0$, then $\partial U(\cdot)/\partial z_i = 0$ if and only if, the indirect utility function (6.4) has the following property:

$$\ell\text{im}_{p_i \to \infty} \frac{\partial V(p_i, \bar{p}, \bar{y}, z_i^0, \bar{z})}{\partial z_i} = 0 \tag{6.13}$$

for all $\bar{p} \geqslant 0$ and $\bar{y} > 0$, where $\bar{p}$ and $\bar{z}$ are row vectors whose elements are the fixed prices of goods x_j and the fixed levels of z_j for all $j \neq i$ respectively. Moreover, z_i^0 denotes the initial level of z_i. *Condition (6.13) simply states that if the price of good x_i is so high that the good is not consumed, then its quality does not matter.*

Using these assumptions, it is possible to derive a money measure of quality changes which can be estimated from market data. Since these calculations are fairly tedious, they have been placed in the appendix to this chapter. The money measure associated with a discrete change in z_i can be written as

$$S_z = -\int_{p_i^0}^{\infty} [x_i(p_i, \bar{p}, \bar{y}, z_i^0, \bar{z}) - x_i(p_i, \bar{p}, \bar{y}, z_i^1, \bar{z})]dp_i \tag{6.14}$$

The right-hand side of (6.14) gives the change in the area to the left of the ordinary demand curve for the ith commodity as it shifts in response to a shift in the quality parameter z_i. This is illustrated in Figure 6.5. A simple example, which may help to clarify this result, can be found in the appendix to this chapter.

Hence, it is possible to infer the value that the consumer places on a change in the quality of a private good or in the supply of complementary public good by calculating the change in the consumer's surplus of a private good. Thus, it is not necessary to derive the underlying utility and expenditure functions, or to estimate complete systems of demand

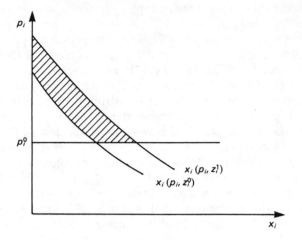

Figure 6.5 The value of a change in the quality attributes of a good (shaded area)

equations. However, as usual, this assumes that the path independency conditions apply.

Equation (6.14) applies to a single consumer, whereas most available demand data refers to the market behaviour of consumers in the aggregate. The market demand function for x_i can be used to measure the effect of a quality change provided all individuals find the good non-essential, and the path independency conditions are satisfied for all H individuals. For example, the latter conditions apply when there are no income effects on demands for goods. Given this assumption, the change in consumers surplus, measured left of the market demand curve, would be an exact measure of the sum of the individual gains.

The assumptions needed to establish this result may seem quite restrictive. None the less, in many circumstances, the availability of a method that only requires data on demand functions for private goods could turn out to be valuable. In particular, the approach does not require the econometric estimation of complete systems of demand equations. The above analysis has demonstrated that the method requires only information on the demand for the single commodity. The approach also suggests a practical methodology for the calculation of so-called hedonic price adjustments. This will be shown in Chapter 7, where different empirical methods are reviewed.

However, before turning to this review, a compensated measure of quality changes in a non-essential good is presented. It should be borne in mind that compensated measures are constructed in such a way that the path independency conditions are satisfied. In general this is not true for uncompensated measures. The compensated measure, which is derived in the appendix to this chapter, can be written as

$$\text{CV}_z = -\int_{p_i^0}^{\infty} [\bar{x}_i(p_i, \bar{\mathbf{p}}, z_i^0, \bar{\mathbf{z}}, \bar{U}) - x_i(p_i, \bar{\mathbf{p}}, z_i^1, \bar{\mathbf{z}}, \bar{U})]dp_i \tag{6.15}$$

This suggests that changes in compensated demand curves can be used to provide a direct measure of the willingness to pay for quality changes or changes in the provision of certain types of public goods or 'bads'. Adding the compensating variations (6.15) for all consumers one obtains the aggregate compensating variation. The error made when the area left of an ordinary demand curve is used instead of the CV or EV measures can be calculated from formulas developed by Willig (1976) and Randall and Stoll (1980).

In closing, it should also be noted that the analysis of quality attributes is easily generalized in diverse directions. For example, each private and public good could be assumed to have certain quality characteristics. These attributes may be affected by, for example, pollution. Cicchetti and Smith (1976) and Stahl (1983c) have developed such a model within the framework of Lancaster's (1966) theory of consumer choice in which the household's utility function is written as $U = U(\mathbf{ax}, \mathbf{bz})$, where $\mathbf{a}$ and $\mathbf{b}$ are vectors of characteristics, i.e. $\mathbf{ax}$ and $\mathbf{bz}$ give the quality-adjusted levels of consumption of private and public goods. The quality attributes are exogenous from the point of view of the household. If the quality of a commodity decreases for one reason or the other, then one unit of the commodity (x_i or z_j) yields less utility than before the deterioriation in quality. The demand functions for private goods are obtained by maximizing the utility function subject to the household's budget constraint (6.2). From a purely formal point of view, the analysis of this model almost parallels the analysis in the previous sections of this chapter. For this reason the interested reader is referred to Stahl (1983c) for a detailed investigation of the properties of a similar model.

Hori (1975) developed a household production model incorporating public goods as inputs to the household production function. The model is used to suggest an approach to the determination of individual demand for public goods from information derived from private goods markets. In order to illustrate the spirit of household production function models, consider the following utility function:

$$U = U(\mathbf{x}, f(\mathbf{X}, \mathbf{z})) \tag{6.16}$$

where $\mathbf{x}$ is a vector of private goods consumed, and $Z = f(\mathbf{X}, \mathbf{z})$ is a good or a service produced by the household using private and public goods as inputs. For example, Z could be a trip to a recreation area which is 'produced' using a car (**X**) and roads (**z**) as inputs. The household maximizes (6.16) subject to the budget constraint $y = \mathbf{p}\mathbf{x} + \mathbf{P}\mathbf{X}$, and the given supply of public goods.

If the production function f( ) is known, the marginal willingness to pay for **z** can easily be calculated once the demand functions $\mathbf{X} = \mathbf{X}(\mathbf{p}, y, \mathbf{z})$ are estimated. In general, however, the functional form of the household production function is unknown. Nevertheless, Mäler (1981) has shown that, by making assumptions about certain broad characteristics of the production function, such as whether an input is essential or not or whether two inputs are substitutes or complements, it is possible to calculate the marginal willingness to pay for **z** from market data. The analysis, which assumes that just two inputs (a private good and a public good) are used to produce Z, largely parallels the above analysis of quality changes and is not performed here. The interested reader is referred to Hori (1975) and Mäler (1981).

In the models discussed so far, the quality attributes, like the prices and income, are exogenous to the consumer, i.e. the analysis focuses on objective measures of quality. Recently, however, Hanemann (1984c) has assumed subjective perceptions of quality, and used Shannon's entropy statistic as a means of measuring the degree of consensus in ordinal ratings of recreation site quality. The advantage of this approach is that differences in choices may be explained by differences in consumer's perception of quality, as well as in their underlying preferences (see Hanemann, 1984c, for details).

Appendix

Some comments on the properties of the EV and CV measures

In order to demonstrate that the EV measure ranks any number of commodity bundles correctly (provided there is a single reference vector), it is sufficient to consider the following example:

$$
\left.
\begin{aligned}
\mathrm{EV}^1 &= e(\mathbf{p}^0, \mathbf{P}^0, \mathbf{q}^0, \mathbf{z}^0, U^1) - e(\mathbf{p}^0, \mathbf{P}^0, \mathbf{q}^0, \mathbf{z}^0, U^0) \\
\mathrm{EV}^2 &= e(\mathbf{p}^0, \mathbf{P}^0, \mathbf{q}^0, \mathbf{z}^0, U^2) - e(\mathbf{p}^0, \mathbf{P}^0, \mathbf{q}^0, \mathbf{z}^0, U^0)
\end{aligned}
\right\} \quad (\text{A}6.1)
$$

where **p** and **P** are vectors of prices, **q** is a vector of rations, **z** is a vector of public goods, and a superscript refers to a particular level of prices, etc. Since the expenditure function is strictly increasing in utility, it follows that $U^2 \geqslant U^1 \geqslant U^0$, then $\mathrm{EV}^2 \geqslant \mathrm{EV}^1 \geqslant 0$, i.e. the EV measure ranks the different bundles in the same order as the underlying utility function.

Consider next the corresponding CV measures:

$$CV^1 = e(\mathbf{p}^1, \mathbf{P}^1, \mathbf{q}^1, \mathbf{z}^1, U^1) - e(\mathbf{p}^1, \mathbf{P}^1, \mathbf{q}^1, \mathbf{z}^1, U^0)$$

$$CV^2 = e(\mathbf{p}^2, \mathbf{P}^2, \mathbf{q}^2, \mathbf{z}^2, U^2) - e(\mathbf{p}^2, \mathbf{P}^2, \mathbf{q}^2, \mathbf{z}^2, U^0)$$

$$\left. \right\} \qquad \text{(A6.2)}$$

Thus, $U^2 \geqslant U^1 \geqslant U^0$ implies that both measures in (A6.2) have non-negative signs. However, it is far from self-evident that $CV^2 \geqslant CV^1$ since the measures are based on different values of $\mathbf{p}$, $\mathbf{q}$ and $\mathbf{z}$. In fact it is fairly easy to demonstrate that the CV measure may fail to rank the changes correctly. For example, using the simple utility function $U = (x_1 z_1 + 1)(x_2 + 1) + (z_1 z_2)^{1/2}$, the reader can easily check that the CV measure fails to correctly rank the three $\mathbf{z}$-vectors $\mathbf{z}^0 = (1,1)$, $\mathbf{z}^1 = (2,1)$ and $\mathbf{z}^2 = (1,994.7)$ for $p_1 = p_2 = 1$, $U^0 = 10$, $U^1 = U^2 \approx 67.5$, and no quantity constraints. This example is sufficient to prove the claim that the CV measure need not rank any three or more bundles correctly.

A utility function that is separable in $\mathbf{z}$ produces a CV measure that provides a correct ranking of any number of $\mathbf{z}$-vectors. This is easily verified using

$$V(\cdot) = f(\mathbf{p}, y) + v(\mathbf{z})$$

$$e(\cdot) = \mathbf{p}\bar{\mathbf{x}}(\mathbf{p}, \bar{U} - v(\mathbf{z}))$$

Moreover, the CV measure associated with the (quasi-linear) utility function

$$V(\cdot) = g(\mathbf{p}, \mathbf{q}, \mathbf{z}) - \mathbf{Pq} + y$$

with $p_n = 1$, is easily shown to rank $\mathbf{p}, \mathbf{P}, \mathbf{q}, y, \mathbf{z}$-vectors correctly.

Using (A6.1) and (A6.2) it can be shown fairly simply that the CV measure, although not necessarily the EV measure, ranks any number of bundles correctly when there are several *initial* bundles but one final bundle. This exercise is left to the reader.

Finally, let us use, for example, the first line of (A6.2) to obtain a money measure that generalizes those derived in Chapters 3, 5 and 6:

$$CV^1 = \int_c [-\bar{\mathbf{x}} d\mathbf{p} + (\mu U_q - \mathbf{P}^0) d\mathbf{q} - \mathbf{q}^1 d\mathbf{P} + \mu U_z d\mathbf{z}] \qquad \text{(A6.2')}$$

where c is some path between initial and final $\mathbf{p}$, $\mathbf{q}$, $\mathbf{P}$, $\mathbf{z}$ vectors, $U_k = \partial U(\bar{\mathbf{x}}, \mathbf{q}, \mathbf{z})/\partial \mathbf{k}$, with $\mathbf{k} = \mathbf{q}, \mathbf{z}$ and $\bar{\mathbf{x}} = \bar{\mathbf{x}}(\mathbf{p}, y - \mathbf{Pq}, \mathbf{q}, \mathbf{z})$. As usual a particular change is evaluated subject to all previously considered changes in prices, rations and the provision of public goods.

Quality changes

In order to derive an observable measure of quality changes, we need the properties of the indirect utility function $V = V(p, \bar{\mathbf{p}}, \bar{y}, z^0, \bar{\mathbf{z}})$, where z^0 denotes the initial level of z_i, and $p = p_i$. For convenient reference, these properties are repeated in a slightly different form here, suppressing the constants $\bar{p}$, $\bar{y}$ and $\bar{z}$ in order to simplify notation

$$\frac{\partial V(p, z^0)/\partial p}{\lambda} = \frac{V_p}{\lambda} = -x(p, z^0)$$

$$\left. \frac{\partial V(p, z^0)}{\partial y} = V_y = \lambda(p, z^0) \right\} \quad \text{(A6.3)}$$

$$\frac{\partial V(p, z^0)/\partial z}{\lambda} = \frac{V_z}{\lambda} = \frac{U_z}{\lambda}$$

First, using the middle expression of the final line in (A6.3) and letting p take values p^0 and p^f respectively, where p^0 is the actual market price of x_i for which $x_i^0 > 0$, and $p^f [p^f \in (p^0, \infty)]$ denotes a price which is so high that x_i is not consumed 'at all', we obtain

$$\frac{V_z(p^f, z^0)}{\lambda(p^f, z^0)} - \frac{V_z(p^0, z^0)}{\lambda(p^0, z^0)} = \int_{p^0}^{p^f} \frac{\partial(V_z/\lambda)}{\partial p} \, dp$$

$$= \int_{p^0}^{p^f} \frac{V_{zp}\lambda - V_z\lambda_p}{\lambda^2} \, dp$$

$$= -\frac{V_z(p^0, z^0)}{\lambda(p^0, z^0)} \quad \text{(A6.4)}$$

where subscripts z and p denote partial derivatives. The final expression follows from the fact that $V_z = 0$ while λ still is positive and finite when $p \geq p^f$ (see Willig, 1978).

Next, the first line in (A6.3) is differentiated with respect to z and both sides integrated between $p = p^0$ and $p = p^f$ to obtain

$$\int_{p^0}^{p^f} \frac{\partial(V_p/\lambda)}{\partial z} dp = \int_{p^0}^{p^f} \frac{V_{pz}\lambda - V_p\lambda_z}{\lambda^2} dp$$

$$= -\int_{p^0}^{p^f} x_z(p, z^0) dp \quad \text{(A6.5)}$$

Comparing the final equalities in (A6.4) and (A6.5), it can be seen that

$$\frac{V_z(p^0, z^0)}{\lambda} = \int_{p^0}^{p^f} x_z(p, z^0) dp \quad \text{(A6.6)}$$

if $V_z\lambda_p = V_p\lambda_z$. which, by invoking (A6.3), can be shown to be the path independency condition. Then (A6.6) gives the change in the area to the left of the ordinary demand curve as it shifts in response to a marginal shift in the quality paramenter z. Integration between z_i^0 and z_i^1 yields the measure discussed in the main text. See also equation (A6.10).

The assumptions made regarding the properties of the utility function, i.e. good x_i is non-essential and $\partial U/\partial z_i = 0$ whenever $x_i = 0$, imply that the expenditure function has the following properties:

$$\ell\text{im}_{p_i \to \infty} e(p_i, z_i^0, \bar{U}) = L < \infty$$

$$\left.\ell\text{im}_{p_i \to \infty} \frac{\partial e(p_i, z_i^0, \bar{U})}{\partial z_i} = 0 \right\} \qquad (A6.7)$$

where all prices and levels of quality attributes except p_i and z_i^0 have been omitted since they remain fixed throughout the analysis. The equations in (A6.7) state that if the price of a non-essential good approaches infinity then expenditure reaches and remains at a finite level L. Moreover, this level is constant with respect to changes in the quality of x_i, because none of the good is consumed.

The (compensating variation) change in the consumer's surplus when p_i is increased from $p_i = p_i^0$ to $p_i \to \infty$, *ceteris paribus*, can be written as

$$CV_p = e(p_i^0, z_i^0, U^0) - e(\infty, z_i^0, U^0)$$

$$= -\int_c \tilde{x}_i(p_i, z_i^0, U^0) dp_i \qquad (A6.8)$$

This measure gives the area to the left of the compensated demand curve for x_i between its intersection with the price axis and the price p_i^0. The fact that the integrand is zero for sufficiently high price levels causes no difficulty in integrating (A6.8).

Differentiating (A6.8) with respect to z_i, using the second property given in (A6.7), we obtain

$$\frac{\partial e(p_i^0, z_i^0, U^0)}{\partial z_i} = -\int_c \frac{\partial \tilde{x}_i}{\partial z_i} dp_i \qquad (A6.9)$$

This result enables us to evaluate marginal quality changes in terms of changes in the consumer's surplus. Integration of (A6.9) between z_i^0 and z_i^1 yields

$$CV_{z_i} = -\int_{p_i^0}^{\infty} \int_{z_i^0}^{z_i^1} [\partial \tilde{x}_i(p_i, \bar{p}, z_i, \bar{z}, \bar{U})/\partial z_i] dz_i dp_i$$

$$= -\int_{p_i^0}^{\infty} [\tilde{x}_i(p_i, \bar{p}, z_i^0, \bar{z}, \bar{U}) - \tilde{x}_i(p_i, \bar{p}, z_i^1, \bar{z}, \bar{U})] dp_i \qquad (A6.10)$$

where previously omitted constants have been inserted. This is the compensated money measure of a change in the quality of a private good discussed in the main text.

An example may be useful. Let us assume that the indirect utility function is

$$V = \ell n\, z_1 - \ell n\, p_1 - \ell n\, p_2 + y + \frac{p_1}{z_1} \tag{A6.11}$$

Taking partial derivatives yields

$$\left.\begin{array}{l} \dfrac{\partial V}{\partial p_1} = -\lambda x_1 = -\dfrac{1}{p_1} + \dfrac{1}{z_1} \\[3mm] \dfrac{\partial V}{\partial z_1} = \dfrac{1}{z_1} - \dfrac{p_1}{z_1^2} \end{array}\right\} \tag{A6.12}$$

The money measure (A6.6) can be written as

$$\int_c \frac{\partial x_1}{\partial z_1} dp_1 = \int_c \frac{1}{z_1^2} dp_1$$

$$= \frac{z_1}{z_1^2} - \frac{p_1^0}{z_1^2} = \frac{\partial V}{\partial z_1} \tag{A6.13}$$

where $c = (p_1^f, p_1^0)'$, and $p_1^f = z_1$ since $x_1 = 0$ if $p_1 \geq z_1$ as can be seen from the first line of (A6.12).

Finally, it should be mentioned that the indirect utility function (A6.11) corresponds to a direct utility function of the form $U = \ell n(z_1 x_1 + 1) + \ell n\, x_2 + x_3$.

'Kinks', 'jump discontinuities', and 'improper integrals'

In Section 5 of this chapter as well as in Chapter 8 we consider demand functions for non-essential commodites that have the property that $x_i > 0$ for $p_i < p_i^f$ and $x_i = 0$ for $p_i \geq p_i^f (p_i^f < \infty)$. The integration over the resulting 'kink' (or point of discontinuity of the unconditional demand function for on-site time in Chapter 8) does not present any difficulties. A function which is continuous in a closed interval, i.e. an interval that contains its end points, is integrable. The same is more generally true of bounded functions that are defined and continuous (in closed or open intervals) with the possible exception of a finite number of points.

Consider the integral

$$\int_{p_i^0}^{p_i^*} x_i(p_i, \bar{\mathbf{p}}, y) dp_i = \int_{p_i^0}^{p_i^f} x_i(p_i, \bar{\mathbf{p}}, y) dp_i + \int_{p_i^f}^{p_i^*} x_i(p_i, \bar{\mathbf{p}}, y) dp_i \tag{A6.14}$$

and assume that $x_i \in C$ on $p_i^0 \leq p_i \leq p_i^f$ and on $p_i^f \leq p_i \leq p_i^*$ but $x_i(p_i^f +, \bar{\mathbf{p}}, y) \neq x_i(p_i^f -, \bar{\mathbf{p}}, y)$, i.e. the function approaches values from the right $(+)$ and left $(-)$ that differ. Thus, there is a discontinuity or finite jump in the integrand at the considered point. Nevertheless, the integral (A6.14) exists as is shown in, for example, Widder (1961, Ch. 5). This result is useful when we integrate the unconditional demand function for on-site time in Chapter 8. The demand functions considered in Section 5 of this chapter, are (kinked but) continuous on $p_i^0 \leqslant p_i \leqslant p_i^*$. This is also true of the conditional demand functions in Chapter 8. Thus, the integration of these functions does not present any difficulties. (Of course, the value of the integral (A6.14) is equal to the value of the first term on the right since

$$\int_{p_i^f}^{p_i} 0 \, dp_i = 0$$

recall that we have assumed that $x_i = 0$ for $p_i \geqslant p_i^f$.)

Suppose next that x_i is positive, continuous, and bounded in the (finite) right half-open interval $[p_i^0, p_i^f)$ but is not necessarily defined or continuous at the end point p_i^f. As a matter of fact, we can assign to x_i any value, e.g. $x_i = 0$, at the end point and still obtain a proper integral, i.e. the first integral on the right-hand side of (A6.14) (see, for example, Courant and John, 1965, Ch. 3, for a proof). Thus, it means no real loss of generality to restrict attention to an open set Ω_I of strictly positive prices and incomes that generates interior solutions, i.e. $\mathbf{x} \gg 0$, as in Chapters 2–5.

In order to illustrate these results we consider the demand function $x_i = (2/p_i) - 1$ defined on $\Omega_p = \{p_i | 0 < p_i < 2\}$. Suppose the interval of integration is $[1, 2]$. We find that

$$
\begin{aligned}
\int_1^2 \left[\frac{2}{p_i} - 1\right] dp_i &= \lim_{\epsilon \to 0} \int_1^{2-\epsilon} \left[\frac{2}{p_i} - 1\right] dp_i \\
&= \lim_{e \to 0} \left[2\ell n(2-\epsilon) - (2-\epsilon) + 1\right] \\
&= 2\ell n \, 2 - 1
\end{aligned}
\tag{A6.15}
$$

Alternatively, since x_i is continuous and bounded in $[1, 2]$ we can assign to x_i any value, e.g. $x_i = 0$, at the right-hand side end point and obtain $\int_1^2 [\quad] dp_i$ directly as a proper integral. If, instead, $\Omega_p = \{p_i | 0 < p_i \leqslant 1.5\}$ and $x_i = 0$ for $p_i \geqslant 1.5$, we obtain a kind of jump discontinuity. The corresponding interval of integration in (A6.15) is $[1, 1.5]$ since $x_i = 0$ for $p_i \geqslant 1.5$. These results illustrate the extensions of the concept of integral discussed above.

Finally, we briefly illustrate two other extensions of the concept of integral. First of all, the integrand in (A6.15) may become unbounded for $p_i \to 0$. If some price approaches zero, the consumer might want an infinite amount of the corresponding good. This explains the fact that it is generally assumed that $p_i > 0$ for all i. Although geometrical intuition suggests that an integral of a function with an infinite discontinuity at the point $p_i = 0$ diverges, such improper integrals may converge, i.e. exist (see, for example, Silverman, 1969, Ch. 13; Widder, 1961, Ch. 9).

Another kind of improper integral involves an infinite interval of integration. For example, the integral

$$- \int_1^A \frac{1}{p_i^n} dp_i = - \frac{A^{1-n}-1}{1-n} \qquad (A6.16)$$

converges if $n > 1$ since

$$\lim_{A \to \infty} A^{1-n} = 0$$

For the case $n = 1$ the integral fails to exist since $\ln A$ tends to infinity as A does. The same result is obtained when $n < 1$. Note that the integrand in (A6.16) can be interpreted as a demand curve that does not intersect the price axis. If the considered commodity is non-essential, then $n > 1$. The Cobb–Douglas demand functions in Section 4 of Chapter 3, on the other hand, correspond to the case $n = 1$.

CHAPTER 7

How to overcome the problem of preference revelation; practical methodologies

Several different practical methods, which can be used to measure the willingness to pay for public goods (bads), have been suggested in the literature. This chapter presents the most frequently used methods (survey techniques, hedonic approaches, and travel costs methods). Each of these methods has its own serious weaknesses. However, apart from a few exceptions, no comprehensive discussion of these problems will be undertaken here. Instead the reader is referred to the references given below which provide an extensive discussion of the shortcomings associated with the different methods. In addition Fisher and Peterson (1976) and Freeman (1979a) present informative reviews of the environment in economics. Comparisons of methods for valuing environmental commodities can be found in Brookshire *et al.* (1981), Johnson *et al.* (1983), Knetsch and Davis (1966), Mäler (1974), Shapiro and Smith (1981), and Schulze *et al.* (1981).

1 Survey data

Direct demand-revealing methods for public goods have been suggested and also used by several authors.[1] Roughly speaking these approaches collect preference information by asking the consumers how much they are willing to pay for some change in the provision of a public good or an environmental service, or about the minimum compensation consumers require if the change is not carried out. For example, the following questions may be asked of the respondent

(CV) Suppose the provision of z is increased from z^0 to z^1. What is the most you would be willing to pay for this increase?

(EV) Suppose that the government refrains from increasing the provision of z. What is the minimum compensation you would need in order to be as well off as after an increase in z?

See Figure 6.2 in Chapter 6 for a graphical illustration of these concepts.

The most well-known problem associated with such methods is 'the free rider problem'. This is as follows: if consumers have to pay on the basis of their stated willingness to pay, they may try to conceal their true willingness to pay in order to qualify for a lower price. On the other hand, if consumers believe that the price (or the tax) charged is unaffected by their response, they may have an incentive to overstate their willingness to pay in order to secure a large supply of the public good.

However, Peter Bohm, in a series of articles, has argued that the free rider problem can be handled in quite a simple way. The following example is adapted from Bohm (1979). Suppose two large samples of the population are confronted with the task of revealing their true willingness to pay for a public good project, such as improved environmental quality. If the project were to be carried out, people in the first sample would pay an amount related to their stated willingness to pay. People in the second sample pay nothing or possibly a symbolic sum of money. If the average willingness to pay coincides for the samples, the hypothesis that there are incentives to misrepresent the willingness to pay, so-called strategic bias, is not supported.

If the average willingness to pay differs between the samples the results can be used to locate an interval in which the true willingness to pay must fall. This is the case at least if people in the first sample, i.e. those paying, have incentives to understate their true willingness to pay while the opposite holds for people in the second sample, i.e. those not paying.

Because of the hypothetical nature of the survey technique, several other potential biases may also occur. The following example is adapted from Schulze *et al.* (1981) who compare six different studies that all use the same survey technique, the contingent bidding survey approach. This technique is characterized by the fact that the valuation is contingent on the specific hypothetical change identified through photographs, brochures, or other means and was first empirically applied by Randall *et al.* (1974). One of the studies, reported in Rowe *et al.* (1980) and assessed in Schulze *et al.* (1981), was the so-called Farmington Experiment, which attempted to establish the economic value of visibility over long distances for Farmington residents and recreators at Navajo Reservoir (where visibility was threatened by power plant emissions).

The interviewee was shown a set of pictures depicting visibility ranges. The pictures were of views in different directions from one location (the San Juan Mountains and Shiprock). A sequence of questions on maximum willingness to pay and minimum compensation were then asked.

For strategic bias investigation, the survey instrument was structured so that the individual was told he would have to pay the average bid, not his own. It is difficult for individuals to bid strategically to achieve a specific outcome in such a case. For instance all previous and future bids must be known. The results also suggested that individuals do not act strategically in order to bias the outcome.

With regard to so-called information bias, it was suggested to the individual that his or her bid was not sufficient to keep power plant emissions at present levels for sustained high quality ambient air. One-third revised their bids when confronted with the possibility that their bids were insufficient. This result indicates that new information may affect bidding behaviour.

Furthermore, so-called instrument bias was addressed in this study. It was observed that the higher the starting bid suggested by the interviewer, the higher the maximum willingness to pay. Also individuals were willing to pay more when confronted with a payroll tax than with an increase in entrance fees.

These (and other) results reported by Schulze *et al.* (1981) indicate that one must be very careful with both the instrument used for payment and the amount and quality of information given to the interviewee at initiation of the interview. Nevertheless, the Farmington Experiment demonstrated reasonable consistency with other similar studies. Moreover, the detailed comparisons of studies in Schulze *et al.* (1981) and in Cummings *et al.* (1986) suggest that the survey technique yields values that are well within one order of magnitude in accuracy. After this brief sketch of the survey technique, we now turn to a more detailed presentation of a study, concerned with air pollution in Norway, based on this technique.

2 *A study based on the bidding technique*

Industry located in the Grenland area south west of Oslo, the capital of Norway, is a heavy polluter of the air. Although the emissions have been reduced during recent years, pollution is still causing problems, in particular through reduced visibility (haze). Therefore, the Norwegian Environmental Protection Agency is interested to 'know' whether further reductions of emissions are called for. For this reason, Hylland and Strand (1983) were asked to estimate the benefits and costs of such reductions in order to arrive at the societal gain or loss of improved air quality in the Grenland area. As a measure of the benefits, Hylland and Strand used the CV measure, not the EV measure, since their aim was to see if the total willingness to pay of the Norwegian population was sufficiently high to cover the costs of reducing/eliminating air pollution in the Grenland area.

In order to estimate the benefits of an improved air quality, two samples of persons were investigated. First of all, a sample of the population in the Grenland area was interviewed using the contingent bidding survey approach. Secondly, a sample of the Norwegian population (except those living in the Grenland area) was asked a number of questions regarding their valuation of improved air quality in the Grenland area. There are at least two reasons for including the whole population in the study. Some of those who are living in other parts of the country may, at some future date, visit Grenland, and, hence impute a value to an improved air quality in Grenland. Even those who do not expect to visit Grenland may impute a value to the existence of good air quality in the area. A reason for this attitude may be that they are concerned about the well-being of others. In particular, they may be willing to reduce their standard of living if this contributes to an improved and more healthy environment for future generations.

The sample of Norwegians

The main question asked to a sample of Norwegians was the following one.

Q1 The Grenland district, i.e. the area around Skien and Porsgrunn, is the industrial area in Norway that has been worst affected by air pollution. A reduction in air pollution to the levels prevailing in other Norwegian towns would require a once-and-for-all expenditure of 1,000 million NEK. Let us assume that this expenditure is financed by means of a one year special surcharge levied on the incomes of all Norwegians. This tax surcharge would be equivalent to approximately 0.6 per cent of annual income, i.e. a person who earns 100,000 NEK would pay 600 NEK while a person who earns 50,000 NEK would pay a tax surcharge of 300 NEK.
Do you support this measure to reduce air pollution if it is financed in this manner?

This question, and a number of questions concerning age, sex, income, home town, and so on, were answered by around 1,000 Norwegians as a part of a nationwide Gallup poll carried out monthly. About 56 per cent of the answers were yes responses. Obviously, the answers cannot be used to calculate the distribution of the maximum willingness to pay (the CV) for improved air quality. We only know that some people are willing to pay a once and for all amount corresponding to 0.6 per cent or more of

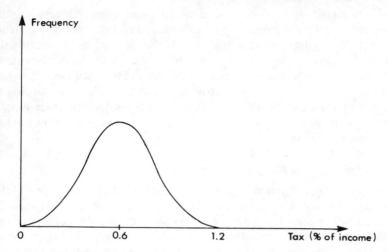

Figure 7.1 The normal distribution

their current yearly income, while others are not willing to pay this much. (The reason for not asking further questions was probably limited financial resources. The authors wanted to concentrate on a detailed investigation of the attitudes of those living in the polluted area.)

In order to arrive at a rough estimate of the aggregate willingness to pay, Hylland and Strand used two different methods. According to the first approach, they simply added 0.6 per cent of the annual income of each person who voted 'yes'. The total willingness to pay of the population is obtained by multiplying the resulting amount of money by the raising factor total population/sample size. The second approach employs Bowen's (1943) median voter theorem. This theorem states that the median voter can be replaced by the average voter provided, in this case, willingness to pay is symmetrically distributed among the population, as in Figure 7.1. Since around 50 per cent voted yes and 50 per cent voted no to question Q1 stated above, Hylland and Strand obtained the total willingness to pay by multiplying 0.6 per cent of the average annual income by the number of people (voters) in the population. Hence, according to this approach, total willingness to pay among the population for improved air quality in the Grenland area is 0.6 per cent of national income.

However, total willingness to pay is underestimated, since more than 50 per cent (56 per cent) voted yes and Bowen's approach also ignores that there may also be those who are prepared to pay more than 1.2 per cent of their income. This applies at least if the population is close to normally distributed around the assumed mean value. Otherwise, the calculated total willingness to pay may exceed or fall short of the 'true' amount. This latter amount is equal to the sum of each individual's maximal willingness to pay for an improved air quality in the Grenland area. In any case, it should be mentioned that the total willingness to pay is about 630 million Norwegian crowns (about $80 million) according to the first approach employed by Hylland and Strand, while their second approach yields a total willingness to pay amounting to 1,050 million Norwegian crowns.

The sample of those living in the Grenland area

A much more detailed investigation was carried out in order to reveal the attitudes of those living in the Grenland area, i.e. those who are directly affected by the considered air pollution. More than 1,000 persons out of 68,000 adults were interviewed using the contingent bidding survey approach. The interviews were based upon three pictures depicting visibility ranges. Picture A shows the selected area, a day with heavy haze; about every tenth day is that hazy. Picture B depicts the same area on an average day, while the range of visibility in Picture C is so good that only every fifth day is that clear.

The interviewees were divided into three subsamples of equal size. One subsample, S1, was shown pictures A and C, a second subsample, S2, was shown pictures B and C, and the third subsample, S3, was shown, or asked to compare, pictures A and B and then B and C. There are at least two reasons for this approach. First of all, the approach allows the calculation of the 'marginal' willingness to pay for an improved air quality over a certain range, i.e. for an improvement from A to B and for the further improvement to C. Second, the approach opens up a possibility to check if the answers are 'path independent'. Reasonably, one should obtain approximately the same willingness to pay for a change from A to C regardless of whether we go directly from A to C or from A to B to C.

In order to make the interviewees familiar with the considered hypothetical changes in the environment, they were asked to estimate the number of days per year which are as hazy as pictures A and B, respectively. Then the following question was asked.

Q2   It is impossible to eradicate all of the fog since part of it is caused by natural conditions. However a reduction in the discharge of industrial waste would undoubtedly lead to much cleaner air.

A reduction in the discharge of industrial waste may be financed by the company itself, the local population, society in general or by all three categories on a joint basis. In order to establish whether a further reduction in air pollution is desirable, it is essential to examine the effect of cleaner air on the welfare of the local population. One measure of this improvement in welfare is the maximum amount that an individual is willing to pay in order to receive a given improvement in visibility, provided that the local population and local companies are themselves required to meet a substantial share of the costs involved. In this study, we are interested in finding out how *individuals* themselves evaluate the advantages of cleaner air. Let us assume that it is possible to halve the number of days of type (A) and instead have a level of visibility approximating to type (B). It is further assumed that a proportion of the expenditure on the reduction of air pollution is financed jointly by means of a general income tax on all income-earners in the district. It is not easy to determine in advance the actual level of expenditure required by these improvement measures.

Would they themselves be prepared to pay ( ) per cent of their income towards such a project in the coming years if all of the other income-earners in the area were also prepared to do the same thing? It should be noted that a 1 per cent tax for an individual who earns 100,000 NEK per annum is equivalent to 1,000 NEK per annum or 2.70 NEK per day. Similarly a 5 per cent tax is equivalent to 5,000 NEK per annum or 13.70 NEK per day.

This question was the first one in a series of questions. The highest tax increase accepted by the respondent was considered to be his bid (CV). In order to be able to address the instrument bias issue, different parts of the sample were confronted with different starting bids and/or sequences of bids, e.g. the bid was raised from 1 per cent to 3 per cent to 5 per cent or, say, directly from 3 per cent to 5 per cent. The choice of starting bids was based on results obtained when testing the survey instrument on a small sample.

Subsamples S1 and S2 answered question Q2 while subsample S3 in addition was asked the following question.

Q3 Let us assume that further measures are taken to reduce air pollution. As a result the number of days where visibility corresponds to type A were reduced by half. The new improved situation is depicted by photograph C. Such measures would be more expensive than those first envisaged. Would they be prepared to pay additional taxation of ( ) per cent in order to obtain this additional reduction in air pollution?

Table 7.1   *Willingness to pay as per cent of annual income for an improved air quality in the Grenland area*

Tax (%)	Sequence of pictures (subsample)				
	AB (S3)	BC (S2)	AC (S1)	BC|AB (S3)	AB+BC (S3)
0	59	60	59	77	58
0.5–6	41	40	41	23	40
7–8	0	0	0	0	2
Average tax (%)	1.0	0.9	0.9	0.3	1.3
No. of observations	334	336	334	334	334

The results are summed up in Table 7.1. It is noteworthy that around 60 per cent of the respondents are not willing to pay at all for an improved air quality in the area. None in the sample was willing to pay more than 8 per cent of his annual income. The average willingness to pay for a change from A to C is 0.9 per cent for subsample S1 and 1.3 per cent for subsample S3. In relation to these results three points can be made.

Firstly, the willingness to pay of subsample S2 for an improvement from B to C exceeds the corresponding willingness to pay of subsample S3. A possible reason is that the latter sample already has 'paid' for an improvement from A to B. That is, the change from B to C is evaluated conditional on the change from A to B. This should reduce the willingness to pay, a hypothesis that is confirmed by the results presented in Table 7.1. This can also be seen by noting that for subsample S2, Hylland and Strand in fact calculate the following individual compensating variation measure:

$$CV(BC) = e(\mathbf{p}, z^B, U^B) - e(\mathbf{p}, z^C, U^B) \qquad (7.1)$$

where a superscript B (C) denotes the initial (final) level of pollution z. The corresponding measure for subsample S3 reads as follows:

$$CV(BC|AB) = e(\mathbf{p}, z^B, U^A) - e(\mathbf{p}, z^C, U^A) \qquad (7.2)$$

If air quality is a 'normal' public good, then the CV in (7.1) exceeds the one in (7.2) since utility level B is higher than utility level A; compare Figure 6.4 in Chapter 6. As a comparison of columns 2 and 4 in Table 7.1 reveals, this is also the result obtained by Hylland and Strand.

Secondly, one would expect the compensating variation of a shift from A to C to be independent of the particular path chosen. Table 7.1 shows that this is not the case in the Hylland–Strand study. Those who were asked to compare A and C are on average willing to pay 0.9 per cent, while those who were confronted with a shift from A to B and then from B to C are prepared to pay 1.3 per cent for an improvement from A to C. Unfortunately, there seems to be no simple or straightforward interpretation of this bias. The reader may suspect that the bias is due to the fact that the CV measure fails to correctly rank certain changes, as was discussed in Chapter 6. Fortunately, this is not the source of the bias. This can be checked by defining CV measures for the changes from A to B and from A to C, respectively, and invoking equations (7.1) and (7.2). Possibly, however, some individuals may not have fully understood the conditional assumption invoked in question Q3 and therefore overestimate their willingness to pay for the improvement from B to C.

Thirdly, as mentioned earlier, the instrument bias issue was addressed by Hylland and Strand. It turns out that the final bids are influenced by the magnitude of the starting bids. For example, given a starting bid of 1 per cent, the average willingness to pay is 0.6 per cent. Those who were confronted with a starting bid of 3 or 5 per cent, on the other hand, are prepared to pay more than 1 per cent. The starting point bias problem can be avoided by allowing the individual to specify a maximum willingness to pay, instead of giving one of two responses, yes or no, to a sequence of bids. Alternatively, the respondent is confronted with a single bid which he has to accept or reject; but different subsamples are offered (asked to pay) different amounts of money. In fact, Hylland and Strand also use a variation of this latter closed-ended approach, as is illustrated below. The problem, however, is that there is some empirical evidence which indicates that the open-ended method provides significantly lower estimates of average willingness to pay than the closed-ended approach. See Seller *et al.* (1985) for a discussion of this issue, and Boyle *et al.* (1985) for a detailed examination of the starting point bias issue.

Next, let us turn to the aggregation issue. Hylland and Strand use two methods to obtain the total annual willingness to pay for clean air. If the estimates obtained for the various subsamples are consistent estimates of the corresponding population values, the total willingness to pay is easily calculated by multiplying the estimates by the appropriate raising factors. Using this approach, Hylland and Strand find that the adult population in the Grenland area is willing to pay 35–50 million Norwegian crowns a year for the change from air quality level A to air quality level C.

Hylland and Strand suggest another way to arrive at an aggregate willingness to pay. In particular, they want to get rid of the starting point bias problem. Therefore, they exploit the fact that not all respondents were confronted with the same starting bid when answering question Q2. Three different starting bid levels, 1, 3, and 5 per cent, were used. Hylland and Strand begin by estimating the proportion of yes answers on

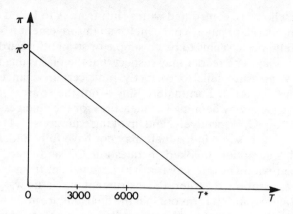

Figure 7.2 The frequency of yes answers on the starting bid as a function of the magnitude of the starting bid

the starting bid as a linear function of the tax corresponding to the starting bid and various other independent variables. For example, the following equation was obtained:

$$\pi = 25 +0.01y - 4.3T \qquad (7.3)$$
$$\quad (18.2) \qquad (29.1)$$

where π is the proportion (%) yes answers on the starting bid, y is household income, T is the tax corresponding to the starting bid (in thousands of Norwegian crowns), and F-statistics are shown in parentheses. For any given y, the relationship is the one depicted in Figure 7.2. Integrating between zero and T^* yields a measure of the expected willingness to pay, i.e. area $0-\pi^0-T^*$. Intuitively, each tax amount is multiplied by the probability that the respondent accepts that he should pay this particular amount of money to secure clean air. Summing (integrating) the resulting weighted amounts, one obtains the expected willingness to pay. Finally, multiplying by the number (in hundreds) of adults in the area yields an estimate of the total willingness to pay for clean air in the area. See Sections 6 and 7 of Chapter 8 for further discussion of this kind of approach to the estimation of consumer surplus measures.

Hylland and Strand argue that there can hardly be any starting point bias if only the frequency of yes answers on the starting bid is used. What the magnitude of the starting bid can affect is the size of the final bid accepted. Nevertheless, there is the problem that there are no observations far to the right in Figure 7.2. Recall that there are only three different starting bids. For this reason, and to obtain 'conservative' estimates, Hylland and Strand (arbitrarily) assume that the willingness to pay is zero for taxes exceeding 6,000 and 3,000 crowns respectively. This reduces the total willingness to pay from about 100 million crowns to 95 and 60 million crowns respectively. Still, however, these figures are much above the one, i.e. 35–50 million crowns, obtained when using the traditional aggregation procedure. Hylland and Strand suggest that the latter procedure is the most appropriate one if there is no starting point bias. On the other hand, in the presence of such bias the approach illustrated in Figure 7.2 may be the appropriate one. This applies at least where it can be assumed that the respondents do not systematically misrepresent their preferences when accepting or rejecting the starting bid.

The total willingness to pay

In order to arrive at an estimate of the total benefits of clean air in the Grenland area, it is necessary to specify a time horizon. Recall that question Q2 requires the respondent to pay the accepted bid during an unspecified number of years. Unfortunately, there is no accepted theoretic foundation or even rule of thumb for the choice of time horizon. Moreover, in general, future benefits and costs must be discounted since a consumer must normally receive a positive minimum compensation before he will postpone a dollar's worth of consumption in a period. Hylland and Strand use a time horizon of 20 years and calculate present values given discount rates of 5 per cent, 10 per cent, and 15 per cent. In this way, they find that 400 million crowns is a reasonable lower bound for the present value of the willingness to pay of the adult population in the Grenland area. Adding to this amount, the 600 million crowns that those living in other parts of the country may be willing to pay, the total benefits of clean air (a change from situation A to situation C) amounts to at least 1 billion crowns. Provided the unknown cost of cleaning the air falls short of this amount of money, the suggested improvement is worthwhile for society. At least this would be the case provided that we can simply add individual benefits and costs, regardless of the distribution of income/welfare between individuals.

In any case, the results reported here illustrate that it is far from a trivial matter to construct a survey instrument. Even though surveys, and the contingent valuation approach in particular, are widely applied, questions obviously remain about the appropriate method of asking the central valuation question.

3 *Hedonic prices*

There has been a growing interest in using property values as a source of information on the benefits of controlling environmental disamenities. The idea is that differences in environmental quality variables are reflected in housing sale prices. The most popular approach is probably the hedonic price technique developed by Griliches (1971) and Rosen (1974). This is a method that is used to estimate the implicit prices of the characteristics which differentiate closely related products. Closely following Freeman (1979a; 1979b), suppose any unit h of housing can be completely described by j locational, K neighbourhood and m environmental characteristics. Then the price of this housing unit is a function of these characteristics:

$$P_h = f_h(S_{h1}, \ldots, S_{hj}, N_{h1}, \ldots, N_{hK}, Z_{h1}, \ldots, Z_{hm}) \quad \text{for all } h \qquad (7.4)$$

where S denotes locational, N neighbourhood and Z environmental characteristics. This is the hedonic or implicit price function.

In fact, this function is a locus of household equilibrium marginal willingnesses to pay. In order to illustrate this, let us write the utility maximization problem of a representative household in the following way:

$$\max_{a} U(\mathbf{x}, \mathbf{S}, \mathbf{N}, \mathbf{Z})$$

$$\text{s.t. } y = \mathbf{px} + h(\mathbf{S}, \mathbf{N}, \mathbf{Z}) \qquad (7.5)$$

where $\mathbf{a} = (\mathbf{x}, \mathbf{S}, \mathbf{N}, \mathbf{Z})$, all variables are assumed to be continuous, and $c = h(\ )$ is rent or periodic cost of housing corresponding to P_h in equation (7.4). This simple form of modelling the problem is sufficient for our limited purposes, although the model is not necessarily in each respect the one underlying equation (7.4).

By examining the first-order conditions associated with an interior solution to this utility maximization problem, it can be easily verified that the marginal implicit prices (e.g. $\partial h/\partial Z_m$), associated with the housing bundle actually chosen must be equal to the correpsonding marginal willingness to pay ($\partial U/\partial Z_m \lambda$) for those characteristics. Inserting the optimal levels of S, N and Z into the rent function yields the rent paid by the utility maximizing household. This explains that equation (7.4) is interpreted as a locus of household equilibrium marginal willingnesses to pay.

Suppose that a (non-linear) version of (7.4) has been estimated for housing in an area. The coefficient(s) for the partial derivative with respect to environmental characteristic Z_m

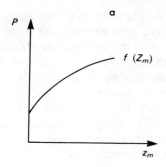

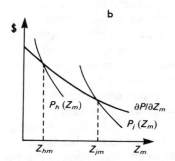

Figure 7.3 (a) the partial relationship between P_h and Z_m; (b) the marginal implicit price of Z_m and the inverse demand curves for two households

$$\frac{\partial P}{\partial Z_m} = f_z(Z_m) \qquad (7.6)$$

where constant characteristics have been suppressed, indicates the increase in (equilibrium) expenditure on housing that is required to obtain a house with one more unit of Z_m (see Figure 7.3). As can be seen from Figure 7.3b, each household chooses a location where its marginal willingness to pay for Z_m is equated with the marginal implicit price of Z_m.

The question is if (7.6) can be interpreted as an inverse demand function for Z_m. The answer is positive if all households have identical utility functions and incomes. These assumptions ensure that all individuals have identical demand functions, implying that all observations in Figure 7.3b must lie on the same (inverse) demand curve.

If individuals are not alike, the supply side of the housing market must be considered. If the supply of houses with given bundles of characteristics is perfectly elastic, then the implicit price of a characteristic is exogenous to the individual household. Since we can observe Z_m for each household and the implicit price can be calculated from (7.6), a regression of observed quantities of Z_m against implicit prices and other independent variables, such as income and other socioeconomic characteristics, should identify the demand function for Z_m.

On the other hand, if the supply of a characteristic is fixed, individuals can be viewed as bidding for the characteristic in question. Then, we can use (7.6) to calculate the implicit price paid by each household, and regress this variable on observed quantities of Z_m and various socioeconomic variables. As a result, the inverse demand curves for different households do not generally coincide, implying that (7.6) cannot be interpreted as an inverse demand curve unless households are identical in every respect. This is illustrated in Figure 7.3b, where the marginal willingness to pay curves of two different households are drawn.

In the intermediate case, where supply adjusts, but not infinitely rapidly, a simultaneous equation approach must be used. Hence, we must specify equations for the supply side as well as for the demand side, and estimate these simultaneously.

Thus no simple conclusion emerges, apart from the possibly trivial one that in empirical studies using the property value approach, one must carefully examine the supply side of the housing market. Nevertheless, once the (inverse) demand function has been estimated, the area under the demand curve between two values of the characteristic determines the change in uncompensated consumer surplus caused by a changed quantity of the characteristic. Adding across households yields the aggregate change in consumer surplus. However, the (lack of) proportionality between this measure and the underlying utility changes is the usual one described in the previous chapters.

4 *A property value study*

In order to illustrate how property values can be used to derive willingness to pay measures for environmental quality, this section summarizes a study by Brookshire *et al.* (1981) that analysed the housing market within a sample plan of communities of the South Coast Air Basin in Southern California. Specifically, Brookshire *et al.* considered whether households actually pay for cleaner air through higher property values for homes in clean air communities.

The data base contains information on 719 owner-occupied single-family residences in 14 communities sold in the January 1977–March

Table 7.2 *Variables used in analysis of housing market*

Variable	Definition (assumed effect on housing sale price)	Units	Econometric equation
Dependent			
Sale Price	Sale price of owner occupied single family residences.	($1,000)	
Independent-Housing			
Sale Date	Month in which the home was sold (positive, indicator of inflation).	January 1977=1 March 1978=15	0.018 (10.1)
Age	Age of home (negative, indicator of obsolesence and quality of structure).	Years	−0.003 (−3.5)
Bathrooms	Number of bathrooms (positive, indicator of quality).	Number	0.148 (9.3)
Living Area	Living area (positive, indicator of the quantity of home).	Square feet	0.000 (14.0)
Pool	Zero–one variable which indicates the presence of a pool (positive, indicator of quality).	Zero=no pool One=pool	0.090 (4.2)
Fireplaces	Number of fireplaces (positive, indicator of quality).	Number	−0.104 (7.8)
Independent-Neighborhood			
Distance to Beach	Distance to the nearest beach (negative, indicator or relative proximity to main recreational activity).	Miles	−0.014 (−9.1)
School Quality	School quality as measured by student percentile scores on the California Assessment Test-12th grade math. (positive).	Percentile ×100	0.001 (2.0)
Ethnic	Ethnic composition – percent white in census tract(s) which contain sample community (positive).	Percent ×100	0.008 (1.3)
Population Density	Population density in surrounding census tract (negative, indicator of crowding).	People per square mile	−0.000 (−7.8)
Housing Density	Housing density in surrounding Census tract (negative, indicator of crowding).	Houses per square mile	
Distance to Employment	Weighted distances to eight employment centers in the South Coast Air Basin (negative indicator of proximity to employment).	Miles/Employment Density	−0.270 (−11.7)
NO$_2$	Nitrogen dioxide concentrations.	Parts per hundred million (pphm)	−0.001 (−2.7)
TSP	Concentrations of total suspended particulates.	Micrograms per cubic meter (μg/m^3)	—
Independent-Community			
Public Safety Expenditures	Expenditures on public safety per capita (positive, indicator of attempt to stop criminal activity).	$/People	0.000 (5.1)
Crime	Local crime rates (negative, indicator of peoples' perception of danger).	Crime/People	−2.280 (−2.4)
Tax	Community tax rate (negative, measurers cost of local public services.	$/$1,000 of home value	−0.031 (−1.8)

Source: Brookshire *et al.* (1981) pp. 157–8, 164.

1978 time period. Table 7.2 contains a detailed description of the data employed in the study (and a regression equation to be discussed below). Needless to say, housing data of such quality are rarely available for studies of this nature. Usually only aggregated data, i.e. census tract averages, are available. The Brookshire *et al.* study therefore gives an idea of what can be but is not usually achieved using housing market data.

The study encompasses two separate but related approaches. The first approach involves a comparison of average housing values in pairs of communities, standardizing only for house size. Provided the variation between pairs of houses is minimal with respect to all characteristics other than air quality, any sale price differential will reflect individual willingness to pay for clean air. The second approach, which is reported here, uses a multistep econometric procedure, originally developed by Harrison and Rubinfeld (1978), which allows air pollution abatement to be valued differently by households.

The first step in this approach is to estimate a hedonic housing value equation of the kind stated in (7.4). It turned out that non-linear functional forms perform somewhat better than the linear form, at least if measured by R^2. One of the estimated equations, with the logarithm of home sale price as dependent variable and based on 719 observations, is shown in the final column of Table 7.2. All coefficients have the expected signs, and all, except ethnic composition, are statistically significant at the 5 per cent level; *t*-statistics are shown in parentheses in the table. Note that Brookshire *et al.* include the squared pollution term (and the logarithm of taxes). It was found that this formulation performed (insignificantly) better than either the first-order or cubic terms.

It is important to note that this regression equation is a locus of equilibrium values. By inserting, the actual values of the various independent variables for any home in the sample, one should derive, at least in theory, the actual sale price of that home. Thus, the considered regression equation cannot be used to directly identify the individual's valuation of changes in air pollution. Recall the discussion in Section 3.

The second step is to calculate the marginal willingness to pay for improved air quality of the average household in each community. Taking the partial derivative of the regression equation in Table 7.2 with respect to the air pollution variable, i.e. the concentration of nitrogen dioxide, yields the (negative of) marginal willingness to pay for a change in NO_2. Since the formulation in Table 7.2 assumes a non-linear relationship, i.e. is of the form

$$\ell n\, P = a + bZ^2 + \ldots \tag{7.7}$$

where Z is the nitrogen dioxide concentration, the magnitude of $\partial P/\partial Z$ ($=2bPZ$) depends on the level of all independent variables. Thus, the marginal willingness to pay for improved air quality varies between communities. Brookshire *et al.* calculate community specific values by assigning to the variables their community mean values.

The third step is to regress the marginal willingness to pay variable on community average income and pollution levels. This procedure should make it possible to identify an inverse demand function. Thus, Brookshire *et al.* treat the supply of houses with given bundles of characteristics as fixed. Recall the discussion in Section 3. Linear as well as log-log forms were estimated. The linear formulation, based upon the 14 community observations, yields the following result:

$$MWP = -1601 + 0.05y + 162.7Z \quad R^2 = 0.86 \tag{7.8}$$
$$(8.3) \quad (3.8)$$

where MWP is marginal willingness to pay in dollars, y is community income, and t-statistics are shown in parentheses. Varying Z with income fixed identifies an inverse demand curve for improved air quality.

The final step is to integrate (7.8) between initial and final pollution levels, assigning the income variable its mean value, to obtain

$$\int MWP dZ = (-1601 + 0.05\bar{y})\triangle Z + \frac{162.7(Z_1^2 - Z_0^2)}{2} \tag{7.8'}$$

where a subscript refers to a particular pollution level, $\triangle Z = Z_1 - Z_0$, and $\bar{y}$ is average community income. Brookshire *et al.* find that an improvement in air quality from poor to fair is valued at $5,800 per home.[2] The value which corresponds to the fair-good change is $4200. The total benefits for the total number of affected homes are around $10 billion. In annual terms, total benefits amount to $0.95 billion, which corresponds to $510 per home. These figures are much lower than those obtained by a comparison of average housing values in a pair of communities, standardizing only for house size. In other words, the latter approach probably attributes to the environmental variable a willingness to pay, which in part is due to other variables than air quality.

Equation (7.8') is an uncompensated money measure of utility change. In order to get an idea of the magnitude of the relative error when an uncompensated measure is used instead of CV or EV, Willig's formula, as defined in equation (4.13) of Chapter 4, can be used. Since air quality is a public good, the income elasticity η in Willig's formula should be replaced by the price flexibility of income, which, using (7.8) is defined as $\epsilon = (\partial MWP/\partial y)(y/MWP)$ when the consumer has y units of money to spend on other goods. Since the price flexibility seems to be rather close to one, assuming that the (unreported) average household income is $35,000, to a first approximation the error is less than 1 per cent ($-510/2 \times 35,000$). For convenient reference, we state, without proof, the following more exact error bound formula:

$$A \geqslant [(1+(1-\epsilon_U)\frac{S}{y^0})^{1/(1-\epsilon_U)} - 1 - \frac{S}{y^0}]\frac{y^0}{|S|} \tag{7.9}$$

where $A = (CV - S)/|S|$, $|S|$ is the absolute value of the ordinary money measure, and ϵ_U is the calculated upper bound on ϵ. Replacing ϵ_U by the lower bound ϵ_L reverses the inequality (7.9), i.e. yields an upper bound, instead of a lower bound, of the percentage error in using S to approximate CV. By reversing the signs of the terms $(1-\epsilon)$ and S/y a formula is obtained for the percentage error in estimating EV. See Cornwall (1984, pp. 634–5) for a derivation of (7.9) and a correction of an error in Randall and Stoll (1980). These formulas can be used for public goods as well as rationed private goods.

In interpreting the results reported by Brookshire *et al.* it should also be noted that they ignore the effect of real property and income taxation on property values. The sign of the net effect of ignoring taxation in calculating benefits is generally ambiguous, as is shown in Freeman (1979a). Nevertheless, a properly conducted study should account for the effects of taxation.

Brookshire *et al.* estimate separate equations for the nitrogen dioxide and total suspended particulate variables. The reason for not including both pollutants in one and the same regression equation is collinearity in the data set. Multicollinearity among attributes is, beside specification errors, one of the most serious problems in the estimation of implicit prices. Multicollinearity, while not resulting in biased estimates, can be the source of wrongly signed coefficients. It should also be mentioned that Halvorsen and Pollakowski (1981) have developed a general 'quadratic Box–Cox functional form' for hedonic price equations which incorporates, as special cases, the functional forms that are normally used in empirical hedonic analyses (linear, log-linear, semi-log, etc; see the informative table in Freeman (1979a, pp. 156–60) for the key features of a number of air pollution–property value studies). However, although a study may make proper use of the Box and Cox (1964) technique to estimate hedonic regressions, it is not unusual that the ordinary least squares procedure is used in order to find the maximum likelihood estimates of the regression coefficients. For example, this seems to be the case in the study by Brookshire *et al.* (1981). However, they do not report the actual method of estimation or indeed the general approach that has been adopted. Spitzer (1982) has shown that OLS estimates of coefficient variances are biased downwards, thereby yielding t-statistics for individual parameters which have an upward bias in absolute terms. Since importance is usually attached to the significance of individual site characteristics, the estimation of accurate t-statistics for indivdiual parameters is crucial. (See Blackley *et al.* (1984) for details and some empirical evidence of the magnitude of the bias of OLS variances.)

In addition, Brown and Rosen (1982) have stressed that one will fail to identify the structural demand functions, i.e. (7.8), unless prior, possibly arbitrary, restrictions on functional form are imposed or marginal prices are estimated from equations fitted separately for spatially distinct markets. For example, the reader can easily verify that if (7.7) is replaced by the price function $P = a + bZ^2$, then estimation of (7.8) would be meaningless. Brookshire *et al.* (1981) avoid estimating an identity by choosing such a functional form that the marginal price function for Z, obtained from (7.7), cannot be expressed as some exact combination of the arguments of (7.8).

In sum, this section has demonstrated that households' aggregate benefits from a public good, in this case clean air, can be measured indirectly from market data. In the cases where property values are available, the property value approach is of great importance because it is much less expensive than the survey method (but see Mäler (1977) for a critical assessment of the property value method). The main drawback of the property value method is the fact that property values are of no relevance when dealing with many types of public goods, i.e. national parks, endangered species, nationwide acid rains, and so on. Moreover, a comparison of money measures of utility change calculated from property values and those measures obtained by other methods still requires to be carried out. This important issue is addressed in the next section.

5 *A comparison of survey and hedonic approaches*

In a recent study Brookshire *et al.* (1982) report on an experiment designed to validate the survey approach by direct comparison to the hedonic property value study presented in the previous section. The Los Angeles metropolitan area was chosen for the experiment because of the well-defined air pollution problem and because of the existence of detailed property value data.

Brookshire *et al.* (1982) start from a simple theoretical model in order to obtain testable hypotheses regarding the sign of the difference between the marginal willingness to pay from survey responses and the rent differential associated with air quality improvement from hedonic analysis of property value data.

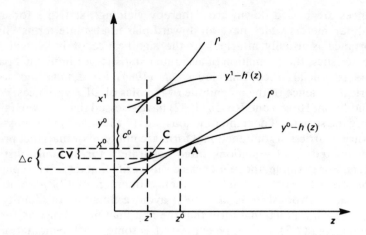

Figure 7.4 The relationship between the rent differential $\triangle c$ and the marginal willingness to pay CV for improved air quality
Source: Brookshire *et al.* (1982, p. 168)

Consider a household which acts as if it maximizes utility

$$U = U(x, z) \tag{7.10}$$

subject to the budget constraint

$$y - px - h(z) = 0 \tag{7.11}$$

where x is a composite good, z is the level of air pollution, and $c = h(z)$ is rent or periodic cost of housing. It is assumed that $\partial U/\partial x > 0$, while $\partial U/\partial z$, $\partial h/\partial z < 0$. This latter assumption means that lower rents will be paid for homes in more polluted areas.

Figure 7.4 illustrates, graphically, the solution of this maximization problem. Given income y^0, the household would maximize utility at point A along indifference curve I^0, choosing to locate at pollution level z^0, consume x^0, and pay rent c^0. If income increases to y^1 the household would relocate, choosing point B on indifference curve I^1, at a lower pollution level z^1 with higher consumption x^1.

The household in equilibrium at point A in the figure was asked how much x it would forgo to experience z^1 rather than z^0 while maintaining the same utility level. Since the household is indifferent between points A and C it would be willing to pay CV dollars to achieve the considered reduction in air pollution.

The hedonic rent gradients $h(z)$ themselves only provide point estimates of the marginal rates of substitution between pollution and other goods for individuals with possibly differing preferences and income. However, the change in rent $\triangle c$ between locations with air quality levels z^0 and z^1 in Figure 7.4, must for any household located at point A be no less than the bid CV. This can be checked by using the second-order conditions for utility maximization. Note that the rent gradient $h(z)$ need not be strictly concave or convex, but must lie below the relevant indifference curve.

Brookshire *et al.* (1982) go on to show that the above result, i.e. $\triangle c \geqslant CV$, holds even in the case of multiple housing attributes, e.g. attributes such as the square footage of the home, number of bathrooms, fireplaces, and neighbourhood characteristics (compare equation (7.5) in Section 3). Thus, their first hypothesis for testing the validity of the survey technique is: for each household in a community, $\triangle c \geqslant CV$. In turn this implies that the average rent differential across households $\triangle \bar{c}$, must be at least as large as the average willingness to pay $\bar{CV}$ for an improvement in air quality. The second hypothesis formulated by Brookshire *et al.* (1982) is that, given the political history of air pollution control in the State of California, mean bids in each community are non-negative, i.e. $\bar{CV} \geqslant 0$, although, to a European, this seems to be quite a superfluous hypothesis.

An hedonic rent gradient was estimated in accordance with the approach summarized in Section 4. Housing sale price is assumed to be a function of housing structure variables, neighbourhood variables, accessibility variables, and air quality as measured by total suspended particulates or nitrogen dioxide. Implicit or hedonic prices for each attribute are then determined by examining housing prices and attribute levels. Recall Table 7.2 in Section 4 of this chapter.

The survey approach followed the works summarized in Sections 1 and 2 of this chapter. The hypothetical market was defined and described both in technical and institutional detail. Air quality was described by the survey instrument to the respondent in terms of easily perceived levels of provision such as visual range through photographs and maps depicting good, fair, and poor air quality levels over the region. The respondent was asked to react to alternative price levels posited for different air quality levels. Payment mechanisms were either of the lump-sum variety, or well-specified schemes such as tax increments or utility bill additions.

Brookshire *et al.* (1982) tested the two specified hypothesis, i.e. $\triangle \bar{c} \geqslant \bar{CV}$ and $\bar{CV} \geqslant 0$, using the *t*-statistic. The hypotheses tests indicate that the empirical analysis is entirely consistent with the theoretical structure given by equations (7.10) and (7.11). However, the results, like those reported by Bishop and Heberlein (1979), indicate that survey estimates of willingness to pay might be biased downward by about 50 per cent. Nevertheless, in situations where market data for hedonic analysis is difficult to acquire, the survey approach is preferable to no information at all on which to base the decision-making process. In particular this is the case when the (underestimated) benefits exceed the costs.

6 *Utility functions and demand equations*

Another approach sometimes used in order to estimate the valuation of public goods/bads is to assume that the utility functions take a particular form and estimate complete demand systems. Recently, McMillan (1979) has used the translog utility function to establish a system of demand equations for housing characteristics.[3] In a sense, however, McMillan's approach consists of two steps. Households first decide on how much they will allocate to housing and then they decide on the combination of housing characteristics they want to acquire. Hedonic prices are used to create a system of budget share equations for housing characteristics so that the demand for environmental characteristics can be estimated within the housing budget constraint.

Assuming a Cobb–Douglas utility function within each considered income group, Polinsky and Rubinfeld (1975) estimate willingness to pay for changes in air quality. However, as noted in Chapter 4, once a particular form of utility function is assumed, the change in utility can be calculated directly, i.e. it seems superfluous to estimate money measures which in general are not proportional to the change in utility.

In order to illustrate this point, and also some of the methods discussed in Chapter 6, a recent study by Shapiro and Smith (1981) is described. They applied a slightly different method than that of Bradford–Hildebrandt–Mäler–Willig, described in Section 5 of Chapter 6, to data characterizing 28 counties in the southern half of California and obtained implicit prices for four 'environmental' goods: rainfall, temperature, public expenditures, and pollution.

The specification of the indirect utility function used by Shapiro and Smith (1981) is similar to the translog function, except that variables are not taken in their log form

$$V\left(\frac{\mathbf{p}}{y}, \mathbf{z}\right) = -\sum_i \alpha_i \hat{p}_i - \sum_i \sum_j \beta_{ij} \hat{p}_i \hat{p}_j - \sum_i \sum_k \gamma_{ik} \hat{p}_i z_k \qquad (7.12)$$

where $\hat{p}_i = p_i/y$, and z_k denotes an environmental quality variable ($k = 1, \ldots, m$). Using (7.12), assuming $\beta_{ij} = \beta_{ji} = 0$ for all i and j, which makes preferences homothetic in the market commodities, one can easily derive expenditure share equations

$$\frac{p_i x_i}{y} = (\alpha_i p_i + \sum_k p_i \gamma_{ik} z_k)/(\sum_j \alpha_j p_j + \sum_j \sum_k \gamma_{jk} p_j z_k) \tag{7.13}$$

Estimation of this expenditure share system (or the demand equations) yield parameter values that may be used to calculate the implicit prices of environmental quality variables

$$\frac{(\partial V/\partial z_k)}{V_y} = \sum_i \gamma_{ik} p_i / \sum_j (\alpha_j p_j + \sum_k \gamma_{jk} p_j z_k) \tag{7.14}$$

Hence, the calculation of the implicit prices depends only upon the parameters that are able to be estimated using the expenditure share system (7.13). The estimation of the prices of environmental goods was carried out in two stages using maximum likelihood techniques. Firstly, parameter estimates were obtained from $(n-1$ of$)$ the market share equations (7.13). Secondly, these estimates were used to estimate the prices of environmental goods using equations (7.14). Obviously, however, the parameter estimates can also be used to estimate the indirect utility function, and hence, can be used to calculate the change in utility of changes in prices, income and environmental goods.

In spite of the use of extremely aggregated data, e.g. only three classes of private goods, were employed to estimate the implicit prices, Shapiro and Smith found several indications that the analysis might be on the right track (see Shapiro and Smith, 1981, pp. 116–19). Moreover, the technique has the advantage of being able to be carried out with less expense than any other except the traditional hedonic price technique.

7 *The travel cost method*

The services of a recreation site are usually provided at a low price. Although this is efficient in the absence of congestion, it makes estimation of demand functions difficult. However, every user pays a price measured by his travel costs. Suppose the estimated relationship between visit rates x and travel cost p is given by $x = x(p)$. Then the change in consumers' surplus resulting from, say, a polluted stream which is cleaned up to permit its use for sport fishing is

$$S = -\sum_j n_j \int_{p_j^0}^{p_j^1} x(p)dp \tag{7.15}$$

where n_j is the population in zone j, p_j^0 is the travel cost for fishing trips from zone j to streams situated farther away, and p_j^1 is the new travel cost. This method, proposed by Hotelling in a letter in 1947, was first

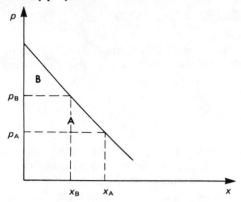

Figure 7.5 Illustration of the travel cost method

used by Clawson (1959). For a recent application of the method to the problem of valuing a day's fishing, the reader is referred to Vaughan and Russell (1982).

The basic idea of the approach is illustrated in Figure 7.5. Suppose, for simplicity, that there is a single stream that can be reached by individuals living in the considered area. The number of trips originating from zone A, expressed as a percentage of the total population living in the zone, is x_A. The average travel cost for these fishing trips is $\$p_A$. From zone B, which is situated farther away from the stream than zone A, x_B trips per capita are recorded. The average travel cost amounts to $\$p_B$. Given a number of such observations, a distance decay equation for fishing trips, like the one in Figure 7.5, can be estimated with travel costs and, say, socioeconomic characteristics as independent variables. A fisherman from zone A earns a consumer surplus equal to area A+B per trip. Multiplying by the number of trips from the zone yields the total consumers' surplus accruing to zone A. Similarly, multiplying area B in the figure by the number of visits from zone B gives the consumers surplus assigned to zone B. Summing all zones, one obtains a measure of total consumer surplus. Figure 7.5 can also be used to derive a demand curve for fishing. First, by assumption, the actual number of fishing trips is known. Second, introduce an admission fee and assume that fishermen respond to an increased fee in the same way as they, according to Figure 7.5, respond to an increased travel cost. That is, if the fee increases from zero to $\$(p_B - p_A)$ per fisherman, the proportion of the zone A population travelling to the stream falls from x_A to x_B, and so on. Summing all zones, a point on the demand curve is derived. Other points on the curve are found by further variations in the entry fee.

It should also be observed that the quality change measure (6.14) in the previous chapter is useful here. This is the case at least if fishing trips are a non-essential commodity. In this situation, we simply interpret x_i in equation (6.14) of Chapter 6 as the number of fishing trips to the stream under consideration, p_i as the travel cost, and z_i as a measure of the degree of pollution of the stream. We are thus equipped with a willingness to pay measure of quality changes which can, at least in principle, be calculated on the basis of market (travel costs) data. The reader is also referred to Bowes and Loomis (1980) who use the expenditure function to show that an increase in travel costs is equivalent to an increase in entry prices provided fishing trips are a non-essential commodity.

The remainder of this section is devoted to a presentation of a recent application of the simple or pure travel cost method. In March 1983 it was suggested that a Nature Reserve, protected from forest harvesting, be created in the Vålå Valley (the V Valley for short) in Northern Sweden. A conflict arose between the Swedish Forest Service, on the one hand, and tourism, nature conservation, and reindeer husbandry interests, on the other. In particular, the Swedish Nature Conservation Movement, supported by quite a few researchers within the field, argued that reforestation is impossible in mountainous areas such as the V Valley. In such areas, cutting may cause more or less irreversible damage to the environment. For this reason, the Swedish Environment Protection Agency initiated a social cost–benefit analysis of the two considered development scenarios. This section briefly presents one particular part of the study, namely a travel cost approach to the estimation of the environmental values involved (see Bojö, 1985, for a full presentation of the results).

The V Valley is an attractive area for tourism, in particular for skiing activities. A total of 282 households were interviewed while visiting the Valley during February to April in 1985. Separate surveys were directed at the local population and local commercial interests, but these will not be reported here.

The sample of respondents was not chosen randomly from the population of visitors since such an approach turned out to be impossible to use from a practical point of view. Instead, the selection of respondents was governed by the possibility of contact with adult visitors. The survey was carried out during the second part of each week selected for the study. Most visitors stay one full week, thus they are quite familiar with the area by the end of the week. The survey instrument, directed at the visitors, consists of six parts: a written introduction presenting the study; a map of the county showing the Nature Reserve; a questionnaire to be filled in by the respondent; a large map of the Nature Reserve, where forests and potential cutting areas are marked in clear colours; a commentary to the map, explaining how the proposed cutting activities will affect different parts of the reserve; and a personal interview to locate the willingness to pay for a preservation of the area.

Since our concern is with the travel cost method, we will focus on the questionnaire filled in by the respondents. The questionnaire covered, for example, the following subjects: home area, means of travel, travel costs, length of stay, main activities during the stay, valuation of the trip to the area as well as the area itself, alternative recreation sites, and disposable household income. Using this information, estimates were made of the following function:

$$H_i = f(p_i, y_i, s_i, D_i) \tag{7.16}$$

where H_i is the number of visitors from zone i, expressed as a proportion of the total number of inhabitants in that zone, p_i is travel costs per household from the origin zone to the V Valley and return, y_i is average disposable household income in zone i, s_i is an index of alternative recreation sites, and D_i is a dummy variable referring to transportation mode. Each of these variables will be briefly discussed in turn.

The numbers H_i were calculated in several steps. Firstly, the respondents were stratified according to home county. Secondly, it was assumed that the distribution of the sample of visitors by home county does not significantly deviate from the corresponding distribution of the total population of visitors during a typical year. Given information on the total number of visitors, it is then a relatively simple matter to calculate the number of visitors from county i as a proportion of the population in that county.

The V Valley can be reached by car, train, bus, and aeroplane. As only a couple of the respondents had come by bus or aeroplane, they had to be excluded from the study since the results would have been too unreliable if these visitors had been included. Furthermore, sportsmen and business men whose trips were not paid by themselves were excluded (although these may earn a 'rent' during their stay). Multiple site visitors were also excluded due to the joint cost problem, i.e. the problem to allocate the travel costs between the different sites.

In order to calculate the travel costs of those visitors travelling by car or train, two different methods were used. The respondents were asked to estimate the money cost of the trip. If travelling by car, the travel costs were considered to approximate to the costs of petrol. Repairs and maintenance costs were not included since the respondent was expected to have difficulties in estimating the magnitude of such costs. This complication is also noted by Seller *et al.* (1985). The second method of calculation of the travel costs is to use stereotyped rules, e.g. $0.1 per mile for those travelling by car, and economy class fare, times family size, for those travelling by train.

In addition, there is an opportunity cost for the time spent on a trip to the recreation site. As a first approximation, the after tax wage rate can be used to calculate this opportunity cost. This is because the travel time reduces working time and/or leisure time. At the margin, the latter 'crowded-out' activities are valued at the after tax wage rate by the individual, neglecting any distortions such as unemployment or fixed numbers of working hours. However, this approach assumes that the trip *per se* does not affect utility. Depending on the circumstances, one can imagine that a household derives positive or negative satisfaction from the trip to a recreation site. In the former (latter) case, the sum of money costs of the trip plus travel time costs evaluated at the after tax wage rate overestimates (underestimates) the true or full travel cost. However, there seems to be little empirical evidence in this respect. Available studies of work travel time, as summarized, for example, in Cesario (1976), indicate that the shadow price of such travel time is much lower than the wage rate. Needless to say, there is no strong case for believing that households consider travels to work and trips to recreation sites as equivalent 'commodities'.

In any case, neglecting the non-monetary parts of the travel costs can lead to biased estimates. In particular, if the non-monetary cost or net opportunity cost of the time spent in travel is strictly positive, then a failure to account for this cost will cause the aggregate consumer surplus to be underestimated, *ceteris paribus*. In terms of Figure 7.5, the estimated curve will be located inside and be less steep than the 'true' one, except possibly for those living very close to the recreation site, since the underestimation of costs increases in relation to distance from the visitor's zone of origin.

For similar reasons, a failure to correctly account for the opportunity cost of time on site may cause a bias. This is so at least if on-site time varies systematically with the distance to the recreation site. On the other hand, if on-site time is a constant, it does not matter whether an opportunity cost is included or not.

In the study summarized in this section, no travel time costs were included. This, of course, probably implies an underestimation of the costs. It should be noted, however, that almost 80 per cent of the respondents found the trip to the V Valley to be a positive experience. This indicates that the underestimation of total travel costs is somewhat less serious than appears to be the case at first sight. Regarding on-site time, no evidence was found that it varies with the zone of origin of the visitor.

In part, differences between zones in visit frequences may be due to differences in income. For this reason, the analysis includes an income variable. The income variable does not relate to the visitor but to the home county of the visitor. The income concept used is disposable household income.

The analysis must also take account of the fact that there may be several recreation sites which are substitutes for one another. For example, the variation in the relative number of visitors from different zones of origin may in part be due to a difference in the availability of similar recreation sites close to the zone of origin. For this reason, Bojö (1985) constructed a kind of substitute availability index. This index is defined as

$$s_i = \sum_{j=1}^{n} \frac{p_i W_j}{p_j} \tag{7.17}$$

where p_i is the travel cost per household from the origin zone to the V Valley and return, p_j is the corresponding travel cost to the jth substitute site, and W_j is a measure of the degree of substitutability between sites i and j.

Since (7.17) reduces to a constant (W_j) for a site situated close to the V Valley, all sites in that county were excluded from the analysis. Three groups of domestic substitute sites, situated far away in three different parts of the country, remain. According to the views expressed in the questionnaire, one of these three groups of sites was the main alternative for about 55 per cent of the respondents. Less than 15 per cent suggested a foreign site, e.g. the Alps, so this substitute was excluded by Bojö; the basic problem being that it turned out to be impossible to construct a reliable index for such sites.

Four functional forms for (7.16), linear, quadratic, semi-logarithmic, and logarithmic, were chosen for examination. In general, the results were far from encouraging. The following linear distance decay function yields the most reasonable result:

$$H_i = 4.1 - 1.4p_i - 43.4y_i - 5.7s_i + 518.5D_i \quad R^2 = 0.43 \tag{7.18}$$

where $D_i = 1$ if the household travels by train, and $D_i = 0$ otherwise. All coefficients, except the income variable, are significant at the 5 per cent level. Thus, equation (7.18) confirms what one would expect, namely that an increase in travel costs reduces the proportion of visitors from a particular zone.[4] Moreover, the supply of similar sites in other parts of Sweden affects H_i in the expected way. Disposable household income, on the other hand, has no significant influence on the relative number of visitors from a particular zone.

Bojö (1985) does not indicate which estimation procedure is used. However, note that estimating (7.18) by OLS may result in heteroscedasticity. As is demonstrated by Bowes and Loomis (1980), one should expect that the larger the origin's population, the smaller the variance of the visits per capita variable H_i. To show this, Bowes and Loomis define the variance of H_i as σ^2/N_i, where σ^2 is the variance of the individual visitation rate, assumed to be constant between zones, and N_i is zone population. One possible way of eliminating this heteroscedasticity problem is by estimating (7.18) by generalized least squares (GLS). See Johnston (1984, Ch. 8) for a detailed investigation of the properties of the OLS and GLS estimators in the presence of heteroscedastic disturbances in cross section studies. Unfortunately, there is also the problem that the variance σ^2 need not be independent of the distance to the site. Therefore, no simple solution to the heteroscedasticity problem in travel cost models seems to be available. For further discussion of this issue, the reader is referred to Bowes and Loomis (1980; 1982), Christensen and Price (1982), and Vaughan *et al.* (1982).

Taking the partial derivative of (7.18) with respect to p_i, a linear curve, like the one depicted in Figure 7.5, is obtained for any given (average) values of the remaining independent variables in (7.18). Proceeding along the lines discussed in relation to Figure 7.5, the aggregate consumer surplus is easily calculated. Adding somewhat speculative figures for excluded groups of visitors (those travelling by bus or aeroplane, sportsmen not paying for their stay themselves, etc.) Bojö arrives at a total consumer surplus amounting to around 1 million Swedish crowns (about $0.13 million). It has been argued that converting the examined area to forestry use causes irreversible damage to the environment. Thus, it is reasonable to argue that a closure of the recreation site causes a yearly loss of 1 million Swedish crowns forever, assuming, of course, that the sum does not vary over time. Using a discount rate of 5 per cent, Bojö arrives at a present value of about 25 million crowns.

Finally, it should be mentioned that the travel cost method produces approximately the same consumer surplus estimate as the contingent valuation method; Bojö (1985) used an open-ended bidding game approach similar to the one presented in Section 2 above. Seller *et al.* (1985) report similar results. They, however, argue that one should expect the travel cost method to produce higher benefits than a contingent valuation method, at least in the case of small income effects; recall that the former approach gives an uncompensated measure while the latter gives a compensated measure. Even in the case of zero income effects a difference would be expected to occur since the travel cost method gives a measure of the valuation of the total recreation experience, while the contingent valuation method usually provides an estimate of a particular attribute or characteristic, e.g. skiing. However, enquiring about the amount that the respondent would pay in order to prevent an area from being 'destroyed', as Bojö did, one would rather expect the reverse outcome. In particular, this is because the respondent may attribute to the resource an existence value, a value that is not captured by the travel cost method. Further work in comparison of the methods is needed before ultimate conclusions can be drawn regarding their relative reliability.

8 *Some further notes on the travel cost method and similar approaches*

A variant of the travel cost approach was applied by Pearse (1968) to big-game hunting in Canada. Hunters were stratified on the basis of income. The person with the highest costs within a stratum was considered a marginal user who had received no net benefits. All others within the same stratum were assumed to have obtained net benefits equal to the difference between their costs and those of the specified marginal user. In this way a consumer surplus measure was obtained for each stratum (see Pearse, 1968, for details).

Recently, Burt and Brewer (1971) and Cicchetti *et al.* (1976) have used an extended variation of the travel cost method to estimate the increment to consumer surplus resulting from the introduction of a new ski site. The approach taken by these authors is in a sense more general than the single equations approach presented in the previous section. Basically, these authors estimate a (linear) system of demand equations for existing sites:

$$\mathbf{x} = \mathbf{a} + \mathbf{bp} \tag{7.19}$$

where $\mathbf{x}$ is an $m \times 1$ vector of visitation rates for each of m existing sites, $\mathbf{p}$ is an $m \times 1$ vector of travel costs to each of the sites, $\mathbf{a}$ is an $m \times 1$ vector of coefficients, and $\mathbf{b}$ is an $m \times m$ vector of coefficients.

Once this system is estimated, the authors select the site which is supposed to be the closest substitute for the new still undeveloped, recreation site. The benefits, i.e. reductions in travel costs, resulting from the introduction of this new site are measured in the following way. First evaluate (7.19) for the given travel costs for all existing sites. Then, evaluate (7.19) with the travel costs measured for the substitute site replaced by those to the new site.

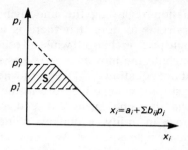

Figure 7.6 Consumers surplus gain due to a fall in travel costs from p_i^0 to p_i^1

The consumer surplus measure, corresponding to (7.15), for this single price reduction from, say p_i^0 to p_i^1, is written as

$$S = -\int_{p_i^0}^{p_i^1} x_i dp_i$$
$$= p_i^0 \left(a_i + \sum_{j \neq i} b_{ij}p_j + \frac{b_{ii} p_i^0}{2}\right) - p_i^1 \left(a_i + \sum_{j \neq i} b_{ij}p_j + \frac{b_{ii}p_i^1}{2}\right) \quad (7.20)$$

This measure, which is illustrated in Figure 7.6, indicates the change in consumer surplus due to reduced travel costs if a new recreation site is introduced. This is the case at least if the demand function for the substitute site i coincides with the demand function for the hypothetical new site. Note that this measure is, in a sense, more general than the one in (7.15) since demand now depends not only on the own price but also on the levels of other prices (travel costs). In any case, Burt and Brewer (1971) and Cicchetti *et al.* (1976) do not use the measure (7.20). Instead they use the whole system (7.19) to obtain the line integral

$$S = \left(\mathbf{a}'\mathbf{p}^0 + \frac{\mathbf{p}^{0'}\mathbf{b}\mathbf{p}^0}{2}\right) - \left(\mathbf{a}'\mathbf{p}^1 + \frac{\mathbf{p}^{1'}\mathbf{b}\mathbf{p}^1}{2}\right) \quad (7.21)$$

where, in the single price change case, only p_i differs between the price vectors $\mathbf{p}^0$ and $\mathbf{p}^1$, and primes denote transposed vectors.

It should be emphasized that both approaches yield the same 'answer' in the single price change case if the cross-price terms $\partial x_i/\partial p_j = b_{ij}$ are symmetrical, i.e. $b_{ij} = b_{ji}$. That is, in this case (7.21) reduces to (7.20), as is easily demonstrated by expanding (7.21). Hof and King (1982), who clarified these issues, also pose the question of what happens if cross-price terms are not symmetrical. In Chapter 3 it was demonstrated that symmetry of the cross-price effects is a prerequisite for path independency in the multi-price change case. In cases where this condition is not met, areas to the left of ordinary demand curves, i.e. the measure (7.21), provide no information regarding the underlying change in utility. However, it is important to note that there is no path dependency problem if just a single price is changed while all other prices and income are held fixed throughout the movement. As was shown in Chapter 3, equation (7.20), but not equation (7.21), except when $b_{ij} = b_{ji}$, yields the ordinary consumer surplus change measure in the single price change case. This measure has the same sign as, but need not be proportional to, the underlying change in utility. From this point of view then, it is sufficient to estimate a single equation. Whether one actually decides to estimate a single equation or a whole system of equations is a question of data collection costs and data quality, on the one hand, and econometric considerations, on the other.

The approaches discussed thus far aim at valuing a specific site. Even if site-specific bundles of characteristics are included so as to characterize each site, as in Burt and Brewer (1971), Cicchetti *et al.* (1976), Morey (1981), and Smith and Desvousges (1985), it is sites, not the separate characteristics of those sites which are valued. In contrast, Brown and Mendelsohn (1984) use a hedonic travel cost method in order to value specific characteristics. As Brown and Mendelsohn (1984, p. 427) put it, the travel cost method can measure the value of the Colorado River, the hedonic travel cost method can value scenic quality, fish density, crowdedness, etc. Basically, the hedonic travel cost method resembles the property value method, but with property values replaced by travel costs. For this reason, there will be no further discussion of the hedonic travel cost method.

Another possible approach is the household production function technique outlined in Chapter 6. This method values the outputs of households rather than an input, e.g. a recreation site. A recent application to congestion and participation in outdoor recreation is given by Deyak and Smith (1978). The method, however, is associated with econometric difficulties because of, among other things, joint production and non-linear output prices. The conditions under which the use of the household production function yields identifiable and unbiased estimates of the parameters of demand functions turn out to be quite restrictive. For a broad discussion of the theory and estimation of the household production function for wildlife recreation, the reader is referred to Bockstael and McConnell (1981).

A final comment relates to the problem of congestion. This problem occurs when the number of users of a recreation facility is 'too large'. Congestion may be interpreted as a kind of rationing and dealt with in the way discussed in Chapter 5. Alternatively, the stock of visitors, X say, is included as a separate argument in the utility functions. If X is reasonably small, it may have no or even a positive influence on utility because of the opportunities for social interaction. If the number of visitors is large, an increase in X may cause congestion and so decrease the marginal utility of a visit. Also, in an uncertain world, a household's decision whether or not to visit a particular site may be influenced by the household's expectations of the number of visitors. See the discussion on state dependent preferences in Chapter 10. In any case, in calculating willingness to pay measures, it is important to address the congestion issue. Several of the studies referred to in this chapter include congestion variables in the regression equations (see, for example, Brown and Mendelsohn, 1984; Cicchetti *et al.*, 1976; Vaughan and Russel, 1982, for details).

CHAPTER 8

Discrete choice models and environmental benefits

There are important situations in which consumers face a discrete rather than a continuous set of choices. For example, a household cannot simultaneously visit two different recreation sites. Quality changes, such as pollution or the development of new sites, may induce households to switch from trips to one area to trips to another. In order to cope with such discrete choice situations, the continuous choice models of the previous chapters must be modified.

To my knowledge, no general discrete choice theory is available for use in deriving consumer surplus measures. A few authors, notably Mäler (1974) and Small and Rosen (1981), have rigorously derived surplus measures for particular classes of discrete choices. Mäler considers a good which must be purchased in a given quantity or not at all. Small and Rosen concentrate on the case when two goods are mutually exclusive, but also briefly discuss other kinds of discrete choice situations. By contrast, Hau (1985) considers the case where the consumer does not know in advance which good he will choose, except up to a probability distribution. Recently, Hanemann (1984a) has developed a unified framework for formulating demand models which are suitable for empirical application.

This chapter concentrates on a case which is slightly different from those cases dealt with by the mentioned authors, but the analysis is much inspired by the work of Small and Rosen (1981). A household is assumed to have the option to visit a particular recreation site. This is the discrete part of the choice. However, if the household decides to visit the site, it is free to choose the on-site time subject to the budget and time constraints. Later, the option to choose among several different sites is introduced. Finally, we deal with the formulation and estimation of relationships that involve qualitative or binary variables.

1 *Behaviour functions when some goods are mutually exclusive*

The household consumes ordinary consumer goods, and divides its time between work and leisure. Leisure time in turn is split between visits to a recreation site and other leisure activities. A trip to the site requires inputs in the form of time and market goods, such as a car and gasoline. The trip is viewed as an all-or-nothing activity, i.e. the household either makes one trip or no trip at all. However, given a decision to make a trip, the household can freely choose the on-site time within the limits set by the total time available.

In order to produce a trip to the recreation site, time and, in general, market goods inputs are needed. This is represented by a production function

$$N = f(L, q) \tag{8.1}$$

where N is the number of trips, L is time taken for trips, and q is a composite market good input. In order to simplify the exposition, we will only consider the case where N take on values of zero or unity (represented by a delta δ below). In the former case $L = q = 0$, while in the latter case at least one input must take on a strictly positive value (and the isoquant is assumed to be strictly convex to the origin). For example, if the household walks to the recreation site, L is strictly positive while q may be equal to zero (although it is hard to visualize a successful trip without a 1974 Château La Mission Haut Brion or possibly a 1973 Dom Pérignon Moët et Chandon, depending on the specific form of the preference ordering). On the other hand, if the household travels by car, both L and q are strictly positive.

The decision problem of the household can be formulated in the following way. Assume that the household acts as if it maximizes a nicely behaved utility function

$$U = U(\mathbf{x}, \ell_0, \delta\ell_1, \mathbf{z}) \tag{8.2}$$

subject to

$$y + (T - \ell_0 - \delta\ell_1 - \delta L)w - \mathbf{px} - \delta P_\ell \ell_1 - \delta Pq(L, 1) = 0 \tag{8.3}$$

where all goods including leisure time are normal so that a lower price always implies more demand; $\mathbf{x}$ is a vector of consumer goods; $\mathbf{p}$ a vector of prices of such goods; δ is zero or unity; ℓ_1 is time at a recreation site; ℓ_0 is the time spent on other leisure activities; $\mathbf{z}$ is a vector of quality variables to be discussed later; y is a fixed income; T is total time; L is the time required for a trip to the recreation site; w is the wage rate; P_ℓ is a fee or price charged per unit of on-site time; q is a composite market good input to a trip to the site; P is the market price of this composite input; and equation (8.1) has been used to solve q as a function of the time on the trip, conditional on a decision to make a trip. In order to simplify the exposition, it is assumed that on-site time is a non-essential commodity having the property that the (conditional) demand is equal to zero if its price exceeds some finite level. For other possible assumptions, the reader is referred to Hanemann (1984a).

In this model, the benefits of the trip are an increasing function of on-site time. The characteristics of the site, such as the length of the downhill runs and the lifts available in the case of a ski site, are constants included in the vector z. Hence, if the household is thought of as producing recreation, the only variable input, besides the decision on inputs in the travel production function, is on-site time. Moreover the satisfaction gained from recreation is assumed to be strictly increasing in time spent on site. There is, of course, a cost associated with additional on-site time, since other leisure activities and (or) working time must be reduced.

The formulation of the decision problem in (8.2) and (8.3) implies that a trip to the recreational site *per se* does not positively contribute to the utility of the household; the trip is only a necessary input in the production of recreation or on-site time. However, note that the household is charged a uniform price per unit of on-site time, an assumption which may seem a bit unrealistic but will turn out to be a useful analytical tool. In fact, this charge implies that the model does impute different values to different (marginal) uses of leisure time; see equations (8.4) below. A further generalization can be attained by imposing a quantity constraint on the number of working hours. This, i.e. underemployment, implies that the current wage overestimates the value of marginal leisure time. Another possibility, following Hanoch (1980), would be to distinguish between leisure on workdays and non-workday leisure. Such generalizations, however, seem to add few additional insights in the present context. Instead, they tend to add to the complexity and detract from the interest of the model. Furthermore, note that the household cannot choose among different recreation sites. However, such generalizations of the model will be considered later.

In order to simplify the exposition, we will consider two different maximization problems. First *assume* that $\delta = 1$ so that the household visits the recreation site. Then, the first-order conditions for utility maximization are written as

$$\frac{\partial U}{\partial \mathbf{x}} - \lambda \mathbf{p} = 0$$

$$\frac{\partial U}{\partial \ell_0} - \lambda w = 0$$

$$[\frac{\partial U}{\partial \ell_1} - \lambda(w + P_\ell)]\delta = 0 \qquad (8.4)$$

$$-\lambda(w + P\frac{\partial q}{\partial L})\delta = 0$$

$$y + (T - \ell_0 - \delta\ell_1 - \delta L)w - \mathbf{px} - \delta P_\ell \ell_1 - \delta Pq(L, 1) = 0$$

where it is assumed that the price–income vector is such that $\mathbf{x} \geqslant 0$, ℓ_0, $\ell_1, L > 0$, and λ denotes the Lagrange multiplier of the budget constraint.

Next, the maximization is repeated but now conditional on $\delta = 0$. The resulting system of first-order conditions for an interior solution consists of equations parallel to those contained in the two first and the final (with $\delta = 0$) lines of (8.4). Of course, the commodity bundle $(\mathbf{x}, \ell_0)$ associated with these new conditions need not coincide with the bundle associated with $\delta = 1$ in (8.4).

Solving these two equation systems yields two sets of behaviour functions conditional on $\delta = 0$ and $\delta = 1$ respectively

$$\left.\begin{array}{l} \mathbf{X}^c = \mathbf{X}^c(\mathbf{p}, w, y, \mathbf{z}) \\ (\delta\ell_1^c = \delta L^c = \delta q^c = 0) \end{array}\right\} \quad \text{for } \delta = 0 \qquad (8.5)$$

$$\left.\begin{array}{l} \mathbf{X}^c = \mathbf{X}^c(\mathbf{p}, w, y, P_\ell, P, \mathbf{z}) \\ \ell_1^c = \ell_1^c(\mathbf{p}, w, y, P_\ell, P, \mathbf{z}) \\ L^c = L^c(w, P) \\ q^c = q^c(w, P) \end{array}\right\} \quad \text{for } \delta = 1 \qquad (8.6)$$

where $\mathbf{X}^c = (\mathbf{x}^c, \ell_0^c, L_w^c)'$, superscript c denotes a conditional behaviour function, and $L_w^c = T - \delta\ell_1^c - \ell_0^c - \delta L^c$ is working time.

In the first case, the household does not undertake a trip to the recreation site. Then, the demand functions for goods, (other) leisure activities and work are independent of the prices of inputs needed for a visit to the recreation site. If a commodity is not purchased at all, changes in its price will not affect demand for the goods actually purchased.

On the other hand, if the household makes a trip to the site, all prices are included as arguments in the conditional behaviour functions. This is captured by the equations (8.6). It should be noted, however, that the optimal or cost minimizing input combination used to produce the single trip is determined by the price of time, w, and the price of the composite

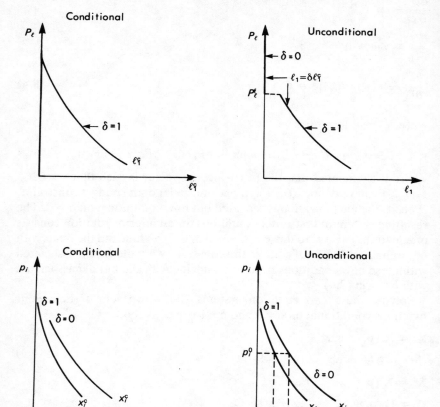

Figure 8.1 Conditional and unconditional demand curves for on-site time and a consumer good. (In drawing the unconditional curves it has been assumed that $\delta = f(P_\ell)$ such that $\delta = 0$ for $P_\ell > P_\ell^f$ and $\delta = 1$ for $P_\ell \leq P_\ell^f$)

market good input, P. The household selects a combination along the isoquant for $N = 1$, and the point of tangency between the isoquant and an isocost line identifies the least cost combination of the two inputs. This is seen by inverting the last but one equation in (8.4) for $\delta = 1$. The travel cost is like a lump sum tax on income conditional on $\delta = 1$. The household can escape the 'tax' by not consuming recreational services, though it then misses the benefits of such services. A utility maximizing household prefers the alternative corresponding to $\delta = 0$ if the travel cost exceeds the recreational benefits but switches to $\delta = 1$ if the price vector is changed so that the benefits exceed the cost.

It is important to note that *unconditional* behaviour functions can also be defined. For example, the unconditional demand function for on-site time is equal to $\delta \ell_1^c(\cdot) = \ell_1(\cdot)$. This function incorporates both the discrete choice itself, i.e. $\delta = 0$ or $\delta = 1$, and the on-site time ℓ_1^c demanded conditional on $\delta = 1$. Figure 8.1 indicates that discreteness introduces a point of discontinuity into (or a shift of) unconditional behaviour functions.

In order to illustrate these results, let us consider the following quasi-linear utility function:

$$U = \ell n\, \ell_0 + \delta \ell n\, (\ell_1 + 1) + x_1 \tag{8.2'}$$

Maximization of this utility function subject to the usual budget constraint yields the demand function $\ell_1^c = [1/(w + P_\ell)] - 1$ for time on site, conditional on $\delta = 1$. For example, if $w = 0.2$, the demand curve intersects the price axis at $P_\ell = 0.8$. In order to arrive at a decision whether to visit the recreation site, the household compares the maximal utility levels obtained for $\delta = 0$ and $\delta = 1$ respectively, and chooses the alternative that yields the highest level of satisfaction. The indirect conditional utility functions corresponding to the considered quasi-linear direct utility function can be written as

$$V = -\ell n\, w - \delta[\ell n(w + P_\ell) - (w + P_\ell - 1) + (wL + Pq)] + y + wT - 1 \tag{8.2''}$$

where $\delta = 0,1$. Suppose that $w = 0.2$, $y = 1$, $T = 24$, $L = 1$, and $Pq = 0.3$. It follows by means of straightforward calculations that the household visits the recreation site if the charge P_ℓ is below \$0.1 per hour, while it refrains from the visit if the charge is raised above approximately \$0.1 per hour. But note that if, for example, the price of petrol is increased so that Pq rises from \$0.3 to \$1, then the household will not visit the site, even if the charge P_l is abolished.

2 *Critical price levels and corner solutions*

The discrete choice, i.e. $\delta = 0$ or $\delta = 1$, is determined by the price–income vector. As is highlighted by the example presented above, there exists a critical entry fee or a reservation price P_ℓ^f per unit of on-site time which, given all other prices and exogenous income, induces the household to switch from $\delta = 0$ to $\delta = 1$. It is assumed throughout that the price–income vector ($\mathbf{p}$, w, y, P) is such that δ switches from $\delta = 1$ to $\delta = 0$ for a strictly positive and finite value of P_ℓ. In order to examine more closely the properties of this critical price level it is useful to derive the (pseudo) expenditure function. Since there are two cases to consider, we obtain two *conditional* expenditure functions

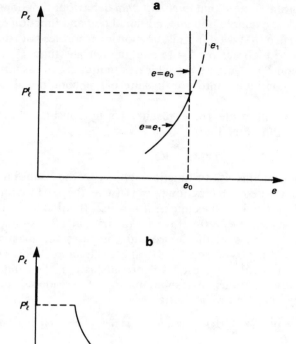

Figure 8.2 The expenditure function and unconditional demand for leisure time at the recreation site as functions of the price paid per time unit at the site

$$e_0(\mathbf{a}) = \mathbf{p}\tilde{\mathbf{x}}(\mathbf{a}) - w\tilde{L}_w(\mathbf{a}) \tag{8.7}$$

and

$$e_1(\mathbf{a}, P_\ell, P) = \mathbf{p}\tilde{\mathbf{x}}(\mathbf{a}, P_\ell, P) + P_\ell\tilde{\ell}_1(\mathbf{a}, P_\ell, P) + Pq(w, P) - w\tilde{L}_w(\mathbf{a}, P_\ell, P) \tag{8.8}$$

where subscripts 0 and 1 refer to $\tilde{\delta} = 0$ and $\tilde{\delta} = 1$ respectively, $\mathbf{a} = (\mathbf{p}, w, \bar{U}, \mathbf{z})$, $\bar{U}$ is the pre-specified utility level, a tilde denotes a *conditional compensated* behaviour function, and $\tilde{L}_w = T - \tilde{\ell}_0 - \tilde{\delta}\tilde{\ell}_1 - \tilde{\delta}\tilde{L}$. The behaviour functions in (8.7) and (8.8) are derived in the usual way by minimizing expenditure subject to the pre-specified utility level. The expenditure functions provide the exogenous income necessary to attain this utility level when the household is allowed to allocate its time between work and different leisure activities conditional on $\tilde{\delta} = 0$ and $\tilde{\delta} = 1$ respectively.

For any P_ℓ, assuming all other prices remain unchanged, the choice between $\tilde{\delta} = 0$ and $\tilde{\delta} = 1$ is made by comparing the corresponding minimal expenditures e_0 and e_1 required for reaching the specified utility level. Hence, we can define an overall or *unconditional* expenditure function as

$$e(\mathbf{a}, P_\ell, P) = \min\{e_0(\mathbf{a}), e_1(\mathbf{a}, P_\ell, P)\} \tag{8.9}$$

A graphical illustration of this result is found in Figure 8.2a. Given the assumptions introduced above, there is a finite price P_ℓ^f such that expenditure is left unaffected when switching from $\tilde{\delta} = 0$ to $\tilde{\delta} = 1$, i.e. when switching from no visit to one visit at the recreation site. In the numerical example of Section 1 this critical level is \$0.1. If P_ℓ is above the critical level, e_0 gives the least cost commodity bundle necessary to attain the specified level of utility, while e_1 gives the least cost combination if P_ℓ is below the critical level P_ℓ^f. This also illuminates the fact that the value $\tilde{\delta}$ takes on (zero or one) is determined by all prices and the income/utility level. Thus a change in say P_ℓ may cause $\tilde{\delta}$ to shift from $\tilde{\delta} = 0$ to $\tilde{\delta} = 1$ or vice versa. (The tilde is there to highlight the fact that the switch need not occur for the same critical price in the compensated as in the uncompensated case.)

The utility function (8.2) is well-behaved when $\delta = 0$ and $\delta = 1$ respectively. This implies that the conditional expenditure functions e_0 and e_1 and the associated conditional compensated behaviour functions are well defined and continuously differentiable. Hence, the unconditional expenditure function has the same convenient properties as in the previous chapters, except at those points for which $e_0 = e_1$. At such points, e is continuous (since $e_0 = e_1$), as can be seen from Figure 8.2a, and right and left differentiable. Hence, taking the partial derivative of the overall expenditure function with respect to P_ℓ yields

$$\frac{\partial e(\mathbf{a}, P_\ell, P)}{\partial P_\ell} = \tilde{\tilde{\ell}}_1(\mathbf{a}, P_\ell, P) \tag{8.10}$$

or

$$\frac{\partial e(\mathbf{a}, P_\ell, P)}{\partial P_\ell} = \left\{ \begin{array}{ll} \dfrac{\partial e_0(\mathbf{a})}{\partial P_\ell} = 0 & \text{for } \tilde{\delta} = 0 \\[3mm] \dfrac{\partial e_1(\mathbf{a}, P_\ell, P)}{\partial P_\ell} = \tilde{\ell}_1 & \text{for } \tilde{\delta} = 1 \end{array} \right\} \tag{8.11}$$

where a double tilde denotes the unconditional compensated demand function for on-site time, i.e. $\tilde{\tilde{\ell}}_1 = \tilde{\delta}\tilde{\ell}_1$. This unconditional compensated demand function, depicted in Figure 8.2b, incorporates both the discrete choice itself and the demand for on-site time conditional on that choice. At the point for which $e_0 = e_1$ the upper and lower expressions are interpreted as right and left derivatives respectively. Recall Figure 8.2a. since the price derivatives are bounded and piecewise continuous they are integrable. At the point for which $e_0 = e_1$ no change in expenditure arises from switching from not consuming to consuming recreation, i.e. integrating over this point of discontinuity does not affect expenditure (see the appendix to Chapter 6). Using the utility function (8.2′), the reader is invited to show that $e_0 = e_1$ (≈ 6.4) for $P_\ell = 0.1$. *Hint*: The expenditure function is obtained by simply replacing y by e in equation (8.2″)!

3 *Consumer surplus measures in the discrete choice case*

Using equation (8.10), the compensating variation measure for a fall in P_ℓ from P_ℓ^0 to P_ℓ^1 is defined as

$$CV_\ell = y^1 - y^0 + e(\mathbf{a}, P_\ell^0, P) - e(\mathbf{a}, P_\ell^1, P)$$

$$= \triangle y - \int_c \frac{\partial e(\mathbf{a}, P_\ell, P)}{\partial P_\ell} \, dP_\ell$$

$$= \triangle y - \int_c \bar{\ell}_1(\mathbf{a}, P_\ell, P) dP_\ell \tag{8.12}$$

where y^0 and y^1 denote initial and final exogenous incomes respectively, c denotes the path of integration, and the household's utility level is fixed at the initial level U^0. This measure gives the area to the left of the income compensated demand curve between initial and final prices (plus the change, if any, in exogenous income). From (8.11) and Figure 8.2a it is seen that $\bar{\ell}_1 dP_\ell = 0$ for prices which exceed the critical level P_ℓ^f since $\delta = 0$ for such prices. It is interesting to note, however, that the techniques for deriving consumer surplus measures used in the previous chapters generalize to the case where there is discreteness.

The discreteness is caused by the travel cost. Loosely speaking, the household visits the recreation site if and only if the surplus gain of on-site time covers the fixed travel cost. In order to show this we first use the conditional expenditure functions to obtain

$$e_1(\mathbf{a}, P_\ell^f, P) = e_0(\mathbf{a}) = (e_0(\mathbf{a}) + C) - C = e_1(\mathbf{a}, P_\ell^*, P) - C \tag{8.13}$$

where C is a sum of money which is equal to the travel cost, i.e. the sum of wage income lost when travelling to the site plus the cost of market goods inputs, and P_ℓ^* ($> P_\ell^f$) is an entrance fee sufficiently high that the *conditional* demand $\bar{\ell}_1$ for on-site time is zero. In the example discussed at the end of Section 1, $P_\ell^* = 0.8$ and $P_\ell^f = 0.1$.

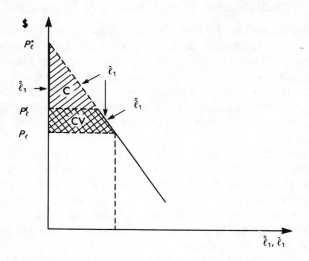

Figure 8.3 The allocation of on-site time as a function of fixed and variable costs

Next, consider the left-hand side term less the right-hand side terms in (8.13). The difference, which of course is equal to zero, can be written as

$$\int_c \frac{\partial e_1}{\partial P_\ell} \, dP_\ell - C = \int_c \ell \, dP_\ell - C = 0 \tag{8.14}$$

where c denotes the path of integration between P_ℓ^f and P_ℓ^*. This result, which is illustrated in Figure 8.3, confirms what one would expect, namely that the household decides to undertake a visit to the recreation site if and only if the associated increase in consumer surplus covers at least the fixed costs of the visit. The critical price P_ℓ^f is the watershed for which the consumer's surplus of on-site time just balances the fixed travel cost and hence makes the household indifferent between zero trips and one trip. If the actual price paid falls short of P_ℓ^f, a trip to the site adds to the consumer's surplus, as is illustrated by the area CV in Figure 8.3. This result can be checked for the utility function (8.2′). Since this utility function is quasi-linear, the ordinary and compensated demand functions coincide. Thus, integrating the ordinary conditional demand function for on-site time, as specified in Section 1, in the interval $0.8 to $0.1, yields a consumer surplus of $0.5, which exactly covers the transportation cost. If the actual charge is below (above) $0.1 per hour, the consumer gains (loses) from undertaking the trip.

4 *The critical price level and the choice of measure*

Following the procedure of the previous section, an equivalent variation measure of on-site time is easily derived. Accordingly this procedure is not repeated. The only difference is that the household now remains at its final utility level, not at the initial level. From previous chapters, it is clear that the CV and EV measures in general impute different money values to the unique change in utility. If the good under consideration is normal, the equivalent variation exceeds the compensating variation for a price change.

This latter property of money measures of utility change means that one would expect the critical price P_ℓ^ζ to be sensitive to the choice of measure. However, a price fall does not require compensation as long as the price exceeds P_ℓ^ζ since no on-site time is consumed. The unconditional ordinary and CV demand curves therefore coincide in this interval. However, this is not true for prices below P_ℓ^ζ unless income effects are zero.

This indicates that if the household consumes on-site time, i.e. $\delta = 1$, and the price rises while the utility level remains fixed, then the critical price for which δ switches from $\delta = 1$ to $\delta = 0$ need not be identical to the aforementioned level P_ℓ^ζ. Recall that P_ℓ^ζ was derived given that the household's utility level is fixed at a level corresponding to zero consumption of on-site time. Hence one would expect the two critical price levels to differ unless the EV and CV demand functions coincide; picture the conventional figure in which the EV demand curve falls outside the CV demand curve. This shows that the 'path-dependency' problem does not disappear just because choice is discrete.

5 *On the relevance of the travel costs method*

In the real world, the individual can often choose among several available recreation sites. At any point in time, however, these are mutually exclusive, since a household cannot simultaneously visit different sites. Suppose for simplicity, that there are only two sites which, from the point of view of the household, are perfect substitutes. However they differ with respect to travel costs, say $C_1 < C_2$. If the price–income vector is such that the household visits a site, it clearly chooses the low cost one. This means that the product of on-site time, $\ell_1 \cdot \ell_2$, at site 1 and site 2 is equal to zero at each point in time.

Next, suppose that the fee, $_1P_\ell$ paid per unit of on-site time at site 1 rises from zero to some strictly positive level while all other prices remain fixed. Three outcomes are possible. As an approximation, if $_1P_\ell\ell_1 + C_1 < C_2$, then the household continues to visit site 1, since this is still cheaper than switching to site 2. However, if $_1P_\ell$ becomes sufficiently high, then the sign of the above inequality is reversed and the household chooses to visit site 2 rather than site 1. Hence, differences in transportation costs can be used to measure differences in the consumer's valuation of the two recreation areas. This assumes, however, that the fee is below the critical level discussed at length in previous sections. If the actual unit price paid for on-site time exceeds the critical level, the household switches to zero consumption of on-site time.

More formally, the household now compares three conditional expenditure functions

$$e_0(\mathbf{a}) = \mathbf{p}\bar{\mathbf{x}}(\mathbf{a}) - w\bar{L}_w(\mathbf{a}) \tag{8.15}$$

$$e_i(\mathbf{a}, {}_iP_\ell, P) = \mathbf{p}\bar{\mathbf{x}}(\mathbf{a}, {}_iP_\ell, P) + {}_iP_\ell\bar{\ell}_i(\mathbf{a}, {}_iP_\ell, P) + Pq_i(w, P) - w\bar{L}_w(\mathbf{a}, {}_iP_\ell, P) \tag{8.16}$$

where $i = 1, 2$ refers to site i. The household may choose not to consume on-site time at all. This choice is made if e_0 gives the least expenditure to attain the specified utility level. Then, $\tilde{\delta}_1 = \tilde{\delta}_2 = 0$. If, on the other hand, e_1 and/or e_2 is smaller than e_0 the household will choose to visit the site for which expenditure is the least, so that either $\tilde{\delta}_1 = 1$, $\tilde{\delta}_2 = 0$ *or* $\tilde{\delta}_1 = 0$, $\tilde{\delta}_2 = 1$.

According to equation (8.14) in Section 3, the household visits a site provided the actual price $P_\ell^\mathfrak{f}$ is below the critical level $P_\ell^\mathfrak{f}$ for which δ switches from $\tilde{\delta} = 1$ to $\tilde{\delta} = 0$. Assume that this condition holds. However, the household now chooses between two sites which are assumed to be perfect substitutes. Using equations similar to equation (8.14) it can be seen that the household visits site 1 if $C_1 < C_2$, i.e. if

$$\int_{c_1}\bar{\ell}_1 d_1 P_\ell - \int_{c_2}\bar{\ell}_2 d_2 P_\ell - (C_1 - C_2) = C_2 - C_1 > 0 \tag{8.17}$$

where $c_1 = (P_\ell^*, P_l^\mathfrak{f})' = c_2$, P_ℓ^* is the price at which the compensated demand curves for on-site time at site 1 and 2, conditional on $\tilde{\delta}_1 = 1$ and $\tilde{\delta}_2 = 1$ respectively, intersect the price axis, and $P_\ell^\mathfrak{f}$ is the price actually charged. The areas under the compensated conditional demand curves are of equal size since the 'commodities' are perfect substitutes by assumption and the actual price charged, $_iP_\ell^\mathfrak{f} \geqslant 0$, is assumed to be the same for both sites. This result can be examined by replacing the second argument of the utility function (8.2') by the argument $\ell\mathrm{n}(\delta_1\ell_1 + \delta_2\ell_2 + 1)$. Apparently, the resulting conditional demand function for on-site time at site 2 is identical to the corresponding function for on-site time at site 1, as specified in Section 1. Thus, if the actual fee charged is the same at both sites and below \$0.1 per hour, the household will visit the low travel cost site.

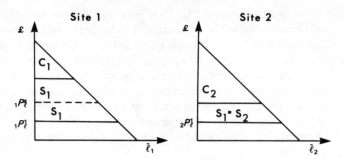

Figure 8.4 The consumer switches from visits to site 1 to visits to site 2 if $_1P_\ell >$ $_1P_\ell^2$ provided that $_1P_\ell^1 = {}_2P_\ell^1$ in the initial situation

Now, assume that $_1P_\ell$ is increased while $_2P_\ell = {}_2P_\ell^1$. From (8.17) it can be seen that there is a price $_1P_\ell^2$ charged for time at site 1 which turns the inequality (8.17) into an equality. If the actual price charged is above this level, the household switches from a trip to site 1 to a trip to site 2, assuming all other prices are fixed. Hence, as is illustrated in Figure 8.4, the area to the left of the conditional demand curve for on-site time at site 1 between the price $_1P_\ell^2$ and the lower, initial price $_1P_\ell^1 = {}_2P_\ell^1$ is equal to the difference in travel costs to the two sites. This implies that the *unconditional* demand $\tilde{\ell}_1$ for on-site time at site 1 will switch to zero at $_1P_\ell^1 = {}_1P_\ell^2$ and not at the higher critical price P_ℓ^c which is relevant when the choice is between a trip to a site or no trip at all (provided, of course, that $_1P_\ell^2 < P_\ell^c$). The area to the left of the unconditional or, equivalently, the conditional demand curve between $_1P_\ell^2$ and the (lower) price actually charged indicates the gain to the household when visiting site 1 rather than site 2. This area is denoted by S_1 in Figure 8.4.

Quality changes of the kind discussed in Section 5 of Chapter 6 (including changes in preferences) are easily generalized to the discrete choice case. Assume that on-site time at site 1 is a non-essential good and that

$$\underset{{}_1P_\ell \to \infty}{\ell\,\mathrm{im}} \ \frac{\partial e(\mathbf{b}, {}_1P_\ell, z_\ell)}{\partial z_\ell} = 0 \tag{8.18}$$

where $e(\cdot)$ is the unconditional expenditure function obtained from equations (8.15) and (8.16), $b = (\mathbf{p}, w, {}_2P_\ell, P)$, z_ℓ is the quality index of site 1, and all prices except $_1P_\ell$ remain fixed. The reader is invited to modify the utility function (8.2') by multiplying ℓ_1 by z_ℓ and derive, for this particular utility function, the results presented in the remainder of this section.

Equation (8.18) states that if the price charged for time spent at site 1 is high enough to prevent the household visiting the site, then the quality of the site does not matter. Of course, the household may be interested in the preservation of a wilderness area even if it does not visit the area. However, this kind of existence value is not considered in this chapter.

Once again the unconditional expenditure function is differentiated with respect to z_ℓ but now the entry fee is held at some lower level $_1P_\ell^1$ for which the good is consumed, and (8.18) is subtracted to obtain

$$\frac{\partial e(\mathbf{b}, {}_1P_\ell^1, z_\ell)}{\partial z_\ell} - 0 = -\int_c \frac{\partial \bar{\bar{\ell}}_1(\mathbf{b}, {}_1P_\ell, z_\ell)}{\partial z_\ell} \, d_1 P_\ell \qquad (8.19)$$

where $c = (\infty, {}_1P_\ell^1)'$. This expression states that the effect on total expenditure of a marginal change in the quality of site 1 can be obtained from market data. The effect on total expenditure equals the change in the area left of the compensated unconditional demand curve for site 1 as it shifts in response to a marginal shift in the quality of the site. (See the appendix to Chapter 6 for a detailed derivation of a similar expression.)

In order to obtain the effect of a discrete change in z_ℓ, say from z_ℓ^0 to z_ℓ^1, the approach used in deriving equation (A6.10) in the appendix to Chapter 6 is applied. After a few manipulations we obtain

$$\text{CV}_z = - \int_c [\bar{\bar{\ell}}_1(\mathbf{b}, {}_1P_\ell, z_\ell^0) - \bar{\bar{\ell}}_1(\mathbf{b}, {}_1P_\ell, z_\ell^1)] d_1 P_\ell \qquad (8.20)$$

A deterioration in quality shifts both the demand curve to the left and lowers the price $_1P_\ell^2$ for which the household switches from a visit at site 1 to a visit at site 2.

Intuitively, if the loss in consumer surplus due to the deterioration in quality exceeds the cost difference $C_2 - C_1$ in equation (8.17) the household switches to site 2. Hence, if the evaluation of the first integral in (8.17), given the new lower quality of the site, indicates a reversal of the sign of (8.17), the household will not continue to visit site 1. In this case, the compensated unconditional demand for on-site time at site 1 will be equal to zero for all positive prices charged, assuming all other prices remain fixed. In less severe cases, e.g. pollution, unconditional demand may be positive for some prices[1] as is illustrated in Figure 8.5.

These discrete choice results lend some support to the Hotelling–Clawson–Knetsch travel cost method (for continuous choice) described in Chapter 7 (Clawson and Knetsch, 1966). In certain circumstances, the change in travel costs correctly measures the change in the consumer's surplus as a new recreation area is developed or an existing one is lost due to pollution. This assumes, however, that the two sites compared, from the point of view of the household, are perfect substitutes. If the sites differ in quality (even in the initial situation) there is no longer any simple

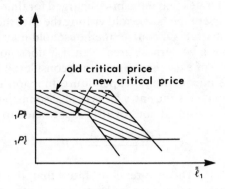

Figure 8.5 Loss of consumer's surplus (shaded area) as the quality of the site reduces

relationship between changes in transportation cost and changes in the consumer's surplus. For example, if site 1 is superior to site 2 from a quality point of view, the consumer may continue to visit site 1 even if the fee rises above $_1P_\ell^s$ in (8.17). Consequently, the loss of the consumer if, for example, site 1 is destroyed by pollution, exceeds the difference in transportation costs to site 1 and site 2.

In any case, it is important to note that results derived for situations in which consumers face a continuous set of choices cannot necessarily be generalized for discrete choice models. For example, Gramlich (1981, pp. 142–3) argues that the loss of a wilderness area through destruction is the usual consumer surplus triangle. That is, the area to the left of the demand curve for the site to be destroyed between the actual price charged and the price for which the curve intersects the price axis. This is a reasonable view if recreational services can be purchased in continuous quantities. On the other hand, if some decisions are mutually exclusive, inspection of Figures 8.3 and 8.4 shows that Gramlich's result must be interpreted with great care. In fact, the upper bound for the loss is given by the area CV in Figure 8.3. The lower bound is given by the change in travel costs, provided that recreation site exists which is a perfect substitute for the one under consideration (assuming that $\triangle C < S$), as is seen from Figure 8.4.

6 *Econometric models*

With regard to the application of the models considered in this chapter, it is important to note that the investigator cannot know with certainty if a particular household will consume on-site time or not. As Small and Rosen (1981) stressed, all that can be assigned is the probability that a good is purchased by a household. Even if the conditional demand functions are identical for all households, the critical price levels may differ across households due to differences in preferences.

Hence, it is useful to replace the choice index δ with a choice probability π. The fraction of the population which consumes the good under consideration can be viewed as a function of prices and income. In order to concentrate on the choice issue, assume that all consumers have identical conditional demand functions for on-site time but differ in their preferences between on-site time and other goods. This last assumption implies that not all households need switch from no visit to a visit at the same critical price level. The aggregate compensated demand for on-site time, assuming only one site is available, is written as

$$\tilde{\tilde{\ell}} = H\tilde{\pi}(\mathbf{a}, P_l)\,\tilde{\ell}_1(\mathbf{a}, P_\ell) \tag{8.21}$$

where H is the number of households, $\mathbf{a} = (\mathbf{p}, w, P, \mathbf{z}, \bar{U}^h)$, a tilde denotes a conditional compensated demand while a double tilde denotes an unconditional compensated demand function.

In (8.21) the fraction $\tilde{\pi}$ consuming on-site time is determined by the price–quality–utility vector. This implies that a change in a price or a quality attribute not only affects the conditional demand for on-site time, but also changes the critical price level for which the choice index δ switches from zero to unity or vice versa. As a consequence, the Slutsky equation for the aggregate demand function is more complicated than in the continuous goods case considered in Section 3 of Chapter 4. Small and Rosen (1981) have demonstrated that a Slutsky-like equation can be obtained

$$\frac{\partial \tilde{\tilde{\ell}}}{\partial P_\ell} = \frac{\partial \ell}{\partial P_\ell} + \ell[\frac{\partial \ell}{\partial Y} - (1-\pi)\frac{\partial \pi}{\partial Y}\frac{Y}{\pi}]/\pi \tag{8.22}$$

where ℓ is the unconditional ordinary or Marshallian aggregate demand function and $Y = Hy^h$ is aggregate income.

If π is constant with respect to changes in income, (8.22) is the usual aggregate Slutsky equation, except that the income effect is divided by $\pi < 1$. Hence, the income effect is larger than in the continuous case. In general, however, one would expect π to increase with income and thus augment the aggregate substitution effect of a price increase through the second term within brackets in (8.22). Hence, one must use caution in interpreting the aggregate effect of a price change in the discrete case. For instance, the own-price slope of the aggregate compensated demand function can no longer be inferred from estimates of the own-price and income slopes of the aggregate Marshallian demand function in the way used in the final section of Chapter 4.

Small and Rosen (1981), following McFadden (1973; 1976), have shown that the bulk of current empirical work on discrete choice is based on conditional stochastic indirect utility models of the form

$$V_i^h(p_i, y^h, z_i) = W^h(y^h) + W_i(p_i, y^h, z_i; \mathbf{J}^h) + \epsilon_i^h \tag{8.23}$$

for all goods i and households h. The function W_i is assumed to be identical for all households. The vector $\mathbf{J}$ contains observable characteristics of the household and ϵ_i^h is a random variable which is independent of the arguments of W_i. See Chapter 10 for definitions.

Assuming a joint probability distribution on $\{\epsilon_i\}$, the probability, conditional on prices etc., that utility is maximized by consuming on-site time is

$$\pi_\ell = \text{prob} \left[\epsilon_i - \epsilon_\ell < W_\ell - W_i, \text{ for all } i \neq \ell \right] \tag{8.24}$$

Intuitively, even if $V_\ell > V_i$ for all i, the problem is that this fact cannot be observed by the researcher. At best, the researcher has information on the magnitudes of W_ℓ and W_i. But knowledge of these magnitudes is not sufficient to determine the sign of the change in utility. Recall the presence of the random terms ϵ_ℓ and ϵ_i in (8.23). At best, we are able to calculate a probability that $V_\ell > V_i$, i.e. the probability that $\epsilon_i - \epsilon_\ell < W_\ell - W_i$ in (8.24). The latter requires that an assumption is made about the probability distribution. For example, assuming a cumulative normal distribution and a binary choice situation, we obtain

$$\left. \begin{array}{l} \pi_\ell = F(W_\ell - W_0) = F(\triangle W) \\ \pi_0 = 1 - \pi_\ell \end{array} \right\} \tag{8.25}$$

where a subscript 0 denotes the second good, and F is the cumulative normal distribution function (see, for example Johnston, 1984; Maddala, 1984; Pindyck and Rubinfeld, 1976). Given specific forms for the observable part of the utility functions, the parameters of $\triangle W$ can be estimated from a sample of observed choices by maximizing the likelihood function associated with (8.25). The probability π_ℓ calculated from (8.25) can be interpreted as the fraction of consumers who will choose good ℓ. Moreover, the measure (8.21) can be computed for any price or quality change.[2] In order to illustrate the approach, the next section presents an empirical application.

7 *Estimating the value of a hunting permit from discrete response data*

In recent years, a few contingent market valuation studies have appeared involving discrete responses which are analysed by, for example, logit or probit techniques. The following example is adapted from Hanemann (1984d), who used data from the Bishop and Heberlein (1979) contingent valuation study of goose hunting in the Horicon Zone of East Central Wisconsin. A sample of hunters were asked if they would be willing to sell their hunting permits for a specified sum of money and, supposing they had not received their permits, if they would have been willing to pay a specified price to obtain one.

The above experiment was purely hypothetical, and no sales or purchases occurred. Bishop and Heberlein also performed a simulated market experiment in which they sent a real offer to a different sample of hunters. About 45 per cent of these actually sold their permits.

In contrast to most other studies, Bishop and Heberlein asked questions with yes or no answers, i.e. their approach involved discrete rather than continuous responses. The sample of hunters was divided into subsamples and each subsample of hunters was offered a specific amount of money ($1, $5, $10, $20, $30, $40, $50, $75, $100, $150, or $200). Bishop and Heberlein correlated the resulting yes and no responses with the amount of money offered to the individual using a logit model, and then derived an estimate of the value of a permit to an average hunter.

In his analysis of how the logit models should be formulated, Hanemann (1984d) assumed the following utility function:

$$V(\delta, y; \mathbf{J}) = W(\delta, y; \mathbf{J}) + \epsilon_\delta \qquad \delta = 0, 1 \tag{8.26}$$

where $\delta = 1$ if the individual possesses a permit to hunt and $\delta = 0$ if he does not, y is income, $\mathbf{J}$ is a vector of observable attributes of the individual which might affect his preferences, and ϵ_0, ϵ_1 are independent and identically distributed (i.i.d.) random variables with zero means. The hunter is assumed to know his utility function, but it contains some unobservable components. These latter components generate the stochastic structure of the model.

Suppose the hunter is offered an amount of money C to forego hunting. The offer is accepted if

$$W(0, y + C; \mathbf{J}) + \epsilon_0 \geqslant W(1, y; \mathbf{J}) + \epsilon_1 \tag{8.27}$$

i.e. if the sum of money C offered is so large that utility with C but without a permit to hunt is at least as high as utility with a permit but without C.

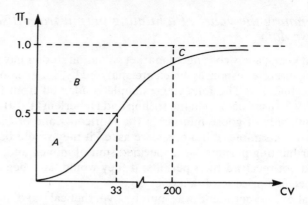

Figure 8.6 Illustration of different willingness to sell measures (the simulated market experiment), where
$\bar{C}V_B = A + B + C$
$\bar{C}V_b = A + B$

The individual hunter knows which choice maximizes utility, but the investigator does not. Hence for the latter, the response is a random variable, whose probability distribution is given by equation (8.24) with $\ell = 1$ and $i = 0$. Assuming a logit model, as Bishop and Heberlein, the willingness to sell probability can be written as

$$\pi_1 = F(\triangle W) = \frac{1}{1+e^{-\triangle W}} \tag{8.28}$$

where $F(\ )$ is the cumulative distribution function of $\epsilon_1 - \epsilon_0$, and $\triangle W = W(0, y, + C; \mathbf{J}) - W(1, y; \mathbf{J})$.

As noted by Hanemann, if a binary response model is to be interpreted as the outcome of a utility maximizing choice, then the argument of the cumulative distribution function must take the form of a utility difference. For example if $W = \alpha_i + \beta(y + \delta C)$, where $i = 0, 1$, and the vector $\mathbf{J}$ is suppressed, then $\triangle W = (\alpha_0 - \alpha_1) + \beta C$. On the other hand, in the logit model employed by Bishop and Heberlein, $\triangle W = \alpha + \beta\ell n\,C$, a particular formula which no explicit utility model (8.27) can generate (Hanemann, 1984d, p. 334). In any case, note that the associated regression equation can be written as

$$\ell n\left(\frac{\pi_1}{1-\pi_1}\right) = \alpha + \beta\ell n\,C \tag{8.29}$$

The dependent variable is simply the logarithm of the odds that the hunting permit is sold. Equation (8.29) is obtained by rearranging the terms in (8.28) and taking logarithms, as is shown in, for example, Pindyck and Rubinfeld (1976, p. 248). The model was estimated using GLS (applying Cox's modification to the odds ratio, a modification described and discussed in, for example, Pindyck and Rubinfeld, 1976, p. 250). Hanemann (1984d) reestimated the model, using the maximum-likelihood method and obtained slightly larger absolute values for the coefficients than Bishop and Heberlein. For a comprehensive discussion of the advantages and disadvantages of various estimation techniques in the case of qualitative dependent variables, the reader is referred to Johnston (1984) and Maddala (1984).

Hanemann proceeds by deriving three different willingness to pay measures. We will not go into the details but only report Hanemann's application, which is illustrated in Figure 8.6. Suppose the hunter's level of satisfaction is held constant at the initial ($\delta = 1$) level. Then, using Bishop and Heberlein's model $\triangle W = \alpha + \beta \ell n \, CV = 0$, i.e. $CV = \exp(-\alpha/\beta)$. Insertion of the estimates of α and β, reported by Bishop and Heberlein, yields point estimates of $CV_A = \$78$ for the hypothetical market experiment ($\alpha \approx -2.8$, $\beta \approx 0.64$) and $CV_B = \$33$ for the simulated market experiment ($\alpha \approx -3.9, \beta \approx 1.11$).

An alternative measure, suggested by Hanemann, is to employ the mean $\bar{C}\bar{V}$ of the distribution of the random variable C. This measure can be written as

$$\bar{C}\bar{V} = \int_c [1 - F(\triangle W)] dC = \int_c (1 + e^\alpha C^\beta)^{-1} dC \qquad (8.30)$$

where $c = (\infty, 0)'$, and $\triangle W = \alpha + \beta \ell n \, C$. Inserting the estimates of α and β yields, according to Hanemann, a point estimate $\bar{C}\bar{V}_B = \$310$, while the integral in (8.30) does not converge for the hypothetical market experiment.

In order to interpret (8.30), let us consider the following expression:[3]

$$\int_0^\infty (1 - F(x)) dx = \int_0^\infty (1 - \int_0^x f(t) dt) dx$$

$$= \int_0^\infty dx \int_x^\infty dt f(t) = \int_0^\infty dt \int_0^t dx f(t)$$

$$= \int_0^\infty t f(t) dt \qquad (8.31)$$

where $x = C$, $f(x)$ is the probability density function, and $F(x)$ is the cumulative distribution function. If (8.31) is absolutely convergent, its value is called the expected value or the mathematical expectation of x. This explains that $\bar{C}\bar{V}$ in (8.30) is interpreted, when it exists, as a mean value.

The money measure actually computed by Bishop and Heberlein

(1979) differed from (8.30) in that they truncated the measure at $C = \$200$. This produces $\bar{C}\bar{V}_a = \$101$ and $\bar{C}\bar{V}_b = \$63$, i.e. a truncation procedure may produce very poor approximations. Nevertheless, other authors (e.g. Seller *et al.*, 1985), who also calculate the measure (8.30) seem to truncate the measure. Moreover, as noted earlier, the model employed by Bishop and Heberlein, and used in deriving (8.30) since no other data were available, is not compatible with utility maximization. Thus, Hanemann's (1984d) study demonstrates that it is important to formulate logit models (and collect data) which are consistent with utility maximization, and to derive consumer surplus measures from the fitted models.

In closing, it should be mentioned that in the case of *continuous* responses, the appropriate approach is to estimate the money measure directly as a function of a set of independent variables (cf. Chapter 7). Nevertheless, suppose that we want to relate the measure, the CV say, to some functional form for the utility function $W(\cdot)$ in (8.26). Then we must insert the chosen function into (8.27) and solve the weak inequality (8.27) for CV, the amount of money that turns (8.27) into an equality. This procedure yields the function to be estimated. Once the equation is fitted to the data, the mean value of the dependent variable is obtained by calculating its expected value. This last step is mentioned simply because a glance at (8.27) shows that the disturbance term may enter the expression for CV in a complicated way (rather than additively, which is the usual assumption in econometrics).

CHAPTER 9

Consumer's surplus in an intertemporal context

Thus far we have dealt exclusively with consumer surplus measures in single-period models. This chapter opens a sequence of chapters that all deal with intertemporal problems. In developing the theory it is as well to discuss the simplest considerations first. For this reason the assumption that agents do not face any uncertainty is retained throughout the present chapter.

Section 1 extends the single-period model described in Chapter 3 to cover optimization for T-period horizons. Overall or lifetime consumer surplus measures are briefly discussed. Such overall measures, however, require huge amounts of information and may be difficult to calculate and estimate. Section 2, therefore, introduces so-called instantaneous consumer surplus measures, and investigates whether the present value of such instantaneous surpluses has the same sign as the lifetime utility change.

The prime attention in this book is focused on consumer surplus measures in atemporal and intertemporal models. However, in some applications, e.g. fishing and hunting, the size of the stock of a natural resource is of importance. Accordingly, the second part of this chapter focuses on models with renewable natural resources. In Section 3 the basic model developed in this chapter is modified so as to include a renewable resource. Section 4 presents a model used by Brown and Hammack (1972) and Hammack and Brown (1974) to analyse the optimal allocation of prairie wetlands in the north-central U.S. and Southern Canada. The main empirical results obtained by Brown and Hammack are reported in Section 5. An important question in studies of projects affecting several generations is how to compare welfare across generations. Therefore, the chapter ends with a brief presentation of different approaches for aggregation of intergenerational welfares.

147

1 *An intertemporal model*

We begin by considering a household with a T-period horizon which acts as if it maximizes a well-behaved utility function

$$U = U(\mathbf{x}^1, \ldots, \mathbf{x}^T) \tag{9.1}$$

subject to its lifetime budget constraint

$$y - \sum_{t=1}^{T} \alpha^t \mathbf{p}_c^t \mathbf{x}^t = 0 \tag{9.2}$$

where $\mathbf{x}^t = (x_{1t}, \ldots, x_{nt})$ is a row vector of goods consumed in the tth period, $\mathbf{p}_c^t = (p_{1t}^c, \ldots, p_{nt}^c)$ is the corresponding vector of prices in current terms, α^t is the present value in period 1 of one dollar in period t at the market rate of interest, and $y = \Sigma \alpha^t y_t$ is the sum of fixed incomes during T periods discounted to the initial period. As usual, primes that denote transposed vectors are suppressed.

Two remarks regarding the budget constraint (9.2) are in order. Firstly, the formulation implies that the household does not plan to leave its heirs assets or debts, although this can be incorporated trivially. Secondly, both borrowing and lending in any amount are allowed at the prevailing interest rate, i.e. capital markets are perfect.

Since the solution of this optimization problem parallels the solution of the optimization problem in Chapter 3 we will turn directly to the indirect utility function. This function is written as

$$V(\mathbf{p}, y) = U(x_{11}(p_{11}, \ldots, p_{nT}, y), \ldots, x_{nT}(p_{11}, \ldots, p_{nT}, y)) \tag{9.3}$$

where prices now are expressed as present values in order to simplify the notation, and $\mathbf{p}$ is a vector of order $1 \cdot (n \cdot T)$. From (9.3) it can be seen that the effects of changes in prices or income in this intertemporal model must be very similar to the effects obtained in the atemporal model investigated in Sections 1 and 2 of Chapter 3. In effect, the results concerning consumer surplus measures derived in Chapter 3 carry over to the intertemporal model, provided the word 'prices' is replaced by the phrase 'the present value of prices'.

Similarly, one may define the compensating variation (and, of course, the equivalent variation). As in the previous chapters, this measure can be derived from the expenditure function. Alternatively, using (9.3)

$$V(\mathbf{p}^b, y^b - \mathrm{CV}) = V(\mathbf{p}^a, y^a) = \bar{V}^a \tag{9.4}$$

where superscript a (b) denotes initial (final) level values, and CV is the overall compensating variation, i.e. the present value of the lump sum income that can be taken from (must be given to) the individual while

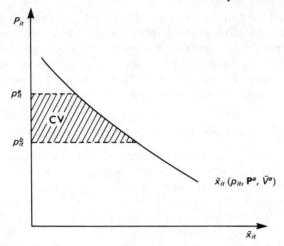

Figure 9.1 The compensating variation (CV) of a price fall in the intertemporal model

leaving him just as well off as he was before a fall (rise) in present value prices **p** and exogenous present value income y.

A graphical illustration of the case where only one price is changed is found in Figure 9.1. The area to the left of the compensated demand curve between the initial and final discounted prices corresponds to the compensating variation in income.

This result can be verified by differentiating the left-hand side of (9.4) with respect to p_{it} and CV, assuming that $\mathbf{p}^a = \mathbf{p}^b$, and noting that lifetime utility remains constant

$$\frac{\partial V}{\partial p_{it}}\, dp_{it} - \frac{\partial V}{\partial y}\, d\text{CV} = -\lambda \tilde{x}_{it} dp_{it} - \lambda d\text{CV} = 0 \qquad (9.5)$$

where $\tilde{x}_{it}(\mathbf{p}^a, \bar{V}^a) = x_{it}(\mathbf{p}^a, y^a)$is a compensated demand function; it should be recalled that the household remains at the prespecified utility level according to (9.4). Rearranging and integrating between initial and final prices yields

$$\text{CV} \equiv \int_c d\text{CV} = -\int_c \tilde{x}_{it}(p_{it}, \mathbf{P}^a, \bar{V}^a) dp_{it} \qquad (9.6)$$

where $c = (p_{it}^b, p_{it}^a)'$, and $\mathbf{P}^a$ is a row vector whose elements are the $nT-1$ fixed prices. The right-hand side of (9.6) gives an area corresponding to the shaded area in Figure 9.1.

All of the results concerning path (in-)dependency of consumer surplus measures derived in Chapter 3 carry over to the simple intertemporal model used in this section. This means, for example, that the CV and EV measures are still path independent. Moreover, areas to the left of ordinary demand curves are proportional to the underlying change in utility if and only if the utility function is such that the marginal utility of income is constant with respect to the prices which change. For further details the reader is referred back to Chapters 3 and 4.

2 *Overall versus instantaneous surplus measures*

The consumer surplus measures discussed in the previous section may be called overall or lifetime measures. Suppose, however, that the consumer's surplus of a price change is, instead, calculated at each point in time, as would probably be the procedure in an empirical study because of the obvious problems entailed in calculating an overall or lifetime measure. Drawing on Blackorby *et al.* (1984), we ask whether the present value of these instantaneous consumer's surpluses has the same sign as the overall utility change.

Some restrictions will be placed on the utility function in this section. Following Blackorby *et al.* (1984), the utility function is assumed to be additively separable

$$U(\mathbf{x}) = \sum_{t=1}^{T} \gamma^t U_t(\mathbf{x}^t) \tag{9.7}$$

where γ^t is a discount factor for period t. It is necessary to assume that the utility function is separable in order to ensure that instantaneous preferences exist, a property which will be needed in this section. The utility function (9.7) represents a special case of separability. (It has been argued that (9.7) is not a very sensible form of modelling behaviour if the discount rate varies over time since the marginal rate of substitution between any two fixed time periods will change as one moves forward through time. This is inconsistent with the existence of a stable underlying preference structure; see Blackorby *et al.* (1973), Deaton and Muellbauer (1983), and Strotz (1956).)

The lifetime indirect utility function is defined as

$$V(\mathbf{p}, y) = \max_{\mathbf{x}} \{U(\mathbf{x}) \mid \mathbf{p}\mathbf{x} \leq y\} \tag{9.8}$$

where $\mathbf{p}, \mathbf{x}'$ are vectors of order $1 \cdot (nT)$, and the lifetime budget constraint corresponds to the one specified in equation (9.2).

Similarly, the instantaneous indirect utility functions are given by

$$V_t(\mathbf{p}^t, y_t) = \max_{\mathbf{x}^t} \{U_t(\mathbf{x}^t) \mid \mathbf{p}^t\mathbf{x}^t \leq y_t\} \quad \text{for all } t \tag{9.9}$$

Note that prices as well as income in (9.9) are expressed as present values in period 1. However, one could equally well multiply through by the scalar $1/\alpha^t$ to obtain prices and income in current terms. This is because the instantaneous demand functions and hence also the instantaneous indirect utility functions are homogeneous of degree zero in prices and income. Moreover, note that the household in (9.9), but not in (9.8), is prevented from borrowing and lending.

Using (9.8) and (9.9) it can be shown that

$$V(\mathbf{p}, y) \geq \Sigma \alpha^t V_t(\mathbf{p}^t, y_t) = F(\{V_t(\mathbf{p}^t, y_t)\}) \tag{9.10}$$

The lifetime utility maximization problem assumes that the household is free to borrow and lend any amount of money at the prevailing market rate of interest. The instantaneous indirect utility functions, on the other hand, assume that the household is constrained by its instantaneous income. Hence, the household is prevented from reallocating its consumption expenditures over time by borrowing and lending. In general, this means that the discounted value of the sum of instantaneous utility levels, i.e. the right-hand side of (9.10), falls short of the maximum lifetime utility level given by the left-hand expression in (9.10). However, if the sequence of y_t is chosen in such a way that saving, even if allowed, equals zero at each point in time, then (9.10) reduces to an equality. Hence

$$V(\mathbf{p}, y) = \max_{\{y_t\}} \{F(\{V_t(\mathbf{p}^t, y_t)\}) \mid \Sigma y_t \leq y\} \tag{9.11}$$

Overall (CV) and instantaneous (CV$_t$) present value compensating variations for a price change from $\mathbf{p}^a$ to $\mathbf{p}^b$ are defined as

$$\left.\begin{array}{l} V(\mathbf{p}^b, y - \mathrm{CV}) = V(\mathbf{p}^a, y) = U^a \\[2mm] V_t(\mathbf{p}^{tb}, y_t - \mathrm{CV}_t) = V_t(\mathbf{p}^{ta}, y_t) = U_t^a \end{array}\right\} \tag{9.12}$$

The overall compensating variation is the maximum amount of present value income or wealth that the household is willing to give up to secure the change. Similarly, the instantaneous compensating variation is the (present value) income in period t that can be taken from the household while leaving it just as well off as prior to the fall in (present value) prices in that period. However it should be remembered that the household in (9.12) is prevented, by assumption, from reallocating its consumption over time.

Now, assume that condition (9.11) holds for the initial price vector $\mathbf{p} = \mathbf{p}^a$. Then, since the household remains at the initial utility level according to (9.12), it must also be the case that

$$V(\mathbf{p}^b, y - \mathrm{CV}) = F(\{V_t(\mathbf{p}^{tb}, y_t^* - \mathrm{CV}_t)\}) \tag{9.13}$$

where an asterisk denotes an optimal income level according to (9.11). However, using (9.10) we obtain

$$V(\mathbf{p}^b, y - \Sigma CV_t) \geq F(\{V_t(\mathbf{p}^{tb}, y_t^* - CV_t)\}) \tag{9.14}$$

Even if the instantaneous incomes are chosen in an optimal way, the household may want to reallocate its consumption over time following the payment of CV_t. The left-hand expression, but not the right-hand expression, in (9.14) permits such reallocations. This explains the weak inequality sign.

Combining (9.13) and (9.14) it follows that $CV \geq \Sigma CV_t$. This indicates that ΣCV_t, the sum of discounted instantaneous compensating variations, can, but need not, have the same sign as the overall measure CV. However, if $\Sigma CV_t \geq 0$ then it must be the case that $CV \geq 0$. In this case, the discounted sum of instantaneous compensating variations ranks the alternatives in the same order as the overall measure.

The present value criterion does not work when $\Sigma CV_t < 0$. Even if the sum of discounted instantaneous compensating variations is negative, the overall compensating variation may be positive. In order to obtain a rule for project rejection, we use the equivalent variation instead, i.e. the minimum amount the household would accept in lieu of the change from $\mathbf{p}^a$ *to* $\mathbf{p}^b$. Overall (EV) and instantaneous (EV_t) equivalent variations are defined as

$$\left. \begin{array}{l} V(\mathbf{p}^b, y) = V(\mathbf{p}^a, y + EV) = U^b \\[2mm] V_t(\mathbf{p}^{tb}, y_t) = V_t(\mathbf{p}^{ta}, y_t + EV_t) = U_t^b \end{array} \right\} \tag{9.15}$$

where U^b and U_t^b denote the final utility levels.

Using equations similar to equations (9.13) and (9.14) reveals that $EV \leq \Sigma EV_t$. Hence, if the discounted sum of instantaneous equivalent variations is negative, then the overall equivalent variation must also be negative. This means that the sum of discounted instantaneous EVs can be used to check whether a project should be rejected.

In short, if the discounted sum of compensating variations (equivalent variations) is positive (negative), then lifetime welfare has increased (decreased). However, ambiguous results occur when the present value of compensating variations is negative and the present value of equivalent variations is positive. This is demonstrated by Blackorby *et al.* (1984). Nevertheless, in many cases the sum of the discounted consumer's surplus should be a useful concept. Assume that we have estimated compensated demand functions for one or more periods. Even if these demand functions, like the demand functions in the previous chapters, only reflect instantaneous utility maximization according to (9.9), some conclusions do emerge. Firstly, if the sum of the discounted instantaneous compensating variations associated with a project is positive, the project is certainly worthwhile. Secondly, if $\Sigma CV_t < 0$, compute the discounted sum of instantaneous equivalent variations. If this discounted sum is negative, the project must be rejected. Although there remains a zone of indeterminacy ($\Sigma CV_t < 0$ while $\Sigma EV_t > 0$), the discounted sum approach greatly simplifies the calculations in the many cases for which definite conclusions emerge.

3 *A model with renewable resources*

In some circumstances, households may be interested in the preservation of a natural resource. For example, some households may assign a value to the blue whales as living creatures in a natural environment. A household owning and harvesting a renewable resource must recognize that if it harvests more than the natural growth of the resource, then the resource will sooner or later be depleted. This latter phenomenon raises the question of the optimal stock of a natural resource. It is outside the scope of this book to deal at length with this issue. However, in calculating, for example, the willingness to pay of hunters, a problem which we will consider in the subsequent sections, the size of the stock of the species is of obvious interest. This is one reason for briefly dealing with this issue. The second reason is that we will deal, in a later chapter, with the benefits of preserving a resource in a risky world. The following discussion may serve as a background to that chapter.

Let us first consider a simple extension of the model presented in Section 1. Assume that the household owns and harvests a renewable resource. The harvest in period t plus what is left to period $t+1$ equals (cannot exceed) what was left over from the previous period plus the growth of the stock in period t

$$s_{t-1} + F_t(s_{t-1}) = h_t + s_t \qquad (9.16)$$

where s_t is the stock at the end of period t, h_t is the harvest in period t, and $F_t(\cdot)$ represents the growth of the resource in period t as a function of the stock at the end of period $t-1$ with $\partial F_t/\partial s_{t-1} \gtreqqless 0$ and $\partial^2 F_t/\partial s_{t-1}^2 < 0$. These properties of the growth function can be visualized by referring to Figure 9.2.

Assume that all markets, including the market for the renewable resource, are perfect, that no value is assigned to the stock of the resource *per se*, and that there are no harvesting costs. Accordingly, the household maximizes

$$L = U(\mathbf{x}) + \lambda[y + \sum_{t=1}^{T} p_{1t}h_t - \mathbf{px}] + \sum_{t=1}^{T} \mu_t[s_{t-1} + F_t(s_{t-1}) - h_t - s_t] \quad (9.17)$$

where $\mathbf{x}$ and $\mathbf{p}'$ are vectors of order $1 \times (n \times T)$, a subscript 1 denotes the

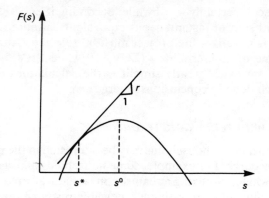

Figure 9.2 The growth function for a renewable resource

renewable resource so that x_{1t} denotes consumption of the resource in the tth period, and λ and μ_t are Lagrange multipliers. This formulation implies that the household sells (buys) $h_t - x_{1t}$ units of the resource in period t. Moreover, there is a constraint on the maximization problem over and above the budget constraint. The new constraint is the constraint on the level of harvest given by equation (9.16).

The terminal value of the stock discounted to the initial period is not included in (9.17). In order to maximize its total utility over an horizon containing T periods, the household must liquidate the stock at the end of period T. However, as T tends to infinity, the present value of this revenue tends to zero. This is why the terminal value discounted to the initial period is not included in expression (9.17) above; it should also be remembered that the management of a renewable resource is ultimately a long-run issue.

Taking partial derivatives of (9.17) with respect to x_{1t}, h_t and s_t, assuming interior solutions, yields

$$\frac{\partial L}{\partial x_{1t}} = \frac{\partial U(\mathbf{x})}{\partial x_{1t}} - \lambda p_{1t} = 0$$

$$\frac{\partial L}{\partial h_t} = \lambda p_{1t} - \mu_t = 0 \qquad\qquad \left.\begin{array}{c}\\[3em]\\\end{array}\right\} \quad (9.18)$$

$$\frac{\partial L}{\partial s_t} = -\mu_t + \mu_{t+1}\left[1 + \frac{\partial F_{t+1}(s_t)}{\partial s_t}\right] = 0$$

In order to interpret these conditions, we focus on a steady-state situation, i.e. where the household harvests the growth in each period so that the stock of the resource remains constant over time. Moreover, this steady-state is taken to imply that the resource price is constant in current terms, i.e. the discounted price decreases over time: $p_{1t} = (1+r)p_{1t+1}$. Using the two last lines of (9.18) respectively for two consecutive periods yields

$$\left. \begin{array}{l} \mu_t = (1+r)\mu_{t+1} \\[2ex] \mu_t = [1 + \dfrac{\partial F(s)}{\partial s}]\mu_{t+1} \end{array} \right\} \qquad (9.19)$$

The conditions in (9.19) imply that a utility maximizing household selects a stock such that marginal growth rate $(\partial F/\partial s)$ equals the market rate of interest (r). This is a well-known result in the economics of renewable resources (see Clark, 1976; Dasgupta, 1982; Dasgupta and Heal, 1979; and Johansson and Löfgren, 1985).

The intuition behind this result is quite simple. If the household reduces the stock by one unit in period t it can earn a once and for all revenue which equals $p_{1t} \cdot 1$. On the other hand, the household loses all future revenues from the harvest of the natural growth of this unit of the stock. If the marginal growth of the resource $(\partial F(s)/\partial s)$ falls short of the interest rate (r) it is profitable to decrease the stock, i.e. to transfer resources to the investment opportunity that gives the highest rate of return. If the marginal growth rate exceeds the market rate of interest, it pays to increase the stock of the resource. Hence, the optimal stock is the one for which the marginal growth rate equals the market rate of interest. As can be seen from Figure 9.2 this optimal stock s^* falls short of the stock s^0 which gives the maximum sustainable yield. It should be emphasized, however, that in more complicated models the optimal stock may exceed the maximum sustainable yield stock. For further information on such models, the reader is referred to Clark (1976), Herfindahl and Kneese (1974), Lecomber (1979), and Siebert (1982).

4 *The Brown–Hammack model for allocation of prairie wetlands*

The renewable resource model discussed in the previous section is a discrete time finite horizon model. Brown and Hammack (1972) have used a continuous time infinite horizon model to examine the optimal allocation of prairie wetlands in the north-central U.S. and Southern Canada.[1] If left in their natural state, these wetlands are essential to migratory waterfowl which are valued hunting objects. On the other hand, the farmers who own the land would prefer to drain the marshes and ponds and convert them to cropland. The Brown–Hammack model and its empirical results will be presented in this and the following section.

The benefits, of preserving the wetlands, are the aggregate consumer's surplus or the willingness to pay of waterfowl hunters while the costs are the opportunity costs or net value of the drained ponds in agricultural production. According to Brown and Hammack, the objective is to choose the bagged waterfowl kill and the number of ponds so as to maximize

$$\int_0^\infty [Hu(x_1(t), x_2(t)) - c(q(t))]\, e^{-rt} dt \qquad (9.20)$$

where H is the number of hunters, $u(\cdot, \cdot)$ is the individual hunter valuation function, $x_1(t)$ is the bagged waterfowl kill at time t, $x_2(t)$ is consumption of other goods (net of goods used as inputs in hunting) at time t, $c(\cdot)$ is the pond cost function, $q(t)$ is the number of ponds at time t, and r is the discount rate.

Brown and Hammack employ a standard assumption in natural resource economics, namely that the utility function is additively separable (which is invariably the case with infinite horizon models). It is important to note, however, that the valuation functions (like the cost functions) are expressed in monetary units and not in 'utils'. Given x_2, the valuation function gives the hunter's willingness to pay for bagged waterfowl. This function is assumed to be concave in the number of waterfowl killed and bagged. Moreover, the valuation function is constant over time, and relates to the 'representative' hunter. The latter explains that we multiply the valuation function by the (constant) number of hunters. The linear or convex cost function in (9.20) indicates the net value of agricultural output forgone as a function of the number of ponds (not drained and converted).

The discount rate in (9.20) ought to reflect the individual's rate of time preference, i.e. the minimum premium the individual must receive before he will postpone a dollar's worth of consumption in one period. Assuming perfect capital markets, it is reasonable to set the rate of time preference equal to the market rate of interest r (see Dasgupta and Heal, 1979, chs 9–10).

It remains to describe the ecological system. The constraint on the waterfowl population is written as

$$\dot{s}(t) = -s(t) + a[I(s(t), q(t)) + bs(t) - cHx_1(t)] \qquad (9.21)$$

where a dot denotes a partial derivative with respect to time, s is the number of mature birds, $I = I(\cdot, \cdot)$ is the number of immature, a is the survival fraction of the fall flight not killed by hunters from September to May, b is the survival fraction of adults from May to September, and c is an adjustment for unbagged kill.

Equation (9.21) describes the evolution over time of the waterfowl population. There is an outflow due to killing and other causes death, and an inflow of immature birds. Note that if the constants a, b, and c are all equal to one, the change over time of the population would simply equal the difference between the number of immature birds (the inflow) and the number killed and bagged by hunters (the outflow). In addition to (9.21), it must also hold that the initial population exceeds the threshold population and that, at any given moment in time, the resource stock and the harvest level cannot be negative.

In order to solve the problem raised by equations (9.20) and (9.21) we will use optimal control theory (see Pontryagin *et al.* 1962). The first step is to formulate the Hamiltonian function

$$L = [Hu(x_1, x_2) - c(q) + \mu(-s + aI(s, q) + abs - acHx_1)]e^{-rt} \quad (9.22)$$

where time indices are suppressed so as to simplify the notation, and μ is a costate variable. Among the necessary conditions for an 'interior' solution are

$$\frac{\partial L}{\partial x_1} = \frac{\partial u}{\partial x_1} - \mu ac = 0$$

$$\left. \begin{array}{l} \dfrac{\partial L}{\partial q} = -\dfrac{\partial c}{\partial q} + \mu a \dfrac{\partial I}{\partial q} = 0 \\[2mm] \dfrac{\partial L}{\partial s} = -\dot{\mu} + r\mu = \mu\left(-1 + a\dfrac{\partial I}{\partial s} + ab\right) \end{array} \right\} \quad (9.23)$$

For purely expositional purposes, let us assume that the constants a, b, and c all equal one. Then, from the first line in (9.23), it can be seen that μ can be interpreted as the marginal value to hunters of waterfowl. A marginal increase in the number of ponds q creates not only a cost in the form of agricultural output forgone, but also a benefit in the form of an increased number of birds (immature) which are valued hunting objects. The second line of (9.23) tells us that the number of ponds should be increased to the point where the marginal cost is equal to the marginal revenue. In order to interpret the final line of (9.23), let us consider a steady state in which the marginal value of waterfowl is constant over time, i.e. $\dot{\mu} = 0$. It then follows that the optimal waterfowl stock is that for which the marginal growth rate $\partial I / \partial s$ is equal to the discount rate; it should be remembered that we have assumed that $a = b = c = 1$. This is exactly the result derived in Section 3.

5 *Estimation of the Brown–Hammack model*

Brown and Hammack made an attempt to estimate the model described in the previous section, and some of their results are reported below. For a detailed presentation the reader should consult Brown and Hammack (1972) and Hammack and Brown (1974). A good summary version of their work is found in Krutilla and Fisher (1975, ch. 9).

In order to obtain information on the hunter valuation function Brown and Hammack used the interview technique (the so-called Davis technique; see Davis, 1964). A sample of waterfowl hunters were questioned concerning the value each attached to hunting. The central question was as follows: 'About how much greater do you think your costs would have had to have been before you would have decided not to have gone hunting at all during that season?' (Hammack and Brown, 1974, p. 92). The resulting willingness to pay amounts were regressed on a number of independent variables to obtain

$$\ell n\, u = 1.5 + 0.4\ell n\, x_1 + 0.4\ell n\, y + 0.2\ell n\, A + 0.1\ell n\, B \quad R^2 = 0.22 \quad (9.24)$$
$$\quad\quad\quad (12.9) \quad\quad (8.4) \quad\quad (4.4) \quad\quad (5.6)$$

where numbers in parentheses are t values, y is income, A is the number of seasons of waterfowl hunting, B is hunter costs for the season, and the number of observations is 1511. Taking the partial derivative with respect to x_1 and rearranging yields

$$\frac{\partial u}{\partial x_1} = 0.4 \frac{u}{x_1} \tag{9.25}$$

This expression indicates the valuation of a marginal unit of bagged kill and can be used to construct a (downward sloping) 'demand' curve for waterfowl kill. Note, however, that (9.25) is not defined for a zero hunting level; in fact, the underlying indifference surface does not intersect the $x_1=0$ hyperplane. Given the fact that the hunter is confronted with a sufficiently high (hypothetical) hunting cost to prevent him from hunting at all, it is not obvious why Hammack and Brown choose a functional form that is not consistent with such behaviour. Compare also equation (A6.16) in the Appendix to Chapter 6.

The growth function $I(s, q)$ was estimated using time series data running from 1955 to 1968. One (out of several different) estimated relationship is

$$\ell n\, I = 1.4 + 0.3\ell n\, s + 0.5\ell n\, q \quad\quad R^2 = 0.83 \tag{9.26}$$
$$\quad\quad (1.6) \quad\quad (6.7)$$

where I is the number of immature birds in September, s is the

Table 9.1 *Economic optimal values and historical values*

	Pond cost			Historical values
	$4.76	$12	$17	
Breeders, s (millions)	33	15	11	8
Ponds, q (millions)	22	6	4	1
Marginal value of waterfowl, μ (dollars)	2	3	4	
Total kill, x_1 (millions)	15	7	5	4

Assumptions: $a = 0.84$, $b = 0.95$, $c = 1.25$, $r = 0.08$ and number of hunters, $H = 0.279$ million.
Source: Krutilla and Fisher (1975, p. 229).

continental breeding population in the preceding May, and q is the number of Canadian prairie ponds in July of the same year.

A number of results are reported in Table 9.1. The cost function $c(q)$ was not estimated. As can be seen from the table, Brown and Hammack assumed that the cost of a marginal pond is constant. Assumptions about the parameters are set out below the table.

It is interesting to note that the economically optimal level of breeding stock far exceeds the one actually observed, at least for reasonable pond cost levels. This result is probably due to the fact that the wetlands are privately owned, i.e. there is a market for wetlands, while there is no market for hunting. In other words, ponds cause a positive external effect which is not reflected in the maximization problems of the landowners.

The results can also be used to calculate the maximum sustainable yield stock of breeders. Differentiating (9.21) with respect to t, with q and x_1 fixed, and setting the resulting expression equal to zero yields

$$-1 + a\frac{\partial I}{\partial s} + ab = 0 \qquad (9.27)$$

This expression can be solved to obtain the steady state stock that gives the highest possible sustainable level of kill. This level corresponds to point s^0 in Figure 9.2. Using the growth function given in (9.26) Brown and Hammack estimated the maximum sustainable yield stock to be 10 million for a pond value of 1.4 million. The corresponding figure for the value of kill is 6 million.

These maximum sustainable yield values are much lower than the economic optima reported in Table 9.1, at least for reasonable pond cost values. The reason is that the maximum sustainable yield values are calculated from the actual number of ponds. The economic optimal solution requires a much larger number of ponds; although a sufficiently high pond cost will reverse the result. Krutilla and Fisher (1975, pp. 231–3) point out that these results illustrate the problems with the biological, or maximum sustainable yield solution, i.e. how the decision maker is to choose the number of ponds. The (bio-)economic approach used by Brown and Hammack, on the other hand, indicates the optimal number of ponds, although this figure, like the rest of the results, must be interpreted with great care. Nevertheless, their approach is an interesting and promising one.

A final comment relates to the fact that the demand derived from the amenity services of a natural area may vary with time. Clearly, such factors as the degree of availability of substitute areas, as measured by cross-price elasticities and travel costs, and the rate of increase in real income, are of critical importance when forecasting demand. Recall the discussion in Chapter 8. Hammack and Brown do not consider such reasons for fluctuations in demand. The reader interested in practical methods used to forecast demand for scarce amenity resources is referred to Krutilla and Fisher (1975), who consider the case of a unique natural area, and Cuddington *et al.* (1981), who deal with the case where the resource in question is not unique but has recognized substitutes. Basically, Cuddington *et al.* multiply the present value of the consumer's surplus in year t by $(1+i)^t$ with i reflecting the rate of increase in real income. Moreover, the size of the surplus depends on the presence of substitute areas, as measured by a cross-price elasticity. Obviously such modifications may have quite an influence on the size of the present value of natural amenities. More generally, variations over time in benefits and/or costs highlight the fact that the decision *when* to undertake a project is of the utmost importance. We will consider this issue in a risky world in Chapter 11. The reader interested in the optimal timing of a reversible development project in situations without uncertainty is referred to Porter (1984).

6 *Aggregation of intergenerational welfares*

In a perfect market economy, the market rate of interest ought to provide a correct reflection of the rate of time preference of present consumers for consumption in the present rather than in the next period. It also indicates the value of using resources in investment projects. In the absence of a perfect market economy, it is well known that the social discount rate may exceed or fall short of the market rate of interest. For a discussion, as well as surveys of different methods for the practical determination of the social discount rate, the reader is referred to any textbook on welfare economics. We will, nevertheless, briefly consider one particular problem, namely the fact that the market rate of interest, even in a perfect market economy, need not accurately reflect society's regard for consumption by future generations.

A particularly important point concerns the fact that, in this chapter, the projects under consideration may affect several generations. It is especially this feature which causes problems in the evaluation of environmental programmes. This section, which draws heavily on Dasgupta and Heal (1979, ch. 9), reviews different frameworks for weighting different generations.

Probably the most influential doctrine is classical utilitarianism. By utilitarianism is meant 'the ethical theory, that the conduct which, under any given circumstances, is objectively right, is that which will produce the greatest amount of happiness on the whole; that is, taking into account all whose happiness is affected by the conduct' (Sidgwick, 1890, p. 409). According to this doctrine, utility is summed across all individuals in all generations without any discounting of future utilities. In point of fact, several utilitarians have found the discounting of future utilities morally objectionable (see, for example, Ramsey, 1928; Harrod, 1948, for discussions of this issue).

However, if there is a positive chance that life on earth will cease to exist, then one may find it defensible to discount future utilities at positive rates. For instance, if it is assumed that the probability π of survival is constant over time, then the probability that the world exists at date τ is $(\pi)^\tau$, which can be written as $(\pi)^\tau = 1/(1+r)^\tau$, where r is an appropriately chosen discount rate. Thus, it would seem to be a legitimate procedure to discount future utilities in a risky world, not because one is myopic, but because there is a positive chance that future generations will not exist. It does not make any sense to save or transfer consumption (resources) to generations that will not exist.

An alternative approach, associated with Harsanyi (1955) and Rawls (1972), is founded on the concept of social contracts. Suppose a particular individual does not know if he belongs to a relatively rich or poor generation. Instead he faces a subjective probability of being a member of any generation t. Accordingly, it is reasonable to choose between two intertemporal consumption programmes on the basis of the expected utility associated with the programmes. If the number of generations is finite, one possibility is to proceed as above. That is, to assume that the probability of doomsday follows a Poisson process so that the probability of survival at date τ is $(\pi)^\tau = (1+r)^{-\tau}$. Thus, there are formal similarities between this approach and the 'modified' utilitarian approach discussed previously. According to both approaches, future utilities are discounted at positive rates. There are, however, also important differences. In particular, the Harsanyi framework assumes that the choosing party satisfies the Neumann–Morgenstern axioms of expected utility (to be discussed in the next chapter). The utilitarian utility functions, on the other hand, are measures of the quantity of happiness of different generations (see Dasgupta and Heal, 1979, pp. 271–3, for a detailed discussion of this issue).

The third approach to the treatment of intergenerational welfare distribution introduces a social welfare function

$$W = W(U_1, \ldots, U_T) \tag{9.28}$$

where, for simplicity, there is only a single (representative) individual in each generation. This welfare function is usually assumed to be continuous and Paretian. The latter means that if two utility sequences have the property that $U_t^a \geqslant U_t^b$ for all t and the strict inequality holds for at least one t, then $W(U_1^a, \ldots, U_T^a) > W(U_1^b, \ldots, U_T^b)$. Moreover, (9.28) is assumed to obey the principle of equal treatment of different generations. Thus, if any two generations are interchanged in (9.28), welfare would be left unchanged.

However, there is no welfare function which is simultaneously continuous, Paretian, and satisfies the equal treatment principle, as is demonstrated in Dasgupta and Heal (1979, pp. 277–80). One way of getting round this problem is to dispense with the equal treatment principle. It is now possible to show that a continuous and Paretian welfare function can be written as

$$W = \sum_{t=1}^{\infty} U_t(1+r)^{-t+1} \tag{9.29}$$

provided the function satisfies the assumptions of independence and stationarity. Loosely speaking, the first assumption means that one treats the well-being of different generations independently of one another. The stationarity assumption means that in the evaluation of two utility sequences, the calendar date for the timing of the utility levels ought not to matter (see Dasgupta and Heal, 1979, pp. 278–80).

In closing, it is interesting to note that several frameworks are consistent with the additive separable form (9.29), with $r \geqslant 0$, which were employed in previous sections of this chapter. One need not appeal to a particular framework, such as the utilitarian one, in order to utilize the simple approach in (9.29). Naturally, it cannot be said that this approach is self-evident in intertemporal studies. On the contrary, the basic issue of the choice of principles for intergenerational aggregation remains unresolved.

CHAPTER 10

Welfare change measures
in a risky world

There are many important situations in which prices, income or preferences are not known with certainty. For example, the waterfowl hunter of Chapter 9 cannot know for sure the number of waterfowl he will kill and bag during the next hunting season. Similarly, the recreationist of Chapter 8 may be uncertain as regards travel costs, entrance fees, and the weather at the site. In such cases it may seem reasonable to distinguish between risk, that refers to situations where probabilities are knowable, and uncertainty proper, which applies to situations where probabilities cannot even be defined. In this book, we will deal exclusively with the former class of situations, although the terms risk and uncertainty are used interchangeably.

Ordinary or compensated demand functions, obtained under certainty, imply very little about a household's attitudes towards risk. This is because the form of demand functions is an ordinal property, while risk aversion is a cardinal property of preferences. Moreover, while conventional demand theory begins with a quasi-concave direct utility function, risk analysis hinges on the stronger assumption of concavity or convexity. The first section of this chapter is devoted to exploring these different concepts.

In Section 2, the welfare change measures derived in previous chapters are modified so as to be able to cope with cases of uncertainty where some decisions must be made before prices are known. These issues are discussed in the context of a simple two-commodity model. Section 3 presents an empirical study involving a discrete choice situation as well as uncertain prices. In Section 4, we introduce the method of backward dynamic programming, which considers future optimal decisions as stochastic depending on new information that is accumulated along the way. In Section 5, this model is used to introduce a few concepts that have been the subject of much discussion among environmental econo-

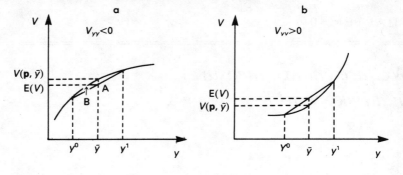

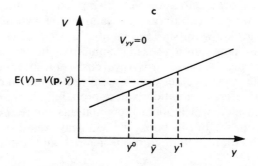

Figure 10.1 (a) A risk-averse, (b) a risk-loving, and (c) a risk-neutral household

mists: expected consumer's surplus, option price, and option value. In terms of the models used in this chapter, the debate concerns the money measure that ought to be used in situations involving changes in future demands which are viewed as random from the standpoint of the present.

1 *Risk measures and the properties of the utility function*

In order to illustrate the meaning of risk attitudes, it is useful to consider a household which faces an uncertain income. Taking partial derivatives with respect to income of a well-behaved indirect utility function $V(\mathbf{p}, y)$ of the form considered in the previous chapters (further assumptions – in particular cardinality – are introduced below) yields

$$
\left.
\begin{aligned}
\frac{\partial V}{\partial y} &= \lambda(\mathbf{p}, y) \\
\frac{\partial^2 V}{\partial y^2} &= \frac{\partial \lambda}{\partial y} = V_{yy}
\end{aligned}
\right\} \tag{10.1}
$$

A household is said to be risk averse with respect to income risk if $V_{yy} < 0$. Conversely, the household is a risk lover if $V_{yy} > 0$, and risk neutral if the expression is equal to zero. Let us consider a Friedman–Savage (1948) diagram such as Figure 10.1 in which utility is depicted as an increasing function of income while all prices are held constant.

Figure 10.1a is drawn on the assumption that $V_{yy} < 0$. Assume that the household receives income y^0 with a probability of one-half, and income y^1 with a probability of one-half. Since the actual outcome is either y^0 or y^1, the expected utility is

$$E(V) = 0.5\, V(\mathbf{p}, y^0) + 0.5\, V(\mathbf{p}, y^1) \tag{10.2}$$

where E is the expectations operator. However, the household clearly prefers to get the expected income $\bar{y}$ rather than the 'gamble', since

$$V(\mathbf{p}, \bar{y}) > E(V) = \Sigma_i \pi^i V(\mathbf{p}, y^i) \tag{10.3}$$

where y^i occurs with probability π^i ($0 < \pi^i < 1$), and $\bar{y} = E y^i$. Such behaviour, i.e. preferring the expected value of a gamble rather than the gamble, is called risk aversion. By moving horizontally to the left from point A towards point B in Figure 10.1a it can be seen that a risk averter is a person who would be willing to forego some part of his income to change a random prospect into a certain one.

Figure 10.1b pictures the case of a risk-loving household ($V_{yy} > 0$). In this case the straight line between y^0 and y^1 is above the corresponding segment of the utility function. Thus the household in Figure 10.1b may prefer a risky prospect to a certain one even if the former gives a lower expected income.

Finally, a risk-neutral household ($V_{yy} = 0$) has a utility function which is linear in income. Clearly, such a household will be indifferent between certain and risky prospects, as is seen from Figure 10.1c.

In the previous chapters it has been assumed that the direct utility function is strictly quasi-concave. The definition of risk attitudes, on the other hand, turns on the stronger assumption of concavity or convexity.

A function is quasi-concave for all commodity bundles $\mathbf{x}^0$, $\mathbf{x}^1$ over a region if

$$U(\pi \mathbf{x}^0 + (1-\pi)\mathbf{x}^1) \geqslant \min \{U(\mathbf{x}^0),\ U(\mathbf{x}^1)\} \tag{10.4}$$

for all $0 \leqslant \pi \leqslant 1$. The function is strictly quasi-concave if the strict inequality holds for $0 < \pi < 1$.

A function is concave over a region if

$$U(\pi \mathbf{x}^0 + (1-\pi)\mathbf{x}^1) \geqslant \pi U(\mathbf{x}^0) + (1-\pi)U(\mathbf{x}^1) \tag{10.5}$$

for all $0 \leqslant \pi \leqslant 1$, and strictly concave if the strict inequality holds for all

$0 < \pi < 1$. By reversing the signs of the inequalities in (10.4) and (10.5) we obtain definitions of quasi-convexity and convexity respectively. Referring back to Figure 10.1, it should be obvious that the measures of risk attitudes are founded on the concept of concavity/convexity, i.e. $V[\mathbf{p}, E(y)] \gtrless E[V(\mathbf{p}, y)]$ when the indirect utility function is strictly concave (convex) in income, a theorem often referred to as Jensen's inequality. Moreover, Hanoch (1977) has shown that risk aversion with respect to income implies and is implied by risk aversion with regard to quantity bundles. Hence, $V_{yy} < 0$ means that the direct utility function is strictly concave.

Measures of risk aversion are defined cardinally, whereas conventional demand theory assumes an ordinal utility function. The latter, i.e. ordinal measurability, means that if a function $U(\mathbf{x})$ is a suitable representation of the household's preference orderings, any other increasing function or monotonic transformation of $U(\mathbf{x})$, say $F(\mathbf{x}) = f(U(\mathbf{x}))$ with $\partial f / \partial U > 0$, will serve equally well. The signs of the first derivatives of an ordinal function are unchanged by a monotonic transformation, but signs of higher order derivatives, e.g. the sign of V_{yy}, can change (since no restriction can be placed upon $\partial^2 f / \partial U^2$).

If the utility function is weakly cardinal, any positive affine transformation of the function, say $G(\mathbf{x}) = a + bU(\mathbf{x})$ with $b > 0$, will serve equally well. Preferences are strongly cardinal if, in addition to being weakly cardinal, the ratio of two magnitudes of preference differences is also a meaningful magnitude of preference. The assumption of strongly cardinal preferences means that it is meaningful to say that $[U(\mathbf{x}^1) - U(\mathbf{x}^0)]/[U(\mathbf{x}^3) - U(\mathbf{x}^2)] = r$ means that a move from $\mathbf{x}^0$ to $\mathbf{x}^1$ is r times preferable to the move from $\mathbf{x}^2$ to $\mathbf{x}^3$ (see Morey, 1984, for details). Furthermore, note that the signs of the partial derivatives of any order, and hence the sign of V_{yy}, are unchanged by any positive affine transformation. In both the cardinal and the ordinal cases, the considered transformations leave the indifference map unchanged.

The magnitude of the second-order derivative V_{yy}, which was used as the risk indicator above, is not invariant under a linear transformation. This is readily verified by multiplying the (cardinal) utility function by a constant and taking the second-order derivative with respect to income. For this reason V_{yy} is not normally used as a measure of risk aversion. The best-known measure, the Arrow–Pratt coefficient of *absolute* risk aversion, is obtained by normalizing by V_y, and reversing the sign

$$R(y) = -\left(\frac{\partial^2 V}{\partial y^2}\right)/\left(\frac{\partial V}{\partial y}\right) = -\frac{V_{yy}}{V_y} \qquad (10.6)$$

Multiplying by income y yields the so-called Arrow–Pratt index of *relative* risk aversion

$$R^R(y) = -y\frac{V_{yy}}{V_y} \tag{10.7}$$

In a cardinal world, the signs of the partial derivatives of these measures with respect to income tell us whether risk aversion is increasing or decreasing when income is increased (see Arrow, 1971; Hey, 1979, 1981; Pratt, 1964).

In conclusion, it is important to emphasize that in analysis of expected utility, only the sub-utility indices $V(\mathbf{p}, y^i)$ need to be cardinally measurable. Expected utility, i.e. $E(V) = \Sigma\pi^i V(\mathbf{p}, y^i)$, on the other hand, is an ordinal concept, i.e. if $E(V)$ maximizes expected utility, so does $f[E(V)]$, where $f[\ ]$ is a monotonic increasing transformation. See Hirshleifer and Riley (1979), Jones-Lee (1976, ch. 3), and Neumann and Morgenstern (1947, ch. 1) for detailed analysis of the axioms underlying the expected utility hypothesis.

2 *Consumer's surplus under price uncertainty*

We now introduce the case where a household must decide upon quantities of commodities before the uncertainty about some prices is resolved. The analysis is performed in terms of a household consuming two (vectors of) normal commodities, x_1 and x_2, respectively. Prices of at least one commodity are random at the time that a decision on x_1 must be taken, but uncertainty is resolved before the decision on x_2 is taken. This last assumption is needed to ensure that the budget constraint is not violated. The fact that decisions are not taken at the same time means that prices are now present value prices, assuming perfect capital markets. However, for reasons which will become apparent, the price of the first commodity, but not the price of the second commodity, is assumed to be stochastic. This makes an interpretation of the model in intertemporal terms somewhat awkward. An explicit intertemporal model is introduced in Section 4.

The utility function of the household is written as

$$U = U(x_1, X_2) = U(x_1, \frac{y-p_1x_1}{p_2}) \tag{10.8}$$

where $X_2 = (y-p_1x_1)/p_2$ from the budget constraint. This and all other utility functions considered in the rest of this book are assumed to be cardinal and well-behaved.[1] For a detailed discussion of these assumptions and their implications the reader is referred to Drèze and Modigliani (1972) and Epstein (1975). Detailed comparative statics examinations of this and similar models can also be found in Block and Heineke (1975), Hey (1979), and Sandmo (1970).

Suppose that p_1 fluctuates randomly ($0 < p_1 < \infty$). If p_1 is a discrete variable, its expected value is a weighted average of all possible price levels. The expected value of a continuous variable is defined in a very similar fashion. In this latter case, we integrate for values of p_1 to obtain

$$E(p_1) = \int_c p_1 f(p_1) dp_1 = \bar{p}_1 \tag{10.9}$$

where the probability density function $f(p_1)$ is the household's subjective probability distribution on p_1, with finite moments of at least first and second order, c is the range of p_1, and a bar denotes an expected value. A simple and commonly used specification is: $p_1 = \bar{p}_1 + \beta\varepsilon$ with $E(\varepsilon) = 0$, where β is the standard deviation. A spread-preserving increase in the price may be represented by an increase in $\bar{p}_1$ and an increase in β may be used to represent a mean-preserving increase in the variability of the price.[2] This particular specification is implicitly employed in this chapter.

The (Neumann–Morgenstern) household is assumed to act as if it maximizes expected utility

$$E(U) = \int_c U(x_1, \frac{y - p_1 x_1}{p_2}) f(p_1) dp_1 \tag{10.10}$$

The problem that confronts the household is to choose the x_1 that will maximize this expression. The first-order condition for an interior solution is

$$E[U_1 - \frac{U_2 p_1}{p_2}] = 0 \tag{10.11}$$

where subscripts 1 and 2 denote partial derivatives with respect to x_1 and X_2 respectively. In principle, (10.11) can be solved to yield the resulting demand function for the first commodity

$$x_1 = x_1(\bar{p}_1, y, \phi) \tag{10.12}$$

where ϕ contains moments about the mean characterizing the stochastic properties of p_1.

Consumption of the second commodity, on the other hand, is a random variable defined by the budget constraint

$$X_2 = \frac{y - p_1 x_1(\bar{p}_1, p_2, y, \phi)}{p_2} = X_2(\bar{p}_1, p_1, p_2, y, \phi) \tag{10.13}$$

As long as the price of the first commodity fluctuates randomly, X_2 is also a random variable (but prices, etc, are assumed to be such that $X_2 > 0$). However, its expected value is obtained by integrating (10.13) over the range of p_1, i.e. replacing p_1 in the middle expression of (10.13) by its expected value $\bar{p}_1$.

Substituting (10.12) and (10.13) into (10.10) yields an indirect expected utility function

$V = \mathrm{E}[v(\bar{p}_1, p_1, p_2, y, \phi)]$

$\qquad = \int_c U[x_1(\bar{p}_1, p_2, y, \phi), X_2(\bar{p}, p_1, p_2, y, \phi)] f(p_1) dp_1$ (10.14)

This function gives the maximum expected utility as a function of p_2 and y, which are known with certainty, and the stochastic properties of p_1. Taking partial derivatives of (10.14) with respect to (the mean of) prices and income yields

$$\left.\begin{array}{l} \dfrac{\partial V}{\partial \bar{p}_1} = - \dfrac{\mathrm{E}(U_2) x_1(\bar{p}_1, p_2, y, \phi)}{p_2} \\[3mm] \dfrac{\partial V}{\partial p_2} = - \dfrac{\mathrm{E}[U_2 \cdot X_2(\bar{p}_1, p_1, p_2, y, \phi)]}{p_2} \\[3mm] \dfrac{\partial V}{\partial y} = \dfrac{\mathrm{E}(U_2)}{p_2} \end{array}\right\} \quad (10.15)$$

This is shown in the appendix to this chapter. Note that the second line does not simplify to anything like the expression in the first line. This is because X_2, but not x_1, is a stochastic variable. We will return to this issue in Section 5.

Using (10.14) one can calculate the compensating variation CV of a *ceteris paribus* change in the mean price. This indicates the non-stochastic amount of money that the household is willing to pay, following a mean price fall, in order to return to the initial expected level of satisfaction

$\mathrm{E}[v(\bar{p}_1^b, \bar{p}_1^b + \varepsilon, p_2, y - \mathrm{CV}, \phi)] = \mathrm{E}[v(\bar{p}_1^a, \bar{p}_1^a + \varepsilon, p_2, y, \phi)] = \bar{V}^a$ (10.16)

where a and b denote the initial and final mean prices respectively, and $\bar{p}_1^i + \varepsilon$ denotes the actual price in 'state' i, where $i = a, b$. For a marginal change in the mean, we obtain from (10.15) and (10.16)

$-\mathrm{E}(\bar{U}_2)\, \tilde{x}_1 d\bar{p}_1 - \mathrm{E}(\bar{U}_2)\, \dfrac{\partial \mathrm{CV}}{\partial \bar{p}_1}\, d\bar{p}_1 = 0$ (10.17)

where a tilde, as usual, denotes a compensated function, and $x_1(\bar{p}_1, p_2, y - \mathrm{CV}, \phi) = \tilde{x}_1(\bar{p}_1, p_2, \bar{V}^a, \phi)$. Note that both the compensated demand function and the marginal compensation are non-stochastic and thus 'factor out' of the expectation. Rearranging and integrating between initial and final mean prices yields

$\mathrm{CV} = -\int_c \tilde{x}_1(\bar{p}_1, p_2, \bar{V}^a, \phi) d\bar{p}_1$ (10.18)

where $c = (\bar{p}_1^b, \bar{p}_1^a)'$, and $\mathrm{CV} = \int_c (\partial \mathrm{CV}/\partial \bar{p}_i) d\bar{p}_i$.

Thus, the compensating variation of a mean price change can be measured left of the compensated demand curve for x_1 corresponding to

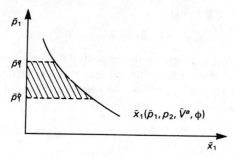

Figure 10.2 The compensating variation (shaded area) of a mean price change

the initial expected utility level. This is illustrated in Figure 10.2. Similarly, the equivalent variation of a subjective mean price change is obtained by fixing the utility level at its final expected value. In general, however, the CV and EV measures will not coincide, unless the underlying utility function is such that income effects are zero for the commodity under consideration. (Compare with the analysis in Chapter 4.)

The above analysis is concerned with a *ceteris paribus* mean price change. The same approach can be used to evaluate changes in higher moments of the probability distribution for p_1. Referring back to the particular specification discussed below equation (10.9), i.e. $p_1 = \bar{p}_1 + \beta\varepsilon$, an increase in β may be used to calculate CV and EV measures of a mean-preserving increase in the variability of the price. Moreover, income uncertainty is easily introduced into the model. It is a straightforward matter to show that x_1 will be a function of expected income $\bar{y}$, provided the uncertainty is revealed after a decision is taken on how much to consume of the commodity. In principle, the model can also be used to consider the effects of policies that affect future prices, i.e. p_2. However, such an investigation is delayed until Sections 4 and 5.

3 *Discrete choice under uncertainty: housing tenure*

In order to appreciate the results derived in the previous sections it is useful to illustrate them by means of an empirical study. Unfortunately, there seem to be no straightforward applications on the consumer surplus issue available. However, there is at least one study that examines a discrete choice situation similar to the one considered in Section 7 of Chapter 8, namely the choice, in a risky world, between owning and renting a house. In Chapter 8, the value of a hunting permit was estimated from discrete response data. The approach implicitly assumes that hunters know the value of a permit with certainty. Similarly, the standard approach to the choice between renting and owning assumes that households have perfect foresight in the sense that they know the true user cost of housing. However, it is highly unlikely that households are able to forecast the fluctuations in this user cost with certainty.

Recently, Rosen *et al.* (1984) have constructed and estimated a model of tenure choice that explicitly allows for the effects of uncertainty. As in Chapter 8, the individual makes his choice by comparing the outcomes of two sub-problems. Let $V(p_1, y)$ be the indirect utility function conditional on owning the house, and $V(p_2, y)$ the indirect utility function when renting is selected. The real cost p_1 of owner-occupation and the real renting price p_2 are both surrounded with uncertainty while income and the (*numéraire*) price of a composite good consumed by the household are known with certainty. The sub-utility functions are similar to those considered in Section 1, the difference being that Rosen *et al.* consider price risk instead of income risk.

An individual elects to own if

$$\triangle V = E[V(p_1, y) - V(p_2, y)] > 0 \tag{10.19}$$

where the expectation is taken with respect to the joint distribution of prices (compare equation 10.27). Equation (10.19) simply states that the individual elects to own if the expected utility of owning exceeds the expected utility of renting. Taking second-order Taylor series expansions around the points $(\bar{p}_1, y)$ and $\bar{p}_2, y)$ respectively yields

$$E[V(p_i, y)] = V(\bar{p}_i, y) + \frac{V_{i1}(\bar{p}_i, y)\sigma_i^2}{2} \qquad i=1,2 \tag{10.20}$$

where a bar denotes an expected price, $V_i E(p_i - \bar{p}_i) = 0$, $V_{i1} = \partial^2 V/\partial \bar{p}_i^2$ and $\sigma_i^2 = E(p_i - \bar{p}_i)^2$. Substituting (10.20) into (10.19) and proceeding in the same way as in Section 7 of Chapter 8, Rosen *et al.* suggest the following specification to be estimated (by OLS)

$$\ell n(\frac{\pi}{1-\pi}) = \alpha + \beta_1 \bar{p}_1 + \beta_2 \bar{p}_2 + \beta_3 \sigma_1^2 + \beta_4 \sigma_2^2 + \beta_5 y + \varepsilon \tag{10.21}$$

where π is the aggregate proportion of home-owners. Thus, in this model, expected prices as well as forecast error variances affect the tenure decision, in sharp contrast to the perfect foresight discrete choice model considered in Chapter 8. It should also be noted that to the extent that the two underlying indirect utility functions are identical (up to an additive constant), expected prices and forecast error variances affect the tenure decision in a symmetrical fashion, i.e. $\beta_1 = -\beta_2$ and $\beta_3 = -\beta_4$. This assumption is employed by Rosen *et al.* when estimating (10.21).

Rosen *et al.* assume that as more information becomes available, individuals employ it when making forecasts, but continue to use old information as well. Basically, they assume (conditional) rational expectations, in contrast to adaptive expectations. According to the hypothesis of rational expectations, which has been proposed by the new classical economists, expectations are formed on the basis of all the available relevant information concerning the variable being predicted. As the originator of the concept, John Muth (1961), suggested, rational expectations are essentially the same as the predictions of the relevant economic theory. This is noted here because in future research on environmental economics, a field which is often concerned with 'long-run' issues, the modelling of expectations will probably be of the utmost importance.

After some preliminary analysis of the time series on prices, Rosen *et al.* (1984, pp 408–9) selected an autoregressive integrated moving-average (ARIMA) process to make forecasts in year τ:

$$p_{it} - p_{it-1} = \phi_i(\tau)(p_{it-1} - p_{it-2}) + \mu_t \qquad i = 1,2 \qquad (10.22)$$

where $t = 0,1,\ldots,\tau-1$, $\phi_i(\tau)$ is the parameter to be estimated, and μ_t is a normally distributed white noise term. This equation is reestimated each year τ with observations from year 0 to $\tau-1$. The estimate of $\phi_i(\tau)$ can be used to solve (10.22) recursively to generate forecasts of the price p_i for as many future years from τ as desired. Rosen *et al.* assume that people form expectations not only for the current year but for the following four years, and base their tenure choice on the five-year average.

Equation (10.22) is also used to produce a series of forecast error variances. However, due to considerations of space, the tedious calculations are not reported here. Instead we turn directly to the results obtained when estimating (10.21) using annual U.S. data for 1956 to 1979, since the results provide a good idea of the interpretation of the model used by Rosen *et al.*

$$\ell n\left(\frac{\pi}{1-\pi}\right)=0.125-4.75(\bar{p}_1-\bar{p}_2)-6.89(\sigma_1^2-\sigma_2^2)+2.04x \quad R^2=0.99$$
$$(10.21')$$

where x is per capita real consumption, the symmetry constraints $\beta_1 = -\beta_2$ and $\beta_3 = -\beta_4$ have been imposed, and all the β-coefficients are statistically significant at conventional levels. When the expected excess of the cost of owning over renting increases, the proportion of owner-occupiers decreases. Similarly, greater uncertainty in the price of owning reduces the proportion of home-owners. Finally, and also as expected, an increase in real consumption, which is used as a proxy for permanent income, increases the proportion of home-owners.

Athough the study reported here refers to the housing market, the approach taken by Rosen *et al.* is also certainly of great interest to environmental economists. For example, a decision whether or not to visit a recreation site may be influenced by expectations of the weather, the rate of congestion, and the size of the travel costs. Similarly, an individual may be uncertain about the true value of preserving a natural area or the value of obtaining a hunting permit, so that his reported willingness to pay is an expected consumer surplus measure. Apparently, in situations where individuals are unable to forecast variables with certainty, it may be quite misleading to use consumer surplus formulas that explicitly or implicitly are based on that particular assumption.

4 *Intertemporal models*

The approach used to derive consumer surplus measures in Section 2 is readily extendable to the multi-period case. Referring back to the T-period horizon model in Section 1 of Chapter 9, we select a *numéraire* commodity, e.g. x_n^T. As in Section 2 the budget constraint is then used to eliminate x_n^T from the utility function. If the household faces random prices, it maximizes the expected value of this T-period utility function.

However, this approach assumes that the subjective distribution of prices is constant over time, i.e. it ignores the possibility that decisions in later periods can be adjusted as more price information becomes available. On the other hand, the dynamic programming technique examined in this section, considers future optimal decisions to be stochastic depending on new information that the household accumulates over time.

In order to illustrate the principles of this technique, we will analyse a form of uncertainty which is probably closer to reality, in many situations, than those considered previously. Current prices are now known with certainty while future prices are random. For the sake of simplicity, let us suppose that the utility function is additively separable

$$U(\mathbf{x}) = \sum_{t=1}^{T} \gamma^t U_t(\mathbf{x}^t) \tag{10.23}$$

where γ^t is a discount factor for period t, and $\mathbf{x}^t = (x_{1t}, \ldots, x_{nt})$ is a vector of goods consumed in period t.

In order to analyse the utility maximization problem in a risky world, Bellman's (1957) technique of backwards induction is used. (A good presentation of this technique is found in Hey (1981, ch. 4).) As this name suggests, the household works backwards. The household decides an optimal strategy in the final period T. In the light of this strategy, the household then selects the optimal strategy in period $T-1$, and so on.

Assume that the household has arrived at the final period. The household's problem is to maximize

$$U_T = U_T(\mathbf{x}^T) \tag{10.24}$$

subject to the budget constraint

$$y_T + z_{T-1} - \mathbf{p}^T\mathbf{x}^T - z_T = 0 \tag{10.25}$$

where z_{T-1} is the amount of money saved and carried over to the final period, and z_T is the end-of-period stock of money. Since period T is the final period, it makes no sense to save, i.e. the optimal value of z_T is zero. For purely expositional reasons, the market rate of interest is set equal to zero in all periods.

An interior solution to the above final period maximization problem yields demand functions of the form

$$\mathbf{x}^T = \mathbf{x}^T(\mathbf{p}^T, y_T + z_{T-1}) \tag{10.26}$$

where z_{T-1} is a predetermined number when viewed from the final period.

The formulation of the maximization problem (10.24) subject to (10.25) implies that decisions are assumed to be taken *after* uncertainty about *current* prices is resolved. In many cases, this is probably a more realistic assumption than the one employed in Section 2, where households were assumed to buy a commodity before the uncertainty about its price was resolved. However, as viewed from period $T-1$ all final period prices may be uncertain, i.e. $p_{iT} = \bar{p}_{iT} + \varepsilon_{iT}$. Hence, the expected maximum value of final period utility, as viewed from period $T-1$, can be written as

$$V_T(z_{T-1}) = \mathrm{E}\{U_T[\mathbf{x}^T(\mathbf{p}^T, y_T + z_{T-1})]\} \tag{10.27}$$

where the expectation is taken with respect to the joint distribution of final period prices, i.e. there is a function $f(p_{1T}, \ldots, p_{nT})$ which gives the consumer's (subjective) probability distribution of final period prices. If some prices are known with certainty, then the distribution is degenerate in those dimensions.

The problem of the household in period $T-1$ is to choose a bundle of goods $\mathbf{x}^{T-1}$ and an end-of-period stock of money z_{T-1} so as to maximize expected utility over the two final periods

$$U_{T-1}(\mathbf{x}^{T-1}) + \gamma V_T(z_{T-1}) \tag{10.28}$$

subject to

$$y_{T-1} + z_{T-2} - \mathbf{p}^{T-1}\mathbf{x}^{T-1} - z_{T-1} = 0 \tag{10.29}$$

where z_{T-2} is the predetermined initial endowment of money, i.e. savings carried over from the preceding period.

The first-order conditions for an interior solution, if such a solution exists, to this maximization problem are

$$\frac{\partial U_{T-1}}{\partial \mathbf{x}^{T-1}} - \lambda_{T-1}\mathbf{p}^{T-1} = 0$$

$$\left.\frac{\gamma\partial V_T}{\partial z_{T-1}} - \lambda_{T-1} = 0 \right\} \quad (10.30)$$

$$y_{T-1} + z_{T-2} - \mathbf{p}^{T-1}\mathbf{x}^{T-1} - z_{T-1} = 0$$

where λ_{T-1} is the Lagrange multiplier of the budget constraint (10.29).

Solving this equation system yields demand functions for goods and an end-of-period stock demand function for money

$$\mathbf{x}^{T-1} = \mathbf{x}^{T-1}(\mathbf{p}^{T-1}, y_{T-1} + z_{T-2})$$

$$\left. z_{T-1} = z_{T-1}(\mathbf{p}^{T-1}, y_{T-1} + z_{T-2}) \right\} \quad (10.31)$$

where z_{T-2} is a predetermined number. See also (10.38) where the dependence on future expected prices is made explicit.

Moving back to period $T-2$, the expected value of the maximum final-two-period utility is obtained by substituting (10.31) into (10.28) and taking expectations with respect to the joint distribution of prices $\mathbf{p}^{T-1}$ in period $T-1$

$$V_{T-1}(z_{T-2}) = \mathrm{E}\{U_{T-1}[\mathbf{x}^{T-1}(\mathbf{p}^{T-1}, y_{T-1} + z_{T-2})] + $$
$$+ \gamma V_T[z_{T-1}(\mathbf{p}^{T-1}, y_{T-1} + z_{T-2})]\} \quad (10.32)$$

Although the household's decisions are taken after the uncertainty about prices is resolved, utility is a random variable as long as future prices are random, i.e. utility will take on different values depending on the values taken by the future period prices.[3] Hence, the relevant concept is expected utility.

The household now continues to work back through the periods. In the first period, the problem of the household can be interpreted as if it maximizes (10.28) subject to (10.29) with time indices $T-1$ and $T-2$ replaced by 1 and 0 respectively. Hence, the expected maximum utility as viewed from the beginning of the first period is

$$V_1(z_0) = U_1[\mathbf{x}^1(\mathbf{p}^1, y_1 + z_0)] + \gamma V_2[z_1(\mathbf{p}^1, y_1 + z_0)] \quad (10.33)$$

where $z_0 \geq 0$ is the initial endowment of money.

It should be emphasized that the function $V_2[\ ]$ in the expression (10.33) implicitly captures all future optimal decisions since it has been obtained by starting at the final period and then moving back period for period towards the present.

The model can now be used to discuss consumer surplus measures. Consider first a change in the price of the ith commodity in the first period. Differentiating (10.33) with respect to p_{i1} yields

$$\frac{\partial V_1}{\partial p_{i1}} = (\sum_{j=1}^{n} U_{j1} \frac{\partial x_{j1}}{\partial p_{i1}} + \gamma \frac{\partial V_2}{\partial z_1} \frac{\partial z_1}{\partial p_{i1}})$$

$$= \lambda_1 (\Sigma p_{j1} \frac{\partial x_{j1}}{\partial p_{i1}} + \frac{\partial z_1}{\partial p_{i1}}) \tag{10.34}$$

where the final expression has been obtained by employing first-order conditions parallel to those stated in (10.30). Using the budget constraint of the first period, it is readily seen that (10.34) can be written as

$$\frac{\partial V_1}{\partial p_{i1}} = -\lambda_1 x_{i1}(\mathbf{p}^1, y_1 + z_0) \tag{10.35}$$

Hence, the same procedure as used in previous chapters can be used to derive consumer surplus measures for changes in first period prices. This is also true for the CV and EV measures. For this reason, the reader is referred to Chapters 3 and 4, where detailed derivations can be found.

5 *Expected consumer's surplus, option price and option value*

We now turn to the case where policy changes affect future prices. This adds a new problem over and above those considered in the previous sections in designing a compensation scheme. This is because future decisions are random as viewed from today. In point of fact, since Weisbrod's (1964) article quoted in Chapter 1, there has been much debate among environmental economists regarding the appropriate money measure in such situations. A common interpretation of the Weisbrod quotation is that, when demand for, say, a park is uncertain, the expected consumer surplus will underestimate the constant maximum payment (option price) that the consumer is willing to make across states (Plummer and Hartman, 1985, p. 2). The difference, it is argued, arises because the option price, which is non-stochastic or state independent, measures both the value of retaining an option to consume the good *and* the expected value of actually consuming the good, i.e. the expected consumer surplus.

Thus, one would expect the difference between option price and expected consumer surplus, called option value, to be positive. Furthermore, if the option value is positive, one would know that the expected consumer surplus was an underestimate of the gain of, for example, preserving a national park. This would greatly simplify cost–benefit analysis in cases where an expected consumer surplus measure, but not option price or option value, is available (at least if the costs fall short of the expected benefits).

In order to illustrate the meaning of the concepts introduced above as well as to examine the sign of option value, we will use a two-period version of our dynamic programming model. First, substitute the right-hand side of (10.27) into (10.28) with $T = 2$, to obtain the first period maximization problem in the following form, i.e. maximize

$$U_1(\mathbf{x}^1) + \gamma E\{U_2[\mathbf{x}^2(\mathbf{p}^2, y_2 + z_1)]\} \tag{10.36}$$

subject to the first-period budget constraint

$$y_1 + z_0 - \mathbf{p}^1\mathbf{x}^1 - z_1 = 0 \tag{10.37}$$

where the expectation is taken with respect to the joint distribution of second-period prices. Note that (10.36) measures expected utility over both periods as a function of consumption $\mathbf{x}^1$ and saving z_1 in the first period, given that the consumption bundle $\mathbf{x}^2$ in the second period is optimally chosen.

Using the first-order conditions (10.30) for utility maximization, with $\partial V_2/\partial z_1$ replaced by $E(\partial U_2/\partial \mathbf{x}^2)\partial \mathbf{x}^2/\partial z_1$, yields first-period and second-period demand functions for goods of the form

$$\left.\begin{array}{l} \mathbf{x}^1 = \mathbf{x}^1(\mathbf{p}^1, \bar{\mathbf{p}}^2, y_1, y_2, \phi) \\[2mm] \mathbf{x}^2 = \mathbf{x}^2(\mathbf{p}^1, \mathbf{p}^2, \bar{\mathbf{p}}^2, y_1, y_2, \phi) = \mathbf{x}^2[\mathbf{p}^2, y_2 + z_1(\mathbf{p}^1, \bar{\mathbf{p}}^2, y_1, y_2, \phi)] \end{array}\right\} \tag{10.38}$$

where a bar above second-period prices denotes expected values, and ϕ contains moments about the mean characterizing the stochastic properties of $\mathbf{p}^2$. Observe that $\mathbf{x}^2$ are stochastic as viewed from the first period. This is because second-period prices are random, i.e. $\mathbf{p}^2 = \bar{\mathbf{p}}^2 + \varepsilon^2$, although uncertainty is resolved before second-period decisions are taken.

Substitution of (10.38) into (10.36) yields an indirect expected utility function

$$V = U_1[\mathbf{x}^1(\mathbf{p}^1, \bar{\mathbf{p}}^2, y_1, y_2, \phi)] + \gamma E\{U_2[\mathbf{x}^2(\mathbf{p}^1, \mathbf{p}^2, \bar{\mathbf{p}}^2, y_1, y_2, \phi)]\} \tag{10.39}$$

where the expectation is taken with respect to the joint distribution of second-period prices. Taking partial derivatives of (10.39) and invoking

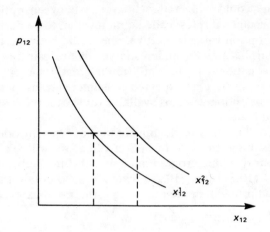

Figure 10.3 The optimal demand for commodity x_{12} is random as viewed from today, where $x_{12}^i = x_{12}^i (\mathbf{p}^1, p_{12}, \bar{p}_{22}, \bar{p}_{22} + \varepsilon_i, y_1, y_2, \phi)$, $i=1, 2$ (in constructing the figure, p_{22}, but not p_{12}, is assumed to be random as viewed from today, and prices $p_{32}, \ldots, p_{n2}$ have been suppressed)

the envelope theorem, this yields, following certain calculations similar to those in the appendix,

$$
\left.
\begin{aligned}
\frac{\partial V}{\partial \mathbf{p}^1} &= -\lambda_1 \mathbf{x}^1(\mathbf{p}^1, \bar{\mathbf{p}}^2, y_1, y_2, \phi) \\[2mm]
\frac{\partial V}{\partial \bar{\mathbf{p}}^2} &= -\gamma E[\lambda_2 \mathbf{x}^2(\mathbf{p}^1, \bar{\mathbf{p}}^2 + \varepsilon^2, \bar{\mathbf{p}}^2, y_1, y_2, \phi)] \\[2mm]
\frac{\partial V}{\partial y_1} &= \lambda_1(\mathbf{p}^1, \bar{\mathbf{p}}^2, y_1, y_2, \phi) \\[2mm]
\frac{\partial V}{\partial y_2} &= \gamma E[\lambda_2(\mathbf{p}^1, \bar{\mathbf{p}}^2 + \varepsilon^2, \bar{\mathbf{p}}^2, y_1, y_2, \phi)]
\end{aligned}
\right\}
\tag{10.40}
$$

The first-period demand functions in the first line of (10.40) are the same as those given by (10.35), although the dependence on future (expected) prices and incomes is made explicit in (10.40).

The second line of (10.40) shows that future optimal demands are stochastic as viewed from today. Figure 10.3 depicts the case where the price of the considered commodity is known with certainty. Nevertheless, the demand for the commodity is uncertain as viewed from today due to uncertainty regarding the price of some other good. In order to illustrate the construction of compensation schemes in such situations, assume that the certain price of commodity x_{12} is changed. From the second line of (10.40), and using a well-known result from mathematical statistics, we have

$$\frac{\partial V}{\partial p_{12}} = -\gamma E(\lambda_2 x_{12}) = -\gamma E(\lambda_2)E(x_{12}) - \gamma \text{cov}(\lambda_2, x_{12}) \tag{10.41}$$

where the expectation is taken with respect to the joint distribution of those second-period prices which are uncertain; at least one second-period price, but not p_{12}, is assumed to be random as viewed from today. Since x_{12}, like λ_2, is a stochastic variable, it does not factor out of the expectation in (10.41). In fact (10.41) illustrates that the expected value of the product of two random variables is equal to the product of their expectations plus their covariance, as is shown in any textbook on mathematical statistics (e.g. Hogg and Craig, 1978). Thus, it is not obvious how to construct a compensation scheme or money measure of utility change. There are, however, two principal candidates, namely stochastic and non-stochastic compensations respectively. In the present context, the stochastic compensation varies with the stochastic second-period prices, while the size of the non-stochastic compensation is independent of any random variations in prices.

In order to illustrate these concepts, let us assume that second-period income is adjusted in such a way that the consumer remains at his initial expected utility level following a change in p_{12}. Denote this (stochastic or non-stochastic as specified below) amount of money by S_ε. Using the second and final lines of (10.40), for a marginal price change we obtain

$$-\frac{\partial \bar{V}}{\partial p_{12}} = \gamma E(\lambda_2 x_{12}) + \gamma E(\lambda_2 S_\varepsilon') = 0 \tag{10.42}$$

where a prime denotes a partial derivative with respect to p_{12}, and $S_\varepsilon = 0$ in the initial preprice-change situation.

Consider first a non-stochastic uniform marginal compensation. Since the compensation, denoted by $OP' = S_\varepsilon'$, is non-stochastic or 'state independent', it factors out of the expectation in (10.42). Using this fact, and rearranging the terms in (10.42), yields

$$OP' = -\frac{E(\lambda_2 x_{12})}{E(\lambda_2)} = -E(x_{12}) - \frac{\text{cov}(\lambda_2, x_{12})}{E(\lambda_2)} \tag{10.43}$$

where the right-hand expression is obtained by using a result discussed below equation (10.41). The amount OP', which is often referred to as an option price, keeps the consumer at the same expected utility level when facing a lower/higher price p_{12} as was achieved at the initial level of p_{12}. Note that the amount OP' is paid/received regardless of the values the

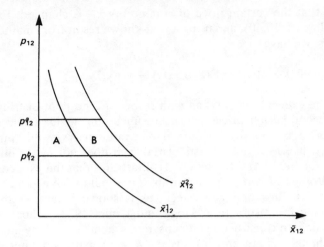

Figure 10.4 Compensating variations, area A or area A + B, depending on the value taken by the stochastic price p_{i2}, $i \neq 1$

stochastic second-period prices actually take on, i.e. it may turn out that the consumer gains or loses from having paid/received \$OP' depending on the realized values of $p_{22}, \ldots, p_{n2}$.

This latter fact hints at another possible compensation scheme, namely one that is constructed in such way that realized or ex post utility is unaffected by the considered change[4] in p_{12}. This amounts to replacing the compensation in (10.42) by compensations which are such that

$$-\frac{\partial \bar{V}}{\partial p_{12}} = \gamma E[\lambda_2(x_{12} + CV'_\varepsilon)] = 0 \tag{10.44}$$

where CV'_ε is a stochastic marginal compensation, and $CV_\varepsilon = 0$ before the change in p_{12}. The amounts CV'_ε fluctuate with those prices that are random as viewed from today in such a way that the sum of the two terms within parentheses in (10.44) is equal to zero for each and every realization of the uncertain prices. This is illustrated in Figure 10.4 for a non-marginal change in p_{12}. Note that the integration between initial and final p_{12}-values is performed inside the expectations operator in (10.44), holding the utility level constant.

An expected compensating variation is obtained by multiplying each amount CV'_ε by the probability that the uncertain prices take on the associated values and summing all such weighted compensations. Thus, in the marginal price-change case, we have

$$E(x_{12}) = -E(CV_\varepsilon') \tag{10.45}$$

In terms of Figure 10.4, the expected compensating variation is equal to π^1 times area A plus π^2 times area A+B, where π^i is the probability that $\tilde{x}_{12} = \tilde{x}_{12}^i$ and $i = 1,2$.

Option value is defined as the difference between option price and expected consumer surplus. A comparison of (10.43) and (10.45) shows that marginal option value OV' can be written as

$$OV' = OP' - E(CV_\varepsilon') = \frac{\text{cov}(\lambda_2, x_{12})}{E(\lambda_2)} \tag{10.46}$$

Thus, the sign of option value is equal to the sign of the covariance between the marginal utility of second period income and the second period demand for the considered commodity. But note that this result holds only as an approximation in the discrete price change case since the expected demands in (10.43) and (10.45) refer to different compensation schemes and therefore need not net out in (10.46).

A useful result derived in Chavas and Bishop (1984) states that the sign of the covariance between two functions $f(\varepsilon)$ and $g(\varepsilon)$ is equal to the sign of the product of their derivatives with respect to ε. Applying this result to (10.46), one finds that option value may be of either sign, even if there is only a single stochastic second-period price. As is shown in Chavas and Bishop (1984), the sign of option value in (10.46) is equal to the sign of the product of the Arrow–Pratt index of relative risk aversion less the income elasticity of the demand for x_{12} times the partial derivative of x_{12} with respect to the uncertain price. Thus, risk aversion *per se* is not sufficient to determine the sign of option value.

Before commenting upon this result, two generalizations of the model and the above result should be mentioned. The model is easily extended in order to cover income uncertainty. Assume second-period income is uncertain about the mean value $\bar{y}_2$. Since, by assumption, second-period consumption is chosen after the consumer knows which state of the world has been realized, y_2 and $\bar{y}_2$ will appear in the behaviour functions (10.40) in a parallel manner to second-period prices. The second-period utility function may also contain a stochastic argument representing, say, the influence of the weather on the satisfaction derived from a trip to a recreation site. Once again, the realized and expected values respectively will appear in the behaviour functions (10.40) in the same way as second-period prices. These results mean that the sign of option value is also governed by (10.46) in the case of income uncertainty and/or state dependent preferences. Thus, regardless of the source of demand uncertainty, option value may generally be of either sign.

This result naturally raises a question regarding the money measure of utility change which would be appropriate in situations involving uncertainty. Unfortunately, there is no simple answer to this question, as will be demonstrated in Section 6 of Chapter 11. Here, only a few brief comments are made. Firstly, it should be observed from equation (10.42) that option price and expected compensating variation are just two out of possibly an infinite number of payment schemes; obviously, one can use (10.42) to construct various intermediate schemes. Secondly, both option price and expected compensating variation in (10.46) have the same sign as the underlying change in expected utility. However, in situations involving more complicated choices, the analysis performed in the next chapter demonstrates that expected consumer surplus measures are not necessarily valid indicators of the sign of the change in expected utility.

Appendix

In this appendix the properties of the indirect utility function (10.14) are derived. First, the expected utility function (10.10) is totally differentiated to obtain

$$E(dU) = E(U_1)dx_1 - \frac{E(U_2 \cdot p_1)dx_1 + E(U_2)x_1 d\bar{p}_1 + E(U_2 \cdot (y - p_1 x_1))dp_2 - E(U_2)dy}{p_2} \quad (A10.1)$$

Next, using the fact that $E(U_1) = E(U_2 \cdot p_1)/p_2$ from the first order condition (10.11), and $X_2 = (y - p_1 x_1)p_2^{-1}$ from the budget constraint, (A10.1) simplifies to

$$E(dU) = - \frac{[E(U_2)x_1 d\bar{p}_1 + E(U_2 \cdot X_2)dp_2 - E(U_2)dy]}{p_2} \quad (A10.2)$$

This equation contains all the properties stated in equations (10.15) in Section 2.

CHAPTER 11

Money measures of the total value of environmental assets

A typical feature of many environmental resources is that they provide many different values. Following Boyle and Bishop (1985) one may distinguish between four more or less distinct values. First of all, there are consumptive use values such as fishing and hunting. Secondly, some resources provide non-consumptive use values. For example, some people enjoy bird watching, while others gain satisfaction from viewing wildlife. Thirdly, a resource may also provide services indirectly through books, movie pictures, television programmes, and so on. Finally people may derive satisfaction from the pure fact that a habitat or species exists.

In this chapter, the tools developed in the previous chapters are put together in an analysis of the total benefits of an environmental asset in a certain as well as in a risky world. Section 1 considers the total value of an environmental asset in a certain world. However, the future availability of a natural resource is frequently uncertain. Section 2 presents different willingness to pay measures that can be used to assess the value of having the supply of a resource stabilized at some arbitrary level. In some cases, a particular project may affect the random variations in the supply of an asset without achieving a certain future supply. Section 3 deals with this case, while Section 4 presents an empirical study concerned with many of the issues considered in this chapter. Then, in Section 5 we turn to decisions criteria in situations involving time as well as irreversible consequences. Section 6 contains a brief discussion of the choice of money measure in situations involving risks, and the chapter is rounded off by indicating a few possible directions for future research.

1 On the total value of a resource

If an environmental asset supplies just a single well-defined service, the associated benefits are generally quite easy to model. For example, if the service is traded in a perfect market, the money measures derived in Chapters 3 and 4 are useful, while a rationed service can be handled by methods assigned in Chapter 5. The benefits of a service which is a pure public good can be evaluated by the money measures presented in Chapter 6.

An environmental asset frequently provides several or all of these different kinds of services. Collecting the different cases, the compensating variation associated with a change in 'environmental quality' can be written as

$$V(\mathbf{p}^1, y^1 - \mathbf{P}^1\mathbf{q}^1 - CV, \mathbf{q}^1, \mathbf{z}^1) = V(\mathbf{p}^0, y^0 - \mathbf{P}^0\mathbf{q}^0, \mathbf{q}^0, \mathbf{z}^0) \tag{11.1}$$

where a superscript 1 (0) denotes final (initial) values, $\mathbf{p}$ is a vector of non-negative prices of unrationed services provided by the considered asset, $\mathbf{q}$ is a vector of rationed services generated by the asset, $\mathbf{P}$ is a vector of prices of rationed services, $\mathbf{z}$ is a vector of public goods provided by the asset, and all prices referring to other commodities in the economy are suppressed. The overall compensating variation defined by (11.1) is the sum of money that makes the consumer as well off with a change in 'environmental quality' as he was before the change. The overall equivalent variation is easily defined by fixing utility at its final level instead of at its initial level.

Several comments to (11.1) are in order. Firstly, a change in the price vector $\mathbf{p}$ covers all kinds of consumptive, non-consumptive, and indirect uses of the asset that are traded in perfect markets. Services that are priced below their market clearing levels and hence are rationed are included in the $\mathbf{q}$-vector. Secondly, the existence value of the asset is included in the $\mathbf{z}$-vector and is therefore treated as a pure public good, a fact that is commented upon below. Furthermore, some non-consumptive uses such as bird watching, and indirect uses, e.g. watching a television programme on blue whales, may be thought of as public goods. Thirdly, a change in income y is included in (11.1) since, for example, if a park is closed and its trees cut down, the income of the considered household may be affected. This is particularly the case when the household owns the land.

In evaluating (11.1), it should be noted that the overall compensating variation is equal to the sum of the changes in compensating variations in the 'markets' where prices, quantity constraints or the supply of public goods change. This assumes, however, that each change is evaluated subject to all previously considered changes holding utility throughout at its initial level, just as was done in Chapters 3–6. See also the appendix to Chapter 6 for a line integral (almost) corresponding to the money measure in (11.1). The practical implication of this result is that one cannot simply ask a respondent about his willingness to pay for the opportunity to fish in a polluted lake that is cleaned up, then ask about his willingness to pay for the scenic beauty provided by the restored lake, and sum these amounts and hope to obtain the total value of the lake. Instead, one may proceed by asking for the maximum willingness to pay for fishing, disregarding any scenic values. Next, the respondent is asked of his maximum willingness to pay for the scenic values provided by the lake, subject to the change in fishing. This 'order of integration', just like the reverse or any intermediate 'order of integration', yields the overall compensating variation. Alternatively, one may simply ask of the total willingness to pay for the improvement in fishing *and* scenic beauty. Using results derived in the appendix to Chapter 6, it is possible to show that this total willingness to pay, which corresponds to the compensating variation in (11.1), has the same sign as the underlying change in utility. However, as usual and contrary to the EV-measure, the CV-measure cannot be used to compare or rank different changes in 'environmental quality'.

In the welfare change measure (11.1), existence value is included as a separate argument. In general, existence value is motivated by some kind of altruistic behaviour. Boyle and Bishop (1985, p. 13), following Bishop and Heberlein (1984), suggest five altruistic motives for existence values.

(i) *Bequest motives*. As Krutilla (1967) argued many years ago, it would appear quite rational to will an endowment of natural amenities as well as private goods and money to one's heirs. The fact that future generations are so often mentioned in debates over natural resources is one indication that their well-being, including their endowments of natural resources, is taken seriously by some present members of society.

(ii) *Benevolence toward relatives and friends*. Giving gifts to friends and relatives may be even more common than making bequests of them. Why should such goals not extend to the availability of natural resources?

(iii) *Sympathy for people and animals*. Even if one does not plan to personally enjoy a resource or do so vicariously through friends and relatives, he or she may still feel sympathy for people adversely affected by environmental deterioration and want to help them. Particularly for living creatures, sympathy may extend beyond humans. The same emotions that lead us to nurse a baby bird or stop to aid a run-over cat or dog may well induce us to pay something to maintain animal populations and ecosystems.

(iv) *Environmental linkages*. A better term probably exists here. What we are driving at is the belief that while specific environmental damage such as acidification of Adirondack lakes does not affect one directly, it is symptomatic of more widespread forces that must be stopped before resources of direct importance are also affected. To some extent this may reflect a simple 'you've-got-to-stop-'em-somewhere' philosophy. It may also reflect the view that if 'we' support 'them' in maintaining the environment, 'they' will support us.

(v) *Environmental responsibility.* The opinion is often expressed that those who damage the environment should pay for mitigating or avoiding future damage. In the acid rain case, there may be a prevalent feeling that if 'my' use of electricity is causing damage to ecosystems elsewhere, then 'I' should pick up part of the costs reducing the damage. (Boyle and Bishop 1985, p. 13.)

Given that an existence value is admitted, this value is often modelled by including the stock of the resource as an argument in the utility functions (see Dasgupta, 1982, ch. 5, for a discussion of this issue). In the case of assets such as air and water, one may instead use visibility measures and water quality indexes respectively. The use of such measures highlights the fact that existence is not normally treated as a binary variable. Rather, it is generally assumed that the marginal existence value is positive but a decreasing function of the size of the stock of the resource (but it is not obvious that this holds for all kinds of 'resources', e.g. mosquito).

Suppose that z_i in (11.1) denotes the current level of the stock of a renewable resource. By taking the partial derivative of the left-hand side of (11.1) with respect to z_i, one obtains the marginal compensating variation or the marginal existence value associated with a small change in z_i. However, as was demonstrated in Chapter 9, there is a close correspondence between the size of the stock of a renewable resource and the size of the steady-state harvest of the resource. In fact, the steady-state harvest is equal to the natural growth of the resource. Therefore, it may be difficult to isolate a pure marginal existence value, beyond, possibly, the short run, i.e. in the long-run most, if not all, elements of the vectors $\mathbf{p}$, $\mathbf{q}$ and $\mathbf{z}$ may be functions of z_i.

These results also highlight that the total value of a resource is difficult to define, even within the simple framework employed in this section. As a first approximation, one may choose a $\mathbf{p}^1$-vector in (11.1) such that the corresponding demands are all equal to zero, conditional on $\mathbf{q}^1 = \mathbf{z}^1 = 0$. The resulting compensating variation is a measure of the total value of the current supply of services of the resource. However, a priori, there is no reason to believe that the current stock of the resource is the optimal one, or even that the current harvest level is a steady-state harvest level. Therefore, one may instead formulate a generalized version of the dynamic model discussed in Chapter 9. In particular, the simple utility function employed in that chapter is replaced by one that covers multiple uses of the resource. Such a model may be used to derive the optimal stock as well as the optimal levels of flow consumptions of the resource. The solution can also be used to calculate a money measure of the total value of the resource. However, this is still an incomplete or partial valuation, since the model neglects any general equilibrium repercussions. We will resist all temptations to try to formulate such models in this book. For some attempts to model multiple use of a resource in a dynamic context, the interested reader is referred to Johansson and Löfgren (1985).

2 *Uncertain supply of an environmental asset*

A concept which has received considerable attention in the literature is Bishop's (1982) supply-side option value. In the case discussed in Section 5 of Chapter 10 uncertainty arises because of uncertainty about 'demand-side' factors such as preferences and income. In many circumstances, however, uncertainty pertains to the environment, or the supply side. The household will demand the good, such as a visit to a natural park, at its current price, but is uncertain about whether the park will be available.

In this section, the analysis of the value of an environmental asset is extended to the case of a risky world. In the option value literature, analyses are usually based on static models, as opposed to the intertemporal models employed in Chapter 10. In order to simplify the analysis, we will follow this tradition here, and use a simple variation of the model of Section 1. The (Neumann–Morgenstern) household is assumed to consume an environmental asset Q and a composite good which serves as the *numéraire*. The smooth indirect utility function of the household is written as $V(y,Q^i)$. There are n states of the world[1] and the probability that state i occurs is denoted by π^i. The analysis is restricted to uncertainty with regard to Q, but the model is easily extended to cover income uncertainty and/or state dependent preferences, i.e. demand-side uncertainty. The reader interested in such analysis is referred to Freeman (1984a), Graham (1981), and Schmalensee (1972), but see also Section 6.

Suppose that there is an opportunity to stabilize the supply of the environmental asset at some level $\bar{Q}$. This level is assumed to be no higher than the highest level attained in the stochastic case. For example, there is perhaps a positive probability that Q, the population of water-fowl say, takes on an extremely high value. A priori, there seems to be no particular reason to believe that 'supply' is always stabilized at this highest attainable level, although this is the special case generally considered in the literature on supply-side option value. The expected gain in going from a stochastic Q to $\bar{Q}$ can be written as

$$\triangle V = V(y,\bar{Q}) - E[V(y,Q^i)] \tag{11.2}$$

where the expectation is taken with respect to the distribution of Q. The household gains from the stabilization if (11.2) has a positive sign, while it loses from the stabiliziation if (11.2) has a negative sign. In particular, a risk-loving household does not view the stabilization with the same eyes as a strongly risk-averse household.

We will consider two different money measures of the utility change in (11.2), namely option price and expected consumer surplus, since these are the measures generally employed in empirical studies. Consider first option price. This is a state-independent payment, denoted OP, which makes the household indifferent between having and not having Q stabilized

$$V(y-OP,\bar{Q}) = E[V(y,Q^i)] \tag{11.3}$$

This expression defines the compensating option price, i.e. the amount the household is willing to pay ahead of time to ensure that Q is stabilized at $Q=\bar{Q}$. Alternatively, one can base the definition on the equivalent variation measure. In any case, substitution of (11.3) into (11.2) immediately reveals that the sign of $\triangle V$ is equal to the sign of OP, i.e. OP is a sign-preserving money measure.

Alternatively, one can define the compensating variation, which is the consumer surplus measure used in this chapter, in state i if the supply of the environmental asset is stabilized

$$V(y-CV^i,\bar{Q}) = V(y,Q^i) \qquad \forall i \tag{11.4}$$

The compensating variation is the amount of income that can be taken from/must be given to the household while leaving it just as well off when consuming $\bar{Q}$ units as when consuming Q^i units of the asset. This compensating variation varies between states since the 'no-stabili-zation' case supply of the asset is state-dependent. Substitution of (11.4) into (11.2), making second-order Taylor series expansions around y, yields

$$\triangle V = E[V(y,\bar{Q}) - V(y-CV^i,\bar{Q})] \approx [E(CV^i) - \frac{V_{yy}E(CV^i)^2}{V_y}]V_y \tag{11.5}$$

where subscripts y denote partial derivatives with respect to income evaluated at $(y,\bar{Q})$, and $E(CV^i)$ is the expected compensating variation.

Two important observations follow from (11.5). Firstly, the expected compensating variation depends only on the ordinal properties of the utility function. In order to see this, suppose the utility function is subjected to a monotone increasing transformation. This transformation affects the Arrow–Pratt index of absolute risk aversion V_{yy}/V_y in (11.5), but leaves the expected compensating variation unchanged. The latter is easily checked by subjecting (11.4) to a monotone transformation. These results highlight Hanoch's (1977) warning, mentioned in the introduction to Chapter 10, that demand functions, obtained under certainty, imply very little with regard to a household's attitudes towards risk. Option price, on the other hand, is sensitive to the cardinal properties of the sub-utility functions since it refers to a particular level of expected utility, as can be seen from (11.3). Secondly, since, depending on the attitudes towards risk, expected utility may increase or decrease following a stabilization of Q, one may suspect that expected consumer surplus measures, such as the one in (11.5), may have the wrong sign. Indeed, in the context of price stabilization, Helms (1985) proves that expected consumer surplus measures may rank changes wrongly. Intuitively, the final term within brackets in (11.5) may have the same sign as $E(CV^i)$ and be so large that the change in expected welfare and the expected compensating variation are of opposite signs. Moreover, just as was the case under certainty, (expected) compensating variation measures cannot be used to rank several different projects.

Supply-side uncertainty, as defined by Bishop (1982), is a special case of the general case considered above. Bishop considers two states, namely, $Q^1 = \bar{Q}$ and $Q^2 = 0$, where, as before, $\bar{Q}$ denotes the proposed level of stabilization. In the absence of 'stabilization', the supply is Q^i with probability π^i for $i=1,2$. In this special case, the expected compensating variation is easily seen to be a sign-preserving measure of utility change. Using (11.3) and (11.5) one obtains

$$\triangle V = \pi^2[V(y,\bar{Q}) - V(y - CV^2,\bar{Q})] = V(y,\bar{Q}) - V(y - OP,\bar{Q}) \quad (11.6)$$

Obviously, the sign of the welfare change in (11.6) must equal the sign of CV^2 and hence the sign of the expected compensating variation $\pi^2 CV^2$, provided utility is increasing in income. Equation (11.6) also illustrates in a simple way that option price is a sign-preserving money measure of the change in expected utility.

Bishop (1982) proceeds by defining a supply-side option value

$$OV = OP - E(CV^i) \quad (11.7)$$

This option value OV is easily proved to be positive for a risk-averse household, zero for a risk-neutral household, and negative for a risk-loving household. (Hint: perform second-order Taylor series expansions of (11.6), or consult Bishop (1982) for a proof.) This is an important relation, which has been elaborated upon by Freeman (1984a) and Smith (1984) who try to provide an analytical bound for option value, useful in empirical investigations. Nevertheless, it should be recalled that Bishop's measure is derived subject to the assumption that $Q^1 = \bar{Q}$ and $Q^2 = 0$. In more complicated choice situations, it may simply be meaningless to define an option value due to the aforementioned deficiencies of expected consumer surplus measures.

3 Access value

Thus far, the value of preserving an environmental asset has been considered in the context of stabilizing supply. Frequently, however, one would expect a policy to affect the probability of a particular event without ensuring a certain outcome. For example, in the hunting study reported in the next section, hunters are bidding on an increased probability of a future suply of endangered animal species. This is the case since a hunter cannot be expected to believe that the considered 'project' ensures with certainty that the hunter will obtain a hunting permit. Thus, using a term due to Galagher and Smith (1985), the project leads to a change in access conditions for an asset whose availability is uncertain.

An access value can be defined by using two different probability distributions for the asset. The change in expected utility associated with a shift in the probability distribution can be written as

$$\triangle V = E_1[V(y,Q_1^i)] - E_0[V(y,Q_0^i)] \tag{11.8}$$

where a subscript refers to a particular probability distribution, and Q_1^i and Q_0^i are assumed to be independently distributed. Performing second-order Taylor series expansions around $(y,\bar{Q}_1)$ and $(y,\bar{Q}_0)$ respectively, just as in equation (10.20) in the previous chapter, gives an idea of the forces that are involved. The expected values $\bar{Q}_1$ and $\bar{Q}_0$, as well as the variations around the expected values affect the sign of (11.8). Expected utility increases if the considered project increases the expected access to the asset, *ceteris paribus*, or reduces the variability of the supply of the resource, *ceteris paribus*. The latter result, however, assumes that the household is risk averse with respect to supply (or price) risk, as can be seen from equation (10.20).

Applying the definition of access value to Bishop's (1982) supply-side model, an access option price AP, i.e. an ex ante state independent uniform payment, can be defined as

$$\sum_{i=1}^{2} \Pi^i V(y-AP, Q^i) = \pi^1 V(y,Q^1) + \pi^2 V(y-CV^2,Q^1) \tag{11.9}$$

where Π^1 is the probability of having access to the asset given that the option is purchased, $\Pi^2 = 1 - \Pi^1$, π^i denotes the corresponding probabilities if the option is not purchased, and equation (11.4) has been used to obtain the final term on the right-hand side of (11.9). Note that if Π^1 is equal to one, then (11.9) reduces to the usual definition of supply-side option price. In the general case, however, it is the expected future availability of the asset upon which the household is bidding. An attempt to estimate AP will be the core of the empirical study summed up in the next section.

A few comments regarding money measures of access values are in order. Firstly access option price is a sign-preserving money measure of utility change. This is seen by substituting the following definition of AP

$$E_1[V(y-AP,Q_1^i)] = E_0[V(y,Q_0^i)] \tag{11.10}$$

into equation (11.8), noting that utility, by assumption, is increasing in income. Straightforward calculations confirm that AP in (11.9) is an increasing function of the probability of having access to the resource. Expected consumer surplus change measures,[2] on the other hand, may fail to correctly rank any two distributions, neither of which are stabilized, as is shown in Helms (1984); recall also the discussion in Section 2 dealing with a special case of the more general case considered here. However, in the simple case considered in equation (11.9), the change in expected compensating variation is simply $(\pi^2 - \Pi^2)CV^2$, a measure which, just like the underlying change in expected utility, has a positive sign if the considered project has a positive impact on the probability of gaining access to the resource. Nevertheless, as is shown in Freeman (1985), even in this simple case it is impossible to determine the sign of access option value, defined as access option price less the increase in expected consumer surplus, without invoking very restrictive assumptions regarding the properties of the utility function. Thirdly, the analysis performed in this and the previous section, can be given an intertemporal interpretation. For example, referring to equation (11.3), the considered project is now interpreted as a more or less permanent stabilization of the supply of the asset when the alternative is that the supply varies randomly from period to period.

4 *Estimating option prices for wildlife resources*

Little research has been devoted to the empirical estimation of option price. However, in recent years a few attempts have been made to estimate option and/or access price. Brookshire *et al.* (1983), Greenley *et al.* (1981), and Walsh *et al.* (1978) constitute interesting initial efforts in this direction.

. This section briefly summarizes the Brookshire *et al.* (1983) study. The focus of their study was on uncertainty of supply. Two wildlife populations, grizzly bears and bighorn sheep in Wyoming, whose future availability is uncertain were selected for analysis.

Approximately 3,000 bighorn-sheep and grizzly-bear survey instruments were mailed to Wyoming hunters (but only 25–30 per cent of these were returned). The respondent was informed that under existing conditions, the probability of any individual obtaining a hunting licence in a year was 10 per cent for bighorn sheep and zero for grizzly bears. A contingent market was established in that new hunting areas were proposed which would be made available for hunting either five or fifteen years in the future (since respondents could not be expected to believe that making a payment this year would immediately result in a larger stock). Exclusion from the market was prescribed since payment each and every year was necessary to qualify the respondent to enter a draw for licences in the future. The method of payment was specified as a grizzly bear or bighorn sheep stamp. The respondent was asked how much he was willing to pay annually for a specified time horizon at four alternative probabilities of future supply. The expected probability of future licence availability is the 'good' for which respondents are bidding. If the probability of licence availability is a 25 per cent chance of future availability, then the individual's bid will represent a Hicksian compensated measure of welfare associated with this chance of future licence availability, i.e. it represents the (compensated) access option price, which is associated with a 0.25 probability of future supply.

The respondent was also questioned as to whether, if a licence was obtained, he would definitely or only possibly hunt the species in question. This allows an analysis of the influence of uncertain demand on the stated access option price.

Figure 11.1 plots the estimated mean values for the access option prices related to the alternative probabilities of future supply. One would expect access option price to be an increasing function of the probability of future availability. This can be checked by using equation (11.9) to calculate the sign of $\partial AP/\partial \Pi$[1]. Such a pattern is, in fact, also present in Figure 11.1, i.e. the mean bids for the option to hunt grizzly bears or

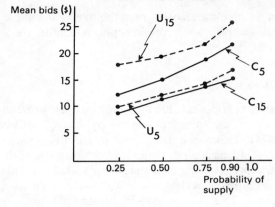

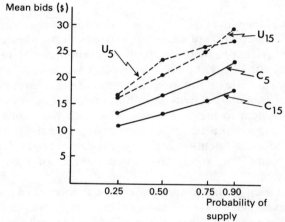

Figure 11.1 (a) Mean grizzly and (b) bighorn bids for certain (C) and uncertain (U) hunting demands for alternative time horizons (5 and 15 years)
Source: Brookshire *et al.* (1983, pp. 8–9)

bighorn sheep both increase as the probability of future availability increases.

One final observation should be made concerning the Brookshire *et al.* (1983) study. A respondent who is certain not to be a hunter may still be willing to pay for the existence of grizzly bears or bighorn sheep or for the option to observe wildlife resources. Therefore, the non-hunter was directed to answer a set of questions concerned with payments to preserve grizzly bears or bighorn sheep. The mean bids for observer access prices are in the range of $20 for both grizzly bears and bighorn sheep. The estimated existence values show more variation, with $24 mean existence value for grizzly bears in the five-year sample and $15 in the fifteen year sample, while the sheephorn results are significantly lower at about $7.

5 *Quasi-option value*

A different concept of option value than the one dealt with thus far in this chapter has been advanced independently by Arrow and Fisher (1974) and Henry (1974). This concept, labelled quasi-option value by Arrow and Fisher (1974), focuses on the intertemporal aspects of development problems (cf. Chapter 10). In particular, it is stressed that environmental decisions concerning the development of resources often involve irreversible consequences. This imposes constraints on the range of subsequent actions.

Fisher and Hanemann (1983, p. 3) note that there are at least two ways in which the preservation of natural resources can contribute to human welfare (over and above their contribution to non-material welfare, such as scenic values). Firstly, by preserving plant and animal populations, one conserves genetic information that may, in the future, be useful in some form of economic activity. Secondly, removal of any one species can cause a system to break down because each has evolved a set of characteristics that make it a unique functional part of the system. It may be possible, to some extent, to replace ecosystem services. However, in general, it seems fair to say that some services of ecosystems are non-substitutable.

The model used in this section to derive the concept of quasi-option value was developed by Hanemann (1984b). Let us consider a planner who has to decide how much of a tract of wild land should be developed in each of two periods, where the first period represents 'today' and the second period represents the uncertain future. It is assumed that development is a binary choice, i.e. either develop fully during a period or do not develop at all. Moreover, any development is irreversible. Let the net benefits of any development program be

$$U = U_1(d_1) + U_2(d, d_2; \theta) \tag{11.11}$$

where $d_t \geqslant 0$ is the amount of land developed in period t $(t = 1, 2)$ $d = d_1 + d_2 \leqslant 1$, θ is a random variable, and $\partial U_t/\partial d_t$, $\partial U_2/\partial d > 0$. Benefits are here measured in 'utils', but they could as well be measured in money. It should also be noted that the discount factor is suppressed in (11.11) in order to simplify notation.

Two scenarios are introduced regarding the behaviour of uncertainty over time. In the first case, no more information about θ becomes available over time. This corresponds to the case considered in Section 2 of Chapter 10, where the household was assumed to choose a vector of actions before the uncertainty about prices was resolved. The second scenario to be considered assumes that the specific value of θ is known at the beginning of period 2. It now makes sense to defer a decision on d_2 to the second period. This corresponds to the case considered in Section 5 of Chapter 10, where the household chose quantities after the uncertainty about prices was resolved.

It should be emphasized that learning[3] here is independent of the amount of land developed in the first period. What has been learned in the first period is exogenous to the model and due to such activities as research. We will discuss subsequently the case in which undertaking some development provides desirable information on the consequences of irreversible development.

The planner (or the household) aims at maximizing the expected benefits over both periods. In the first scenario considered, all development decisions must be taken before uncertainty is resolved. Hence, the planner maximizes

$$\bar{U}(d_1) = U_1(d_1) + \max_{d_2}\,[\mathrm{E}\{U_2(d, d_2; \theta)\}] \qquad (11.12)$$

In order to interpret this expression, and referring back to the method of backward induction used in Section 5 of Chapter 10, we can work backwards. Firstly, the optimal development strategy in the second period is decided, i.e. $d_2 = 0$ or $d_2 = 1$ is chosen, subject to d_1 which is a predetermined number ($d_1 = 0$ or $d_1 = 1$), and subject to $d \leq 1$. Then we move back to the first period. The problem is now to choose d_1 in such a way as to maximize total expected benefits over both periods. This is captured by (11.12), and the maximum value of the expression is denoted $\bar{U}(\bar{d}_1)$, where $\bar{d}_1$ maximizes (11.12) subject to $d_1 = 0$ or $d_1 = 1$. Note, however, that since nothing further is learned about the value of θ by the second period, the decision maker could equally well choose both d_1 and d_2 in the first period (instead of sequentially as above).

Since the choice is between no development and full development, the planner has only to compare $\bar{U}(0)$ and $\bar{U}(1)$. Hence, he chooses not to develop if $\bar{U}(0) \geq U(1)$, and to develop if $\bar{U}(0) < U(1)$.

Turning now to the second scenario, the planner learns the value of the random variable θ by the second period. The decision is now to maximize

$$\bar{\bar{U}}(d_1) = U_1(d_1) + \mathrm{E}\{\max_{d_2} U_2(d, d_2; \theta)\} \qquad (11.13)$$

where the decision on d_2 can be taken after the uncertainty is resolved, but subject to the amount developed in the first period, i.e. $d_1 = 0$ or $d_1 = 1$, and $d_1 + d_2 \leq 1$. The aim of the planner is then to choose d_1 in order to maximize (11.13), given that the amount of development in the second period is optimally chosen. Call this optimal first period amount of development $\bar{d}_1$. This amount is found by comparing $\bar{U}(0)$ and $\bar{U}(1)$ in (11.13). Clearly, it is optimal to refrain from development in the first period if $\bar{U}(0) \geqslant \bar{U}(1)$, and vice versa.

Now, we are ready to define quasi-option value, QV, as

$$QV = \bar{\bar{U}}(0) - \bar{U}(0) \geqslant 0 \tag{11.14}$$

This expression gives the increase in expected benefits of not developing the area in the first period, when the planner can wait to determine d_2 after uncertainty is resolved instead of taking a decision before uncertainty is resolved. The difference between the two terms in (11.14) is known as the expected value of perfect information (conditional on $d_1 = 0$). The sign of (11.14), which in general is strictly positive, can be determined by invoking a theorem originally developed by Marschac (see Hey, 1981, pp. 87–9).

It is possible to correct the inefficiency which follows if decision makers ignore the possibility of improved information by introducing a tax on development. This tax τ should be such that

$$\bar{U}(0) - [\bar{U}(1) - \tau] = \bar{\bar{U}}(0) - \bar{\bar{U}}(1) \tag{11.15}$$

where $\bar{U}(1) = \bar{\bar{U}}(1)$, since, with full development in the first period, new information available by the second period makes no difference. Thus, the tax on development in (11.15) is equal to the quasi-option value defined by equation (11.14).

In closing, three remarks regarding the above analysis are in order. Firstly, Hanemann (1982) has shown that the result $\bar{d}_1 \leqslant \bar{d}_1$ does not follow in the general case where d_1 can take any value in the interval $[0, 1]$. Nevertheless, of course, the value of information is still there. Secondly, development *per se* may provide information, i.e. the problem may allow for active learning in the sense that the amount and types of information gained depend upon the action taken in the first period. This has been stressed by Freeman (1984b) and Miller and Lad (1984). Moreover, as is the case in the Viscusi and Zeckhauser's (1976) analysis, some development can provide information regarding whether development is in fact irreversible. These results mean that development decisions involving a quasi-option are not necessarily more conservationist than decisions without the quasi-option (see also Lohmander, 984, for a similar discussion). Thirdly, the reader interested in interpretations of quasi-option value in terms of expected consumer surplus and option values is referred to Hanemann (1984b) and Mäler (1984). The latter author also deals with the aggregation of option and quasi-option values among individuals.

6 *Some concluding remarks on the choice of money measure in a risky world*

The results concerning the sign of option value are rather devastating. If option value was always positive, at least for a risk-averse household, one could argue that the expected consumer surplus of, for example, preserving a national park, underestimates the true gain. However, as the results of this and the previous chapter make clear, no such simple rule holds.

Ulph (1982) has shown that the kind of option value considered here is due to a distinction between ex ante and ex post welfare; option price is an ex ante measure while expected consumer surplus is an ex post measure. Ulph (1982) holds that even if one were interested in ex ante welfare judgements, there may be situations where one wishes to use ex post compensation measures. For example, a project which is expected to be profitable may actually cause the death of a lot of people and hence result in an outcome that is rather bad. In such situations there is no reason to believe that a uniform ex ante measure, i.e. option price, necessarily leads to the same decision as an ex post compensation measure. Nor is it entirely obvious which welfare change measure is the appropriate one in such situations (see Hammond, 1981, Ulph, 1982, for further discussion of this issue).

The concept of option value is often interpreted as a risk-aversion premium. This interpretation may seem reasonable when viewed in the light of the above distinction between ex ante and ex post welfare, and the discussion of ordinal versus cardinal properties of money measures in Section 2. However, the sign of option value is in general ambiguous, even in the case of risk-averse households. Hanemann (1984b) has shown that even if the individual's utility depends solely on his income, option value (due to income uncertainty) is not strictly the same as a risk premium. Turning to multivariate utility functions, Karni (1983) has shown that there is no longer any simple correspondence between the concavity of the utility function in income and a positive risk premium.

Moreover, option price and expected consumer surplus are just two out of possibly an infinite number of money measures of a unique change in expected utility. To see this, it is useful to consider a simple model with income uncertainty. Following Graham (1981), the willingness-to-pay function associated with a certain change in the supply of Q from Q^0 to Q^1 is defined by the relationship

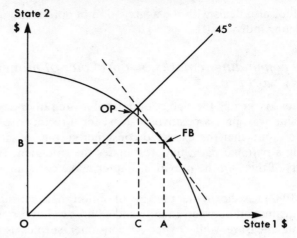

Figure 11.2 Collecting a maximum certain payment OC

$$E[V(y_h^i - S_h^i, Q^1)] = E[V(y_h^i, Q^0)] \qquad \forall h \qquad (11.16)$$

where S_h^i is the payment collected from household h in state i, and the expectation is taken with respect to the distribution of income. For example, both a state-independent payment and expected compensating variation preserve the equality in (11.16). Obviously, however, there are possibly an infinity of other such payment schemes.

Graham (1981) suggests that one should collect the maximum aggregate certain payment subject to (11.16). If this amount of money exceeds the certain costs of the project, then the project is obviously worthwhile whatever state of the world happens to occur. In a single-household context, where risk necessarily must be 'collective', this maximum state-independent payment is equal to option price. This result generalizes to a multi-household society, provided all individuals are similar and everyone experiences the same state of the world, i.e. risk is collective.

At the other extreme, risks are insurable on an individual basis. Suppose that individuals are alike but that $\pi^i H$ individuals experience state i, where $\pi^i < 1$. Consider the two-states case illustrated in Figure 11.2, which is due to Graham (1981). The slope of the willingness-to-pay locus depicted in the figure is obtained by differentiating the left-hand expression in (11.16) (see Graham, 1981, pp. 717–18 for details). By assumption, the probability is π^1 that an individual experiences state 1 and $\pi^2 = 1 - \pi^1$ that he experiences state 2. The maximum aggregate sure payment the society can collect is equal to

$$H(\pi^1 OA + \pi^2 OB) = H \cdot OC \tag{11.17}$$

Thus, by collecting \$OA from each of those π^1 per cent households which experience state 1 and \$OB from each of those π^2 per cent who experience state 2, society can collect a certain payment corresponding to \$$H \cdot OC$. Note that the point FB in the figure denotes the 'fair bet' associated with fair insurance in the insurance literature. The tangent to the willingness-to-pay locus at this point yields alternative payment combinations with the same expected value; the slope of the tangent is equal to $-\pi^1/\pi^2$. Thus, expected values are of interest if the situation involves individual-insurable risks (regardless of whether markets for contingent dollar claims actually exist or not). It is important to stress, however, that option price and the expected compensating variation are lower bounds for the expected value of the fair bet. The latter amount of money can be viewed as obtained by maximizing $E(S_h^i)$ subject to (11.16). This procedure equates the marginal utility of income between all states of nature. The first-order conditions for an interior optimum are $\pi^i = \psi \pi^i \partial V / \partial S_h^i$, for all i, where ψ is a Lagrange multiplier. Substitution of these conditions into the expression for the willingness-to-pay function, assuming two states of the world, yields

$$\frac{dS_h^2}{dS_h^1} = -\frac{\pi^1 (\partial V / \partial S_h^1)}{\pi^2 (\partial V / \partial S_h^2)} = -\frac{\pi^1}{\pi^2} \qquad \forall h \tag{11.18}$$

at the optimum, i.e. at FB in Figure 11.2. The calculation of option price and the expected compensating variation, on the other hand, are based on 'actual' incomes, implying that the possibility of extracting additional payments by equating the marginal utility of income between states is not exploited (although, if fair insurance is available, individuals continuously adjust in order to equate marginal utilities of income between states).

Graham (1981, p. 716) concludes that option price is the appropriate money measure in situations involving identical individuals and collective risk, while expected value calculations are appropriate in situations involving similar individuals and individual risks. Therefore, with the exception of the former case, and possibly option price and expected consumer surplus measures as lower bounds in the other extreme case, there does not seem to be any simple rules of thumb that could be used in empirical investigations. Obviously, it is not an easy task to try to estimate complete willingness-to-pay loci, which can be used to calculate aggregate certain payments in various situations. There are also the problems of ex ante versus ex post utility and the failure of expected consumer surplus measures always to rank correctly alternative regimes.

In addition, most of the literature on option value employ models of atemporal risk, while the considered problems often involve temporal risk, just as the models of Chapter 10 and Section 5 of the present chapter. Therefore, conclusions drawn from the models employed in the option value literature do not necessarily generalize to more realistic and complicated decision problems. On the other hand, modelling temporal risk is a difficult task, and the models easily become too complicated and data consuming to be able to be used in empirical investigations.

In closing, it is important to stress that the ambiguous sign of option value does not mean that the underlying change in expected utility is ambiguous. On the contrary, in all of the cases considered, the change in expected utility is unique.[4] The problems appear when one tries to express the utility change in terms of a money measure. The willingness-to-pay loci employed above indicate that a utility change may be expressed in terms of an infinite number of money measures. Hence it seems unlikely that the controversies about which money measure to use can be solved solely by invoking purely theoretical considerations. The choice of measure must, in general, be made on other grounds, such as the possibility of obtaining sufficient information to calculate one or other measure. Nevertheless, analyses of the relationship between different money measures may be of considerable help in such situations, i.e. such analyses may indicate whether or not the chosen measure over- or under-estimates the true gain from a particular project. The reader interested in further discussion of decision criteria in situations involving risk is referred to Arrow (1964), Arrow and Lind (1970), and Hirschleifer (1965).

7 On directions for future research

The results derived and discussed in this book show that much of the confusion prevailing a decade or so ago regarding the properties of money measures of utility change has been removed. For example, the conditions under which ordinary and various compensated money measures provide a correct ranking of utility changes has been explored. Moreover, appropriate money measures of simultaneous changes in prices, quantity constraints, and the provision of public goods are now available. There are also numerous empirical studies that seek to compare the properties of different empirical methods for estimations of money measures.

In spite of these extensions, much remains to be done. This book is rounded off by indicating a few possible directions, for future research. Firstly, Chapter 8 indicates that situations involving discrete choices are both common and important in environmental economics. Undoubtedly, existing models can be refined and extended so as to be able to deal with more complicated choice situations than is presently the case. In particular, most, if not all, available studies within the field consider binary responses while many real world decisions involve more than two possible responses. Similarly, the econometrics of discrete choices is developing rapidly. In future empirical investigations, it seems probable that the simple logit and probit models currently employed will be replaced by more general econometrical approaches.

Another important feature of choices highlighted in this book is that they are often taken before the agent knows for sure what prices, incomes, and so on, will prevail. Even if the agent knows the prevailing levels of these variables, he cannot be sure of their future values. This general uncertainty regarding the future will affect today's decisions. It is an important task for future research to integrate uncertainty in a way that is suitable for empirical studies. For example, the implications of uncertainty with regards to the formulation of questionnaires remains unclear. Similarly, it remains to integrate discrete choices and uncertainty regarding prices, incomes, and preferences. The empirical study of the housing market presented in Chapter 10, clearly indicates that forecasts of prices and variances are of extreme importance for the individual's decision making in a risky world. Similarly, the analysis performed in this chapter shows that demand functions obtained under certainty imply very little with regard to an individual's attitudes towards risk.

The literature dealing with supply-side option value generally compares a situation where a resource is available at its present level of quality to a situation where the resource is not available at all. The more general and interesting case, however, seems to be the one where a particular project affects the probability distribution, e.g. reduces the chance of bad outcomes and increases the chance of favourable outcomes. As noted in Section 3 of this chapter, ordinary as well as compensated expected consumer surplus change measures may fail to correctly rank such changes. This implies that questions about the willingness to pay, originally formulated for a riskless world, must be used with great caution in situations involving risk. Option price measures, on the other hand, provide a correct ranking of changes in expected utility. Nevertheless, the recent discussion between Mitchell and Carson (1985) and Greenley *et al.* (1985) highlights that it is quite easy to misspecify the questions and that the outcome may be quite complicated to interpret. Their discussion also underscores the importance of carefully deriving money measures when there are several uses of an asset before constructing a survey instrument. Otherwise, the chance of asking the questions in the wrong order and invoking wrong 'subject to' constraints is high (compare Section 1 of this chapter).

A final extension to be mentioned is the combination of expected utility maximization and hedonic housing value analysis. A recent study by Brookshire *et al.* (1985) demonstrates that the expected utility hypothesis may be a reasonable description of the behaviour of individuals who face a low-probability, high-loss natural hazard event. They show that the property value markets for Los Angeles and San Francisco convey hedonic price differentials to consumers that correspond closely to expected earthquake damages for particular homes located in relatively hazardous areas. This approach is an interesting and promising one and can probably also be used for examinations of the reliability of the survey technique in situations involving uncertainty. Moreover, the approach may provide further insight regarding the appropriate treatment of risk in social cost–benefit analysis. Although there is a considerable literature on this issue (e.g. Arrow, 1964; Arrow and Lind, 1970; Hirschleifer, 1965) there are still few applications to environmental problems.

Notes

1. Introduction

1 For a recent and comprehensive survey of the literature the reader is referred to Ekelund and Hébert (1985).
2 See Bailey (1954), Friedman (1949), and McKenzie (1983) for discussions of alternative interpretations of the Marshallian case.

2. Some basic concepts

1 Loosely speaking, continuous means that no gaps exist in the ordering while increasing means that more is preferred to less.
2 $X = \{x | x \geqslant 0\}$, i.e. the set of all x such that x is non-negative.
3 See Section 1 of Chapter 4 for a definition of a non-essential good.

3. The concept of consumer surplus

1 However, in an ordinal world, only the signs of S and $\triangle U$ matter. See the discussion below equation (3.21) and also Section 1 of Chapter 4.
2 Assuming, of course, that at least one price and/or income is fixed since all of the conditions stated in (3.7) cannot hold simultaneously.

4. Topics in the theory of consumer surplus measures

1 See the Slutsky equation (2.11) in Chapter 2.
2 If income elasticities change signs in the considered path, the indicated relationship between the different money measures need not hold; in fact, the three measures could coincide.
3 A comparison of EV in (4.1) and $EV_1 = e(\mathbf{p}^0, U^2) - e(\mathbf{p}^0, U^0)$ establishes this claim.
4 The money measures CV, EV and S are not affected since the demand functions (and hence also the conditions for path independency of the money measures) are unaffected by monotone transformations.
5 Under quasi-homotheticity, the income expansion paths are straight lines but need not go through the origin. The well-known Stone–Geary utility function, associated with the linear expenditure system, provides an example of this case (see Geary, 1949/50; Stone, 1954).

5. Consumer surplus measures in quantity-constrained regimes

1 Any subscripts denoting effective or quantity-constrained functions, as opposed to the notional or unconstrained functions of Chapters 3 and 4, are omitted in order to

simplify the notation. Similarly, primes denoting transposed vectors and matrices are suppressed.

2 If two or more demands are rationed, the argument becomes more complicated since a change in q_1 will affect the virtual prices of other rationed goods. This interaction must be accounted for when considering (changes in) several constraints.

3 This is the case at least where there is just a single *initial* vector of prices, quantity constraints and income. See the appendix to Chapter 6.

6. Public goods and externalities in consumption

1 For more information on the definitions of public goods (and mixed goods which fall between the polar cases of purely public and purely private goods) and external effects see McGuire and Aaron (1969), Milleron (1972); Musgrave (1959), Mäler (1974), Ng (1979), Samuelson (1954; 1955; 1969), and Strotz (1958). For recent surveys of the environment in economics and externalities, respectively, the reader is referred to Fisher and Peterson (1976) and Mishan (1971).

2 The path independency conditions are easily obtained from those stated in the appendix to Chapter 5.

3 In order to show this, we use equation (A6.2) in the appendix to this chapter. Set z^0 equal to a decision to preserve both parks, z^1 equal to a decision to preserve only the first park, and z^2 equal to a decision to preserve the second, but not the first park. The result then follows directly. Moreover, using (A6.1) with $U^2 = U^1 < U^0$, it can easily be shown that the EV measure ranks the alternatives correctly. However, see the appendix for a case where the EV measure, but not the CV measure, fails to rank bundles correctly.

7. How to overcome the problem of preference revelation; practical methodologies

1 See for example Bohm (1972; 1977; 1979; 1984), Clarke (1971), Kurz (1974), Malinvaud (1971), Sinden (1974), and the survey in Schulze *et al.* (1981).

2 Average poor air quality corresponds to 12.38 pphm/day, average fair to 9.55 pphm/day, and average good to 6.9 pphm/day.

3 A translog utility function is written as

$$\ell n \; U = \Sigma_i \; \alpha_i \; \ell n \; x_i + (\Sigma_i \; \Sigma_j \; \beta_{ij} \; \ell n \; x_i \; \ell n \; x_j)\frac{1}{2}$$

where $i, j = 1, \ldots, n$.

4 Bojö (1985) uses standardized estimates of travel costs rather than questionnaire results.

8. Discrete choice models and environmental benefits

1 It is important to note that the critical price levels derived in this section are not, in general, constant with respect to the choice of money measure. See the discussion in Section 4. Also, great care must be shown in using the CV measure for multi-site comparisons. Recall the discussion in Section 4 of Chapter 6.

2 For detailed derivations as well as extensions the reader is referred to Small and Rosen (1981) and, in particular, Hanemann (1984a). Amemiya (1981) presents a survey of the literature on qualitative response models. Recent interesting contributions include the generalized extreme value model and the distribution-free maximum likelihood method, see Small (1982) and Cosslett (1983) respectively, and also Maddala (1984). An application of discrete choice models to outdoor recreation is given by Lundin (1975).

3 See Lindley (1969, p. 59).

9. Consumer's surplus in an intertemporal context

1 Hammack and Brown (1974, pp. 78–83) also formulate a discrete-time, infinite-horizon model, however, the economic interpretation of the continuous time approach is easier to understand because of its notational simplicity.

10. Welfare change measures in a risky world

1 The utility function is assumed to be strongly quasi-concave, i.e. we do not rule out risk loving. See the definition of a well-behaved utility function in Section 1 of Chapter 2. (As was demonstrated in Section 1, $V_{yy} \leq 0$ if the utility function is concave.)

2 For different risk measures see Diamond and Stiglitz (1974) and Rothschild and Stiglitz (1970; 1971).

3 It is assumed that $E(\varepsilon_i^t) = 0$ and $E(\varepsilon_i^t \varepsilon_j^\tau) = 0$ for all commodities i, j ($i \neq j$) and all periods t, τ ($t \neq \tau$). Moreover, all prices and incomes are assumed to be strictly positive and finite.

4 A problem is to design compensation schemes that preserve incentives. See Just *et al.* (1982, pp. 355–6) for a discussion of this moral hazard problem.

11. Money measures of the total value of environmental assets

1 A state of world or nature is a description of the world so complete that, if true and known, the consequence of every action would be known (Arrow, 1971, p. 45).

2 Expected compensating variation, expected equivalent variation, and the expectation of the uncompensated money measure.

3 According to the subjectivist or Bayesian theory of the foundation of probability, there is no need for individual probability beliefs to coincide with either each other or some outside 'objective' standard. Proponents of the rational expectations hypothesis, on the other hand, argue that without some way of inferring what an agent's subjective view of the future is, the Bayesian hypothesis is of no help in understanding the agent's behaviour. For discussion on this point, see Lucas (1977), Sheffrin (1984), Swamy *et al.* (1982), and Zellner (1985).

4 For a critique of the expected utility theory of rationality the reader is referred to Allais and Hagen (1979).

Bibliography

Allais, M. and Hagen, O. (eds.) (1979) *Expected Utility Hypothesis and the Allais Paradox*. Reidel, Dordrecht.

Amemiya, T. (1981) Qualitative response models: A survey. *Journal of Economic Literature* 19, 1483–536.

Arrow, K. J. (1951) *Social Choice and Individual Values*. John Wiley & Sons, New York.

(1964) The role of securities in the optimal allocation of risk-bearing. *Review of Economic Studies* 31, 91–6.

(1971) *Essays in the Theory of Risk-bearing*. North-Holland, Amsterdam.

Arrow, K. J. and Fisher, A. C. (1974) Environmental preservation, uncertainty, and irreversibility. *Quarterly Journal of Economics* 88, 312–19.

Arrow, K. J. and Lind, R. (1970) Uncertainty and the evaluation of public investment decisions. *American Economic Review* 60, 364–78.

Bailey, M. J. (1954) The Marshallian demand curve. *Journal of Political Economy* 63, 255–61.

Barten, A. P. and Böhm, V. (1982) Consumer theory. In Arrow, K. J. and Intriligator, M. D. (eds.), *Handbook of Mathematical Economics*, vol. II. North-Holland, Amsterdam.

Bellman, R. (1957) *Dynamic Programming*. Princeton University Press, Princeton.

Benassy, J. P. (1982) *The Economics of Market Disequilibrium*. Academic Press, New York.

Bergson, A. (1938) A reformulation of certain aspects of welfare economics. *Quarterly Journal of Economics* 52, 310–34.

Bishop, R. C. (1982) Option value: An exposition and extension. *Land Economics* 58, 1–15.

Bishop, R. C. and Heberlein, T. A. (1979) Measuring values of extra-market goods: Are indirect measures biased? *American Journal of Agricultural Economics* 61, 926–30.

(1984) Contingent valuation methods and ecosystem damages from acid rain.

University of Wisconsin-Madison, Dept. of Agricultural Economics. Staff Paper No. 217.

Blackley, P., Follain, J. R. Jr and Ondrich, J. (1984) Box–Cox estimation of hedonic models: How serious is the iterative OLS variance bias? *Review of Economics and Statistics* 66, 348–53.

Blackorby, C., Donaldson, D. and Moloney, D. (1984) Consumer's surplus and welfare change in a simple dynamic model. *Review of Economic Studies* 51, 171–6.

Blackorby, C., Nissen, D., Primont, D. and Russell, R. R. (1973) Consistent intertemporal decision making. *Review of Economic Studies* 40, 239–48.

Blackorby, C., Primont, D. and Russell, R. R. (1978) *Duality, Separability, and Functional Structure: Theory and Economic Applications.* North-Holland, New York.

Block, M. K. and Heineke, J. M. (1975) Factor allocations under uncertainty: An extension. *Southern Economic Journal* 41, 526–30.

Boadway, R. W. (1974) The welfare foundations of cost-benefit analysis. *Economic Journal* 84, 926–39.

(1975) Cost-benefit rules in general equilibrium. *Review of Economic Studies* 42, 361–73.

Boadway, R. W. and Bruce, N. (1984) *Welfare Economics.* Basil Blackwell, Oxford.

Bockstael, N. E. and McConnel, K. E. (1981) Theory and estimation of the household production function for wildlife recreation. *Journal of Environmental Economics and Management* 8, 199–214.

Bohm, P. (1972) Estimating demand for public goods: An experiment. *European Economic Review* 3, 111–30.

(1975) Option demand and consumer's surplus: Comment. *American Economic Review* 65, 733–6.

(1977) Estimating access values. In Wingo, L. and Evans, A. (eds.), *Public Economics and the Quality of Life.* Johns Hopkins University Press, Baltimore.

(1979) Estimating willingness to pay: Why and how? *Scandinavian Journal of Economics* 81, 142–53.

(1984) Revealing demand for an actual public good. *Journal of Public Economics* 24, 135–51.

Bojö, J. (with the collaboration of Hultkrantz, L.) (1985) *A Cost–benefit Analysis of Forestry in Mountainous Areas: The Case of Valadalen.* Stockholm School of Economics, Stockholm (in Swedish).

Bös, D., Genser, B. and Holzmann, R. (1982) On the quality of publicly supplied goods. *Economica* 49, 289–96.

Bowden, R. J. (1978) *The Econometrics of Disequilibrium.* North-Holland, Amsterdam.

(1984) A note on the 'bottom-up' approach to measuring compensating variations. *Metroeconomica* 36, 65–76.

Bowen, H. R. (1943) The interpretation of voting in the allocation of economic resources. *Quarterly Journal of Economics* 58, 27–48.

Bowes, M. D. and Loomis, J. B. (1980) A note on the use of travel cost models with unequal zonal populations. *Land Economics* 56, 465–70.

(1982) A note on the use of travel cost models with unequal zonal populations: Reply. *Land Economics* 58, 408–10.

Box, G. E. P. and Cox, D. R. (1964) An analysis of transformations. *Journal of the Royal Statistical Society* 26 (Series B), 211–52.

Boyle, K. J. and Bishop, R. C. (1985) The total value of wildlife resources: Conceptual and empirical issues. Invited paper, Association of Environmental and Resource Economists Workshop on Recreational Demand Modeling, Boulder, Colorado, 17–18 May 1985.

Boyle, K. J., Bishop, R. C. and Welsh, M. P. (1985) Starting point bias in contingent valuation bidding games. *Land Economics* 61, 188–94.

Bradford, D. and Hildebrandt, G. (1977) Observable public good preferences. *Journal of Public Economics* 8, 111–31.

Brookshire, D. S., D'Arge, R. C., Schulze, W. D. and Thayer, M. A. (1981) Experiments in valuing public goods. In Smith, K. V. (ed.), *Advances in Applied Microeconomics*, vol. 1. JAI Press, Greenwich, Connecticut.

Brookshire, D. S., Eubanks, L. S. and Randall, A. (1983) Estimating option prices and existence values for wildlife resources. *Land Economics* 59, 1–15.

Brookshire, D. S., Thayer, M. A., Schulze, W. D. and d'Arge, R. C. (1982) Valuing public goods: A comparison of survey and hedonic approaches. *American Economic Review* 72, 165–77.

Brookshire, D. S., Thayer, M. A., Tschirhart, J. and Schulze, W. D. (1985) A test of the expected utility model: Evidence from earthquake risks. *Journal of Political Economy* 93, 369–89.

Brown, G. M. Jr. and Hammack, J. (1972) A preliminary investigation of the economics of migratory waterfowl. In Krutilla, J. V. (ed.), *Natural Environments: Studies in Theoretical and Applied Analysis*. Johns Hopkins University Press, Baltimore.

Brown, G. Jr and Mendelsohn, R. (1984) The hedonic travel cost method. *Review of Economics and Statistics* 66, 427–33.

Brown, J. N. and Rosen, H. S. (1982) On the estimation of structural hedonic price models. *Econometrica* 50, 765–8.

Burns, M. E. (1973) A note on the concept and measure of consumer surplus. *American Economic Review* 63, 335–44.

Burt, O. R. and Brewer, D. (1971) Estimation of net social benefits from outdoor recreation. *Econometrica* 39, 813–27.

Caulkins, P. P., Bishop, R. C. and Bouwes, N. W. (1985) Omitted cross-price variable biases in the linear travel cost model: Correcting common misperceptions. *Land Economics* 61, 182–7.

Cesario, F. J. (1976) Value of time in recreation benefit studies. *Land Economics* 55, 32–41.

Chavas, J.-P. and Bishop, R. C. (1984) *Ex-ante Consumer Welfare Evaluation in Cost–Benefit Analysis*. Department of Agricultural Economics, University of Wisconsin, Madison.

Chipman, J. S. and Moore, J. C. (1980) Compensating variation, consumer's surplus, and welfare. *American Economic Review* 70, 933–49.

Christensen, J. B. and Price, C. (1982) A note on the use of travel cost models with unequal zonal populations: Comment. *Land Economics* 58, 395–9.

Cicchetti, C. J. and Freeman, A. M. III (1971) Option demand and consumer surplus: Further comment. *Quarterly Journal of Economics* 85, 528–39.

Cicchetti, C. J. and Smith, K. V. (1976) The measurement of individual congestion costs: An economic application to wilderness recreation. In Lin, S. A. Y. (ed.) *Theory and Measurement of Economic Externalities.* Academic Press, New York.

Cicchetti, C. J., Fisher, A. C. and Smith, V. K. (1976) An econometric evaluation of a generalized consumer surplus measure: The Mineral King issue. *Econometrica* 44, 1259–76.

Clark, C. W. (1976) *Mathematical Bioeconomics: The Optimal Management of Renewable Resources.* John Wiley & Sons, New York.

Clarke, E. (1971) Multipart pricing of public goods. *Public Choice* 8, 19–33.

Clawson, M. (1959) *Methods of Measuring Demand for and Value of Outdoor Recreation.* Reprint 10, Resources for the Future, Washington, D.C.

Clawson, M. and Knetsch, J. L. (1966) *Economics of Outdoor Recreation.* Johns Hopkins University Press, Baltimore.

Cornes, R. and Albon, R. (1981) Evaluation of welfare change in quantity-constrained regimes. *Economic Record* 57, 186–90.

Cornwall, R. R. (1984) *Introduction to the Use of General Equilibrium Analysis.* North-Holland, Amsterdam.

Cosslett, S. R. (1983) Distribution-free maximum likelihood estimator of the binary choice model. *Econometrica* 51, 765–82.

Courant, R. and John, F. (1965) *Introduction to Calculus and Analysis*, vol. 1. John Wiley & Sons (Wiley-Interscience), New York.
  (1974) *Introduction to Calculus and Analysis*, vol. 2. John Wiley & Sons (Wiley-Interscience), New York.

Cuddington, J. T., Johansson, P.-O. and Löfgren, K. G. (1984) *Disequilibrium Macroeconomics in Open Economies.* Basil Blackwell, Oxford.

Cuddington, J. T., Johnson, F. R. and Knetsch, J. L. (1981) Valuing amenity resources in the presence of substitutes. *Land Economics* 57, 526–35.

Cummings, R. G., Brookshire, D. S. and Schultze, W. D. (1986) *Valuing Public Goods: The Contingent Valuation Method.* Rowman and Allanheld Publishers, Totowa, N.J.

Dasgupta, P. S. (1982) *The Control of Resources.* Basil Blackwell, Oxford.

Dasgupta, P. S. and Heal, G. M. (1979) *Economic Theory and Exhaustible Resources.* James Nisbet/Cambridge University Press, Oxford.

Davis, R. K. (1964) The value of big game hunting in a private forest. In Transactions of the twenty-ninth North American wildlife conference. Wildlife Management Institute, Washington, D.C.

Deaton, A. and Muellbauer, J. (1983) *Economics and Consumer Behavior.* Cambridge University Press, New York.

Deyak, T. A. and Smith, K. V. (1978) Congestion and participation in outdoor recreation: A household production function approach. *Journal of Environmental Economics and Management* 5, 63–80.

Diamond, P. A. and McFadden, D. (1974) some uses of the expenditure function in public finance. *Journal of Public Economics* 3, 3–22.

Diamond, P. A. and Stiglitz, J. E. (1974) Increases in risk and in risk aversion. *Journal of Economic Theory* 8, 337–60.

Diewert, W. E. (1982) Duality approaches to microeconomic theory. In Arrow, K. J. and Intriligator, M. D. (eds.), *Handbook of Mathematical Economics*, vol. II. North-Holland, Amsterdam.

Dixit, A. K. and Weller, P. A. (1979) The three consumer's surpluses. *Economica* 46, 125–35.

Domencich, T. A. and McFadden, D. (1975) *Urban Travel Demand. A Behavioral Analysis*. North-Holland, Amsterdam.

Drèze, J. H. and Modigliani, F. (1972) Consumption decisions under uncertainty. *Journal of Economic Theory* 5, 308–35.

Dupuit, J. (1844) De la mesure de l'utilité des travaux publics. Annales des Ponts et Chaussées. Translated by R. H. Barback in *International Economic Papers* 17 (1952), 83–110, Macmillan, New York.

Ekelund, R. B. Jr and Hébert, R. F. (1985) Consumer surplus: the first hundred years. *History of Political Economy* 17, 419–54.

Epstein, L. (1975) A disaggregate analysis of consumer choice under uncertainty. *Econometrica* 43, 877–92.

Fisher, A. C. and Hanemann, M. W. (1983) *Endangered Species: The Economics of Irreversible Damage*. Department of Agricultural and Resource Economics, University of California, Berkeley.

Fisher, A. C. and Peterson, F. M. (1976) The environment in economics: A survey. *Journal of Economic Literature* 14, 1–33.

Fleming, W. H. (1965) *Functions of Several Variables*. Addison-Wesley, Reading, Mass.

Freeman, A. M. III (1979a) *The Benefits of Environmental Improvement. Theory and Practice*. Johns Hopkins University Press, Baltimore.

(1979b) Hedonic prices, property values and measuring environmental benefits: A survey of the issues. *Scandinavian Journal of Economics* 81, 154–73.

(1984a) The sign and size of option value. *Land Economics* 60, 1–13.

(1984b) The quasi-option value of irreversible development. *Journal of Environmental Economics and Management* 11, 292–5.

(1985) Supply uncertainty, option price, and option value. *Land Economics* 61, 176–81.

Friedman, M. (1949) The Marshallian demand curve. *Journal of Political Economy* 57, 463–95.

Friedman, M. and Savage, L. J. (1948) The utility analysis of choices involving risk. *Journal of Political Economy* 56, 279–304.

Gallagher, D. R. and Smith, K. V. (1985) Measuring values for environmental resources under uncertainty. *Journal of Environmental Economics and Management* 12, 132–43.

Geary, R. C. (1949/50) A note on a constant utility index of the cost of living. *Review of Economic Studies* 18, 65–6.

Gerking, S. D. and Weirick, W. N. (1983) Compensating differences and interregional wage differentials. *Review of Economics and Statistics* 65, 483–7.

Graham, D. A. (1981) Cost–benefit analysis under uncertainty. *American Economic Review* 71, 715–25.

(1984) Cost–benefit analysis under uncertainty: Reply. *American Economic Review* 74, 1100–2.

Gramlich, E. M. (1981) *Benefit–cost Analysis of Government Programs.* Prentice-Hall, Englewood Cliffs, N.J.

Greenley, D. A., Walsh, R. G. and Young, R. A. (1981) Option value: Empirical evidence from a case study of recreation and water quality. *Quarterly Journal of Economics* 95, 657–73.

(1985) Option value: Empirical evidence from a case study of recreation and water quality: Reply. *Quarterly Journal of Economics* 100, 292–9.

Griliches, Z. (ed.) (1971) *Price Indexes and Quality Change.* Harvard University Press, Cambridge, Mass.

Halvorsen, R. A. and Pollakowski, H. O. (1981) Choice of functional form for hedonic price equations. *Journal of Urban Economics* 10, 37–49.

Hammack, J. and Brown, G. M. Jr (1974) *Waterfowl and Wetlands: Toward Bioeconomic Analysis.* Johns Hopkins University Press, Baltimore.

Hammond, P. J. (1981) Ex ante and ex post welfare optimality under uncertainty. *Economica* 48, 235–50.

Hanemann, M. W. (1982) *Information and the Concept of Option Value.* Department of Agricultural and Resource Economics, University of California, Berkeley.

(1984a) Discrete/continuous models of consumer demand. *Econometrica* 52, 541–61.

(1984b) *On Reconciling Different Concepts of Option Value.* Department of Agricultural and Resource Economics, University of California, Berkeley.

(1984c) Entropy as a measure of consensus in the evaluation of recreation site quality. *Journal of Environmental Economics and Management* 18, 241–51.

(1984d) Welfare evaluations in contingent valuation experiments with discrete responses. *American Journal of Agricultural Economics* 66, 332–41.

Hanoch, G. (1977) Risk aversion and consumer preferences. *Econometrica* 45, 413–26.

(1980) Hours and weeks in the theory of labor supply. In Smith, J. P. (ed.), *Female Labor Supply: Theory and Estimation.* Princeton University Press, Princeton.

Harberger, A. C. (1971) Three basic postulates for applied welfare economics: An interpretive essay. *Journal of Economic Literature* 9, 785–97.

Harrison, D. Jr and Rubinfeld, O. L. (1978) Hedonic housing prices and the demand for clean air. *Journal of Environmental Economics and Management* 5, 81–102.

Harrod, R. F. (1948) *Towards a Dynamic Economy*. Macmillan, London.

Harsanyi, J. (1955) Cardinal welfare, individualistic ethics, and interpersonal comparison of welfare. *Journal of Political Economy* 63, 309–21.

Hau, T. D. (1985) A Hicksian approach to cost–benefit analysis with discrete-choice models. *Economica* 52, 479–90.

Hause, J. C. (1975) The theory of welfare cost measurement. *Journal of Political Economy* 83, 1145–82.

Hausman, J. A. (1981) Exact consumer's surplus and deadweight loss. *American Economic Review* 71, 662–76.

Helms, J. L. (1984) Comparing stochastic price regimes: The limitations of expected surplus measures. *Economics Letters* 14, 173–8.

   (1985) Expected consumer's surplus and the welfare effects of price stabilization. *International Economic Review* 26, 603–17.

Henderson, A. (1940/1) Consumer's surplus and the compensating variation. *Review of Economic Studies* 8, 117–21.

Henry, C. (1974) Option values in the economics of irreplaceable assets. *Review of Economic Studies Symposium on Economics of Exhaustible Resources*, 89–104.

Herfindahl, O. C. and Kneese, A. V. (1974) *Economic Theory of Natural Resources*. C. E. Merrill Publishing Company, Columbus.

Hey, J. D. (1979) *Uncertainty in Microeconomics*. Martin Robertson, Oxford.

   (1981) *Economics in Disequilibrium*. Martin Robertson, Oxford.

Hicks, J. R. (1939) The foundations of welfare economics. *Economic Journal* 49, 696–712.

   (1940/1) The rehabilitation of consumers' surplus. *Review of Economic Studies* 8, 108–15.

   (1943) The four consumer's surpluses. *Review of Economic Studies* 11, 31–41.

   (1945/6) The generalized theory of consumer's surplus. *Review of Economic Studies* 13, 68–73.

   (1946) *Value and Capital*. Clarendon Press, Oxford.

Hirshleifer, J. (1965) The investment decision under uncertainty: Choice-theoretic approaches. *Quarterly Journal of Economics* 79, 509–36.

Hirshleifer, J. and Riley, J. G. (1979) the analytics of uncertainty and information – An expository survey. *Journal of Economic Literature* 17, 1375–421.

Hof, J. G. and King, D. A. (1982) On the necessity of simultaneous recreation demand equation estimation. *Land Economics* 58, 547–52.

Hogg, R. V. and Craig, A. T. (1978) *Introduction to Mathematical Statistics*, 4th edn, Macmillan, New York.

Hori, H. (1975) Revealed preference for public goods. *American Economic Review* 65, 978–91.

Hotelling, H. (1938) The general welfare in relation to problems of taxation and of railway and utility rates. *Econometrica* 6, 242–69.

(1947) Unpublished letter to Director of National Park Service.

Howard, D. (1977) Rationing, quantity constraints, and consumption theory. *Econometrica* 45, 399–412.

Hurwics, L. and Uzawa, H. (1971) On the integrability of demand functions. In Chipman, J. S., Hurwics, L., Richter, M. K. and Sonnenschein, H. F. (eds.), *Preferences, Utility and Demand*. Harcourt Brace Jovanovich, New York.

Hylland, A. and Strand, J. (1983) *Valuation of Reduced Air Pollution in the Grenland Area*. Department of Economics, University of Oslo, Norway (in Norwegian).

Johansson, P.-O. and Löfgren, K. G. (1985) *The Economics of Forestry and Natural Resources*. Basil Blackwell, Oxford.

Johnson, F. R., Krutilla, J. V., Bowes, M. D. and Wilman, E. A. (1983) *Estimating the impacts of forest management on recreation benefits. Part I: Methodology. Part II: Application with reference to the White Mountain National Forest* (by Johnson, F. R. and Krutilla, J. V.). Multiple Use Forestry Project, Resources for the Future, Washington, D.C.

Johnston, J. (1984) *Econometric Methods*, 3rd edn, McGraw-Hill, Tokyo.

Jones-Lee, M. W. (1976) *The Value of Life*. Martin Robertson, Oxford.

Just, R. E., Hueth, D. L. and Schmitz, A. (1982) *Applied Welfare Economics and Public Policy*. Prentice Hall, Englewood Cliffs, N.J.

Kaldor, N. (1939) Welfare propositions of economics and interpersonal comparisons of utility. *Economic Journal* 49, 549–52.

Kannai, Y. (1977) Concavifiability and constructions of concave utility functions. *Journal of Mathematical Economics* 4, 1–56.

Karni, E. (1983) On the correspondence between multivariate risk aversion and risk aversion with state-dependent preferences. *Journal of Economic Theory* 30, 230–42.

Katzner, D. W. (1970) *Static Demand Theory*. Macmillan, London.

Knetsch, J. L. and Davis, R. K. (1966) Comparisons of methods for recreation evaluation. In Kneese, A. V. and Smith, S. C. (eds.) *Water Research*. The Johns Hopkins University Press, Baltimore.

Knetsch, J. L. and Sinden, J. A. (1984) Willingness to pay and compensation demanded: Experimental evidence of an unexpected disparity in measures of value. *Quarterly Journal of Economics* 99, 507–21.

Krutilla, J. A. (1967) Conservation reconsidered. *American Economic Review* 57, 777–86.

Krutilla, J. V. and Fisher, A. C. (1975) *The Economics of Natural Environments: Studies in the Valuation of Commodity and Amenity Resources*. Johns Hopkins University Press, Baltimore.

Kurz, M. (1974) An experimental approach to the determination of the demand for public goods. *Journal of Public Economics* 3, 329–48.

Laffont, J.-J. (ed.) (1979) *Aggregation and Revelation of Preferences*. North-Holland, Amsterdam.

Lancaster, K. J. (1966) A new approach to consumer theory. *Journal of Political Economy* 74, 132–57.

Lau, L. J. (1969) Duality and the structure of utility functions. *Journal of Economic Theory* 1, 374–96.

Lecomber, R. (1979) *The Economics of Natural Resources*. Macmillan, London.

Lindley, D. V. (1969) *Introduction to Probability and Statistics. Part 1: Probability*. Cambridge University Press, Cambridge.

Lohmander, P. (1984) Diversification in the natural resource enterprise, option values and improved industrial coordination. Department of Forest Economics, Swedish University of Agricultural Sciences. Working Paper No. 40.

Lucas, R. E. Jr (1977) Understanding business cycles. In Brunner, K. and Meltzner, A. (eds.), *Stabilization of the Domestic and International Economy*. Carnegie-Rochester Conference Series in Public Policy. North-Holland, Amsterdam.

Lundin, S. A. G. (1975) A conditional logit analysis of the demand for outdoor recreation. Unpublished Ph.D. dissertation, University of California, Berkeley.

McFadden, D. (1973) Conditional logit analysis of qualitative choice behavior. In Zacembka, P. (ed.), *Frontiers of Econometrics*. Academic Press, New York.

(1976) Quantal choice analysis: A survey. *Annals of Economic and Social Measurement* 5, 363–90.

McGuire, M. C. and Aaron, H. (1969) Efficiency and equity in the optimal supply of a public good. *Review of Economics and Statistics* 51, 31–9.

Mackay, R. J. and Whitney, G. A. (1980) The comparative statics of quantity constraints and conditional demands: Theory and applications. *Econometrica* 48, 1727–44.

McKenzie, G. W. (1983) *Measuring Economic Welfare: New Methods*. Cambridge University Press, Cambridge.

McKenzie, G. W. and Pearce, I. F. (1982) Welfare measurement – A synthesis. *American Economic Review* 72, 669–82.

McMillan, M. L. (1979) Estimates of households' preferences for environmental quality and other housing characteristics from a system of demand equations. *Scandinavian Journal of Economics* 81, 174–87.

Maddala, G. S. (1984) *Limited-dependent and Qualitative Variables in Econometrics*. Cambridge University Press, New York.

Mäler, K.-G. (1971) A method of estimating social benefits from pollution control. *Swedish Journal of Economics* 73, 121–33.

(1974) *Environmental Economics. A Theoretical Inquiry*. Johns Hopkins University Press, Baltimore.

(1977) A note on the use of property values in estimating marginal willingness to pay for environmental quality. *Journal of Environmental Economics and Management* 4, 355–69.

(1981) A note on the possibility of calculating demand for a public good from information on individual behaviour. Research paper 6209, Stockholm School of Economics, Stockholm.

(1984) *Risk, Uncertainty and the Environment*. Stockholm School of Economics, Stockholm.

Malinvaud, E. (1971) A planning approach to the public good problem. *Swedish Journal of Economics* 73, 96–117.

Marshall, A. (1920) *Principles of Economics*, 8th edn, Macmillan, London.

Massell, B. F. (1969) Price stabilization and welfare. *Quarterly Journal of Economics* 83, 284–98.

Mendelsohn, R. and Strang, W. J. (1984) Cost–benefit analysis under uncertainty: Comment. *American Economic Review* 74, 1096–9.

Miller, J. R. and Lad, F. (1984) Flexibility, learning, and irreversibility in environmental decisions: A Bayesian analysis. *Journal of Environmental Economics and Management* 11, 161–72.

Milleron, J.-C. (1972) Theory of value with public goods: A survey article. *Journal of Economic Theory* 5, 419–77.

Mishan, E. J. (1971) The postwar literature on externalities: An interpretative essay. *Journal of Economic Literature* 9, 1–28.

(1976) The use of compensating and equivalent variation in cost–benefit analysis. *Economica* 43, 185–97.

Mitchell, R. C. and Carson, R. T. (1985) Option value: Empirical evidence from a case study of recreation and water quality: Comment. *Quarterly Journal of Economics* 100, 291–4.

Morey, E. R. (1981) The demand for site-specific recreational activities: A characteristics approach. *Journal of Environmental Economics and Management* 8, 345–71.

(1984) Confuser surplus. *American Economic Review* 74, 163–73.

Musgrave, R. A. (1959) *Theory of Public Finance*. McGraw-Hill Kogakuska, Tokyo.

Muth, J. F. (1961) Rational expectations and the theory of price movements. *Econometrica* 29, 315–35.

Neary, J. P. and Roberts, K. W. S. (1980) The theory of household behaviour under rationing. *European Economic Review* 13, 25–42.

Neumann, J. von and Morgenstern, O. (1947) *Theory of Games and Economic Behavior*, 2nd edn, Princeton University Press, Princeton, N.J.

Ng, Y.-K. (1979) *Welfare Economics. Introduction and Development of Basic Concepts*. Macmillan, London.

(1982) Beyond optimality: The necessity of interpersonal cardinal utilities in distributional judgements and social choice. *Zeitschrift für Nationalökonomie* 42, 207–33.

Patinkin, D. (1963) Demand curves and consumer's surplus. In Christ, C. F. *et al.*

(eds), *Measurement in Economics, Studies in Mathematical Economics and Econometrics in Memory of Yehuda Grunfeld*. Stanford University Press, Stanford.

Pearse, P. H. (1968) A new approach to the evaluation of non-priced recreational resources. *Land Economics* 44, 87–99.

Pindyck, R. S. and Rubinfeld, D. L. (1976) *Econometric Models and Economic Forecasts*. McGraw-Hill Kogakusha, Tokyo.

Plummer, M. L. and Hartman, R. C. (1985) Option value: A general approach. Mimeo.

Polinsky, A. M. and Rubinfeld, D. L. (1975) Property values and the benefits of environmental improvements: Theory and measurement. Discussion Paper No. 404, Harvard Institute of Economic Research, Cambridge, Mass.

Pontryagin, L. S., Boltyanski, V. S., Gamkrelidze, R. V. and Mishchenko, E. F. (1962) *The Mathematical Theory of Optimal Processes*. John Wiley & Sons (Wiley-Interscience), New York.

Porter, R. C. (1984) The optimal timing of an exhaustible, reversible wilderness development project. *Land Economics* 60, 247–54.

Pratt, J. W. (1964) Risk aversion in the small and in the large. *Econometrica* 32, 122–36.

Quandt, R. E. Bibliography of rationing and disequilibrium models. Unpublished.

Ramsey, F. (1928) A mathematical theory of saving. *Economic Journal* 38, 543–59.

Randall, A. and Stoll, J. R. (1980) Consumer's surplus in commodity space. *American Economic Review* 70, 449–55.

Randall, A., Ives, B. and Eastman, C. (1974) Bidding games for valuation of aesthetic environmental improvements. *Journal of Environmental Economics and Management* 1, 132–49.

Rawls, J. (1972) *A Theory of Justice*. Clarendon Press, Oxford.

Rogerson, W. P. (1980) Aggregate expected consumer surplus as a welfare index with an application to price stabilization. *Econometrica* 48, 423–36.

Rosen, S. (1974) Hedonic prices and implicit markets: Product differentiation in pure competition. *Journal of Political Economy* 82, 34–55.

Rosen, H. S., Rosen K. T. and Holtz-Eakin, D. (1984) Housing tenure, uncertainty, and taxation. *Review of Economics and Statistics* 66, 405–16.

Rothbarth, E. (1940–1) The measurement of changes in real income under conditions of rationing. *Review of Economic Studies* 8, 100–7.

Rothschild, M. and Stiglitz, J. E. (1970) Increasing risk. I: A definition. *Journal of Economic Theory* 2, 225–43.

(1971) Increasing risk. II: Its economic consequences. *Journal of Economic Theory* 3, 66–84.

Rowe, R., D'Arge, R. C. and Brookshire, D. S. (1980) An experiment on the economic value of visibility. *Journal of Environmental Economics and Management* 7, 1–19.

Roy, R. (1942) *De l'Utilité, Contribution à la Théorie des Choix*. Hermann, Paris.

Samuelson, P. A. (1942) Constancy of the marginal utility of income. In Lange, O., McIntyre, F. and Yntema, T. O. (eds), *Studies in Mathematical Economics and Econometrics in Memory of Henry Schultz*. University of Chicago Press, Chicago.
(1947) *Foundations of Economic Analysis*. Harvard University Press, Cambridge, Mass.
(1950) The problem of integrability in utility theory. *Economica* 30, 355–85.
(1954) The pure theory of public expenditure. *Review of Economics and Statistics* 36, 387–9.
(1955) Diagrammatic exposition of a theory of public expenditure. *Review of Economics and Statistics* 37, 350–6.
(1969) Pure theory of public expenditure and taxation. In Margolis, J. and Guitton, H. (eds.), *Public Economics*. Macmillan, London
(1972) The consumer does benefit from feasible price stability. *Quarterly Journal of Economics* 86, 476–93.
Sandmo, A. (1970) The effect of uncertainty on saving decisions. *Review of Economic Studies* 37, 353–60.
Schmalensee, R. (1972) Option demand and consumer's surplus: Valuing price changes under uncertainty. *American Economic Review* 62, 813–24.
Schulze, W. D., D'Arge, R. C. and Brookshire, D. S. (1981) Valuing environmental commodities: Some recent experiments. *Land Economics* 57, 151–72.
Scitovsky, T. (1941) A note on welfare propositions in economics. *Review of Economic Studies* 9, 77–88.
Seade, J. (1978) Consumer's surplus and linearity of Engel curves. *Economic Journal* 88, 511–23.
Seller, C., Stoll, J. R. and Chavas, J.-P. (1985) Validation of empirical measures of welfare change: A comparison of nonmarket techniques. *Land Economics* 61, 156–75.
Shapiro, P. and Smith, T. (1981) Preferences for non-market goods revealed through market demands. In Smith, K. V. (ed.), *Advances in Applied Microeconomics* vol. 1. JAI Press, Greenwich, Connecticut.
Sheffrin, S. M. (1984) *Rational Expectations*. Cambridge Surveys of Economic Literature. Cambridge University Press, New York.
Sidgwick, H. (1890) *The Methods of Ethics*. Macmillan, London.
Siebert, H. (1982) Nature as a life support system. Renewable resources and environmental disruption. *Zeitschrift für Nationalökonomie* 42, 133–42.
Silberberg, E. (1972) Duality and the many consumer's surpluses. *American Economic Review* 62, 942–52.
(1978) *The Structure of Economics: A Mathematical Analysis*. McGraw-Hill, New York.
Silverman, R. A. (1969) *Modern Calculus and Analytic Geometry*. Macmillan, New York.
Sinden, J. A. (1974) A utility approach to the valuation of recreational and

aesthetic experiences. *American Journal of Agricultural Economics* 56, 61–72.

Small, K. A. (1982) *Ordered Logit: A Discrete Choice Model with Proximate Covariance among Alternatives.* Department of Economics, Princeton University.

Small, K. A. and Rosen, S. (1981) Applied welfare economics with discrete choice models. *Econometrica* 49, 105–30.

Smith, B. and Stephen, F. H. (1975) Cost–benefit analysis and compensation criteria: A note. *Economic Journal* 85, 902–5.

Smith, K. V. (1984) A bound for option value. *Land Economics* 60, 292–6.

Smith, K. V. and Desvousges, W. H. (1985) The generalized travel cost model and water quality benefits: A reconsideration. *Southern Economic Journal* 52, 371–81.

Spitzer, J. J. (1982) A primer on Box–Cox estimation. *Review of Economics and Statistics* 64, 307–13.

Stahl, D. O. II (1983a) Quasi-homothetic preferences, the generalized Divisia quantity index, and aggregation. *Economica* 50, 87–93.

(1983b) A note on the consumer surplus path-of-integration problem. *Economica* 50, 95–8.

(1983c) On cost–benefit analysis with quality attributes. *Zeitschrift für Nationalökonomie* 43, 273–87.

(1984) Monotonic variations of consumer surplus and comparative performance results. *Southern Economic Journal* 51, 503–20.

Stiglitz, J. E. (1969) Behavior towards risk with many commodities. *Econometrica* 37, 660–7.

Stone, R. (1954) Linear expenditure systems and demand analysis: An application to the pattern of British demand. *Economic Journal* 64, 511–27.

Strotz, R. H. (1956) Myopia and inconsistency in dynamic utility maximization. *Review of Economic Studies* 23, 165–80.

(1958) Two propositions related to public goods. *Review of Economics and Statistics* 40, 329–31.

Swamy, P. A. V. B., Barth, J. R. and Tinsley, P. A. (1982) The rational expectations approach to economic modelling. *Journal of Economic Dynamics and Control* 4, 125–48.

Tobin, J. and Houthakker, H. S. (1950/1) The effects of rationing on demand elasticities. *Review of Economic Studies* 18, 140–53.

Turnovsky, S. J., Shalit, H. and Schmitz, A. (1980) Consumer's surplus, price instability, and consumer welfare. *Econometrica* 48, 135–52.

Ulph, A. (1982) The role of ex ante and ex post decisions in the valuation of life. *Journal of Public Economics* 18, 265–76.

Varian, H. R. (1978) *Microeconomic Analysis.* W. W. Norton & Company, New York. (Second edn 1984).

Vartia, Y. O. (1983) Efficient methods of measuring welfare change and compensated income in terms of ordinary demand functions. *Econometrica* 51, 79–98.

Vaughan, W. J. and Russell, C. S. (1982) Valuing a fishing day: An application of a systematic varying parameter model. *Land Economics* 58, 450–63.

Vaughan, W. J., Russell, C. S. and Hazilla, M. (1982) A note on the use of travel cost models with unequal zonal populations: Comment. *Land Economics* 58, 400–7.

Viscusi, W. K. and Zeckhauser, R. J. (1976) Environmental policy choice under uncertainty. *Journal of Environmental Economics and Management* 3, 97–112.

Walsh, R. G., Greenley, D. A., Young, R. A. Mckean, J. R. and Prato, A. A. (1978) *Option Values, Preservation Values and Recreational Benefits of Improved Water Quality: A Case Study of the South Platte River Basin, Colorado.* Department of Economics, Colorado State University, Fort Collins.

Waugh, F. W. (1944) Does the consumer benefit from price instability. *Quarterly Journal of Economics* 58, 602–14.

Weisbrod, B. A. (1964) Collective-consumption services of individual-consumption goods. *Quarterly Journal of Economics* 78, 471–7.

Weymark, J. A. (1985) Money-metric utility functions. *International Economic Review* 26, 219–32.

White, F. C. and Ziemer, R. F. (1983) Disequilibrium prices and economic surplus in the U.S. fed beef market. *Canadian Journal of Agricultural Economics* 31, 197–204.

Widder, D. V. (1961) *Advanced Calculus*, 2nd edn, Prentice-Hall, Englewood Cliffs, N.J.

Willig, R. D. (1973) Consumer's surplus: A rigorous cookbook. Technical report No. 98, Institute for Mathematical Studies in the Social Sciences, Stanford.

(1976) Consumer's surplus without apology. *American Economic Review* 66, 589–97.

(1978) Incremental consumer's surplus and hedonic price adjustment. *Journal of Economic Theory* 17, 227–53.

Zabalza, A. (1982) Compensating and equivivalent variations, and the deadweight loss of taxation. *Economica* 49, 355–9.

Zellner, A. (1985) Bayesian econometrics. *Econometrica* 53, 253–69.

Index